D1535182

Tunisia

Anthony Ham

Abigail Hole

Contents

TUNIS p63

NORTHERN TUNISIA p112

CAP BON p93

CENTRAL WEST & THE TELL p136

KAIROUAN & THE CENTRAL COAST p158

JERBA p237

SOUTHERN TUNISIA p195

Destination Tunisia

Tunisia has it all – it's a small country, but a big destination.

This is a land of myths, from the once-mighty city-state of Carthage to the beautiful island of Jerba, the Land of the Lotus Eaters. It's also a land where 2500 years of history come alive: in the astonishing Roman colosseum at El-Jem; in the ancient cities of Dougga and Sufetula; in charming medinas (old cities) surrounded by crenellated walls; and in the fairytale architecture of the Berbers. In Kairouan, the fourth-holiest city in Islam, foundation myths and towering mosques connect Tunisia to the heart of Islam, while the nation's story is told in intricately woven carpets and a very modern sales pitch in the narrow lanes of the city's enchanting medina.

Tunisia's splendid historical heritage is married to a very modern country of pristine white-sand beaches overlooked by imposing castles and the awe-inspiring open spaces of the Sahara desert, stretching deep into Africa.

Whether you're seeking a week of sunshine along Tunisia's superb Mediterranean coastline or sleeping under the stars on a sand dune, you'll have ample opportunities to escape from the rigours of modern life but with all the comforts you could need – stunning resorts, delicious food and great shopping. Charismatic Mahdia and Le Kef are places to chill, while the palm-fringed oases of Douz and Tozeur are the gateways to a fascinating desert world.

Perhaps more than anything else, it's the hospitable Tunisians, with their feet firmly planted in an ancient, traditional land while rushing headlong into the modern world, who'll provide the highlights. You'd be missing a wonderful experience if you didn't join them.

JANE SWEENEY

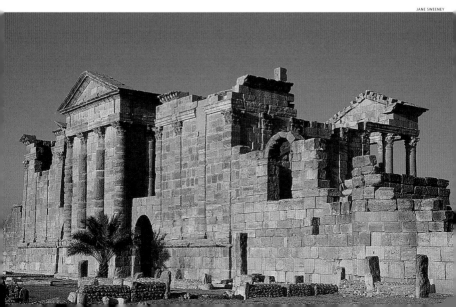

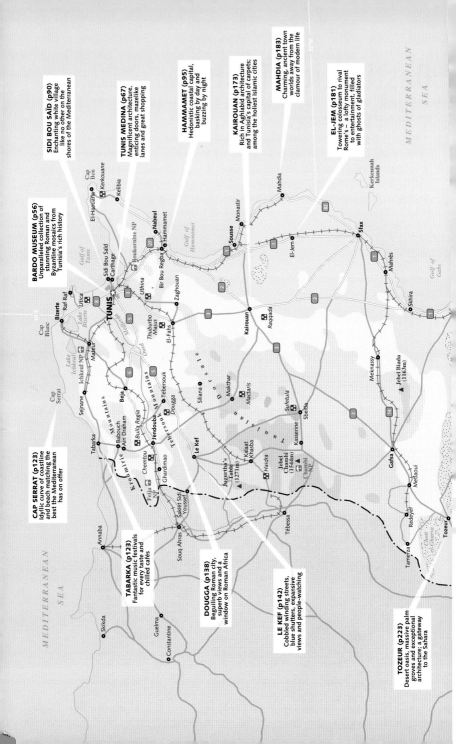

BARDO MUSEUM (p56)
Unparalleled collection of stunning Roman and Byzantine mosaics from Tunisia's rich history

SIDI BOU SAÏD (p90)
Enchanting white village like no other on the shores of the Mediterranean

TUNIS MEDINA (p67)
Magnificent architecture, enticing doors, mazelike lanes and great shopping

HAMMAMET (p95)
Hedonistic coastal capital, basking by day and buzzing by night

KAIROUAN (p173)
Rich in Aghlabid architecture and Tunisia's capital of carpets; among the holiest Islamic cities

MAHDIA (p183)
Charming, ancient town worlds away from the clamour of modern life

EL-JEM (p181)
Towering colosseum to rival Rome's – a lofty monument to entertainment, filled with ghosts of gladiators

CAP SERRAT (p123)
Idyllic curve of coastline and beach matching the best the Mediterranean has on offer

TABARKA (p123)
Fantastic music festivals for every taste and chilled cafés

DOUGGA (p138)
Beguiling Roman city, superb views and a window on Roman Africa

LE KEF (p142)
Cobbled winding streets, blue shutters, expansive views and people-watching

TOZEUR (p223)
Desert oasis, massive palm groves and exceptional architecture; a gateway to the Sahara

MEDITERRANEAN SEA

MEDITERRANEAN SEA

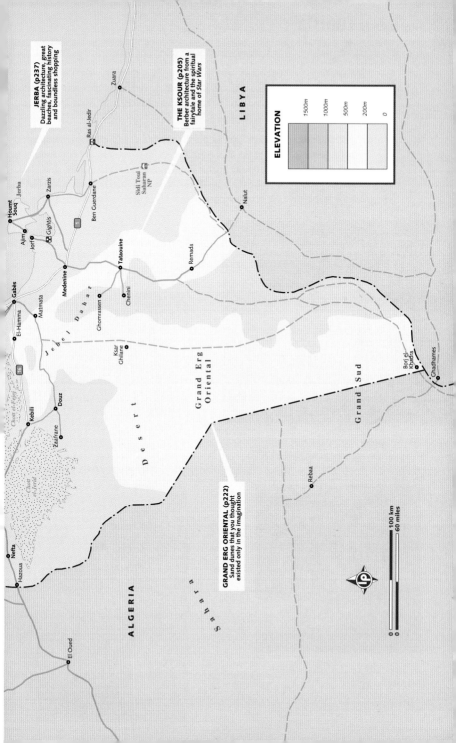

JERBA (p237)
Dazzling architecture, great beaches, fascinating history and boundless shopping

THE KSOUR (p205)
Berber architecture from a fairytale and the spiritual home of *Star Wars*

GRAND ERG ORIENTAL (p222)
Sand dunes that you thought existed only in the imagination

ELEVATION

	1500m
	1000m
	500m
	200m
	0

LIBYA

ALGERIA

Zuara
Ras al-Jedir
Houmt Souq
Jerba
Zarzis
Ajim
Jorf
Gightis
Ben Guerdane
Sidi Toui Saharan NP
Nalut
Gabès
Medenine
Tataouine
Remada
Matmata
El-Hamma
Chenini
Ghomrassen
Jebel Dahar
Kebili
Douz
Ksar Ghilane
Grand Erg Oriental
Zaafrane
Nefta
Hazoua
Chott el-Jerid
El Oued
Desert Sahara
Rebaa
Borj el Khadra
Grand Sud
Ghadhames

0   100 km
0   60 miles

Apart from being home to wonderfully friendly people, Tunisia is a world of ancient cities, idyllic beaches and just about everything in between. Medinas are filled with the abundant architectural heritage of Islam, while the Sahara here is stunning and accessible.

In addition to the highlights on these pages, don't miss the superb beaches at **Cap Serrat** (p123) and **Sidi Ali el-Mekki** (p120), the underground Roman ruins at **Bulla Regia** (p131) and the enchanting medinas of **Mahdia** (p183) and **Sfax** (p186). Inland, you'll find the troglodyte homes and *Star Wars* settings of **Matmata** (p201) and the otherwordly Berber architecture of **the Ksour** (p205).

DAMIEN SIMONIS

See Tunisia's finest example of Islamic military architecture, the Monastir Ribat (p170)

Meet local Berber people – this woman stands outside a traditional ksar in Chenini (p210)

FRANCES LINZEE GORD

SCOTT DARSNEY

Be awestruck by El-Jem's colosseum (p181)

CHRISTOPHER WOOD

Wander past the fishing boats at Bizerte's old port (p117)

Explore the distinctive remains of the Ksar Megabla (p207) in Tataouine

ADRIEN VADROT

DAMIEN SIMONIS

Admire intricate architecture in Kairouan's medina (p175)

Sit back and watch the Gulf of Tunis from Sidi Bou Saïd (p90), a beautiful village dressed in white

GEOFF STRINGER

Come face to face with Berber history in the old walled town of Tamerza (p229)

Take up a position at the Capitol for a view over the old Roman city of Dougga (p138)

Touch the past at the fantastic Bardo Museum (p56) in Tunis

Trek through sand dunes in the Grand Erg Oriental (p219)

Getting Started

Tunisia is well accustomed to tourists and an easy destination to visit, meaning that rather than chasing visas and trying to circumvent other bureaucratic obstacles before you leave, most of your predeparture planning will be spent tracking down a good read or surfing websites to gain an insight into what you can look forward to.

Tunisia is the sort of country where you can soak up your one week of sun in luxury or rough it without spending much money at all; see p6 and p13 for help in planning your itinerary.

WHEN TO GO

In some ways, the choice of when to go is easy. If you're having visions of lying on a beach, the time to visit is July and August when hot sun is guaranteed and cheap European airfare and accommodation packages are on offer in just about every European travel agency. The benefit of visiting at this time is obvious – a memorable Mediterranean beach holiday without European prices. This is when the coastal towns are at their liveliest. It's also when the Tunisian tourist authorities kick into action with a number of superb festivals in old Roman sites; see p17 and p257 for more details.

See Climate Charts (p254) for more information.

The downside of visiting in July and August is that you'll be sharing the beaches with about two million northern European holiday-makers. This is also when high-season prices kick in – fine if you're on a prebooked package but less so for independent travellers for whom rooms can be hard to find, and public transport can get packed out. In July and August, the soaring temperatures also mean that exploring the Sahara desert is really only possible for an overnight expedition.

DON'T LEAVE HOME WITHOUT...

Pack lightly, especially if you don't plan to leave the beach. Apart from anything else, you'll then have room for all the carpets, *sheeshas* (water pipes) and miniature bird cages that you'll surely buy during your stay.

There are some other essential (and some not-so-essential) items that you could consider:

- a small size-three football – a great way to meet local kids (and their families);
- a Swiss Army knife with a bottle and/or can opener in case you buy alcohol from a supermarket and want to actually drink it;
- a hat, sunglasses and sunscreen – essential on the beach and in the Sahara;
- a jacket in winter when even the Sahara can get cold, especially at night;
- a small sewing kit – useful for emergency repairs to backpacks stretched to bursting by souvenir shopping;
- a non-hotmail email address (see p259);
- a small cool pack – wine, beer and bottled water are all much cheaper (and warmer) in supermarkets;
- a sense of perspective – persistent shopkeepers are just trying to make a living and can actually be nice people.

Tampons are usually only found in supermarkets, but most other toiletries are widely available. Condoms are cheap and readily available over the counter at pharmacies.

LONELY PLANET INDEX

Litre of petrol 430 mills

Litre of bottled water
300 mills (supermarkets)
TD0.7-1 (everywhere else)

Beer (the very drinkable
local Celtia brew) TD1.5-2

Souvenir T-shirt TD5

Street treat (the reflective
pleasure of smoking the
sheesha) TD1-2

If your holidays fall at the right time and you're travelling independently, one of the best times to visit is between mid-March and mid-May when the spring days are pleasantly warm and the countryside is at its prettiest after the winter rains. November is the best time for visiting the Saharan south – longer expeditions deep into the desert are possible, the date harvest (which produces some of the best dates in the world) has just finished, prices are generally cheaper and Douz and Tozeur host back-to-back desert festivals (see p257 for more details).

For a detailed summary of what is meant throughout the book by high and low season, see p251.

COSTS & MONEY

Tunisia is an inexpensive country for Western visitors.

If you're counting your dinars, you can get by on TD15 to TD20 a day. This would involve staying in hostels or budget hotels, eating at cheap local restaurants and travelling only every few days. For some of you that will be more of a survival exercise than a holiday, while no doubt others will see it as a badge of honour to do it for less.

The minimum that mid-range travellers can get by on is about TD40 a day. This is enough to get yourself a comfortable room, travel around and enjoy a glass of wine with your evening meal. For TD60 a day, you'll have enough in reserve for the occasional blow-out. Adding a carpet purchase can push it out towards TD80 per day, depending on how long you stay.

It is, of course, possible to spend TD150 on a single night's luxury accommodation.

If you've already paid for a package at a resort, you'll only have to pay for things like meals, excursions, souvenirs and the occasional taxi.

TRAVEL LITERATURE

The following travel writing gives a good sense of what Tunisia's all about; it's ideal for predeparture planning or something to read on the beach.

The Muqaddimah, by Ibn Khaldun, is a masterpiece; this prolific 15th-century traveller ranges across North Africa (including a prolonged stay in Tunisia) with a sharp eye, accessible writing and remarkably sympathetic observations for his time.

Daniel Bruun's *The Cave Dwellers of Southern Tunisia: Recollections of a Sojourn with the Khalifa of Matmata* is a window on a forgotten world with its idiosyncratic portrait of Berber Tunisia before the tourists arrived.

Norman Douglas' *Fountains in the Sand* is a typical stiff-upper-lip, colonial account of a 1912 journey through southwestern Tunisia; entertaining enough as long as you can ignore his intolerance of all things Tunisian.

Among the Faithful, by Dahris Martin, offers a unique portrait of Kairouan by a young American woman who lived there in the 1920s; easy to read and sympathetic.

Behind Closed Doors: Women's Oral Narratives in Tunisia, by Monia Hajaiej, is a precious insight into the lives of Tunisian women from a local female perspective; this is less travellers' stories than essential reading.

Barnaby Rogerson's *A Traveller's History of North Africa* includes some good essays on the history of Tunisia placed within the wider North African context.

HOW MUCH?

Hammam from TD2
(basic scrub)

International newspapers
TD2-6

Bottle of Tunisian wine
from TD4 (supermarkets)
from TD9 (restaurants)

Entry ticket to ancient
sites TD1.1 (most)
TD5.4 (the biggies)

Sunset over the Mediteranean or Sahara – money
can't buy

TOP 10S
ARCHITECTURAL TREASURES

- Punic city of Kerkouane (p108)
  The best preserved and most
  evocative of the Punic sites

- Roman city of Dougga (p138)
  Perched on a hilltop, fascinating
  like no other Roman city

- Great Mosque of Kairouan (p175)
  Austere Aghlabid exterior and
  extravagant prayer hall

- Ksar Ouled Soltane (p211)
  The best of the fantastical fortified
  granary stores of the Berbers

- Medina at Sfax (p189)
  The medina least touched by tourism
  and built according to classic medina layout

- Roman Colosseum at El-Jem (p181)
  An astonishing monument to
  pleasure rising up from the plains

- Ribat at Monastir (p170)
  The best of Tunisia's fortresses and
  favourite of film directors

- Village of Chenini (p210)
  Crumbling hilltop Berber village
  built into the mountain

- Troglodyte houses, Matmata (p202)
  Underground Berber houses in a
  real-life *Star Wars* set

- Ville nouvelle of Tunis (p73)
  Elegant French-Tunisian fusion with
  extravagant neo-classical façades

RELAXING EXPERIENCES

- Watching the sunset from the Guellala
  Mosque on the island of Jerba (p247)

- Leaving Kairouan without having
  purchased a carpet (p179)

- Stretching out on the sand under the
  stars in the Sahara desert (p222)

- Overlooking the Mediterranean in
  Sidi Bou Saïd (p90)

- Contemplating the sunset at the remote
  Roman city of Haidra (p155)

- Sipping a coffee in the Place du
  Caire in Mahdia (p183)

- Watching the sunset from the sand
  dunes and *Star Wars* sets at Ong Jemal (p230)

- Sipping your wine in a Parisian-style
  pavement café in cosmopolitan Tunis (p77)

- Downing a beer in the underground *Star
  Wars* bar in Matmata (p201)

- Soaking in the hot springs at Ksar Ghilane
  after your first ride on a camel (p222)

TUNISIAN MUSIC CDS

- Anouar Brahem Trio – *Le Pas du Chat
  Noir* (2002) Soulful oud (lute) with
  piano and accordion

- Dhaffer Youssef – *Electric Sufi* (2002)
  Contemporary jazz with traditional
  instruments and resonant voice

- Lotfi Bouchnak – *Live in Berlin* (2002)
  Good recording by one of the old-school
  malouf singers

- Latifa – *Mawkatash: Love Songs* (2000)
  A good introduction to arguably Tunisia's
  foremost diva

- Sonia M'Barek – *Takht* (1999) A classic of
  modern *malouf* with great vocals backed
  by terrific ensemble

- Anouar Brahem Trio – *Astrakan Café* (2000)
  Oud, *bendir* (wooden tambourine) and *dar
  bouka* (clay drum)

- Amina – *Nomad: The Best of Amina* (2003)
  Techno and electronica meets Arab pop by
  one of Tunisia's most popular female singers

- Ghalia Benali & Timnaa – *Wild Harissa* (2002)
  Seductive CD accessible to Western ears and
  with extraordinary voice

- *La Sulamiyya: Chants Soufi de Tunis* (1999)
  Sombre recording by one of Tunisia's best
  Sufi ensembles

- *Tunisie: Anthologie du Malouf* (1993) The five-
  CD set is perfect for lovers of *malouf*; one CD
  is enough for those who just want a taste

Paul Theroux's *The Pillars of Hercules* contains a frustratingly brief chapter on Tunisia; his stories include an amusing encounter with a carpet tout, as well as descriptions of his visit to Sfax and the Kerkennah Islands.

Michael Palin's *Sahara* is more entertaining than in-depth and covers, without Theroux's grumpiness, Jerba, Matmata, El-Jem, Sousse and Sidi Bou Saïd, including some old movie sets from *Monty Python's Life of Brian*.

Robert D Kaplan's *Mediterranean Winter: The Pleasures of History and Landscape in Tunisia, Sicily, Dalmatia, and Greece* was due for release in 2004; it should be good for placing Tunisia within its historical Mediterranean perspective.

INTERNET RESOURCES

The Internet is a great place to find out more about Tunisia, and many of the hotels in Tunisia now have email addresses and/or websites. Remember, though, that information is closely monitored by the Tunisian government.

Adventures of Tunisia (http://lexicorient.com/tunisia/index.htm) A comprehensive site with information and photos for over 100 Tunisian destinations.

Film Scouts (www.filmscouts.com/scripts/matinee.cfm?Film=eng-pat&File=locatns) A good summary of Tunisian sites used in filming *The English Patient*.

Lonely Planet (www.lonelyplanet.com) Succinct summaries on travel in Tunisia, postcards from other travellers and the Thorn Tree bulletin board.

Travel & Tourism Guide to Tunisia (www.tourismtunisia.com) Good website of the Tunisian National Tourist Office; includes festival dates, hotel details and destination summaries.

Tunisia Online (www.tunisiaonline.com) Government-run site with good sections on the environment, women in Tunisia, history and tourism as well as Tunisian news in English, French and Arabic.

University of Pennsylvania Tunisia Page (www.sas.upenn.edu/African_Studies/Country _Specific/Tunisia.html) An extensive set of links to web pages about Tunisia from academic and human rights sites to travel information and photos.

Itineraries

CLASSIC ROUTES

MOSQUES, MEDINAS & THE COLOSSEUM · 12 days / Tunis to Sfax

Tunis (p63) is a great place to start your sojourn, with the exceptional **Bardo Museum** (p56) and World Heritage–listed **medina** (p67). This laid-back city with its cafés and sophisticated ville nouvelle is a good base for day trips to the ruins of **Carthage** (p84) and the enchanting white village of **Sidi Bou Saïd** (p90); staying at the latter is a great alternative. Allow three to four days in and around Tunis, then head south to **Sousse** (p160) where the medina hosts some of Tunisia's finest architecture as well as a buzzing ville nouvelle stretched along a popular beach. You can use Sousse as a base for day trips to **Monastir** (p170) with its superb *ribat* (fortified monastery) and mausoleum to Habib Bourguiba; **Kairouan** (p173), with its splendid Islamic architecture; and the incredible Roman colosseum at **El-Jem** (p181). Alternatively, you can stay overnight or longer at any of these towns. **Mahdia** (p183) provides the perfect antidote to the clamour of the resorts and larger towns and is definitely worth at least an overnight stay. Further down the coast, **Sfax** (p186) is home to Tunisia's most authentic medina and a reminder of what the other coastal towns must have been like before the tourists arrived.

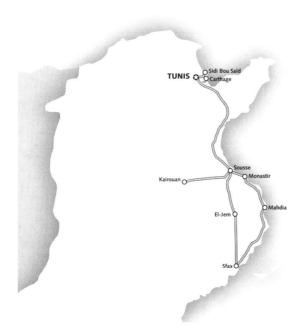

This 300km route wends its way from Tunisia's largest city to its second largest, past an astounding array of architectural forms and fascinating ruins. It takes between 10 days and two weeks.

JERBA, BERBERS & THE SAHARA   10 days / Jerba to Ong Jemal

The island of **Jerba** (p237) is home to distinctive and whitewashed fortress-like architecture (see the boxed text, p242) which you could easily spend a couple of days exploring. **Houmt Souq** (p240) is a wonderful town with covered souqs, good restaurants and vine-covered squares, not to mention accommodation in enchanting restored *funduqs* (inns; p243), so factor in at least one (preferably more) nights sleeping here. Sidi Mahres beach (p248) on the island's east coast is a great place to relax for a couple of days.

Jerba's a good base for exploring the south, including the underground Berber houses at **Matmata** (p201) and the picturesque Arab-Berber **ksour district** (p205) set in the heart of *Star Wars* country around Tataouine. If you devote three or four days, exploring each of these areas more fully carries rich rewards, not least among them the stunning abandoned Berber villages of **Chenini** and **Douiret** (p210) and the improbable **Ksar Ouled Soltane** (p211). From anywhere around here and with your own 4WD vehicle, you can push south to **Ksar Ghilane** (p222) on the edge of the **Grand Erg Oriental** (p214) with its incomprehensible seas of sand dunes, although the best places from which to launch a Saharan expedition are the laid-back town of **Douz** (p215) or **Tozeur** (p223), both of which are set amid enormous palm groves. Tozeur is also a good launching pad for the exploration of the *Star Wars* Mos Espa set at **Ong Jemal** (p230) or the **oasis villages** (p223) close to the Algerian border.

It takes a week or two to travel the 540km from the sunny coast to the desert interior via Berber villages, oasis towns and seas of sand dunes.

ROADS LESS TRAVELLED

NORTHERN LANDSCAPES   10 days / Bizerte to Haidra

It's difficult to get off the beaten track in a country the size of Tunisia, but it is possible. Your best chance is an exploration of the north, with its rugged coastline, lush mountains and relatively few foreign visitors. You could start your journey in **Bizerte** (p115), a large town with an old-world feel, before moving on (preferably not at weekends) to the largely empty and quite beautiful beaches at **Sidi Ali el-Mekki** (p120), **Raf Raf** (p120) and **Cap Serrat** (p123). **Tabarka** (p123), another chilled, café-filled town that escapes the crowds (except during its many wonderful music festivals), is a good place to break the journey. Then push up into the hills to the seductive charms of **Ain Draham** (p128), deep in the forests of the Kroumirie Mountains. To get further away from it all, go trekking (p128 and p253) from Ain Draham in the green, green hills. On your way south, spend as long as you can at charming and evocative **Le Kef** (p142). South into Tunisia's central plains, there are a few opportunities to leave the crowds behind; try the historically significant (see p24) and spectacular natural fortress of **Jugurtha's Table** (p157) and the remote Roman site of **Haidra** (p155). Covering all these sites could stretch from one to two weeks depending how long you laze on the beach or lose yourself in the hills.

This route takes you away from the crowds to quiet beaches, forested mountains and remote archaeological sites. It will take a week or two, and covers 430km.

TAILORED TRIPS

THE BEST TUNISIAN BEACHES

You'd need to work harder than a beach lover should to see all of Tunisia's best beaches on one trip.

On the northern coast, **Cap Serrat** (p123) is the pick with a glorious sandy bay that's all but deserted much of the time. Another good choice in the same area is **Montazah Beach** (p125) at Tabarka, with a backdrop of densely wooded mountains. Other northern beaches worth seeking out are at **Raf Raf** (p120) and **Sidi Ali el-Mekki** (p120).

On the central coast, it's hard to go past the busy beach at **Hammamet** (p95); it's not hard to see why they built the resorts here. Nearby **Nabeul** (p101) is similarly good. **Mansourah Beach** (p106) at Kélibia is long and lovely. Sousse's **Boujaffar Beach** (p165) is reclaimed by locals in the evening when the whole world comes out to play, while for a slightly different experience, the **Monastir City Beach** (p172) lets you emerge from the waves to the sight of Tunisia's most imposing *ribat*. Basically, anywhere along this coast is a good spot to lay out your towel.

There are few better beaches than **Sidi Mahres Beach** (p248) with its great sweeps of sand along the east coast of the delightful island of Jerba.

TUNISIA FOR KIDS

Tunisia has a wealth of activities for kids (see also p253). Starting from Tozeur, swimming at the waterfalls in the otherwise barren landscape around **Tamerza** (p229) is great fun, while exploring an old *Star Wars* set amid the sand dunes of **Ong Jemal** (p230) will win smiles of recognition and incredulity. Chances are also that they'll never forget riding a camel in the **Sahara desert** (p222). While you're exploring the south, paddling in the hot springs at **Ksar Ghilane** (p222) is the kind of deep-desert experience of which dreams are made, while going underground in search of *Star Wars* landmarks in **Matmata** (p201) or being led around the fairytale hilltop Berber village of **Chenini** (p210) by a local child guide is a great way to see Tunisia through a child's eyes. The nearby ksour (p208) look like they could have been conceived by a playful, childlike imagination.

On your way north, detour to **Jerba** to the impressive models of the Museum of Guellala (p247), while *The Thousand and One Nights* will come alive under the guidance of the mischievous Ali Baba (p247). The otherwise unspectacular **Kerkennah Islands** (p192) have shallow waters like a massive baby pool. The *ribat* at **Monastir** (p170) is ripe for exploring with its corridors, staircases and cubbyholes, as is the colosseum at **El-Jem** (p181).

For information about activities for children in Tunis, see p75.

ROMAN & PHOENICIAN TUNISIA

Any tour of Tunisia's ancient sites must start at **Carthage** (p84); the setting in the northern suburbs of Tunis overlooking the Mediterranean is delightful. From there you can branch out onto the Cap Bon Peninsula to the remote Punic city of **Kerkouane** (p108) – evocative, relatively intact and not to be missed. Turn your attention to the Romans and head west into the Roman heartland of the Tell, where you'll find one of Rome's most unusual legacies – **Dougga** (p138) – with the usual ordered Roman town planning replaced by ruins twisting around the hill. A detour to the underground Roman villas of Bulla Regia (p131) is definitely worth the effort. Further to the south, **Sbeitla (Sufetula)** (p152) is also well preserved (as it's best in the early morning light, an overnight stay is recommended). Its temples are among the finest in North Africa.

Among the highlights of what remains, stop off at the minor site of **Cillium** near Kasserine (p154) and then head out to the remote and charming site of **Haidra** (p155) before continuing your loop back to the north with a stop in **Mactaris** (p150) on the way. Because transport is not particularly frequent in Tunisia's Central West, the above itinerary could take two weeks, although with your own car, a week to 10 days is possible, depending on your level of interest.

FOLLOWING THE FESTIVALS

Music lovers should definitely plan to be in Tunisia in summer, although you'd need to stick around for a couple of months to catch everything. Tabarka is the hub of the music festival calendar with the **Rai Festival** (p126) in late June showcasing the best of rai from just across the border, followed soon after by the world renowned **Tabarka International Jazz Festival** (p126) in July. By the middle of July, the **El-Jem International Symphonic Music Festival** (p182) is underway with classical music finding its atmospheric home in the Roman colosseum at El-Jem. Around the same time, the **Festival of Malouf** (p257) at Testour showcases Tunisia's most enduring religious traditions, while there's no better place to watch classical drama than the Roman theatres of Carthage and Dougga for the **International Festival of Carthage**. It's followed soon after by the **Hammamet International Festival** (p98) with a mix of international film, music and theatre groups. If you're still around, Tabarka again takes centre stage with a **World Music Festival** (p126) at the end of August, followed by the **Festival of Latin Music** (p126) in early September.

If you've missed all of this, November is the best time to visit the south when Douz hosts the **Sahara Festival** (p217), a local festival that pre-dates tourism, followed almost immediately by the **Oasis Festival** (p257) in Tozeur.

Precise dates change from year to year so check out the ONTT's website (www.tourism tunisia.com/culture/festivals). For a fuller listing of festivals, see p257.

STAR WARS – A DEVOTEE'S GUIDE

Southern Tunisia is the country's *Star Wars* heartland, having provided the backdrop to the canon with its strange podlike architecture, custom-built sets and wild desert-scapes. You could conceivably see all these sites in a week to 10 days.

Use Tozeur as a base for visiting **Ong Jemal** (p230), 30km northwest of town: it was Darth Maul's lookout in *The Phantom Menace,* and the place where he tussled with Qui-Gon. Nearby **Mos Espa** (p230) is a weird and wonderful village construct in the middle of the desert used for the prequel films. **Sidi Bouhlel**, east of Tozeur on the edge of Chott el-Jerid, has been nicknamed Star Wars Canyon; it's where jawas parked their sand-crawlers, R2D2 trundled plaintively along, Luke was attacked by Tusken raiders, and Ben and Luke overlooked Mos Eisley. Tour operators in nearby Tozeur (p226) can help you track it down. West of Nefta, a stretch of the **Chott el-Jerid** (p225) saw Luke contemplate two suns while standing soulfully at the edge of a crater. The landscape around its fringes doubled as Junland Wastes populated by Krayt dragons and sand people. Ask at the syndicat d'initiative in Nefta (p230) for directions.

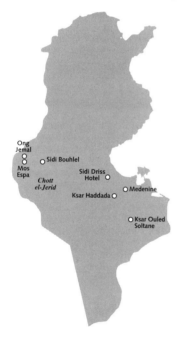

Further east, the famous **Sidi Driss Hotel** (p203) in Matmata is one of the best sites, having been used in all four movies, including for interior shots of the Lars family homestead in *Star Wars*; the dining room is where Luke tucked into blue milkshakes and went head to head over the harvest with his Uncle Owen. Anakin Skywalker's *Phantom Menace* slave-quarters home is off bustling av 7 Novembre in **Medenine** (p212), while the fabulous **Ksar Haddada** (p208) was the location for the Mos Espa slave quarters and is where Qui-Gon learned the truth about Anakin's parentage in *The Phantom Menace.* South of Tataouine, **Ksar Ouled Soltane** (p211) doubled as more evocative and easily recognisable slave quarters.

Among the many websites detailing *Star Wars* locations, one of the best is Star Wars Traveller (www.toysrgus.com/travel/tunisia.html), while the UK-based Tataouine Tours (www.tataouinetours.com) specialises in *Star Wars* tours to Tunisia.

The Authors

ANTHONY HAM   Coordinating Author, Central West & the Tell, Kairouan & the Central Coast, Southern Tunisia, Jerba

Anthony worked as a refugee lawyer in Australia for three years, during which time he represented asylum seekers from across the Middle East and Africa and completed a Masters degree in Middle Eastern politics. Tiring of daily battles with a mean-spirited Australian government, he set off to write and photograph his way around the world. He has travelled extensively throughout Africa, and wrote Lonely Planet's guide to neighbouring *Libya*. Based in Madrid, he spends part of every year in North and West Africa, and is writing a book about the Sahara.

My Favourite Trip

Jerba has something special – it's a place of beauty and refuge like nowhere else in Tunisia. The child in me is drawn again and again to the ksour around Tataouine. Next stop Douz, a laid-back and hospitable desert town, the perfect place to organise my trip into the Sahara (especially Ksar Ghilane and the Grand Erg Oriental). There's nothing comparable to watching the sunset from high on a sand dune, enveloped in silence. Tozeur, with its old town and massive *palmeraie* (palm grove), would also be high on my list. Then I'd work my way north (via El-Jem, Mahdia, Kairouan and Le Kef) to take in any of Tabarka's great music festivals.

ABIGAIL HOLE   Tunis, Cap Bon, Northern Tunisia, Central West & the Tell

Abigail is from London and worked in publishing in London and Hong Kong before joining Lonely Planet, first as an editor and then as a full-time writer. Shortly after spending months in Africa researching Mali, Mauritania, Egypt and Tunisia for Lonely Planet's *Africa on a Shoestring*, she returned to Tunisia to research this book, where she diligently checked out the warmth of the sea and the wondrous white-sand beaches, and danced badly at brilliant music festivals.

My Favourite Trip

I'd start in peaceful, perfect Sidi Bou Saïd, tearing myself away from the blue shutters and bougainvillea to travel north to Bizerte, an unspoilt old port with a long balmy corniche for evening promenading. Next I'd go west, and camp out at the magical little beach at Cap Serrat for a couple of days or weeks. I'd make it to laid-back Tabarka in time for one of the music festivals, then head up into the hills around Ain Draham. A journey across to castle-crowned Le Kef would allow a stop to see the underground villas of Bulla Regia. After wandering around the alleys of Le Kef long enough to become a local character, I'd head back to Tunis, not missing the Roman city of Dougga at dusk on the way.

CONTRIBUTING AUTHORS

Rafik Tlatli wrote the Food & Drink chapter. Rafik is the head chef and hotelier of Hotel Les Jasmins and Restaurant Slovenia in Nabeul. He has written *Saveurs de Tunisie*, *Delice de Tunisie* and many books of recipes, and made regular radio and TV broadcasts on cooking in France, Italy and Russia as well as Tunisia. He is the founder and president of the national association of chefs in Cap Bon. Rafik has organised a master chef competition in Tunis for the past 10 years, an annual gastronomic conference in Tunis since 1998, and has also run seminars on Tunisian cuisine in countries ranging from Japan to Sweden.

Dr Caroline Evans wrote the Health chapter. Having studied medicine at the University of London, Caroline completed general practice training in Cambridge. She is the medical adviser to Nomad Travel Clinic, a private travel-health clinic in London, and is also a GP specialising in travel medicine. Caroline has acted as expedition doctor for Raleigh International and Coral Cay expeditions.

Snapshot

Tunisia is an ancient land moving to a very modern beat; a crossroads of civilisations where the great questions of the new millennium are hotly debated. Tunisians inhabit many worlds, belonging as much to the pleasure-filled Mediterranean as to Africa, the Middle East and the world of Islam.

Expect frequent conversations about the 'war on terror' and its many offshoots. In an age of media soundbites and cultural stereotypes, such conversations can go a long way towards ameliorating the misunderstandings that abound about Islam and about the West. Tunisians are well aware (and appalled) that Islam has been typecast as a result of so-called fanatics out to terrorise the West, particularly since 11 September 2001 – the vast majority of Tunisians abhor terrorism as much as anyone. Further, and not without some justification, if the West is offended by the anti-Western rhetoric of the radical minority, many Muslims see Western policies, particularly the hostility towards Iraq and the Palestinians, and support for Israel, as a direct attack on Islam.

It's worth remembering that any hostility is overwhelmingly directed at Western governments. Individuals are far more likely to be overwhelmed by hospitality, and rarely is a Western visitor to Tunisia judged on the basis of his or her nationality or religion.

If the West's understanding of Islam and Muslims is deeply flawed, so too is the understanding many Muslims have of the West, particularly the freedoms enjoyed by women. Fed on a satellite diet of Hollywood promiscuity, some Tunisian men are genuinely surprised that female tourists don't want to sleep with them.

Public debate doesn't extend to domestic politics; don't expect Tunisians to be candid about such matters unless you're in the company of trusted friends. With just two presidents, routinely elected with over 99% of the vote, in almost 50 years of independent history, Tunisia is not a place where people are free to speak their minds. However, given the relative openness and prosperity in other areas of Tunisian life, many people grudgingly accept this sequestration of freedoms as a necessary trade-off in avoiding the fates of their neighbours – Algeria's civil war and Libya's erstwhile pariah status.

Tunisia's economic wellbeing remains at once dependent upon and vulnerable to the vagaries of the outside world; the economy is heavily reliant on tourism and remittances from nationals working abroad. A job in Europe is a prize sought by many; throughout your stay you'll be asked almost as often about the job prospects in your country as you'll see Tunisians home for the holidays and driving around in French-licensed cars.

That said, the Tunisian economy is very much on the upswing, with modern infrastructure, a growing private sector and strong links to Europe. Even as they keep one eye on Europe in case opportunity presents (the queue at the French embassy in Tunis is invariably long), Tunisians are proud of their modern, stable and self-consciously secular country.

FAST FACTS

Population: 10.012 million

Unemployment: 15.6%

Inflation: 4%

GDP per capita: US$6363

There are 70 doctors and 286 nurses per 100,000 people compared with 303 and 497 in France

Life expectancy for Tunisian women is 75 years (up from 51 years in 1966); men can expect to live 72 years (around 10 years less than French women and men)

Once the breadbasket of Rome, Tunisia now has to import almost 40% of its food

The main crops are wheat, barley, maize, sorghum, dates, olives and oranges

Petrol and petroleum products account for about 25% of Tunisian exports

Mahdia was used to film the Tobruk scenes of *The English Patient*

History

Tunisia is a land where the great sweeps of history endure. Some of history's greatest empires have come, gone and left their mark, leaving clear footprints that are still visible to the modern visitor. Tunisia was home to the mighty city-state of Carthage which flourished and then yielded to its archenemy Rome. Much later, it lay in the path of the conquering armies of Islam who swept aside the old order and drew Tunisia into the Arab sphere of influence. Later still, the French joined the European scramble for African possessions and made Tunisia a colony before acceding to the voice of a people clamouring for independence. The empires of legend gave way to home-grown leaders of renown; in almost 50 years as an independent state, Tunisia has had just two presidents – Habib Bourguiba and Ben Ali – whose stamp upon modern Tunisia is difficult to overstate. And through it all, Tunisia's oldest inhabitants – the Berbers – have endured, watching invasion follow conquest, resisting the occupation of their land. If the Berbers of Tunisia tell you that they've been here for a long time, believe them because they are the only witnesses to the whole of Tunisia's epic history. In short, they've seen it all.

The boundaries of modern Tunisia are, apart from the Sahara, remarkably similar to those ruled by Carthage 2500 years ago.

FIRST PEOPLES

A mere 200,000 years ago, stone-age cultures eked out an existence using primitive stone tools near the southern oasis town of Kélibia, although you won't see any evidence of this when you visit. These were the days when the Sahara was covered in forest, scrub and savannah grasses – a picture that defies comprehension if you find yourself standing too far south of Douz in mid-August.

Some 8000 years ago, at the end of the last Ice Age, the rains stopped and the Sahara began to dry out, effectively cutting Tunisia off from the rest of Africa. People began arriving from the east; among the most significant were the Capsians. Named after finds of finely sculpted stone and bone implements near the city of Gafsa (ancient Capsa), the Capsian people lived in southern Tunisia until about 4500 BC. Some mosaics from ancient Capsa are on display in the museum in Gafsa (see p233). Waves of migration from southern Europe continued until around 2500 BC.

It is from these Neolithic peoples that the Berbers are thought to descend.

THE RISE & FALL OF CARTHAGE

The name that looms largest in Tunisian history is Carthage. Now a well-heeled northern suburb of Tunis but still an evocative site (see p84), Carthage was once a Phoenician trading post that emerged to dominate the western Mediterranean in the 6th century BC.

The Phoenicians were first drawn to the Tunisian coast in search of staging posts along the trade route between their mother city of Tyre (in modern Lebanon) and the silver mines of southern Spain. Their first settlement in Tunisia was at Utica, about 35km north of Tunis, in 1101 BC – the ruins of this landmark port are still visible today (see p120). Utica

1101 BC	814 BC
Phoenicians found first settlement in Tunisia at Utica	City of Carthage founded by Phoenicians

soon became one of a chain of port settlements that stretched the length of the North African coast. They included Hadrumètum (Sousse), Hippo Diarrhytus (Bizerte) and Thrabaka (Tabarka).

Carthage was founded in 814 BC by the Phoenician queen Elissa (Dido), whose story is told in the city's elaborate foundation myth (see the boxed text, p86). A reaction to the growing Greek presence in the region, Carthage was intended as the start of a more permanent Phoenician presence in Tunisia.

While Tyre suffered at the hands of the Assyrians in the 7th and 6th centuries BC, Carthage went from strength to strength. By the end of the 6th century BC it had become the main power in the western Mediterranean, controlling the North African coast from Tripolitania (western Libya) to the Atlantic and with colonies in the Balearic Islands, Corsica, Malta, Sardinia and Sicily.

Phoenician civilisation in North Africa came to be called 'Punic', a derivation of both the Latin *Punicus* and Greek *Phoinix*. The Punic city of Carthage rapidly grew into the metropolis of the Phoenician world, recording an astonishing population of around 500,000 at its peak. Its wealth was protected by a powerful navy who patrolled one of the greatest commercial empires in world history. During the 5th and 4th centuries BC, Carthage turned its attentions to expanding its empire in Africa, carving out a territory that ran from Tabarka in the northwest to Sfax in the southeast. This new territory included the fertile lands of the Cap Bon Peninsula and the Medjerda Valley, supplying Carthage with a large agricultural surplus to export.

It was inevitable that this regional primacy would lead to conflict with the other great powers of the Mediterranean; first Greece and then Rome. Carthage fought numerous wars with the Greeks over Sicily, just 80km northeast of Carthage, most notably in 310 BC. By the time the Carthaginians finally took control of the island in the middle of the 3rd century BC, they found themselves squaring off against an expansionist Rome.

The scene was set for the first of the Punic Wars that would preoccupy the two powers for the next 100 years. Rome launched the first war in 263 BC with a campaign to win control of Sicily. Roman successes on land and the supremacy of Carthage's navy ensured a stalemate that dragged on for the next 20 years.

Rome finally secured a breakthrough when its fledgling navy destroyed the Carthaginian fleet off Trapani (eastern Sicily) in 242 BC. Navyless and close to broke, Carthage was forced to accept Roman terms and abandon Sicily, followed by Sardinia and Corsica in 238 BC. Trouble at home grew as unpaid mercenaries revolted, sparking a bitter conflict, the savagery of which inspired Gustave Flaubert's over-the-top novel *Salammbô* (1862).

Carthage's defeat in the Battle of Zama meant that it again had to relinquish its overseas territories. Over the next 50 years it nonetheless reestablished itself as a commercial centre despite losing much of its former territory in Africa to the Numidian king Massinissa, whose cavalry had fought for the Romans alongside Scipio at Zama (see the boxed text, next page). The city's revival fostered increasing unease in Rome. Whipped up by men like Cato the Elder, an eminent statesman and writer, Rome launched the Third Punic War with the intention of settling the issue

Carthage, A History, by Serge Lancel, is a detailed but accessible history of the Punic state from its foundation to its ultimate destruction by Rome in 146 BC.

263–242 BC	218–202 BC
First Punic War between the Romans and the Phoenicians (Carthaginians)	Second Punic War; the glory years and decline of the Carthaginian general, Hannibal

HANNIBAL BARCA

Acclaimed by some as the finest military leader in history, the great Carthaginian general Hannibal Barca came within a whisker of erasing the emerging Roman Empire from the history books in the course of the Second Punic War (218–202 BC).

He was born in 247 BC, the son of Hamilcar Barca, Carthage's leading general during the First Punic War. The Carthaginian surrender that ended the war left Hamilcar thirsting for revenge.

Frustrated by Carthage's powerful merchant lobby, which preferred trade to war, Hamilcar established an alternative power base in Spain where he made the nine-year-old Hannibal swear an oath of eternal enmity to Rome at the altar of Carthage's great Temple of Baal.

Having assumed control of Carthaginian forces in Spain in 221 BC, Hannibal set off three years later at the head of an army of 90,000 infantry backed by 12,000 cavalry and 37 elephants. Hannibal's journey took him across hostile Gaul before an epic crossing of the Alps that saw him descend into the plains of northern Italy in the spring of 217 BC. Only 17 elephants survived the crossing, and his army had shrunk to just 23,000.

His finest hour came the following year at the Battle of Cannae (216 BC), where Hannibal virtually annihilated a Roman army of 80,000 despite being vastly outnumbered. His tactic of employing a 'soft centre' to his line, which lured the Romans forward into a trap, makes this one of the most studied battles in history.

Despite his success on the battlefield, he was unable to break Rome. More than a decade of hide-and-seek followed as Rome sought to contain Hannibal without engaging him in battle. Finally Rome sent Scipio Africanus to retake Spain and attack Carthage in 204 BC, forcing the recall of Hannibal from Italy. They met at the Battle of Zama (near Siliana) in 202 BC; it was Hannibal's only defeat.

After the war Hannibal moved briefly into politics before he was forced by a plot to flee. He spent the last years of his life touting his skills as a military adviser around the eastern fringes of the Roman Empire before committing suicide in 183 BC when he was betrayed to the Romans.

Hannibal remains a popular figure in Tunisian lore; his rugged features adorn the TD5 note.

once and for all. In 149 BC, the Roman army again landed in Utica and laid siege to Carthage for three years. When the city finally fell in 146 BC, the Romans showed no mercy. The city was utterly destroyed, the people sold into slavery and the site symbolically sprinkled with salt and damned forever.

The Carthaginians had been great traders and merchants, but they were also ruthless rulers who alienated the indigenous Berber peoples around them. It is often claimed that the Berbers learnt advanced agricultural methods from the Carthaginians but many were simply forced into the desert and mountain hinterland. It is unlikely that many mourned Carthage's demise.

Hannibal Barca
and the Punic Wars
(www.barca.fsnet.co.uk/)
Good historical site covering all things Carthaginian and the epic struggle between the Romans and the Punic armies led by Hannibal.

ROME – FROM NEGLECT TO FULL CONTROL

With Carthage in ruins and Roman expansionary priorities lying elsewhere, Rome seemed at a loss as to what to do with its new acquisition. It was happy to leave most of the country to the Numidians and doubtless they were in turn happy to be left alone after centuries of Carthaginian oppression. Under Massinissa, the Numidians had established a kingdom that stretched from western Algeria to Libya. Its major towns included

146 BC	44 BC
Carthage destroyed, sprinkled with salt and damned by the Romans who took control of Tunisia	Julius Caesar resettles Carthage as a Roman city

THE ORIGINS OF 'AFRICA'

Once the Romans had completed their destruction of Carthage, they looked around for a name for the territory they had acquired.

The search ended about 50km to the west, in the band of low hills running north from the Medjerda River between the towns of Membressa (modern Mejez el-Bab) and Matar (Mateur). This was the homeland of the Afri, a Berber tribe whose loyalty the Romans were keen to cultivate in their efforts to create a buffer against the Numidian kingdom further to the west.

The new province of Africa occupied the northeastern third of modern Tunisia. The name spread as the boundaries of Roman control were extended east and west along the north coast, until eventually the name became synonymous with the entire continent, which the Romans scarcely knew.

Sicca Veneria (Le Kef; p142), Thugga (Dougga; p138) and Vaga (Béja; p130). On Massinissa's death in 148 BC Rome attempted to cut the kingdom down to size by dividing it up between his three sons.

The tactic worked until the kingdom was reunited by Massinissa's grandson Jugurtha, whose massacre of a Roman company sparked a war from 112 to 105 BC. His mountain base at Jugurtha's Table (see p157) is still an impregnable natural fortress where the success of the resistance against the world's most powerful empire is more easy to understand. Jugurtha was eventually betrayed by his father-in-law, King Bocchus I of Mauretania, and captured.

Rome, benevolent as it saw itself to be, was prepared to give the Numidians another chance. It split the kingdom into a western half centred on Cirta Regia (in modern Algeria) and an eastern half based at Zama, near Siliana. The last of the Zama kings, Juba I, backed the wrong side in the Roman civil war (based on the power struggle between Julius Caesar and Pompey) and was trounced by Julius Caesar at the Battle of Thapsus in 46 BC.

Rome was now firmly in control of its African outpost and Roman settlement began in earnest. Julius Caesar re-established Carthage as a Roman city in 44 BC and it became the capital of the expanded colony of Africa Proconsularis.

By the 1st century AD, the wheat-growing plains of the Medjerda Valley and the Tell Plateau were supplying more than 60% of the Roman Empire's grain requirements. Africa also supplied the wild animals used in amphitheatre shows, as well as gold, olive oil, slaves, ivory, ostrich plumes and *garum* (a fishpaste delicacy). The great cities built by the Romans on the backs of this prosperity – Dougga (p138), Sufetula (p152), Thuburbo Majus (p146), Haidra (p155), Thysdrus (El-Jem; p181) with its enormous amphitheatre and Bulla Regia (p131) – are now among Tunisia's principal tourist attractions.

The Romans, smitten by the Tunisian coastline, also unwittingly started the trend towards Tunisia being a place of relaxation for sun-starved Europeans when they established a string of coastal colonies for army veterans. Berber communities prospered and some Berbers were granted Roman citizenship. It was these wealthy citizens who donated the monumental public buildings that graced the Roman cities of the region.

Rome's Africa colonies became so influential that Septimius Severus, from Leptis Magna and known as 'The Grim African', became emperor of Rome in AD 193.

AD 439–533	533–647
Decline of Rome and occupation of North Africa by the Vandals	Tunisia comes under renascent Byzantine Empire

THE VANDALS & THE BYZANTINES

By the beginning of the 5th century AD, Roman power was in terminal decline and the Vandal king Gaeseric (or Genseric), who had been busy marauding in southern Spain, decided that Rome's North African colonies were there for the taking. He set off across the Straits of Gibraltar in AD 429, bringing the entire Vandal people (about 80,000 men, women and children) with him in one of history's most astonishing invasions. Within 10 years, the Vandals had fought their way across to Carthage, which they made the capital of a short-lived empire.

The Vandals lived up to their reputation. They helped themselves to what they found, built no great monuments and left virtually no trace of their rule, which had accelerated North Africa's economic decline.

The Byzantine emperor Justinian, based in Constantinople (modern Istanbul), had in the meantime revived the eastern half of the Roman Empire and had similar plans for the western territories. His general Belisarius defeated the Vandals in AD 533, ushering in 150 years of Byzantine rule. Like most occupiers before them, the Byzantines lived in a state of constant siege, with Berber chiefs controlling the bulk of the country. They built with their customary zeal, however, and many of Tunisia's Roman sites feature later Byzantine modifications. Churches and forts, in particular, were added.

THE ARRIVAL OF ISLAM

In the early 7th century AD, the armies of the new religion of Islam (see p36 for more information about the origins of Islam) swept out from Arabia to irretrievably alter the face of North Africa. Islam's green banner was flying over Egypt by AD 640, and, soon after, Tripoli was in Muslim hands. The Arabs defeated the Byzantine armies (see p152) in Tunisia but largely withdrew with their spoils, allowing the Byzantines to hold on to their possessions in the north.

It was not until nearly 30 years later that Islamic rule was secured. For three years, beginning in AD 669, Okba ibn Nafaa al-Fihri swept across the top of the continent, stopping on the way to establish Qayrawan (Kairouan), Islam's first great city in the Maghreb and still one of the holiest cities of Islam (see p173).

The Berbers adopted the religion of the invaders readily enough but did not accept Arab rule, and in AD 683 the Arabs were forced to abandon North Africa after Okba was defeated and killed by a combined Berber-Byzantine army. The victors were led by the Berber chieftain Qusayla, who then established his own Islamic kingdom based at Kairouan.

The Arabs soon regrouped. They retook Kairouan in AD 689 and dislodged the Byzantines from Carthage in AD 698, but continued to encounter spirited resistance from Berbers who had rallied behind the legendary princess Al-Kahina (see the boxed text, p204). She defeated the Arabs at Tébessa (Algeria) in AD 696, but was eventually cornered and killed after a legendary last stand at El-Jem in AD 701 (see p181). North Africa, with Kairouan as its capital, became a province of the rapidly expanding Islamic empire controlled by the Umayyad caliphs, based in Damascus.

Arab World Wide Web Directory (www.arabinfoseek.com /tunisia-history.htm) Patchy links to articles (which range from the facile to the comprehensive) about Tunisia's ancient history.

647	669–672
First Islamic conquest of Tunisia	Second Islamic conquest of North Africa by armies of Okba ibn Nafaa al-Fihri

Meanwhile, the tyrannical behaviour of Arab troops stationed in North Africa had pushed the Berbers to the brink of yet another rebellion. They were drawn to the teachings of the Kharijites, a puritanical Islamic sect whose egalitarian beliefs contrasted sharply with the arrogant and worldly ways of the Umayyad elite whom they continued to resist.

ISLAMIC DYNASTIES

Tunisia, like much of North Africa, was always too geographically distant from the great centres of Islamic power to be ruled directly and this gave rise to a succession of local Islamic dynasties.

Ibrahim ibn al-Aghlab was appointed Abbasid governor of Ifriqiyya (Tunisia and parts of Libya) in AD 797. Operating from Kairouan, he soon secured control of an area covering western Algeria, Tunisia and the Libyan province of Tripolitania. He was rewarded for his efforts by being made hereditary emir, and was the founder of the successful Aghlabid dynasty that ruled for over a century and left Tunisia with arguably its most enduring Islamic architectural legacies. The Great Mosque in Kairouan (p175) and the *ribats* (forts) at Sousse (p162) and Monastir (p170) were all built during the Aghlabid period.

Next came the Fatimids, a group of Berber Shiites (see p36) from the Kabylie region of central Algeria on a mission from God to depose the Abbasid caliphate and declare their leader, Obeid Allah, as caliph. Through alliances with disaffected Berber tribes, the Fatimids quickly conquered North Africa. The Aghlabids were defeated in AD 909, and a year later Obeid Allah was declared the true caliph at Raqqada, south of Kairouan. Anticipating reprisals, the Fatimids built a new capital, Mahdia (see p183), on a small, easily defended coastal headland and set about plotting the capture of Egypt, a plan that was complicated by a Kharijite uprising in AD 944 which captured Kairouan and laid siege to Mahdia before being driven off by Berber tribesmen led by Ziri ben Manad.

A new dynasty, the Zirids, arose but pressure began to mount for a return to religious orthodoxy. In 1045 the Zirids caved in and officially returned to the Sunni mainstream in open defiance of the Fatimids. The reply from Fatimid Cairo was devastating: the Bani Hilal and Bani Sulaim tribes of upper Egypt invaded the Maghreb en masse. The 200,000-strong Bani Hilal in particular completed a conquest which made the Vandals look like a small raiding party. Over the following century North Africa was slowly reduced to ruins.

The power vacuum was eventually filled by the Almohads, who came to power in Morocco at the beginning of the 12th century. They completed their conquest of North Africa with the capture of Mahdia in 1160, but the empire almost immediately began to crumble. The Maghreb split into three parts: Ifriqiyya (Tunisia) came under the Hafsids until the 16th century; Algeria came under the Banu Abd al-Wad; and Morocco came under the Merenids. Although borders have changed and rulers have come and gone, this division remains more or less intact today.

THE OTTOMAN TURKS

While the Ottoman Turks and the Spanish fought for control of the Mediterranean – yet another conflict not of Tunisian making – local resistance

A History of the Arab Peoples, by Albert Hourani, is a sweeping and nuanced history of the Arab World and Islam and infinitely preferable to books which try to get inside 'the Arab mind'; essential reading.

came from Muslim corsairs, or pirates. The most famous were the Barbarossa brothers, Aruj and Khair ed-Din, who had established themselves on the island of Jerba. Aruj captured Algiers from the Spanish but was killed when they retook the city in 1518. Khair ed-Din turned for help to the Turks, who jumped at the chance. He was given the title of *beylerbey* (governor) and supplied with troops.

Tunis was to change hands four more times before Sinan Pasha finally claimed it for the Turks in 1574, forcing the last of the Hafsids into exile. Tunis became a *sanjak* (province) of the Ottoman Empire.

In 1591, soldiers staged a coup, massacring their senior officers. They took the process a stage further in 1598 when Othman Dey seized power, downgrading the Ottoman pasha to a figurehead. The dey ruled Tunis, Kairouan and the major coastal towns, but control of the interior was put in the hands of a provincial governor, called the bey.

Internecine warfare and endless power struggles persisted until the early 18th century when Hussein ben Ali, the son of a Turkish janissary (infantryman) from Crete, came to power. He turned back the Algerians and founded the Husseinite line of beys, who survived until Tunisia became a republic in 1957.

> *The Sultan's Admiral,* by Ernie Bradford, is a suitably lively biography of the famous 16th-century pirate Khair ed-Din, who terrorised Christian shipping in the western Mediterranean and paved the way for the Ottoman conquest.

THE FRENCH PROTECTORATE

By the beginning of the 19th century, France had become the new power in the western Mediterranean. Piracy was outlawed in 1816 and slavery was abolished in 1846. These Western reforms exacted a heavy toll on the country's limited finances, necessitating heavy borrowing in the form of high-interest loans from European banks. By 1869 the country was broke. Control of its finances was handed over to an international commission, an ignominious state of affairs for this once-prosperous trading nation.

A final attempt to hold off European control was made by a short-lived ministry led by the reformer Khaireddin (1873–77), but he was forced from office and his plans were scuttled. In 1881 the French sent 30,000 troops into Tunisia on the pretext of countering border raids by Tunisian tribesmen into French-occupied Algeria. They stayed. The bey was forced to sign the Treaty of Kassar Saïd which acknowledged the sovereignty of the bey, but effectively put power in the hands of a French resident-general.

> The first constitution *(destour)* in the Arab world was proclaimed in Tunisia in 1861.

The 1883 Convention of La Marsa established co-sovereignty and parallel justice systems. Under this arrangement, Europeans were judged under French law and locals under a modified form of Islamic law. The protectorate, or rather the European population of Tunisia, prospered under French rule.

The French went about the business of land acquisition more discreetly than they did in neighbouring Algeria. In Tunisia, the French managed to get their hands on the best of the fertile land without confiscating property from individuals; they simply took over the large tracts of the Cap Bon Peninsula and the Medjerda Valley that had previously been controlled by the bey or used by nomads for grazing their animals. The citrus groves of Cap Bon are a legacy of this time, as are the vineyards that provide the bulk of the country's wine grapes.

The south was too arid for agriculture and was largely left alone until the beginning of the 20th century when it was discovered that the hills

Late 11th century	12th–16th centuries
Bani Hilal and Bani Sulaim tribes settle across North Africa	Hafsids rule over Tunisia after demise of Moroccan Almohads

west of Gafsa were made of phosphate. The massive mining operation begun by the French remains an important export earner for the modern Tunisian economy.

In 1920 the first nationalist political party, the Destour (Constitution) Party, was formed. The party's demands for democratic government, though supported by the bey, were ignored by the French, and the nationalist movement soon lost its way.

THE ROAD TO INDEPENDENCE

In 1934 a young, charismatic Sorbonne-educated lawyer, Habib Bourguiba, led a breakaway movement from the Destour Party. He founded the Neo-Destour Party, which soon replaced the old guard of the Destour. Support for the party quickly spread. On 9 April 1938, dozens of people were reported killed when the French turned their guns on demonstrators in Tunis. The party was banned, and Bourguiba was arrested and removed to France.

War in Europe once again drew Tunisia within the influence of other peoples' wars. In 1942 the Germans landed in Tunis in the hope that they could turn back the Allied advances from east and west. The campaign in Tunisia raged for six months and the Allies lost more than 15,000 men before they captured Bizerte on 7 May 1943.

In the same year, the Germans allowed the Neo-Destour leaders to return to Tunisia, where a government with Neo-Destour sympathies was formed by Moncef Bey.

When the French resumed control after the war, they were as uncompromising as ever. The bey was deposed and Bourguiba was forced to flee to Cairo from where he organised a successful propaganda campaign aimed at bringing Tunisia's position to international attention. By 1951 the French were ready to make concessions. A nationalist government was set up and Bourguiba was allowed to return. No sooner had he returned than the French changed their minds – Bourguiba was exiled for a third time. Violence followed, and the country was soon in a state of complete disarray.

In July 1954, the French president announced negotiations for Tunisian autonomy. In June 1955 an agreement was reached, and Bourguiba returned to Tunis to a hero's welcome.

Tunisia was formally granted independence on 20 March 1956, with Bourguiba as prime minister. Within a year, the last bey was deposed, the country became a republic and Bourguiba was declared Tunisia's first president.

HABIB BOURGUIBA

If Carthage is the dominant 'personality' of ancient Tunisian history, Habib Bourguiba is the enduring symbol of modern Tunisia, having dominated the Tunisian political landscape for almost 50 years.

Bourguiba had made his name resisting the French; his early years as president continued in the same vein, which endeared him greatly to the Tunisian people. In 1958, France bombed the Tunisian border village of Sakiet Sidi Youssef, claiming that Tunisian-backed Algerian rebels had crossed into Tunisian territory. Bourguiba demanded that France

In addition to Habib Bourguiba's exile from Tunisia, he was also exiled to Tabarka, Remada and, for two years, the island of Galite.

The 1959 constitution of the Republic of Tunisia states that the president must be a Muslim.

1574	1598
Sinan Pasha claims Tunisia for the Turkish Ottoman Empire	Othman Dey seizes power

evacuate their military base at Bizerte. Tunisian troops opened fire on the French, prompting a bloody retaliation in which more than 1000 Tunisians died. In an important victory for Bourguiba, the French finally withdrew in 1963.

Bourguiba was quick to introduce sweeping political and social changes, looking to Westernisation as the way to modernise. His ideals were socialist and secular, and he regarded Islam as a force that was holding the country back.

He set about reducing the role of religion in society by removing religious leaders from their traditional areas of influence. Probably his most significant moves were towards women's emancipation (see p40) and the abolition of religious schools. This latter move deprived religious leaders of their grass-roots educational role in shaping society. The religious school at the Zitouna Mosque in Tunis, a centre of Islamic learning for centuries, suffered the indignity of being incorporated into the Western-style University of Tunis.

The Sharia'a (Quranic law) courts were also abolished, and more than 60,000 hectares of land that had financed mosques and religious institutions were confiscated. Not surprisingly, religious leaders vehemently opposed the changes and for a time resistance flared, particularly in Kairouan. Bourguiba responded by removing troublesome clerics from office.

Despite his autocratic style and frequent prolonged absences through ill health, Bourguiba managed to keep the bulk of the population on his side. In 1974 the National Assembly made him president for life.

THE ISLAMIC OPPOSITION

Bourguiba's assault on the religious establishment planted the seeds of modern Tunisia's most enduring fault line – the tension between the rise of militant Islam and the protection of individual freedoms.

The 1970s were significant for the gradual emergence of an Islamic opposition in the form of the Islamic Association, led by the popular preacher Rashid Ghannouchi. Disillusionment with Bourguiba and his recast Parti Socialiste Destourien (PSD) increased dramatically following the use of the military to crush a general strike called by Tunisia's first trade union federation, the Union Générale des Travailleurs Tunisiens (UGTT) in January 1978.

Under increasing pressure at home and abroad, Bourguiba called the first multiparty elections in 1981. The Islamic Association became the Mouvement de Tendance Islamique (MTI; Islamic Tendency Movement), and advocated a return to Islamic values. Bourguiba, who never had much time for opposition of any sort, was certainly not prepared to tolerate an Islamic party and refused to license the MTI.

The National Front (an alliance between the PSD and the UGTT) took all 136 seats on offer, drawing cries of foul play.

After the elections, Bourguiba cracked down hard on the MTI. Ghannouchi and its other leaders were jailed and remained so until 1984, when riots were sparked by the withdrawal of a bread subsidy. The rioting lasted six days and stopped only when Bourguiba resumed the subsidy. The riots were notable for the shouting of slogans such as 'God is Great' and 'Down with America'. Eventually the MTI leaders were freed to ease tensions.

Modern Tunisia, by Andrew Borowiec, is one of the more readable modern histories of Tunisia with a particular focus on its battle against Islamic fundamentalism; essential reading.

Habib Bourguiba of Tunisia: The Tragedy of Longevity, by Derek Hopwood, is probably the best account of the Bourguiba years with the right mix of criticism and an understanding of the nation's hagiography.

Mid-19th century	1881
French arrive in Tunisia	Treaty of Kassar Saïd signed granting power to French resident-general

Anxious to preserve its power and desperate to avoid the upheaval caused by Islamic militancy in Algeria and Egypt, Bourguiba's government spent much of the '80s conducting a repressive clampdown on the Islamic opposition – death sentences and other severe punishments were the norm.

THE DECLINE OF BOURGUIBA

While this struggle for the heart and soul of Tunisia was occurring, Bourguiba's decades-long reign was otherwise stagnating. Bourguiba was seen to be more and more out of touch with his subjects. In 1986 he sacked Prime Minister Mohammed Mzali, just weeks after naming Mzali as his successor. Mzali's replacement, Rachid Sfar, lasted only a year before making way for Zine el-Abidine ben Ali, the tough minister for the interior and former army general.

As minister for the interior, Ben Ali had presided over the crackdown on the Islamic opposition, which had produced more than 1000 arrests. In September 1987, 90 of those held, including Ghannouchi, were put on trial on charges ranging from planting bombs (12 tourists had been injured in blasts at hotels in Sousse and Monastir) to conspiring to overthrow the regime.

The trial produced seven death sentences, while Ghannouchi was given hard labour for life. Bourguiba demanded the death sentence for all the

Les Trois decennies Bourguiba (www.bourguiba.net/) Quite extensive French-language site covering the life and political career of Tunisia's founding father.

THE FATHER OF MODERN TUNISIA

Like so many great figures of history, Habib Bourguiba was a man of legend. The man who stood at the helm of Tunisian politics for 50 years may have been born in 1903 but no-one is really sure of the date and he always kept his age a well-guarded secret. More certain is the fact that no person did more than Bourguiba to shape modern Tunisia, from leading the country to independence from the French to forging the nation's secular identity.

Early evidence of his unconventional and inventive approach came in 1960 when Bourguiba urged workers to ignore the Ramadan fast, which he regarded as economically damaging because of its effect on productivity. He met serious opposition from religious leaders, but he mounted an ingenious argument against the fast, declaring that Tunisians were exempted because they were waging a jihad (holy war) against poverty – and that the Prophet Mohammed himself had excused warriors engaged in a jihad from fasting so that they could be at full strength to tackle the enemy.

Even as he did battle to free the country from what he saw as the perils of Islamic tyranny, his repressive measures in doing so and in suppressing all political opposition made his mission a perennially contradictory one. He nonetheless fostered a strong national identity and the development of a standard of living that puts Tunisia at the top of the pile in the developing world.

After his toppling in 1987, Bourguiba was held for some time in detention in his palace at Carthage before being shunted off to 'retirement' in another palace outside Monastir, the town of his birth, where he remained until his death in April 2000. Even from beyond the grave, Bourguiba cast a long shadow. The charismatic father of the nation caused his successor no end of discomfort when he died. As many as 120,000 people lined the streets to bid farewell. Official attempts to play down the occasion inflamed crowds, who responded with taunts of 'Long live Bourguiba'. The bronze door of his mausoleum, which should not be missed (see p172), is marked with the words: 'The Supreme Combatant, the Liberator of Women, the Builder of Modern Tunisia'.

1920	1934
First political party (Destour) formed in Tunisia	Habib Bourguiba forms Neo-Destour Party and begins struggle for independence

accused and was furious at the outcome, insisting that Ghannouchi and 15 others be executed by 16 November 1987.

It was against this backdrop that Ben Ali made his move. The arrest of Ghannouchi had sparked street battles, and there were fears that executions could lead to a popular uprising. On 7 November 1987, Ben Ali seized power in a palace coup. He assembled a group of doctors who were asked to examine the 83-year-old president, who, predictably, was declared unfit to carry out his duties.

PRESIDENT BEN ALI

President Ben Ali now looms almost as large over Tunisia as his predecessor, a fact you'll never be allowed to forget as his smiling face features on posters throughout the country (a failure to display his picture can cause problems for businesses from the police).

The early years of his rule seemed to indicate that little had changed. Between 1990 and 1992, some 8000 alleged fundamentalists were imprisoned. Human rights groups such as Amnesty International and, for a time, the French government, led the way in calling for greater freedoms. In response, the government banned the broadcasting of French television programmes, a move still lamented by Tunisians. It reached the stage where Tunisia became something of a pariah state, although never on the scale of neighbouring Libya.

Having torn the heart out of the Islamic opposition, Ben Ali moved cleverly to appease its remnants and the wider population. He headed off on a heavily publicised pilgrimage to Mecca to establish his own credentials as a good Muslim, and ordered that the Ramadan fast be observed. He also promised a multiparty political system, although he baulked at legalising the MTI – which had by now changed its name to Hizb al-Nahda (Renaissance Party).

Political prisoners were released, the State Security Court was abolished and police powers of detention were limited. Political exiles were invited to return, and many decided that it was safe to do so.

However, the general elections held in April 1989 didn't exactly reflect a new liberalism. Ben Ali's Rassemblement Constitutionel Democratique (RCD), as the PSD had become known, won all the seats amid charges of vote rigging. In the presidential elections, Ben Ali was re-elected with 99.27% of the vote. Hizb al-Nahda was not allowed to contest the poll, but many of its candidates stood as independents. Estimates of their share of the vote varied from 13% up to 40% in some urban areas.

This result, coupled with the successes of the Islamic Salvation Front (FIS) in municipal elections in Algeria, prompted Ben Ali to rule out official recognition of the Hizb al-Nahda.

Tunisia officially supported the US-led alliance in the 1991 Gulf War, but popular sentiment was very much behind Iraq. In May 1991, the government announced that it had uncovered a Hizb al-Nahda plot to establish an Islamic state by force. A sizeable number of those arrested were members of the military.

Ben Ali confirmed his hold on power at elections in 1994 and 1999. The 1999 elections left the ruling RCD with 150 seats in the Chamber of Deputies. The official opposition, the Mouvement des Democratiques

President Ben Ali must rule until 2018 to match Habib Bourguiba's period in office (32 years); he is only the 15th longest-serving African leader.

Socialistes (MDS), won 13 seats. Four other parties share the remaining 22 seats. Ben Ali retained the presidency with a Soviet-style 99.44% of the vote.

There is no suggestion that the government is anything other than in complete control. Politics is not a popular (or advisable) topic of conversation, although many Tunisians express what could be genuine admiration for Ben Ali's leadership.

For all of Ben Ali's repression of political and religious freedoms, Tunisians are proud of their country's reputation for stability in a volatile region. Many Tunisians have also turned away from Islamic groups, angered by the killing of at least 19 people in a bomb blast at a synagogue in Jerba in April 2002 (see the boxed text, p246). Both Bourguiba and Ben Ali also strongly supported popular Arab causes: Tunisia was home to the Arab League for most of the 1980s; and the Palestine Liberation Organisation (PLO) was based at Hammam Plage, just south of Tunis, after it was forced out of Lebanon by the Israelis in the early 1980s until mid-1994 when Yasser Arafat and the PLO returned to the Israeli-controlled occupied territories.

The second major reason for Ben Ali's survival is an economy which is among the most successful in the developing world. Despite high unemployment, international agreements enabled Tunisia to become, in 1995, the first Arab state to be integrated into the European Economic Area. Agreements with Italy to allow Tunisians to work in its agricultural sector also contribute to an economy which is growing steadily and cementing Tunisia's reputation as a stable and relatively prosperous modern nation.

Tunisian government Internet censors are among the strictest in the world; Internet journalist Zouhair Yahyaoui is serving a two-year prison sentence for spreading false information.

---

7 November 1987

Ben Ali ousts Habib Bourguiba in bloodless coup to become Tunisia's second president

April 2000

Death of Habib Bourguiba in Monastir

The Culture

THE NATIONAL PSYCHE

Tunisians cast their eyes in many directions: to Europe, the economically dominant neighbour; to the east and the lands of Islam; to Tunisia's traditional Berber heartland; and to the villages where many city-dwellers were born.

Tunisian proverbs include: 'Good reputation is better than wealth', 'High prices attract buyers' and 'The door of the shop is open and in God we trust'.

Perhaps more than anywhere else in the Arab world, it is in Tunisian cities that the modern triumphs, most obviously in the Tunisian women and men mingling easily with each other and with all the nations of the world who've come to visit them. In rural areas, tradition holds sway and family life is all-important; those returning home from the city, from their life in Europe with their European values, learn again that theirs is a schizophrenic existence. The most enduring emblems of the many worlds that Tunisians inhabit are visible on almost any city street: a mother wearing a *hejab* (headscarf), her daughter walking alongside in the latest (often revealing) Western fashions, while the unemployed urban poor mill around on street corners watching the cars with European number plates glide past.

This is a people reflecting the aspirations of the African continent, forging an economy of relative prosperity, yet all the while planning their escape to Europe.

This is a nation on the doorstep of the West, for which there is widespread admiration even as they express considerable anger over the perceived injustices done in the West's name elsewhere in the region. Tunisia shares with the Arab world a history of invasion and colonial meddling which has somehow morphed into a tradition of gracious hospitality that has its roots in the nomadic Bedouin traditions of refuge and hospitality; there are also many references to providing hospitality to strangers in the Quran. It may even occasionally survive in the souqs (markets) where souvenirs are sold, but only after the salesmen remain true to the old Tunisian proverb – 'Consider me as your brother but let's settle our accounts as partners'.

Around 18% of the national budget involves government spending on education, compared with just 6% for health and 5% for defence (1990–2001).

Tunisia is baseball caps and straw hats; mobile phones ringing in the midst of the ancient, serious and exuberant art of conversation; men overflowing with testosterone who don't shirk from wearing jasmine behind the ear; a nation proud of its modernity and filled with men grumbling about how women are favoured and how dangerous it is – for the women, you understand – to give them such freedom; a people who are quick to point to the freedoms they enjoy and to profess a love for President Ben Ali, a more hushed and lingering admiration for Habib Bourguiba and a whispered admission that they can't say what they really think.

Lion Mountain, by Mustapha Tlili, offers a powerful and timely fictional account of the disasters wrought upon a remote village by progress and tourism; not available from Tunisian bookshops.

LIFESTYLE

Tunisian society has changed beyond all recognition in the course of the last century. There are now two parallel societies: the modern, Western-leaning, cosmopolitan society of big cities like Tunis and Sousse, and the traditional society of the smaller towns and villages.

Traditional society is based on the family. In rural areas, it is still common to find three generations living under one roof, and social life (especially for women) is restricted largely to the extended family.

Although Islam's role in public life has been severely curtailed by the government, religion continues to mark the important events of life. When a baby is born, the first words uttered to it are the call to prayer. A week later this is followed by a ceremony in which the baby's head is shaved and an animal sacrificed. The major event of a boy's childhood is circumcision, which normally takes place sometime between the ages of seven and 12. When a person dies, a burial service is held at the mosque and the body is then buried with the feet facing Mecca.

Over 51% of students in secondary schools in 1999–2000 were girls, while 51.9% of university students in 2000–2001 were women.

The absence of any government unemployment benefits also contributes to the enduring strength of family ties: the unemployed survive thanks to the support of family members and often one working adult has to provide for four or five other adults. Social security does, however, provide old-age and disability pensions, free health care and education.

INSIDE A TUNISIAN WEDDING

If you visit Tunisia in summer, expect your sleep to be disturbed by processions of cars through the streets, horns blaring, and loud music continuing until the early hours of the morning. What you're hearing is the joy of a Tunisian wedding.

The process starts months (even years) before the actual event. When their children reach marriageable age, parents begin the search for prospective sons- and daughters-in-law. It is rumoured that mothers often go to the *hammam* (bathhouse) on scouting expeditions for their sons, to find the most beautiful women, after which they conduct discreet research into the woman's family background, her job prospects and other aspects of eligibility. When the parents have made their choice (increasingly after having consulted their daughter), the girl is asked for her agreement. Under Tunisian law, she has a right to refuse, which is respected by most families.

If the girl agrees, a meeting between the two families is arranged – quite a formal and awkward occasion, according to most Tunisians with whom we spoke. If all goes well, contracts are exchanged and the legal formalities completed. Between then and the wedding, the couple is allowed a series of meetings. Again, they're not exactly intimate occasions as they're usually accompanied by family members in all but the most liberal families; anything (from gossip to illicit acts) could be fatal to a woman's honour and hence her marriage prospects.

Weddings traditionally last three days, for the duration of which the woman is secluded from public view with the women of her family.

On the first day of the wedding, the groom does the rounds of town with his male friends, purchasing gifts (clothes, jewellery, perfumes) for his wife. He then, with great ceremony, delivers these gifts to the eagerly awaiting women of the wife's family who then carefully scrutinise the gifts to determine the financial means of the husband who is under enormous pressure to outdo all expectations.

On day two the husband and wife remain with their families and enjoy an evening of feasting in the company of an all-male or all-female cast of family members. It is also on the second day that the man shaves off his beard (which he has been growing for a month) and the woman goes to the *hammam* and allows a beautician to remove all the hair from her body.

The night of the third day is the culmination of months of hopes, expectations and gossip and, as such, is a time of great celebration. In the early evening, the cars begin gathering to begin the noisy procession of friends and family through the streets, announcing the joyful news to the whole town. In the south, revellers traditionally passed through town on foot, alongside the bride astride a camel but concealed by a canopy.

And there is a party to end all parties, a time of feasting, music and dancing.

At the end of the night, the husband and wife retire to the man's house (nowadays this is often a hotel), alone together for the first time for one week's seclusion and consummation of the marriage. Thankfully, the older women no longer wait outside for the blood-stained sheet as proof of the woman's virginity.

POPULATION

Almost 98% of Tunisia's population is Arab-Berber – after 14 centuries of intermarriage, the line between the two is practically nonexistent. You're more likely to find people claiming a purely Berber heritage (see the boxed text, p204) in the south of the country along the northern fringe of the Sahara. Europeans and Jews make up the remaining 2%.

Around 30% of the Tunisian population is under the age of 15.

The government's family-planning programme has slowed the population growth rate to 1.6%, but having such a young population places a great strain on social services, particularly with their need to find employment. Although the overall population density is around 62 people per sq km, the actual population distribution varies from more than 2500 per sq km in Tunis to less than 10 per sq km in the south; two-thirds of Tunisians live in urban areas.

MEDIA

Tunisian television, radio and newspapers are the sole preserve of the government and its supporters. Perhaps that's why so much that you'll see reads or sounds like a presidential press release; rest assured that Tunisians find the front-page news that the president met the ambassador for Bahrain every bit as dull as you do.

For television, there are only two (Arabic-language) channels, both controlled by a government intent on protecting itself from criticism and its citizens from anything even vaguely corrupting. Most Tunisians get around dull local programming by purchasing satellite dishes (often smuggled in from Algeria) and watching international programmes in the privacy of their own homes.

There's more variety to be found in the realm of newspapers (French and Arabic), but they're still heavily censored. The music radio stations are less potentially subversive (at least in the government's eyes) and therefore far more entertaining.

The Colonizer and the Colonized, by Albert Memmi, is a classic study of the effects of colonisation, drawing on the political, social and sexual impact of the French occupation of Tunisia.

As for new media, numerous Internet sites are blocked by the government, including hotmail, some political sites and most pornography.

And one tip: if you're watching Tunisian TV in Sousse and you see pictures of the president waving to crowds in Sousse, don't expect a handshake; chances are that it's file footage being shown to throw potential troublemakers off the scent that he's in Tunis.

RELIGION

Islam is the state religion in Tunisia, although most Tunisians are quite relaxed in their approach to religion or prefer to practise their faith in private, perhaps in part because the government has spent much of the last five decades cracking down hard on those who wish to mix religion with politics (see p30). Tunisia is a liberal and tolerant society.

Tunisian Jews (www.harissa.com) Homepage of Tunisian Jewish community and diaspora – easy to negotiate and informative.

In addition to the more than 95% of Tunisians who are Sunni Muslim (the orthodox majority in Islam), there are small communities of Kharijites (see the boxed text, p39), Jews (see the boxed text, p246) and Roman Catholics.

Islam

THE BIRTH OF ISLAM

The Prophet Mohammed was born into one of the trading families of the Arabian city of Mecca (in present-day Saudi Arabia) in AD 570 and began to receive revelations in AD 610. After a time he started imparting the content of Allah's message to the Meccans. Its essence was a call to submit to God's will ('Islam' means submission).

Mohammed gathered quite a following against the idolaters of Mecca, and his movement especially appealed to the poorer levels of society. The powerful families became increasingly outraged and, by AD 622, had made life sufficiently unpleasant for Mohammed and his followers; they fled to Medina, an oasis town some 300km to the north and now Islam's second holiest city. (This migration – the Hejira – marks the beginning of the Islamic calendar, year 1 AH or AD 622.) In Medina, Mohammed continued to preach.

By AD 632, Mohammed had revisited Mecca and many of the tribes in the surrounding area had sworn allegiance to him and the new faith. Mecca became the symbolic centre of the faith, containing as it did the Kaaba, which housed the black stone supposedly given to Ibrahim (Abraham) by the angel Gabriel. Mohammed determined that Muslims should face Mecca when praying outside the city.

On Mohammed's death in AD 632, his followers quickly conquered the areas that make up modern Syria, Iraq, Lebanon, Israel and the Palestinian Territories. This was accomplished under Mohammed's four successors, the caliphs (or Companions of Mohammed).

Islam quickly spread west, first taking in Egypt and then fanning out across North Africa. By the end of the 7th century, the Muslims had reached the Atlantic and thought themselves sufficiently in control of the Gezirat al-Maghreb (Island of the West, or North Africa beyond Egypt) to march on Spain in AD 710.

Islam Online (www.islamonline.net /English/index.shtml) World news from an Islamic perspective as well as interesting information about Islamic rituals and even an 'Ask a scholar' enquiry line.

THE QURAN

Islam shares its roots with the great monotheistic faiths that sprang from the harsh land of the Middle East – Judaism and Christianity – but it's considerably younger. The holy book of Islam is the Quran. It contains many references to the earlier prophets of both the older religions – Adam, Abraham, Noah, Moses and Jesus are recognised as prophets in a line that ends definitively with the greatest of them all, the Prophet Mohammed.

For Muslims, the Quran is the word of Allah, directly communicated to Mohammed in a series of revelations.

Most Tunisians are Sunnis (the orthodox bedrock of Islam) belonging to the Malekite school of Quranic interpretation, which is somewhat less rigid in its application and interpretation of the Quran than the other schools.

The Quran is the Islamic holy book and considered the highpoint of Arabic literature; it should be read by anyone interested in learning about Islam from the source.

THE FIVE PILLARS OF ISLAM

In order to live a devout life, Muslims are expected at least to observe the Five Pillars of Islam:

Shahada This is the profession of faith, Islam's basic tenet: 'There is no god but Allah, and Mohammed is the Prophet of Allah' *(Allahu akbar, Ashhadu an la Ilah ila Allah, Ashhadu an Mohammed rasul Allah)*. It is a phrase commonly heard as part of the call to prayer and at many other events, such as births and deaths. The first part has virtually become an exclamation good for any time of life or situation.

Sala Sometimes written 'salat', this is the obligation of prayer, ideally five times a day, when muezzins (mosque officials) call the faithful to pray. Although Muslims can pray anywhere, it is considered more laudable to do so together in a mosque.

Zakat Giving of alms to the poor was from the beginning an essential part of the social teaching of Islam, and was later developed in some parts of the Muslim world into various forms of tax to redistribute funds to the needy. The moral obligation towards one's poorer neighbours continues to be emphasised at a personal level.

Sawm Ramadan, the ninth month of the Muslim calendar, commemorates the revelation of the Quran to Mohammed. In a demonstration of Muslims' renewal of faith, they are asked not to let anything pass their lips, and are expected to refrain from sex, from dawn to dusk for a month. For specific dates of the month of fasting, see p258.

Haj The pinnacle of a devout Muslim's life is the pilgrimage to Mecca. Ideally, the pilgrim should go to Mecca in the last month of the year, Zuul Hijja, to join Muslims from all over the world.

Muslims traditionally attribute a place of great respect to Christians and Jews as *ahl al-kitab*, the 'people of the book'.

THE CALL TO PRAYER

The first slivers of dawn are flickering on the horizon, and the deep quiet of a city asleep is pierced by the cries of the muezzin exhorting the faithful to the first of the day's prayers:

> Allahu akbar, Allahu akbar
> Ashhadu an la Ilah ila Allah
> Ashhadu an Mohammed rasul Allah
> Haya ala as-sala
> Haya ala as-sala

Of all the sounds that haunt the ears of the first-time visitor to Tunisia, it's possibly the call to prayer that leaves the most indelible impression. Five times a day, Muslims are called, if not actually to enter a mosque to pray, at least to take the time to do so where they are. The midday prayers on Friday, when the sheikh of the mosque delivers his weekly *khutba* (sermon) are considered the most important. The mosque also serves as a kind of community centre, and often you'll find groups of children or adults receiving Quranic lessons, people in quiet prayer and others simply sheltering in the tranquil peace of the mosque.

Islam: A Short History, by Karen Armstrong, provides a contemporary and sympathetic study of Islam from its birth to its modern struggle against misrepresentation.

THE MOSQUE

All mosques *(masjid)* are based on the layout of the house belonging to the Prophet Mohammed in Medina. The original setting was an enclosed, oblong courtyard with huts (housing Mohammed's wives) along one side wall and a rough portico, or *zulla*, providing shade at one end for the poorer worshippers.

The courtyard has become the *sahn*, the portico the arcaded *riwaqs* and the houses the *haram* or prayer hall. The prayer hall is usually divided into a series of aisles that segregate the sexes. Running down the middle is a broad aisle which leads to the mihrab, a vaulted niche at the centre of the qibla wall. Built to face Mecca, this wall indicates the direction of prayer. It's also the site of the minbar, a pulpit raised above a narrow staircase and from where the *khutba* is delivered.

The courtyards of many mosques in Tunisia are open to non-Muslims, but nowhere will you be allowed into the prayer hall.

Almost every mosque (Sousse's Great Mosque is an unusual exception; see p161) have a minaret (from the word *menara*, meaning lighthouse) – the tower at one corner of the mosque from where Muslims are called to prayer. Attached to many mosques are elaborately decorated *medersas* (Quranic schools) which served as residential colleges where theology and Muslim law were taught. They comprise an open-air courtyard, with an ablutions fountain in the centre and a main prayer hall at the far end, surrounded by an upper gallery of student cells. The Medersa Bachia and Medersa Slimania in the Tunis medina (see p69) can both be visited by non-Muslims.

The many small whitewashed domes which you'll see all over Tunisia are the tombs of marabouts, Muslim holy men (see the boxed text, p232). A *zaouia* is an expanded version of a marabout's tomb and typically contains a prayer hall and accommodation for visitors. Some of the best are in Kairouan.

THE IBADIS

Jerba is home to one of the last remaining communities of Ibadis, an offshoot of the Kharijites. The word 'Kharijite' means 'those who go out to fight jihad (holy war)'. The Kharijites separated from other Islamic doctrines in the years after Islam was born when they accepted the legitimacy of the first two caliphs but held all others to be in error. Indeed, some argue that the Kharijites were responsible for the death of Ali (the fourth caliph, whose followers founded the Shiite Islamic sect).

When Islam spread across North Africa in the 7th century AD, the rebellious Berber tribes accepted the new religion, but typically were drawn to sects, such as the Kharijites, which rejected the prevailing hierarchies.

The Ibadis believe that the imam or head of the Muslim community should be the most worthy candidate, regardless of their origin or family background. The imam, chosen by the community, can also be removed if he fails to adhere to the Islamic principles of his office. The Ibadis even believe that it is not necessary for there to be an imam at all times. Again this suited the Berbers who would sometimes appoint an imam to mediate between the disparate tribes during times of conflict only to dispense with his services when he was deemed no longer necessary.

Under the Ottomans, the Ibadis, who lived under a council of learned elders, were tolerated and left to their own devices, but their unorthodox beliefs have always made them vulnerable to attack from zealots, hence their retreat to a few well-defended refuges like Jerba.

ISLAMIC CUSTOMS

When Muslims pray, they must follow certain rituals. First they must wash their hands, arms, feet, head and neck in running water before praying; all mosques have an area set aside for this purpose. If they are not in a mosque and there is no water available, clean sand suffices; and where there is no sand, they must go through the motions of washing.

Then they must face Mecca (all mosques are oriented so that the mihrab, or prayer niche, faces Mecca) and follow a set pattern of gestures. You regularly see Muslims praying by the side of the road as well as in mosques. In everyday life, Muslims are prohibited from drinking alcohol and eating pork (considered unclean).

ISLAMIC HOLIDAYS

The principal religious holidays in Muslim countries are tied to the lunar Hejira calendar. The calendar is about 11 days shorter than the Gregorian (Western) calendar, meaning that in Western terms the holidays fall at different times each year; see p258 for a table of dates of Islamic holidays. These holidays are far from universally observed in Tunisia, particularly in tourist areas.

Ras as-Sana New Year's day, celebrated on the first day of the Hejira calendar year, 1 Moharram.

Moulid an-Nabi This is a lesser feast celebrating the birth of the Prophet Mohammed on 12 Rabi' al-Awal. In the Maghreb this is generally known as *mouloud*.

Ramadan & Eid al-Fitr Most Muslims, albeit not all with equal rigour, take part in the fasting that characterises the month of Ramadan, a time when the faithful are called upon as a community to renew their relationship with God. Ramadan is the month in which the Quran was first revealed. From dawn to dusk, a Muslim is expected to refrain from eating, drinking, smoking and having sex. This can be a difficult discipline, and only people in good health are asked to participate. Those engaged in exacting physical work or travelling are considered exempt. Every evening during Ramadan is a celebration; *iftar*, the breaking of the day's fast, is a time of animated activity, when the people of the local community come together not only to eat and drink but also to pray. Non-Muslims are not expected to participate, even if more pious Muslims suggest you do. Restaurants and cafés that are open during the day may be harder to come by, and at any rate you should try to avoid openly flouting the fast. The end of Ramadan, or more accurately the first days of the following month of Shawwal, mark the Eid al-Fitr, the Festival of Breaking of the Fast (also known as the Eid as-Sagheer, the Small Feast), which generally lasts for four or five days, during which time everything grinds to a halt. This is not a good time to travel, but can be a great experience if you are invited to share in some of the festivities with a family. Ramadan is widely observed in Tunisia, although it was forbidden during the reign of Habib Bourguiba.

Haj & Eid al-Adha The fifth pillar of Islam, a sacred duty of all who can afford it, is to make the pilgrimage to Mecca – the haj. It can be done at any time, but at least one should be accomplished in Zuul Hijja, the 12th month of the Muslim year. The high point is the visit to the Kaaba, the stone of Ibrahim in the centre of the haram, the sacred area into which non-Muslims are forbidden to enter. The faithful, dressed only in a white robe, circle the Kaaba seven times and kiss the black stone. The haj culminates in the ritual slaughter of a lamb (in commemoration of Ibrahim's sacrifice) at Mina. This marks the end of the pilgrimage and the beginning of the Eid al-Adha, or Feast of the Sacrifice (aka the Grand Feast, or Eid al-Kebir). Throughout the Muslim world the act of sacrifice is repeated, and the streets of towns and cities seem to run with the blood of slaughtered sheep.

Kasbah
(www.kasbah.com
/vitalstats/travellers
/womans_resources
/tunisia_tunisia_1.htm)
Contains useful contact details for women's organisations in Tunisia as well as some statistics.

WOMEN IN TUNISIA

One of the many titles which Habib Bourguiba, Tunisia's first president, awarded to himself during his reign was 'The Liberator of Women'. Many Tunisian women agree, and conditions for women in Tunisia are better than just about anywhere in the Islamic world – to Western eyes, at least. Bourguiba, whose first wife was French, was a staunch supporter of women's rights, and it was one of the first issues on his agenda after independence. His 1956 Personal Status Code banned polygamy and ended divorce by renunciation. It also placed restrictions on the tradition of arranged marriages, setting a minimum marriage age of 17 for girls and giving them the right to refuse a proposed marriage.

Some 24% of Tunisian magistrates are women, while women represent 22% of Tunisian lawyers, 26.2% of journalists and 33% of teachers.

Bourguiba was outspoken in his criticism of the *hejab* (the veil worn by Muslim women), which he regarded as demeaning. He called it an 'odious rag', and banned it from schools as part of a campaign to phase it out. It is now unusual to find them worn by women under 30, many of whom consider not wearing the *hejab* to be an expression of their liberty. However, a backlash from conservative elements (fuelled in part by global events and a desire among some Muslims to embrace more strongly their Muslim identity) has led to it being worn more than perhaps it otherwise would be.

Among the statistics relating to women in Tunisia are:

- School enrolment of girls six years old – 99.1% (2000–01)
- Female literacy – up from 24% (1966) to 69.9% (2000–01)
- Percentage of women in working population – 23.8%
- Proportion of municipal council seats held by women – 20.6%
- Proportion of Chamber of Deputies seats held by women – 11.5%

Tunisia Online
(www.tunisiaonline.com
/women/index.html)
Government site with an impressive summary of Tunisian women's participation in public life.

For all that, many Tunisian women live dual lives – encouraged to participate by relatively favourable legal and socio-economic conditions, yet restricted by traditional family values that limit their involvement in public life. Away from the more cosmopolitan city centres such as Tunis or the beachside resort towns, the public social domain remains that of the man, while women largely remain in the home. It's quite common to hear Tunisian men grumbling about how women are favoured by the government and its legal framework. It doesn't take too much of a cognitive leap to realise the limitations this attitude may place upon women away from the public spotlight.

ARTS
Literature

There are countless streets in Tunisian towns named after Tunisia's national poet, Abu el-Kacem el-Chabbi (also spelled Abdulkacem Chebbi), whose poem *Will to Live* is taught to every schoolchild. As a result, he is one of the best-known literary figures among Tunisians.

Most Tunisian writers live and work in Europe where the financial rewards are greater and the dangers arising from offending the government are much diminished.

Few Tunisian writers have been translated into English. Among those novelists whose work is available internationally are Mustapha Tlili and the internationally acclaimed Albert Memmi, who lives in Paris and writes in French about the identity crisis faced by North African Jews like himself. Other well-known novelists whose works have been translated into English include Hedi Bouraoui *(Return to Thyna)* and Sabiha Khemir *(Waiting in the Future for the Past to Come)*.

Writers of short stories include Ali Duaji, Hassouna Mosbahi (who was shortlisted for the 2001 Caine Prize for African writing) and Habib Selmi, who doubles as a translator for Gabriel García Márquez.

Sleepless Night, by Ali Duaji, is an engaging collection of short stories and sketches about life in and around Tunis during the first half of the 20th century.

Cinema

Tunisia is often used as a setting for international film makers, but it also has a small and internationally renowned film industry of its own; a couple of directors have won critical acclaim in Europe in recent years. They include Ferid Boughedir, whose *Halfaouine* featured at the Cannes Film Festival in 1990. Female director Moutfida Tlatli won a special prize at the 1994 festival for her film *Silence of the Palace*.

The biennial Carthage International Film Festival offers a good opportunity to view the latest work from Tunisian and regional directors.

Keswa: Le Fil Perdu (1999) is directed by Kalthoum Bornaz, a renowned female director, whose satirical portrayal of a young Tunisian woman defying her family's wishes for an arranged marriage is at once funny and thought-provoking.

Music

Western ears may need a little time to adjust to Tunisian music; while Western music is based on the octave, Arabic music uses a scale based around 24 quarter notes. *Malouf* (which means 'normal') is a form of traditional Arab-style music that has become a national institution in Tunisia. It was introduced into Tunisia in the 15th century by Andalusian refugees and consists of instrumental pieces, which serve as preludes and breaks, and vocal works performed in a set sequence, called a *nouba*, which has nine distinct parts. Traditionally, *malouf* was performed by small ensembles using a *rbab* (a kind of two-stringed violin), *oud* (lute) and *darbuka* (drum, usually made of terracotta with a goatskin cover on one side), with a solo vocalist. Today, ensembles are more likely to be made up of large instrumental and choral groups, playing a mixture of Western and traditional Arabic instruments.

Traditional *malouf* was superseded by a new, lighter style of music introduced from Egypt in the mid-1920s, but underwent a revival in the 1930s when Baron Erlangen, a musicologist living in the Tunis suburb of Sidi Bou Saïd, founded the Rachidia Ensemble, which became the official centre for *malouf* music; this is where most of Tunisia's leading musicians have trained.

After independence, *malouf* was adopted as a symbol of national identity. Since then, it has become institutionalised to a great extent, with the government offering courses in *malouf* at the National Conservatory of Music in Tunis and an annual cycle of festivals and competitions culminating in the International Festival of Malouf held in July in Testour.

A Summer in La Goulette (1994), directed by Ferid Boughedir, one of Tunisia's premier directors, is a comedy set in 1967 Tunis where three daughters seek Muslim, Christian and Jewish boyfriends at the time of the Arab–Israeli war.

Stars of the *malouf* scene include the El-Azifet Ensemble (an exclusively female orchestra).

Tourist restaurants often put on live performances of traditional music; the restaurant M'Rabet in the Tunis medina (see p78) plays *malouf*, although it's a bit staged for tourists. Other good restaurants in Tunis for traditional music (though not necessarily *malouf*) are La Mamma (p79) and Lucullus (in La Goulette; p84).

During the summer, there are weekend free concerts on Ave Habib Bourguiba, as well as classical music concerts at the Centre of Arabic and Mediterranean Music in Sidi Bou Saïd and at L'Acropolium in Carthage. Tabarka also hosts some outstanding music festivals (see p257 and p126 for details).

Most of the music you'll hear as you travel around is classical Arabic, usually love songs performed by some raven-haired songstress from Cairo, or Algerian dance music known as *rai* which is a special favourite of louage (shared taxi) drivers – a good barometer of popular (male) taste. Among the more popular modern Tunisian singers are Sabar Rbaï and Salma Echarfi.

For our pick of the top 10 Tunisian music CDs, see p12.

Music From Tunisia (www.focusmm.com /tunisia/tn_musmn.htm) Contains a short summary of the main themes of Tunisian music and links to songs from musicians little known outside Tunisia.

Architecture

Tunisia boasts an exceptional range of architectural styles signposting more than 2500 years of history.

One of the highlights of visiting Tunisia is getting lost in the ancient medinas. For an explanation of medina and residential architecture, see the boxed text, p187.

Further south, the Berbers were responsible for some of the most astonishing and other-worldly forms of indigenous architecture anywhere in the world. Not surprisingly, they have become a favourite of the makers of the *Star Wars* movies (see p18). See also the boxed texts on p202, p209 and p211. Also worth seeking out is the traditional relief brickwork found in Tozeur and Nefta, which uses protruding bricks to create intricate geometric patterns.

Jerba's highly distinctive fortress architecture reflects the island's long history as a stronghold of the fiercely autonomous Kharijite sect. The buildings were all designed with defence in mind, and the landscape is dotted with what look like battlements, all painted a brilliant white. See the boxed text on p242 for more details.

Most pervasive and formidable of all is the architecture of Islam which ranges from the austere functionality of the early Aghlabids to the exuberant work of the later Andalusians and Ottomans.

For our favourite highlights of Tunisian architecture, see the boxed text on p12.

ISLAMIC MILITARY ARCHITECTURE

Walls were constructed of rock set in clay, and also served as barracks, granaries and arsenals. Towers, or small turrets, were placed at regular intervals around the perimeter, while the top of the wall featured crenellations to provide shelter for defenders. The best examples, in Sfax and Sousse, were both built by the Aghlabids in the 9th century.

The Islamic gate, or *bab*, centred around two crenellated, stone-block towers which flanked the central bay in which the gate was set. The horseshoe arch was the most common design, enclosed by multifoil curves. The gates were usually highly decorated with friezes, using geometric, flower-and-foliage or shell motifs. Favourites include those of Sfax, Kairouan and

---

TUNISIA'S WORLD HERITAGE–LISTED SITES

Tunisia has eight sites recognised by Unesco for their world cultural, historical and architectural significance:

- The colosseum at El-Jem (p181)
- The Punic/Roman ruins of Carthage (p84)
- The Tunis medina (p67)
- Lake Ichkeul National Park (p121)
- The Punic ruins of Kerkouane (p108)
- The Sousse medina (p161)
- The city of Kairouan (p173)
- The Roman ruins at Dougga (p138)

Monastir. Another form of gate is the *skifa*, such as the Skifa el-Kahla at Mahdia (p183), which features a long, vaulted passageway protected by a series of gates.

In Tunisia, a kasbah refers to the principle fortress guarding a medina and was usually built astride the city's walls, or positioned in a commanding corner. No kasbah occupies a position as commanding as the one that towers over the ancient fortress city of Le Kef (p144).

A *borj* was a smaller fort added to bolster a medina's defences at key points, such as the Borj Ennar in Sfax (p190). It also described free-standing forts like the Borj Ghazi Mustapha on Jerba (p243).

A *ribat* was a cross between a fort and a monastery. They were occupied by Islamic warriors, who divided their time between fighting and quiet contemplation of the Quran. Most have now disappeared, with the notable exceptions of the *ribats* of Sousse (p162) and Monastir (p170).

Visual Arts
MODERN PAINTING
Introduced by the French, painting is now a well-established contemporary art form in Tunisia. It ranges from the highly geometric forms of Hédi Turki to Western styles that aim to encapsulate the essence of Tunisian daily life and culture, including scenes of cafés, *hammams* and music and dance performances. The work of Yahia Turki (widely considered to be the father of Tunisian painting) and Ammar Farhat, in particular, fall into this last category. Other well-known names within Tunisia include the artists Jellal Ben Abdallah, Zoubeir Turki and Abdelaziz Gorgi.

Under the French, the ambient lifestyle of Tunisia attracted European artists who were entranced by the North African light and architecture. Most famously, Tunisia was a source of inspiration to the Swiss expressionist Paul Klee, who visited the country in 1914.

In the 1940s, a collection of professional and amateur artists established the nationalist École de Tunis as a counterpoint to French dominance. It was responsible for popularising Tunisian life as a subject matter for painting.

Modern art galleries in Tunisia are mainly confined to Tunis and its wealthy suburbs, especially the traditional artist's haven of Sidi Bou Saïd. The inside back page of the English-language weekly *Tunisia News* has a list of exhibitions. Galerie Alif, behind the French embassy in Tunis, has a vast collection of art books and regular exhibitions in the basement.

Designs and Patterns from North African Carpets and Textiles, by Jacques Revault, is the essential companion for those thinking of buying a carpet in Tunisia and a handy weapon against the touts.

Espace Diwan 9, in the Tunis medina at 9 Rue Sidi ben Arous, also has a good selection.

Other places in Tunis that may be worth checking out include Galerie Yahia, in the Complex Palmarium, 64 Ave Habib Bourguiba; Galerie Artémis at 30 Rue 7232, El-Menzah IX; Galerie des Arts at 42 Complex Jamil, El-Menzah VI; and Galerie Gorgi at 31 Rue Jugurtha, Le Belvédère.

Calligraphy is a primary art form in Islamic cultures because representations of the human form are considered to be heresy.

CALLIGRAPHY

Calligraphy is an art form with a long history in the Islamic world, stemming from the belief that Arabic is a holy language revealed by Allah to the Prophet Mohammed in the form of the Quran. Early calligraphers used an angular script called Kufic that was perfect for stone carving; the eastern wall and minaret of the Great Mosque in Sfax (p189), and above the entrance to the Mosque of the Three Doors in Kairouan (p177) are among the finest examples. Among modern calligraphists, Nja Mahdaoui is renowned for his free-flowing style.

MOSAICS

Mosaic is an ancient technique which was popular during the time of the Roman Empire. The mosaics found in Tunisia date mainly from the 2nd to 6th centuries AD. Those from the 3rd century onwards show a distinctive African style, characterised by large dramatic compositions with vigorous colour and realistic subjects such as amphitheatre games, hunting and scenes of life on the African estates.

Most mosaics are the type known as *opus tessellatum*, in which patterns are formed out of little squares or pieces of stone called *tesserae* (from the Latin, meaning cubes or dice). The technique involved laying out a setting bed of mortar in which the *tesserae* were placed. Mosaics were distributed throughout public baths and private houses, with the most elaborate being found in the main reception rooms, to impress visitors and clients.

The mosaics at the Bardo Museum (p56) in Tunis form an exceptional collection.

Theatre & Dance

Performances of traditional Berber dancing are a popular form of entertainment at the country's resort hotels. These dances date back to pre-Islamic times. They include the dramatic Dance of the Vases, performed by dancers with vases balanced on their heads. This is also a highlight of the Festival of the Ksour, held around Tataouine in November.

Environment

Tunisia was once a lush green country, a home to the great animal species of Africa. Whereas much of Europe was shivering under a blanket of Ice-Age snow, the Sahel and the Sahara were lands of savannah, vast lakes, rivers and forests. The forests and the animals have now all but gone, leaving behind an environment in urgent need of protection from climate change, careless waste disposal and the excessive demands of ill-conceived tourist infrastructure.

Cap Blanc, northwest of Bizerte, is the northernmost point of the African continent, more than 8000km (5000 miles) north of the continent's southernmost tip.

THE LAND

Tunisia looks smaller than it is (164,150 sq km or 63,360 sq miles) because it borders Algeria to the west and Libya to the southeast. Measuring 750km from north to south but only 150km from east to west, Tunisia is a fraction larger than England and Wales, and about the same size as Washington state in the USA, or Victoria in Australia. Sicily is the closest European landfall, just 80km to the northeast.

The ragged and irregular 1400km Mediterranean coastline forms Tunisia's eastern and northern boundaries.

The main mountain range is the Tunisian Dorsale, which represents the easternmost folds of Algeria's Saharan Atlas and the High Atlas Mountains of Morocco. The Dorsale runs northeast from Tébessa in Algeria to Zaghouan, just south of Tunis, and includes Tunisia's highest mountain, Jebel Chambi (1544m). After Zaghouan, the mountains taper off to form the Cap Bon Peninsula.

Sahara, by Marq de Villiers and Sheila Hirtle, markets itself as the biography of the world's greatest desert and doesn't do a bad job; little specifically on Tunisia but essential for lovers of the desert.

The majority of the country's arable land lies north of this line. These agricultural regions cover the high plains known as the Tell, and the fertile valley of the Oued Medjerda. The Medjerda, which rises near Souq Ahras in eastern Algeria, is the country's only permanent river. To the north of the Medjerda are the Kroumirie Mountains.

Directly south of the Dorsale is a treeless plain, 200m to 400m above sea level, which drops down to a series of *chotts* (salt lakes) before giving way completely to desert. The *erg* (sand sea) that completely covers the southern tip of Tunisia is the eastern extremity of the Grand Erg Oriental, which also covers a large area of Algeria.

WILDLIFE
Animals

North African forest elephants, the smaller cousins of modern African elephants, were once abundant, as were the great cats, including lions and cheetahs. Most disappeared when the Romans began clearing the forests of the interior to grow wheat.

The only large mammal still present in high numbers is the wild boar, but the prospects of seeing this shy creature are somewhat akin to those of spotting President Ben Ali sunning himself on the beach at Sousse. Sightings of mongoose, porcupine and genet (an arboreal, catlike carnivore) are even rarer. All live in the last vestiges of northern forest. Jackal are more widely distributed and striped hyena are occasionally found in the south.

Desert regions are home to privately-owned camels (there are no wild camels), gerbils, hares and the cute, squirrel-like suslik.

There's more chance of spotting the desert varanid (lizard) – a smaller member of the family that includes Australia's goanna and Indonesia's Komodo dragon – snakes (including horned vipers) and scorpions.

Lions were still present in Tunisia until the mid-19th century, when the last was shot near Haidra.

ENDANGERED SPECIES

Several species were hunted to the brink of extinction by (mostly European) shooters. Those that survived are now under government protection in national parks (see below). Protected species include the addax (an antelope species with impressive spiral horns), maned mouflon, oryx, ostrich, serval and fennec (a nocturnal desert fox with enormous, radarlike ears and fur-soled feet to protect against scorching sands). Sadly the monk seal has probably disappeared from the Cap Bon coast.

The elephants used by Hannibal to cross the Alps, and thousands of big cats shipped off to provide entertainment at the Colosseum in Rome, came from Tunisian forests.

BIRDS

More than 200 species have been recorded in Tunisia. They include storks, hawks and eagles in spring and autumn; colourful bee-eaters and rollers; and a host of wading birds and waterfowls.

The number of resident bird species is comparatively small, but millions of migrating birds use the country en route between Europe and sub-Saharan Africa in spring and autumn. Having survived the formidable barrier of the Sahara and hunters' guns in Sicily and Malta, landfall in Tunisia provides a welcome respite.

See p252 for information about bird-watching, as well as the boxed text on p122.

Plants

The Kroumirie Mountains are densely forested with evergreen holm oak and cork oak. The strawberry tree is another common species, so-called for the striking red fruit that ripen in November/December; just as striking are the fragrant white flowers that cover the tree in autumn.

Only small pockets of the Tell's ancient forests of Aleppo pine remain (between Siliana and Makthar) while further south, the *Acacia raddiana* forest of Bou Hedma National Park is all that's left of Tunisia's savannah.

The semi-arid Sahel region is dominated by olive trees, cultivated since before Roman times. If you fly between Jerba and Tunis in daylight, you'll see the enormous area under cultivation. Another feature of this area is *Opuntia tomentosa*, better known as the prickly pear; it's a popular roadside snack.

The treeless plains of the south support large areas of the multi-use esparto grass (see the boxed text, p154).

In the far south, the Jericho rose rolls around the desert, carried by the wind, with its branches curled up in a tight ball that encloses its seeds. It opens only on contact with moisture. In the oases, towering date palms provide shelter for a surprising variety of fruit trees.

NATIONAL PARKS

The government has set aside nine national parks (more are planned), each protecting a surviving remnant of a typical ecosystem.

The only park with facilities for visitors is Ichkeul National Park (see p121), 30km southwest of Bizerte, which protects Lake Ichkeul. The others are difficult to get to, and some double as military areas.

For the record, other national parks include:

Bou Hedma National Park About 85km east of Gafsa, protects the last 16,000 hectares of Tunisia's once-extensive acacia forests. A number of species previously extinct in Tunisia are being reintroduced, including addax, maned mouflon, oryx and ostrich.

Boukornine National Park About 18km south of Tunis at Hammam Lif, Boukornine (1900 hectares) surrounds Jebel Boukornine (576m). Home to wild boars, jackals, porcupines and the military.

Chambi National Park About 15km west of Kasserine, these 6700 hectares of forest surround Tunisia's highest mountain, Jebel Chambi. Most of the forest is Aleppo pine, but there's also a pocket of cork oak and juniper. Animals include mountain gazelles and striped hyenas.

Tunis International Centre for Environmental Technologies (www.citet.nat.tn) Organisation set up after 1992 Rio conference; seeks change through education and adoption of Western technology to expand the reach of environmental protection programmes.

Feija National Park Near the Algerian border, 20km northwest of Ghardimao, this park covers 2600 hectares of oak forest. Animals include Barbary deer, wild boar and jackal, while serval are being reintroduced.

Orbata National Park West of Gafsa, this new park covers 3000 hectares including desert mountain habitat for the mouflon sheep.

Sidi Toui Saharan National Park About 50km south of Ben Guerdane, Sidi Toui (6300 hectares) covers arid plains and dune country; home to gazelle, jackal, and the successfully reintroduced fennec fox.

Zagouan National Park About 60km south of Tunis, this new 2000-hectare park is home to the rare golden eagle.

In 2002 a joint project between the Tunisian government and the World Bank was initiated to improve the management of the parks, including opening them up for organised eco-tourism projects. Although things are progressing slowly, visiting the parks may soon become a lot easier.

ENVIRONMENTAL ISSUES

Environmental degradation isn't just a modern phenomenon. The Romans' agricultural expansion destroyed most of Tunisia's forests (down from an estimated 30% in pre-Roman times to less than 2% now) with an attendant loss of biodiversity. The ecology of the high plains has been destroyed forever and Tunisia loses around 23,000 hectares of arable land to erosion every year. The wheat-growing regions of the Tell are scarred by massive erosion gullies and much former agricultural land is suitable only for grazing.

Water shortage is a real problem. The huge water requirements of the tourist industry have depleted artesian water levels and dried up springs. This is nowhere more evident than in Jerba, where the water needs of the island's resort hotels have threatened the existence of agriculture on the island and made the water undrinkable. Dam construction ensures that most places in the north receive adequate supply.

Westerners are often shocked by the depressing amount of litter in the countryside; it's not unusual to see rubbish being thrown from cars or buses. Government campaigns appear to be having some success in educating people about responsible garbage disposal, but it's a slow process. You'll find rubbish bins in most medium-sized towns, and the government has invested a lot of money in clearing beaches of rubbish.

Pollution from heavy industries has caused widespread damage to the marine environment of the shallow Gulf of Gabès. The gulf's fishing stocks (and the livelihood of local fishermen) are also under threat.

The government has developed a national strategy for sustainable development, but legislation has been slow in coming, while the resources and political will necessary to enforce the environmental programmes have taken a back-seat to economic imperatives.

National Office of Sanitation (www.onas.nat.tn) Government organisation which focuses on pollution and water resources in the context of urban, tourist and industrial developments.

Tunisia Online (www.tunisiaonline.com /environment) Government site with quite detailed section on environmental programmes and links to organisations.

DOING YOUR BIT

There are a few things that you can do to minimise the impact of your stay and preserve what's left of the country's natural resources. Taking as few showers as possible and never leaving the water running while you soap yourself or shave can save a surprising amount of water. Wherever possible, drink tap water, and if you buy bottled water, refill the bottle with tap water (many hotels have fridges). If you're camping, avoid the use of firewood (carry with you a small gas stove for cooking) and if you go out into the desert, always burn your rubbish, including cigarette butts and toilet paper. When walking in the countryside, stick to established paths to reduce your contribution to erosion.

Food & Drink by Rafik Tlatli with Abigail Hole

Rafik Tlatli is the head chef and hotelier of Hotel Les Jasmins and Restaurant Slovenia in Nabeul. He has written a number of books, and made regular radio and TV broadcasts on cooking in Europe and Tunisia.

Tunisians like their food hot – this usually gentle race equates this preference with their passionate temperament. They also get hungry when they see red on their plate – the colour of appetite, passion and tomatoes. With abundant local fresh produce, Tunisian cooking is packed with sun-focused flavours, and based around grains, fresh vegetables and fruits, fish and olive oil – the locally profuse foodstuffs celebrated in many a Roman mosaic.

The cooking of early dwellers was limited by their circumstances, often nomadic, and the cooking pots they could take with them. Many dishes, such as *tajine* (different from the Moroccan dish of the same name, this is an omelette with meat, egg, cheese and vegetables), stem from those days on the move: the Berbers, who dominated Tunisia originally, cooked good plain food and introduced couscous. Centuries of immigrants colonised the cuisine as well as the country, bringing Roman, Arabic, Jewish, Turkish, Andalusian and French tastebuds into the equation. And Tunisia's importance during the early spice trade meant that caraway, saffron, mustard, cayenne, ginger, cinnamon, black pepper and sugar all floated through its harbours and onto its plates.

STAPLES & SPECIALITIES

The Momo Cookbook: A Gastronomic Journey Through North Africa, produced by the London restaurant, has recipes, covers background to cookery culture and has delectable photography.

Tunisians refuel regularly – at least three times daily, often starting off with a street snack around 9am or 10am (or at any peckish point). But the day revolves around the three old favourites: breakfast *(ftour sbah)*, lunch *(ftour)* and dinner *(ashaa)*.

Breakfast consists of milk, coffee, eggs, *assida* (a pudding made with flour or ground semolina, olive oil and dates), fritters, *sohlob* (sorghum, sugar, cinnamon and ginger), or *hsou* (a spicy soup with a base of semolina and capers). The morning routine differs in the countryside. Farmers wake up early (5am or so), have a pre-work coffee, and at about 9am eat a solid meal, whereas most town dwellers will skip the 5am slot for mysterious reasons.

For the two main meals, the star of the show is couscous, a stew or pasta, often given sterling support by soups, salads, vegetable dishes, *tajine* or fish.

You'll be surprised to see how much tinned tuna features in Tunisian meals, vying with *harissa* (chilli paste) for the most-used ingredient award: in sandwiches, dolloped on a salad, and alongside *harissa* as hors d'oeuvres.

Harissa

www.harissa.com Website dedicated to Tunisian Jews, with weird syntax, but some good stuff on dishes and background.

Tunisian cuisine revolves around *harissa*, a fire-red chilli concoction made from crushed dried red peppers, garlic, salt and caraway seeds. Hot peppers were introduced by the Spanish, and the word comes from the Arabic meaning 'break into pieces', as the paste is traditionally made by pounding red chillies in a mortar. Tunisians associate its heat with passion, and an old tale says that a man can judge his wife's love by the amount of spice in his food – if it's bland then romance is dead.

Bread

Bread is eaten with every meal; it's usually a heavy baguette (long crusty French loaf), but often, particularly in the countryside, it's *tabouna*. This traditional Berber bread is flat, round and heavy, flavoured with *hab hla-*

oua (aniseed), and named after the traditional clay-domed ovens in which it's baked. The price of bread is subsidised and controlled – riots resulted from price rises in 1984.

Seafood

Fish are abundant and often flavoured with garlic, saffron, cumin, paprika, turmeric or dried rosebuds. Fried fish is traditionally accompanied by *tastira*, a delicate mixture of fried tomatoes and eggs, stirred together, cut into fine pieces, and seasoned with caraway seeds, salt and olive oil. *Kabkabou* is a baked dish with saffron, preserved lemons, tomatoes and capers.

Also popular are mussels, clams, calamari and oysters, as well as crayfish and lobster (particularly around Tabarka), which are boiled and often served with a roux (white sauce made from butter and flour) and mayonnaise.

Prawns are expensive for Tunisians, but they are very fond of them. *Chevrettes* are very small, and usually boiled and served with mayonnaise. The succulent larger varieties are grilled, sautéed with garlic and parsley, or simmered in a *gargoulette* (clay cooking pot).

Briq

The stolidly named *briq* is extremely addictive; it's of Middle Eastern origin, but the Tunisians have taken the *briq* to their hearts and stomachs. It's a flaky deep-fried envelope of pastry that's usually filled with a satisfying, tie-splattering slurp of egg (skilfully rendered so that the white is cooked and the yolk is runny). It might also be stuffed with lightly cooked onions, parsley, potato, capers, tuna, egg, seafood, chicken or meat.

Briqs aren't just confined to savoury delights, but can be stickily sweet too, often filled with almond or sesame paste and covered in honey for good measure.

Couscous

The national dish, couscous (semolina granules) is eaten by rich and poor alike – it's more versatile than a show-jumping saxophonist, with more than 300 ways of serving it up. It's eaten at festivals and family celebrations – people eat it communally, delving into a shared large single deep bowl.

Couscous is prepared by wetting the grains and steaming them in a *couscoussière*, a two-piece pot. The upper part is lined with a sieve, which holds the couscous grains, while the sauce is cooked slowly in the lower part, and aromatic steam from this rises up through the sieve to cook the couscous – the grains expand up to three times their original size.

Couscous is served topped by a sauce that could harbour vegetables, chickpeas, beef, chicken, lamb or fish.

Kemia

Kemia are appetisers – an array of small tasty dishes that are usually served with alcoholic drinks or when you sit down to eat. They're a version of Middle Eastern mezze, and similarly social: it's often the custom to get together for drinks and *kemia*. At such a gathering you might be offered nuts, olives, *poutargue* (mullet roe), sliced dried fish, spiced octopus, squid and shrimps, crushed carrots, pumpkin or courgette mixed with spices and *harissa*, *imalah* (pickled carrots and cauliflower), persimmons, sesame sticks and relishes. Then would come salads, corn on the cob, or *tajine*, mini *briqs*, *salade meshouia* (blended roasted peppers, served cold) and *omni houria* (cooked carrots mashed with garlic and olive oil).

The Great Book of Couscous: Classic Cuisines of Morocco, Algeria and Tunisia, by Copeland Marks, includes recipes, visits to markets and chefs' homes and comparisons of the North African cuisines.

www.globalgourmet.com/destinations/tunisia Gastronomic morsels – both recipes and cultural.

DID YOU KNOW?

Tunisia is unusual in North Africa in that it often serves couscous with fish.

TRAVEL YOUR TASTEBUDS

The most eagerly anticipated dish at any informal drinks party will be *akoud*: a glutinous dish of bull's genitals and tripe in garlic and cumin sauce.

The thinking person's *ojja* (tangy tomato and garlic sauce mixed with lightly scrambled egg) is the variety spiced up with brains.

Often eaten to celebrate Eid al-Adha, *daouara* is a type of sausage made of sheep liver and lungs, spiced with parsley and mint, served with couscous or rice.

Mloukhia is a pungent beef or lamb stew, simmered until the meat almost disappears into the sauce, with powdered *corète* (aka *mloukhia*; a herb). It has a unique, some might say slimy, taste.

People often have a milk drink – *lben* – when eating couscous: another acquired taste that's worth sampling.

We Dare You...

...to try a Barbary Fig (aka Cactus Fruit or Prickly Pear). Introduced by the Spanish in the 16th century, these are covered in fine spines that'll leave your hand like a cactus if you try to pick one up. They are plump, juicy red-orange fruits, in season October to December. Tip: get the vendor to peel it for you.

Some Tunisian cakes are so well-sugared they make your teeth curl. See how sweet you can go, washing them down with a cup of mint tea with 10 sugars.

Fruit & Nuts

Tunisia has wonderful seasonal fruit. Ripened in the Tunisian sun, it has a flavour that's a glorious surprise to those used to buying imported foodstuffs. Grapes are at their best at the end of August – try delicious white muscats from around Kélibia, or *razzegoui*, a large white grape, shaded pink. Summer sees roadsides stacked with succulent *della* (melon). Fresh *tmer* (dates) appear from October – there are over 100 types, but finest of all, with almost translucent flesh, are called *deglat ennour* (finger of light). *Mishmish* are apricots with an extraordinary delicate flavour; you might want to couple them with some crunchy *inzas bouguidma* (miniature pears). From around September, pomegranates start to join the dessert menu, their deep blush-red fruit often covered in sugar, so specify if you want them without *(sans sucre)*. Fresh almonds are in season in July and August (their pods are pale green and suedelike) – crack them open to find a gleaming pale kernel. Other nuts frequently used in desserts or eaten as appetizers are hazelnuts, pistachios and cashews.

Couscous mein Leibgericht, by Mme Klementine Konstantini, is available in French and German. Tunisian specialities are described and recipes supplied.

DRINKS

Cafés deck every corner, crammed with people (usually male) drinking *ahwa arbi* (Turkish coffee) fragrant with orange blossom or rose water, *express* (espresso coffee), *café direct* (coffee with milk), or *capucin* (espresso with a dash of milk). Mint tea is also popular; in touristy places it's often served with pine nuts, which react with the hot tea to create a delectable buttery taste – some people add fresh almonds, which have the same delicious effect.

Although Tunisia is a Muslim country, alcohol is easily available. A popular aperitif is *boukha* – a gloopily sweet, aromatic spirit made from distilled figs, served at room temperature or chilled, and often mixed with Coke. Also popular are aniseed drinks such as Pastis – a French relic – and whiskey, which appeals for its snobbish value. *Thibarine* is herb based, made from an ancient recipe in the Thibar region near Dougga. *Sarabi* is as sweet as you'd expect a liqueur distilled from dates to be; it's from Soukra (near Tunis).

Saveur de Tunisie by Rafik Tlatli, in French, supplies innovations in Tunisian cooking.

Laghmi, fermented palm sap, is found in the southern oases, and can be powerful – check the quality before surrendering your stomach.

Celtia is the local brand of beer. It's a drinkable lager – and also the cheapest. French Lowenbrau is also brewed locally.

Tunisia has had some practice in wine-producing: Dionysus, god of wine, staggers joyously all over Roman mosaics, and Magon, contemporary to the Phoenicians, wrote about techniques of production still used today.

Tunisia's wines come from its northern vineyards, from varied grapes such as shiraz, merlot, cabernet and sauvignon blanc. Reds tend to be heavy but a safer bet than the whites.

Délice de Tunisie, edited by Rafik Tlatli, is a French book that brings together specialities of 10 different regions, chosen by Tunisian chefs.

CELEBRATIONS

Festivals and occasions are a chance to chow down in earnest; you can measure the importance of the event by the number and variety of dishes.

There are many dishes specific to certain times, such as at the birth of a child, when it's traditional to eat *zrir* (nut paste served in small glasses) – it's thought this will help revitalise the mother.

Marriage

Marriage is the ultimate opportunity for families to show off their hospitality with a huge spread. The festivities last seven days, with the culinary part kicking off on the fourth day, known as Outia Sghira. During the evening, a bull is slaughtered in front of the bride's house. Its meat is used to make dishes for the ensuing days, but that evening it's vegetable couscous for dinner. The fifth day is Outia Kbira, and guests dine on meat and chickpea couscous followed by tea and *baklaoua* (vanilla slice stuffed with almonds). On the sixth day is a big feast when friends are given *tajine*, *market ommalah* (meatball stew), *salade meshouia* and *klaya* (meat and paprika stew).

Finally, it's the big day: lunch is pasta with meat sauce, and *mloukhia*. In the evening everyone eats couscous again, and finishes with fruit, leaving a bit of room for *baklaoua* and other sweets during the evening's celebrations.

Ramadan

The flipside of the Muslim holy month, with its daylight fasting, is night-time no-holds-barred feasting.

Each night, people start Ramadan breakfast by drinking a glass of water and eating a date. Afterwards they tuck into a hearty bowl of *shorba* (spicy soup) and an egg *briq*. Next on the menu is couscous or pasta.

Once the day's hunger has been sated, people socialise at home until late, topping up on fruits, sweets and cakes, and sipping tea or coffee.

Before sunrise, people wake to eat *shour*, a light meal, and energise for the day's fast by snaffling some *mesfouf*, an elaborate couscous dessert, with dates, raisins, grilled chopped almonds, sugar and cannelle, and covered in hot or cold milk.

So the holy month is not only a time of abstinence, but also sees the most extravagant and varied meals of the year. The feasts unite the family and the country, as most people will be settling down to eat these traditional dishes at exactly the same time.

La cuisine tunisienne d'Ommok Sannafa, by Mohamed Kouki, is a French and Arabic classic on Tunisian cooking.

Eid al-Fitr

Eid al-Fitr – the lesser *eid* – marks the end of Ramadan. This small festival is big on Tunisian cakes, such as *baklaoua*, *ghraïba* made from fine semolina, or *makhroud* – Kairouan's speciality, a semolina cake packed with dates and almond paste.

For three days families visit each other bearing sweet confections. Children not only get to enjoy this sugar fest, but are dressed in brand-new clothes.

250 Recettes Classique de Cuisine Tunisienne, by Edmond Zeitoun, has mouthwatering Jewish-Tunisian recipes.

Eid al-Adha

Eid al-Adha is the greater *eid*, taking place 70 days after Eid al-Fitr. It's a bad time for sheep as each family slaughters an animal and serves it up in different guises for at least a week as, for example, *m'rouzia*, a stew with raisins and chestnuts, or *daouara* (see the boxed text, p50).

Ras as-Sana

Ras as-Sana is the first day of the lunar or Hejira year. People always prepare, among other things, the dark-green dish of *mloukhia* (see the boxed text, p50) – it's prepared because the year is green.

In the Nabeul region, a special couscous dish, *kadid* (salted dried meat conserved since Eid al-Adha) is prepared, decorated by a hard-boiled egg, raisins, chickpeas, sweets and dried fruit. Giving the decoration a final flourish is a doll made from coloured sugar, unique to the area.

Mediterranean Cooking Revised Edition, by the expert Mediterranean cookery writer Paula Wolfert, pays particular attention to Tunisian specialities and traditions, laying emphasis on healthy but robust eating.

Moulid an-Nabi

Moulid an-Nabi commemorates the birth of the Prophet Mohammed, and in the morning everyone tucks into *assida*, which can be made two ways: the simple version is made of fine semolina or flour, sprinkled with oil or butter and honey. The more refined, Ottoman-influenced sort is a pudding made of crushed pine seeds, topped with cream and hazelnuts, pine seeds, pistachios and crushed almonds. Again it's sweet-toothed Kairouan that excels in its preparation.

WHERE TO EAT & DRINK

Tunisia's eateries are firmly divided – the cheaper places are basic, don't usually serve alcohol and are regular local haunts. Some of these are known as *gargottes*; they're small, with quick service, serving sandwiches and meals such as grilled chicken, fish, stew and couscous. They're cheap but may be heavy on the spice. *Rôtisseries* are even cheaper and serve up mainly fried meats. Fast-food places serve hamburgers, chips and various sandwiches. *Meshoui* are roadside joints selling barbecued meat – usually spotted in clusters and identifiable by hulking hanging carcasses and smoking barbecues.

Restaurants touristiques are more formal. Despite the name, they're not just for tourists – one of the legacies of the French is that people eat out a lot more than is traditional in Arabic countries. These restaurants are assessed by the ONTT (national tourist office) and marked with one to three forks. They serve Tunisian and international specialities, usually

---

TUNISIA'S TOP FIVE

Chez Nous (see p79) Excellent roast veal, sautéed prawns and grilled fresh fish.

Slovenia (see p104) Restaurant that produces innovative Tunisienne cuisine, such as succulent *couseïla* (couscous with seafood, fish, lamb and chicken).

Les Emirs (see p170) Serves delicious Tunisian specialities, such as couscous with stuffed calamari, lamb (*a la gargoulette*) and Berber *mechoui*.

De La Medina (see p100) Renowned for its *tajine*, *koucha* with saffron and *bouza* with dried fruit.

Restaurant Haroon (see p245) Supplies the best fresh fish, Jerban couscous and lamb *(a la gargoulette)*.

DOS & DON'TS

- You should always eat or pass things with your right hand – your left hand is reserved for less salubrious tasks like wiping your bottom.
- Make sure you eat up all your food, and don't refuse if someone offers you more.
- If you drop a piece of bread on the floor, you should pick it up and kiss it.
- It's OK to burp, but you should ask God's pardon: *Astakhfirou allah*.
- Don't start eating before the father of the family.

---

have a set three-course menu (TD9 to TD12), and serve a range of wines, aperitifs and digestifs.

You can eat in many hotels even if you're not a guest; however, the hours are strict – 12.30pm to 2.30pm and 7pm to 9pm.

There are a variety of cafés – some small, standup places fit for a swallow of caffeine and a pastry, others leisurely and dominated by men gossiping and playing dominoes and cards. *Sheeshas* – tobacco water pipes – are often in evidence at the latter. These contraptions cool the fragrant smoke, making for a gentle puff with attendant musical gurgle; you can have *mwassi* (honey-soaked) or *tufa* (apple flavoured). Some cafés are mixed, particularly in Tunis, and there are also a few all-women places tucked away.

www.paula-wolfert.com
Recipes from this North
African culinary specialist.

Most bars are boozy, raucous dives, unsuitable for women as it's a male-dominated scene. If women want to drink, it's best to head for a reputable hotel bar, or drink at a restaurant. Liquor stores and supermarkets sell alcohol, but put your bottles in bags when carrying them around in public and hide the bottles or cans if you are drinking in public places like the beach.

Quick Eats

Tunisians have developed snacking into a fine art, with countless solutions for a hungry rumble.

Popular on winter mornings, particularly with labourers, is *lablabi*. This steamy, set-you-up-for-the-week soup is based on chickpeas. It's served in distinctive terracotta bowls (you'll see them stacked up where it's sold) that are filled with pieces of bread with soup poured over the top, spiced with *harissa* and cumin. Sometimes egg and tuna are stirred in too.

A favourite savoury is a *casse-crôute*, a half-baguette stacked in jaw-challenging style with *harissa*, *meshouia*, cucumber, tomato, fried egg, tuna, olives and a few chips on top. Another temptation is a *fricasse* – a folded piece of leavened bread stuffed with *harissa*, potatoes and tuna, and fried.

An important part of life is the doughnut (*yoyo* or *beigent*), eaten fresh and hot in the morning. They're made of soft yielding dough dipped in oil, served with sugar or enveloped in honey. *Babalouni* or s*hishi* are large doughnuts, fried and rolled in sugar. These are an afternoon snack – so don't try getting yourself a big doughnut in the morning.

Recette de Couscous, by
Magali Morsy, includes
couscous recipes from all
over North Africa.

VEGETARIANS & VEGANS

The thought that people might not eat meat through choice is a strange one for Tunisians, and veganism an unheard-of curiosity. But fruit, vegetables, grains and nuts are the staples of Tunisian cuisine, so you'll have no cause to go hungry. Lots of starters are meatless: salads appear on every menu – *salades Tunisienne* or *meshouia* are delicious and ubiquitous, though you'll have to ask that they hold the tuna. The *briq* is often free of meat, and *ojja*, *shakshouka* and *tajine* are other options if you check what's going into them – often a meat stock will be used. Vegans will find eating out in Tunisia difficult, and will have to self-cater most of the time, though salads and *lablabi* may be good options. Otherwise you can buy your food fresh from colourful food markets – every town has a market day.

WHINING & DINING

Tunisians adore children, and your offspring will be welcome everywhere. *Gargottes* are noisy, lively places and so children slot in fine – the food might be spicier, but you can ask for less piquant portions. Many restaurants are aimed at families and so don't serve alcohol – some of those that do are quasi-bars and are male-dominated, smoky and not so child-friendly. Tunisia's sublime climate means that you'll often be eating outside, which is ideal for little ones. Pasta dishes, chips, hamburgers, grilled chicken, salads, and, of course, cakes are all good staples you'll find everywhere.

HABITS & CUSTOMS

Some families eat sitting around a *mida*, a round, low table on which the food is served in a big communal dish. If the family is religious, meals start with the words *bis millah* – invoking Allah – and end with thanks: *al-hamdu lillah*. Don't be surprised if at the end of the meal the women leave the table and the men stay (Western women will be treated as honorary men). Table manners apply above all when you are guest in someone's house.

EAT YOUR WORDS
Useful Phrases
What do you recommend?
 Ash noua tansahni.
Not too spicy, please.
 Moush haar.
Could you please bring me some/more?
 Zidni shouaïa, min fadhlek.
Thanks, that was delicious.
 Baraka la houfik, bnin barsha.
I'm a vegetarian.
 Ana ma nakolsh kan el khodhra hlib oua adham.
I'm a vegan, I don't eat meat or dairy products.
 Ana végétalien ma na kolsh l'ham, ma na kolsh halib oua. Moushtakkatou.
I have a wheat/nut allergy.
 Ana andi hassassia lil kamh oua el boufrioua.

Menu Decoder
brochette – meat or fish kebab
kammounia – meat stew with lots of cumin
keftaji – spicy ratatouille usually served with meatballs
kousha – lamb seasoned with rosemary, mint and turmeric and baked in a clay pot with potatoes, tomatoes and capsicum
loup à la sfaxienne – perch baked with tomatoes, onions, peppers, garlic and capers
merguez – spicy seasoned lamb or goat sausages, eaten hot or cold
mérou au citron – grouper poached in a sauce of lemon, harissa, and cumin, with slices of lemon between each morsel of fish
meshoui – grilled meat
ojja – fresh tomatoes and chillies blended into a spicy sauce – often prawns, merguez or brains are added – with eggs stirred in at the last minute

ragoût de gnaouia – meat and vegetable stew, rich red in colour and eaten with bread
salade meshouia – grilled peppers and tomatoes with olive oil and garlic; served cold garnished with olives or tuna
salade Tunisienne – peppers, tomatoes, cucumber, chopped small and seasoned with lemon juice, olive oil and mint
shakshouka – vegetable dish of mostly peppers, onions and tomatoes
shorba – spicy soup, usually oily, made from meat or chicken and celeriac with pasta
tajine – unlike its Moroccan namesake, this is an omelette that may contain white beans or potatoes, breadcrumbs, chopped meat, cheese and egg; it's usually made from leftovers

English-Arabic Glossary

BASICS

bill/check	al-fatura
breakfast	ftour sbah
dinner	ashaa
fork	farshita
knife	sekina
lunch	ftour
oil	zit
olives	zitoun
spoon	mirafa
sugar	sukar

STAPLES

beer	birra
bread	khobz
butter	zebda
chicken	djej
chips	batata maklya
eggs	adham
fruit	ghilla
lamb	alloush
mineral water	madabouza
rice	rouz
wine	shreb

FISH

bream	dorade
crawfish	langouste
grouper	mérou
mullet	mullet
octopus	pulpe
perch	loup de mer
prawns	crevettes
red mullet	rouget
swordfish	espadon
tuna	thon

COOKING TERMS

barbecued	meshoui
fried	mukli

Bardo Museum   متحف باردو

The **Bardo Museum** (☎ 513 650; admission TD4.2, plus camera TD1; ⏰ 9.30am-4.30pm mid-Sep–Mar, 9am-5pm Apr & Jun–mid-Sep) is Tunisia's finest museum. It's essential and fantastic to visit. If you go to any of Tunisia's ancient sites, the Bardo's collection fills in the picture of what they contained. Most famous is its superb collection of mosaics that adorned Roman Africa's sumptuous villas – an incredible document of Roman obsessions, lifestyle and beliefs. There's stunning marble statuary too, though any protruding bits were bashed in by the Vandals, which explains the lack of noses and genitals. The Bardo also houses the Islamic museum, forming a dramatic contrast to all these portraits, as Muslim art eschews the figurative and concentrates on the purely decorative.

> **The museum would be worth a visit even without its exhibits**

The museum would be worth a visit even without its exhibits. In the suburb of Bardo, about 4km west of the Tunis city centre, it occupies the former official residence of the Husseinite beys. The first palace was commissioned by the Hafsid sultan Al-Mustansir (1249–77), who was responsible for restoring and diverting the Zaghouan-to-Carthage aqueduct to supply the palace and the medina with water. The present extravaganza was built in the late 17th century, and was steadily enlarged by a succession of Husseinite occupants – there are some particularly lively ceilings. It became a museum in 1888.

PRACTICALITIES

You can get here by taxi – about TD3 from the centre of Tunis, or by métro léger (Tunis' tram network) to Le Bardo station on line 4 (TD0.5). The entrance is on the northern side (rue Mongi Slim), while the station is on the museum's southern side (blvd du 20 Mars 1956).

Another option is the yellow city bus No 3 (TD0.5) from Tunis Marine or Hôtel Africa Méridien. It stops around the corner on ave de l'Union de Maghreb Arabe.

If you want to avoid the tour groups, it's best to arrive early, late or at lunch time. In summer, it's a good idea to start on the 2nd floor, as it gets hot in the afternoon. It'll take at least half a day to see everything, and it's worthwhile making two visits so that you can see everything without suffering museum overkill.

Most of the labelling is in Arabic and French, but the bookshop sells an English museum guide (TD12.5).

GROUND FLOOR
Room 1, Prehistoric

Early Palaeolithic (200,000 to 100,000 BC) to Neolithic times are summed up in this interesting room. Displays include a re-creation of the Hermaion d'El Guettar, a religious monument with a striking resemblance to a heap of rubble, discovered near Gafsa. It is thought to be 40,000 years old and probably the world's oldest spiritual monument.

Room 2, Baal Hammon

This room is named after a small terracotta statue of the Punic god seated on a throne, his arms resting on sphinxes. It also houses an extraordinary lion-headed representation of the goddess Tanit, which has an almost cartoonish quality. Her feather dress also shows an Egyptian influence. Both were found at Thinissut, near Bir Bou Regba, and date from the

BARDO MUSEUM

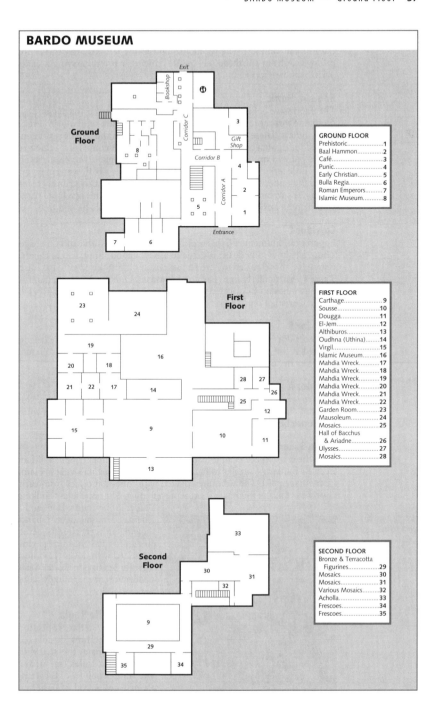

Ground Floor

Exit

Bookshop

Corridor C

Gift Shop

3

Corridor B

8

Corridor A

4

2

5

1

Entrance

7   6

GROUND FLOOR

First Floor

23

24

19

16

20   18

21   22   17   14

15

9

13

28   27

26

25

12

10   11

FIRST FLOOR

Second Floor

33

30

31

32

9

29

35   34

SECOND FLOOR

1st century AD – proof that Punic religious practices continued long after the Roman conquest. The room also houses the famous 3rd-century BC priest stele from Carthage (see p89), showing a priest carrying a child, perhaps to be sacrificed.

Room 4, Punic

The expressive collection of clay funeral masks from Carthage (see p84) dominate this room, grimacing and smiling alongside similarly grotesque tiny amulets. These bizarre, contorted faces – male and female – were intended to frighten bad spirits away from the dead. A couple of fragmented masks painted on ostrich eggshells are also on display. There's an interesting little terracotta figure thought to depict either a bath scene or a voyage to the underworld. Punic ceramics include a gloriously grumpy-faced jar, and a surreal terracotta lamp in the shape of a man's head: the flame would come out of his beard, which merges into the shape of a frog.

Corridor C

Funerary monuments fill this area, with works from Korba and Carthage. These all show how death is actually a really good thing, where the deceased is either elevated to hero status, or standing at the gates of paradise. There's a particularly fine marble nine muses. One piece – the epitaph of Gatosus – has an inscription that begins with a pagan formula and ends with a Christian one, showing the merging of the faiths.

Corridor B

This corridor is lined with a collection of elaborately decorated stelae unearthed at the minor site of Macota, near Makthar, with several different panels – the top ones bounce with dolphins, suns and flowers.

Corridor A

Rare fresco fragments from Carthage, Gigthis and Bou Grara line this corridor, indicating how colourful the walls of the Roman villas must have once been.

Room 5, Early Christian

Here the centrepiece is an unusual 6th-century cruciform baptismal font from El-Kantara – similar to the bath in George Sebastian's villa in Hammamet (see p97). The walls are covered with funeral mosaics from early churches. Among them is a vivid representation of a nonchalant-looking Daniel in the Lion's Den, and a schematic mosaic from Tabarka showing an early church – even down to its mosaic paving decorated with doves. The short corridor leading to Room 6 has a collection of charmingly naïve terracotta tiles.

Detail of a mosaic from Bulla Regia (Room 6).
CHRISTOPHER WOOD

Room 6, Bulla Regia

This has a stellar collection of Roman statues discovered at Bulla Regia – the site with underground villas (see p131). The statues hail from the Temple of Apollo, god of light and music, and the dominant figure is, naturally, the god himself, holding a lyre. He's huge, languorous and sensual, with how-does-it-stay-on drapery. He is flanked by figures of Minerva and Saturn. All around the room are representations of Ceres, goddess of the earth, particularly popular in the Tunisian wheat belt. The room also contains a mosaic of Perseus gripping a Gorgon's head while rescuing Andromeda from a sea monster.

Room 7, Roman Emperors
The walls are lined with a motley-looking crew of broken-nosed Roman emperors. They include a cherubic Augustus, known as the father of Roman Tunisia. Septimus Severus, the only African-born emperor, has very Roman features, while the Gordian sports a two-day growth and looks suitably depressed – he became emperor only in his 80s, and reigned for three weeks before Carthage fell and he committed suicide.

Room 8, Islamic Museum
This section was being renovated at the time of research.

FIRST FLOOR
The stairway up to the first floor from Room 5 is lined with Christian funerary mosaics, with some touching inscriptions such as: 'Rogata lived four years, 11 months, three days and seven hours'. They sometimes supply information such as occupation, providing a brief insight into ancient economic activities.

Islamic Museum
A right turn leads to an older section of the palace, housing the second part of the Islamic Museum. Around a central courtyard, the rooms include a little coffee-making room and formal reception rooms. They are furnished in the 19th-century Husseinite style, with coloured glass and stucco; black-and-white arches contrast with the elaborate coloured tiling.

Room 9, Carthage
On the left at the top of the stairs, this grand, colonnaded reception room has an icing-sugar ceiling and is devoted to some triumphant statuary from Roman Carthage (see p84). Two beautiful black marble busts were found in the Antonine Baths. The statues are arranged around large floor mosaics from Oudhna (Uthina; see p149), including an industrious portrait of 3rd-century farm life in Roman Africa (remarkably similar to today), and another of Dionysus offering a vine to Ikarios, both from the Laberii house.

Room 10, Sousse
From the Sousse villa of a wealthy horse breeder, an enormous floor mosaic covers nearly 140 sq metres, surrounding a central medallion representing the Triumph of Neptune (the sea god was a popular theme in coastal towns) riding in a chariot drawn by sea horses. The Lord Julius mosaic in this room is famous for its depiction of life on a wealthy lord's estate.

The giant sandalled foot and head by the doorway leading to the Dougga room belong to a statue of Jupiter from the Capitol of Thuburbo Majus (see p147). Their size suggest the statue stood a ludicrous 7.5m high.

The ceiling in this room has a tremendous interlocking pattern.

ROOM 6 HIGHLIGHT

A glorious Roman statuary with a mammorth, sensual Apollo as the centrepiece.

ROOM 9 HIGHLIGHT

Huge mosaics from Oudna overlooked by black and white marble statues.

ROOM 10 HIGHLIGHT

A wealthy horse-breeder's show-off mosaic covers 140 sq metres.

Room 11, Dougga

This room contains several fine mosaics from Tunisia's most beautifully set Roman site (see p138), including the celebrated work depicting huge dark-skinned cyclops working Vulcan's forge, from the site's Cyclops Baths. However, the highlight comes from seaside La Chebba: an incredibly fine piece depicting the Triumph of Neptune. He is surrounded by the four seasons, represented by rushes, vines, ears of wheat and olive branches. The work is so well preserved, it appears years rather than millennia old, and the composition and sense of movement is unparalleled. This room's ceiling is an exuberant mass of painted garlands.

ROOM 11 HIGHLIGHT

Several virtuoso mosaics including the unusual Cyclops piece.

Room 12, El-Jem

El-Jem is famed for its huge Roman amphitheatre (see p181), and was a hedonistic town if its mosaics are anything to go by: this selection is centred on the Triumph of Bacchus, a hungover-looking god of wine, riding a chariot pulled by two tigresses. The corners are filled with vines sprouting forth from vases. Other small pieces continue the consumption theme: a hare, a fish and a bunch of grapes.

Room 13, Althiburos

ROOM 13 HIGHLIGHT

A mosaic details an extraordianary 25 types of boat in a room that feels like you've stepped into a music box.

Room 13 hosted palace concerts, and it feels as if you are inside a music box, with brightly painted interlocking patterns and galleries either end. The remote site of Althiburos, about 30km south of Le Kef, yielded one of the museum's more extraordinary finds – a mosaic featuring 25 different types of boat, crewed by an assortment of cupids. The room also features an interesting fishing mosaic found near Menzel Bourguiba, with an unfortunate swimmer being devoured by a sea monster. Another meal scene shows an innovative banquet where the guests sit on benches rather than reclining on couches.

Room 14, Oudhna (Uthina)

This grand salon devoted to Oudhna (Uthina; see p149) was the palace's dining room. One wall is covered by a large 4th-century mosaic of Orpheus charming the beasts. Although parts are badly damaged, the artistry of the surviving detail is astonishing. Next to it is a small mosaic fragment with a rare depiction of a Carthaginian war elephant. The room also features finds from the site's House of the Laberii, including the depiction of the moon goddess Selene gazing on the sleeping figure of Endymion, a handsome shepherd boy granted eternal youth by Jupiter. There are some fine still-life mosaics – one of seafood, one of bread and butter – the depiction is almost painterly as such small fragments have been used to make up the picture. There's also a striking black-marble bust with a Libyan hairstyle.

Room 15, Virgil

ROOM 15 HIGHLIGHT

The only known portrait of the poet in one of the palace's finest rooms.

Room 15 was once part of the bey's private apartments, and is elaborately tiled and stuccoed. The star piece is a 3rd-century mosaic of Virgil from Sousse – the oldest known portrait of the poet. Virgil is seated holding a copy of his *Aeniad*, flanked by two Muses – a nervous-looking Clio (history) and more-composed Melpomene (tragedy). The room splits into four sections – one contains terracotta pieces, another, coins: Punic, Numidian, Roman, Vandal, Byzantine, Arab, Spanish and Ottoman. At the centre is a Zaghouan mosaic showing zodiac signs and gods for the days of the week; the background mimics much-prized Chemtou marble (see p134).

Rooms 17–22, Mahdia Wreck

These six rooms show finds from a ship that went down off Mahdia in the 1st century BC, loaded with decorative objects intended for a Roman villa: it was an impressive cargo of then extremely fashionable Greek statuary. The Bronze Hall displays what was considered hot in home décor in the 1st century BC, including some creepy dancing dwarves. In the Beds Hall, reconstructed beds give an idea of the domestic interior of the villa. The Medallions Hall is lined by stone *tondi* – sea-scarred busts, including one of Aphrodite. This is followed by the remains of the mighty columns in the Architectural Hall – 60 such columns remain underwater. The immense decorated capitals show the scale of the ship's haul.

Room 23, Garden Room

This room's layout shows the importance of the garden to the Italian-style villa, and it's interesting, despite the use of some tacky plastic plants. A 4th-century polygonal mosaic from Carthage spreads across all four walls and features nereids (sea nymphs) and cupids swimming in a sea full of monsters and abundant fish.

Room 24, Mausoleum

The centrepiece here is a 2nd-century stucco tomb from Carthage, from the official's cemetery. A mosaic from Thuburbo Majus (see p146) concentrates on the popular theme of abundance – of both fish and sea beasts. Some stone tiling from the same site is an unusual feature here, showing how the Romans made the most of natural pattern and colour.

Room 25, Mosaics

More of a corridor than a room, this features a curling composition of acanthus flowers surrounding peacocks and other birds, from a *frigidarium* at Thuburbo Majus. It fills up one wall – evidently at this time floridity was in fashion.

Room 26, Hall of Bacchus & Ariadne

The main feature in this room is a large mosaic of the same name from Thuburbo Majus. Small, muscular wrestlers, from Gightis, decorate two other pieces.

Room 27, Ulysses

The room is named after an expressive Ulysses mosaic from the House of Ulysses at Dougga. The wandering hero – with a real look of wonder on his face – is strapped to his shipmast so he might listen to the Sirens without being lured towards them – the dangerous creatures are lined up stage right, while the other sailors are looking away (the story goes their ears are stopped with wax). Alongside is another great piece showing Dionysus as a nipper and a worried-looking aged Silenus vanquishing some pirates who have picked on the wrong boat and are getting turned into dolphins. Above the door is a crowning of Venus that appears to be the product of a disturbed imagination. There's also a beautiful fountain from Thuburbo Majus, featuring Neptune with a watery beard. Above is a finely balanced piece of frivolity from El-Jem, showing a music competition between Apollo and a satyr, with Minerva as judge. A huge Utica mosaic stretches all the way to the floor above, featuring Neptune, Amphitrite and lots of evil sea monsters.

ROOM 27 HIGHLIGHT

A brilliantly expressive mosaic of Ulysses tied up and tempted by Sirens.

Room 28, Mosaics

The star here is a large, peculiar mosaic of Venus (always the vamp), with perfect orbs for breasts, flanked by two female centaurs from Elles, near Makthar, while an El-Jem piece shows a wild boar hunt – an ancient African passion.

SECOND FLOOR
Room 29, Bronze & Terracotta Figurines

A gallery overlooking Room 9, this gives a great view of its floor mosaics. The glass cases mostly feature funerary pottery from Carthage and Sousse. Look out for the bronze statue of a drunken Hercules looking decidedly unheroic.

Room 30, Mosaics

Wild beasts are prominent here, with an unlikely ostrich scene from Le Kef and ferocious bears from Korba. There's a labyrinth from Thuburbo Majus and an unusual panther skin from 4th-century Carthage.

Detail of a mosaic (Room 30).

CHRISTOPHER WOOD

A typically louche piece from El-Jem shows a drunken Dionysus. A 2nd-century Thuburbo Majus mosaic centres on a poet looking dolefully creative, accompanied by two masks – proof that African mosaics occasionally celebrated intellect as well as hunting. Cabinets contain small terracotta figures, contrasting with the show-off scale of the mosaics. There are erotic scenes from El-Jem and inventive pieces such as a vase from Sousse in the shape of a gurning actor's head.

Room 31, Mosaics

From this room you get a good view of the upper part of the Neptune and Amphitrite mosaic (see p61); an untriumphant-seeming Oceanus overlooks the proceedings. A portrayal of Diana, goddess of hunting, riding a stag – again from Thuburbo Majus – shows the goddess as an inset surrounded by stylised wild beasts.

Room 32, Various Mosaics

There are some beautiful floral designs on the walls leading to Room 32, no more than a tiny gallery containing geometric mosaics.

Room 33, Acholla

The minor, yet wealthy Roman port of Acholla, 40km north of Sfax, yielded some fine mosaics that are some of the oldest found in Africa. Many of the pieces come from the Trajan Baths, and give an idea of the scale of decoration in such places. The finest depicts a sea centaur carrying off a nymph.

Rooms 34 & 35, Frescoes

Both rooms were being renovated at the time of research.

Tunis تونس

CONTENTS

Tunis is a curious hybrid, its easiness mocking the frantic nature of other Arabian capitals. Sunglass-sporting city slickers swish past elderly men wearing red felt hats, women wrapped in headscarves link arms with their dressed-to-kill daughters, and artisans blowtorch metal in backstreet hole-in-the-wall workshops as people throng to glittering shopping malls. In the French ville nouvelle, boulevards and cafés are overlooked by graceful 19th-century buildings, with wedding-cake hotels and houses blinkered by tall shutters and bustling palm-lined streets filled with takeaway patisseries and busy restaurants. This profoundly European, eminently straightforward street grid is countered by the twisting allure of the medina – a vast, enchanting maze of arched alleys, delicate mosques, kaleidoscopic-tiled coffeehouses, giant keyhole-shaped studded doors and scattering stray cats.

Tunis is not heavily on the tourist trail. It's a place where you can just wander, but alongside the intrigue of everyday life it offers magnificent things to see and do: the medina's Islamic splendour, narrow alleyway communities and historic *hammams* (bathhouses); the ruins of ancient Carthage, set among the great white villas of the Tunis upper classes; the astoundingly complete Roman mosaics in the palatial Bardo Museum; and the blue-and-white, flower-laden clifftop village of Sidi Bou Saïd.

It's a sociable, small-scale capital, and you're never far from a beach, however urban it might feel compared with the rest of the country. The suburbs of Tunis stretch endlessly out along deep-blue seafronts, where in summer everyone walks in search of a breeze.

HIGHLIGHTS

- Exploring **Carthage** (p84), with its history, mythology and coastal views
- Following small winding streets in the **medina** (p67)
- Admiring **Sidi Bou Saïd** (p90): being this good-looking should be illegal
- Seeing the Roman mosaics at the palatial **Bardo Museum** (p56)

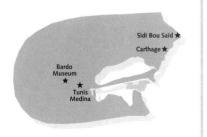

- TELEPHONE CODE: 71
- POPULATION: 700,000

TUNIS

HISTORY

Tunis (ancient Tynes) has existed since the earliest days of Carthaginian expansion. The name features on 5th-century BC maps, and the Roman general Regulus camped here in 255 BC during the First Punic War.

The Romans ignored Tunis after the defeat of Carthage, but after ousting the Byzantines from Carthage in AD 695, the victorious Arab Hassan bin Nooman decided to build again at Tunis, which he felt was in a better defensive position. The medina was sited on a narrow band of high ground flanked by the Sebkhet Sejoumi (salt lake) to the southwest and Lake Tunis to the east. A deep-water channel was dug across the lake to allow access to the sea.

The birth of the city can be dated to the building of the Zitouna (Great) Mosque (see p67) in AD 732, although it was in the 9th century, when Aghlabid ruler Ibrahim ibn Ahmed II moved his court here, that it became the seat of power.

It fell from favour under the Fatimids, who chose Mahdia as their capital in the 10th century, and escaped the subsequent ravages of the Hilalian invasion in the 11th century, emerging again as the capital following the conquest of North Africa by the Almohads in 1160.

The city flourished under the Hafsids, who ruled from 1229 to 1574. The population more than tripled (to about 60,000). Souqs (markets), mosques and *medersas* (Quranic schools) were built, trade boomed and the Zitouna Mosque university was established.

Tunis suffered badly during Turkish-Spanish tussles, which gave rise to the fall of the Hafsids. Much of the city was destroyed and the population fled. Tunis was finally secured for the Ottomans by Sinan Pasha in 1574, and people began to return. Their number was swollen by the arrival of refugees fleeing religious persecution: Moorish Andalusians from Spain and Jews from Livorno in Italy. Many were fine artisans, who played an important role in the city's reconstruction.

The colonising French created a new heart to the city, building their elegant ville nouvelle (new town) just east of the medina on land reclaimed from Lake Tunis.

ORIENTATION

Almost everything of importance to travellers is within the ville nouvelle.

The city's main east–west thoroughfare is ave Habib Bourguiba, running from Lake Tunis to place de l'Indépendance, with the walled medina at its western end. A causeway at the eastern end carries road and light-rail traffic east across Lake Tunis to La Goulette, and then north along the coast to the affluent beach suburbs of Carthage, Sidi Bou Saïd, La Marsa and Gammarth.

The main north–south thoroughfare is the street known as ave de Carthage to the south of ave Habib Bourguiba and as ave de Paris to the north. Ave de Carthage runs southeast to place Barcelone, hub of the city's excellent métro léger (tram network). The train station is on the square's southern side.

TUNIS IN...

Two Days
Spend the morning exploring the **medina** (p67). Head to the **Bardo** (p56) in the afternoon, returning for a promenade along **ave Habib Bourguiba**. Finish up at **Dar el-Jeld** (p78), eating fine traditional Tunisian food in glorious surroundings. The next day head out to **Carthage** (p84). Afterwards take the TGM to **Sidi Bou Saïd** (p90), wandering around the whitewashed backstreets, drinking in the views at the **Café Sidi Chabaane** (p91) and having dinner at one of the village's restaurants.

Four Days
Follow the two-day itinerary, but on the third day visit the extraordinary azure-edged coast near **Korbous** (p111), and splash around where a scaldingly hot spring empties into the sea. On the fourth day explore more of the **medina**, and steam in one of its historic **hammams**. In the evening go to **Gammarth** (p92) for a meal by the sea, and to sample some of its nightlife.

For the 8km trip from the airport into town, take a taxi (TD3.5) or one of the half-hourly No 35 buses to ave Habib Bourguiba (TD0.6).

Maps

The tourist office hands out a good, free map. The best maps are produced by the **Office de la Topographie et de la Cartographie** (☎ 891 477), including *Tunis – Ariana/Bardo*, covering the city centre, and *La Marsa, Sidi Bou Saïd, Carthage & La Goulette*, showing the coastal suburbs. Both are on a scale of 1:10,000 and cost TD8.

These maps are on sale at Espace Diwan 9 (see following).

INFORMATION
Bookshops

Al-Kitab (Map pp70-2; 43 ave Habib Bourguiba) This has maps and travel guides, and a few English titles.

Espace Diwan 9 (Map pp70-2; 9 rue Sidi ben Arous) Has a good selection of books about Tunisia.

Libraire Claire Fontaine (Map pp70-2; 14 rue d'Alger) Has a small English-language section that includes Penguin Classics.

Second-hand bookshop (Map pp70-2; rue d'Angleterre) Has some English titles, owner will buy and exchange books.

Cultural Centres

British Council (Map pp70-2; ☎ 259 053; 5 place de la Victoire)

Centre Culturel de la Russe (Map p68; ☎ 780 953; ave de la Liberté)

Centre Culturel Français (Map p68; ☎ 787 701; 87 ave de la Liberté)

Goethe Institut (Map p68; ☎ 848 266; 6 rue du Séngal)

Institut Cervantes (Map p68; ☎ 788 847; 120 ave de la Liberté)

US Information Resource Center (☎ 107 000; Zone Nord-Est des Berges du Lac)

Emergency

Police (Map pp70-2; ☎ 197) The most central police station is on rue Jamel Abdelnasser; a couple of the officers speak English.

Internet Access

Publinet (Map pp70-2; TD1-2 per hr) Branches at 28 ave Habib Bourguiba, ave de la Liberté, rue de Gréce, rue Mokhtar and rue de Russe. The best is on rue Mokhtar.

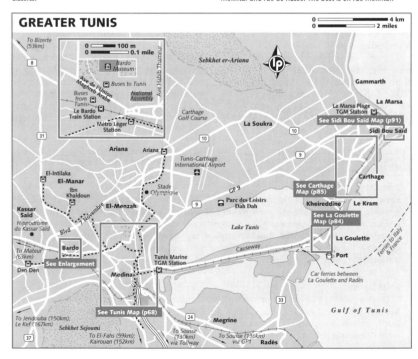

GREATER TUNIS

Laundry
Lavarie Tahar (Map pp70-2; 15 rue d'Allemagne) Charges TD6 to wash and dry 5kg of clothes.

Medical Services
Local paper *La Presse* has the details of late-night chemists.
Hôpital Charles Nicolle (Map p68; ☎ 662 275; blvd du 9 Avril)

Money
The major banks are along ave Habib Bourguiba; most have ATMs. There are also banks and an ATM at the airport.

Post
Main post office (Map pp70-2; rue Charles de Gaulle; ☼ daily) Poste restante (TD0.4 per item).

Tourist Information
Tourist office (Map pp70-2; ☎ 341 077; 1 ave Mohammed V; ☼ 8am-6pm Mon-Sat, 9am-noon Sun) Has a map of Tunis, a road map of Tunisia and brochures on Carthage and the medina (all free). Other branches at the train station (same hours) and airport.

Travel Agencies
There are lots of travel agencies around the centre. Try **Carthage Tours** (Map pp70-2; ☎ 347 015; ave Habib Bourguiba).

DANGERS & ANNOYANCES
Tunis is a safe city, though you should beware of pickpockets in the medina. It's also best to avoid the medina and Halfaouine district after dark, as muggings are not unknown.

Scams
Touts and shopkeepers will try all sorts of cunning ruses to get you into their shop. In the medina you'll be invited to see the view from a rooftop – passing through a shop on the way (it can be more tricky getting out). You'll also be told that you're in luck, as there's a festival, today only, an unmissable celebration of Berber craft. Even Paul Theroux, been-everywhere travel writer, got caught out by this one, as he describes in *The Pillars of Hercules*.

SIGHTS
Many sights are within the medina's tangled streets, but there's also the fantastic Bardo Museum to the northwest (see p56), and the

ancient remains of Carthage and charming Sidi Bou Saïd to the north.

Medina   Map pp70-2
Wandering through the medina, a World Heritage site, is extraordinary. The architecture has been added to over centuries, but it feels magically complete, a maze of tunnels and alleys dotted with hidden mansions. The huddled architecture is ideal for the climate, as the narrow streets are cool in summer and warm in winter. The lanes around the Zitouna Mosque are packed with souvenir shops, but away from these you will find arched winding streets, backstreet workshops, local markets and children playing football.

It was founded in the late 7th century AD (shortly after the Arab conquest), and was the city's focal point for over a thousand years – until the arrival of the French, who developed the ville nouvelle, depriving the medina of its role so that it slipped into decline. Today, less than 15,000 people live here, and the main trade is in souvenirs.

Large parts of the northern section were demolished in the 1930s and 1940s under a programme of slum clearance that was designed to improve vehicle access. Fortunately, the demolition days are done.

ZITOUNA (GREAT) MOSQUE
Also known as the Great Mosque or Mosque of the Olive Tree, the **Zitouna Mosque** (admission free; ☼ non-Muslims 8am-noon) is the medina's focal point. The first mosque on this site was built in AD 734, but it was rebuilt in the 9th century by the Aghlabid ruler Ibrahim ibn Ahmed (AD 856–63) in typically austere fashion, and resembles the Great Mosque in Kairouan in design. The builders recycled 200 columns salvaged from the ruins of Roman Carthage for the central prayer hall. In the 10th century, a second cupola, porticos, a minaret and the arched walkway were added.

The mosque's theological faculty was an important Islamic learning centre until it was closed down by President Bourguiba shortly after independence to try to reduce the influence of religion on society. The faculty was re-opened in 1987. Non-Muslims are allowed in as far as the courtyard.

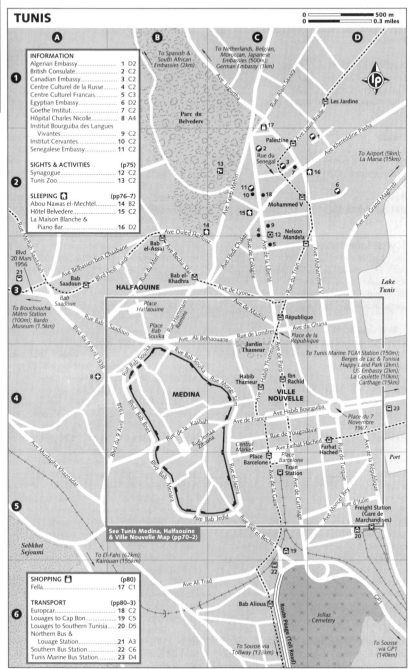

TUNIS

0 _____ 500 m
0 _____ 0.3 miles

INFORMATION
Algerian Embassy.................... 1 D2
British Consulate.................... 2 C2
Canadian Embassy.................... 3 C2
Centre Culturel de la Russe.... 4 C2
Centre Culturel Francais.......... 5 C3
Egyptian Embassy.................... 6 D2
Goethe Institut........................ 7 D2
Hôpital Charles Nicolle.............. 8 A4
Institut Bourguiba des Langues
    Vivantes............................... 9 C2
Institut Cervantes.................... 10 C2
Senegalese Embassy................ 11 C2

SIGHTS & ACTIVITIES (p75)
Synagogue............................... 12 C2
Tunis Zoo................................. 13 C2

SLEEPING (pp76–7)
Abou Nawas el-Mechtel............ 14 B2
Hôtel Belvedere....................... 15 C2
La Maison Blanche &
    Piano Bar.............................. 16 D2

SHOPPING (p80)
Fella... 17 C1

TRANSPORT (pp80–3)
Europcar.................................. 18 C2
Louages to Cap Bon................. 19 C5
Louages to Southern Tunisia.... 20 D5
Northern Bus &
    Louage Station...................... 21 A3
Southern Bus Station................ 22 C6
Tunis Marine Bus Station.......... 23 D4

To Spanish &
South African
Embassies (2km)

To Netherlands, Belgian,
Moroccan, Japanese
Embassies (500m);
German Embassy (1km)

Parc du
Belvedere

Les Jardine

To Airport (5km);
La Marsa (15km)

Palestine

Rue du
Senegal

Mohammed V

Nelson
Mandela

Lake
Tunis

Blvd
20 Mars
1956

Bab
Saadoun

Bab
Saadoun

To Bouchoucha
Métro Station
(100m); Bardo
Museum (1.5km)

Bab
el-Assal

Bab el-
Khadra

HALFAOUINE

Rue de Lyon

République

Ave du Ghana

Place
Halfaouine

Place
Bab
Souika

Jardin
Thameur

Place de la
République

To Tunis Marine TGM Station (150m);
Berges de Lac & Tunisia
Happy Land Park (2km);
US Embassy (2km);
La Goulette (10km);
Carthage (15km)

Habib
Thameur

Ibn
Rachid

MEDINA

**VILLE
NOUVELLE**

Ave Habib Bourguiba

Place du 7
Novembre
1987

Ave Farhat Hached

Farhat
Hached

Central
Market

Place
Barcelone

Place
Barcelone

Train
Station

Port

Ave Mustapha Khaznadar

Sebkhet
Sejoumi

Freight Station
(Gare de
Marchandises)

See Tunis Medina, Halfaouine
& Ville Nouvelle Map (pp70–2)

To El-Fahs (62km);
Kairouan (155km)

Ave Ali Trad

Bab Alioua

Jellaz
Cemetery

To Sousse via
Tollway (133km)

Route Péage (Toll Road)

To Sousse
via GP1
(140km)

OTHER MOSQUES

There are mosques all over the medina; the interiors are off-limits to non-Muslims. The finest include:

Kasbah Mosque (place de la Kasbah) dates from the 13th century. From here the call to prayer is quietly signalled by a white flag hung from the minaret.

Mosque of Youssef Dey (Souq el-Berka) was Tunis' first Ottoman-style mosque (1616), and was surrounded by Turkish souqs. It was designed by the Andalusian architect Ibn Ghalib in a colourful mishmash of styles. Look out for a characteristic octagonal minaret crowned with a miniature green-tiled pyramid. The different style of architecture served as propaganda for the new masters, demonstrating their ascendancy.

Hamuda Pasha Mosque (rue Sidi ben Arous) is a 17th-century, harmonious, richly decorated building, with an elegant witch's-hat minaret, decorated by tiles and black and white stones.

Mosque of Sidi Mahres (rue Sidi Mahres), built in 1675, is named after Tunis' patron saint, who saved the city after it was captured by Abu Yazd during a rebellion against Fatimid rule in AD 944. His tomb lies opposite the entrance to the mosque, in the **Zaouia of Sidi Mahres**. The mosque is ranked as one of the city's finest Ottoman buildings, with a fine white topping of curvaceous cupolas and half-cupolas surrounding the central dome. You can get a good view of these from Halfaouine.

Mosque of the Dyers (rue des Teinturiers) was built in 1716 by Hussein ben Ali, founder of the Husseinite line of beys. It has an adjoining mausoleum and *medersa*, and another Ottoman octagonal minaret.

Youssef Sahib Mosque (place Halfaouine) was started in the 19th century but only finished in 1970. It's almost Venetian looking; the railings and black marble were imported from the continent.

MEDERSAS

Medersas are schools for study of the Quran. The following fine examples are clustered around the Zitouna Mosque.

With an ornately studded door, the **Medersa Mouradia** (37 Souq el-Leffa; admission free; ⏰ 9am-4.30pm Mon-Sat) was built in 1673 on the ruins of a Turkish barracks destroyed during a

rebellion. It's used to train apprentices in traditional crafts.

The oldest is the **Medersa of the Palm Tree** (11 Souq des Libraires; closed to public), still a Quranic school, built in 1714 on the site of a *funduq* (travellers' inn) and named after a long-gone tree.

The **Medersa Bachia** (19 Souq des Libraires) is identifiable by the small public fountain beside the entrance, and has striking striped arches. A construction by Husseinite bey Ali Pasha from 1752, it now houses an artisans' school.

Ali Pasha also built **Medersa Slimania** (Souq des Libraires & Souq el-Kachachine) in 1754, to commemorate his son Suleiman, who was poisoned by his brother. Some rooms are now occupied by the Tunisian Medical Association, but the remainder is open to the public.

SOUQS

Traditionally markets were divided up into different areas of commerce. The most refined trades were those closest to the Zitouna Mosque, while dirtier businesses such as the tanners or blacksmiths were on the outskirts. The markets are either named after the trade or their founding community, such as **Souq el-Grana** – the Livornese Jews' Souq.

The main markets include the **Souq el-Attarine** – the Perfume Makers' Souq, dating from the 13th century, near the Zitouna Mosque. Although today it's not all perfume, there are plenty of essential oils to keep you going. Also near the mosque is the **Souq des Libraires**, the Booksellers' Souq, also 13th century.

Souq el-Attarine leads into the **Souq el-Trouk**, the Turkish Souq – traditionally the tailors' souq, but now mainly souvenirs.

One of the biggest souqs is the **Grand Souq des Chechias**, where dusty shopfronts are brimful with blood-red hats, and you can see them being shaped and hammered. In the 17th century, this was one of Tunisia's biggest industries. A million red felt skullcaps (known as fezzes in the West and *chechias* in Tunisia) were made annually by 15,000 craftsmen, and exported worldwide.

Souq el-Berka dates from Ottoman times: this was the slave souq where prisoners of Muslim corsairs (pirates) were brought to be sold. It's now a goldsmith's market.

TUNIS MEDINA, HALFAOUINE & VILLE NOUVELLE

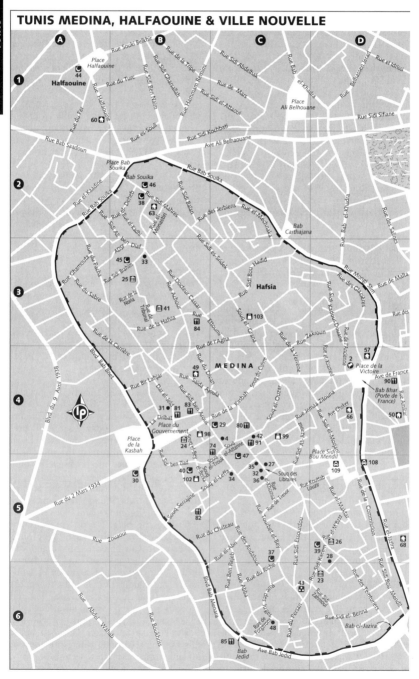

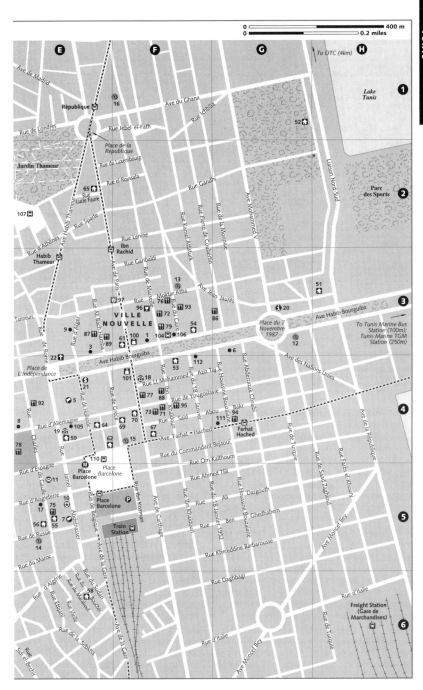

TUNIS

MUSEUMS, MAUSOLEUMS & PALACES

The **Tourbet el-Bey** (admission TD1.6, plus camera TD1; 9.30am-4.30pm) has green fish-scale domes typical of mausoleums. A weird mishmash of tiles and intricate stucco, it was built during the reign of Ali Pasha II (1758–82) and many of the subsequent Husseinite beys, princesses, ministers and trusted advisers ended up here. The male tombs are topped with strange, anonymous marble renditions of their preferred headgear, be it turban or *chechia*, with the number of tassels showing their importance.

Built in 1796, a former palace is now the **Dar Ben Abdallah Museum** (Centre for Popular Arts & Traditions; Impasse Ben Abdallah; admission TD1.6, plus camera TD1; 9.30am-4.30pm Mon-Sat). It was renovated in the 19th century in the Italianate style that was all the rage, and this influence is visible in the stucco, ceramics and carved decoration. Four of the rooms have been used to create scenes of 19th-century bourgeois life, using dummies dressed in

traditional costumes – some sporting ridiculous beards.

The **Dar Lasram Palace** (24 rue de Tribunal; admission free; 8.30am-1pm & 3-5.30pm Mon-Sat) is one of the medina's finest buildings and home of the Association de Sauvegarde de la Medina, the organisation that takes care of conservation. The interior has rooms and courtyards tiled in intense colours and patterns. Medina maps, plans and photographs are displayed.

Musée de la Ville de Tunis (rue de Tribunal; admission free; 10am-5pm Mon-Sat) is hidden away in the crumbling Palais Khereddine, facing a pretty, palm-shaded square; one day it will house the Museum of Tunis, but until then it hosts excellent temporary free exhibitions.

Dar Othman (rue el-M'Bazz) was built by Othman Dey in the early 17th century. The palace is a magnificent example of period architecture, distinguished by its exuberantly busy façade. Some rooms are now offices, but you are welcome to visit the courtyards.

Mosaic detail, Bardo Museum (p56)

Roman mosaics, Bardo Museum (p56), Tunis

Roman busts (p59), Bardo Museum

Venus mosaic, Bardo Museum (p56)

GEOFF STRINGER

Alleyway, Tunis medina (p67)

Doorway detail, Tunis medina (p67)

CHRISTOPHER WOOD

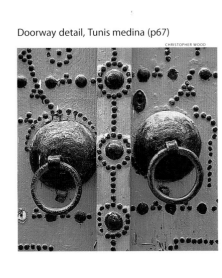

Statue on Byrsa Hill (p87), Carthage

JANE SWEEN

STEAM & SOCIABILITY

You haven't fully experienced Tunisia until you've been scrubbed down with an oven scourer by an enthusiastic elderly masseur. The oldest and most atmospheric *hammams* (bathhouses) are in the medina, which is packed with places to keep residents steamed and cleaned. Often recognisable by their candy-striped red-and-green doorways, they feel as if they haven't changed (or been cleaned much) for hundreds of years. It's an amazingly exotic, sensual and relaxing experience. You'll need a towel, and you might want a scrubbing mitt, shampoo and soap. To avoid undue attention, be aware that people don't bathe naked, but wear their underwear (men wear shorts). It usually costs TD1, while a massage costs another TD1. There are bucketloads to choose from, but the following (all on Map pp70-2) are all favourites:

- **El-Kachachine** (30 Souq des Libraires) One of the medina's finest, this is for men only.
- **El-Methihra** (11 rue el-Methira; ☺ women afternoons, men evenings) This friendly place is ancient, small scale and tiled, with lots of places to lie down and recuperate.
- **Sahib** (Halfaouine; ☺ women afternoons, men evenings) With echoing domed rooms, this glorious, dilapidated set of baths was immortalised in the film *Halfaouine*.
- **Zitouni** (rue des Juges) Women only, this is clean, with a good hot room; it's newer than the others, with freshly white-painted walls.

Ville Nouvelle   Map pp70-2

The ville nouvelle is lined with buildings with tall shuttered windows, wrought-iron balconies, cafés and patisseries. There are some fine examples of colonial architecture, ranging from the exuberant to the bizarre.

Cathedral of St Vincent de Paul (place de l'Indépendance) sits comfortably in the bizarre camp. The architects of this 1883 cathedral obviously thought 'Why plump for boring old one style?', and the result is a melding of Gothic, Byzantine and Moorish elements. The main doors are normally locked, but there is a side entrance on rue d'Alger.

The statue opposite the cathedral is of Ibn Khaldun, the great Tunis-born Islamic teacher and philosopher.

There are some fabulously ornate façades around. Supreme examples include the **National Theatre** (ave Habib Bourguiba), which has a meringue-sculpted frontage that looks as if you could crack it off and eat it. The **Hôtel Majestic** (36 ave de Paris) is another splendid almost-edible confection.

Other grand structures such as the post office and the French embassy were designed for the colonial power to assert its authority via its impressiveness – a trend that's been throwing up imposing architecture here since Roman times.

Beaches

The beaches of Tunis are all accessible by TGM suburban train from Tunis Marine station (Map p82). For details see Around Tunis, p83. La Marsa is the best and less crowded than those at La Goulette and Carthage (but note the patch nearest the president's palace at Carthage is quite pristine).

WALKING TOUR   Map p74

This tour takes in all the medina's main sights, and stops at its finest, most atmospheric cafés.

Start at the **Bab Bhar** (Porte de France or French Gate). This huge freestanding arch was the medina's eastern gateway until the surrounding walls were demolished by the French to create place de la Victoire. From here head along rue Jemaa Zitouna, the main tourist drag. Nestled between the stuffed camels are jewellery, ceramics, glassware and eager shopkeepers. Near the top, at number 73, you'll pass the fine **National Library (1)**, once a set of barracks. Your first opportunity for a sit-down is **Café Ez-Zitouna (2)**, where beautifully tiled arched rooms, full of *sheesha* pipes and fragrant smoke, open onto the street. Next, head up to the **Zitouna Mosque (3**; p67). Another great stop to the north is **M'Rabet (4**; p78). This traditional Turkish café is packed with pillars painted in stick-of-rock stripes, with rush-matted seating on raised platforms, and there's a leafy courtyard.

Amble southwards along **Souq des Libraires (5**; p69). The western side is lined with medersas (6; p69) formerly linked to the Zitouna Mosque theological faculty. Carry on along rue el-Khomsa, then turn right at rue de Tresor and go south along rue des Teinturiers – street of the dyers. On the corner is the extravagant **Mosque of the Dyers** (7; p69). Opposite, an archway leads to rue el-M'Bazz and the **Dar Othman** (8; p72).

Bear right along rue Sidi Kacem and you'll hit the **Dar Ben Abdallah Museum** (9; p72). Further on are the green fish-scale domes of the **Tourbet el-Bey** (10; p72). From here head north along the rue Tourbet el-Bey. If you like, you could make a detour, turning left down rue des Juges, then right along **rue des Forgerons** (11) – the blacksmiths' street – full of noisy dark workshops and

figures blackened by smoke. A right at the end will take you to **Bab Jedid** (12), one of three gates built by the Hafsids, and the only one still standing. There is a restaurant, **Granada** (13; p78), under the arches of the gate.

Retrace your steps back to the main route: following rue Tourbet el-Bey; at No 41 is the **Mosque of M'sed el-Kobba** (14), aka Kuttab Ibn Khaldoun (a *kuttab* is a Quranic primary school). The famous historian Ibn Khaldun (1332–1406) was born at No 33 and taught briefly at the mosque before leaving for the bright lights of Cairo. When you reach the Zitouna Mosque again, go west along the Souq el-Leffa: on the corner is **Medersa Mouradia** (15; see p69). Along this street

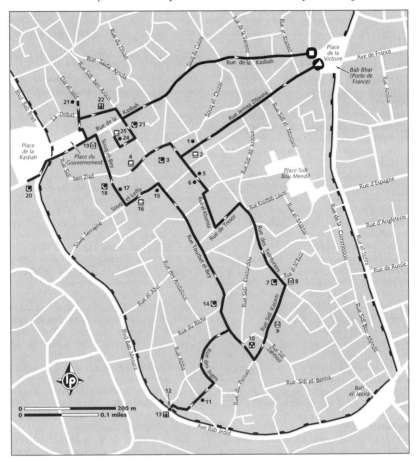

several shops allow access to their rooftops for a view over the medina.

By this time you'll be gagging to get into **Café dar Mnouchi (16)** (Souq el-Leffa), a tranquil courtyard that's a balm after the busy souqs, with tiling patterns like exploding flower displays and rejuvenating milkshakes.

Next, turn north along **Souq el-Berka (17**; p69). You'll see the **Mosque of Youssef Dey (18**; p69). Nose out along Souq el-Bey and you'll come out at the peaceful place du Gouvernement, a shady square. The **Dar el-Bey (19)**, on the south side of the square, is a former palace guesthouse that's now the prime minister's office. The guards don't like having their picture taken. West of the Dar el-Bey is the place de la Kasbah, once overlooked by the old kasbah, which was destroyed by the French in 1883. The **Kasbah Mosque (20**; p69) is to the southwest.

Take Dar el-Jeld northwards and you can look around immaculately restored **Le Diwan (21)**, an 18th-century mansion that's now an upmarket craft shop and banqueting hall. This corner of the medina is particularly well kept, with whitewashed façades, trailing flowers and big doors. Nip back up Dar el-Jeld and take a left past its eponymous huge-doored restaurant. Head down the pretty little alley, where you can stop at **Dar Hamouda Pacha (22**; p78). With whitewashed alcoves around small, calm courtyards, and mute-coloured sofas, this is the chichi way to smoke your *sheesha*, and has good coffee. Following the alley further, you'll come out at rue Sidi ben Arous. Turn right. You'll see the Hamuda Pasha Mosque (**23**; p69).

Now, it's time you bought one of those traditional red-felt hats. You'll look like Tommy Cooper, but is that so bad? Turn right into the **Souq des Chechias (24)**. One of the oldest medina coffeehouses is **Café Chaoechin (25)**, another good place to stop. *Sheeshas* gurgle among the ornate cubbyholes of the hatmakers' souq, with rickety painted tables under tiled arches. From here you can return along rue Sidi ben Arous (turning right) then turn left, walking along rue de la Kasbah to reach Bab Bhar.

COURSES
Language
Institut Bourguiba des Langues Vivantes (Map p68; ☎ 832 418; www.iblv.rnu.tn; 47 ave de la Liberté) Courses in classical and Tunisian Arabic.

Dance
During winter, the Ecole Serguei Diaghilev de Ballet et Danse Classique at the **Centre Culturel de la Russe** (Map p68; ☎ 780 953; ave de la Liberté) gives lessons in classical and Tunisian dance.

TUNIS FOR CHILDREN
If there's one thing Tunisians like more than *harissa* it's children. As Tunis is so laid-back and small, it's an easy place to be with kids. There's also quick access to beaches if sightseeing seems too much like hard work, and they are welcome in restaurants.

The entertaining **Tunisia Happy Land Park** (Dah Dah; Berges de Lac; 12 tickets TD5, one ticket TD0.5; ☼ 6am-10pm Mon-Fri, 10am-10pm Sat & Sun) has lots of flashing lights and various rides for different age groups. It's part of the new district of Berges de Lac, where people go to see and be seen, and there's a lively corniche (coastal road) to wander up and down. A taxi from the centre costs about TD3.5.

Tunis Zoo (Map p68; Belvedere Park; adult/child TD0.4/0.2 ☼ 9am-6pm Tue-Sun) is another good place for children in a shady, peaceful park with some interesting animals including monkeys and some wonderfully colourful parrots, though some cages look cramped.

Some children will like the **Bardo Museum** (see the special section, p56) with its mosaics – the pictures tell stories and feature lots of animals, and Romans are big in children's historical consciousness. Some will also be happy exploring the medina in small doses, and the **Dar Ben Abdallah Museum** (p72) with its waxwork figures. Another good place is **Sidi Bou Saïd** (p90), with its relaxing pace, marina, beach and elaborate mansions. In Carthage there's a tiny beach and the **Oceanographic Museum** (p89) with an aquarium.

If all fails, many of the upmarket hotels also provide babysitting services.

TOURS
Tours around Tunis do not run from Tunis, but from the coastal resorts. However, if you want to go on a tour encompassing the medina, Bardo Museum, Carthage and Sidi Bou Saïd, contact **Carthage Tours** (Map p70-2; ☎ 344 066; 59 ave Habib Bourguiba), which will arrange for you to join one, at a cost of around TD35.

FESTIVALS & EVENTS

Tunis' main event is the **Carthage International Festival** (www.festival-carthage.com.tn) in July and August (for details see p89). Carthage is also the setting for the biennial **Carthage International Film Festival**.

Sidi Bou Saïd also has a festival called Kharja, held in July or August in honour of the Muslim saint who lived there.

You'll find information about these festivals in the local press or at the tourist office.

SLEEPING

Tunis has a good choice of accommodation for all budgets. The medina is an exciting place to stay, but has only budget hotels, many of which include six-legged friends and a soundtrack of bodily functions in the price. Aimed at visiting labourers rather than tourists, medina hotels are usually unsuitable for lone women (unless otherwise stated). The ville nouvelle contains most of the mid-range, old French hotels, characterised by tall ceilings, balconies and good value, and there are numerous lusher, newer places. There are also some lovely options that offer serenity and occasional sea views out in the northern suburbs.

Medina & Halfaouine

Hôtel Maison Doreé (Map pp70-2; ☎ 240 632; 3 rue el-Koufa; s/d with shower TD26/29, with private bathroom TD33/36; ⚙) Maison Doreé is charming: simple and spotless with an old-fashioned French-feeling formality, its rooms (varied in shape and atmosphere; ask to see a couple) have shuttered balconies and comforting 1950s furnishings; the restaurant is also good.

Hôtel Majestic (Map pp70-2; ☎ 332 848; www.majestic hotel.com.tn; 36 ave de Paris; s/d/tr with private bathroom TD35/50/65; ⚙) A glorious piece of fading,

flouncy grandeur, this is the kind of place that should be inhabited by old ladies with toy poodles. Rooms vary in size and attractiveness so ask to see a few.

Auberge de Jeunesse (Map pp70-2; ☎ 567 850, 25 rue Es-Saida Ajoula; dm incl breakfast TD6) In the thick of the medina, this occupies the 18th-century Dar Saida Ajoula palace and has single-sex dorms. It has a surfeit of regulations and management seems to get its kicks from enforcing them (closed 10am to 2pm, a 10pm curfew, no showers between 7.30pm and 9am). However, it's still a bargain: clean, and the large dorm has fine murals.

Hôtel Marhaba (Map pp70-2; ☎ 354 006; 5 rue de la Commission; s/d with shared bathroom TD8/12) At the medina's edge, central and clean, though not much else, this is always busy and is fine for lone women. Hot showers cost TD1.

Hôtel de la Medina (Map pp70-2; ☎ 327 497; 1 rue des Glaciéres; d/tr with shared bathroom TD12/15) Many of the spartan, whitewashed, blue-shuttered rooms here have great views over the square. This is OK for lone women, and has clean-ish showers (TD1).

Hôtel les Amis (Map pp70-2; ☎ 565 653; 7 rue el-Monastiri; s/d with shared bathroom TD4/8) At the northern edge of the medina, this all-male preserve has some small, prettily tiled rooms and some plain ones. The bathroom has no shower, but a hybrid bath-sink.

Hôtel des Amis (Map pp70-2; rue Halfaouine; s/d with shared bathroom TD5/10) Around a courtyard, this is quite clean and airy. It's a popular hangout for patients being treated at the nearby hospital.

Ville Nouvelle

BUDGET

Hôtel de Savoie (Map pp70-2; ☎ 253 780; 13 rue de Boucher; s/d/tr with shared bathroom TD5-6/10/12) This is a basic little oasis on a local narrow street, centred on a small courtyard with a large tree. Rooms are upstairs, the shower downstairs and all is overseen by the careful owner.

Hôtel Cirta (Map pp70-2; ☎ 321 584, 42 rue Charles de Gaulle; s/d with shared bathroom TD10/12) Rather grubby and dingy, with lumpy beds, this at least has some atmosphere and balconies over the street. Showers cost TD1.

Hôtel Grand Victoria (Map pp70-2; ☎ 342 862; 79 ave Farhat Hached; s/d with shared bathroom TD10/15) Overlooking place Barcelone, this has impoverished garret-type rooms that are pretty clean.

THE AUTHOR'S CHOICE

La Maison Blanche (Map p68; ☎ 844 718; www.bestwestern.com/tn/lamaisonblanche; 45 ave Mohamed V; s/d TD195/220; ⚙) The glorious five-star White House has elaborate furnishings in light, bright rooms with curvaceous windows. The piano bar is darkly Art Deco, while the restaurant serves refined Moroccan and Tunisian food amid appropriately complicated inlaid furnishings. The hotel sometimes offers discounts of around 30%.

Hôtel de Suisse (Map pp70-2; ☎ 323 821; 5 rue de Suisse; s/d with shower TD10/20) The rooms here are spartan but fairly clean, with showers in a corner alcove. The 1st-floor rooms are so low that standing on the balcony is like standing on the pavement.

MID-RANGE

Grand Hôtel de France (Map pp70-2; ☎ 326 244; hotelfrancetunis@yahoo.fr; 8 rue Mustapha Mbarek; s/d with shared bathroom TD17/19, with shower TD23/17) This has faded elegance; it's airy and light, with a wooden coffinlike lift and lots of wrought iron. The best rooms are top-floor ones with balconies and good views. However, single women have reported feeling uncomfortable here.

Hôtel rue de Russie (Map pp70-2; ☎ 328 883; 18 rue de Russie; s/d with private bathroom TD35/50) With an explosion of flowers outside, this is an attractive, newish good-value place with smart rooms that overlook either the street or the leafy interior courtyard.

Hôtel Salammbô (Map pp70-2; ☎ 337 498; hotel.salammbo@gnet.tn; 6 rue de Grèce; d with shared/private bathroom TD17/20) Salammbô has spic-and-span, basic rooms with lurid bedspreads. Some have balconies, there are lots of hallway murals and the staff are friendly and efficient.

Hôtel Transatlantique (Map pp70-2; ☎ 240 680; 106 rue de Yougoslavie; s/d with shared bathroom TD19/26, with private bathroom TD25/30) This hotel is distinguished by its elaborate tiling in the reception. The rooms are plain and clean, with high ceilings and lots of light.

Hôtel de l'Agriculture (Map pp70-2; ☎ 326 394; 25 rue Charles de Gaulle; s/d with private bathroom TD20/30) Rooms here are small and stuffy, but clean and brightly painted in blue and white, with neat little bathrooms.

Hôtel Carlton (Map pp70-2; ☎ 330 664; carlton@planet.tn; 31 ave Habib Bourguiba; s/d/tr with private bathroom TD47/74/89; ▨) This small, immaculately maintained three-star hotel is friendly and has well appointed but quite worn and plain rooms with satellite TV. Rooms at the front have balconies but are noisy as they overlook Tunis' main street.

Hôtel Belvédere (Map p68; ☎ 782 214; 10 ave des Etats Unis d'Amérique; s/d TD57/67) This is a four-star, quiet, comfortable business hotel, situated in a tranquil street, with good views from the rooms over the surrounding old colonial buildings.

Hôtel Omrane (Map pp70-2; ☎ 345 277; www.hotel-omrane.com.tn; 65 ave Farhat Hached; s/d TD 45/65) Central, rooms are smartish but a tad drab, with TV. This is more comfortable than others at the same price, but with less character.

TOP END

Grand Hôtel du Lac (Map pp70-2; ☎ 336 100; ave Mohammed V; s/d TD70/116) This bizarre, inverted pyramid is thought by some to have been the inspiration for the sandcrawler in *Star Wars*. Whatever, it's a monument to the 1970s, complete with the ashtray architecture of the lobby chandelier. To stay here you should wear an open-necked nylon shirt, shades, and lots of chest hair. The rooms are fusty pastel but have great views. They'll drop prices faster than you can ask for a Campari and soda.

Hôtel Africa Méridien (Map pp70-2; ☎ 347 477; 50 ave Habib Bourguiba; s/d TD220/230) Refurbished and plush, this is a flash deep-pile business-traveller-oriented place, with fantastic views that stretch out across Tunis and the lake.

Hôtel Abou Nawas Tunis (Map p68; ☎ 350 355; www.abounawas.com; place des Droits de l'Homme, ave Mohammed V; s/d TD220/240; ▨ ▨) Overlooking Lake Tunis, this has good views and predictably plush rooms: it's a five-star business option, with all the personality and comfort that implies.

Abou Nawas el-Mechtel (Map p68; ☎ 783 200; 3 ave Ouled Haffouz; s/d TD175/200; ▨ ▨) South of Parc du Belvedere, this round-windowed branch of the luxury chain is similarly well run and luxurious, but has only four stars and so is cheaper.

EATING

The medina may be full of cheap hotels, but Tunis' swankiest restaurants are also to be found within its walls (it also has lots of hole-in-the-wall places for the hungry but hard up). The lively heart of the ville nouvelle has plenty of mid-range eateries (as well as loads of patisseries, *rôtisseries* and sandwich/pizza joints), with finer places scattered around the embassies to keep the diplomatic staff sated. The new development at Berges de Lac – by the lakeside – is a popular evening hangout, with some flashy cafés. Even more choice can be found by heading out to the city's delightful seafront suburbs (see p83). Restaurants all open for lunch and dinner daily unless otherwise specified.

TUNIS

Dar el-Jeld (Map pp70-2; ☎ 560 916; 5-10 rue Dar el-Jeld; meal around TD35) This is special from the moment you knock on the grand arched doorway, which opens into an immaculately restored, elaborate 18th-century tiled and stuccoed mansion. The magnificent main dining room is in a covered central courtyard, but there are also private alcove tables around the edge, ideal for scheming or romancing, or a spot of both. A good way to start is with the mixed hors d'oeuvres, then try delicious traditional Tunisian dishes such as *kabkabou* (fish with fresh tomatoes, capers and olives).

Medina   Map pp70-2

Mahdaoui (2 rue Jemma Zitouna; dishes TD2-8) At the heart of the medinaand is popular for lunch, the tables fill a narrow alley by the Zitouna Mosque. The daily blackboard menu offers couscous, fish and chicken – scrumptious and cheap despite its central location.

Fast Food (rue Ettoumi) This popular pocket-sized place does great sandwiches for around TD1.5.

M'Rabet (dishes around TD8) Above the busy traditional café, this is a swanky popular tourist stop in distinguished rooms with good views of the Zitouna Mosque; there's live traditional music and dance in the evening.

Dar Essaraya (☎ 560 310; www.essaraya.com; 6 rue Ben Mahmoud; meals around TD30) Southwest of Zitouna Mosque, this place has extravagant food matched by over-the-top decoration.

Dar Bel Hadj (☎ 200 894; 17 rue des Tamis; dishes TD25) North of the Zitouna Mosque, this is less well known: another grand traditional restaurant with delicious food in an elaborate 17th-century mansion.

Dar Hamouda Pacha (☎ 561 746; 56 rue Sidi ben Arous; mains TD12.5-18) This is an intimate, elegant restaurant with chairs scattered among white arches and small courtyards. Cuisine is Tunisian French.

Granada (Bab Jedid) Under the dramatic arches of a city gate, this offers simple dishes and an array of snacks.

The **central market** (rue Charles de Gaulle) is the place to stock up on food, with a mouth-watering selection of local cheeses, cold meats, fresh bread, *harissa*, olives and pickles as well as fruit and veg.

Central supermarkets include **Monoprix** (rue Charles de Gaulle/ave de la Liberté) and the **Magasin Général** (ave de France). Both stock a range of local wines.

Ville Nouvelle   Map pp70-2
BUDGET

Carcassonne (8 ave de Carthage; 4-course set menu TD4). The value offered at this small, popular, friendly place is remarkable, with good-quality food in pleasant, relaxed surroundings. Service is fast.

Istanbul (3 rue Pierre de Coubertin; set menu TD4.5, dishes TD2.5-4.5) This small place, with the classic tiles-and-TV combination of most cheap Tunisian restaurants, has simple Sfaxian (spicy) dishes and a good set menu.

Abid (☎ 257 052; 98 rue de Yougoslavie; mains TD2.5-5) With a TV, flickering neon and simple Tunisian staples, this is a good-value neighbourhood favourite.

Capitole (mains TD4.8-11, 3-course menu TD5.5) This long-standing place has cheap, pretty palatable food but on a quiet night you can feel like you're in an out-take from *The Shining*, and there's no alcohol to take your mind off it.

MID-RANGE

Capri (☎ 257 695; 34 rue Mokhtar Attia; dishes TD2-7.8) Small to the point of being oppressive, on two levels, this is a lively place that is popular with a male crowd, with pine inside and outside, serving alcohol and good simple seafood.

Margaritas (☎ 240 632; Hôtel Maison Doreé; 3-course menu TD12) You get good service for the price here; it's reasonably formal, but brightly lit. The three-course menu is good value but with small portions.

Tontonville (☎ 253 918; 96 rue de Yougaslavie; dishes TD3-9, set menu TD7; ✆ lunch & dinner Mon-Sat) This buzzing place is heavily curtained from the street, serves alcohol and has lots of good fish. The *mouchaia* that comes with the dishes also comes with a kick.

L'Orient Tunis (☎ 252 062; rue Ali Bach Hamba; dishes TD7-18) Tall ceilings, brick arches, swords, shells, and tiling sporting yellow-and-green swirling tendrils, give this a strong Andalusian flavour, matched by the seafood slant of the menu.

Le Carthage (☎ 255 614; 10 rue Ali Bach Hamba; mains TD9-17; ✆ lunch & dinner Mon-Sat) With prize-winning couscous, white tablecloths and kitsch classical statuary, this is an intimate, popular choice.

Bolero (☎ 245 928; 6 Passage el-Guattar; mains TD4.5-7.5; set menu TD7) This small cosy place with red tablecloths and low lighting is a great favourite with Tunis businessmen, who retreat here for long lunches to peruse the long wine list. It specialises in grilled meats and seafood. The set menu is a sweet deal.

La Mamma (☎ 241 256; rue de Marseille; dishes TD7.2-16.5; ✎ lunch & dinner Sep-Jul) La Mamma has a red interior, plastic flowers, dishes such as barbecued octopus, and good live musicians who look like moonlighting snooker players.

Al-Mazar (☎ 340 423; 11 rue de Marseille; most mains TD4.9) Al-Mazar has a good atmosphere, as befits a bar cunningly disguised as a restaurant; lone women might find it intimidating. With paintings on the walls and big globe lightshades, you might think yourself in Paris. The food is excellent, with special mention going to the *harissa* and to the chocolate mousse.

Chez Nous (☎ 243 043; 5 rue de Marseille; main dishes TD9-18, fixed menu TD10) This simple back room feels like it could be an Italian-American mobsters' favourite place; there's nothing fancy, but the food is good, and there are faded black-and-white photos of faded stars on the walls.

Andalous (☎ 241 756; 13 rue de Marseille; mains TD8.5-12.5) Dimly lit by ornate lanterns, this has a somewhat Moroccan feel, a discreet TV in the corner, affable waiters and tasty seafood and meat dishes.

Neptune (☎ 254 820; 3 rue de Caire; dishes TD3-5; ✎ noon-10pm) With its metallic chairs, Formica tabletops and wicker-framed mirrors that could have been plucked from 1970s suburbia, this place has simple Tunisian favourites.

Theátre de l'Etoile du Nord (☎ 255 242; www.etoiledunord.org; 41 ave Farhat Hached; snacks TD1-3, set menu TD4.5) This is an unusually artsy café-bar, spacious and theatrical, with neon lighting. It occasionally hosts fringe theatre and other events but mainly serves as a meeting place for a mixed crowd of men and women.

Café-Patisserie Zem-Zem (rue Charles de Gaulle) This tiny place has freshly squeezed orange juice (TD0.6), excellent coffee and a good range of pastries.

Berges du Lac

La Croisette (☎ 963 287; Corniche du Lac, Les Berges du Lac; ✎ noon-midnight) The Berges du Lac development is trendy and prices reflect this, but this popular *salon de thé*-restaurant has a lovely waterside setting and is surrounded by fairy lights; service is slow.

DRINKING

Most of the city-centre bars are raucous all-male preserves. For more refined nightlife, head out to the northern suburbs, particularly La Marsa (see p92).

Bar Jamaica (Map pp70-2; Hotel El-Hana International, ave Habib Bourguiba) On the 10th floor, this small bar is a quiet haven. The rooftop views across the central streets are unmatched.

El-Hana Brasserie (Map pp70-2; Hotel el-Hana International, ave Habib Bourguiba) This has a good pavement location for a prime view of the avenue's parade of people.

Oscars (Map pp70-2; rue de Marseille) The vaguely cine-themed bar-restaurant upstairs is fun, though not for single women (the women here are usually working). There's live music and dancers at the weekend.

Piano Bar (Map p68; La Maison Blanche, 45 ave Mohamed V) A good place for a refined and quiet drink, this five-star hotel bar is Art-Deco and dark-wood heaven.

Le Palais (Map pp70-2; ave de Carthage) This is the kind of heartwarming hangout where people order a bottle of Johnny Walker with their snack. It's sleazy and seedy, but it's open late and there are a few (working) women customers.

Wealthy Tunisians and tourists are most likely to be getting down at any of Tunis' clubs, which are mainly attached to hotels. The best are out in the northern suburb of La Marsa: try the club at the Hotel Plaza Corniche (p92).

ENTERTAINMENT
Cinemas

There are plenty of cinemas, mainly showing Egyptian films or Bollywood-style action movies in Arabic, but you'll also find the latest Hollywood offerings, dubbed into French.

The local press has listings. Admission costs around TD3 at plush places such as **La Parnasse** and **Le Capitole** (both ave Habib Bourguiba), though older films are often cheaper. The only arthouse cinema is **Maison de la Culture Ibn Khaldoun** (Map pp70-2; ave de Paris).

Live Music & Dance

There are traditional live music and dance displays at restaurants M'Rabet (p78), La Mamma (p79) and Lucullus (p84). The upstairs bar at Oscars Hotel (p79) has lively entertainment at weekends. In the summer, there are weekend free concerts on ave Habib Bourguiba. Look out for classical music concerts at the Dar Ennejma Ezzahra (Centre of Arabic & Mediterranean Music; p90) in Sidi Bou Saïd and at L'Acropolium (p87) in Carthage. Big stars dazzle at Carthage's amphitheatre during the International Festival.

Sport

Five of the 14 soccer teams in the Tunisian first division are from Tunis, including archrivals Club Africain and Espérance Sportive de Tunisie. Both use Stade Olympique in El-Menzah as a home ground. Admission starts at TD7 and matches are usually at 2pm on Sunday. To get there, take métro léger line 2 from République and get off at Cité Sportive.

You'll find fixture details in the Saturday press. The teams are referred to by their initials – CA for Club Africain, and EST for Espérance Sportive de Tunisie. Other clubs from around Tunis are Stade Tunisien (ST) and Club Olympique de Transports (COT) from the western suburbs; Avenir Sportif de La Marsa (ASM) from La Marsa; and Club Sportif de Hammam Lif (CSHL), from the southern suburbs.

SHOPPING

The medina is packed with shops selling everything a tourist needs, from fine handicrafts – jewellery, perfume, carpets, ceramics, brass and glassware – to stuffed camels and throwaway fashion. Prices can start ludicrously high, so put on your haggle hat.

Société de Commercialisation des Produits de l'Artisanats (Map pp70-2; Socopa; ave Habib Bourguiba) This has a selection of good-quality crafts and prices are fixed. Here you can get an idea of costs before heading into the medina.

Mains des Femmes (Map pp70-2; 1st fl, 47 ave Habib Bourguiba) This shop is the fixed-price outlet for handicrafts produced by rural women's cooperatives, with rugs, including kilims and *mergoums* (woven carpets with geometric designs), embroidered blankets, wooden toys, dolls and jewellery. Prices are reasonable, and the money goes to a good cause.

Hanout Arab (Map pp70-2; 52 rue Jemaa Zitouna) On the main tourist drag, this is an unusual, lovely fixed-price shop with distinctive Tunisian crafts, including pottery, textiles and jewellery.

Fella (Map p68; ☎ 785 924; 9 place Pasteur) This fixed-price chichi boutique is housed in a small whitewashed domed building, and has kept stars from Umm Kolthum to Princess Grace in handmade floaty robes and household ornaments.

GETTING THERE & AWAY

Air

Tuninter flies to Jerba, Tozeur and Sfax. Getting a booking in the middle of summer can be hard.

Tuninter tickets can be bought from **Tunis Air** (Map pp70-2; ☎ 330 100; 48 ave Habib Bourguiba), or from any travel agent. Tuninter also has a special reservations service (☎ 701 717).

For details of international flights to and from Tunis, see p268.

Airline offices in Tunis include:

Air France (☎ 355 422; 1 rue d'Athènes)

British Airways (☎ 330 046; 17 ave Habib Bourguiba)

EgyptAir (Map pp70-2; ☎ 341 182; 1st floor, Complexe el-Hana International, 49 ave Habib Bourguiba)

Lufthansa Airlines (Map pp70-2; ☎ 941 344; Complexe el-Mechtel, ave Ouled Haffouz)

Swiss International Air Lines (☎ 781 003; Tunis-Carthage International Airport)

Tunis Air (Map pp70-2; ☎ 330 100; 48 ave Habib Bourguiba)

Boat

Ferries from Europe arrive at La Goulette, at the eastern end of the causeway across Lake Tunis. A taxi to the city centre costs about TD4, which is a good investment as it's quite a long walk to La Goulette Vieille station.

In summer, reserve as early as possible, especially if you want to take a vehicle.

The **Compagnie Tunisienne de Navigation** (Map pp70-2; CTN; ☎ 322 802; 122 rue de Yougoslavie) handles tickets for ferries operated by CTN and its French partner SNCM to Genoa and Marseilles. **Carthage Tours** (Map pp70-2; ☎ 344 066; 59 ave Habib Bourguiba) handles tickets for Tirrenia Navigazione to Trapani, Naples and La Spezia.

See p271 for full details on the range of ferries to and from France and Italy.

Bus

Tunis has two intercity bus stations – one for departures to the south of Tunis and another for departures to the north.

French-language *La Presse* carries details of SNTRI departures from both bus stations daily. It should be noted that these schedules list only final destinations and not the places en route.

SOUTHERN BUS STATION

Buses to the south leave from the **southern bus station** (Map p68; ☎ 801 333; Gare Routière Sud de Bab el-Fellah), situated just south of the centre opposite the huge Jellaz Cemetery. You can walk, or catch métro léger line 1 to Bab Alioua, which is 200m beyond the bus station.

Services from the southern bus station include:

destination	fare	duration	frequency (per day)
Ben Guerdane	23 TD	8 hrs	3
Douz	23 TD	8 hrs	3
El-Haouaria	4.3 TD	2 hrs	7
El-Jem	9.5 TD	3 hrs	4
Gabès	17 TD	6½ hrs	10
Gafsa	15.5 TD	5 hrs	8
Hammamet	3 TD	1¼ hrs	hourly
Jerba	23 TD	8 hrs	3
Kairouan	7.5 TD	3 hrs	hourly
Makthar	7.7 TD	3 hrs	8
Matmata	18.6 TD	8 hrs	1
Medenine	18.4 TD	7 hrs	7
Nabeul	3.1 TD	1½ hrs	half-hourly
Nefta	20 TD	7 hrs	2
Sbeitla	11 TD	4 hrs	3
Sfax	11.8 TD	5 hrs	8
Sousse	6.8 TD	2½ hrs	8
Tamerza	22 TD	7 hrs	2
Tataouine	22.4 TD	8 hrs	3
Tozeur	18.9 TD	7 hrs	5
Zaghouan	3 TD	1¼ hrs	9

NORTHERN BUS STATION

Buses to the north leave from the **northern bus station** (Map p68; ☎ 562 299; Gare Routière Nord de Bab Saadoun), about 2km northwest of the city centre.

The easiest way to get there is by métro léger line 4 to Bouchoucha station. The métro léger station is about 150m west of the bus station on blvd 20 Mars 1956.

Services from the northern bus station include:

destination	fare	duration	frequency (per day)
Ain Draham	9 TD	4 hrs	4
Bizerte	3.1 TD	1 hrs	half-hourly
Jendouba	7.5 TD	3 hrs	6
Kalaat Kasba	10.8 TD	5 hrs	4
Le Kef	8 TD	3 hrs	hourly
Tabarka	8.3 TD	3½ hrs	6
Tebersouk	4.8 TD	2½ hrs	hourly

Car

All the major car rental companies have offices at the airport and in town. These include:

Avis 90 ave de la Liberté (☎ 788 563); Tunis Hilton lobby (☎ 787 167)
Europcar (Map p68; ☎ 340 303; 17 ave Habib Bourguiba)
Express (☎ 259 954; 39 ave Farhat Hached)
Hertz (Map pp70-2; ☎ 256 451; 29 ave Habib Bourguiba)
Topcar (☎ 800 875; 7 rue de Mahdia)

Louage

Tunis has three main louage (shared taxi) stations. Louages to Cap Bon leave from opposite the southern bus station, and services to other southern destinations leave from the station at the eastern end of rue El-Aid el-Jebbari, off ave Moncef Bey. Louages to the north leave from near the northern bus station.

The louage station at place Sidi Bou Mendil in the medina is for services to Libya, and services to Algeria leave from nearby.

Train

Tunis Ville train station (Map pp70-2; ☎ 241 858) is on place Barcelone. The most useful route is the line south to Sousse (TD6, two hours, 10 daily), El-Jem (TD8, three hours, five daily), Sfax (TD9.15, 3½ hours, six daily) and Gabès (5½ hours, four daily). One train daily branches inland to Gafsa (TD13.4, 7½ hours) and Metlaoui (TD14.4, eight hours).

There's also a train to Monastir (TD7.4, three hours, one daily) and on to Mahdia (TD7, four hours); otherwise change at Sousse.

Trains head to Hammamet (T3.5, 1½ hours, nine daily) and Nabeul (TD3.5, 1¾ hours). Only one is direct, the other services involve changing trains at Bir Bou Regba.

Bizerte (TD3.5, 1½ hours, three daily), Jendouba (TD5.85, 2¾ hours, four daily), Ghardimao (3¼ hours, three daily) and Kalaat Kasba (five hours, one daily) are also served.

The trains can get crowded in summer, especially going south. To get a seat, it's a good idea to make a reservation the day before. There's a discount of 15% on return tickets.

GETTING AROUND
To/From the Airport

Tunis-Carthage International Airport is 8km northeast of the centre: a taxi costs around TD3.5, or bus No 35 heads to/from ave Habib Bourguiba (TD0.6, half-hourly 6.30am to 5.30pm). Note that the TGM L'Aeroport station is not near the airport.

Bus

Yellow city buses operate to all parts of the city, but you'll mainly need them to get to the airport, the Bardo Museum or the northern bus station. The destination, point of origin and route number are displayed in Arabic on a board by the back door.

Routes of interest to tourists have the destination marked in Latin script as well. The basic fare is TD0.5 on most routes, and you buy your ticket on the bus.

There are three main bus terminuses: Tunis Marine, which is near the TGM station at the causeway end of ave Habib

MÉTRO LÉGER & TGM ROUTES

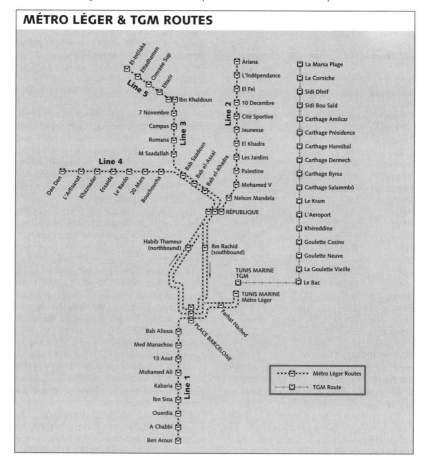

Bourguiba; place Barcelone; and Jardin Thameur, just off ave Habib Thameur. Tunis Marine is the starting point for the No 3 bus to the Bardo Museum via the northern bus and louage stations, and for the No 35 bus to the airport.

Métro Léger

The métro léger tram network is much easier to use than the buses. There are five main routes running to various parts of the city – see map opposite. There are route maps in Arabic and French inside the trams.

Tickets are sold at the small kiosks at the entrance to each station. They must be bought before you travel. The basic fare is TD0.6.

Services using lines 3, 4 and 5 between République and place Barcelone travel south along ave de Paris and ave de Carthage and north on rue de Hollande and ave Habib Thameur.

Taxi

Taxis are extremely cheap by European standards and are all fitted with meters. On the day rate, a short hop will cost you around TD1; a longer trip such as out to the Bardo will cost TD3.5, to Sidi Bou Saïd will be around TD6.5. The evening rate is pricier, but shorter journeys still work out cheap. Other than at the airport, where some drivers are intent on negotiating a set fare, drivers always use the meter. Taxis are especially good if you are visiting embassies, as the drivers know where they are and can save you a lot of slogging. The only problem with taxis is that there aren't enough of them. During peak hours this is a real problem; you just have to be patient and lucky. Taxis can also be booked by phone – ask at your hotel reception.

TGM

The TGM is a suburban train line that connects central Tunis with the beachside suburbs of La Goulette, Carthage, Sidi Bou Saïd and La Marsa. It's fast, cheap and convenient, although it can get crowded; avoid the rush hours (7.30am to 8.30am and 5pm to 6.30pm). The first train leaves Tunis Marine at 5am, and the last train at midnight. Departures range from every 12 minutes during peak hours to every 40 minutes. First class is well worth the extra cost. It costs TD0.65

to La Goulette (20 minutes) and TD0.9 to Carthage (30 minutes), Sidi Bou Saïd (35 minutes) and La Marsa Plage (45 minutes).

AROUND TUNIS

Until the arrival of the French at the end of the 19th century, La Goulette, Carthage, Sidi Bou Saïd, La Marsa and Hammam Lif were distinct villages and towns, quite isolated from the capital. This changed with the building of the causeway across Lake Tunis.

They remain, however, quite different. Each has a unique atmosphere – from the majestic World Heritage–listed Carthage, one of the greatest cities of the ancient world, to the lively day-trip bustle of La Goulette, the flower-covered white-and-blue patchwork of Sidi Bou Saïd, the luxury villas and white-sand coast of La Marsa and Gammarth, and the seedy splendour of Hammam Lif.

LA GOULETTE   حلق الواد

The old port of La Goulette, 10km from the centre, is popular with locals, who flock to the fish restaurants, cram the beach and revel in the summer breezes. It's the first stop east of the causeway across Lake Tunis. The suitably down-to-earth name means 'the gullet' in French – this refers to its position on the narrow channel connecting Lake Tunis to the open sea. It has a past-its-best feel reminiscent of English seaside towns and the traffic tends to turn you off the pavement seating, but there's a big range of restaurants, and a night-time buzz.

It remains a major port, handling cargo as well as passenger ferries from Europe. The principal monument is the massive fort – the Ottoman Borj el-Karrak, which is closed for renovations.

History

La Goulette was developed as a port by the Arabs after their capture of Tunis at the end of the 7th century, and it became a strategic defensive outpost. Its importance can be gauged from the dimensions of the 16th-century Ottoman fort here, built on the ruins of an earlier Spanish effort.

The eventual Ottoman victory heralded a golden age for La Goulette, which became

LA GOULETTE

0 — 100 m
0 — 0.1 miles

INFORMATION
Banque de Tunisie..................1 A3
BNA Bank...............................2 A4
Police Station.........................3 A3
Post Office..............................4 A3
UIB Bank................................5 A3

SIGHTS & ACTIVITIES   (p83)
Borj el-Karrak.........................6 A3
Mosque...................................7 A3

SLEEPING ⌂   (p84)
Hôtel La Jetée.........................8 B3

EATING ⫟   (p84)
L'Aquarius...............................9 B3
La Cordoue............................10 B3
La Victoire.............................11 B3
Le Chalet...............................12 B2
Le Monte Carlo......................13 B2
Lucullus.................................14 B3
Stambali................................15 B3

To Carthage (4km); Sidi Bou Saïd (6.5km)

La Goulette Vieille

Market

To Arch (50m); US Embassy (8km); Tunis (10km)

Place 7 Novembre

Gulf of Tunis

Port

To Ticket Office (50m); Customs (100m); Embarkation Hall (400m)

To Fishing Port (300m)

---

home to one of the state-approved corsair fleets which preyed on Christian shipping in the Mediterranean. The kasbah was used to imprison the hundreds of slaves needed to row corsair galleys. The riches they brought back led to the emergence of a small, walled town west of the kasbah that housed a substantial Jewish community. In colonial times, many Italians moved in, developing the area known as Little Sicily to the north. Today, both communities have moved on.

Sleeping & Eating
If you fancy a chock-a-block seaside scene and you want to be a stone's throw from a (rubbish-cluttered but lively) beach, there are a few hotels and restaurants. Most eateries are clustered around place 7 Novembre and ave Franklin Roosevelt. They seem legally bound to have similar menus and prices.

Hôtel La Jetée (☎ 736 000; 2 rue de la Grand Mosquée; s/d Jan–mid-Jun & mid-Sep–Dec TD55/80; mid-Jun–mid-Sep TD70/100; ❄ ⌘) This is a fairly new four-star hotel, with comfortable rooms that have balconies overlooking the busy beach, and staff are friendly.

La Victoire (☎ 735 398; 1 ave Franklin Roosevelt; starters TD3-5, mains TD6-14) This has a large air-con room, with the atmosphere of a Rotary Club function room – however, it's a good place for watching the action on the street without any traffic fumes, and the fish is tasty.

L'Aquarius (☎ 737 750; 2 ave Habib Bourguiba; starters TD2.5-9, mains TD7.5-18) A popular place, this has outside seating and a Liberace-style interior, with plaid walls, fairy lights and cosy booths.

Lucullus (starters TD3-7, mains TD7-13) The most upmarket joint around, this has traditional music and a dancer each evening out on the large terrace – inside the walls are white and there's plenty of good fish and seafood.

La Cordoue (☎ 735 476; 13 ave Franklin Roosevelt; starters TD3-8, mains TD7-16, 3-course lunch TD12) This has sticky plastic seats and won't win any décor prizes, but the food has a good reputation.

Stambali (☎ 738 506; dishes TD0.5-6) This is your cheap-and-simple option, where you can tuck into *lablabi* and all the other old favourites, and sit indoors or outside in a Formica environment.

Le Chalet (☎ 735 138; 42 ave Franklin Roosevelt; starters TD3-10, mains TD7-14, 3-course meal TD9) This is a more refined-feeling place than many of the others, with the advantage that the outside tables are set back from the road, under white canopies, surrounded by geraniums.

Getting There & Away
Train is the easiest way to travel. The TGM journey from Tunis Marine to La Goulette Vieille costs TD0.66 and takes about 15 minutes. A taxi to the city centre costs TD4 to TD6, depending on the time of day.

CARTHAGE   قرطاج
Home of military superstar Hannibal, and setting for the tragic romance between Carthaginian Dido and Roman Aeneas in Virgil's *Aeneid*, Carthage was one of the

greatest cities of the ancient world. It has a historic and poetic resonance that captures the imagination, and a past endowed with the operatic combination of lust, riches, honour, destruction and ambition. The founders of the city, the economically savvy Phoenicians, were exceptionally wealthy – the historian Pliny rather generously credits them

with inventing trade, which is an indication of how their business skills were regarded.

On the World Heritage list, the site today preserves its natural splendour, with lush vegetation and superb views over the gulf, and although the remains are patchy and spread out, enough is left to evoke (with a dose of imagination) Carthage's epic past.

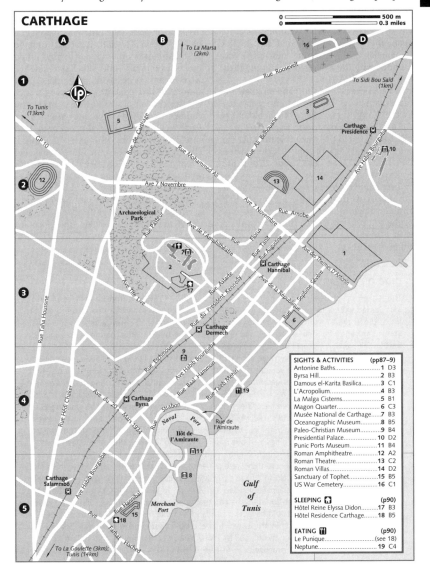

CARTHAGE

0 ———— 500 m
0 ———— 0.3 miles

SIGHTS & ACTIVITIES	(pp87–9)
Antonine Baths	1 D3
Byrsa Hill	2 B3
Damous el-Karita Basilica	3 C1
L'Acropolium	4 B3
La Malga Cisterns	5 B1
Magon Quarter	6 C3
Musée National de Carthage	7 B3
Oceanographic Museum	8 B5
Paleo-Christian Museum	9 B4
Presidential Palace	10 D2
Punic Ports Museum	11 B4
Roman Amphitheatre	12 A2
Roman Theatre	13 C2
Roman Villas	14 D2
Sanctuary of Tophet	15 B5
US War Cemetery	16 C1

SLEEPING	(p90)
Hôtel Reine Elyssa Didon	17 B3
Hôtel Residence Carthage	18 B5

EATING	(p90)
Le Punique	(see 18)
Neptune	19 C4

The highlights are the museum and excavated quarter that top Byrsa hill, the impressive Antonine Baths, the Punic ports, the Roman amphitheatre and the Sanctuary of Tophet. However, all the sites are worth a visit if you have the time.

History

The Phoenicians founded Carthage, legend has it, in 814 BC. Their power, based in the city of Tyre in modern Lebanon, was at its peak, and it seems that Qart Hadasht (the Phoenician name meaning 'new city') was founded with the aim of consolidating their hold on North Africa.

It had an ideal seafaring and strategic location: a narrow, hilly promontory flanked by the sea on three sides – the Sebkhet er-Ariana, the salt lake to the north of Tunis, was connected to the sea at this time. At the centre of a network of routes, it dominated the Mediterranean and trade from the continent.

Tyre came under increasing threat from the Assyrians during the 7th century BC, and Carthage took over as the major city of the Phoenician world. Its epic conflicts with Rome are covered in the History chapter (p22).

Colourful legends surround the demise of the Punic city during the third war with Rome. After a furious fight, 50,000 Carthaginians were taken away to slavery and 1000 remained defiantly besieged. Their commander, Hasdrubal, surrendered, his wife and children committed suicide by leaping into a fire, and the site was levelled and symbolically sprinkled with salt.

In 44 BC Julius Caesar re-established the city, and it became a provincial capital in 29 BC. Within 200 years, it had grown to be the third-largest imperial city behind Rome and Alexandria, with 300,000 residents, three forums, a circus holding 70,000, and mammoth baths and amphitheatre.

After the fall of the Roman Empire, the Vandals and Byzantines both ruled from Carthage, but the city slipped back into obscurity following the Arab conquest. The area returned to agriculture as its chief activity; in the 16th century Leo the African reported its production of peaches, pomegranates, olives and figs.

Now the most exclusive suburb in Tunis, Carthage retains its significance – the palace of the president is here, in a location chosen for its symbolic as well as its natural advantages.

DIDO ON THE MOVE

The legend surrounding the founding of Carthage in 814 BC evolved from the efforts of Greek and Roman writers to come up with a suitably aristocratic background for one of the great cities of the ancient Mediterranean world. They based the story on the few facts known to them about Carthage's Phoenician origins, and emphasised the blue-blooded nature of the link. The best-known version features in Virgil's epic poem, the *Aeneid*.

The story begins in the Phoenician capital of Tyre in the time of King Pygmalion. According to Virgil, Pygmalion coveted the wealth of the high priest Sichaeus, who was married to his sister, Princess Elissa. Pygmalion arranged for Sichaeus to be murdered and, concealing his involvement from Elissa, attempted to lay his hands on the loot. The ghost of Sichaeus, however, told Elissa what had happened and advised her to flee – as well as revealing the location of his treasure. Elissa decided to take his advice, and tricked Pygmalion into providing her with ships on the pretext of moving to a new palace down the coast, away from the memory of her husband. Thus she was able to load up all her belongings without raising Pygmalion's suspicions. At the last moment, she was joined by 80 noblemen, including her brother Barca.

They fled first to Cyprus, where they were joined by 80 suitable wives and the island's high priest, before setting sail for North Africa. By now Elissa had become Elissa Didon (aka Queen Dido), meaning 'the wanderer' in Phoenician. On arriving in North Africa, Elissa set about the job of acquiring land on which to found the city that would become Carthage. She struck a deal with the locals whereby she could have as much land as could be covered with an ox hide. The wily Elissa cut the hide into thin strips, which she used to surround the hill that became the Byrsa. (This final part of the legend is seen by many as a snide Roman dig at the Carthaginians' reputation for sharp business practices.)

Sights

The sights include Byrsa Hill and the museum, the Roman amphitheatre, the Roman theatre and villas, the Antonine Baths, the Punic ports, the Sanctuary of Tophet, the Paleo-Christian Museum, the Malga Cisterns and the Damous el-Karita Basilica.

A multiple-entry ticket valid for one day only (TD5.2, plus camera TD1) allows entry to all the above sights, which are open from 8.30am to 5pm from mid-September to March, and 8am to 7pm from April to mid-September.

The sights are spread over a wide area. From the Sanctuary of Tophet in the south to the Antonine Baths in the north it's 2km. You can use the TGM to cover larger distances and walk between some sites – to see them all, your best bet may be to make several visits, finishing up your day at reviving Sidi Bou Saïd. If you have only a few hours, limit yourself to the museum and the surrounding Punic ruins on the slopes of Byrsa Hill, then walk downhill to the Roman amphitheatre and the Antoine Baths.

Also at Carthage are the Cathedral of St Louis, Oceanographic Museum and American Military Cemetery.

BYRSA HILL

Getting off the TGM at Carthage Hannibal, it's a short walk to the top of Byrsa Hill. The entire site is visible from the summit (inside the museum compound) with amazing views across the excavated fragments, down through cypress trees and today's extravagant villas, to the distinctive shapes of the ancient Punic ports and the intense blue of the Gulf of Tunis.

The hill was the spiritual heart of the ancient city. In Punic times, it was occupied by a temple to the Carthaginian god Eschmoun; the Romans destroyed most of the Punic structures and levelled off the top to create a space large enough – 336m by 323m – to hold their capitol and forum. These in turn were destroyed as the fall of Rome unleashed a free-for-all for building materials, but the foundations were left, which have allowed archaeologists to work out the layout and scale of the buildings.

The area outside the museum is chock full of architectural bric-a-brac, and contains a small section of a residential quarter of the Punic city that was buried – and thus

preserved – during Roman levelling operations. The remains of the houses date from the 3rd-century BC – they're neat, careful structures that open onto two streets.

Musée National de Carthage

The ground level features some fine, louche 5th-century AD mosaics featuring lots of peachy bottoms, and a Roman sculpture of a boozy Silenus and Maenad continues the sensual theme. There are lamps dating from the 4th century BC to the 7th century AD, some still blackened by smoke. Particularly striking among the Punic remains are the domestic objects – masks painted on fragile ostrich shells and a bronze jug with two male figures as the handle that date back to the 5th or 6th century BC, some beautiful engraved 3rd-century razors with duck-shaped handles, and a 4th-century BC terracotta baby bottle in the shape of a bird. There's also a fragment of a Punic town-planning inscription.

Upstairs you are first greeted by a mammoth, blank-eyed bust of Roman royalty. The displays are divided into different themes, one of which describes the final siege of Punic Carthage (149–146 BC) and shows the Punic terracotta bullets and the Roman lead ones. With a few centuries' worth of hindsight, the Roman versions look more lethal. There is some beautifully worked jewellery from a Punic tomb, and many more fragments from daily life and work more than 2000 years ago, such as amphorae and fishing bits and bobs.

L'Acropolium

The French-built **L'Acropolium** (Cathedral of St Louis; admission TD2.5; ☼ 9am-6pm), constructed by the French in 1884, is a Gothic extravaganza that was dedicated to the 13th-century French saint-king who died on the beach at Carthage in 1270 during the ill-fated Eighth Crusade. The deconsecrated cathedral's ice-cream interior has been restored and houses frequent, interesting exhibitions and concerts (hence the name change).

ROMAN AMPHITHEATRE

The Roman amphitheatre is on the western side of the Byrsa, about a 15-minute walk down from the museum. It was once one of the largest theatres in the Roman Empire, with a capacity for 40,000. Today only the neat overgrown oval of the stage remains, but it's an evocative place, with a sinister exposed subterranean passage where victims and performers would once hang out. Most of its stones were stolen for other building projects in later centuries.

LA MALGA CISTERNS
Across the road is an impressive huge 2nd-century pipe network – remains of the voluminous cisterns northeast of the amphitheatre that were the main water supply for Carthage in Roman times. The reservoir was nearly 1km long and was fed by a huge aqueduct that ran 132km across the country, carrying mountain spring water from Zaghouan (see p148).

US WAR CEMETERY
Around 750m along the road from the cisterns, a neat forest of plain white crosses (rue Roosevelt) bears testament to the Americans who were killed in North Africa during World War II. There are 2840 graves here, and a Wall of Remembrance to 3724 others who were never found. It's moving: like all war cemeteries its dignified simplicity quietly underlines the horror of so many lives lost.

DAMOUS EL-KARITA BASILICA
You may want to take a cab to reach this monumental church, as it's around 1km via road from the cemetery. The basilica was 65m by 45m, with nine aisles, and the remaining lines of broken grey columns clearly stake out this huge scale. Steps lead into a well-preserved underground rotunda, 9.5m in diameter, which was used to display saints' relics.

ROMAN THEATRE & VILLAS
You can walk to the Roman theatre, which has been almost completely reconstructed, forming an impressive though not Roman (some scant remains are visible) venue for the annual Carthage International Festival (see p76).

The Roman villas are just east of the theatre, accessed from rue Arnobe. Most of the site is heavily overgrown. The centrepiece is the Villa of the Aviary, with marble tiling and mosaics; you get a sense of refined Roman life from the over-reconstructed house. The views over the gulf are wonderful.

ANTONINE BATHS
Across the road and down on the seafront, these monumental baths have a sublime seaside setting. Built in the middle of the 2nd century, they were once the third largest in the Roman Empire, again supplied with water by the great Zaghouan aqueduct. The *frigidarium* at the centre was 22m by 42m, with eight colossal pillars. The size of what is left is awesome, and it's just the foundations. A lonely 15m-high column gives a sense of the sometime height, and huge fragments of marble inscription supply a taste of the décor. The baths were destroyed by the Vandals doing what they did best in AD 439, and the stone reused by the Arabs during the construction of Tunis.

The shady palm-filled garden contains other remains too, including a tiny early Christian mosaic-floored funerary chapel forming a telling contrast to the aggrandising size of the baths.

Nearby are the remains of a 2000-year-old association headquarters, with a mosaic outside featuring cherubic boys and garlands, as well as some pits where Punic pottery kilns were discovered.

MAGON QUARTER
The Magon Quarter is a few blocks south of the Antonine Baths along rue Septime Sévère (the street opposite the baths entrance). Excavations have uncovered a small area of Roman workshops superimposed on the ruins of an earlier Punic residential area, which are now surrounded by a garden. There's not much to see but it's a pretty promenade along the seafront.

PALAEO-CHRISTIAN MUSEUM
Near Carthage Dermech TGM station, this small museum has good displays on the Punic ports and on excavation methods at the site. First-century AD buckles, tacks, forceps and needles are among its relics.

The museum grounds include the ruins of the city's most important Byzantine church, the 6th-century Basilica of Carthagenna. The foundations show that it had three naves, and some evocative mosaic fragments are scattered among the ruins.

PUNIC PORTS
Close to Carthage Byrsa TGM station, these two ancient ports retain their shape, and it's

SACRIFICING THE TRUTH?

Ancient Greek and Roman spin doctors had a hand in propagating stories of the Phoenicians' propensity for child sacrifice – it might have happened, but not as commonly as they would have had people believe. Evidence comes from classical sources: Plutarch and Diodorus claimed child sacrifice was common at Carthage, and the remains at the Sanctuary of Tophet seem to support this view, but some claim that the offerings to the gods were children who were stillborn or who had died of natural causes. Certainly, the Punic people were continually painted as tainted – it was claimed that they traded and stole children as well as performing human sacrifices. If a Roman said that you had *fides punica*, he would mean you were mighty unreliable. These qualities nicely set off the classical Western civilisations as noble and free of such gruesome practices (they just threw people to wild beasts).

strange to imagine today's serene ponds as they once were – the basis of Carthage's power and prosperity. The southern harbour was for commercial shipping, linked by a channel to the circular northern basin, the military base, with moorings for an incredible 220 ships. This arrangement made the naval base secure and private as only the commercial port had access to the sea.

It was filled in by Scipio after the destruction of Carthage in 146 BC, but in the 2nd century the Romans reinvented the islet as a circular forum, with two temples. Today the Îlot de l'Amiraute, at the centre of the naval basin, has a miniscule museum. It houses an interesting reconstruction of the Punic dockyards that once occupied the island (then completely surrounded by water) as well as a depiction of the equally impressive Roman port complex.

Nearby, the **Oceanographic Museum** (Dar el-Hout; ☎ 730420; 28 rue 2 Mars; admission TD1; ⏱ 10am-1pm & 3-6pm Tue-Sat, 10am-6pm Sun) contains enthusiastic displays of model boats, stuffed birds, conservation techniques and suspended model fish. Downstairs is an aquarium with some disconsolate fish including a strikingly alien-looking octopus.

SANCTUARY OF TOPHET

The chilling **Sanctuary of Tophet** (rue Hannibal), just east of Carthage Salammbô TGM station, was first excavated in 1921. The amateur French archaeologists responsible for the dig were curious about the source of a number of ancient grave stelae that were being offered for sale, and began to explore their source. Their excavations uncovered a sacrificial site and associated burial ground where it is commonly believed Carthaginian children were sacrificed to the deities Baal

Hammon and Tanit. The stick-drawing symbol representing Tanit is hauntingly like a simplistic children's cartoon. The name Tophet is Hebrew for 'place of burning' and comes from Bible references to child sacrifice, such as in Jeremiah: '(people of Judah) have built the altar called Tophet... and there they burn to death their little sons and daughters.'

More than 20,000 urns have been discovered at the site, each containing the ashes of a child and marked with a stele. Many also contained the burned bones of lambs or kids. The majority of them have been dated to the period between the 4th and 2nd centuries BC when Carthage was embroiled in numerous wars and rebellions, and the need to appease the gods was at its greatest. However, there is some controversy about interpretations of the site – see the boxed text, above.

Among the discoveries was the famous stele, now in the Bardo Museum, showing a priest holding an infant – it's thought he is carrying the child off to be slaughtered.

Local guides are enthusiastic about the site's morbid side and can be prone to exaggeration.

Festivals & Events

Carthage International Festival (www.festival-carthage.com.tn) is held in July and August. It features music, dance, theatre and international stars, in the spectacular open-air setting of the Roman theatre.

The biennial **Carthage International Film Festival**, held in the city's major cinemas, concentrates on Middle Eastern and African cinema. The two-week festival is next due in October 2005 – every other year it takes place in Burkina Faso.

Sleeping & Eating

Hôtel Residence Carthage (☎/fax 731 799; 16 rue Hannibal; s/d with private bathroom & breakfast TD57/80) A quiet place 100m from the Tophet, this has a chintzy feel. The smartish though ordinary rooms have TV and overlook the garden. Its Moroccan Restaurant, **Le Punique**, is flouncy but highly regarded.

Hôtel Reine Elyssa Didon (Byrsa Hill) This modern building, with huge windows, is superbly located on Byrsa Hill. It was closed at the time of research for renovation, which should see it re-open as a five-star hotel.

Neptune (☎ 731 456; starters TD2-7.5, mains TD5.5-13.5) Seating at this restaurant is on a fantastic small seaside terrace, a lovely calm and breezy spot to sit on a hot day or evening. It serves upmarket fish and seafood dishes.

Getting There & Away

The journey from Tunis Marine to any of the six Carthage TGM stations costs TD0.9 in 1st class (a worthwhile choice at busy times) and takes about 30 minutes. See p83 and Map p82.

SIDI BOU SAÏD   سيدي بو سعيد

Set high on a cliff, the village of Sidi Bou Saïd is all white angles and curves, bulging curved blue window grills and crisscrossed fretwork. As you stroll around the narrow lanes, blissful views open up over the fierce blue of the Gulf of Tunis. Flaming-red geraniums and shocking-pink bougainvillea pour over the walls and fill courtyards. The buildings cluster around the Mosque and Zaouia of Sidi Bou Saïd, the 13th-century Sufi saint after whom the place is named – there is a festival devoted to him in August. The distinctive architecture is Andalusian-inspired, a result of the influx of Spanish Muslims in the 16th century. Longstanding local families and moneyed expats have ensured that the buildings retained their character; the village was given protected status in 1915. It has attracted numerous painters and writers, including Paul Klee, Auguste Macke, André Gide, Michel Foucault, and Osbert and Edith Sitwell.

The centre of activity is the small, cobbled main square, place Sidi Bou Saïd, lined with cafés, sweet stalls and souvenir shops. Although it's every tourist's favourite stop, the daily hubbub gives it a lively buzz, and by the evening it quietens down and empties out.

Sights

The **lighthouse** above the village stands on the site of an ancient *ribat* (fort), built in the early 9th century as part of a coastal early-warning system that included the *ribats* of Sousse (see p162) and Monastir (see p170).

Dar el-Annabi (rue Habib Thameur; admission TD3; ☯ 9am-6.30pm) is a family home that is open to the public. Built at the end of the 18th century, it's vibrantly tiled and centred around several courtyards filled with jasmine, henna and bougainvillea. Rooms on display include a prayer room, reception rooms and a lovely little library, all carefully presented, with some grand wax figures, and black-and-white family photos on the walls that add a sense of authenticity. The superb panorama from the top terrace sweeps across the village, bay and across to Carthage.

Dar Ennejma Ezzahra (Centre of Arabic & Mediterranean Music; ☯ 9am-noon & 4-7pm Tue-Sun Apr-Sep, 2-5pm Tue-Sun Oct-Mar), an exquisitely grand house built by Rodolphe d'Erlanger, is a classic example of oriental fantasy through a Western looking glass. It has a display of instruments, and occasionally hosts much-recommended performances of rare classical music.

The street heading off to the right at the top end of the main square takes you to the top of a steep path leading down through pine forest to the marina and a small beach. From here it is possible to follow the road around and back up the hill to emerge near Carthage Amilcar TGM station. The walk from Sidi Bou Saïd takes about an hour.

Sleeping

Despite a certain lack of imagination when it comes to names, there are some exceedingly lovely hotels here.

Hôtel Dar Saïd (☎ 729 666; rue Toumi; r from TD205; ☯ ☯) This boutique four-star hotel has to be one of the country's most charming, and has been rated one of the best 50 hotels in the world. It's in a converted grand (but not imposing) villa, centred around pretty, tiled courtyards and with views filled with piercing-blue sea and pink bougainvilleas. The small pool and gardens overlook the bay, the food is good, and the service is welcoming yet relaxed (you never have to sign for anything) and makes you feel at home (if only home were like this).

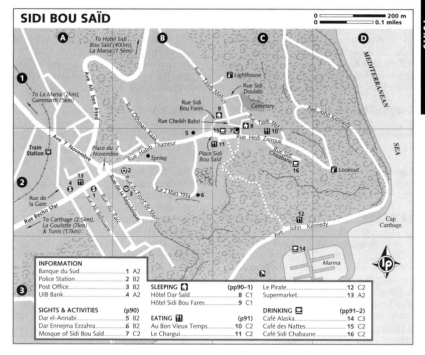

SIDI BOU SAÏD

Hôtel Sidi Bou Fares (☎ 740 091; 15 rue Sidi Bou Fares; s/d TD28/50, d with private bathroom TD65) Simple, barrel-vaulted rooms surround a courtyard full of blooming shrubs and vines, and the friendly owner speaks excellent English.

Hôtel Sidi Bou Saïd (☎ 740 711; s/d Nov-Feb TD73/102, Mar-Jun & Sep-Oct TD83/115, Jul-Aug TD99/147) About 1km north of Sidi Bou Saïd off the road to La Marsa, this is set high up and has sweeping views across the bay and luxurious rooms.

Eating
RESTAURANTS

The cheaper places to eat are around place du 7 Novembre, near the TGM station. There are several small places here selling sandwiches and pizza by the slice. A popular stall around the corner from Café des Nattes sells *bombalouni* (doughnuts) and almond *briqs*.

Au Bon Vieux Temps (☎ 744 733; 56 rue Hedi Zarrouk; starters TD6-14, mains TD14-20) This small, much-recommended place has a beautiful, quite ridiculously romantic small terrace overlooking the sea, delectable French and

Tunisian food and has fed such luminaries as the Portuguese president and Miss France (they weren't together).

Le Chargui (☎ 740 987; mains TD5-10) This is the cheapest of the restaurants in the centre, and has a big open-air courtyard with moulded whitewashed seating, and a rooftop terrace with great views.

Le Pirate (☎ 748 266; ave John Kennedy; starters TD4-20, mains TD10-20) By the marina, this is another upmarket place with candlelit garden seating under palm trees and white canopies, serving excellent seafood, such as lovely *mérou brochettes*; piped music lends it a dash of cheese.

CAFÉS

Café de Nattes (place Sidi Bou Saïd) This is right at the heart of the village, and has steep steps and small terraces that are perfect for checking out who's strolling up and down the cobbled catwalk of the street, while sipping mint tea with pinenuts.

Café Sidi Chabaane (rue Sidi Chabaane) One of the prettiest café settings around, with layers of terraces cut into the cliff and rush matting on its whitewashed edges. It's an ideal place to watch the sunset, with high-up views over the blue-green limpid sea, yacht-stuffed marina and sandy swathe of beach.

Café Alaska (Marina) Yachts bob up and down in the water edged by this large café that's a busy local option in the evening.

Getting There & Away

It's about 17km northeast of Tunis. The easiest way to travel is by TGM train from Tunis Marine (TD0.7; 35 minutes). It's a 15-minute walk from the station up to the top of the hill and the centre of the old part of the village. A taxi during the day costs around TD7 (around TD10 after 7pm).

LA MARSA المرسى

La Marsa, once the summer base of the beys, is an exclusive beachside suburb at the end of the TGM line from Tunis. A 19th-century palace remains, and most of the houses are grand villas. The sweeping, palm-lined beach stretches north around a great bay that finishes beneath the cliffs of the five-star resort village of Gammarth. The beach is relatively uncrowded during the week, but gets packed out at weekends.

Pension Predl (☎ 749 529; s/d TD15/30) This is an unusual place in that it's a pension in a home, with basic but clean rooms off an striking tall-ceilinged central room.

Hôtel Plaza Corniche (22 rue du Maroc; ✖ ✿) American-owned and eccentrically decorated, with plastic palms, lots of kitsch and flower-sprigged bright rooms with balconies, this is a popular place for a poolside evening drink, though drinks are expensive. There's also a popular disco – reputedly one of Tunis' best.

Les Ombrelles (☎ 742 964; ave Taieb M'hiri; starters TD7, mains TD9-18) Right on the seafront, with the waves lapping against the shore, this has tasty, straightforward seafood. The interior dining room is a warm yellow and the whole place is candlelit at night.

Au Bon Vieux Temps (☎ 774 322; starters TD6-14, mains TD14-20) Another branch of this refined French restaurant sits under an explosion of flowers near the TGM station.

There is a cluster of cafés and restaurants around the TGM station, and a couple of fish restaurants on the beach during summer.

GAMMARTH قمّرت

Beneath the cliffs of Cap Gammarth, 2km north of La Marsa, this is a rich, leafy suburb with lots of sleek seaside villas, a graceful curve of coast, some excellent restaurants and a mixed bag of five-star hotels.

Abou Nawas Gammarth (☎ 741 444; s/d Jan-Dec TD180/190, Jul-Aug TD210/230; ✖ ✿) With sea views and all the luxury and comfort you might expect, this is smaller and so a bit more personable than its central sisters.

Les Dunes (☎ 743 379; 130 ave Taieb M'hiri; starters TD3-8, mains TD10-18; ✋ lunch & dinner Tue-Sat) A graceful white-painted villa, this has a terrace overlooking the sea and good seafood.

You can walk around the bay from La Marsa, which takes about 45 minutes, unless you stop for a swim on the way. A cab from La Marsa will cost around TD1.

HAMMAM LIF

This southern suburb has been a spa resort for thousands of years. In colloquial Arabic, Lif means 'nose', as the baths here are reputedly good for clearing the sinuses. Bou Kornine – a mountain with twin peaks (the name means two humps) – looms over Hammam Lif. Somewhat down-at-heel, it's one of the most popular places to promenade along the seafront and search out a breeze (or even leap in the sea) of a summer's evening, with interesting buildings and loads of food stalls, candy floss and opportunities to survey your fellow citizens – the corniche is busy until at least 1am. You can reach here by train from Tunis Ville (20 minutes, five daily), or by taxi (TD4).

Cap Bon الوطى القبلي

The Romans called Cap Bon the 'beautiful peninsula' (Pulchri Promontorium) and the name still fits. With a spine of rocky hills, and velvet bone-white beaches wrapping its coast, this lush and fertile crooked thumb of land points towards Sicily, only 140km away, and has long had close links with Europe – geologists speculate that the land masses were once joined, split by the rising Mediterranean 30,000 years ago.

Crowded with citrus trees and vineyards, the region is a major producer of delicious fruit and is famous for its wine, particularly the fragrant muscat. Easygoing Cap Bon, with its gentle climate, also happens to be Tunisia's main tourist magnet; they're particularly drawn to the mesmerising long white-sand beaches around Hammamet and Nabeul, with resulting masses of hotels, restaurants, markets and shops concentrated along the east coast. The pace slows as you head northeast to Kélibia, with its almost empty balmy beach, small port and mighty fortress. Nearby, perched above the warm azure ocean, are the unique ruins of Punic Kerkouane – the most complete remains of this ancient civilisation. The small town of El-Haouaria, skirted by more white sand at the peninsula's northern tip, feels even more remote – a world away from the commercialism further south – and is near coastal quarries that date back more than 2500 years.

The west is much more rugged and isolated, difficult to get around (it's easier to reach from Tunis than to cross the peninsula), with scattered lonely villages. A dramatic road clinging to the rocky, glorious coast leads to the stuck-in-time spa of Korbous, where a scalding hot spring spills directly into the sea, as if performing a magic trick.

HIGHLIGHTS

- Exploring the magnificent fortress and long, long beach at **Kélibia** (p106)
- Enjoying days on the beach and nights on the town in **Hammamet** (p95)
- Unwinding at **Korbous** (p111), where a hot spring pours into the ocean
- Unravelling Punic mysteries at **Kerkouane** (p108)

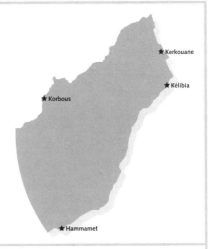

- TELEPHONE CODE: 72

History

Cap Bon was under Carthaginian control by the early 5th century BC, keeping the Punic capital in fruit and veg and forming a key part of its defence system, centred on fortified Aspis (Kélibia). Geographically vulnerable, Cap Bon was the route chosen by both Agathocles of Syracuse (in 310 BC) and the Roman general Regulus (in 256 BC) during their respective assaults on Carthage. Each time Aspis was sacked. Kerkouane survived Agathocles, but was trashed by Regulus and abandoned forever.

Aspis went on to become the important Roman settlement of Clypea. Neapolis (Nabeul) was the other big town, and the countryside is dotted with relics of other settlements. Rich under the Romans, its prosperity continued until the Arabic conquest. Clypea became a Byzantine stronghold that held out against the Arabs until the late 7th century AD, long after the rest of Tunisia had fallen. Piracy and unrest in the region led to its decline in the 14th to 16th centuries. Cap Bon was constantly threatened from the sea, forcing many coastal communities to shift – thus Nabeul and Kélibia town centres are a few kilometres inland.

A wave of Andalusian immigrants revitalised the area, and it was favoured by European settlers during the French era: the countryside is dotted with the ruins of old, red-tiled farmhouses. The French developed the vast citrus groves around Beni Khalled and Menzel Bou Zelfa and the vineyards around Grombalia.

An exclusive kind of tourism took off in the 1920s, triggered largely by Romanian millionaire George Sebastian building his luxurious villa outside Hammamet. Less-welcome visitors took over the villa in 1943 when Axis forces retreated to Cap Bon and ran their campaign from there, until the surrender that ended the North African phase of WWII.

Climate

Cap Bon has a mild climate – as a coastal region it is cooler during the summer and warmer in winter than other parts of Tunisia.

Getting There & Away

The nearest airport is Tunis-Carthage. There are many buses and louages (shared

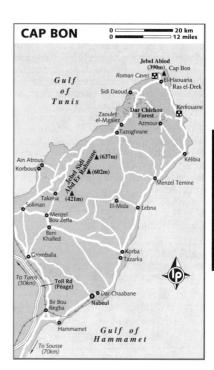

taxis) serving the region with Hammamet and Korbous around an hour from the capital. Nabeul and Hammamet are also connected to Tunis by train.

Getting Around

Louages and buses connect the coastal towns. It's more difficult to cross the peninsula – Soliman and Korbous are better reached from the capital than from Cap Bon's southern coast.

HAMMAMET   حمّامات

☎ 72 / pop 52,000

Hammamet ('the baths' in Arabic) is Tunisia's busiest resort, a holiday heaven that is blessed with a soft curve of amber-sand beach, and edged by the densely blue Mediterranean Sea surreally dotted by galleon-style tourist boats. Early planning constraints said hotels should not over-reach the height of a tree, and though there are some broad interpretations of this, the buildings in Hammamet are relatively restrained. The small centre is packed with restaurants and shops, overlooked by its

Disney-perfect medina, and the evenings usher in a carnival atmosphere. But if your idea of a break is escaping bright lights and burgers, and facility-fat hotel complexes don't rock your world, then head for the smaller resorts on the northern coast or further up the Cap Bon.

The metamorphosis from quiet fishing village began in the 1920s when Hammamet was the playground of the European jet set, led by millionaire George Sebastian. Today, hotels stretch all the way to the fantasy tourist zone of Yasmine Hammamet, 5km to the south.

George Sebastian's incredible villa is now home to Hammamet's International Cultural Centre.

Orientation

Hammamet's medina is central, overlooking the sea on a small spit of land jutting out into the Gulf of Hammamet. There are two main streets in the town: ave Habib Bourguiba, which runs north from the medina and links up with the road to Hammamet Sud and the new development of Yasmine Hammamet; and ave de la République, which heads northeast from the medina to Hammamet Nord and on to Nabeul.

Information

EMERGENCY

Infirmary (☎ 282 333; 29 ave Habib Bourguiba)
Police (Map p96; ☎ 280 079; ave Habib Bourguiba)

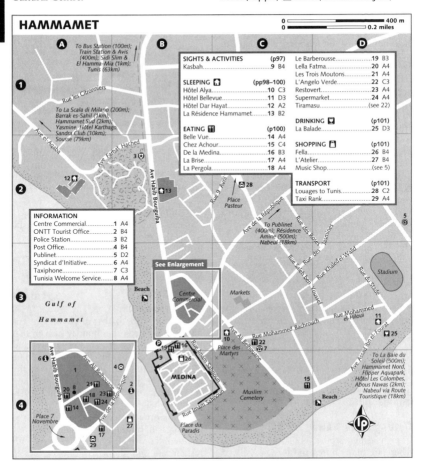

HAMMAMET

0 — 400 m
0 — 0.2 miles

SIGHTS & ACTIVITIES (p97)
Kasbah...9 B4

SLEEPING (pp98–100)
Hôtel Alya....................................10 C3
Hôtel Bellevue............................11 D3
Hôtel Dar Hayat.........................12 A2
La Résidence Hammamet..........13 B2

EATING (p100)
Belle Vue.....................................14 A4
Chez Achour................................15 C4
De la Medina...............................16 B3
La Brise..17 A4
La Pergola....................................18 A4

Le Barberousse...........................19 B3
Lella Fatma..................................20 A4
Les Trois Moutons......................21 A4
L'Angelo Verde...........................22 C3
Restovert......................................23 A4
Supermarket.................................24 A4
Tiramasu...................................(see 22)

DRINKING (p101)
La Balade......................................25 D3

SHOPPING (p101)
Fella..26 B4
L'Atelier.......................................27 B4
Music Shop...............................(see 5)

TRANSPORT (p101)
Louages to Tunis.........................28 C2
Taxi Rank.....................................29 A4

INFORMATION
Centre Commercial.......................1 A4
ONTT Tourist Office......................2 B4
Police Station................................3 B2
Post Office....................................4 B4
Publinet..5 D2
Syndicat d'Initiative.....................6 A4
Taxiphone......................................7 C3
Tunisia Welcome Service..............8 A4

To Bus Station (100m); Train Station & Avis (400m); Sidi Slim & El Hamma-Mia (1km); Tunis (63km)

Rue les Citronniers

To La Scala di Milano (200m); Barrak es-Sahil (1km); Hammamet Sud (2km); Yasmine, Hôtel Karthago, Sandra Club (10km); Sousse (79km)

Ave el-Aqaba

Ave Farhat Hached

Ave Habib Bourguiba

Rue 9 Avril

Place Pasteur

Ave de la République

To Publinet (400m); Résidence Amine (500m); Nabeul (18km)

Rue des Roses

Rue des Jasmines

Rue Sidi ben Youssef

Rue Khaled el-Walid

Rue du Stade

Stadium

See Enlargement

Beach

Centre Commercial

Markets

Rue Mohammed Bachrouch

Rue Mohammed el-Hiloui

Gulf of Hammamet

Ave Ali Belhouane

Place des Martyrs

Muslim Cemetery

Beach

To La Baie du Soleil (500m); Hammamet Nord, Flipper Aquapark, Hôtel Les Colombes, Abous Nawas (2km); Nabeul via Route Touristique (18km)

Ave Assad Ibn el-Fourat

MEDINA

Rue Imam Sahnoun

Place du Paradis

Ave Habib Bourguiba

Ave Ali Belhouane

Ave de la République

Place 7 Novembre

INTERNET ACCESS
Publinet (Map p96; 117 ave de la Liberation; 163 ave Habib Bourguiba; ave Taieb Azzazi) All charge TD2 per hour.

MONEY
The banks, with ATMs, are concentrated around the junction of aves Habib Bourguiba and de la République.

Many hotels and shops can also change cash and travellers cheques.

POST
Main post office (Map p96; ave de la République) Near the centre.

TOURIST INFORMATION
ONTT ave de la République & ave Ali Belhouane (Map p96; ☎ 280 423; ☼ 7.30am-8pm Jul-Aug, 8am-6pm Mon-Sat & 9am-noon Sun Sep-Jun); Yasmine Hammamet (☎ 249 103; ☼ 8.30am-1pm Mon-Sat, 3-5.45pm Mon-Thu) A source for maps of Hammamet and Nabeul, and there's usually someone around who speaks English.
Syndicat d'Initiative (Map p96; ☎ 262 891; ave Habib Bourguiba; ☼ 8am-noon & 3-6pm Mon-Sat, 7.30am-8pm Jul-Aug) This small office carries similar items to the ONTT.

Sights
MEDINA
The Hafsids built this sandcastle medina (1463–74), using the site of a 9th-century Aghlabid structure. Souvenir shops have swallowed the weblike old souqs, but the southern residential district is particularly well preserved.

Kasbah (Map p96; admission TD1.6, plus camera TD1; ☼ 8.30-6pm mid-Sep–Mar, 8am-7pm Apr-Jun, 8am-8pm Jul–mid-Sep) An immaculate building in the northwestern corner, it has fortifications that signify the town's defensive past. There are sweeping views across the coast and tangled medina from a small ramparts café.

INTERNATIONAL CULTURAL CENTRE
Hammamet's bewitching **International Culture Centre** (Map p98; admission TD1; ☼ 8am-6pm Feb-Sep, 8am-5pm Oct-Jan) was designed and built by George Sebastian from 1920 to 1932. Frank Lloyd Wright said it was one of the most beautiful places he knew: the appreciative architect was just one of Sebastian's many illustrious, bohemian guests. It's the ultimate party house, with a central colonnaded swimming pool, huge black marble dining

table, and baptistery font-style four-seater bath. Nazi Erwin Rommel used it as an Axis headquarters during WWII, and after the war British Prime Minister Winston Churchill stayed here.

Sebastian's innovative yet traditional whitewashed arches and angles can be seen echoed in countless Hammamet hotels. The house feels unloved, but its faded airs only evoke more strongly a sense of good times past. It now hosts interesting displays of art. The terrace faces a rich view of flowers, greenery and sea-flooded horizon, and you can walk down to the beach.

The grounds include a Roman-style amphitheatre, used during July and August to stage Hammamet's annual International Cultural Festival, with entertainment ranging from classical theatre to Arabic music. Tickets are sold at the tourist office and at the door. A neighbouring Sebastian-built domed building opens as a café during the festival.

The place is 3km northwest of the town centre – a taxi will set you back TD1 (collective TD0.5).

PUPPUT بوبات
The Roman site of **Pupput** (Map p98; admission TD1.1; ☼ 9am-5pm mid-Sep–Mar, 8am-7pm Apr–mid-Sep) is 6.5km southwest of the Hammamet town centre. It was once a staging post on the Roman road from Carthage to Hadrumetum (Sousse). The name suggests that it occupies the site of an earlier Punic settlement. Now the remains are scant, but still interesting, with some dating from Byzantine and Roman times. The 5th-century House of Figured Peristyle retains a couple of columns and some mosaic flooring, but the most vivid are the bleached-out Byzantine tomb mosaics that are displayed on a wall.

Activities
BEACHES
Hammamet is all about beaches. The best one stretches northwest from the medina, though you'll be happy to get to know the beach running towards Nabeul too.

DIVING
A couple of hotels have diving centres, offering certification courses (around TD325), and sets of six dives (TD195). There are

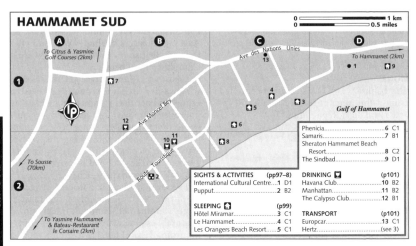

HAMMAMET SUD

0 ————— 1 km
0 ————— 0.5 miles

To Citrus & Yasmine
Golf Courses (2km)

Ave des Nations Unies

To Hammamet (2km)

Gulf of Hammamet

To Sousse
(70km)

To Yasmine Hammamet
& Bateau-Restaurant
le Corsaire (2km)

SIGHTS & ACTIVITIES	(pp97–8)
International Cultural Centre	...1 D1
Pupput	...2 B2

SLEEPING	(p99)
Hôtel Miramar	...3 C1
Le Hammamet	...4 C1
Les Orangers Beach Resort	...5 C1

Phenicia	...6 C1
Samaris	...7 B1
Sheraton Hammamet Beach Resort	...8 C2
The Sindbad	...9 D1

DRINKING	(p101)
Havana Club	...10 B2
Manhattan	...11 B2
The Calypso Club	...12 B1

TRANSPORT	(p101)
Europcar	...13 C1
Hertz	(see 3)

some WWII wrecks and sea life to explore, but Tabarka's sites and centres are better.

Samira Club (☎ 226 484)

Venus (☎ 227 211)

Port Yasmine Diving Centre (☎ 319 741)

FLIPPER AQUAPARK

A water park in Hammamet Nord, **Flipper Aquapark** (☎ 261 800; admission adult/child TD14/8; 10am-7pm) has lots of winding slides and splashy features for small and big kids.

GOLF

Golf is big business, with two clubs to the west of town.

Citrus (☎ 226 500), beside the main Tunis–Sousse road, is a huge complex laid out among citrus and olive trees. Built in the early 1990s, it includes two demanding 18-hole courses and a nine-hole short course. **Yasmine** (☎ 227 665), about 2km to the north, has an 18-hole course and a nine-hole for beginners.

Both clubs demand proof of handicap (better than 36 for Citrus). Green fees cost TD35/64 for 9/18 holes.

HORSE-RIDING

Numerous places offer horse riding for one or two hours in the surrounding hills or out to the Berber villages. Most hotels will arrange this for you, or try **Club Equestre el-Mrezgua** (☎ 261 645) which has camels and horses in Hammamet Nord, opposite Hôtel Club Les Colombes.

Tours

Lots of tour companies offer excursions, including a half-day tour to Berber villages, Takrouna, Zriba and Jeradou, and one-day tours whizzing round Carthage, Sidi Bou Saïd and the Bardo Museum. Try:

Hammamet Travel Service (☎ 280 193; ave Dag Hammarskjold)

Tunisia Welcome Service (Map p96; ☎ 280 766; www.tunisia-orangers.com)

Festivals & Events

The International Festival takes place in July and August with impressive local and international acts – music, dance, theatre and cinema – all taking place in the seaside amphitheatre at the International Cultural Centre.

Sleeping

Three-star-plus places usually offer air-con, a pool and sizeable rooms. Such is Hammamet's capacity that you can usually walk up and get a room, and discounts (always worth a try) if business is slack. Prices plummet in winter. Rates here include breakfast, and children under 12 cost 30% to 50% less.

CENTRE

If you want to be near the best restaurants and a stuffed-camel's throw from the medina, this is where to stay.

Résidence Amine (☎ 765 500; ave de la Libération; s/d with private bathroom TD15/30) Friendly and spotless, affably run, and a good budget choice, with some big rooms.

La Résidence Hammamet (Map p96; ☎ 280 733; 54 ave Habib Bourguiba; s/d/tr/q with private bathroom & kitchen TD17/28/36/42; ✕ ⬛) A central bargain, with a range of comfortable studio apartments, around a leafy courtyard.

Hôtel Alya (Map p96; ☎ 280 218; ave Ali Belhouane; s/d Nov-Mar TD15.5/25, Apr-Oct TD24.5/35, Jul-Aug TD44.5/55) This good, central little two star has airy white-and-blue rooms with balconies, some with medina views.

Hôtel Bellevue (Map p96; ☎ 281 121; ave Assad ibn el-Fourat; s/d Jul-Aug TD35/64, Apr-Jun & Sep-Nov TD25/35, Dec-Mar TD15/25) Overlooking the beach, an appealing though slightly rundown choice with breezy sea-facing rooms and welcoming staff.

Hôtel Dar Hayat (Map p96; ☎ 260 824; ave el-Aqaba; s/d Nov-Feb TD62/124, Oct, New Year, Mar-Jun TD85/170, Jul-Aug TD120/240; ✕ ⬛) A graceful, boutique five star, with bright, elegant rooms, sea views and an unusual amount of charm.

La Baie du Soleil (☎ 280 511; ave Assad Ibn el-Fourat; s/d Oct-Mar TD12/24, Apr-Sep TD20/32, Jul-Aug TD49/68) Simple holiday-camp-style pod-like rooms are a bit worn but good value; they're packed with children in July and August.

NORD
The beach here is lovely and quieter than the south, but the hotels are a bit old and tired.

Abou Nawas (☎ 281 344; Route Touristique el-Merezka; Nov–mid-Mar s/d TD41/54, mid-Mar–Jun & mid-Sep–Oct TD70/100, Jul-Sep TD96/132, Aug TD128/186; ✕ ⬛) This is up to the usual luxurious standard of the Abou Nawas chain, with attractive, comfortable rooms overlooking the beach and gardens, and friendly service.

Hôtel Club Les Colombes (☎ 280 777; Route Touristique el-Merezka; full board s/d Nov-Mar TD27/44, Apr-Oct TD43/72, Jul TD66/92, Aug TD70/112; ✕ ⬛) Right on the beach, a well established hotel with a staid, quiet atmosphere. The rooms have good sea views.

SUD
The south not only has the balmy curve of beach but also the bulk of the nightlife.

Samaris (Map p98; ☎ 226 353; r with private bathroom TD15; camping adult/child/tent/car/van/hot shower TD2.8/2/2/2/2.8/2.3) It's surprising to go from the busy road into this leafy courtyard-centred, tranquil place, a few kilometres

from the beach. The campsite is shady, and pretty too. Breakfast isn't included, but there's a restaurant.

The Sindbad (Map p98; ☎ 280 122; ave des Nations Unies; s/d Nov-Mar TD49/68, Apr-Oct TD68-96, mid-Jul–Aug TD161/202; ✕ ⬛) The Sinbad is a five-star hotel with excellent service, a rare intimate atmosphere, pretty rooms decorated in warm yellows with shady terraces, and a lush pool.

Hôtel Miramar (Map p98; ☎ 280 344; s/d Nov-Mar TD45/62, Apr–mid-Jun & mid-Sep–Oct TD69/120, mid-Jun–Sep TD115/176; ✕ ⬛) At this big four star, the normal rooms are jaded but have balconies either facing the sea or garden, while the lush suites with two terraces are Sebastian inspired.

Sheraton Hammamet Beach Resort (Map p98; ☎ 226 555; www.sheraton.com; ave Moncef Bey; s/d Jan–mid-Mar, Nov & Dec from TD90/120, mid-Mar–Jun, Sep & Oct from TD120/180, Jul-Aug from TD160/260, Xmas & New Year from TD110/160; ✕ ⬛) A tasteful, beachside place with an excellent reputation; whitewashed, simple, yet luxurious bungalows are set in lush gardens.

Phenicia (Map p98; ☎ 226 533; s/d Nov-Mar TD75/110, Apr-Jun, Oct, Xmas & New Year TD85/130, Jul-Aug TD130/200; ✕ ⬛) Built in the '70s by the presidential architect, this has been refurbished with impressive flair, style and strong colours.

Les Orangers Beach Resort (Map p98; ☎ 280 144; www.orangers.com.tn; s/d Nov-Mar TD36.5/50, Apr-Jun, Sep & Oct TD70/94, Jul & Aug TD116/152; ✕ ⬛) A family-oriented four star, this is large and comfortable, with old-fashioned rooms and pools with slides.

Le Hammamet (Map p98; ☎ 280 344; rue Nevers; s/d Nov-Mar TD26/32, Apr-Oct TD43/64, Jul & Aug TD67/102; ✕ ⬛) Despite the impersonal architecture this has good service, pleasant gardens and comfortable rooms, as well as a good spa and a 'Queen Vic' pub.

YASMINE
The newest area of development, this is cheek-by-jowl four and five star. It's on a different scale, with palm-lined boulevards, a newish marina, and a spanking-new medina, which adds a touch of Vegas-style weirdness and encompasses souqs, restaurants and housing. Special mention should also go to five-star neo-castle Lella Baya for out-and-out architectural eccentricity and absurdity.

Hôtel Karthago (☎ 240 666; s/d Nov-Mar TD62/84, Apr-Oct TD88/116, Jun-Aug TD135/190; 🔲 🗩) This marina-side five star is stylish, with a cream-coloured gold-studded central atrium reminiscent of a very swish '70s cruise liner. The rooms echo this design, and there's a classy spa. There's an ice rink next door.

Sandra Club (☎ 248 441; min 5 nights s/d Jun TD35/40, Jul TD45/60, Aug TD50/70, Sep TD40/50, Xmas & New Year TD40/70; 🗩) One of the more attractively designed and furnished hotels, with simple traditional whitewashed arches, this has a cheery all-in package feel.

Flora Park (☎ 227727; www.solmelia.com; s/d TD65/80; 🔲 🗩) Unusual in this area, this is a boutique hotel, a bit away from the beach, but with an intimate feel, nice spa and tasteful rooms.

Hasdrubal Thalassa (☎ 248 800; www.hasdrubal-hotels.com; s/d Jan-Mar TD150/210, Apr-Oct TD230/320; 🔲 🗩) One of the Leading Hotels in the World group, this is suitably lush, with lots of marble, ostentatious pool and super spa.

Eating

RESTAURANTS

There are lots of good restaurants, all open for lunch and dinner daily unless otherwise stated.

Les Trois Moutons (Map p96; ☎ 280 981; Centre Commercial; starters TD4-19, mains TD9-17.5) Rated among the country's best restaurants, with an interior like a conservatory stage set and lots of classy seafood.

Chez Achour (Map p96; ☎ 280 140; rue Ali Belhouane; starters TD3-11, mains TD7.5-20) A long reputation and the seafood is good, if not outstanding. Seating is in a garden courtyard decorated by white lanterns.

El Hamma-Mia (☎ 279 128; off ave du Koweit; starters TD6-18, mains TD8.5-20) A sumptuously decorated place which serves upmarket traditional food, and has seating in a lovely little grassy garden.

Sidi Slim (☎ 279 124; www.sidislim.com; 156 ave du Koweit; starters TD4-16, mains TD8.5-17) With fussy décor that involves some crazy-paving arches, Sidi Slim has good seafood and meat dishes.

La Brise (ave de la Republique; starters TD1.4-4.5, mains TD3.5-10) The best of the cheapies. A wipe-clean tiled place with some outside tables and nice food in hearty portions.

La Pergola (Map p96; ☎ 261 751; Centre Commercial; starters TD3.5-15, mains TD6.5-17; set menu TD12) The best of the central restaurants, with a lat-

ticed, leafy, candlelit terrace, and live folk music nightly, but haphazard service.

La Scala di Milano (Map p96; ☎ 98 618 713; La Corniche; starters TD4-12, mains TD10-16) A bit out of the way, but produces excellent pasta and has an outside terrace. Was fugitive Italian ex-prime minister Bettino Craxi's favourite restaurant and La Scala de Milano has his chair enshrined to prove it.

Restovert (Map p96; ☎ 278 200; rue du Stade; dishes TD1.8-6.8; 🕘 9am-1am) Plastered with film posters, this is a popular hangout for young Hammamet, with a good balcony for street-surveillance and lots of tasty snackfood.

L'Angolo Verde (Map p96; ☎ 262 641; ave de la République; dishes TD2.8-14.5) Under the same management (who also own the Havana Club), this is popular and good for children, with some tree-shaded pavement seating, good pizzas and pasta (no alcohol). Next door is tucked-away **Tiramasu** (Map p96) with killer ice cream.

Bateau – Restaurant Le Corsaire (☎ 240 323; Port Yasmine Hammamet; starters TD4-13, mains TD10.5-18) An upmarket small boat restaurant floating in the marina, here you can sit on the top deck and tuck into top seafood.

Also recommended:

Lella Fatma (Map p96; ☎ 280 756; ave Habib Bourguiba; starters TD3.5-8.5, mains TD7.5-16.3) Good location and reliably palatable food.

Belle Vue (Map p96; ☎ 280 825; starters TD3.5-8, mains TD5.5-13.5) Much the same as Lella Fatma.

De la Medina (Map p96; ☎ 281 728; starters TD2-4, mains TD3.5-12, 3-course set menu TD9) Seating on medina ramparts.

Le Barberousse (Map p96; ☎ 280 037; starters TD3.5-6, mains TD9-12) Also on the medina walls, the view is again the main attraction.

SELF-CATERING

Self-caterers can stock up on fruit and veg at the markets between ave de la République and rue des Jasmines. The small supermarket at the medina end of ave de la République also sells a good selection of local wines.

Drinking

The good discos are in Hammamet Sud, bumping and grinding on two parallel streets, so if you get hacked off with one you can head elsewhere. They peak on Friday and Saturday, charge around TD10, which includes one drink, and open till 4am or 5am.

Havana Club (Map p98; ave Moncef Bey) Aka Buena Vista, this has Cuban pictures, a fantastic atmosphere and good tapas. It plays Latino house and Arabic pop (with rock on Monday and jazz on Thursday), with some live acts. It's partly open-air.

Manhattan (Map p98; ☎ 226 226; ave Moncef Bey) Several people assured us this is Africa's best disco, and the seventh best in the world; we're not sure who judged this, but it has big flashing lights and plays pop house.

The Calypso Club (Map p98; ☎ 227 530; ave Mohamed Bey) This is the haunt of Tunisia's loaded youth and has pricey drinks and the most see-and-be-seen atmosphere.

La Balade (Map p96; Belle Vue; snacks TD2-4, mains TD4-14; ☾ to 3am) Near the centre, this is a lovely place for a drink, with tables covered by white canopies, overlooking the beach.

Shopping
Jewellery, leather, clothes, ceramics, and carpets are sold in and around the medina, with lots of choice, though you'll get better deals elsewhere.

Fella (Map p96; ☎ 280 426; Medina) Sophia Loren, Umm Kolthum, Princess Grace, and Greta Garbo have all stepped out in Fella at some point. The boutique is housed in a pretty white building, with immaculate handmade dresses, jewellery and bits and pieces.

L'Atelier (Map p96; ☎ 261 918; rue Ali Belhaouane) This small gallery has stunning original, metal-framed etchings by Baker Ben Fredj.

Music Shop (Map p96; ave Taieb Azzabi) At this hole-in-the-wall place you can record compilation CDs of Arabic and Western music.

Getting There & Away
BUS
There are buses to/from Nabeul (TD0.6, 30 minutes, half hourly) and Tunis (TD3, 1½ hours, hourly, five daily) and Sousse (TD4.8, 1½ hours, two daily), from near the train station.

CAR
Car rental agencies include:
Avis (☎ 280 164; rue de la Gare)
Europcar (Map p98; ☎ 280 146; rue des Hôtels)
Hertz (Map p98; ☎ 280 187; rue des Hôtels)

LOUAGE
Louages to Tunis (TD3.53, one hour) leave from Place Pasteur, about 800m northeast of the medina. Other louages, to Sousse (TD3.7, 1½ hours) and Kairouan (TD4.5, 1¾ hours), leave from Barrak es-Sahil, 2km northwest of town.

TRAIN
There are trains to/from Nabeul (20 minutes, 12 daily) and Bir Bou Regba (seven minutes), where services connect with trains heading north to Tunis, or south to Sousse, Sfax and beyond.

There's a direct service to/from Tunis (1½ hours, one daily). The station is about 1.5km from the centre, at the northern end of ave Habib Bourguiba.

Getting Around
The main taxi rank is by the medina, and it costs TD3.5 to Hammamet Sud. A 'toy-town' train calls at all the major hotels, and buses run from here to Yasmine Hammamet (TD0.5, half-hourly).

NABEUL   نابل
☎ 72 / pop 57,400

Nabeul, 18km north of Hammamet, is a laid-back town, one of Tunisia's major ceramics centres, with a fine white-sand beach and a frantic Friday market. But the town doesn't feel entirely devoured by tourism – it's the administrative centre of Cap Bon. Quieter than Hammamet, it has a unique line in kitsch roundabout architecture. An arts festival with lots of traditional music is held in late July and early August.

Orientation
Nabeul is spread out. The centre is about 1.5km inland – a legacy of the 16th century when pirates terrorised the coast, forcing towns to shift away from the sea. Now the pirates have gone, the town has slowly spread back towards the coast.

The two areas are linked by ave Habib Bourguiba, which runs through the middle from the northwest (the road from Tunis), and finishes by the beach. The town is centred around the intersections of ave Habib Bourguiba, ave Habib Thameur and rue Farhat Hached (Souq de l'Artisanat).

Information
EMERGENCY
Hospital (Map p103; ☎ 285 633; ave Habib Thameur)
Police (Map p103; ☎ 285 474; ave Habib Bourguiba)

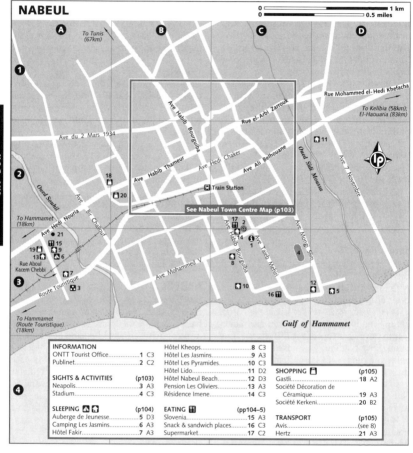

NABEUL

To Tunis (67km)

Rue Mohammed el- Hedi Khefacha

To Kelibia (58km); El-Haouaria (83km)

Ave Habib Bourguiba
Rue el-Arbi Zarrouk
Ave du 2 Mars 1934
Ave Hedi Chaker
Ave Habib Thameur
Ave Ali Belhouane
Oued Sidi Moussa
Ave 7 Novembre
Train Station

See Nabeul Town Centre Map (p103)

To Hammamet (18km)
Oued Souhili
Ave Hedi Nouria
Bir Challout
Rue Aboul Kacem Chebbi
Ave Mohammed V
Ave Mongi Slim
Ave Taieb Mehiri
Ave Habib Bourguiba
Route Touristique

To Hammamet (Route Touristique) (18km)

Gulf of Hammamet

0   1 km
0   0.5 miles

INFORMATION		
ONTT Tourist Office	1	C3
Publinet	2	C2
SIGHTS & ACTIVITIES		**(p103)**
Neapolis	3	A3
Stadium	4	C3
SLEEPING		**(p104)**
Auberge de Jeunesse	5	D3
Camping Les Jasmins	6	A3
Hôtel Fakir	7	A3
Hôtel Kheops	8	C3
Hôtel Les Jasmins	9	A3
Hôtel Les Pyramides	10	C3
Hôtel Lido	11	D2
Hôtel Nabeul Beach	12	D3
Pension Les Oliviers	13	A3
Résidence Imene	14	C3
EATING		**(pp104–5)**
Slovenia	15	A3
Snack & sandwich places	16	C3
Supermarket	17	C2
SHOPPING		**(p105)**
Gastli	18	A2
Société Décoration de Céramique	19	A3
Société Kerkeni	20	B2
TRANSPORT		**(p105)**
Avis	(see 8)	
Hertz	21	A3

INTERNET ACCESS

Publinet (Maps p102 & p103; ave Hedi Chakar; ave Taieb Mehiri; TD2 per hr).

MONEY

There are plenty of banks with ATMs; mostly along aves Habib Thameur and Habib Bourguiba.

POST

Main post office (Map p103; ave Habib Bourguiba)

TOURIST INFORMATION

ONTT (Map p102; ☎ 286 800; ave Taieb Mehiri; ☯ 8.30am-1pm & 3-5.45pm Mon-Thu & 8.30am-1.30pm Sat Sep-Jun, 7.30am-1.30pm & 5-9pm Mon-Sat & 9am-noon & 5-9pm Sun Jul-Aug) Has maps of Nabeul and Hammamet.

Syndicat d'Initiative (Map p103; ave Habib Bourguiba; ☯ 9am-1pm Mon-Sat year-round, 4-8pm Jul-Aug) Small, supplies similar stuff to the ONTT.

Sights & Activities
MARKET

Nabeul's bustling, buzzing Friday market is, for mysterious reasons, a major tourist event. Thousands of day-trippers turn up to tussle over jewellery, leather, glass, brass and ceramics. Unsurprisingly, prices are high; stallholders are used to people with much more money than time.

Rues Farhat Hached (Souq de l'Artisanat) and el-Arbi Zarrouk get packed. They're busiest between 9am and noon; by 2pm, life is slowly returning to normal.

BEACHES

Long and sandy, the beach is nearly all that beaches should be – it's cleanest in front of the resort hotels.

MUSEUM

Nabeul's small, well-laid-out **museum** (Map p103; ave Habib Bourguiba; admission TD1.1, plus camera TD1; ☻ 9am-1pm & 3-7pm Apr–mid-Sep, 9.30am-4.30pm mid-Sep–Mar) covers Cap Bon's history and displays artefacts such as Punic jewellery. The statues from Thinissut, an open-air sanctuary, are particularly impressive. They include a life-size terracotta lion-headed goddess, sphinxes and the nurturing goddess – an ancestor of the Madonna and child. There's also information on local Roman site Neapolis, with well-restored mosaics and displays on Tunisia's fish-salting factories, which produced the yummy-sounding *garum* sauce (made from fermented fish guts).

NEAPOLIS   نيابوليس

Ancient Neapolis, meaning 'New City' in Greek, is about 1.5km southwest of the centre. The Punic settlement, established in the 5th century BC, was invaded by Agathocles in 310 BC, and destroyed by Roman forces during the Third Punic War. It was later re-established as a Roman town, and a major producer of fishy *garum* sauce, which must have made for fragrant streets. Several full amphorae were unearthed in the 1960s. It's closed while excavations continue; Nabeul museum displays information about the site.

Courses

Espace Sarra Sport (Map p103; ave Habib Bourguiba) offers Tunisian dance lessons. One-hour beginner sessions take place on Tuesday, Thursday and Saturday morning.

Tours

Delta Travel (Map p103; ☎ 271 077; 113 ave Habib Bourguiba) runs excursions to Dougga and so on, and longer trips down south.

Sleeping

Nabeul has lots of character-filled family-run pensions and several mid-range hotels.

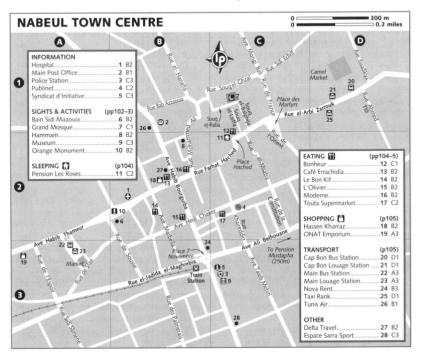

NABEUL TOWN CENTRE

INFORMATION	
Hospital	1 B2
Main Post Office	2 B1
Police Station	3 C3
Publinet	4 C2
Syndicat d'Initiative	5 C3
SIGHTS & ACTIVITIES	(pp102–3)
Bain Sidi Maaouia	6 B2
Grand Mosque	7 C1
Hammam	8 C3
Museum	9 C3
Orange Monument	10 B2
SLEEPING	(p104)
Pension Les Roses	11 C2

EATING	(pp104–5)
Bonheur	12 C1
Café Errachidia	13 B2
Le Bon Kif	14 B2
L'Olivier	15 B2
Moderne	16 B2
Touta Supermarket	17 C2
SHOPPING	(p105)
Hassen Kharraz	18 B2
ONAT Emporium	19 A3
TRANSPORT	(p105)
Cap Bon Bus Station	20 D1
Cap Bon Louage Station	21 D1
Main Bus Station	22 A3
Main Louage Station	23 A3
Nova Rent	24 B3
Taxi Rank	25 D1
Tunis Air	26 B1
OTHER	
Delta Travel	27 B2
Espace Sarra Sport	28 C3

0 — 300 m
0 — 0.2 miles

BUDGET

Camping Les Jasmins (Map p102; ☎ 285 343; ave Hedi Nouria; adult/child/tent/caravan/vehicle/hot shower TD2.8/2./2.5/2/2.3; ⚑) Les Jasmins is next to the hotel (see mid-range), has shady sites beneath old olive trees, and is a five-minute walk from an uncrowded stretch of beach.

Auberge de Jeunesse (Map p102; ☎ 285 547; ave Mongi Slim; dm TD5, camping person/tent/caravan TD1/5/5) On the beach, this has a great location, and separate spic-and-span single-sex dorms in barrel-ceilinged *ghorfas* (rooms), each with their own bathroom. The hostel also has a camping area with a washing block.

Pension Les Roses (Map p103; ☎ 285 570; Place Hached; s/d with shared bathroom TD8/16, plus hot showers TD1) In souq central, Les Roses feels like a step back in time – with tall blue-shuttered windows, basic, clean rooms and enigmatic landlady.

Pension Mustapha (☎ 222 262; rue Habib el-Karma & ave Ali Belhouane; s/d with private bathroom TD11.5/20 Nov–mid-Mar, TD12.5/22 mid-Mar–Oct) Although by a busy junction, this is friendly and clean; prices include breakfast and rooms have fans and some balconies.

MID-RANGE

Hôtel Les Jasmins (Map p102; ☎ 285 343; off ave Hedi Nouria; hotel.jasmines@gnet.tn; s/d Nov–Mar TD27/42, Apr–Oct TD34/52, Jul–mid-Sep TD50/78; ⚑) This has a relaxed atmosphere and attractive architecture. Rooms have balconies, and you can eat meals on tables set amid trees, or there's Slovenia (see Eating, this page) next door.

Pension Les Oliviers (Map p102; ☎ 286 865; rue Aboul Kacem Chebbi; s/d with private bathroom Nov–mid-Mar TD20/25, mid-Mar–Oct TD25/32, Jul–mid-Sep TD37/45) This is a gem with simple rooms with balcony surrounded by olive and citrus groves, near the beach. The charming owners, ex-high-school teachers, both speak excellent English.

Hôtel Fakir (Map p102; ☎ 285 477; s/d Nov–Aug TD20/30, Nov–Mar TD10/15, Apr–Oct TD15/25) Nearby, this has large bright white airy rooms with small wooden furniture, some with outlooks over pine trees and a glimpse of the sea.

Hôtel Les Pyramides (Map p102; ☎ 285 775; ave Habib Bourguiba; s/d Nov–Mar TD18/21, Apr–Oct TD27/34, Jul TD44/56, Aug TD53/66; ⚑) This package place has nothing-special rooms with small balconies, but facilities include tennis courts and disco.

Hôtel Lido (Map p102; ☎ 362 988, ave 7 Novembre; s/d/2-/4-person bungalow Nov–Mar TD28/42/45/60,

Apr–Jun TD52/74/72/90, Sep & Oct TD73/106/100/150; ⚑) A good three-star hotel with some bungalows, lush grounds and lots of sports facilities. Breakfast not included.

Hôtel Nabeul Beach (Map p102; ☎ 286 111; ave Taieb Mehiri; full board s/d Nov–mid-Mar TD64/108, mid-Mar–Oct TD100/160, Jul–mid-Sep TD140/240; ⚑) Plain but pleasant rooms, overlooking a nice pool and by the beach. Massive discounts may be available.

Hôtel Kheops (Map p102; ☎ 285 444; ave Habib Bourguiba; s/d Nov–Mar TD40/48, Apr–Oct TD74/98, Aug TD125/140; ⚑) One of Nabeul's most up-market places, with a '70s reception, pleasingly plain rooms with good views and a mammoth pool.

Residence Imene (Map p102; ☎ 222 310; ave 7 Novembre; s/d Apr-Sep TD32/50, Oct–Mar TD24/48; ⚑) A bit nondescript, but a comfortable place with a convenient location midway between the beach and the centre.

Eating

Try the cluster of snack bars serving sandwiches and *lablabi* (thick soup) near the seafront on ave Taieb Mehiri, and lots of good restaurants around town; all open lunch and dinner daily.

Slovenia (Map p102; ☎ 285 343; Hôtel Les Jasmins, starters TD3.5-8, mains TD10.8-16) Perhaps Nabeul's finest restaurant, run by one of Tunisia's best chefs, Rafik Tlatli (see the boxed text, p52). The menu is innovative with Tunisian, Indonesian, Andalusian and Slovenian influences, and dishes such as an oil-less *briq* (pastry) or delicious fish cooked in an earthenware pot. Seating is in a lowlit leafy garden or cosy interior.

Bonheur (Map p103; rue Farhat Hached; starters TD1-3, mains TD3-6) The best of the cheapies, this has the requisite tiled walls and TV, very fast service and simple dishes such as couscous and *brochettes* (kebabs) – it also serves beer.

Moderne (Map p103; rue Farhat Hached; starters TD1-2, mains TD3-7) This is a cheap local restaurant that also serves alcohol.

L'Olivier (Map p103; ☎ 286 613; ave Hedi Chaker; starters TD4-12, mains TD4.5-18) Cosy, on two levels, and has a good reputation.

Le Bon Kif (Map p103; ☎ 222 783; 25; ave Marbella; starters TD3.5-10, mains 4.5-18) A pretty good choice, with the regular menu of couscous, seafood and meat dishes. It has a pleasant tiled courtyard at the back, with a trickling water feature.

Ottoman fort (p120), Ghar el-Melh

Narrow street, Bizerte (p115)

Fishermen near Les Aguilles (The Needles; p125), Tabarka

JANE SWE

Old port (p117), Bizerte

CHRISTOPHER WOOD

House of the Hunt (p132), Bulla Regia

Locally made pottery (p105), Nabeul

JOHN BRE

POT TILL YOU DROP

Traditionally known for their fine Punic and Roman-influenced pots and vases, and for the ornate decoration introduced by 17th-century Andalusian immigrants, Nabeul potters turn out astounding (some in the worst sense) ceramics. There are some beautiful examples of traditional work, particularly bowls and tiling pictures. If you want to buy, but are unsure of prices, go first to the **ONAT emporium** (Map p103; ave Habib Thameur) to get an idea – there are artisan's workshops at the back too.

You'll find massive choice at the Friday market, or try the following shops, where you can see the artists and potters at work.

■ **Société Décoration de Céramique** (Map p102; ave du Grand Maghreb) A home-based workshop, this has a good range and you can watch the all-women team paint the pots.

■ **Société Kerkeni** (Map p102; 121 ave Habib Thameur) Some gloriously exuberant designs and a huge range to choose from.

■ **Gastli** (Map p102; ave Habib Thameur) Across the road from Société Kerkeni, this also has a good array.

■ **Hassen Kharraz** (Map p103; ave Habib Thameur) The most upmarket, this is where to go if you've got a gilt craving.

Café Errachidia (Map p103; ave Habib Thameur) The best place for people-watching on the porch with a *sheesha* (water pipe) and a mint tea, this serves up delicious biscuits too.

Self-caterers should head for the **Touta supermarket** (Map p103; ave Hedi Chaker) or the **supermarket** (Map p102; ave Habib Bourguiba).

Getting There & Away

AIR
Tunis Air (Map p103; ☎ 286 092; 178 ave Habib Bourguiba) faces the post office. The nearest airport is Tunis-Carthage.

BUS
The bus station is on ave Habib Thameur. Buses go to Hammamet (TD0.6, 30 minutes, half-hourly 5.30am to 9pm, to 11pm July and August), Tunis (TD3.1/5.7 normal/comfort, 1½ hours, half-hourly 6am to 8pm). Other services include Zaghouan (TD3.5, 1½ hours, seven to nine daily), Sousse (TD5, two hours, three daily Monday to Saturday) and Kairouan (TD5, 2¼ hours, three daily).

Buses for the rest of Cap Bon leave from rue el-Arbi Zarrouk. There are buses to/from Kélibia (TD3, 1¼ hours, 13 daily) and El-Haouaria (TD3.5, 1¾ hours, hourly) – you may have to change at Kélibia. For information, head to the main bus station.

CAR
There are lots of rental agencies, including: **Avis** (Map p102; ☎ 286 555; Hôtel Kheops)

Hertz (Map p102; ☎ 285 327; ave Habib Thameur)
Nova Rent (Map p103; ☎ 222 072; 54 ave Habib Bourguiba)

LOUAGE
There are two louage stations. Services to other parts of Cap Bon including Kélibia (TD2.75, one hour), El-Haouaria (TD5) and Korba (TD0.85) leave from next to the bus station on rue el-Arbi Zarrouk. Other ervices leave from behind the main bus station on ave Habib Thameur; destinations include Tunis (TD3.4), Kairouan (TD5.25), Sousse (TD4.7) and Zaghouan (TD3.25).

TAXI
If you take a shared taxi to Hammamet, it should only cost TD1 to TD2 – one all to yourself will set you back around TD8.

TRAIN
The station is central, on ave Habib Bourguiba. There are trains to/from Hammamet (TD0.55, 20 minutes, nine to 12 daily), Tunis (TD3.4/4.5 2nd/1st, 1½ hours, six daily), Sousse (TD4.8/6.35, six to eight daily) and Sfax (TD8.6/11.45, one to two daily).

Getting Around
Nabeul is reasonably spread out, and in summer it's an effort to walk from the centre to the beach. A taxi costs about TD1 (TD0.5 shared); you can take a *calèche* (horse-drawn carriage), but bargain hard and agree on a price before setting off.

AROUND NABEUL
Dar Chaabane   دار شعبان

This small village, 4km northeast of Nabeul on the road to Kélibia, is Tunisia's stonework capital. Most people here are masons, and the main street is lined with workshops, carving out everything from ashtrays to replicas of famous statues. If you need a couple of monumental lions for the entrance to your country estate, this is the place to go. Workshops can arrange international delivery.

Any bus heading north can drop you here, or you can take a local bus from the beach (TD0.25, hourly 9.30am to 6.30pm July and August). A taxi costs about TD2.5 from Nabeul.

Ben Khiar

This village, about 2km east of Nabeul, is a weaving centre and has a cooperative that welcomes visitors and sells its goods – bags, blankets, carpets and coats – at low fixed prices. It's a fascinating place, the all-male workers skilfully operating the ferociously complex looms and spinning wool. Some have worked here for more than 30 years.

You can walk here; there are buses (TD0.25; hourly 10am to 6pm, to 8pm Sunday July and August) from the beach, or a taxi costs about TD2.5.

Korba Lagoon   قربة

A long, narrow lagoon that follows the coast for 15km, this is one of the finest birdwatching areas in Tunisia – the wetlands attract a spectacular wealth of birdlife. In winter, the lagoon becomes dappled in pink as flamingos amass; the juveniles can be seen all year.

It begins at the little town of Korba – whose main business is producing tomatoes – 19km northeast of Nabeul, and gets more tranquil and scenic the further north you head.

The main road to Menzel Temine and Kélibia runs parallel to the lagoon, so any bus or louage travelling north can drop you where you choose. Buses to Korba leave about hourly (TD1, 15 minutes).

KÉLIBIA   قليبية

☎ 72 / pop 36,000

Kélibia, 58km north of Nabeul, sits near an exhilarating, endless silvery powder beach edged by translucent sea, overseen by a towering fort. Developers haven't yet got far: the town continues to survive on fishing and servicing the surrounding farmland. The centre, a mix of functional shops and men-packed cafés, is 2km inland, while the attractions are all on the coast to the east, where you'll find a small beach, the picturesque port and a few low-key resort hotels. The town's also famous for Muscat Sec de Kélibia, a fragrant dry white wine.

At the end of July Kélibia hosts an international film shorts festival, which is well worth a look.

History

Kélibia began life as a Berber settlement, but little is known about the town until the arrival of the Carthaginians in the 5th century BC. They called it Aspis, meaning 'shield', either reflecting its defensive status or the shape of the land. Whatever the reason, the fort they built was a key part of Carthage's defence. It proved ineffective against both Agathocles and Regulus, but the town made it through to be reborn as Roman Clypea, traces of which are scattered around town in excavated fragments, including mosaics. It remained one of Tunisia's major cities until the 11th century, but was later damaged by Sicilian pirate attacks, and even moved inland to escape raids.

Orientation & Information

Most travellers will arrive at the bus and louage station on ave Ali Belhouane. The centre is just east of here around the junction of rue Ibn Khaldoun and ave Habib Bourguiba. To get there, head north along ave Ali Belhouane (towards El-Haouaria) from the bus and louage station, and then turn right into rue Ibn Khaldoun. There is no tourist office. There are a couple of banks and a supermarket on rue Ibn Khaldoun, and the post office is on ave Habib Bourguiba. The fort and port are 2km east of here along ave des Martyrs.

There's a **publinet** (59 rue des Martyrs), charging TD2 per hour.

Sights & Activities
BEACHES

Mansourah Beach, 2km to the north, is glorious. It's a bit exposed but otherwise brilliant, with only a few buildings.

The beach at Kélibia itself is very small and not that flash.

FORT

The fabulous polygonal **fort** (admission TD1.1; ☺ 9am-5pm mid-Sep–Mar, 8am-7pm Apr–mid-Sep) dominates the harbour, with views so broad that the horizon appears to curve like the rim of a vase. Built by the Carthagians, the fort was dismantled in the 3rd century BC, during the first Punic War, but reconstructed after the war ended. In the 2nd century, the Romans razed it, and political unity in the Mediterranean meant there was no need for fortifications here. In AD 580, the Byzantines set up their usual small fort within the old walls, still visible at the centre, and it was their last refuge when driven out of Carthage in AD 698. It became important following the Arabic conquest, and today's huge fortress was built to defend against the Normans. From the 13th to 16th centuries it became a Sufi religious centre, seeing action again in the 16th century during battles between the Turks and Spanish and when bombarded by the French in the 17th century. The most recent additions are gun emplacements, built by German forces during WWII.

A road leads up to the fort from opposite the Maison des Jeunes on the Mansourah road.

Sleeping

Kélibia doesn't have many hotels; most are at the beach by the harbour.

Maison des Jeunes (☎ 296 105; dm TD5) The usual institutional blue-and-white building supplies the usual basic place to lay your head. It's often full in summer so call ahead.

Hôtel Florida (☎ 296 248; Kélibia Plage; s/d with private bathroom Apr-Oct TD25/35, Nov-Mar TD19/33) Built in 1946, this is a slightly shabby favourite; it has a nice shaded terrace by the water's edge that's particularly beloved by Kélibia's locals.

Hôtel Palmarina (☎ 274 062; Kélibia Plage; s/d Oct-Mar TD32/56, Apr–mid-Jul TD44/68, mid-Jul–Aug TD46/72; ✷ ☎) This three-star place has a pool and pleasant rooms with shady, sea-facing balconies, but despite being fairly new, is fraying at the edges and lacks much care. The air-con barely functions.

Pension Anis (☎ 295 777; ave Erriadh; s/d with shared bathroom TD20/30, with private bathroom TD30-35/45; ✷) Halfway between the beach and the town, this friendly place has pristine rooms, some of which are huge. There's an excellent restaurant (see under Eating, this page).

Hôtel Mamounia (☎ 296 088; s/d with private bathroom Nov–mid-Mar TD32/44, Jul TD50/70, Aug TD63/86; ☎) An older package resort, features rooms with balconies, a fine edge-of-the-sea setting and a pool, but is a bit overpriced.

Club Kélibia (☎ 277 777; s/d full board Apr-Jun & Sep TD95-104/150-168, Oct TD86/132, Jul-Aug TD120/200; ☺ Apr-Sep only; ✷ ☎) Out at Mansourah, this is as yet the only hotel – a mustard-coloured carbuncle, but with big, nicely decorated cream and blue rooms, spa and pools. No phone bookings.

Eating

A small but good array of restaurants; all open for lunch and dinner daily.

De la Jeunesse (☎ 277 777; starters TD3-7, mains TD5-16) On the main road, this has a terrace with a barbecue, and air-conditioned seating downstairs. It's a longstanding reasonable favourite.

Pension Anis (☎ 295 777; starters TD2.85-6.85, mains TD7.35-11.2) Kélibia's best restaurant with an unusually wide range of dishes. The intimate interior is divided by wooden lattices, and there is a good wine list.

Le Goéland (☎ 273 074; Port de Kélibia; starters TD2.5-12, mains TD7.5-14) At the port, with a lovely seaside location and reliable food – the traditional Tunisian options, and pizzas. Next door is **Café Sidi el-Bahri** (☎ 296 675; starters TD0.8-4.2, mains TD2.2-10) another great setting and popular at night, though the food is run of the mill. Neither serves alcohol.

El-Mansourah (☎ 295 169; El-Mansourah Plage; starters TD2.5-8.5, mains TD7-17, 3-course set menu TD15-20) A magnificent setting on a small headland at the south of Mansourah Beach; some tables are set into rocks in the sea. The food is reasonably good with lots of fresh fish.

Les Arcades (Hôtel Palmarina; starters TD3-8.5, mains TD5-16) A good reliable restaurant with tasty salads and hearty fish and meat dishes. It's airy and quiet, decorated by some kitsch stained glass.

Café el-Borj A little domed place just below the fort: colourful rugs are spread over the steep steps that lead down into trees. The views over the rocky bays and olive groves make this a great place for a cuppa and a *sheesha*.

Getting There & Away

Buses and louages leave from ave Ali Belhouane. There are buses to/from Tunis

(TD4.31, 2¼ hours, hourly), to/from Nabeul (TD2.38, 1¼ hours, hourly), and El-
Haouaria (TD1, 40 minutes, hourly). There
are also regular louages to these destinations. There's a bus to Kairouan at (TD7.2,
3½ hours), Sousse (TD6.7, three hours) and
Monastir (TD7.14, 3½ hours).

Getting Around
The bus station is 2.5km from the harbour
and beach. A taxi to the bus station costs
about TD1.5 (shared TD0.5). Buses go to/
from El-M beach hourly from 10.30am to
6.30pm (TD0.3).

KERKOUANE   كركوان
The remote Punic settlement of **Kerkouane**
(admission TD2.1, plus camera TD1; ☉ 9am-4pm Tue-Sun
mid-Sep–Mar, 9am-6pm Tue-Sun Apr–mid-Sep) is set on
a dazzling curve of turquoise coast 12km
north of Kélibia, and is one of Tunisia's
most remarkable ancient sites. Abandoned
in its prime in the middle of the 3rd century
BC and never reoccupied, it offers a unique
insight into all things Punic.

The site is clearly signposted off the road
between Kélibia and El-Haouaria. Buses and
louages can drop you at the turn-off, leaving
a pleasant walk of 1.5km to the site.

History
Little is known of the town's history, not
even its name. Kerkouane was coined by
French archaeologists, who stumbled on
the site in 1952.

Finds suggest it was an established Berber
town when the Phoenicians arrived in the
8th century BC, but Berber and Phoenician
cultures blended and it evolved into a Punic
town. The oldest remains date to the early
6th century BC, but the ruins today are
mainly 4th- to 3rd-century BC.

Although ancient writers waxed about
the fertility of the peninsula, no evidence
of agricultural activity has been found here.
Kerkouane, it seems, was home to an urban
elite of merchants and craftsmen. Excavations have uncovered pottery workshops
and kilns, as well as evidence of jewellery
and glass making, and stone carving. The
town also produced a prized dye known as
Tyrian purple (after the Phoenician capital, Tyre). It was extracted from murex, a
species of shellfish once plentiful along
the coast.

The large necropolis has yielded many
decorative and precious objects, indicating
the town's wealth and tastes, though many
tombs were ransacked and damaged by
treasure hunters in the early 20th century.

An earlier plunderer was Agathocles in
310 BC, but the town recovered – only to
be burnt by Roman general Regulus in 256
BC during the First Punic War. This time
the site was abandoned and overgrown by
dwarf palms and drowned by sands until
uncovered during excavations from 1957
to 1961. The most intact vestiges of Punic
civilisation in existence are here, and Kerkouane was added to the World Heritage
List in 1982.

Sights
Kerkouane was a harmoniously laid-out
town, protected by double fortifications
around 15m wide. The outer wall was built
after Agathocles' attack.

Cap Bon was much exalted in ancient literature, and although exaggeration played
its part, there is no doubt it was a region
of plenty: historian Diodorus wrote of Agathocles' invasion: 'all the lands that he had
to cross were set with gardens and orchards
watered by numerous springs. There were
well-constructed country houses, built with
lime...' To protect this good life, forts and
towers were added: such as the small square
coastal **fort** on the northern side and the fortifications around the south gate. None of
which did any good when Regulus went on
the rampage.

The main entrance was through the distinctive **west gate**, also known as the Port
du Couchant (Sunset Gate), built into an
overlap between the walls. It is the houses
that are the main attraction, particularly
those of the wealthy northeastern quarter,
with some wonderful examples of opus
signinum flooring – scatter-pattern mosaic. Check out 3 rue de l'Apotropaïon,
better known as the **House of Tanit**, which
features a beautiful, simple white Tanit
sign set into the floor, suggesting that the
sign served as a kind of talisman or protec-
tive symbol.

The town's finest address was 35 rue de
l'Apotropaïon, with a sublime seafront setting. It has a peristyle (colonnaded) courtyard and an impressive bath, with a seat and
armrests, decorated with white mosaic.

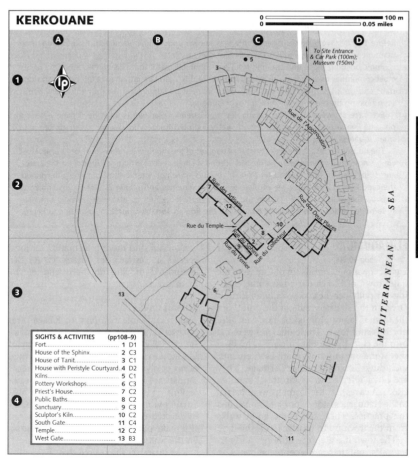

KERKOUANE

0 — 100 m
0 — 0.05 miles

To Site Entrance
& Car Park (100m);
Museum (150m)

Rue de l'Appropriation

Rue des Artisans

Rue du Temple

Rue des Deux Places

Rue du Sphinx

Rue du Verrier

Rue du Collecteur

SEA

MEDITERRANEAN

CAP BON

SIGHTS & ACTIVITIES	(pp108–9)	
Fort	1	D1
House of the Sphinx	2	C3
House of Tanit	3	C1
House with Peristyle Courtyard	4	D2
Kilns	5	C1
Pottery Workshops	6	C3
Priest's House	7	C2
Public Baths	8	C2
Sanctuary	9	C3
Sculptor's Kiln	10	C2
South Gate	11	C4
Temple	12	C2
West Gate	13	B3

The town also had **public baths**, on rue des Artisans. These are small scale and functional – contrasting with the Roman attitude to architecture – and probably used by the workers to clean up. It's possible that they were near the temple so that people could cleanse themselves pre-worship.

The remains of the principal **temple** run west from rue du Temple. Along one side **pottery workshops** used to produce votive objects have been discovered. The temple was the scene of one of the site's strangest finds: a small cache of Roman lamps and bowls that had been hidden away, dating from the 3rd century AD – 500 years after the town was abandoned. West of the temple, at 2 rue du Sphinx, is the **Priest's House**. In its centre, pro-tected within a small room, is a circular bread oven, like the *tabounas* still used here.

Rue du Sphinx is named after a sphinx on a solid gold ring found at No 1, which has a fine bathroom with a double bath.

MUSEUM

The museum has some startling finds from the site necropolis, particularly the Woman of Kerkouane, a wooden sarcophagus cover carved from cypress, thought to represent the goddess Astarte. There are also some beautiful pieces of gold jewellery, everyday objects such as razors, kohl pots and tweez-ers, and delicate funerary statues. Imported Greek pottery demonstrates the sophistica-tion of the residents' taste.

PUNIC ARCHITECTURE

Before the discovery of Kerkouane, little was known about Punic architecture: knowledge had been gleaned from sites rebuilt by successive civilisations.

Punic building techniques ranged from *pisé* (rammed earth) to precision masonry. One of the most common is opus Africanum, which features rubble walls strengthened at intervals with stone slabs and uprights. This Punic technique was adapted by Roman and Byzantine builders, and is seen holding up the walls of the Capitol of Dougga.

Evidence shows that Kerkouane's layout was carefully planned: it must have been a serene place to live, a pleasant backwater, with well-appointed houses along wide streets dotted with small squares.

The houses represent the oldest known examples of the modern Tunisian courtyard home. Most were single storey, with rooms arranged around a small central atrium, a corridor to the street, and steps leading to a rooftop terrace. The houses were not ostentatious, but finely decorated, their red floors delicately inset with white-stone fragments, and ornate plaster friezes and carvings on the walls and ceilings. The site is particularly famed for its elaborate, private armchair-style baths, which form a striking contrast to the Roman sociable approach to getting lathered.

EL-HAOUARIA   الهوّارية
☎ 72 / pop 10,300

Under the mountainous tip of Cap Bon, the quiet town of El-Haouaria has some enticing unspoilt beaches, especially at Ras el-Drek on the southern side of the point. But the town is famous for its coastal caves, 3km northwest of town. These quarries were cut into the cliffs by the Phoenicians, who used the stone in building many settlements, including Kerkouane and Carthage. They are often referred to as Grottes Romaines (Roman caves), as the Romans were partial to El-Haouaria's stone too, and continued the practise. There are some good walks from the town up to nearby Jebel Abiod.

The town has a choice of hotels and restaurants, and there are a couple of banks on the main street.

Sights
JEBEL ABIOD
It's worth the effort to climb this peak (390m), north of town; there are magnificent, blustery views out along the coast, and it's a good bird-watching spot. It represents the northeastern tip of the Tunisian Dorsale, a prime migration route for thousands of raptors travelling between Africa and Europe. In May and June, the skies can be thick with birds waiting for the thermals that will carry them across the Straits of Sicily.

Access to the mountain is by a road that leads north of rue Ali Belhouane in the town centre. The road finishes at a telecommunications tower at the summit.

You can find more information on local species at **Les Amis des Oiseaux** (☎ 269 200), signposted off the northern end of the main street.

ROMAN CAVES
This remarkable complex of **Roman caves** (admission TD1.1; 🕑 9am-5pm mid-Sep–Mar, 8am-7pm Apr–mid-Sep) is on the coast to the west of El-Haouaria. The cliffs here are formed of an easily worked, highly prized yellow sandstone, and the Carthaginians began exploiting this in the 6th century BC. Small pyramid-shaped shafts remain, lit by hacked-out oblong skylights; you can still make out the marks of quarrying tools on the walls.

The quarriers discovered that the quality of the stone was much better at the base of the cliff than on the surface, and opted to tunnel into the cliffs rather than to cut down. The end result after almost 1000 years of quarrying were caves stretching almost 1km along the coast. It was a highly sophisticated operation. The cut stone was dragged out through the caves and loaded onto ships for transportation.

The caves are signposted 3km west of town. It takes about 45 minutes to walk here, but there's plenty of passing traffic for hitchers.

Festivals & Events
El-Haouaria has a tradition of falconry, and it stages an annual **Festival d'Epervier** in May or June, with demonstrations of the birds

near the caves, and live music and market stalls in the town.

Sleeping

Pension Dar Toubib (☎ 297 163; s/d with private bathroom Apr-Aug TD20/32, Sep-Mar TD8/16) With a tiled entrance on a quiet street, this has small, basic rooms. To get here, follow the 'Hotel' signs from the main square out towards the mountain. It's a 10-minute walk.

Hôtel L'Epervier (☎ 297 017; 3 ave Habib Bourguiba; s/d Nov-Mar TD20.4/30.8, Apr-Oct TD30.8/44) In the middle of town, this friendly two star has a variety of comfortable, old-fashioned rooms with small terraces.

Pension Les Grottes (☎ 269 072; www.centregrotte .com.tn; Route les Grottes; s/d Sep-May TD35/50, Jun-Aug TD45/70) Although this has a good hilltop position and small pool, the bungalow architecture is not that attractive and makes little of the views.

Eating

There are several basic *gargottes* (cheap eateries) opposite the Hôtel L'Epervier. **Hôtel L'Epervier** (3 ave Habib Bourguiba; starters TD2-8, mains TD8-15, set menu TD8) has tree-shaded courtyard seating, and **Pension Les Grottes** (Route les Grottes; starters TD3.5-10, mains TD6-13) has a reasonable restaurant. Both serve alcohol.

La Daurade (☎ 269 080; starters TD2.5-6, mains TD5-12) Out by the caves, this friendly place has an incredible position overlooking the sea, and excellent seafood. There are lovely open terraces, and the seating reaches down to the water's edge. No alcohol is served.

Getting There & Away

El-Haouaria is well served by public transport. There are buses travelling along the north coast to Tunis (TD4.26, two hours, five daily), via Soliman, and to Kélibia (TD0.94, 40 minutes, eight daily). There are regular louages to Kélibia (TD1.2), and less frequent ones to Tunis (TD4).

SOLIMAN

☎ 72

Soliman, 10km southwest of Korbous, is quick to access from Tunis, and the white-sand beach is framed by shadowy mountains, but it has a slightly desultory feel.

Hôtel Soliman (☎ 200 105; www.solymar.com; s/d with private bathroom Apr-Oct TD29/38, Jul-Aug TD34/48, Nov-Mar TD26/32; 🏊) Right on the beach, this

package-heavy three star has nice little rooms opening onto a sea-facing terrace.

Buses and louages run to/from Soliman (TD 2.5, one hour) from Tunis. You can then catch a shared taxi to the beach (TD0.5).

KORBOUS قربص

☎ 72

Korbous is an old-fashioned, faded but enormously popular beauty spot. It's all arches and stripes, centred around a little clock, squeezed into a narrow ravine and surrounded by steep cliffs; it's also famous for its hot springs. The approach to Korbous from Soliman is spectacular, especially the final 6km when the road hugs the coastal cliff-face. At Ain Atrous, about 1.5km north of Korbous, a hot spring empties itself directly into the sea, providing a small patch of heated ocean that's always jostling with people. Next to the spring there are a few small restaurants specialising in grilled fish priced from around TD4.

There are only two hotels in Korbous. At **Residence de Thermes** (☎ 284 664; ave 7 Novembre; s/d with private bathroom Apr-Sep TD35/50, Oct-Apr TD30/ 40; 🏊) some of the simple white-walled rooms are better than others and there's a pleasant warm-yellow restaurant (three-course set menu TD8) across the street. A better option is **Hôtel Les Sources** (☎ 284 540; ave 7 Novembre; s/d Nov-Oct TD41/62, Jul–mid-Sep TD49/76; 🏊), a three star with unintentionally funky '70s textiles in the rooms, good views and a pool. The bar is popular and there's a restaurant (three-course set menu TD9). On the same street is **Restaurant Dhib** (☎ 284 523; ave 7 Novembre; starters TD1-3, mains TD2.5-6), with the usual menu and outdoor sidewalk seating.

In the centre is **Les Stations Thermales et Touristiques** (☎ 284 645; 🕑 8am-8pm), offering some daunting-sounding water treatments and more-relaxing massages.

Getting There & Away

It's much easier to get to Korbous from Tunis than from the resorts on the southern side of Cap Bon. There are frequent buses to Korbous (TD2, one hour) from the southern bus station in Tunis, as well as regular louages (TD2.5) from Tunis, or from Soliman (TD1.5).

Services between Korbous and Nabeul operate via Soliman.

Northern Tunisia

CONTENTS

Northern Tunisia is a mesmerising surprise. It's a rolling, golden, magnificently lush region, edged by the glinting blue Mediterranean and long serene white-sand stretches. The beaches at Sidi Ali el-Mekki, Raf Raf and Cap Serrat are among the most beautiful in the country, and, best of all, are hidden away and unpopulated (apart from at weekends).

But the north also harbours some charismatic towns. The region bordering Algeria has a particular character born both out of this proximity and the hilly landscape that divides up the territory. Backed by diving, forested hills, Tabarka is a charming, slow-moving seaside spot, with tree-shaded cafés, good beaches and lively summer music festivals. Further up into the Kroumirie Mountains, thick with tall pines, lies Ain Draham – a dramatically situated red-roofed village that's high enough to get snow in winter. Narrow winding roads lead from settlement to settlement in this seemingly epic and remote area, long popular for hunting. The northern hills allow vast views and hide the incredible Roman site of Bulla Regia, with uncannily preserved subterranean villas, and the evocative, huge quarries of Chemtou.

Back on the coast, Bizerte has a picturesque ancient port lined by a golden kasbah, long promenade and handsome beaches, and it shuffles at a pace that's stuck midway through the last century. Nearby is Lake Ichkeul, a World Heritage–listed national park.

Although the area is no secret to Tunisians, who head to the hills to escape the summer heat, or come here for weekends away from the city, the region hasn't been much discovered by foreign tourists.

NORTHERN TUNISIA

HIGHLIGHTS

- ■ Relaxing on the **beaches** at Sidi Ali el-Mekki (p120) and Cap Serrat (p123)

- ■ Mixing with the fishermen at the enchanting **old port** (p117) in Bizerte

- ■ Enjoying the cafés, beaches and summer live music in **Tabarka** (p123)

- ■ Exploring the elaborate underground Roman villas of **Bulla Regia** (p131)

- ■ Walking through rolling peaks coated in cork forest around **Ain Draham** (p128)

History

Northern Tunisia has been much fought over – not only because of its geographical advantages, but also as one of the country's richest agricultural regions. It was first settled in 6000–2500 BC by European migrants; later the Phoenicians gained their first footholds, setting up at Utica in 1100 BC. During the Second Punic War, the Roman General Scipio landed at Utica in 204 BC. The Romans gained power a century later, but they were content to let the Numidians rule. One of their main bases was at Beja (Vega). The Romans rebuilt the previous Punic settlements, and made the most of the region's capacity for wheatgrowing – hence the glory of such settlements as Bulla Regia. The Vandals overran the area but left little mark, and with the coming of the Arabs and Islam the seat of power moved southwards to Kairouan. The Spanish and the Ottoman Turks played pass-the-parcel with the region's strategic points in the 16th century, and piracy was rife.

In the 19th century, the French focussed on the northern riches – Bizerte was such a successful port that they refused to leave until seven years after independence.

During WWII the north was once again a battleground, as testified by the many war cemeteries in the area.

Climate

Summers are very hot and dry, with temperatures peaking in July and August. Up in the Kroumirie Mountains it's a few degrees cooler in summer, and cold in winter, with snow in the highest spots.

National Parks

Near Bizerte is the limpid Lake Ichkeul, with a unique ecosystem of salt and fresh water that ensures a mass of birdlife, and also home to an unlikely herd of water buffalo. Near the border with Algeria is the Feija National Park, forested and hilly, with wild gazelles.

Getting There & Away

There are airports at Tunis-Carthage and Tabarka. Buses and louages (shared taxis) for the north leave from Tunis' northern

NORTHERN TUNISIA

bus station (see p81). There are also trains to Bizerte.

Getting Around

The transport system is not that well integrated, and in smaller places buses and louages tend to stop around 7pm. However, with patience and a bit of time, you can reach all but the most remote places by public transport.

BIZERTE بنزرت

☎ 72 / pop 113,400

Bizerte is a bewitching port city, sitting on a canal that links silvery saltwater Lake Bizerte and the glimmering Mediterranean. The old port, lined with cafés, pastel harbour buildings, bobbing fishing boats and the golden fortifications of the kasbah, feels like 1950s France or Italy, the only glitch being a couple of saggy apartment blocks. An unassuming tourist strip stretches out along the corniche (coast road), and sandy beaches flank the town. From here you can also visit Raf Raf and Sidi Ali el-Mekki, and the reflective expanses of Lake Ichkeul.

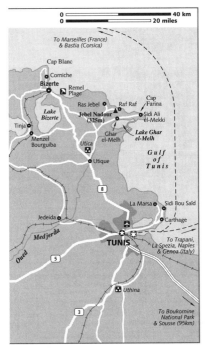

History

Bizerte's strategic location has landed it an eventful history.

The Phoenicians founded the port in the 8th century BC as Hippo Zarytus, and later built the first canal connecting Lake Bizerte to the sea – opening up one of the finest harbours in the western Mediterranean. The Romans in 146 BC destroyed the city to avenge its part in the Punic Wars. Rebuilt 100 years later as Roman Hippo Diarrhytus, it was later occupied by the Vandals and the Byzantines.

In AD 678, the Arabs captured the town and renamed it Bizerte. The Spanish and the Turks were next to tussle over it: the Spanish occupied the town from 1535 to 1570, then the Ottomans took over and it became the principal port for the Muslim corsairs (pirates) preying on Christian shipping in the Mediterranean.

Bizerte declined until the opening of the Suez Canal in 1869 gave the port renewed significance. The French transformed the town, and developed a major naval base at nearby Menzel Bourguiba, on the southwestern edge of Lake Bizerte. They dug a new canal, completed in 1895, to handle modern shipping and filled in the old canal, dug by the Carthaginians, to build their ville nouvelle (new town).

Such was the French attachment to Bizerte that they refused to leave after independence in 1956. The Tunisians did not get them out till 15 October 1963, by which stage more than 1000 Tunisian lives had been lost (see p29).

Today Bizerte continues to be dominated by its busy port rather than by tourism.

Orientation

The modern centre is the French ville nouvelle, north of the shipping canal. The town planners had a crazy time with the grid system here – inserting a few disorienting diagonal streets. Some street signs are in Arabic only, which adds to the challenge of getting around.

The old Arab quarter is north of the ville nouvelle and borders the old port. Blvd Hassen en-Nouri runs north from the ville nouvelle to the beaches of the corniche.

The shipping canal is spanned by a modern bridge; across it is the main road south to Tunis.

BIZERTE

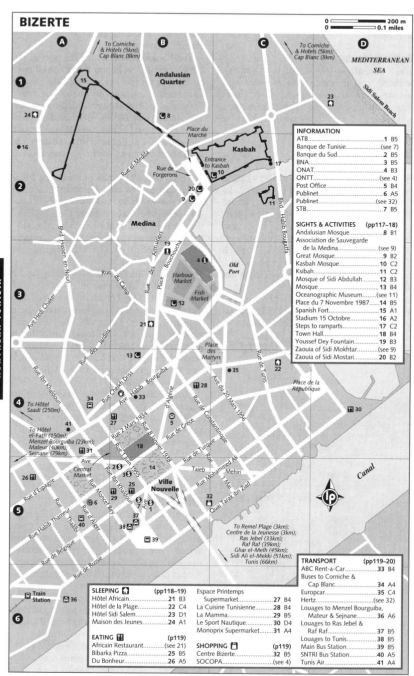

To Corniche & Hotels (5km); Cap Blanc (8km)

Andalusian Quarter

To Corniche & Hotels (5km); Cap Blanc (8km)

MEDITERRANEAN SEA

Sidi Salem Beach

0   200 m
0   0.1 miles

24

16

15

Place du Marché

8

23

Rue el-Medda

Rue de Forgerons

Entrance to Kasbah

Kasbah

17

20

9

10

11

Medina

Blvd Habib Bougatfa

Rue des Armuriers

Place Bouchoucha

19

4

Old Port

Harbour Market

Fish Market

12

Blvd Hassen en-Nouri

Ave Hedi Chaker

Rue du Camp

Rue des Jardins

21

13

Place des Martyrs

35

22

Rue de Tunis

Place de la République

To Hôtel Saadi (250m)

Rue Ibn Khaldoun

34

27

41

To Hôtel el-Fath (150m); Menzel Bourguiba (23km); Mateur (40km); Sejnane (79km)

31

26

Rue Cheikh Driss

Ave Habib Bourguiba

33

28

5

Rue d'Algérie

Rue de Grèce

Ave du 20 Mars 1956

Rue de Constantinople

30

Ave 2 Mars 1934

18

Rue Bizerte 1938

Rue de Turquie

Rue 1er Juin 1955

14

Taieb Mehiri

Rue Mohammed Ali

Ave Central Market

25

29

6

37

38

40

39

Rue d'Espagne

Rue Moncef Bey

Rue d'Alger

Rue Habib Thameur Thaalbi

Ville Nouvelle

32

Quai Tarak Ibn Ziad

Canal

To Remel Plage (3km); Centre de la Jeunesse (3km); Ras Jebel (33km); Raf Raf (39km); Ghar el-Melh (45km); Sidi Ali el-Mekki (51km); Tunis (66km)

Rue de Belgique

Rue de Russie

Train Station

36

INFORMATION
ATB...**1** B5
Banque de Tunisie...................(see 7)
Banque du Sud.......................**2** B5
BNA...**3** B5
ONAT..**4** B3
ONTT......................................(see 4)
Post Office................................**5** B4
Publinet.....................................**6** A5
Publinet...................................(see 32)
STB..**7** B5

SIGHTS & ACTIVITIES   (pp117–18)
Andalusian Mosque...............**8** B1
Association de Sauvegarde
  de la Medina........................(see 9)
Great Mosque..........................**9** B2
Kasbah Mosque.....................**10** C2
Ksibah.....................................**11** C2
Mosque of Sidi Abdullah......**12** B3
Mosque...................................**13** B4
Oceanographic Museum.......(see 11)
Place du 7 Novembre 1987....**14** B5
Spanish Fort...........................**15** A1
Stadium 15 Octobre..............**16** A2
Steps to ramparts.................**17** C2
Town Hall...............................**18** B4
Youssef Dey Fountain............**19** B3
Zaouia of Sidi Mokhtar..........(see 9)
Zaouia of Sidi Mostari...........**20** B2

SLEEPING   (pp118–19)
Hôtel Africain.........................**21** B3
Hôtel de la Plage....................**22** C4
Hôtel Sidi Salem....................**23** D1
Maison des Jeunes.................**24** A1

EATING   (p119)
Africain Restaurant..............(see 21)
Bibarka Pizza..........................**25** B5
Du Bonheur............................**26** A5
Espace Printemps
  Supermarket........................**27** B4
La Cuisine Tunisienne...........**28** B4
La Mamma...............................**29** B5
Le Sport Nautique.................**30** D4
Monoprix Supermarket.........**31** A4

SHOPPING   (p119)
Centre Bizerte.........................**32** B5
SOCOPA...................................(see 4)

TRANSPORT   (pp119–20)
ABC Rent-a-Car.......................**33** B4
Buses to Corniche &
  Cap Blanc...............................**34** A4
Europcar..................................**35** C4
Hertz.......................................(see 32)
Louages to Menzel Bourguiba,
  Mateur & Sejnane................**36** A6
Louages to Ras Jebel &
  Raf Raf..................................**37** B5
Louages to Tunis....................**38** B5
Main Bus Station...................**39** B5
SNTRI Bus Station.................**40** A5
Tunis Air.................................**41** A4

NORTHERN TUNISIA

Information

INTERNET ACCESS
Publinet (rue Habib Thameur; Centre Bizerte, Quai Tarak ibn Ziad; TD2 per hr)

MONEY
There are lots of banks around place du 7 Novembre 1987 and along ave Habib Bourguiba, some with ATMs.

POST
Main post office (ave d'Algérie) In the centre.

TOURIST INFORMATION
ONTT (☎ 432 897; ✆ 8.30am-1pm & 3-5.45pm Mon-Thu, 8.30am-1.30pm Fri & Sat) By the Socopa shop, next to the old port.

Sights & Activities

OLD PORT, PLACE BOUCHOUCHA & MEDINA
The old port has a captivating atmosphere, with blue-shuttered windows, cafés and multicoloured fishing boats making squiggling reflections in the water.

With the old port to the east and the medina to the west, place Bouchoucha connects the old and new towns. In 1881, this area was the western channel of the canal system connecting Lake Bizerte with the sea. It rejoined the eastern channel at ave Habib Bourguiba, creating an island where the European merchants and town elite once lived. This area now hosts lively markets: spice sellers cluster near the mosque, selling, among other things, dried chameleons on sticks (and luckier live ones).

East of the square is **Youssef Dey fountain**, built in 1642. It has an Andalusian inlaid arch around an inscription inviting users to drink here until the waters of paradise become available. The medina's most important buildings are nearby. The **Zaouia of Sidi Mokhtar** now houses the Association de Sauvegarde de la Medina, the group responsible for medina conservation, with a fascinating map showing how the town looked in 1881.

To the north is the 1652 **Great Mosque**, best viewed from rue des Armuriers. Its striking pointed octagonal minaret is patterned with tiling. Although the medina was damaged during WWII, its alleys are worth a wander, with blue grills and studded keyhole-shaped doors, irregular arches and shadows. The tiny rue de Forgerons is still full of cluttered blacksmith workshops and men with blackened hands. It's off a quiet timeless square that borders the kasbah, with a couple of cafés.

KASBAH
Heavy, golden crenellated walls make their defensive statement by the port entrance. The kasbah was originally a Byzantine fort, built in the 6th century AD to guard the port along with its kid brother, the *ksibah* (small fort), on the southern side. Today's kasbah was built by the Ottomans in the 17th century.

The fortifications are 10m high and up to 11m thick, to withstand artillery bombardment, and enclose narrow, winding streets pivoting the kasbah mosque. The only entrance is through the western gateway. There are **steps** (adult/child TD0.5/0.25; ✆ 9am-12.30pm & 3-8pm) up to the ramparts from outside the eastern buttress. On the top is a café, a couples' favourite, with chairs and tables nestling next to shrubs.

SPANISH FORT
Actually Turkish, this misleadingly named fort peers over the town from north of the medina. It was built between AD 1570 and 1573 by Ulj Ali, the military ruler of Algiers, after he had booted out the Spanish. All that remains of the wall are two sections on either side of the fort, but the views across the town are stupendous and take in the old Andalusian quarter with its whitewashed mosque.

Below it is a modern amphitheatre.

KSIBAH & OCEANOGRAPHIC MUSEUM
A squat little fort, the *ksibah* was modified by the Aghlabids, who added the attractive arched *skifa* (gate) and a courtyard with a set of cells – not for prisoners but for silent Quran study.

Also known as Fort Sidi Henni, it now houses a small **Oceanographic Museum** (adult/child TD0.5/0.25; ✆ 9am-12.30pm & 3-8pm), a grand description for a glum-looking turtle and small collection of fish not much more exciting than your goldfish back home. There's a small rooftop café with good views over the narrow streets and old port.

BEACHES
The beaches north of town are sweeping and balmy, but hotel-ridden for the first few

kilometres. They're backed by the corniche, *the* place for an evening promenade.

The coast road finishes about 8km north of town at Les Grottes; it's a bit of breezy Italian-feeling coast with a dramatic small beach protected to the west by the white cliffs of Cap Blanc, one of the northernmost points of the African continent. If you catch the No 2 bus from town, you will have to walk or hitch the last 2km or so; tell the driver you're aiming for Les Grottes and they'll let you off at the turn-off. A return taxi fare costs TD7.

Remel Plage, 3km east of Bizerte, is the best of the local beaches, with a pine-forest backdrop, rows of straw sunshades and some shipwrecks sprinkling the sea. Any bus heading east, or local bus No 8, can drop you off at the turn-off, from where it's a 15-minute walk; a cab costs TD3.

Sleeping

Bizerte's budget options are all central, while its choicer places are spread along the corniche – mostly mid range, with a couple of top-enders.

BUDGET

Hôtel Saadi (☎ 422 528; rue Salah Ben Ali; r with shared bathroom TD14) Opposite the football stadium, 400m from the centre, this is the best cheapie. A pleasant, plain and clean little place, its best rooms are airy and have balconies.

Hôtel de la Plage (☎ 436 510; 34 rue Mohamed Rejiba; s/d with private bathroom TD15/30, Jul & Aug TD18/36) Clean, simple and friendly, this has a good central location. The rooms are small, with blue-shuttered windows over the street.

Centre de la Jeunesse de Remel Plage (☎ 440 804; dm TD13, campsite/person TD6.5/1) This good campsite and basic hostel is a beach-ball lob from Remel Plage. The bathrooms can get a bit grubby, but there are shady sites beneath the large pines. Buses eastwards from Bizerte can drop you at the Remel Plage turn-off, but it's easier to spend TD3 on a taxi. If you're visiting between October and March, phone first to check it's open.

Hôtel el-Fath (☎ 430 596; 136 ave Habib Bourguiba; s/d with shower TD15/30) This has some large rooms with windows, but although it's cleanish and welcoming, you might share your room with the odd cockroach.

Maison des Jeunes (☎ 431 608; dm TD4) Signposted off blvd Hassen en-Nouri near the Spanish Fort, this friendly places is a basic block with standard uncushy dorms.

Hôtel Africain (☎ 434 412; 59 rue Sassi el-Bahri; s/d with shared bathroom TD5-7/10-14) The Africain has spartan but spic-and-span rooms, some with windows that open into the hallway. The bathroom is clean, but down a flight of stairs.

MID-RANGE

Prices in this section include breakfast.

Hôtel Le Petit Mousse (☎ 432 185; corniche; s/d Sep-Jun TD40/60, Jul & Aug TD50/80) Small-scale and dating from 1946, this is an unusually intimate corniche hotel, 4km from the centre, and has a good restaurant (see Eating & Drinking).

Hôtel Nador (☎ 443 022; corniche; s/d Nov-Mar TD25.5/50, Sep & Oct TD38/54, Jul & Aug TD57/82; ⚆ ⚇) With rooms off long walkways in a kind of housing-estate arrangement, this two-star is a couple of kilometres along the corniche, set in lush gardens, and has arched rooms with balconies. It's the Italians' favourite. The pool's big but a tad shabby.

Hôtel Sidi Salem (☎ 420 365; s/d with private bathroom Nov-Mar TD35/60, Apr-Oct TD55/90; ⚆ ⚇) Near the kasbah, Sidi Salem, aka the bungalows, has large rooms facing a wide sandy beach, and facilities coming out of its ears.

Hôtel Corniche (☎ 431 844; corniche; s/d Nov–mid-Mar TD40/60, d mid-Mar–Oct TD80, Jul–mid-Sep TD120; ⚆ ⚇) This three-star place is friendly and has very comfortable rooms with good views, a lovely pool and is set by a prime stretch of beach. It has a moribund disco, which gets busy in the summer.

Residence Ain Meriem (☎ 7243 1912; corniche; 3/5/7-person apartment Nov-Mar TD50/60/80-100, Apr-mid-Jul & end-Aug–mid-Sep TD70/80/100-130, & mid-Jul-end-Aug TD150/160/190-230; ⚆ ⚇) About 2km from town, this has well-decorated white-walled apartments in inoffensive domed buildings.

Hôtel Club Jalta (☎ 443 100; corniche; www.hoteljalta.tourism.tn; s/d Nov-Mar TD23/36, Apr & May & mid-Sep–Oct TD35/50, d Aug–mid-Sep TD76; ⚆ ⚇) This is 3km to the north: though it's in an unsightly white-painted block, it's centred on a plant-filled courtyard and has a big pool, and some balconies have good sea views.

TOP END

Bizerta Resort (☎ 436 966; fax 422 955; corniche; s/d Jan-Mar TD71/80, Apr-Jul, Sep & Oct TD87/96, Aug TD102/120;

⊠ ⊠) This four-star, 500m north of the Hôtel Sidi Salem, feels the most luxurious on the strip, in a business-hotel kind of way. Views from the back are over the large pool and prime stretch of beach.

Residence Essada (☎ 423 535; corniche; 2-4/4-6/6-8 person apartments Nov-Mar TD50/88/120, Apr-Jun, Sep & Oct TD54/72/132, Jul & Aug TD110/130/160; **⊠ ⊠**) Another corniche four-star, this has smart apartments with dark furnishings, white walls and balconies, arranged around a large pool.

Eating & Drinking

Le Sport Nautique (☎ 431 495; Quai Tarak ibn Ziad; starters TD2.5-12, mains TD5.5-18) One of Bizerte's best restaurants, with a lovely setting overlooking the port and shimmering stretch of water. It specialises in dishes such as squid cooked in ink, and serves alcohol.

Le Petit Mousse (☎ 432 185; corniche; starters around TD4, mains around TD14) This is the corniche's most upmarket place, with balmy, candle-lit terrace or garden seating. The mainly French food is pretty good, and there's a varied choice of Tunisian wines.

Du Bonheur (☎ 431 047; 31 rue Thaâlbi; 4-course menu TD13.5-14.5, starters TD3.8-7.8, mains TD6.8-12) This has two sections: one is a simple front bar and a back restaurant; next door you have to knock on the door and inside it's divided into intimate booths, and there is an elaborately painted ceiling. Food is tasty Tunisian.

La Belle Plage (☎ 431 817; corniche; starters TD3-7, mains TD9-20) Another recommended corniche place, this overlooks the sea, is famed for fish and serves alcohol.

Eden (☎ 439 023; corniche; starters TD3.8-14.2, mains TD6.5-14) Opposite the Hôtel Corniche, with a small outdoor terrace, this also does good seafood and serves booze.

La Cuisine Tunisienne (rue 2 Mars 1934 & rue de Constantinople; starters TD0.9-2, mains TD2.4-4) This is a friendly, popular spot, a cheap-and-cheerful, plastic-table-filled eatery with a good choice of traditional standards.

Bibarka Pizza (☎ 443 315; rue Ibn Khaldoun; dishes TD1.4-6.1) This tiled place serves mainly pizza among plastic plants and tablecloths. The low-ceilinged upstairs section has wooden bench seats in semi-booth style.

La Mamma (☎ 435 719; 17 rue Ibn Khaldoun; dishes TD1-7) Another pizzeria, this is again more intimate upstairs, complete with a glowing

picture of the intact Twin Towers. The fish is recommended.

Cap Blanc (corniche; starters TD4.7-15, mains TD4.2-15) This corniche garden is a good place to go for a drink (beer is served in pottery tankards to preserve family sensibilities); the food is OK – the usual Tunisian dishes and pizza. There is live traditional music most weekends, and often people get up to shake their thing.

Hôtel Nador (see Sleeping) Of the hotel bars, this is the most popular: seating is around the pool.

Self-caterers should check out the markets in place Bouchoucha. There are several supermarkets in the ville nouvelle.

Shopping

There's a good branch of **Socopa** (☎ 439 684) by the old port, selling fixed-price traditional crafts.

Getting There & Away

AIR

Tunis Air (☎ 432 201; 76 ave Habib Bourguiba) has an office, but the nearest airport is Tunis-Carthage.

BUS

There are buses to Tunis (TD3.3, 45 minutes to one hour, half hourly), Ras Jebel (TD1.6, 45 minutes, hourly), the connecting point to Raf Raf, and a lone 6am departure to Ain Draham (TD8, three hours) via Tabarka (TD8, three hours) and Menzel Bourguiba (TD0.8, 15 minutes, half hourly), from the main bus station at the end of ave d'Algérie.

Houmt Souq (Jerba), Kairouan, Sfax and Sousse buses leave from the SNTRI bus garage on rue Habib Thameur.

Buses heading east, such as local bus No 8, can drop you at the Remel Plage turn-off for the beach and camp site (TD0.3, every 15 minutes).

CAR

ABC Rent-a-Car (☎ 434 624; 33 ave Habib Bourguiba)
Europcar (☎ 431 455; 19 rue Rejiba, place des Martyrs)
Hertz (☎ 438 388; Centre Bizerte)

LOUAGE

Louages to Tunis (TD2.25) have a red stripe and leave from opposite the bus station. Around the corner, blue-striped ones zoom to Ras Jebel (TD1.6), Raf Raf (TD2.5) and Ghar el-Melh (TD1.2). Blue-striped louages to Menzel Bourguiba (TD1) and Mateur (TD1.5), and yellow-striped ones to Sejnane (TD3) and Tabarka (TD8), go from opposite the train station.

TRAIN
There are trains to Tunis (TD3.5, 1½ hours, four daily), via Tinja and Mateur. The train station is by the shipping canal at the south-western end of rue de Russie.

Getting Around
Bus Nos 2 and 21 to the corniche (half-hourly) stop at the corner of blvd Hassen en-Nouri and ave Habib Bourguiba. Bus No 2 can drop you at the turn-off to Les Grottes beach.

AROUND BIZERTE
Raf Raf   رفراف
Raf Raf has one of the best beaches in the country: a long pale brushstroke fringed by pine trees, set beneath the rugged escarp-ment that runs east from Jebel Nadour (325m) for about 2km to Cap Farina. It's often speckled with debris and people, but weekdays are quiet.

Raf Raf town is about 1km inland, but there's not much to it. The main road from Ras Jebel bypasses the centre and heads straight for the beach.

Hôtel Dalia (☎ 441 688; s/d Nov-Jun TD30/60, Jul-Sep TD35/70) The only option is tiny, modern Dalia with small bright rooms and little balconies. It's to the left of the main road leading down to the sea, and it has a restaurant.

Restaurants line the main road along the seafront, serving fresh fish and pizza.

Public transport operates via Ras Jebel, 6km west of Raf Raf. Buses to Ras Jebel leave from the bus stop on the main street 50m before the beach. There are regular buses and louages from Ras Jebel to Bizerte.

Ghar el-Melh   غار الملح
The village of Ghar el-Melh, on the south-ern side of Jebel Nadour, snoozes between the hillside and a silted-up lagoon. It's only a few kilometres south of Raf Raf, but almost 20km by road. There are an unlikely three Ottoman forts in the village. The little fish-ing port is somnolently calm, with a relax-ing little café.

Ghar el-Melh was founded during the reign of Osta Murad Dey (1637–40) as the pirate base of Porto Farina. Its notoriety was such that in 1654 it was attacked and temporarily knocked out of action by the celebrated English naval heavy Sir Francis Drake. After privateering was abolished at the beginning of the 19th century, the Hus-seinite beys attempted to turn the port into a major naval base. During his reign, Ahmed Bey (1837–55) ordered the construction of two new forts, a surrounding defensive wall and a new port flanked by armouries. His efforts were soon defeated by the silt-laden waters of the Oued Medjerda, which began to clog the lagoon. Attempts to dredge the lagoon failed, and the port was abandoned in favour of La Goulette (Tunis). Today the lagoon is more like a coastal swamp, and only tiny fishing boats can use the narrow channel between the port and the sea.

You can get to Ghar el-Melh by bus from Bizerte (TD1.5, one hour, two daily) and there are occasional louages. There's no public transport making the trip to Sidi Ali el-Mekki.

Sidi Ali el-Mekki
سيدي علي المكّي
Sidi Ali el-Mekki could throw its hat in the ring as Tunisia's finest beach. It's an unspoilt strand backed by hills and just a few buildings, fronted by a calm jump-in-me stretch of green-blue sea. It's deserted during the week, but gets crammed at the weekend.

The only accommodation is some two-room straw **shacks** (weekdays/weekends TD10/15). Camping is OK too.

Cap Farina (☎ 72 448 757; fish TD12, prawns TD17; ☺ lunch, dinner) This serves delicious seafood, barbecued on pine cones. You sit on a sim-ple terrace on the beach. Bookings are es-sential. At the weekend there are foodstalls serving up sandwiches too.

It's 6km east of Ghar el-Melh on the southern side of Cap Farina. You can take a bus or louage to Ghar el-Melh, then walk or hitch the last stretch.

Utica   أوتيكا
The ruins of **Utica** (admission TD2.1, plus camera TD1; ☺ 8.30am-5.30pm Tue-Sun mid-Sep–mid-Mar, 8am-7pm Tue-Sun mid-Mar–mid-Sep) are sparse compared with other Tunisian Roman sites, but it's

a tranquil flower-filled place, and has an important history. You'll come to the small museum first on the left, 2km from the main road. In its grounds is a 2nd-century AD fountain with a mosaic of a sad-eyed Neptune made with continental marble and Egyptian turquoise, and the remains of a 1st-century AD *hammam* (bathhouse), with nonslip terracotta flooring. The mosaic that gave the site's House of the Hunt its name is also displayed.

Inside, the Punic room shows everyday objects found in the site necropolis, including makeup utensils, razors and some beautiful jewellery. There's also a gruesome pile of bones in an infant tomb that the curator will be delighted to show you. Imported Greek pottery indicates the sophistication of the Punic settlement, while the Roman room shows that the craze for marble garden statuary was big 2000 years ago.

The site itself is 500m further along the road. The main attraction is the House of the Cascade, with a central patio; it's named after a mosaic-decorated fountain in a northern room with a fishing scene. One glorious basin mosaic shows a fishing cupid in a boat, and the triclinium (dining room) is floored in green (from Greece) and golden (from nearby Chemtou) marble, in striking geometric patterns. To the north, the public baths were by the old shoreline, and covered nearly 3 sq km – the remains are scant and overgrown. A mammoth mosaic with a sea-god theme from Utica is on display at the Bardo Museum (see p56).

Utica was once a thriving port and city at the mouth of the Oued Medjerda. It was founded by the Phoenicians in about 1100 BC, 300 years before Carthage. Utica remained important and a rival to Carthage for more than 1000 years, building grand monuments to challenge its rival.

Having defected to the Roman camp before the Third Punic War, Utica became the capital of the Roman province of Africa after the destruction of Carthage in 146 BC. Caught up in the Roman civil war in the 1st century BC, Utica supported Pompey. When the ruler, Caton, realised it was a lost cause he committed suicide rather than be captured – becoming a local hero the hard way – and Julius Caesar entered the city.

Under Hadrian the city continued its success. A new aqueduct was built, along with a forum, huge baths and some elaborate residences. Utica's days were numbered, though, by the waters of the Oued Medjerda. Silt levels in the river rose dramatically in Roman times because of the huge increase in wheat cultivation. By the beginning of the 2nd century AD, the port had been rendered useless, and the river was no longer navigable. Carthage was back in favour and had again become the capital, while Utica declined, though it continued to be inhabited into the Arab era.

These days, the site occupies a low hill overlooking rich farmlands. The coast is now some 8km to the east, where the port of Ghar el-Melh has become similarly clogged.

GETTING THERE & AWAY
The turn-off is signposted to the east from the small, modern village of Utique, 33km north of Tunis on the road to Bizerte.

If you haven't got your own transport, you'll have to ask a louage or bus on the Tunis to Bizerte route to drop you on the main road and walk the last 2km.

NORTH COAST
Between Bizerte and Tabarka the coastline is rugged and rural, with sparkling blue bays and some secluded villages. The largely uninhabited coast is only accessible at certain points, and this is a good area to get off the beaten track and jump in the sea. The main road winds inland through fields and forests, and much of the coast is covered with tree plantations. Louages run to the coastal settlements but you'll need patience to get to them via public transport.

Lake Ichkeul   بحيرة اشكل
This World Heritage–listed **national park** (admission free; ۞ 7am-7pm) encompasses a huge ochre marsh and shallow lake surrounded by the snaking trunks of olive groves, fierce dry cacti and brown-orange rocks. It's 30km southwest of Bizerte, and covers Lake Ichkeul and the peak Jebel Ichkeul (511m). It's worth visiting for the scenery alone, but it's also birdwatcher heaven: from October to February the waters and surrounding marshes are home to more than 200,000 migratory waterfowl from all over Europe (see the boxed text, next page).

There's a small ecomuseum that explains the unique ecosystem – the waters are

---

LAKE ICHKEUL BIRDLIFE

Lake Ichkeul is a haven for water birds. Some hunt along the shoreline or probe the soft mud at the water's edge; others stride on long legs into deeper water to seek prey. The brightly coloured kingfisher is a diving jewel, while warblers, finches and rails dart about the dense vegetation surrounding the lake.

Ichkeul's shores are thronged with stilts, sandpipers and stints. Aptly named wagtails strut about; and grey herons and little egrets stalk the shallows for fish and frogs. In spring, thousands of 'passage migrants' arrive from south of the Sahara, stopping briefly to replenish their energy before flying on to fan out across Europe.

The resident species are joined by migrants, such as squacco herons, white storks and cattle egrets. In the reed beds, the bittern, a well-camouflaged relative of the heron, is more often heard than seen, and Cettis, great reed warblers and moustached warblers make a riot of territorial sound. The purple gallinule pokes among the vegetation on long, splayed toes; its bright-blue plumage and red bill make it virtually unmistakable, especially when picked out by sunrays.

The greater flamingo loves shallow lakes. As they are nomadic, huge gatherings are not guaranteed, but if you're in luck you'll see one of Tunisia's ornithological highlights, a mass of pink above the shimmering waters.

As summer wanes and autumn draws on, the summer 'shift' of migrants disperses south again to be replaced by birds escaping the northern winter. Chief among these are the ducks and geese. For sheer numbers of these, Lake Ichkeul has few rivals. Ducks, such as wigeons, teals, gadwalls, pintails and, farther out, pochards, come in hoards. As many as 15,000 greylag geese have been spotted wintering at Ichkeul. Other waterfowl specialities include white-headed ducks and marbled teals, and countless coots.

---

saline in summer and diluted by freshwater in winter. Environmental pressures – there are several dams – have reduced the influx of freshwater in winter, affecting the ecology and future of the park, but authorities postulate that this can be maintained by artificial methods. Animals living in the environs include mongoose, porcupine, jackal, wild boar and, somewhat out of context, a herd of water buffaloes – descendants of a pair given to Ahmed Bey in 1840. They live in the marshes around the lake – a long way from home but in a suitably exotic landscape.

There's no accommodation, and camping is not permitted. The best time to spot wildlife is early morning or dusk.

Access to the park is from the southeastern side of the lake, 10km north of Mateur. Coming from Bizerte, follow the main road south to Menzel Bourguiba for 21km, continue to the village of Tinja and fork right onto the Mateur road. The turn-off to the park is signposted on the right after 9km. This road runs dead straight along a causeway for 7km to the base of Jebel Ichkeul and the park entrance. Officials will check you in and out 3km before the car park and information centre.

Buses and louages between Bizerte and Mateur can drop you at the park turn-off, but you will have to walk or hitch from there (a bike would come in handy). There's very little traffic, except at weekends.

Sejnane   سجنان

The small town of Sejnane is set among smooth field-covered hills, grey-green trees and spiky outcrops of cactus. It's halfway between Mateur and Tabarka, and famous for the primitive, moulded pottery known as Sejnane ware.

The techniques used by the potters of the Berber villages around here date back to Neolithic times. Clay is hand-moulded into assorted unusual animal figurines and bowls of different shapes and sizes, then open-fired on mounds of glowing coals before being decorated with rusty reds and deep browns. You'll find the ceramics on sale at tourist shops countrywide, as well as at roadside stalls. There are lots of them about 6km northeast of town on the road to Bizerte, and others on the road to Mateur.

Sejnane itself is a small service town clustered around the junction of the roads to Bizerte, Mateur and Tabarka. Storks' nests are everywhere – check out the roof of the train station, towards Tabarka on the western side of town. There are dozens more nests on the abandoned mining rig behind the station.

There are a couple of *gargottes* (cheap restaurants), but no accommodation.

The main junction also serves as the bus and louage station. SNTRI buses travelling the northern route (via Mateur) between Tabarka and Tunis can drop you at Sejnane. There are regular local buses and louages to and from Mateur (TD2.4), Tabarka (TD3.5), Bizerte (TD3.5) and Sidi Mechrig (TD1). The train station is for freight services only.

Cap Serrat   كاب سرات

Cap Serrat is dazzling, serene and remote. The road to it snakes through eucalyptus plantations filled with beehives – in summer you can buy honey from the roadside. For much of the year the beach is deserted, with just a few campers in summer.

There are several small café/restaurants cooking up fresh fish; ask at the beach restaurants. Several have rooms (TD50/150-180 per week/month). Showers are available (TD0.25), as is boat hire (TD20 per day).

It's 27km north of Sejnane. The access road to Cap Serrat is signposted 11km north of Sejnane along the back road to Bizerte (which skirts the northern edge of Lake Ichkeul). From the turn-off, the road winds through the forest before emerging in a small valley dotted with a few scattered farmhouses. The road continues north to a tiny settlement at the base of the peninsula, and ends at a parking area behind the beach. The area is no longer undiscovered, but there is not much public transport, which keeps numbers down. There are infrequent louages from Sejnane (TD1).

A rough road hugs the coast from Cap Serrat to Sidi Mechrig, some 20km to the west – it requires a 4WD as some sections are sandy.

Sidi Mechrig   سيدي مشرق

Sidi Mechrig is a tiny coastal settlement with one hotel, a small new fishing port and a stretch of sandy beach overlooked by a complete Roman arch – the remains of an ancient bathhouse. It's usually approached from the village of Tamra, 9km west of Sejnane; from here it's another long, winding 17km to the coast.

Hôtel Sidi Mechrig (s/d with shared bathroom & breakfast TD10/20) has a great location overlooking the beach and arch, and small tiled rooms, which were being renovated at the time of research. It also has the only bar between Tabarka and Mateur, guaranteeing a steady stream of customers. There's a restaurant with terrace seating overlooking the sea, which is a great spot to munch grilled fish, chips and salad (TD7.5), washed down with a cold beer.

Public transport is limited. In July and August, there are three buses (TD1) daily to and from Sejnane; the rest of the year about four buses run to cater for students. There are also louages and *camionnettes* (pick-ups) from Sejnane.

TABARKA   طبرقة

☎ 78 / pop 13,600

Tabarka, 22km from Algeria, is set at the base of evergreen mountains, and pervaded with flooding, shimmering sunlight. It's a lovely laidback coastal town, where people sit for hours at tree-shaded cafés. The little bay to the north is watched over by an impressive Genoese fort on Tabarka Island (now linked by a causeway), while a long stretch of beach curves away eastwards towards Cap Nègre. Popular with Tunisians, unlike other resorts it's not dominated by Europeans, but has an expanding zone touristique with comfortable hotels and a golf course. During the summer Tabarka hosts several fabulous music festivals.

History

Like so many North African coastal towns, Tabarka began life as a Phoenician settlement. Originally called Thabraca (Shaded Place), it remained a minor outpost until Roman times, when it became a major port exporting Chemtou marble. It was also the exit point for many African big cats en route to the colosseums of Rome and elsewhere.

In the 16th and 17th centuries, Tabarka became one of the ports used by the Muslim corsairs. They included the notorious Khair ed-Din Barbarossa, who was obliged to hand over Tabarka Island to the Genoese in the 1540s as ransom for the release of his cohort, Dragut. The castle built by the Genoese enabled them to hold out against the Ottomans until 1741, when it fell to the bey of Tunis.

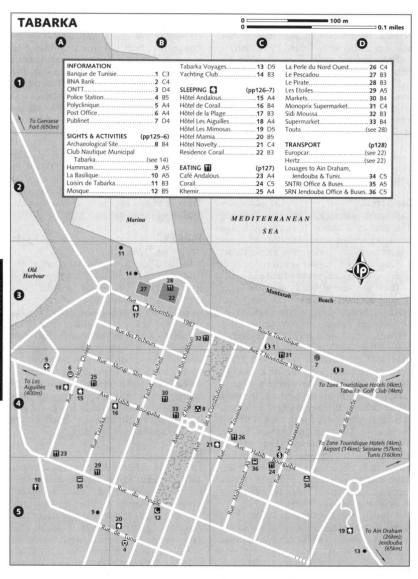

TABARKA

0   100 m
0   0.1 miles

INFORMATION	
Banque de Tunisie	1 C3
BNA Bank	2 C4
ONTT	3 D4
Police Station	4 B5
Polyclinique	5 A4
Post Office	6 A4
Publinet	7 D4

SIGHTS & ACTIVITIES	(pp125–6)
Archaeological Site	8 B4
Club Nautique Municipal Tabarka	(see 14)
Hammam	9 A5
La Basilique	10 A5
Loisirs de Tabarka	11 B3
Mosque	12 B5

Tabarka Voyages	13 D5
Yachting Club	14 B3

SLEEPING	(pp126–7)
Hôtel Andalous	15 A4
Hôtel de Corail	16 B4
Hôtel de la Plage	17 B3
Hôtel Les Aiguilles	18 A4
Hôtel Les Mimosas	19 D5
Hôtel Mamia	20 B5
Hôtel Novelty	21 C4
Residence Corail	22 B3

EATING	(p127)
Café Andalous	23 A4
Corail	24 C5
Khemir	25 A4

La Perle du Nord Ouest	26 C4
Le Pescadou	27 B3
Le Pirate	28 B3
Les Etoiles	29 A5
Markets	30 B4
Monoprix Supermarket	31 C4
Sidi Moussa	32 B3
Supermarket	33 B4
Touta	(see 28)

TRANSPORT	(p128)
Europcar	(see 22)
Hertz	(see 22)
Louages to Ain Draham, Jendouba & Tunis	34 C5
SNTRI Office & Buses	35 A5
SRN Jendouba Office & Buses	36 C5

The French built the modern town and the causeway connecting the island to the mainland. Despite these developments, Tabarka was considered to be enough of a backwater to be a suitable place of exile for Habib Bourguiba in 1952. He spent a short time here, staying at the Hôtel Les Mimosas and the Hôtel de France (now Hôtel Andalous).

Today it's tourism that shores up the local economy, while the modern port handles tonnes of cork harvested from the Kroumirie forests. The red coral, found just offshore, is still exploited for the jewellery trade – and it's worth considering the environmental effects of this before investing in any.

Orientation

The small centre is the usual French grid, bisected by the main street, ave Habib Bourguiba.

Ave Habib Bourguiba begins at the large roundabout at the town's southeastern edge and ends at the old harbour. The causeway to Tabarka Island leads off from here, with a small beach to the west and the marina and port to the east.

The southeastern roundabout is at the junction of the roads south to Ain Draham and east to Sejnane. The zone touristique is 4km east of town, signposted off the road to Sejnane.

Information

EMERGENCY
Polyclinique (☎ 671 200; ave Habib Bourguiba) Open 24 hours for medical emergencies.

INTERNET ACCESS
Publinet (route Touristique; TD2 per hr)

MONEY
Most of the banks are on ave Habib Bourguiba, some with ATMs.

POST
Post office (ave Hedi Chaker) Opposite Hôtel Les Aiguilles.

TOURIST INFORMATION
ONTT (☎ 673 555; ave 7 Novembre 1987; ☺ 8.30am-1pm & 3-5.45pm Mon-Thu, 8.30am-1.30pm Fri & Sat Sep-Jun, 7.30am-1.30pm & 2-8pm Mon-Thu, 9am-2pm Fri-Sun Jul-Aug) Occupies the old train station.

Sights & Activities

BEACHES
Tabarka has two beaches. The causeway that links Tabarka Island to the mainland created the central sheltered bay known as Old Harbour, while Montazah Beach is a great sweep of white sand stretching east (the further from the marina the cleaner it is). The zone touristique hotels nab their own enclosures but it's easy to wander in.

GENOESE FORT & LES AIGUILLES
The magnificent Genoese fort, long occupied by the military, is intended to house Tabarka's museum sometime in 2004 and will be open to the public.

Until then, the best views are from Les Aiguilles (Needles), spiky pinnacles of rock on the western side of Old Harbour Bay, and a popular early evening spot and photo backdrop.

LA BASILIQUE
This small church was built by French missionaries at the end of the 19th century and occupies an old Roman cistern. It was the home of the town's museum until it closed for repairs several years ago, never to re-open. It makes a superb venue for concerts at the Tabarka festivals.

DIVING
Tabarka has Tunisia's best diving, with more than 10 excellent sites. For experienced divers, these include the colourful Grouper Rock, where you can meet large groupers, the Tunnels, with more grouper, octopus and many others, and the Colours, with technicolour rocks and sealife. For beginners, sites include Pigeon Cave, with lots of little fish and calm waters, Cap Tabarka, brilliantly coloured with shoals of fish, and the Swimming Pool, a popular, sheltered site.

Club Nautique Municipal Tabarka (☎ 671 478) Operating from the marina yachting club, this club goes back over 20 years and organises trips, rents equipment and offers accreditation courses for beginners (TD310) and packages of 1/6/10 dives (TD21/110/190). It also arranges boat trips (two hours TD15).

Loisirs de Tabarka (☎ 670 664; diving.tunisie@planet.tn; rue Ali Zouaoui) This newer place is also marinaside and offers CMAS level 1 to 2 (TD300 to TD380), or 1/6/10 dives (TD25/120/180), rents equipment and is the only place that runs trips to the protected Galite islands, with fantastic sealife, about 2½ hours away (TD70 per person).

Méhari Diving Centre (Hôtel Riu Mehari) This hotel centre offers CMAS-PADI-SSI courses levels 1 to 4 (TD230 to TD400) and one-month instructor courses (TD600), or 1/6/10 dives (TD25/132/200). You can also hire equipment and snorkelling stuff.

GOLF
Tabarka Golf Club (☎ 671 031; zone touristique) has a fine 18-hole layout (9/18 holes TD28/48). Be warned the fairways are carved out of dense coastal scrub that swallows up nearly every stray ball.

NORTHERN TUNISIA

It's one of the few Tunisian clubs that welcomes hackers; there's no need to show proof of handicap.

HORSE RIDING

Horse riding can be arranged through the **Hôtel Golf Beach** (☎ 673 002; zone touristique) near the golf course. The stables are run by Fershishi Rahim (TD20 for two hours).

Tours

Tabarka Voyages (☎ 673 740; 13 route de Ain Draham) combines Bulla Regia, Chemtou and Le Kef for TD50 for a full day trip.

Tunisie Voyages (Hôtel Riu Mehari) has lots of tours for a minimum of six people, such as Dougga and Chemtou (TD46) or a half-day at Bulla Regia (TD25).

Festivals & Events

Tabarka has a brilliant, burgeoning array of music festivals – chances for throngs of people to dance wildly on the terraces of La Basilique. The big one is the weeklong jazz festival in July, with acts playing at Café Andalous and La Basilique. The Rai Festival is at the end of June and showcases some of the best in Algerian music. At the end of August it's the turn of world music and in early September Tabarka goes Latin. In July and August there's an international festival, with a chance to see traditional local music. Concerts usually start around 10pm and continue till after midnight. Tickets cost about TD4; some of the jazz events cost up to TD20.

Sleeping

Tabarka has lots of mid-range accommodation in town and more luxurious options along the zone touristique (around 1km to 4km from the town centre), but budget options are scarce.

BUDGET

Hôtel de Corail (☎ 673 789; rue Tazarka; s/d with shared bathroom TD7/14) This has old-fashioned rooms with high ceilings and balconies. However, the bathrooms are not completely clean, and it's cold in winter, hot in summer.

Hôtel Mamia (☎ 671 058; 3 rue de Tunis; s/d with shared bathroom TD15/18) With rooms set around a courtyard, this is clean, but the windows only open onto the courtyard and showers are feeble and the management may make you feel as if you're inconveniencing them.

MID-RANGE

Hôtel Les Mimosas (☎ 673 018; s/d Nov-Mar TD27.5/40, Apr-Jun, Sep & Oct TD35/50; 🌣 🖭) This elegant, good-value, three-star place has wonderful views over the bay and town. It's like a cartoon French villa with bright-yellow shutters – ask for a room with a balcony as the views are impeccable. Bourguiba spent some time here. The spacious, lovely pool overlooks the panorama, set in perfect lawns ideal for an evening drink. The aircon doesn't work too well though.

Hôtel de la Plage (☎ 670 039; 11 ave 7 Novembre 1987; s/d Jul–mid-Sep with shared bathroom TD20/40, with private bathroom TD25/50, mid-Sep–Jun TD15/30, TD20/40) Clean, small and central, the nicest rooms here have balconies overlooking the street. The entrance has some crazy fibreglass seashell action, but the reception is otherwise dour.

Hôtel Les Aiguilles (☎ 673 789; 18 ave Habib Bourguiba; s/d Apr-Jun & mid-Sep–Oct TD22/34, Jul–mid-Sep TD40/60, Nov-Mar TD18.28; 🌣) This friendly place is in an old colonial building, originally a bank, converted into a comfortable, but slightly overpriced two-star hotel.

Hôtel Andalous (☎ 670 600, 25 ave Hedi Chaker; s/d Apr-Jun & mid-Sep–Oct TD40/70, Jul–mid-Sep TD65/100, Nov-Mar TD 35/60; 🌣) Opposite Les Aiguilles is this renovated three-star, with a popular pavement café that adjoins the tastiest *shwarma* stall. The rooms are smart but a bit pricey, even if they do have TV, balconies and good views over the bay.

Hôtel Novelty (☎ 670 176; ave Habib Bourguiba; s/d Nov-Mar TD31/46, Apr-Jun & mid-Sept–Oct TD43/60, Jul–mid-Sep TD65/90) With unusually shaped white-painted bright and airy rooms and slightly shabby but clean bathrooms, this is a respectable choice. The best views are from the top floor and there's heating.

Residence Corail (☎ 670 370; 2/4/6-person apartments Apr-Jun & mid-Sep–Oct TD46/80/100, Jul–mid-Sep TD80/125/175, Nov-Mar TD40/70/85) Self-catering apartments by the marina, these are spacious, good value and smart – the studios are particularly good. They have big windows and balconies although the views aren't great and the fountain in the central courtyard is positively dodgy.

Hôtel Dar Morjane (☎ 643 411; zone touristique; s/d Nov-Mar TD24/38, Apr-Jun & Sep-Oct TD41/61, Jul & Aug TD68/96; 🌣 🖭) This corniche three-star is friendly, with good views and a big pool; however, it's showing its age a bit.

TOP END

All these top-enders are along the zone touristique.

Dar Ismail (☎ 670 188; s/d Nov–mid-Mar TD52/80, mid-Mar–Oct TD72/108; ✖ ⊋) Nearest the town and a glitzy tangerine of a building with peachy, comfortable rooms, this has a big pool and all comforts.

Robinson Club (☎ 670 302; www.robinson.de; s/d TD120/200; ✖ ⊋) This is the furthest (about 4km), newest and swankiest kid on the block. Luxurious rooms have the softest pillows, the views back across the bay are lovely, and there's all the glass and chrome you could want. The pool is on two levels and there's a dive club. Its clientele is mainly German.

Hôtel Riu Mehari (☎ 670 184; www.riu.com; s/d Nov-Dec & Jan-Mar TD51/78, Apr-Jun & Sep-Oct TD71/124, Jul & Aug TD103/162; ✖ ⊋) Though it is a bit impersonal, rooms here have good views of the beach and landscaped pool, and there's an indoor pool, a dive club and lots of stuff for kids.

Residence Riu Mehari (☎ 670 184; 2-person studios/ 4-person apartments Nov-Jun TD80/125, Jul-Aug TD130/195; ✖ ⊋) Opposite the hotel of the same name, with similarly well-appointed self-catering apartments in bungalows among trees.

Abou Nawas (☎ 673 532; s/d Nov-Mar TD44.5/52, Apr-Jun & mid-Sep–Oct TD73/94, Jul–mid-Sep TD129.5/167; ✖ ⊋) This is as smart as you could expect from the luxury chain, in an attractive irregular white building with red slanted roofs. The tasteful rooms have small balconies overlooking the garden. The pool is huge and there's entertainment such as tennis courts and poolside aerobics – scary or fun depending on where you're coming from.

Royal Golf (☎ 673 664; s/d Apr-Jul & mid-Sep–Oct TD70/80, Aug–mid-Sep TD100/140, Nov-Mar TD50/65; ✖ ⊋) Further from the sea than the others, this has good views of the mountains and sea, and rooms are decked out in green-stained wood. The atrium looks like it's housing a curly-wrought-iron convention. The pool is tiptop, with views of the green hills around.

Eating

CAFÉS

Café Andalous (ave Hedi Chaker) With chairs and tables all over the pavement, this is a classic coffeehouse – the elaborately tiled interior is chock-a-block with Ottoman bric-a-brac, such as spiky antlers, and men playing cheq-

uers. During the jazz festival, this is one of the venues for live music.

RESTAURANTS

There is lots of excellent seafood here; many small places serve barbecued fish for about TD2.5 – look for the charcoal grills, particularly around rue du Peuple and ave Farhat Hached. All these open for lunch and dinner daily.

Les Etoiles (rue du Peuple; dishes TD1-5) One of many similar simple but tasty places on this street, this has outside tables, a nice local feel and does a mean barbecued fish.

Sidi Moussa (ave 7 Novembre & ave d'Algérie; meals TD5) A small, welcoming place, with some outside seating, this offers good fresh fish with chips, salad and fruit.

La Perle du Nord Ouest (☎ 670 164; ave Habib Bourguiba; starters TD2.5-4, mains TD2.5-5) A busy bar and restaurant, La Perle has red-and-yellow canopies and a background of dramatic traditional music.

Corail (ave Habib Bourguiba; starters TD1.5, mains TD5.5, 3-course set menu TD7) This cheap-and-cheerful place has a good set menu, some outside tables and jolly management.

The mid-range restaurants are also reasonable. **Hotel Les Aiguilles** and **Hotel Novelty** offer three-course deals for TD10. **Les Mimosas** is better and charges TD12 – and eating here qualifies you to use the (very nice) pool.

Khemir (ave Habib Bourguiba; starters TD2-4, mains TD6-10) This has pavement tables and a good range of seafood.

There's a cluster of restaurants serving alcohol and good fish by the marina.

Le Pirate (☎ 670 061; marina; starters TD3.5-5, mains TD3.8-14; ✖ 9am-midnight Mar-Nov) Set on a shrub-encircled terrace, across the road from the beach, this has tasty fresh fish.

Touta (☎ 671 018; starters TD3-8, mains TD4.5-13) This recommended place is another restaurant that serves up good seafood and has a nice setting by the port.

Le Pescadou (☎ 9823 7996; starters TD2.5-4, mains TD7-10) Another place with a good port setting, one of the specialities here is *bouillabaisse*.

SELF-CATERING

Self-caterers can stock up at the **Monoprix supermarket** (ave 7 Novembre 1987). You'll find fresh fruit and vegetables, and local fish, at the markets behind the smaller supermarket by the central roundabout.

Getting There & Away

AIR
Tabarka has an international airport, but little happens apart from the occasional European charter flight (no domestic flights).

BUS
The SNTRI office and bus station are on rue du Peuple. There are services to/from Tunis (TD8.1, 3¼ hours, six daily), Le Kef (TD5.3, three hours, two daily), Ain Draham (TD1, 45 minutes, 11 daily) and Jendouba (TD2.8, 1½ hours, five daily).

SRN Jendouba, on ave Habib Bourguiba at the junction with rue Mohammed Ali, has buses to Jendouba (TD2.8, 1¾ hours, four daily) and Ain Draham (TD1.3, 40 minutes, 11 daily). The 6.15am and 9.30am services to Jendouba continue to Le Kef (TD5.2, 3½ hours). It also has a service to Bizerte (TD6.1, 3¼ hours) at 7am.

SRT Bizerte has a daily service to Bizerte at 2.45pm, leaving from outside the Monoprix supermarket.

LOUAGE
Louages leave from ave Habib Bourguiba for Ain Draham (TD1.1), Jendouba (TD2.8) and Tunis (TD7.5).

Getting Around
A taxi to/from the airport costs around TD5. The town is too small to warrant local buses, so you can either walk or take a taxi. In summer, a 'toytown' train shuttles between the Porto Corallo complex and the zone touristique.

CAR
Car-hire companies in town:
Europcar (☎ 670 834; Porto Corallo complex)
Hertz (☎ 670 670; Porto Corallo complex)

TABARKA TO AIN DRAHAM
The road that goes south from Tabarka to Ain Draham, 26km inland, has to be one of Tunisia's most beautiful routes. It climbs through rich countryside, from the coastal plain into the huge forests of the Kroumirie Mountains. The road winds up into the hills, with immense views opening and closing through the dense forests.

The climb begins a few kilometres south of Tabarka, with views back over the piercing blue coast. The road then starts to twist

and turn its way up the valley of the Oued Kebir, and the paddocks give way to forest. The predominant species is the cork oak; you'll see deep-red, tannin-stained trunks of freshly harvested trees stacked beside the road.

At the small village of Babouch, 21km from Tabarka, there is a turn-off to the Algerian border. The border is 3km to the west, and it's another 28km from there to the coastal town of El-Kala.

AIN DRAHAM عين دراهم
☎ 78 / pop 15,300
Ain Draham is Tunisia's hill station, created as a retreat by the French. It has slanted red roofs and haunted-looking houses spilling down the western flank of Jebel Biri (1014m), the highest peak of the Kroumirie Mountains. All around are rolling hills covered in cork forest. Shops display faded cassette boxes and more carvings of stags than is strictly necessary. At an altitude of around 900m, it usually snows in winter, and offers welcome respite from the summer heat. It's a great base for mountain walks.

The town was popular with colonial hunters – the last of Tunisia's lions and leopards were shot around here early last century. Hunting continues to be an attraction, with wild boars now the prime target, but most visitors come to relax and escape the summer heat.

Orientation & Information
The main road through town becomes the main street, blvd de l'Environment. It dips into a small valley as you come into town from Tabarka, then climbs steeply through the centre and continues towards Jendouba.

The bus and louage stations are just west of the main street at the bottom of the hill, while everything else of importance is up the hill towards Jendouba. There's a couple of banks (BNA and STB), a post office, Taxiphone offices and a **syndicat d'initiative** (☎ 655 222).

Trekking
The surrounding hilly forests have great potential as a trekking destination, and are largely unexplored.

The absence of decent maps makes it difficult to trek independently, although there are

LES TAPIS DE KROUMIRIE

Carpets and kilims (woven rugs) are woven in Ain Draham by a small women's cooperative called Les Tapis de Kroumirie, a project launched in the 1980s by two French doctors. Operated with the help of the Ain Draham Centre d'Action Sociale, it aims to provide employment for local women and revive local carpet-making traditions.

It's an interesting place to visit. The produce is sold from the workshop, where about a dozen looms are in operation. The carpets are the thick-pile Berber type known as *alloucha*, produced in natural tones and decorated with simple, traditional Berber motifs. The wool is all spun by hand. Prices are fixed, but they're not high.

To get there, turn right at the bottom of the steps opposite the *syndicat d'initiative*. The co-operative is above the Ministère des Affaires Sociales, about 50m on the right. The carpets are also sold in Tunis by Mains de Femmes (47 ave Habib Bourguiba).

some good short walks close to town. One easy option is the Col des Ruines – walk out along the Tabarka road to the Hôtel Nour el-Ain and then take the well-trodden forest track that leads back to town. The circuit takes about two hours. You can also walk to the top of the other nearby summit, Jebel Biri. It's about a three-hour return journey; the path starts near the Hôtel Rihana.

Hôtel Rihana (☎ 655 391) has long specialised in organising winter wild-boar hunts and uses the same guides to lead trekking groups in spring and autumn. It offers guided treks for small groups for about TD50 each per day.

Sleeping

Maison des Jeunes (☎ 647 087; dm TD5) Cold in winter; basic rooms are on offer at the top end of town, on the road to Jendouba.

Hôtel Beauséjour (☎ 655 363; d with private bathroom from TD47) A green-shuttered former hunting lodge, this feels like the setting for an Agatha Christie novel. Perhaps it's the dive-bombing boars on the walls. The restaurant does a set menu (TD15) and serves beer.

Résidence Le Pins (☎ 656 200; s/d with private bathroom Oct-Jun TD25/35, Jul-Sep TD29/48) Modern and clean, with sweeping views, particularly from the roof.

Hôtel Nour el-Ain (☎ 655 000; Col des Ruines; 🍽 🏊) This three-star, 2km to the north, has rooms with balconies and views over to Tabarka or Ain Draham. There's a big tiled *hammam* and indoor pool. President Ben Ali's holiday chalet is a stone's throw away.

Hôtel Rihana (☎ 655 391; s/d from TD42/64) Big with hunters and training sportspeople, Rihana has a masculine feel, with pictures of dead boars in reception, a red velvet bar and an indoor pool; the views from the old-fashioned rooms are wonderful.

Hôtel Les Chênes (☎ 655 315) About 7km along the road to Jendouba, tucked into trees, is the two-star Les Chênes, an old white trophy-decorated hunting lodge dating back to the 1920s. It was closed for refurbishment at the time of research.

Hôtel La Forêt (☎ 655 302; s/d/ste TD105/150/230; 🍽) This newish four-star is 8km south of Ain Draham and has comfortable rooms with striking black-and-white tiling, and the inevitable great views. The suites have spa baths. An indoor pool is planned.

Eating

The possibilities for dining out are limited to a couple of basic places with little to choose between them. **Restaurant la Casa** has some outside tables and good sandwiches.

The **Hôtel Beauséjour** has the best restaurant in town, and a bar.

Getting There & Away

BUS

There are regular buses to Jendouba (TD2, one hour, seven daily) and Tabarka (TD1, 40 minutes, 11 daily), Le Kef (TD4, three hours, nine daily), Tunis (TD9.1, 4½ hours, four daily) and Hammam Bourguiba (TD1, two daily). Regular louages go to/from Tabarka and Jendouba, and occasionally Tunis, Beni Matir and Hammam Bourguiba.

LOUAGE

Louages leave from outside the bus station. There are regular services to Tabarka and Jendouba, and a few to Tunis.

NORTHERN TUNISIA

AROUND AIN DRAHAM
Hammam Bourguiba

حمّام بورقيبة

☎ 78

An enchanting winding drive through forested hills takes you to this resort village, 15km southwest of Ain Draham. In a small valley near the Algerian border, it feels on the edge of something and in the middle of nowhere. The hot springs here are renowned for their health benefits. There is a dirty but prettily located *hammam*, a hotel and a huge new hotel under construction. It was a favourite retreat of former president Habib Bourguiba.

SLEEPING

El Moradi (☎ 610 552; s/d TD47/74, full board TD52/84; 🕸) has accommodation in smart bungalows among landscaped gardens that are framed by beautiful countryside. There's a clinical feel – with white walls and staff in neo-nurse gear. The *hammam* (TD7) hot room is a muscle-melting blast, and there are lots of reasonably priced massage, rheumatism and respiratory treatments (some of which involve comic tubes up noses).

GETTING THERE & AWAY

To get there, take the road that leads to the Algerian border from Babouch and turn left after about 1km. There are two daily buses from Ain Draham (TD1), or you can take a taxi (TD5). There are also infrequent louages.

Beni Metir

بني مطير

The village of Beni Metir, 10km southeast of Ain Draham down a winding road, feels French as a baguette, with red-roofed houses in among the trees, sloping down to the lake. The village centres around a small crossroads, with a quaint mosque the main sign that you're in Tunisia. Beni Matir was built by the French in the 1950s to house the workers who constructed the dam that is the reason for the village's existence. Once work was completed, the village was handed over to the locals.

The area is popular with families at weekends. The large lake created by the dam is surrounded by forest.

There's a 60-bed **maison de jeunes** (dm TD5, full board TD15). Built by the French, this is a friendly, clean place; there is also a house to rent that sleeps 10.

Public transport is restricted to occasional louages or *camionnettes* – ask around at the bus station in Ain Draham or outside the *maison des jeunes* in Beni Metir. Or you can take a taxi from Ain Draham (TD6).

BÉJA

☎ 78 / pop 56,400

Not many tourists make it to Béja, a solid small town set in curvaceous grain hills, but

---

KILLING FIELDS

The painful progress of WWII's North African campaign is marked by Tunisia's military cemeteries. Axis forces landed in Tunisia in November 1942 to counter the Allied armies based in Morocco. Conditions were difficult – it was cold and rainy, with long supply lines, and there was a stalemate until February. As the rains ceased, some movement began, and Axis forces finally surrendered on 12 May 1943.

Many of the cemeteries are the work of the Commonwealth Commission and are designed to evoke home. Native plants are used: geraniums and lawns provide a surprising, moving, immaculately maintained corner of British pastoral.

In all the war cemeteries, the headstones have an elegiac uniformity. When remains were identified, the headstone was marked with a name. Other remains were lost or not identified, and this horror is underlined by the numerous anonymous stones. Most who lost their lives were in their early 20s.

The largest Commonwealth cemetery is 3km outside Medjez el-Bab, where a shocking 2906 soldiers are buried in a simple field neatly decked in geraniums: the birdsong in the surrounding trees seems appropriately haunting and chaotic. There are others at Béja (see p130), Massicault, Ras Rajal, Oued Zarga, Thibar, Enfida and Sfax. The American Military Cemetery at Carthage commemorates US soldiers (see p88). There are French cemeteries at Enfida and Gammarth (see p92) and a German cemetery at Borj Cedria.

it's worth a short stop, with a whitewashed and tiled medina, some interesting religious buildings and a small war cemetery. The main road from Jendouba, ave Bourguiba, leads to the main central square, place du 7 Novembre. Walking north of here, up rue Khereddine, you'll enter the medina and reach the **Great Mosque** with its terracotta-coloured minaret. Slightly further north is the fishscale dome of the **Zaouia of Sidi Abdel Kader**. Working your way east through the medina's narrow streets, on the outskirts is the **shrine of Marabout Sidi Boutef Faha**. Inside you can see henna handprints left prior to circumcision and marriage ceremonies. Northeast of here is the **Commonwealth War Cemetery**, a chillingly neat field of 394 graves, contrasting with the wildly overgrown colonial cemetery next door.

Hôtel Phenix (☎ 450 188; 37 ave de la République; d TD30) is southeast of place de 7 Novembre, with big bright rooms. The front ones are best, with little balconies over the street. The **restaurant** (starters TD2.5-7, mains TD7.5-11) is recommended.

There are good connections from here. The train station is on ave Habib Thameur, with the bus station behind it. Louages stop just off ave Bourguiba, but pick up from ave M'Ben Kahla. They regularly serve Tebersouk (TD2.3, 45 minutes) and Medjez el-Bab (TD1.2, 45 minutes).

BULLA REGIA بولّا عيعيا

The only example of a subterranean classical city, this remarkable **Roman site** (admission TD1.6, plus camera TD1; ☼ 7am-7pm Apr-Sep, 8.30am-5.30pm Oct-Mar), 9km north of Jendouba, is famous for its extraordinary underground villas, which echo the troglodyte Berber homes at Matmata. To escape the summer heat, the ever-inventive Romans retreated below the surface, but these are no burrows; they're extensive, elegant homes of the moneyed, complete with colonnaded courtyards. They're named according to their mosaic subjects: some stunning works have been removed to the Bardo Museum (p56) in Tunis, but many remain in place. For once it's a chance to walk into a complete Roman room, rather than trying to imagine one from ankle-high walls.

History

The dolmens (Neolithic tombs) that dot the surrounding hills show that the area was inhabited long before the Romans arrived. The town of Bulla emerged in about the 5th century BC as part of Carthage's move to develop the Medjerda Valley as a wheat-growing area. 'Regia' was added later when it became the capital of one of the short-lived Numidian kingdoms tolerated by Rome following the destruction of Carthage.

The town flourished under Roman rule, with its citizens growing rich on wheat – and making sure their neighbours knew it through grand constructions. It reached the peak of its prosperity in the 2nd and 3rd centuries AD, and most of the site's buildings belong to that era.

Bulla Regia was subsequently occupied by the Byzantines, who added their inevitable fort, but it was abandoned after the Arab conquest in the 7th century.

Sights

It's a most evocative experience to wander through these silent structures. You can start at the small museum, which supplies some background.

Just to the right of the site entrance are the **Memmian Baths**, named after Julia Memmia, wife of Emperor Septimius Severus. The most extensive of the remaining aboveground buildings, its walls are impressively high, with rooms surrounded by arched service areas – a reminder of the slaves keeping such baths going.

Walking northwards, you will reach the first of the underground villas – the city's wealthy quarter. Seven have been excavated, and several others remain unexplored. The villas vary in their level of sophistication, but are all built to the same basic plan. Above ground, they would have resembled any contemporary Roman villa. The surface structures were built around a central courtyard, open to the sky, below which lay underground rooms.

The first is the small **House of Treasure**, named after a store of Byzantine coins discovered here. You can feel the drop in temperature as you descend underground. A large dining room is decorated with a geometrically patterned mosaic and next door is a bedroom.

Continuing north above ground, you pass some Byzantine churches, with some columns as well as a walk-in cross-shaped baptistery font. North of here is the next

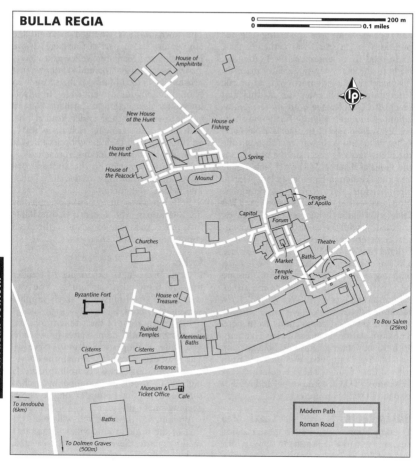

BULLA REGIA

0 ——— 200 m
0 ——— 0.1 miles

House of
Amphitrite

New House
of the Hunt

House of
Fishing

House of
the Hunt

Spring

House of
the Peacock

Mound

Temple
of Apollo

Capitol

Forum

Churches

Theatre

Market

Baths

Temple
of Isis

Byzantine Fort

House of
Treasure

To Bou Salem
(25km)

Ruined
Temples

Memmian
Baths

Cisterns

Cisterns

Entrance

Museum &
Ticket Office

Cafe

To Jendouba
(6km)

Baths

Modern Path
Roman Road

To Dolmen Graves
(500m)

subterranean villa – the rather unloved-feeling **House of the Peacock** – named after a mosaic that's now in the Bardo.

Across the road is the incredibly complex **House of the Hunt**. This is centred on an underground eight-pillared colonnaded hall – seemingly decorative hexagonal holes at the top cleverly reduce the weight of the structure. Off this courtyard is a huge mosaic-floored dining room, an indication of the inhabitants' entertaining lifestyle. Upstairs are some typically neat latrines side by side, next to the building's private *hammam* – this homestead was really state of the art.

Next door, the hunting mosaic has been left in situ at the **New House of the Hunt**. Large

chunks are missing, but there's still plenty left to view, including the obligatory lion hunt. Underground is a five-column hall with a swirling geometric floor.

From here take the path north and descend into the **House of Amphitrite**. The mosaic in here is exquisite – a perfectly preserved portrait of Venus flanked by two centaurs, one shocked (having his hair tugged), the other quizzical. At the base are some lively cupids riding dolphins – one of them is checking himself out in a mirror at the same time. Leaping fish add to the vibrancy and balance of the piece.

Heading south from here you reach the **House of Fishing**, the earliest of the villas. This had a fountain in the basement, and a small room contains a mosaic on the eponymous fishing theme. After this, you'll pass on your left the spring that once supplied the ancient city with water – and still delivers its cool waters to nearby Jendouba. Take the path leading west – you will pass a small mound that's worth climbing to the top for a fine panorama.

From here, retrace your steps south then take the path leading east to the **forum**, surrounded by the ruins of two temples – the **capitol** to the west and the **Temple of Apollo** to the north. This yielded the truly godlike statue of Apollo displayed at the Bardo, among others.

Just south of here is the marketplace, and a little further down there is a small but beautifully preserved **theatre** with a large mosaic of a not-very-fierce bear. The seating here is in particularly good condition. Note that the front three tiers are extra wide and separated from the rest by the remains of a low wall – VIP seating. Southwest are the remains of a small **Temple of Isis**, in honour of the Egyptian goddess, who was a fashionable addition to the Roman pantheon.

The hill behind the museum is covered with Neolithic tombs and is worth a stroll.

Getting There & Away
The turn-off to Bulla Regia is 6km north of Jendouba on the road to Ain Draham. Any bus or louage travelling between the two can drop you off here. Hitching along the 3km from the turn-off to Bulla Regia is easy enough, but it's also a pleasant walk if it's not too hot.

Most people visit the site from Jendouba. A taxi costs about TD3.5 (TD0.5 if shared).

JENDOUBA   جندوبة
☎ 78 / pop 44,700
The sedate regional centre of Jendouba, 153km west of Tunis, is regarded by most as pretty dull, but it has a gentle feel, comes alive somewhat in the early evening, and it's hard to avoid if you want to visit Bulla Regia. It's an important transport hub.

Orientation & Information
Most important things are around the central square, including the post office, banks (including STB with an ATM), supermarket, train station and police station.

The bus and louage stations are at the major roundabout on the western side of town. To get there, follow the main street (ave Hedi Chaker) west from the central square for about 500m. The roundabout is at the intersection of the roads going north to Ain Draham, northeast to Tunis (bypassing the city centre), south to Le Kef and west to Ghardimao.

Sleeping & Eating
The best plan is to time your comings and goings so you don't need to stay overnight, but there are a few options.

Hôtel Atlas (☎ 603 217; rue 1 Juin 1955; s/d TD18/25) Just off the central square behind the police station, this has simple, formica-filled rooms, a lively public bar and a quieter one for residents. The set menu costs TD8.

Hôtel Simitthu (☎ 604 043; blvd 9 April 1938; s/d TD24/32) Opposite the SRN Jendouba bus station at the roundabout, this is a clean, modern two-star hotel, with traditional rooms and a good restaurant (set menu TD10).

There are a several small restaurants and *rôtisseries* around the central square, or you can eat at the hotel restaurants.

Getting There & Away
Jendouba is an important regional transport hub with good links to all the major centres of the north.

BUS
SNTRI has buses to/from Tunis (TD6.5 to TD7.5, four hours, six daily). SRN Jendouba has buses to/from Tabarka (TD2.8, 1¾ hours, 11 daily) via Ain Draham, Ghardimao (TD1.35, 40 minutes, two daily summer and six daily winter) and Le Kef (TD 2.3, 1½ hours, 10 daily). To get to Bulla Regia, take any bus going to Ain Draham and ask to be let out at the turn-off, or take a taxi (TD3 or TD1 if shared).

LOUAGE
Louages leave from by the bus station. The main destinations are Ain Draham, Ghardimao, Le Kef, Tabarka and Tunis.

TRAIN
If you're travelling to Tunis, the train is the way to go. There are around five departures daily, the first at 5.20am and the last at 5.30pm (2nd/1st TD5.85/7.35, 2¾ hours).

CHEMTOU شمتو

Chemtou is a unique Roman site. Its quarries were the source of an unusual pink-veined yellow marble that was prized throughout the Roman world as the exotic stone that most resembled gold.

The ancient quarries are great yellow streaky hollowed-out hills, set in timeless rolling pastoral. The work that went into carving out and transporting the huge blocks of stone is a daunting thought. The site is brought to life by the excellent museum.

History

The site, on the Oued Medjerda's northern bank, was originally the Numidian settlement of Simitthu. Its marble was used to construct the celebrated Monument of Micipsa at Cirta (modern Constantine in Algeria) in 130 BC.

The region came under Roman control after the battle of Thapsus in 46 BC, when Caesar defeated the combined forces of Pompey and the last Numidian king, Juba I. Its marble became *the* material to indicate Roman superiority – not only was it golden, but it expressed the empire's domination over exotic lands. After Caesar's assassination, a 6m Chemtou column was erected in his honour in Rome's forum.

The Roman settlement was founded during the reign of Augustus (27 BC–AD 16) and due to the marble craze, it quickly developed into an important town. The quarrying operation here was said to be the most sophisticated in the Roman world. Each block of marble carried the stamp of the emperor of the day, that of the proconsul for Africa and the quarry supervisor, and a reference mark. The workers were slaves – contemporary convicts either got sentenced to be torn apart by wild beasts at the amphitheatre or work in the mines or quarries, which gives an idea of how much fun the work was.

Initially, the blocks were hauled to the Oued Medjerda on rollers and floated downstream to the port of Utica on barges. By the beginning of the 2nd century, rising levels of silt had all but closed the river to barge traffic, obliging the Romans to build a special road across the Kroumirie Mountains to link the quarries with the port of Thabraca (Tabarka).

The quarries were worked until Byzantine times, but were abandoned following the 7th-century Arab invasion.

Sights

The **site** (admission TD2.1, plus camera TD1; ⏲ 8am-7pm May-Sep, 8.30am-5.30pm Oct-Apr) sprawls over a wide area, sandwiched between the Medjerda and a band of low hills that were the source of the town's marble wealth.

Despite the town's proximity to the river, water was brought to the town by aqueduct from a spring in the hills 30km to the north. If you arrive from the north, the first ruins you see are the remains of this aqueduct advancing across the land. The aqueduct ends at the ruins of the old **baths**, on the right of the entrance road. The road continues past a somewhat better-preserved Roman **theatre** and stops outside the museum and ticket office.

This excellent **museum** is the star attraction, and the best place to start your visit. Built with German assistance, it displays finds unearthed by a German/Tunisian team which has been excavating the site since 1992. Labelling is in Arabic, French and German, but the layout is clear enough to get the gist even if you can't read any of these. As well as a comprehensive explanation of the site and the quarrying operation, it has re-creations of the Monument of Micipsa, a section on Numidian history and a working model of the ancient flour mill that once stood on the river banks. It's interesting to see how the Romans used stone as propaganda.

One of the most dramatic finds at the site was a haul of 1648 gold coins that are pictured here (they're kept in a bank vault), showing the town's sometime wealth. It seems that they were buried before the Vandal invasion.

The museum flanks a small excavated section of **Roman road**. Excavations elsewhere have concentrated on the nearby **forum**, and have revealed that it was built on the foundations of a Numidian temple.

The site is quite spread out, so it's good to drive or get your taxi to shift you between points of interest. The land's quite rough so it's advisable to wear trainers.

The **quarries**, three in all, are opposite the museum. They are impressive, daunting holes, visible from far away, like bites out of the hills. The warm colour of the rock is striped and makes for beautiful walls; a spooky low shaft leads off them.

A path leads up to the ruins of a **temple** on top of the easternmost hill. It was originally a Numidian site before being converted first into a temple to Saturn by the Romans and then a Byzantine church.

Check out the remains of a **Roman bridge** over the Medjerda just downstream from the modern ford crossing. Judging by the massive piers, the Romans took the river more seriously than locals do today. Downstream from the bridge are the ruins of a **mill**.

Getting There & Away

There is no public transport to the site. The easiest solution is to strike a deal with a taxi driver in Jendouba or Ghardimao. Reckon on paying about TD20 to get there and back, with a couple of hours at the site.

If your budget doesn't stretch to chartered taxis, you can catch any bus or louage travelling between Jendouba and Ghardimao and ask to be dropped at the Chemtou turn-off, just east of the village of Oued Melliz. That will leave you with a 3km walk. The only problem is that you will have to ford the Oued Medjerda. The flow is not much more than a trickle for most of the year, but it can become a mighty torrent after winter rains.

If you have your own vehicle, the approach is via the C59 loop road that runs north of the Oued Medjerda. This road begins at the Bulla Regia junction north of Jendouba and emerges just west of Ghardi-mao. Chemtou is clearly signposted from the Bulla Regia end.

GHARDIMAO خارديماو

☎ 78 / pop 19,400

Ghardimao has an almost appealingly dead-end feel, with a brooding, still atmosphere that in a Western movie would precede a shoot out. It really is the end of the line, especially since the suspension of the Al-Maghreb al-Arabi (Trans Maghreb Express) train service that once linked Tunisia with Morocco via Algeria.

The countryside around is beautiful, tempered by the tension of the frontier. There's a forest-filled national park 20km away, near the border, that's certainly off the beaten track.

If you get stuck here there is only one place in town, **Hôtel Tebornik** (☎ 660 043; s/d with shared bathroom TD7/14, with private bathroom TD10/20), opposite the train station in the middle of town. Half the letters on the hotel sign have fallen off, reflecting a general air of dereliction, but the rooms are reasonable, some with balconies. The **restaurant** (starters TD1-1.5, mains TD3) is surprisingly good. The hotel also has the only bar in town, a popular local bolthole.

Getting There & Away

Trains go to/from Tunis (3¼ hours, four daily) via Jendouba (25 minutes) between 5.30am and 4.30pm. Buses and louages leave from next to the railway line, about 200m towards Jendouba from the station. Jendouba is the main destination. There is one direct bus a day to Tunis (TD8, 3¾ hours).

Central West & the Tell

Tunisia's Central West provides a fantastic opportunity for visitors to get away from the coastal crowds. The Tell, which covers the high plains of the Tunisian Dorsale, was the granary of ancient Rome, and the Romans bequeathed to this region the greatest concentration of ancient cities in Tunisia, which are now in ruins but filled with countless signposts to a prosperous past.

Dougga is the undoubted highlight with a setting unlike any other city of ancient Rome, overlooking the plains and devoid of the uniformity which characterised most other Roman cities. Sufetula (Sbeitla) is also spectacular, and this scarcely visited site captures the sense of a Roman frontier town; it is especially magical in the early-morning light.

The other Roman cities of Mactaris and Haidra evocatively convey the sense of abandonment and isolation that the remote Roman outposts left behind, providing a poignant counterpoint to a bleak, eroding landscape whose most fertile and forested days have long passed. As you cross these plains, the landscape tells the story – a lonely, sense of being left behind by history with stunning reminders of a glorious past.

Not far away, Jugurtha's Table is a beautiful, remote and historically significant site where Berber resistance to Roman rule enjoyed its proudest hour before being swept away.

Perhaps even more enchanting than all of these, charming Le Kef captures the spirit of this part of Tunisia – rarely visited but with a feel unlike any other place in the country. With its cobbled streets, cafés that time forgot and stunning setting, it should be on every visitor's itinerary and could just be Tunisia's best-kept secret.

HIGHLIGHTS

- Seeing **Roman temples** (p152) at Sbeitla, magical in the early morning light
- Discovering **Jugurtha's Table** (p157), a remote and spectacular natural fortress
- Soaking up glorious golden **Dougga** (p138), Tunisia's most spectacular Roman site
- Chilling in **Le Kef** (p142), a seldom-visited hilltop town with attitude and atmosphere

★ Dougga
★ Le Kef
★ Jugurtha's Table
★ Sbeitla

History

After Rome defeated Carthage in the 2nd century BC, the hinterland of its new African provinces was largely left to the Berber tribes of the interior, most notably the Numidians who accommodated Roman rule even as they rebelled against it. The final Berber resistance came at Jugurtha's Table, the legendary stronghold and scene of Numidian king Jugurtha's last stand at the end of the 2nd century BC. Roman towns then grew prosperous on the proceeds of agricultural production and as staging posts along lucrative trade routes. After the Roman departure, the area slid into obscurity.

Climate

This desolate terrain briefly comes to life in spring with spectacular displays of wildflowers. The summers are impossibly hot, whereas the winters are cold and bleak.

Getting There & Away

Most towns, even the smallest in the Tell, have at least one daily bus to Tunis. Le Kef

and Dougga are much better served with connections elsewhere.

Getting Around

This is one of the more time-consuming places to get around in Tunisia. Louages (shared taxis) are quite plentiful, but few go very far, involving considerable time hopping on and off transport. It's difficult to visit Haidra and Jugurtha's Table without your own transport.

DOUGGA   دقة

The ancient site of **Dougga** (admission TD2.1, plus camera TD1; ⊙ 8am-7pm Apr-Sep, 8.30am-5.30pm Oct-Mar) is a Roman city with a view. Built of golden stone, it mirrors the cornfield and ochre landscape of the Kalled Valley and Tebersouk Mountains. The remains are startlingly complete, giving a beguiling glimpse of how Romans lived their lives, flitting between the baths, the theatre, and temples (21 have been identified). One of the most magnificent Roman monuments in Africa, its mighty capitol, surges up from the site.

The theatre has been extensively renovated, and is a superb setting for classical drama during the Dougga Festival in July and August. Travel agencies in Tunis and major resort areas organise festival excursions.

The city was built on the site of ancient Thugga, a Numidian settlement, which explains why the streets are so uncharacteristically tangled. The 2nd-century BC Libyo-Punic Mausoleum is the country's finest pre-Roman monument.

The best time to visit is early morning, or late in the day – ideally when the summer dusk is flooding the stone and the site is almost deserted.

Trainers are good for the old Roman roads and rough paths that crisscross the site. There's not much shade, so in summer you'll need a hat, sunscreen and water. There's a café selling snacks, but it's a magical setting for a picnic.

History

This prime site, with natural springs, has been occupied since the 2nd millennium BC, judging by the dolmen graves on the ridge above the ruins.

It was already a substantial settlement by the time Carthage advanced into the

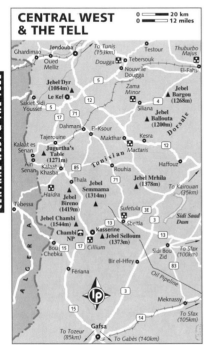

DOUGGA

0 _____ 100 m
0 _____ 0.1 miles

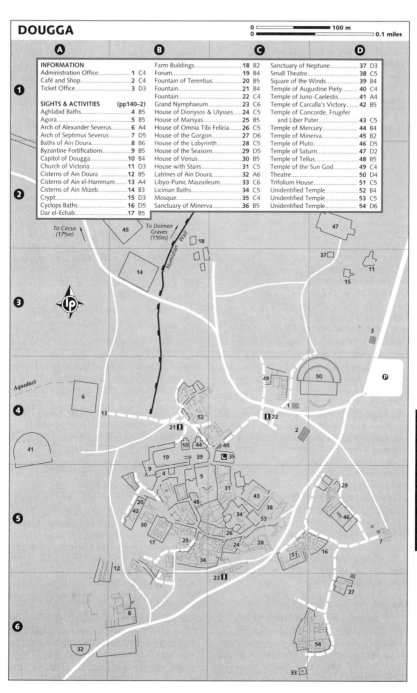

INFORMATION
Administration Office.................. 1 C4
Café and Shop............................ 2 C4
Ticket Office.............................. 3 D3

SIGHTS & ACTIVITIES   (pp140–2)
Aghlabid Baths........................... 4 B5
Agora.. 5 B5
Arch of Alexander Severus.......... 6 A4
Arch of Septimus Severus........... 7 D5
Baths of Ain Doura..................... 8 B6
Byzantine Fortifications.............. 9 B5
Capitol of Dougga..................... 10 B4
Church of Victoria..................... 11 D3
Cisterns of Ain Doura 12 B5
Cisterns of Ain el-Hammam....... 13 A4
Cisterns of Ain Mizeb............... 14 B3
Crypt....................................... 15 D3
Cyclops Baths........................... 16 D5
Dar el-Echab............................ 17 B5

Farm Buildings......................... 18 B2
Forum...................................... 19 B4
Fountain of Terentius................ 20 B5
Fountain.................................. 21 B4
Fountain.................................. 22 C4
Grand Nymphaeum................... 23 C6
House of Dionysos & Ulysses..... 24 C5
House of Marsyas...................... 25 B5
House of Omnia Tibi Felicia....... 26 C5
House of the Gorgon................. 27 D6
House of the Labyrinth.............. 28 C5
House of the Seasons................ 29 D5
House of Venus......................... 30 B5
House with Stairs...................... 31 D3
Latrines of Ain Doura................ 32 A6
Libyo-Punic Mausoleum............ 33 C6
Licinian Baths.......................... 34 C5
Mosque................................... 35 C4
Sanctuary of Minerva................ 36 B5

Sanctuary of Neptune............... 37 D3
Small Theatre........................... 38 C5
Square of the Winds.................. 39 B4
Temple of Augustine Piety......... 40 C4
Temple of Carcalla's Victory....... 42 B5
Temple of Concorde, Frugifer
     and Liber Pater.................... 43 C5
Temple of Juno-Caelestis........... 41 A4
Temple of Mercury................... 44 B4
Temple of Minerva.................... 45 B2
Temple of Pluto....................... 46 D5
Temple of Saturn...................... 47 D2
Temple of Tellus....................... 48 B5
Temple of the Sun God.............. 49 C4
Theatre.................................... 50 D4
Trifolium House........................ 51 C5
Unidentified Temple.................. 52 B4
Unidentified Temple.................. 53 C5
Unidentified Temple.................. 54 D6

To Circus
(175m)

To Dolmen
Graves
(150m)

Numidian Wall

Aqueduct

CENTRAL WEST & THE TELL

HIGHLIGHTS

It will take you at least three hours to explore the site properly, though you could do a cursory tour in about an hour if you are really pushed. The following is a list of must-see sights:

- Theatre – drama with a view; this was built to hold 3500 spectators
- Capitol – Africa's most magnificent Roman edifice
- Licinian Baths – a complex worthy of the site's prosperity
- Libyo-Punic Mausoleum – a rare and spectacular 21m-high 2nd-century BC monument

---

interior in the 4th century BC. The town stayed under Carthaginian control throughout the 3rd century BC, but became part of the kingdom of the Numidian king Massinissa at the end of the Second Punic War.

Thugga lay outside the boundaries of the first Roman province of Africa, which was created after the destruction of Carthage in 146 BC, and remained a Numidian town until 46 BC – when the last Numidian king, Juba 1, backed the wrong side (Pompey) in the Roman Civil War.

Thugga became Dougga, part of the expanded province of Africa Nova, and the slow process of Romanisation began. Dougga's prosperity peaked between the 2nd and 4th centuries when it was home to an estimated 5000 people.

The town declined during the Vandal occupation, and the population had all but disappeared by the time the Byzantines arrived in AD 533 and set about remodelling Dougga as a fort. The ruins of an Aghlabid bathhouse, east of the capitol, show that the site was still inhabited in the 10th century.

People continued to live among the ruins until the early 1950s when the inhabitants were moved to Nouvelle Dougga.

Sights

It will take three to four hours to take in the highlights, beginning and ending at the Tebersouk entrance. If time is short, you could skip the northern part north of the theatre – although it's a shame to miss the glorious views from the Temple of Saturn.

THEATRE

The amazing **theatre** is nestled into the hillside to the west of the car park. Built in AD 188 by one of the city's wealthy residents, Marcus Quadratus, its 19 tiers could accommodate an audience of 3500. The theatre has been extensively renovated, and is a superb setting for classical drama during the Dougga Festival in July and August. Travel agencies in Tunis and major resort areas organise festival excursions.

From the theatre, head south and follow the Roman road that leads downhill towards the capitol, passing the ruins of a small **fountain**. The road emerges at the **Square of the Winds**, bounded by temples and named after the large circular engraving by the capitol listing the names of the 12 winds. You can make out some of the names, including Africanus (the sirocco). The square's function is unclear, but it was probably a marketplace, used in conjunction with the **agora** to the south.

TEMPLES

The town is dominated by the imposing hilltop **Capitol of Dougga** (AD 166), a monument that makes you feel as if you've shrunk. It's in remarkable condition, with 10m-high walls, and six mighty, show-off fluted columns supporting the portico. The massive walls are the finest known example of a construction technique called *opus africanum*, which uses large boulders to strengthen walls built of rubble.

The walls enclose the temple's inner sanctum. The three large niches in the north wall once housed a giant statue of Jupiter (his oversized head and sandalled foot are in the Bardo Museum in Tunis) flanked by smaller statues of Juno and Minerva. The carved frieze shows the emperor Antonius Pius being carried off in an eagle's claws, with an inscription dedicating the temple to the gods Jupiter, Juno and Minerva.

The Byzantines were responsible for the fortifications that enclose the capitol and the **forum**, built on the orders of the General Solomon, and constructed using stones filched from surrounding buildings. Look out for the stones bearing the dedication from the **Temple of Mercury**, which have wound up at knee height on the eastern wall, facing the Square of the Winds.

The Temple of Mercury's meagre remains are to the north of the square. To the east are four square pillars belonging to the tiny 2nd-century **Temple of Augustine Piety**. The small stone **mosque** next door stands on the rectangular base of a former Temple of Venus.

BATHS

If you head south along the path running past the **House with Stairs**, so called because of the many stairs, you reach a large but poorly preserved temple complex dedicated to **Concorde**, **Frugifer** and **Liber Pater**. Beyond is a **small theatre** facing southeast towards the valley. It's alongside the **Licinian Baths**, their size further indication of the town's prosperity. The walls of this extensive complex remain largely intact, particularly those surrounding the grand central *frigidarium* (cold room). A tunnel for the slaves, who kept the baths operating, is a reminder of how all this good life was maintained.

Heading east, and straight ahead over the staggered crossroads, you come across an unusual solid square doorframe to the south. It marks the entrance to an unidentified temple referred to as **Dar el-Echab** after the family who once occupied the site. Carry on past Dar el-Echab, and then head south. The route turns into a rough path that winds downhill past the ruined **Cisterns of Ain Doura** to the **Baths of Ain Doura**, the city's main summer baths.

If you head back uphill from here along the dirt road that crosses the site, you'll pass the **grand nymphaeum** on the left. This huge, partly restored fountain is thought to have been supplied with water by an underground conduit from the Cisterns of Ain el-Hammam, 300m northwest.

Continue along the road for another 75m, then turn right, descending the steps leading to **Trifolium House**. This is believed to have been the town brothel – the discreet name was inspired by the small clover-leaf-shaped room in the northwestern corner of the house.

Next door are the **Cyclops Baths**, named after the remarkable mosaic found here (now in the Bardo). The baths themselves are in disrepair, except for the sociably horseshoe-shaped row of 12 latrines just inside the entrance.

ARCH OF SEPTIMIUS SEVERUS

From here you can head east along the paved Roman road that leads downhill to the ruins of the **Arch of Septimius Severus**, built in AD 205 to honour Rome's first African-born emperor.

Turn right before the arch and follow the path that winds south past the **House of the Gorgon** to the **Libyo-Punic Mausoleum**. This triple-tiered monument stands an amazing 21m high, crowned by a small pyramid with a seated lion at the pinnacle. It was built during the reign of Massinissa at the beginning of the 2nd century BC. It is dedicated, according to a bilingual (Libyan and Punic) inscription, to 'Ateban, son of Ypmatat, son of Palu'. The inscription once occupied the vacant window at the base. It was removed by the British consul to Tunis in 1842, who destroyed the rest of the monument in the process. The stone was taken to England (where it is now in the British Museum), although the monument was rebuilt by French archaeologists in 1910.

Retrace your steps towards the Arch of Septimius Severus and then head north past the scant ruins of the **Temple of Pluto** and **House of the Seasons**. Cross the dirt road and climb the steps leading to a welcome café.

From here you can cut across the site to the well-preserved **Arch of Alexander Severus**, built between AD 222 and 235 to mark the city's western entrance. A path leads southwest from here through olive trees to the roughly contemporary **Temple of Juno-Caelestis**, dedicated to the Roman version of the Carthaginian god Tanit. Its construction was funded by a resident, who was made a *flamen* (a Roman priest) in AD 222. It was adapted as a church in the 5th century. The pillar-surrounded sanctuary retains an impressive portico, and is reached via a flight of steps.

CISTERNS

Immediately west of the Arch of Alexander Severus are the cavernous **Cisterns of Ain el-Hammam**, added during the reign of aptly named Commodius (AD 180–192) to meet the city's growing demand for water. They were supplied via **aqueduct** from springs 12km to the southwest. Sections are visible among the olive trees west of the cisterns.

A rough path leads north through the trees from here, emerging after 150m in front of the nine **Cisterns of Ain Mizeb**. These were the city's main water supply, fed by a spring some 200m to the west. They remain in excellent condition and are used for storage by the site authorities.

Follow the dirt road that leads northwest, and then cut across the fields to the **Temple of Minerva**. Looking northwest of here it's possible to discern the outline of the **circus**, now an elongated wheat field filling a saddle between two hills.

Turn right and aim for the rocky ridge to the northeast, which is dotted with dozens of primitive **dolmen graves**. These are just north of the so-called **Numidian Wall**, which protected the city in pre-Roman days. Cross the wall and follow the paths that curve across the hill towards the **Temple of Saturn**.

This great temple must have been a magnificent sight after its completion in AD 195, but only six stunted columns remain. Built on a platform facing east over the valley of the Oued Kalled, it would have dominated the ancient city's northern approach. The temple stands on the site of an earlier temple to Baal-Hammon, the chief deity of the Punic pantheon adopted by the Numidians. Baal-Hammon became Saturn in Roman times, and was the favoured god of Roman Africa.

The reconstructed apse south of the temple is all that remains of the **Sanctuary of Neptune**.

The ruins of the Vandal **Church of Victoria**, on the slope east of the sanctuary, are the only evidence of Christianity at Dougga. The church was built in the early 5th century using stone pinched from the surrounding temples. The small **crypt**, next door, is packed with large stone sarcophagi, and retains the saint's relics.

From here, you can follow the path south to the theatre.

Getting There & Away

Dougga is 6km west of Tebersouk. Frequent buses or louages between Tunis and Le Kef stop at Tebersouk, and it's easy to visit the site on a day trip from either city – or en route between the two. You can leave your luggage at a local business. From Tebersouk, you can hire a *camionnette* (TD5) to take you there and back. If you're coming from Le Kef, you can get off the bus at the Nouvelle Dougga turn-off on the main road.

From here it's a 3km walk, but, again, locals will offer to take you there and pick you up later for TD5.

TEBERSOUK   تبرسوق
☎ 78 / pop 12,700

This small town has a fine setting high up in yellow-green hills. It's an attractive place, though there's nothing specific to see here. Market day is Thursday and a buzzing time to be in town.

You might want to stay overnight to get to the ruins at Dougga before the crowds arrive, or stay late after they've gone.

Hôtel Thugga (☎ 466 647; s/d TD29/42; 🏊) If you're gagging to get to the ruins early or stay there late, this overpriced two star is comfortable enough. The food in the restaurant is reasonable – there's an attractive terrace too. The hotel is about 2km out of town, down by the main Tunis–Le Kef road.

Getting There & Away

All SNTRI services operating between Tunis (TD5, 1¾ hours) and Le Kef (TD3, 1¼ hours) call in at Tebersouk, meaning that there are services in each direction roughly every hour. There are regular louages between here and Béja, Tunis and Le Kef, but they will stop running by about 7pm.

LE KEF
☎ 78 / pop 46,000

High in the hills, Le Kef (El Kef, Arabic for 'rock') feels enclosed and defensive, piled up the southern flank of Jebel Dyr (1084m) and topped by a storybook kasbah. It's only 45km from Algeria. The old city's made up of narrow, hilly, cobbled streets and blue-shuttered buildings, centred on a scoop of park, with stunning views across the mass of golden and green fields that spread out in all directions, with hills rising up like islands from the plains. The town still largely subsists on agriculture, and there's a feeling of killing time in the air. However, the town is one of Tunisia's best-kept secrets, with its views, honey-coloured walls, winding narrow alleys, and sense of community. It's cold in winter, and oven-hot in the summer.

History

The first town on this strategic site was known as Sicca, established in about 500 BC

LE KEF

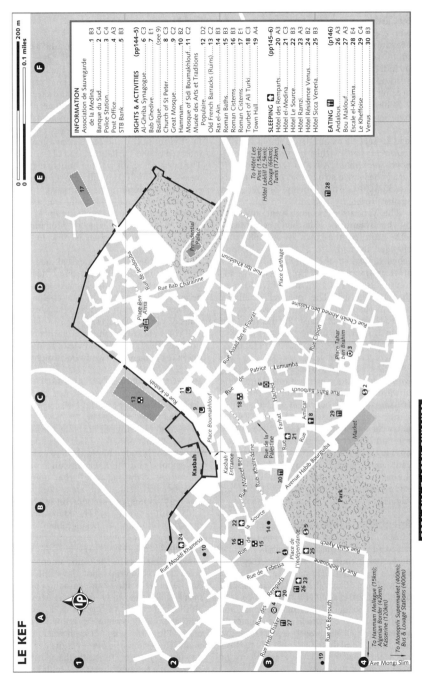

by Carthage to protect the west of its newly won empire. It was known for the temple prostitutes who hung out at its sanctuary to the goddess Astarte, whose portfolio included love. In Roman times, the sanctuary was dedicated to Venus, and the town became Sicca Veneria.

When Carthage couldn't pay its mercenaries, they were sent here and rose in revolt, whereupon more mercenaries were sent to sort them out, triggering a horrific four-year battle (this inspired Flaubert's novel *Salammbô*). After the fall of Carthage, Le Kef became a stronghold of the Numidian king, Jugurtha, during his rebellion against Rome.

The Vandals came and went, followed by the Byzantines and then the Arabs – who captured the town in AD 688 and changed its name to Shaqbanaria. Locals rebelled against the central government at every opportunity before becoming autonomous after the Hilalian invasions of the 11th century. The town fell briefly to the Almohads in 1159, but soon returned to its independent ways. By the time the Ottomans arrived in the 16th century, the region had become the private fiefdom of the Beni Cherif tribe.

Le Kef prospered under the Ottomans, who rebuilt its fortifications, and this upward spiral continued under the beys. Hussein ben Ali, who founded the Husseinite line of beys, was born here.

Under the French, it retained its military role, but the colonial power concentrated on the agricultural plains to Kef's disadvantage. However, during WWII, it was the provisional capital. Its significant situation has made it party to struggles within Algeria.

Orientation & Information

Most things of importance to travellers are found near place de l'Indépendance, below the kasbah in the town centre. The exceptions are the bus and louage stations, side by side on ave Mongi Slim, about a 15-minute walk downhill from place de l'Indépendance.

There is no tourist information centre, but try the staff at the **Association de Sauvegarde de la Medina** (☎ 201 148; place de l'Indépendance) or the museum (see Sights). The post office is on rue Hedi Chaker, and there are plenty of banks around the centre.

Sights
KASBAH
The grand crenellated crown of the **kasbah** (◷ 8am-5pm) dominates the city. The main draw is the great views across the city and the rolling blue, green and gold landscape. A fort of some sort has occupied the site since the 5th century BC; today's edifice represents 2500 years of constant remodelling by a succession of owners. It was built by the Byzantines in the 6th century, and reinforced by the Turks at the end of the 16th. The latest occupant was the Tunisian army, based here until 1992. It left its exercise equipment behind in the courtyard.

A second, smaller kasbah was added within the outer walls of the main kasbah in 1679, during the time of Mohammed Bey. This second kasbah is now in very poor condition.

The guardian appreciates baksheesh (a tip) for accompanying you around the main points of interest – the Turkish mosque, prison cells, a bronze cannon left behind by the Dey of Algiers in 1705, several gates and walls of various vintages.

If you walk around the small gardens outside the walls, you get great views across the town; it's a magical place to be at night.

MUSEUM OF ART & POPULAR TRADITIONS
The well-laid-out **Musée des Arts et Traditions Populaires** (admission TD1.1, plus camera TD1; ◷ 9.30am-4.30pm mid-Sep–May, 9am-1pm & 4-7pm Apr–mid-Sep) is housed in the beautiful former Zaouia of Sidi Ali ben Aissa dating from 1666. It's all whitewashed spaces and tall ceilings, and the museum concentrates on culture of the region's Berber nomads, complete with tent. There are also utensils, jewellery, looms and sections on medicine and traditional crafts. The staff are extremely helpful and knowledgeable.

MEDINA
The medina's principal monuments are around place Boumakhlouf, down the steps on the eastern side of the kasbah. The **Basilique** is also known as the Great Mosque, although it ceased to operate as a mosque long ago. No-one seems to know what its original function was – or even when it was built. The cruciform design indicates that its role was connected with the Christian church. It's thought that it was built by the

Byzantines in the 6th century, and was possibly a monastery. Converted into a mosque in the 8th century, after the Arab invasion, it's now a mini museum, filled with some local photographs and various carvings.

Next to the Great Mosque is the enchanting little **Mosque of Sidi Boumakhlouf**, with gleaming white cupolas surrounding an octagonal Ottoman minaret. The mosque was built at the beginning of the 17th century and named after the town's patron saint, who is buried next to the mosque along with his family. Just outside, a café occupies the steps in front of the mosque, and this tree-shaded square is bewitchingly pretty.

The **Tourbet of Ali Turki** (rue de Patrice Lumumba) houses the tomb of the father of Hussein ben Ali, founder of the Husseinite line of beys, who ruled Tunisia for 250 years (1705–1957) until independence.

The ancient **Al-Ghriba synagogue** (rue Farhat Hached), is at the heart of the former Jewish quarter, the Harah. Information about the history of the Harah is hard to find. Early 19th-century travellers reported finding a thriving Jewish community, and there is a sizeable Jewish cemetery east of the Presidential Palace. The synagogue is a curiosity, paying tribute to a vanished part of local culture. As well as the restored interior, there are fragments of newspapers and old manuscripts. The caretaker will let you in; you should give him a tip.

CHURCH OF ST PETER

The remains of this 4th-century church, also known as the Dar el-Kous, are on rue Amilcar just south of the synagogue. It contains a remarkably well-preserved apse that was added in Byzantine times. It's often locked.

RAS EL-AIN

The town owes its very existence to the Ras el-Ain spring, located in the heart of town on place de l'Indépendance. Its waters once supplied the huge Roman bath complex next door which was discovered during a recent archaeological dig. The spring also supplied the Roman cisterns, opposite the baths on the northern side of rue de la Source.

BAB GHEDIVE

Stepping through this preserved gate – the sole remaining door – is like a journey through the looking glass, from the city to the countryside. By the gate is a huge Roman underground cistern – a spooky, gloomy cavern that's popular with secret boozers after dark. Small red cliffs form a backdrop to the town – villagers walk down from here with their donkeys to collect water from the pump. Southeast of the cisterns is an old Christian cemetery, with wrought-iron grave decorations perhaps influenced by garden furniture, and cracked, uneven earth creepily reminiscent of Michael Jackson's *Thriller*. Further down towards the wall is a large Jewish cemetery with graves dating to Roman times.

Sleeping

Le Kef has a good array of budget accommodation and a couple of mid-range places.

BUDGET

Hôtel el-Medina (☎ 204 183, 18 rue Farhat Hached; s/d with shared bathroom TD10/15) Reliable and pretty clean, this is bang in the centre. It's cold in winter, hot in summer, but there are good views from the rooms at the back.

Hôtel Le Source (☎ 204 397; s/d TD15/25) Run by a real character, this place has some attractive rooms with balconies, though bathrooms are not always gleamingly clean. The best room has a private bathroom and is brilliantly tiled, with an elaborate stuccoed domed ceiling – it's the closest you'll get to bedding down in the Mosque of Sidi Boumakhlouf.

MID-RANGE

Hôtel-Résidence Venus (☎ 204 695; rue Mouldi Khamessi; s/d TD25/36) Nestled beneath the outer walls of the old kasbah, this is a small, friendly pension with comfortable rooms. It's the same management as Les Pins and if you ask nicely they'll let you use the pool there. The breakfast is good too.

Hôtel Ramzi (☎ 203 079; rue Hedi Chaker; s/d TD12.5/7) This has nice little clean and tiled rooms, and the restaurant is good too.

Hôtel Sicca Veneria (☎ 202 389; place de l'Indépendance; s/d TD22/36) The Sicca is very central, but the rooms are a bit drab, although some have balconies.

Hôtel Les Pins (☎ 204 021; s/d TD30/42; ⟦⟧) About 1.5km east on the road to Tunis, Les Pins is good value and lovely, clean and bright, with lots of colourful tiling, surrounding a courtyard pool. All rooms have nicely tiled bathrooms and some have good views.

Hôtel des Remparts (☎ 202 100; 5 rue des Remparts; s/d with shared bathroom TD16/30) On a quiet street with bright, fairly clean rooms, some with big windows. The restaurant serves beer.

Hôtel Leklil (☎ 204 747; s/d TD30/40; ✕) A new three-star hotel is in an old-fashioned-style building, with big terraces, and has a wonderful quiet setting amid trees out of town, but the windows don't make the most of the views.

Eating

Bou Maklouf (rue Hedi Chaker; dishes TD1-2) An excellent cheapie, very popular, with the town's best chicken and chips and a whole range of other specials, *lablabi* (soup) and so on, as well as salads.

Venus (☎ 200 355; rue Farhat Hached; starters TD2.5-3.5, mains TD5.5-11) Operated by the owners of the Résidence Venus, this has good food – lots of mixed grills and meat dishes – and the atmosphere of a low-lit, convivial bar. It's male dominated but not too raucous.

Andalous (rue Hedi Chaker; dishes TD1-3) This is a simple place with a good reputation, although the more squeamish might want to give the lamb's head a miss and go for the fish – there's a good fishmongers nearby.

Le Kheffoise (☎ 203 887; ave Habib Bourguiba; pizza TD2) This good, very clean little bakery and pizzeria has seating on a small interior balcony, and the pizzas are fine.

Escale el-Khaima (ave Habib Bourguiba; pizza TD2.5-5, dishes TD1-7; ✕ Apr-Oct) On the road heading out towards Dougga, there are several open-air cafés that overlook the endless plains. Escale el-Khaima is the best of the bunch – a fantastic setting and a busy evening option.

Getting There & Away

BUS

SNTRI has buses to/from Tunis (TD8, three hours, hourly), travelling via Nouvelle Dougga (TD3, one hour) and Tebersouk (TD3, 1¼ hours; change at either for Dougga).

There are buses to/from Jendouba (one hour, two daily), and occasional services to/from Kairouan (via Makthar), Kasserine and Tabarka.

LOUAGE

The louage station is next to the bus station. There are frequent louages to Tunis (TD7.5). Other destinations include Jen-douba, Kasserine and Makthar. There are no louages to Tebersouk.

AROUND LE KEF
Hammam Mellegue حمّام ملأق

At Hammam Mellegue, 15km west of Le Kef, you can have a real Roman bath, in a spectacular setting. The baths are hidden away at the base of a dramatic, sheer escarpment and hills with moss-green hardy trees, overlooking a broad sweep of the Oued Mellegue – a greenish-banked murky ochre river.

Although much of the 2nd-century complex now lies in ruins, the **caldarium** (hot room; TD1) is still used as a *hammam* (bathhouse). It's an extraordinary place that remains almost unchanged after more than 1800 years. A large timber door opens onto a cavernous, steam-filled, subterranean chamber, lit by skylights set into the arched ceiling. Stone steps lead down to a large pool fed by hot springs, with its slightly saline waters emerging from the ground at 50°C. People loll around in the shallow pool. There are separate male and female rooms for bathing.

GETTING THERE & AWAY

The turn-off to Hammam Mellegue is about 3km southwest of Le Kef, near the junction of the main roads to Tunis, Dahmani and Sakiet Sidi Youssef. If you're coming from Le Kef, follow the signs to Sakiet Sidi Youssef. The turn-off is opposite a military base on the edge of town. Look for a sign to the Forêts du Kef, above a distance marker to Hammam Mellegue (12km). Don't go wandering off the beaten track here – those skull-and-crossbone signs indicate that there are mines in the vicinity.

They are the only indication you're on the right track as the gravel road heads west across rolling wheat country. The first 10km is in good condition; the final 2km is dodgy as the road descends an escarpment to the Oued Mellegue. The road was passable (cautiously) in the smallest car.

THUBURBO MAJUS طبربو ماجوس

Roman **Thuburbo Majus** (admission TD2.1, plus camera TD1; ✕ 8.30am-5.30pm mid-Sep–Mar, 8am-7pm Apr–mid-Sep) has a prosperous, wealthy air, even in its ruinous state, still surrounded by the shimmering wheat fields that made its fortune. About 60km southwest of Tunis, near the small town of El-Fahs, it's a typical Roman provincial town, with a capitol designed to impress, baths, villas and cisterns. In the 2nd century the town had 10,000 inhabitants, the wealthiest of whom outdid each other with public buildings and fine mosaics – many of which are on display at the Bardo Museum in Tunis (see p56).

History

The town was here long before the Romans arrived – this ancient Berber settlement was one of the first to come under Carthaginian control during Carthage's drive to build an African empire in the 5th century BC. It remained loyal to Carthage until the bitter end that followed the conflict with Rome.

Forced to pay tribute after the fall of Carthage in 146 BC, it became something of a backwater until it was declared a municipality following a visit by the Emperor Hadrian in AD 128. The town soon developed into an important trading centre for local agricultural produce – oil, wheat and wine. Most of the buildings date from the second half of the 2nd century, although there was a second phase of construction at the end of the 4th century. By the 5th century the town was no more than a village.

Sights

CAPITOL & FORUM

The capitol dominates the site, raised high above the surrounding residential ruins on a giant stone platform, with four giant pillars of pink limestone marking the entrance to the temple. Built in AD 168, it is reached by a wide flight of stairs leading up from the forum to the southeast – there are great views from the top. The capitol was dedicated to two emperors, Marcus Aurelius and Commodus, and was under the protection of the ancient trinity of Jupiter, Minerva and Juno. The giant sandalled foot and head of an enormous statue of Jupiter, estimated to have stood 7.5m high, were found here. The oversized fragments now reside at the Bardo Museum in Tunis.

The ruins of a Byzantine **olive press** occupy the space beneath the capitol. As elsewhere,

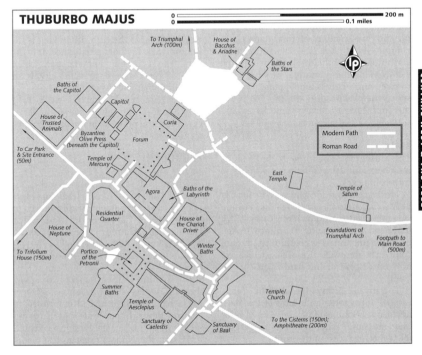

THUBURBO MAJUS

0 — 200 m
0 — 0.1 miles

To Triumphal Arch (100m)
House of Bacchus & Ariadne
Baths of the Stars
Baths of the Capitol
Capitol
House of Trussed Animals
Curia
Byzantine Olive Press (beneath the Capitol)
Forum
To Car Park & Site Entrance (50m)
Temple of Mercury
Modern Path
Roman Road
East Temple
Temple of Saturn
Agora
Baths of the Labyrinth
Residential Quarter
House of the Chariot Driver
House of Neptune
Foundations of Triumphal Arch
Footpath to Main Road (500m)
To Trifolium House (150m)
Portico of the Petronii
Winter Baths
Summer Baths
Temple of Aesclepius
Sanctuary of Caelestis
Sanctuary of Baal
Temple/ Church
To the Cisterns (150m); Amphitheatre (200m)

Byzantine builders showed themselves willing to adapt any available structure, cleverly making use of what was a bathing pool to catch oil.

The capital overlooks the forum, an essential feature of any Roman town. It was built in AD 161–2, so it predates the dominating capital. It is colonnaded on three sides; the columns were erected in 182 BC.

TEMPLE OF MERCURY, MARKET & HOUSE OF NEPTUNE

The Temple of Mercury, on the southwestern side of the forum, abuts the market – Mercury was the god of trade as well as messenger of the gods. It has an unusual circular design. The stalls of the market can be discerned on three sides of the courtyard below the temple. Directly behind the market is a very un-Roman tangle of residential streets, which were obviously in existence before the Romans arrived. Beyond is the spacious House of Neptune, where excavations are ongoing, with some impressive geometric-patterned mosaics.

PORTICO OF THE PETRONII

The Portico of the Petronii is named after the family of Petronius Felix, who paid for the construction of this gymnasium complex in AD 225. It was surrounded by Corinthian columns, built of an unusual yellow-veined grey marble, of which one row remains. This is where people played sports before heading to the baths. In the southeastern corner some letters are carved – part of a game.

BATHS

The citizens of Thuburbo Majus had no reason to complain, with no fewer than five bath complexes.

The biggest bath complex was the **Summer Baths**, adjacent to the Portico of the Petronii, covering 2800 sq m. The **Winter Baths**, 150m to the east, features a grand entrance flanked by four veined marble columns. Both bath complexes were full of mosaics, which are now on display in the Bardo Museum in Tunis.

The smaller **Baths of the Labyrinth**, southeast of the agora, and **Baths of the Stars**, northeast of the capitol, are named after their mosaics. Lastly, there are the **Baths of the Capitol**, just west of the capitol.

SANCTUARY OF BAAL & SANCTUARY OF CAELESTIS

The Sanctuary of Baal is a small square temple and is easily identified by the two pillars at the top of its steps. Baal was the chief god of the Punic pantheon, but his cult survived (in Romanised form) long after the fall of Carthage. That of Caelestis, with its complete yellow-stone arch, was for another adapted god – this time the Roman version of Tanit. The temple was later converted into a Byzantine church, the traces of which can still be seen.

OTHER SITES

A rough path leads southeast from the Sanctuary of Baal towards the ruins set into the hills of the massive arched **cisterns** which once supplied the town with water. The mound beyond the cisterns marks the site of a small **amphitheatre**. Another rough path leads north from here to a low hill topped by the remains of a **Temple of Saturn**.

Getting There & Away

Thuburbo Majus is just west of the Tunis–Kairouan road, 3km north of El-Fahs. There is no public transport to the site, but any bus operating between Tunis and Kairouan can drop you at the turn-off, leaving a 15-minute walk to the site entrance and car park. The sight of a triumphal arch, which marks the northern edge of the city, is an indication that you're getting close.

There are regular louages to El-Fahs from the Cap Bon louage station in Tunis (TD2.95), and buses from the southern bus station.

ZAGHOUAN زكوان

☎ 72 / pop 15,800

This beautifully set, sleepy town is tucked beneath the foot of the rugged Jebel Zaghouan (1295m) and surrounded by hills. It used to supply ancient Carthage with fresh water. During Hadrian's reign, from AD 120–31, a 132km-long aqueduct was built with typical confidence and ambition. Long stretches (in remarkably good condition) can still be seen – solid arches that seem to stride across the countryside – along the Tunis–Zaghouan road. Septimus Severus had it restored in 203 and although the Vandals, as usual, did their best to trash it, the Byzantines rebuilt it. Hassan Ibn Nooman damaged it again, during the siege of Carthage in AD 698, but it was then reconstructed in the 10th and 13th centuries. The springs are still used today by local residents; there are a couple of gushing outlets on strategic corners in the town. There are markets here on Thursday afternoon and Friday morning.

Also built under Hadrian, the **Nymphaeum**, or Temple des Eaux, is a once-grand fountain, a shrine to the spring that kept Carthage in water, surrounded by 12 niches that once held statues depicting each month. It has a fine setting, with a backdrop of hills, and there's an attractive garden café.

Restaurant la Source (☎ 675 661; ave 7 Novembre; starters TD1.5, mains TD4-9) has a terrace with excellent views, and inside is air-conditioned and filled with dark wood, with sections that can be screened off for extra intimacy. The menu is simple but the food is good.

Getting There & Away

Public transport leaves from the middle of town. There are buses to El-Fahs (TD1.3, four daily) and Tunis (TD2.75, two daily) and to Nabeul/Hammamet (TD2.95) and Sousse (TD3.75), as well as louages to these destinations.

Louages to Zaghouan (TD2.75, one hour) leave from the Cap Bon station in Tunis.

OUDHNA (UTHINA)　　أوتينا

Oudhna – ancient Uthina – is a fascinating and not-much-visited site, about 30km south of Tunis, just east of the aqueduct that once supplied fresh water from Zaghouan to Carthage. It is dominated by the dramatic hilltop capitol that has been converted into a farmhouse, with enormous Byzantine cellars, and a well-restored amphitheatre.

History

The Roman historian Pliny mentions this as the Berber settlement of Adys and one of the first Roman colonies in Africa. It was the site of a major battle between Carthage and the Roman general Regulus during the first Punic War in 255 BC. Regulus reported that it was an important walled town, although no evidence for this exists today.

Uthina was founded by the emperor Augustus at the beginning of the 1st century AD, and settled with army veterans. They had little clue how to work the land, and Uthina struggled to survive until the land was bought up by real farmers. Like many Roman towns in Africa, its prosperity peaked in the 2nd and 3rd centuries – it was one of the areas where the Roman presence was the strongest in Africa, at the centre of a fertile agricultural region. Christianity took a powerful hold here and it was home to many bishops. It declined after the Vandal conquest, but survived into Byzantine times and was later occupied by the Arabs.

The site was a munitions dump during WWII, which damaged several monuments.

Sights

The site is large, and continues to be excavated. It is set in a lovely rural landscape, covered in olive groves and cypress trees. The access road stops at a low hill at the centre of the site topped by a dramatic old colonial farmhouse that is still occupied and seems to rear up from the earth. Known locally as El-Kalaa (the fortress), this was once the **capitol**.

The farmhouse stands on the site of the Capitoline temple. The **forum**, identifiable to the south, is now a farmyard surrounded by outbuildings and populated by chickens. The restored steps leading to the capitol mount the rocky slope between the farmyard and the farmhouse and are worth climbing for a good view across the site.

Beneath the capitol is a pristine, magnificent, vaulted series of chambers, built in Byzantine times.

South of the forum are the remains of a **reservoir**, standing at the end of an **aqueduct** that supplied water from springs at nearby Jebel Rassas. Most of the water was delivered to a network of enormous arched **cisterns** 200m south of the reservoir. Some have collapsed although others remain in remarkably good condition – huge, dank watertight rooms.

The sections of collapsed masonry east of the capitol mark the site of the main **public baths**, nicknamed Touir Ellil – the bat tunnel. In contrast to the chaos above ground (damaged by explosions when it was used as an arms depot during WWII), the subterranean level is in good condition. During excavations a beautiful black marble bust with a Libyan hairstyle was discovered, now displayed in the Bardo Museum in Tunis.

North of here, beside the access road, are the **Baths of the Laberii** – the mosaic of Orpheus charming the animals, now in the Bardo, was found here, and the baths take their name from the inscription on the mosaic. During the Byzantine period the northeast part was a pottery workshop, and many Christian artefacts were discovered here. The baths stand beside the remains of the celebrated **House of the Laberii**, or of Ikarios (named after a mosaic showing Ikarios giving a vine to the king of Attica), a sumptuous villa of over 30 rooms, and probably the best house in town – you can see the remains of a colonnade that surrounded a garden. All the rooms were paved with mosaics, the finest of which are now on display at the Bardo.

The **amphitheatre**, west of the access road, could cater for crowds of more than 10,000 and is a good indication of the stature of the Roman town. Once known as El-Habs, meaning the prison – as well as a place of entertainment it contained cells for the criminals and wild beasts who were the unfortunate entertainers. It was being restored at the time of research.

Getting There & Away

There is no public transport to the site. It's clearly signposted 28km south of Tunis on the road to El-Fahs and Kairouan. It's another 2km to the site, which is close to the modern village of Oudna. The station here is for freight trains only. Or you could go to El-Fahs and negotiate with a louage driver to take you to Thurburbo Majus and Oudna, then back to Tunis – the whole trip will cost about TD15 to TD20.

MAKTHAR (MACTARIS)   مكثر
☎ 78 / pop 9000

The ruins of ancient Mactaris are a worthwhile stopover on the road between Kairouan (114km to the east) and Le Kef (69km northwest), but don't plan to stay here for the night as the modern town is bleak and the only accommodation option similarly unappealing.

History

Ancient Mactaris was one of many native towns incorporated into the Carthaginian Empire at the end of the 5th century BC as part of Carthage's push to control the hinterland. It was captured by the Numidian king Massinissa before the Third and final Punic War, and remained in Numidian

hands until the beginning of the 1st century AD, when Rome began to take the settlement of Africa seriously.

The Roman town reached the peak of its prosperity in the 2nd century. The Vandals and the Byzantines both left their mark in subsequent centuries, and the town continued to be occupied until the 11th century, when it was destroyed during the Hilalian invasions.

Orientation & Information

The ancient site is on the southeastern edge of town at the junction of the roads to Kairouan and Le Kef.

If you're visiting the site in the winter, come suitably dressed. At an altitude of more than 1000m, the winds that blow off the surrounding hills can be bitterly cold.

Ancient Mactaris

The entrance to **Mactaris** (admission TD2.1, plus camera TD1; ☎ 8am-6pm summer, 8.30am-5.30pm winter) is through the **museum**, which houses some interesting old gravestones as well as Roman busts, lamps and old coins. Immediately south of the museum are the remains of the town's small **amphitheatre**, built in the 2nd century AD and looking in remarkably good condition after recent restoration.

The site's main path runs south from the amphitheatre towards the crumbling remains of the enormous **Trajan's Arch**, built in AD 116 and dedicated to Emperor Trajan. The arch overlooks the **Roman forum**, built at the same time. The four columns at the northeastern corner of the forum mark the location of the town's **market**. The foundations south of the arch belong to a 6th century Byzantine tower.

A path leads northeast from the forum to the scanty remains of the **Temple of Hotor Miskar**, dedicated to the Carthaginian god of the same name. Nearby are the remains of a Roman villa known as the **House of Venus** named after the mosaic of Venus found there, now in the museum.

The group of columns south of Trajan's Arch belong to a small **Vandal church**, built in the 5th century AD. The baptistery font, hidden behind the apse at the eastern end, still has traces of the original mosaics.

The jumble of arches and columns standing at the southwestern corner of the site was once the home of the town's **schola juvenum**,

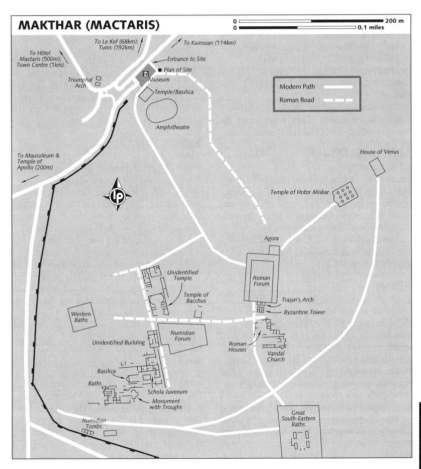

MAKTHAR (MACTARIS)

To Le Kef (68km);
Tunis (192km)

To Kairouan (114km)

To Hôtel
Mactaris (500m);
Town Centre (1km)

Entrance to Site

Plan of Site

Triumphal
Arch

Museum

Temple/Basilica

Amphitheatre

Modern Path
Roman Road

To Mausoleum &
Temple of
Apollo (200m)

House of Venus

Temple of Hotor Miskar

Agora

Unidentified
Temple

Temple of
Bacchus

Western
Baths

Unidentified Building

Numidian
Forum

Roman
Forum

Trajan's Arch

Byzantine Tower

Roman
Houses

Vandal
Church

Basilica

Baths

Schola Juvenum

Monument
with Troughs

Numidian
Tombs

Great
South-Eastern
Baths

a youth club where local boys learned how to be good Romans. It was converted into a church in the 3rd century AD. It's a pleasant, shady spot. The area just south of the schola was the town's **cemetery** and is dotted with Numidian tombs.

The southern part of the site is dominated by the massive walls of the **Great South-Eastern Baths**. Built in the 2nd century AD, it was later converted into a fortress by the Byzantines in the 6th century. The baths here are nonetheless among the best preserved in Tunisia. The star feature is the extraordinary blue and green mosaic floor of the central room.

The ruins of the **Temple of Apollo** are about 800m southwest of town and signposted from the museum. It was the town's principal temple in Roman times and was built on the site of an earlier Carthaginian temple to the god Baal Hammon. Adjoining the site are the crumbling remains of the Roman aqueduct that once supplied water to the town.

Sleeping & Eating

Makthar's only hotel, the tiny **Hôtel Mactaris** (☎ 876 465; d TD10), is about 500m from the ancient site on the road into town and is only for the desperate. The three very basic rooms are above the only bar in town, and you'd need to drink a skinful before you even considered lying down on one of the saggy old iron beds. It also has a cheap restaurant serving grilled food and salads.

Getting There & Away

Buses leave from the T-junction 100m north of the Hôtel Mactaris. There are five buses a day to Le Kef (TD3, 1¼ hours) and two to Kairouan (TD4.6, 1¾ hours). SNTRI operates three buses a day to Tunis (TD7.7, three hours).

You can also get to Tunis, Le Kef and Kairouan by louage. They leave from the main street in the middle of town.

SBEITLA (SUFETULA) سبيطلة

☎ 77 / pop 7500

Stuck out in the middle of nowhere on the plains 107km southwest of Kairouan, Sbeitla is home to the wonderful ancient town of Sufetula, famous for its remarkably well-preserved Roman temples.

The modern town has very little going for it, although it does at least have a few decent hotels.

History

It is assumed that Roman Sufetula followed an evolutionary path similar to other Roman towns in the region, such as Ammaedara and Mactaris, and was established at the beginning of the 1st century AD on the site of an early Numidian settlement.

The surrounding countryside proved ideal for olive growing, and Sufetula quickly developed into a wealthy town. The temples were built when Sufetula was at the height of its prosperity in the 2nd century. Its olive groves ensured that the town continued to prosper long after other Roman towns slipped into decline, and it became an important centre of Christianity in the 4th century.

The Byzantines made Sufetula their regional capital, transforming it into a military stronghold from which to tackle the area's rebellious local tribes. It was here in AD 647 that Prefect Gregory declared himself independent of Constantinople. His moment of glory lasted only a few months before he was killed by the Arabs, who at the same time destroyed much of Sufetula. The Arab victory is celebrated at the Festival of the Seven Abdullahs, held in the last week of July.

Orientation & Information

The ruins of **Sufetula** (admission TD2.1, plus camera TD1; ☎ 7am-7pm summer, 8.30am-5.30pm winter) are 1km north of the modern town centre, on the road to Kasserine. The site entrance is opposite the museum.

The best time to visit the site is very early in the morning, which means spending the night at one of the nearby hotels. It's well worth it, though, for the spectacular sight of the temples glowing orange in the early morning sun.

Sights

TEMPLES

The celebrated **temples** hold centre stage, towering over the surrounding ruins.

The wall that surrounds the temples was built by the Byzantines in the 6th century AD. The entrance is on the southeastern side of the complex through the magnificent triple-arched **Antonine Gate**, built in AD 139 and dedicated to Emperor Antoninus Pius and his adopted sons Marcus Aurelius and Lucius Verus. It opens onto a large paved **forum** flanked by two rows of columns which lead up to the temples. There are three temples, each dedicated to one of the three main gods of the Roman pantheon. The **Temple of Jupiter**, in the centre, is flanked by slightly smaller temples to his sister deities Juno and Minerva.

GREAT BATHS

The ruins of these extensive **baths** are to the southeast of the temples. They are remarkable mainly for the complex under-floor heating system used in the hot rooms, easily distinguishable now that the floors themselves have collapsed.

THEATRE

The ancient **theatre**, just east of the Great Baths, has a prime position overlooking the Oued Sbeitla. Built in the 3rd century AD, not much remains except for the orchestra pit and a few scattered columns, but it's worth visiting for the views along the Oued Sbeitla which is particularly picturesque in spring.

CHURCH OF ST SERVUS

The four precarious-looking pillars of stone on the left as you walk between the temples and the Great Baths mark the site of the **Church of St Servus**, built in the 4th century AD on the foundations of an unidentified pre-Roman temple.

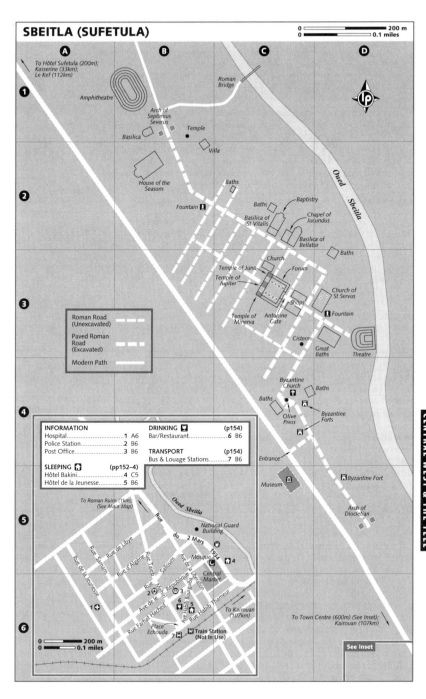

SBEITLA (SUFETULA)

0 — 200 m
0 — 0.1 miles

A **B** **C** **D**

To Hôtel Sufetula (200m);
Kasserine (33km);
Le Kef (112km)

Roman
Bridge

Amphitheatre

Arch of
Septimius
Severus

Temple

Basilica

Villa

House of the
Seasons

Baths

Oued Sbeitla

Fountain

Baths

Baptistry

Basilica of
St Vitalis

Chapel of
Jucundus

Basilica of
Bellator

Baths

Church

Temple of Juno

Forum

Temple of
Jupiter

Church of
St Servus

Shops

Temple of
Minerva

Antonine
Gate

Fountain

Cistern

Great
Baths

Theatre

Byzantine
Church

Baths

Baths

Olive
Press

Byzantine
Forts

Entrance

Byzantine Fort

Museum

Arch of
Diocletian

Roman Road (Unexcavated)
Paved Roman Road (Excavated)
Modern Path

Inset

INFORMATION
Hospital.............................1 A6
Police Station.....................2 B6
Post Office.........................3 B6

SLEEPING (pp152–4)
Hôtel Bakini.......................4 C5
Hôtel de la Jeunesse.............5 B6

DRINKING (p154)
Bar/Restaurant....................6 B6

TRANSPORT (p154)
Bus & Louage Stations..........7 B6

To Roman Ruins (1km);
(See Main Map)

Oued Sbeitla

National Guard
Building

Rue du 2 Mars 1934

Rue Salmm

Rue de Libye

Rue de la Jeunesse

Rue d'Algérie

Rue Taïeb

Rue Salloum

Mosque

Ave de la Libération

Rue de la République

Rue Mongi Slim

Central
Market

Ave de le U

Ave Habib Bourguiba

Rue Habib Thameur

Rue Farhat Hached

Place
Echouda

Train Station
(Not In Use)

To Kairouan
(107km)

To Town Centre (600m) (See Inset);
Kairouan (107km)

See Inset

0 — 200 m
0 — 0.1 miles

CENTRAL WEST & THE TELL

ESPARTO GRASS

One of the few plants that thrives in the harsh conditions of the Tunisian interior is a wiry, narrow-bladed native grass known as esparto *(Stipa tenacissima)*.

Left to its own devices, it grows into dense clumps topped by graceful, feathered seed heads, making it a popular garden plant in some parts of the world. In Tunisia, it's too valuable just to be admired.

In ancient times, it was gathered and woven into a host of household items, such as matting and baskets. It was tough enough to produce crude ropes, animal harnesses and saddle bags.

These days, esparto is exploited primarily for the production of high-quality paper. Large areas of the countryside around Kasserine and Sbeitla are devoted to its cultivation. You'll often see long rows of women working their way across fields of esparto armed with small sickles. The cut esparto is bailed up and trucked off to a modern paper factory in Kasserine.

Esparto grass also grows in abundance near Matmata.

BASILICA OF BELLATOR

This is the first of a row of ruined churches about 100m east of the temples on the main path leading northwest towards the Arch of Septimius Severus. It was built at the beginning of the 4th century AD on the foundations of an unidentified pre-Roman temple.

BASILICA OF ST VITALIS

This was built in the 6th century AD as a bigger and grander replacement for the Basilica of Bellator. The basilica itself doesn't amount to much now, but hidden away in the baptistery at the back is a beautiful baptismal basin that has been left in situ. The rim is decorated with an intricate floral mosaic in brilliant reds and greens.

MUSEUM

The only exhibits worth seeking out at the museum are the statue of Bacchus reclining on a panther, which was discovered at the site's theatre, and the mosaics.

OTHER SITES

The path running northwest from the churches crosses a neat grid of unexcavated streets before arriving at the remains of the **Arch of Septimius Severus**. To the west before you reach the arch are the meagre remains of the **House of the Seasons**, named for a mosaic now in the Bardo Museum in Tunis.

A rough path continues north from the arch, past the ruins of a small basilica, to the site of the town's **amphitheatre**, which has yet to be excavated and is so overgrown that you have to look hard to find the outline. Another path leads east from the arch down to a restored **Roman bridge** over the Oued Sbeitla.

Sleeping & Eating

Hôtel de la Jeunesse (☎ 466 528; ave Habib Bourguiba; s/d TD10/14) The only option for budget travellers is a friendly place with simple rooms.

Hôtel Sufetula (☎ 465 074; fax 465 582; s/d with breakfast TD35/50; ❄ 🍽) Overlooks the ancient site from its hilltop location 1.5km north of town. It's a comfortable, modern hotel with pleasant rooms and the restaurant does a perfectly adequate three-course menu for an extra TD5 per person.

Hôtel Bakini (☎ 465 244; rue du 2 Mars; s/d with breakfast TD28/40; ❄) The only alternative is uninspiring but adequate at the eastern edge of town.

The **bar/restaurant** on ave Habib Bourguiba is more bar than restaurant, but it does serve basic grilled food like brochettes, salad and chips for TD2.8.

Getting There & Away

Buses and louages leave from a dusty vacant lot on the southern edge of town, off rue Habib Thameur.

SNTRI has three buses a day to Tunis (TD11, four hours) via Kairouan (TD5.8, 1½ hours). Regional services include frequent buses to Kasserine (TD1.5, 45 minutes). There's a direct daily bus to Le Kef (TD6.7, three hours); otherwise change at Kasserine.

There are louages to Kasserine and Kairouan.

KASSERINE   القصرين

☎ 77 / pop 38,000

Kasserine, 38km southwest of Sbeitla, would be a strong contender in any poll to nominate the dullest town in Tunisia. It does, however, make a useful base for exploring the remote western reaches of the country as it has some useful transport connections.

Kasserine's main industry is the production of high-quality paper from esparto grass (see boxed text, left) – you'll see a mountain of the stuff, piled up waiting to be processed, at the factory in the centre of town.

If you come to Kasserine in winter, come suitably dressed. The town is just east of Tunisia's highest mountain, Jebel Chambi (1544m), and gets desperately cold.

Orientation & Information

Everything of importance here is found on the extended main street, blvd de l'Environnement.

The town centre is the main square, place de l'Independence, which is commonly known as place de l'Ancienne Gare. The **post office** is nearby and there are several **banks** around the square.

Sights

The minor Roman site of **Cillium** (admission free) was, like Kasserine today, an important regional centre. The ruins are spread over a wide area, but are centred on a low hill overlooking the broad bed of the Oued Dhrib on the southwestern edge of town. This area is enclosed and watched over by a guardian.

The main features are a well-preserved **triumphal arch** and a large **theatre**, which is carved into the hillside. Both date from the 3rd century, when Cillium was at the height of its prosperity. The **capitol** and **forum** are also identifiable, as are the main **baths**. The site is signposted to the east of the road to Gafsa, about 250m south of Hôtel Cillium.

Cillium's most famous monument is the **Mausoleum of the Flavii**. This triple-tiered monument to Flavius Secundus and his family stands by the roadside at the western end of blvd de l'Environnement. It looks stunning at night when spotlights sometimes highlight the 110 lines of poetry inscribed on the bottom tier.

Sleeping & Eating

Hôtel de la Paix (☎ 471 465; blvd de l'Environnement; s/d with breakfast TD9/16; half board TD11.5/21) This friendly place, 50m east of the central square, is the best budget choice. The popular downstairs restaurant/bar serves meals from TD2.5.

Hôtel Pinus (☎ 470 164; blvd de l'Environnement; s/d TD20/30) Located 700m further out towards Sbeitla, the Pinus is overpriced and drab.

Hôtel Cillium (☎ 474 406; fax 473 682; s/d TD35/50; half board TD40/60) Kasserine's only upmarket choice is thankfully good and just south of the roundabout on the western side of town. In winter you might end up sitting at the bar with a bunch of elderly European men dressed up in paramilitary costumes; they're hunters who come here to go pig-hunting in the surrounding forests.

Getting There & Away

The bus and louage stations are about 1km east of the town centre on the road to Sbeitla.

SNTRI has four buses a day to Tunis (TD11.8, 4½ hours), via Kairouan. Regional services include buses to Sbeitla (TD1.5, 45 minutes), Gafsa (TD4.6, 1¾ hours), and north to Le Kef (TD5.4, 2½ hours) via Kalaat Khasba (TD2.8, 1¼ hours).

Travelling by louage around here involves lots of short journeys and frequent vehicle changes. There are frequent services to Sbeitla (TD1.5), but travelling south to Gafsa involves changing louage at Fériana; travelling north to Kalaat Khasba or Le Kef involves a change at Thala.

HAIDRA   حادرة

The remote border village of Haidra, 69km to the northwest of Kasserine, is the site of ancient Ammaedara, one of the oldest Roman towns in Africa. It's a wonderfully evocative site, spread along the northern bank of the Oued Haidra. The problem is that it's a difficult place to get to without your own transport, especially if you want to stick around for the fabulous sunsets. The sun sets slowly behind the mountains of Algeria to the west, bathing the site in a rich orange light.

Modern Haidra is little more than a customs post on the road to the Algerian town of Tébessa, 41km to the southwest. There are shops and a café, but no restaurants and no hotels. The closest accommodation is in Kasserine or Le Kef, 78km to the north.

History

Ammaedara is a Berber name, although the only evidence of pre-Roman occupation is the foundation of a Carthaginian temple to

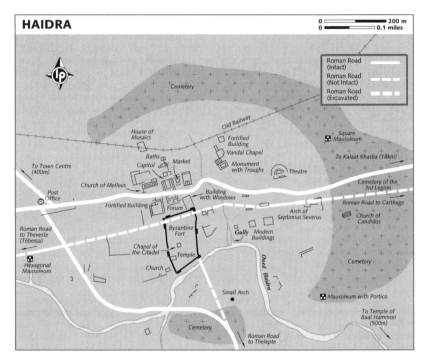

the god Baal-Hammon, overlooking the Oued Haidra to the southeast of the site.

The first Roman settlement here was established by the troops of the Augustine Third Legion at the beginning of the 1st century AD as a base during their campaign to suppress a rebellion by the Numidian chief Tacfinares. Only a cemetery near the Arch of Septimius Severus survives from this period. After Tacfinares was defeated, Ammaedara was repopulated with retired soldiers and became a prosperous trading town.

Ancient Ammaedara

The road from Kalaat Khasba passes right through the middle of the site, which is not enclosed and can be visited at any time. Admission is free, but the amiable custodian appreciates a tip.

The site is dominated by the walls of an enormous **Byzantine fort**, built in AD 550. It straddles the old Roman road and runs down to the banks of the Oued Haidra. The ruins of an earlier Roman temple are incorporated into the southwestern corner.

The principal Roman monument is the extremely well preserved **Arch of Septimius Severus**, which stands on the eastern edge of the site. It was built in AD 195, and remains in good condition because it was protected for centuries by a surrounding Byzantine wall. About 300m south of here, the **mausoleum** with portico stands silhouetted on a small rise overlooking the *oued* (river).

The modern road passes over the old forum, although a single giant **column** marks the site of the great temple that once stood at the capitol. Around the capitol are the remains of the old baths and the market.

Although the site is dotted with the ruins of numerous small churches, the only one that warrants serious inspection is the partially reconstructed **Church of Melleus**, just west of the forum. Originally built in the 4th century, it was later expanded by the Byzantines

Getting There & Away

Visiting Haidra without your own transport is a challenge, but can be achieved with a bit of determination.

You can get to Kalaat Khasba, 18km northeast of Haidra, on any bus travelling between Kasserine and Le Kef. There's also a daily train from Tunis (TD9.7, five hours).

From Kalaat Khasba, you'll find occasional louages out to Haidra (900 mills, 15 minutes). The alternative is to hitch from the roundabout on the main road at the southern side of town. Whatever you do, you'll need to set out early; public transport dries up by mid-afternoon.

JUGURTHA'S TABLE   جفرنة ةلواط
☎ 78

Jugurtha's Table (1271m), close to the Algerian border near the small town of Kalaat es-Senan, 85km northwest of Kasserine, is a spectacular flat-topped mountain that rises sheer from the surrounding plains.

The mountain is named after the Numidian king Jugurtha, who used it as a base during his seven-year campaign against the Romans from 112 BC to 105 BC. Its sheer, impregnable walls make it a superb natural fortress. The only access to the summit is by a twisting set of steps hewn into the escarpment at the eastern end. The Byzantines added the small gate at the base of the steps.

The turn-off is about 5km east of Kalaat es-Senan on the road to Kalaat Khasba. The steps are steep, and awkward enough to require caution in places.

The reward for those who climb to the top is a spectacular view over the surrounding countryside. The hills you can see to the west are across the border in Algeria. There's little else to see apart from a small shrine of a marabout (holy man), a network of low stone walls and a few curious cows.

If you're in the mood for a walk, you can start your hike to the steps from the small village of Ain Senan, on the western side of the mountain 3km southeast of Kalaat es-Senan. The return walk from Ain Senan takes about two hours; take sufficient water because there's none to be found along the way. Tourists are supposed to register at the National Guard office on the main street of Kalaat es-Senan before they set out, and check back afterwards to announce their safe return.

Sleeping & Eating

There's very basic accommodation at the **Hôtel Kalaat Senan** (☎ 286 356; per person TD2.5, r TD7.5), next to the National Guard office on the main street of town. The hotel also doubles as the only bar in town, and has a small restaurant where you can get a plate of grilled chicken, chips and salad for TD3. The closest decent rooms are in Le Kef.

Getting There & Around

There are good sealed roads connecting Kalaat es-Senan with Kalaat Khasba, 28km to the southeast, and Tajerouine, 25km to the northeast, with occasional louages from both towns. Tajerouine is 35km south of Le Kef on the main road to Kasserine.

A taxi from Kalaat es-Senan to Ain Senan costs TD1.5.

Kairouan & the Central Coast

CONTENTS

The central coast of Tunisia and its hinterland is home to the country's most diverse range of attractions: fortified medinas, which protected cities from invasion and grew wealthy on the trade of the Mediterranean and the Sahara; beach resorts catering to the modern pursuit of sun and surf; and the single most impressive Roman monument in Africa. It's also Tunisia's Islamic heartland, with Kairouan ranking only behind Mecca, Medina and Jerusalem as one of the holiest cities of Islam.

In Sousse these different worlds meet with one of the finest medinas in the country, with its labyrinthine grandeur just a few hundred metres from the water's edge where Europeans and Tunisians fill the beaches to overflowing in summer. North of Sousse, Port el-Kantaoui is a classy playground of resorts set around a luxury yachting harbour, while to the south, Monastir has perhaps the finest *ribat* (fortified monastery) in the country and somehow escapes the clamour of Sousse.

It's from Monastir and Sousse that most travellers visit Kairouan, a beguiling Islamic city which is home to splendid and distinctive medina architecture and the Great Mosque, while El-Jem's colosseum rises from the plains in an astonishing reminder of the legacy left by the Romans.

Further down the coast, Mahdia has a charm all its own with an old town that bewitches all who visit, while Sfax is different again – rarely visited by tourists but the perfect place to see a medina as they were before the tourists arrived.

HIGHLIGHTS

- Wandering around Monastir's magnificent **ribat** (p170), military architecture at its most photogenic and favourite of film directors

- Meandering through Mahdia's ancient **medina** (p170), a maze of vine-shaded squares and narrow cobbled streets

- Standing fearless in El-Jem's **colosseum** (p181), the most impressive Roman monument in Africa

- Basking in the energy of **Sousse** (p161), the quintessential Tunisian resort town with a great medina

- Exploring the medina in **Sfax** (p189), the best living and working medina in Tunisia and the least touched by tourism

- Soaring though the skies on a magic carpet ride after carpet-shopping in the holy Islamic city of **Kairouan** (p180)

KAIROUAN & THE CENTRAL COAST

History

The Sahel, the large coastal bulge between the Gulf of Hammamet and the Gulf of Gabès, has always been a battleground for other people's wars. Sousse, the home base of Hannibal in the Carthaginian battles against the Romans, again found itself on the losing side when Pompey made it his headquarters in his doomed civil war against Julius Caesar (based at Monastir). It was finally destroyed by the first wave of Islamic armies that swept across North Africa in the 7th century. These Islamic armies founded the holy city of Kairouan and ushered in the reign of Islamic dynasties, the most productive of which were the Aghlabids (who left a splendid architectural legacy in all of the coastal towns) and the Cairo-based Fatimids whose mark can still be seen in Mahdia.

For some reason, the indigenous Berbers took umbrage at their traditional land being taken over by foreigners. Whether confronted with the Roman Empire from the north or the Muslim dynasties from the east, they fought them all, mounting rebellion after rebellion, one of which destroyed Kairouan while during another they held out against vastly superior numbers in the colosseum of El-Jem.

In modern Tunisian history, Monastir is revered as the birthplace of the nation's founder, Habib Bourguiba.

Climate

Tunisia's central coast gets very hot in summer (after all, that's why many of you have come) but you're never too far from a sea breeze. The further you go inland, the hotter it gets – Kairouan and El-Jem bake in summer, but can be quite cold in winter.

Getting There & Away

All the towns covered in this chapter are well-connected to the rest of the country by bus, louage (shared taxi) and (apart from Kairouan) train. Most people prefer louages or trains as many buses heading north or south originate elsewhere and are often full by the time they arrive here.

Getting Around

Again, louages or train are the easiest ways to get around. There are no direct connections between Kairouan and either El-Jem or Mahdia, while visiting El-Jem at sunset requires some planning (see the boxed text, p182).

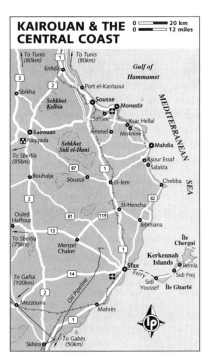

SOUSSE

سوسة

☎ 73 / pop 158,000

From the beach to the medina, Sousse is a great place to take the pulse of modern Tunisia. It's at once quintessentially Tunisian and the sort of place where tourists come to surround themselves with reminders of home. The mix doesn't always work, but Sousse does have a natty charm.

By day, Sousse is a beach resort looking to sun and sea for inspiration, with Boujaffar Beach thronging as much with Tunisian tourists as sun-starved Europeans. The ville nouvelle streets are lined with hotels and restaurants all eager for their cut. The further you go from the water, the slower the beat until you lose yourself in the medina's quiet, winding streets. Here, there's a sense of entering a different, altogether quieter world where nothing happens in a hurry.

By early evening, the medina falls silent while Sousse's student population and local residents reclaim the waterside promenade to the extent that it can seem as if the whole world is out to stroll and watch the world go by. You'd be crazy not to join them.

History

Sousse was founded in the 9th century BC as the Phoenician outpost of Hadrumète, and fell under the sway of Carthage from the middle of the 6th century BC. The famous Carthaginian general Hannibal used the town as his base against the Romans in the final stages of the Second Punic War in 202 BC.

The town allied itself with Rome during the Third and final Punic War (see History, p160), but Hadrumètus, as it became known, later chose the wrong side when it became Pompey's base during the Roman civil war, and suffered badly after his forces were defeated by Julius Caesar at the Battle of Thapsus in AD 46. Sousse's formidable defences proved of little use when it was levelled, wall and all, by Okba ibn Nafaa al-Fihri, falling to the Arabs in the late 7th century. Rebuilt as the Arab town of Soussa, it became the main port of the 9th century Aghlabid dynasty based in Kairouan.

By the time the French arrived in 1881, it had declined to a modest settlement of just 8000 people.

Orientation

Life in Sousse revolves around two axes. The first, running from place Farhat Hached, along ave Habib Bourguiba to the beach and then north along ave Hedi Chaker and rue de la Corniche, is home to banks, hotels and restaurants and is the heart of the ville nouvelle. The second is the medina which contains the main sites of historical interest and a good selection of hotels.

Information

INTERNET ACCESS

Publinet rue Remada (Map pp164-5; 8am-midnight; TD2 per hr); ave Mohamed Maarouf (Map pp164-5; 8am-1am Mon-Sat, 3pm-1am Sun) The latter, near the post office, is bigger.

Rib@t Net (Map pp164-5; medina) Keeps irregular hours.

MEDIA

You'll find international newspapers for sale in the lobbies of the bigger hotels.

MEDICAL SERVICES

Clinique Les Oliviers (242 711) North of town; it is more used to dealing with insurance forms.

Farhat Hached University Hospital (Map p163; 221 411; ave Ibn el-Jazzar) The city's main hospital, northwest of the medina.

MONEY

The banks are concentrated along ave Habib Bourguiba and some have ATMs, although don't expect all of them to work all of the time. STB has a branch (but no ATM) in the medina just west of the Grand Mosque. There's also an ATM at the post office on ave Mohamed Maarouf.

POST & TELEPHONE

Main post office (Map pp164-5; ave Mohamed Maarouf) Just up from place Farhat Hached.

There are many Taxiphone offices around the city centre and along rue de la Corniche.

TOURIST INFORMATION

Syndicat d'initiative (municipal tourist office; Map pp164-5; 220 431; place Farhat Hached; 8am-7pm) Occupies the nearby Zaouia of Sidi Yahia near the entrance to the medina.

Tourist office (Map pp164-5; 25 157; fax 224 262; 1 ave Habib Bourguiba; 7am-7pm Mon-Sat & 9am-noon Sun summer, 8.30am-1pm & 3-5.45pm Mon-Thu & 8.30am-1.30pm Fri-Sat winter) Unusually efficient branch, on the north side of place Farhat Hached. Useful notice board with timetables for buses and trains and opening hours of local attractions. Staff speak a variety of languages, including English.

Sights & Activities

MEDINA

The walls of Sousse's fine old medina stretch 2.25km at a height of 8m and are fortified with a series of solid square turrets. They were built by the Aghlabids in AD 859 on the foundations of the city's original Byzantine walls. Within the walls are 24 mosques (12 for men and 12 for women) and a wealth of historical landmarks well worth seeking out.

The main entrance to the medina is at the northeastern corner at place des Martyrs. The area was created when Allied bombs blew away this section of the wall in 1943. Of the other gates, the most historically interesting is **Bab el-Finga** (*finga* means 'blade' in Arabic); the French set up their guillotine outside the gate.

Great Mosque

The **Great Mosque** (Map pp164-5; admission TD1.1; 8am-2pm Sat-Thu, 8am-1pm Fri) is a typically austere Aghlabid affair. It was built, according to a Kufic (early Arabic) inscription in the courtyard, in the year AD 851 by a freed slave called Mudam, on the instructions of the Aghlabid ruler Abul Abbas. Mudam adapted an earlier kasbah, which explains the mosque's turrets and crenellated wall, as well as its unusual location; the great mosque is usually sited in the centre of a medina. The mosque is also unusual in that it has no minaret; its proximity to the *ribat* meant that the latter's tower could be used to call the faithful to prayer. The structure underwent 17th-century modifications and 20th-century restoration.

Non-Muslims aren't allowed beyond the courtyard but from there you can see the grand barrel-vaulted prayer hall.

Ribat

The **ribat** (Map pp164-5; admission TD2.1, plus camera TD1; ☻ 8am-7pm summer, 8am-5.30pm winter) is northwest of the mosque and is the oldest monument in the medina, built in the final years of the 8th century AD.

The entrance is through a narrow arched doorway flanked by weathered columns salvaged from the ruins of Roman Hadrumètum. The small ante-chamber was the last line of the building's defences – from high above the columns projectiles and boiling liquids were rained down on intruders. A vaulted passage opens out into a courtyard surrounded by porticos. The *ribat*, designed principally as a fort, was garrisoned by devout Islamic warriors who would divide their time between fighting and silent study of the Quran in the tiny, cell-like rooms built into the walls. The prayer hall on the first floor has an elegant vaulted ceiling and reflects this dual purpose with a simple mihrab (one of the oldest in North Africa) and fortified windows that were used by archers.

Scramble up the narrow 76-step spiral staircase of the nador (watch tower), which was added by the Aghlabids in AD 821, for unparalleled views over the medina up the hill to the kasbah and down into the courtyard of the Great Mosque.

Zaouia Zakkak

The splendid octagonal stone minaret at the junction of rue Dar Said and rue de Tazerka belongs to the 17th century **Zaouia Zakkak** (Map pp164-5), the medina's leading example of Ottoman architecture. Non-Muslims can do no more than admire from the street the

minaret with its wonderful blue-green stone and tile work, with its echoes of Andalusia.

Sofra Cistern

This great underground **cistern** (Map pp164-5), once the medina's principle water supply, was created in the 11th century by enclosing a large Byzantine church. It's an eerie place with the columns of the church rising from the black waters. The entrance is on the northeastern side, but the battered old metal door is often locked.

Souq er-Ribba

This souq is the closest Sousse comes to a medieval bazaar. The roof is unmistakably modern, yet the sales-pitch beneath it is age-old. Far from the tranquillity of the southern medina, **Souq er-Ribba** (Map pp164-5) forms the commercial heart of the medina. The place is a riot of colour, packed with haggling merchants, browsing tourists and barrow boys trying to squeeze through with their improbably overloaded carts. This is not the world's most evocative bazaar but worth exploring nonetheless.

Kalaout el-Koubba

The **Koubba** (Map pp164-5; ☎ 229 574; rue Zarrouk; adult/child TD2/1, plus camera/video TD1/3; ☻ 9.30am-1pm daily, 4-6.30pm Sat-Thu) was an ancient *funduq* (caravanserai or inn) and the rooms surrounding the courtyard are now given over to mannequin displays of day-to-day life under the Ottomans. It's thought to have been built in the late 11th century AD. The most striking feature is the cupola with its remarkable zigzag ribbing; the fluted interior is just as impressive.

Sousse Archaeological Museum & Kasbah

Sousse's excellent archaeological **museum** (Map pp164-5; ☎ 227 256; ave du Maréchal Tito; admission TD2.1, plus camera TD1; ☻ 9am-noon & 2-6pm Tue-Sun summer, 9am-noon & 3-7pm Tue-Sun winter) occupies the southern section of the old kasbah.

One of the best collection of mosaics in the country is housed in the rooms around the kasbah's two main courtyards. The highlight is the room on the northern side of the entrance courtyard with exceptional exhibits, including the *Triumph of Bacchus*, which depicts the Roman god of wine riding in a chariot at the head of a parade of satyrs, as well as many superb fishing scenes.

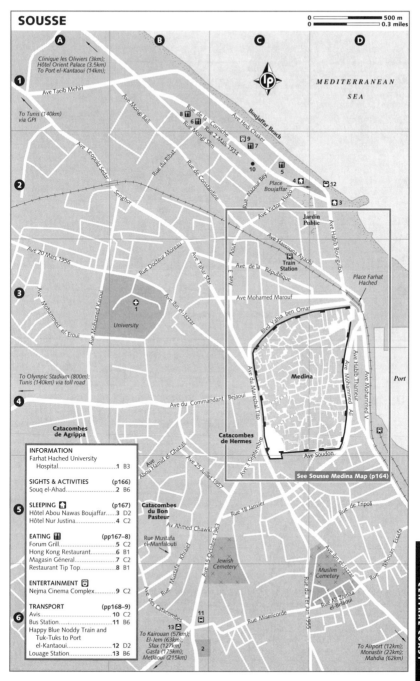

SOUSSE

0 — 500 m
0 — 0.3 miles

MEDITERRANEAN SEA

Clinique les Oliviers (3km);
Hôtel Orient Palace (3.5km);
To Port el-Kantaoui (14km);

Ave Taeib Mehiri

To Tunis (140km)
via GP1

Ave Mongi Bali

Ave Léopold Sédar

Senghor

Rue du Ribat

Rue de Constantine

Rue de la Corniche

Rue 2 Mars 1934

Rue Mongi Slim

Boujaffar Beach

Ave Hedi Chaker

Ave 20 Mars 1956

Rue Docteur Moreau

Ave Tahar Sfar

Ave Ibn el-Jazzar

Ave Mohammed Karoui

Ave Mohammed el-Eroui

University

To Olympic Stadium (800m);
Tunis (140km) via toll road

**Catacombes
de Agrippa**

Ave du Commandant Bejaoui

Rue Nazeur Bey

Place
Boujaffar

Ave Victor Hugo

Ave Hassouna Ayachi

Ave de la République

Ave 3 Août

Ave Mohamed Marouf

Blvd Yahia ben Omar

Medina

Catacombes
de Hermes

Ave 3 Septembre

Ave du Maréchal Tito

Jardin
Public

Train
Station

Place Farhat
Hached

Ave Habib Bourguiba

Ave Habib Thameur

Ave Mohammed Ali

Ave Mohammed V

Port

Ave Soudon

See Sousse Medina Map (p164)

Ave Abou Hamid el-Chazali

Ave 25 Juillet 1957

**Catacombes
du Bon
Pasteur**

Av Ahmed Chawki

Rue Mustafa
el-Manfalouti

Rue Mustafa Kharaf

Ave 15 Octobre 1963

Jewish
Cemetery

Rue 18 Janvier

Rue de Tripoli

Ave Ibn el-Jazzar

Muslim
Cemetery

Rue Nichan Essafa

Rue Ali Zouma
el-Belaoui

Rue Misericorde

Rue du 1er Juin 1955

Ave les Catacombes

To Kairouan (57km);
El-Jem (63km);
Sfax (127km);
Gasfa (175km);
Metlaoui (215km)

To Airport (12km);
Monastir (22km);
Mahdia (62km)

INFORMATION
Farhat Hached University
  Hospital.................................**1** B3

SIGHTS & ACTIVITIES   (p166)
Souq el-Ahad..............................**2** B6

SLEEPING   (p167)
Hôtel Abou Nawas Boujaffar......**3** D2
Hôtel Nur Justina......................**4** C2

EATING   (pp167–8)
Forum Grill................................**5** C2
Hong Kong Restaurant..............**6** B1
Magasin Géneral.......................**7** C2
Restaurant Tip Top....................**8** B1

ENTERTAINMENT
Nejma Cinema Complex............**9** C2

TRANSPORT   (pp168–9)
Avis...**10** C2
Bus Station...............................**11** B6
Happy Blue Noddy Train and
  Tuk-Tuks to Port
  el-Kantaoui............................**12** D2
Louage Station..........................**13** B6

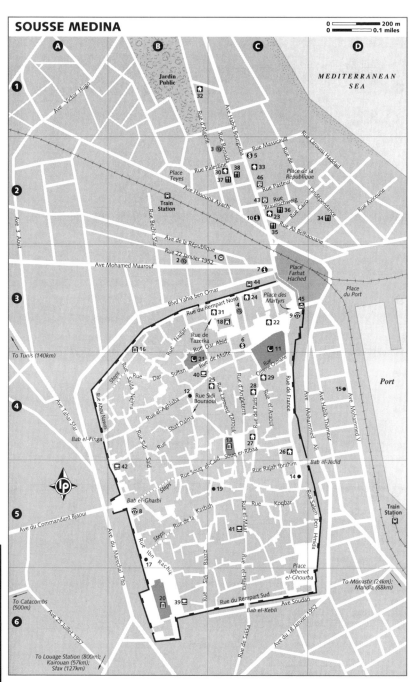

SOUSSE MEDINA

0 ————— 200 m
0 ——— 0.1 miles

MEDITERRANEAN
SEA

Jardin
Public

Place
Teyes

Train
Station

Place de la
République

Place
Farhat
Hached

Place
du Port

Place des
Martyrs

Port

To Tunis (140km)

Bab el-Finga

Bab el-Gharbi

Train
Station

Bab el-Jedid

Place
Jebenet
el-Ghourba

To Monastir (24km);
Mahdia (68km)

To Catacombs
(500m)

Bab el-Kebli

To Louage Station (800m);
Kairouan (57km);
Sfax (127km)

Other rooms contain a collection of funerary objects from a Punic grave beneath the museum and a resident artist demonstrating the patient and painstaking artistry of mosaic-making.

Standing at the high point of the médina, the kasbah was built onto the city walls in the 11th century. It incorporates the imposing square **Khalef tower**, built by the Aghlabids in AD 859 at the same time as the city walls, and superseded the *ribat* as the city's watchtower. It's now a lighthouse.

Note that there is no entrance from inside the medina walls.

Museum Dar Essid

This small, private **museum** (Map pp164-5; ☎ 220 529; 65 rue du Remparts Nord; admission TD2, plus camera TD1; ☼ 10am-7pm summer, 10am-6pm winter) is also not to be missed. In a quiet part of the medina, it occupies a beautiful old home furnished in the style of a well-to-do 19th-century Sousse official and his family. The dimensions of the elaborately decorated, arched door are the first indication of the owner's status. It opens into a small anteroom for meeting strangers, and then into a tiled courtyard surrounded by the family rooms. A plaque in the courtyard reveals that the house was built in AD 928, making it one of the oldest in the medina. There's an extravagance reflected in the Andalusian tiled façades and items ranging from European antique furniture to traditional perfume bottles, from decorative plaster work to a 700-year-old wedding contract and marble from Carrara in Italy. Check out the Roman lamp with the graphic depiction of a copulating couple; it's by the master bed to remind the husband to demonstrate his control and stamina until the lamp went out.

The upstairs area, reached by a heavily restored staircase, is the old servant's quarters and there's a pleasant café with splendid panoramic views. It's a good place to catch the breeze.

CATACOMBS

The **catacombs** (Map pp164-5; ave des Catacombes; admission TD1.1; ☼ 8am-noon & 3-7pm Tue-Sun summer, 9am-noon & 2-6pm winter) include an estimated 5.5km of tunnels containing the graves of more than 15,000 local Christians, mostly from the 4th and 5th centuries AD. The only section open to the public is about 100m of the Catacombes du Bon Pasteur, named after an engraving of the *bon pasteur* (good shepherd) found inside. Most of the graves have been bricked in; a couple have glass fronts, revealing skeletal remains.

BOUJAFFAR BEACH

Sousse's **Boujaffar Beach** (Map p163) is named, somewhat incongruously, after a local Muslim holy man. It's a decent strip of sand which can get ridiculously crowded in summer. The beach is divided into public and private sections run by the beachfront hotels. Although it doesn't always work this way, there is a disturbing trend towards the roped-off private sections being the domain of Westerners sunbathing on sun lounges under 'parasols' while Tunisians crowd into what's left. Entry to the roped-off areas is generally open to non-hotel guests (TD2 per person); these areas sometimes allow free entry in the late afternoon. You'll find all sorts of water-sports equipment for hire along the beach.

Petty theft seems to have become a problem, so don't leave valuables lying around unattended.

In summer, the beachfront is packed with people sitting in the cooler evening air or strolling along the waterfront – a wonderful way to pass a summer's evening.

MARKETS
Sousse's weekly market is held on Sunday in the **Souq el-Ahad compound** (Map p163) just south of the bus and louage stations. It's a chaotic affair, with stalls spilling out into the surrounding streets. You'll find everything from handicrafts to livestock.

Sleeping
BUDGET
For cheap hotels, head to the medina where you'll find no pretensions to comfort but decent budget value.

Hôtel Ahla (Map pp164-5; ☎ 220 570; place de la Grande Mosque; per person TD7.5) In a great location opposite the entrance to the Great Mosque, the Ahla's beds on tiled elevated platforms are a nice touch, although the walled shower receptacles with no shower are less explicable. The shared showers are passably clean and the toilets are far less grim than they look. Not a bad choice.

Hôtel Gabès (Map pp164-5; ☎ 226 977; 12 rue de Paris; mattress on roof TD5, s with shared bathroom TD6, tr with toilet TD22) Another fine choice. The staff are efficient and the rooms are simple, tidy and very good value. The roof terrace is small but a wonderful place to pass the time.

Hôtel el-Aghlaba (Map pp164-5; ☎ 211 024; rue Laroussi Zairouk; s/d/tr TD8/12/15) This place is also good. The woman owner runs a tight ship and the rooms are well kept. The renovated interior suggests this was once a fine old medina home. The saggy mattresses in some rooms are something of a let-down.

Hôtel Ezzouhour (Map pp164-5; ☎ 228 729; 48 rue de Paris; s with shared bathroom TD7.5, d TD15-18) South of the Great Mosque, this is an eclectic place. The reception area speaks of a graceful old medina home, the bare singles on the first floor have an African boarding house ambience and the rooms on the top floor are quite attractive.

MID-RANGE
Hôtel de Paris (Map pp164-5; ☎ 220 564; fax 219 038; 15 rue du Rempart Nord; s/d TD14/22) Just inside the medina's north wall, the atmosphere here is more pleasant than the rooms which are clean but bare and hot. The roof terrace is a big selling point and the owner's friendly.

Hôtel Medina (Map pp164-5; ☎ 221 722; fax 221 794; 1 rue Othene Osmane; s/d TD22/41; ⚌) This labyrinthine place on the southern side of the Great Mosque has large, refurbished rooms which are reasonable value if not quite the four-stars the manager promises. Bargaining may be worth the managerial scowls as everybody seems to pay a different price.

Hôtel Emira (Map pp164-5; ☎ 226 325; 52 rue de France; s/d with breakfast TD19/27) Some of the spacious, well-maintained rooms here have a small terrace and all have character, with the judicious use of tiles.

Hôtel Residence Safra (Map pp164-5; ☎ 227 737; rue du Rempart Nord; s/d TD15/25) This is a relatively new place and it shows. The spick-and-span rooms are pleasantly decorated, comfortable and, importantly, come with good mattresses. They don't get many Western tourists but the service is willing.

Hôtel Residence Monia (Map pp164-5; ☎ /fax 210 469; rue Remada; s/d with breakfast TD25/45) The Monia is an excellent family-run place and one of the best choices in this price range. There's an intimate feel here (it's the sort of place where they remember your name) and the rooms are good value. Get here early or book ahead, especially if you want a room with a balcony.

Hotel Sousse Azur (Map pp164-5; ☎ 227 760; fax 228 145; 5 rue Amilcar; s/d with TV TD30/50, 4-bed apartment TD60; ⚌) Close to the beach but set back a bit from the clamour, the rooms here are spacious and tastefully decorated if a touch overpriced.

Hôtel Claridge (Map pp164-5; ☎ 224 759; fax 227 277; 10 ave Habib Bourguiba; s/d with breakfast TD12.5/25) The long-standing Claridge is a friendly place where the simple if uninspiring rooms (some with balcony) are about the right price. Some rooms at the front can be noisy.

TOP END
The beachfront north of Sousse has been transformed into a row of big hotels that stretches as far as the eye can see. Most of them are booked out in summer, so aren't an option anyway. There are some cheap deals to be found in winter. Prices include breakfast.

Hôtel Nur Justina (Map p163; ☎ 226 866; fax 225 993; 4 ave Hedi Chaker; s/d TD35/50; ✗ ⚗) The rooms here are more comfortable than luxurious and some have good views.

Hotel Sousse Palace (Map pp164-5; ☎ 219 220; www.soussepalace.com; ave Habib Bourguiba; s/d TD102/148; ✗ ⚗) A very popular place in the heart of town, its facilities are legion, from a private beach away from the crowds to aerobics classes and beauticians. It's usually booked out in summer and exceptional value in winter (TD36/52).

Hôtel Abou Nawas Boujaffar (Map p163; ☎ 226 030; boujaafar@abounawas.com.tn; ave Habib Bourguiba; s/d summer TD68/136, winter TD48/96; ✗ ⚗) Four-star and semiluxurious, the Abou Nawas has spacious rooms with a few nice decorative touches; ask for one with a sea view as they cost the same.

The hotels get steadily bigger and smarter as you head up the beach, culminating in the five-star **Hôtel Orient Palace** (☎ 242 888; fax 243 345; s/d TD110/160; ✗ ⚗), 4km north of town. Facilities here include no less than three swimming pools, tennis courts, a fitness centre and disco.

Eating

In the beachfront area, you're more likely to find schnitzel and spaghetti than a decent *tajine* (stuffed omelette) or *lalabi* (thick soup). The further you go from the beach, the better your chances of finding anything different than you can find at home. All places here are open for lunch and dinner unless stated.

RESTAURANTS

Rue Remada is the place to go for a good cheap feed. You'll find half a dozen small restaurants bunched together, all advertising very similar menus at similar prices. Places like the **Restaurant el-Ons** offer good, no-nonsense traditional food at great prices: a range of salads for TD1 and hearty main courses (chicken with rice or couscous are the staples) from TD2.2.

Restaurant el-Najm (Map pp164-5; rue Braunsch-weig; ⏱ 6am-10pm) El-Najm is a great no-frills place for hearty Tunisian meals. From 6am to 9.30am, labourers flock here for reputedly the best *lalabi* in town (TD1). The rest of the day, the *shakchouka* (vegetable dish; TD2) is very tasty and the sheep's head (TD3 for half a head) is definitely an acquired taste. This is a great place to get a break from spaghetti and pizza. Signed only in Arabic, it's 50m southeast of ave Bourguiba.

Restaurant Le Peuple (Map pp164-5; ☎ 220 564; rue de Rempart Nord; salads TD1.8-2.5; mains TD3-6) A deservedly popular place just inside the medina, Le Peuple gets good reviews from readers. Service is fast and friendly and the *briqs* (pastries) here (TD1.4) are as good as you'll get in Sousse.

Forum Grill (Map p163; ☎ 228 399; ave Hedi Chaker; starters TD1.5-2.8, mains TD4.5-9) Forum Grill bucks the beachfront trend by combining multi-lingual menus, reasonable prices and predominantly Tunisian cuisine. They do the *briqs* (TD1.5 to TD2.4), salads and *tajines* (TD5.8 to TD6) especially well and the lamb or fish *shorba* (soup; TD2.8) is a sensation. The service is attentive and slow enough for you to rediscover the lost art of conversation; the clientele is a mix of Tunisian and European.

There are dozens of upmarket restaurants along the northern section of ave Habib Bourguiba and on rue de la Corniche. You'll

---

JASMINE – IT'S A BOY THING

Sitting in any restaurant in Sousse can involve saying no to a seemingly endless stream of men selling jasmine. Any look around will tell you that the main buyers aren't tourists but other Tunisian men.

According to some locals, there's a strict delineation of how to wear your jasmine. If you wear it behind your left ear, you have a girlfriend and want to advertise that happy fact to all the world. Wear it in the right ear and chances are that you don't have a girlfriend but would very much like one. Some men buy the jasmine as a gift for women. If they accept the gift, many women will wear it on their shirt or collar, although solely for decorative purposes, not to signify anything.

Of course not all Tunisians agree that the humble jasmine carries such weighty significance. The most common reason given to us by Tunisian men was the simple and unarguable 'because it smells nice'.

find menus in three or four languages and waiters who can speak all of them. The dishes here are predominantly Western approximations.

Restaurant Tip Top (Map p163; ☎ 226 158; 73 rue de la Corniche) Tip Top gets consistently good reports and the street-front dining area has more character than most. Seafood is a prominent (though expensive) feature of the menu, and it's possible to eat well for about TD25 per person.

Restaurant Marmite (Map pp164-5; ☎ 226 728; 8 rue Remada; mains around TD10-12) The Marmite is a cosy place where you can eat well for TD20 per person, plus wine. The name of the restaurant, incidentally, has nothing to do with the popular English savoury sandwich spread; a *marmite* in Tunisia is a large urn-shaped cooking pot.

Hong Kong Restaurant (Map p163; ☎ 221 366; 4 rue de Rabat; starters TD3-6, mains TD8-15) This is one of but a handful of Chinese restaurants in the country. It has an extensive menu of nearly 200 items, including a full range of pork dishes (think about it). Reckon on TD25 for two, plus wine. The wood-panelled dining room is more pleasant when they open the windows.

SELF-CATERING

The **Magasin Général** (Map pp164-5; blvd Abdelhamid el-Kahdi) is the best supermarket with a good selection of Tunisian wine. There is also a **Monoprix supermarket** (Map pp164-5; cnr ave Habib Bourguiba & rue Ali Belhaouane).

The main produce markets are in the medina, just inside the Bab el-Jedid.

Drinking

Summer in the medina can get pretty warm so it's worthwhile stopping off for a mint tea or cool drink at some points along the way. In the southern stretches of the medina between the Dar Essid Museum and the Kasbah, the best is probably the **Restaurant-Café Seles** (Map pp164-5). Hard up against the Kasbah wall, the **Café des Nomades** (Map pp164-5) has great views from the roof terrace.

Elsewhere in the medina, try **Café Sidi Bouraoui** (Map pp164-5; rue el-Aghlaba) or the unnamed café along rue el-Maar.

Most restaurants here serve alcohol, and the only habitable nightclubs are in the big hotels.

Getting There & Away

AIR

Sousse is served by Monastir's airport, but only by international flights. The **Tunis Air** office (Map pp164-5; ☎ 227 955) is at 5 ave Habib Bourguiba.

BUS

Buses leave from blvd Yahia ben Oma, just outside the medina, heading for Monastir (No. 52, TD0.85, 40 minutes, every 30 minutes), Mahdia (TD2.5, 1½ hours, every 45 minutes) and Port el-Kantaoui (Nos 12 and 18, TD0.5, 20 minutes, every 30 minutes).

Buses to all other destinations depart from the new bus station at Souq el-Ahad, 800m southwest of the medina.

Destination	Fare	Duration	Frequency (per day)
Douz	TD2	6½ hrs	16.6
El-Jem	TD8	1¼ hrs	3.2
Gabès	TD8	4¼ hrs	11.1
Hammamet	TD2	1½ hrs	4.8
Jerba	TD2	7 hrs	16.5
Kairouan	TD2	1½ hrs	3.4
Kebili	TD2	6 hrs	15.1
Nabeul	TD3	2 hrs	5
Sfax	TD8	2½ hrs	6
Tozeur	TD1	5¾ hrs	14.7
Tunis	TD8	2½ hrs	6.8

There are also local buses to Kairouan (TD3) every 30 minutes from 6am to 7pm.

SRTG Nabeul operates three services a day to Hammamet (TD3.5, 1½ hours) and Nabeul (TD3.9, two hours).

LOUAGE

The louage station is opposite the bus station at Souq el-Ahad. Major destinations include El-Jem (TD3.3), Hammamet (TD3.7), Kairouan (TD3.5), Mahdia (TD2.9), Monastir (TD1.4), Sfax (TD5.6) and Tunis (TD6.8). Tickets for Sfax, and Gabès need to be purchased from the ticket office.

TRAIN

The mainline station is conveniently central. There are ten trains a day north to Tunis (TD6, two hours, 2¼ hours) and six to Nabeul (2nd/1st class TD3.4/4.5). There's only one convenient departure time (8.01am) for

Interior of the Great Mosque (p175), Kairouan

DAMIEN SIMONIS

Colosseum (p181), El-Jem

DAMIEN SIMONIS

Street leading to the Mosque of Sidi Boumakhlouf, Le Kef (p142)

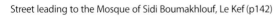

JANE SWEENEY

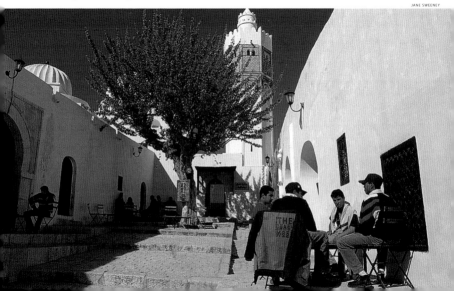

JANE SWEE

Roman theatre (p140), Dougga

JANE SWEENEY

Carved tablet at the ruins of
Sbeitla (Sufetula; p152)

WAYNE WALTON

Ribat (fortified monastery; p162), Sousse

Beachfront, Monastir (p170)

JOHN BRETT

Sfax (1¾ hours) and Gabès (3¾ hours). The only train to Gafsa (5¾ hours) and Metlaoui (6¼ hours) departs at 11.23pm.

There are also frequent services on the branch line to Monastir (TD1.3/0.9 in 1st/2nd class, 35 minutes) and Mahdia (TD3.3/2.5, 1¾ hours) with 16 services between 6am and 8pm in summer. They leave from Bab el-Jedid station, by the port near the southeastern corner of the medina.

Getting Around
TO/FROM THE AIRPORT
The airport is 12km south of town, TD6 by taxi from the town centre. You can also get there by train (920/690 mills in 1st/2nd class, 20 minutes) on the metro branch line between Sousse and Monastir. From Sousse there are 20 departures between 6am and 8pm, whereas services from the airport start around 5am.

BUS
The local bus network operates from just north of the medina on Blvd Yahia ben Omar. Useful services include Nos 8, 21, 22, which all travel past the bus and louage stations at Souq el-Ahad (280 mills).

TAXI
There are lots of taxis, particularly in the main tourist areas; you'll struggle to run up a fare of more than TD3 around the city.

TRAIN & TUK-TUK
Believe it or not, there's a 'Happy Blue Noddy Train' that runs up and down the main road of the tourist strip. It goes from the northern end of ave Habib Bourguiba to Port el-Kantaoui, 14km to the north. It leaves ave Habib Bourguiba on the hour, returning on the half-hour. The fare is TD3.5/2.5 one way per adult/child and TD5/4 return. It operates from 9am to 11pm in summer, to 6pm in winter. From the same point, five-wheel motorcycle 'tuk-tuks' (one way/return TD2/3) do the same journey quicker and cheaper although with a touch less novelty.

AROUND SOUSSE
Port el-Kantaoui   عناء القنطاوي
Port el-Kantaoui is a place apart – a luxury marina complex grafted onto the Tunisian coast 14km north of Sousse. Touted as 'the pleasure port of the Mediterranean', it's an expansive and classy custom-built village of hotels, restaurants and souvenir shops clustered around a large yachting harbour. It would be possible to spend your entire holiday here without leaving. There are beaches, mock pirate ships, glass-bottom boats, diving schools (from TD20 per dive, around TD300 for a course), floating restaurants, banks, international newspapers, an aromatic garden and zoo (entry TD2.5), a manicured golf course (count on TD60 including club hire), nightclubs and amusement parks (TD7 to TD12) for children and the young-at-heart. The architecture is Andalusian, the food spans the full range of European and local cuisine and the atmosphere is thoroughly multinational.

What saves it from becoming a European enclave is the fact that it's invariably filled with Tunisian day-trippers and tourists from around the Arab World, particularly the Gulf States. There may be no feeling of being in Tunisia here, but there *is* a seductive sense of internationalism; it's a good place to spend your one week in the sun and it has more life than the zones touristique elsewhere.

Everything comes at a price. The hotels are unashamedly geared towards the package tour market and rates can be prohibitive (and, in summer, rooms unavailable) for the independent traveller. Nonetheless, everyone should at least visit Port el-Kantaoui. Depending on your perspective, you'll feel like you've stumbled onto a movie set or found the last word in luxury.

SLEEPING & EATING
You could take your pick here and you're unlikely to be disappointed. Most places are within walking distance of the marina, but the hotels listed below are the closest.

Hannibal Palace (☎ 348 577; fax 348 321; s/d TD141/196; ✷ ☎) The closest five-star place to the marina (around 200m) and one of the original Port el-Kantaoui hotels, this has most of the luxury bells and whistles you'd expect for the price, but with impersonal service.

Among the four-star places within striking distance are: **Hadstrubal** (☎ 348 944; fax 348 969; s/d TD112/160; ✷ ☎) which is central yet somehow without the clamour; **El Kanta Residence** (☎ 348 666; fax 348 656; s/d TD119/148; ✷ ☎), which is comfortable and welcoming; and **Marhaba**

Palace (☎ 347 071; fax 347 077; s/d TD112/160; 🔀 🖳), which is similarly good. For self-catering apartments, try **Les Maisons de la Mer** (☎ 348 799; fax 348 961; 2/4/6 persons TD90/130/160; 🔀 🖳).

Most of the hotels try and steer you towards their own restaurant. The restaurants around the marina and the hinterland are all fairly similar in terms of what's on the menu, and are of a reasonably high standard. The choice of where to eat is more a question of what ambience and view you're after; wander around until one takes your fancy. Expect to pay a minimum of TD25 per person plus drinks. One place that has been recomended is **Les Emirs** (☎ 240 865; marina), with Tunisian specialities including lamb *á la gargoulette*.

GETTING THERE & AWAY

There are ample transport options to/from Sousse – see p168 for details.

From Port el-Kantaoui, all buses, tuk-tuks and 'noddy trains' leave from the station around 150m west of the marina.

MONASTIR المنستير

☎ 73 / pop 60,000

In the Middle Ages, it was said that a visit to Monastir was a first step on the road to paradise. Nowadays, the town, on a headland some 20km south of Sousse, may not quite live up to that, but the beach, the superb *ribat* and the Mausoleum of Habib Bourguiba definitely warrant a day trip from Sousse.

History

Monastir was founded as the Phoenician trading settlement of Rous, living then (as now) in the shadow of its larger and more illustrious neighbour, Hadrumete (Sousse).

It briefly took the limelight in AD 46 when Julius Caesar based himself here before defeating Sousse-based Pompey at the Battle of Thapsus, the decisive moment of the Roman civil war. It subsequently became the Roman town of Ruspina.

Two millennia later, Habib Bourguiba was born here and lived on the outskirts of town until his death in April 2000.

Information

INTERNET ACCESS

Publinet La Gare (☼ 8am-8pm; TD2 per hr) At the train station.

MONEY

There are branches of all the major banks on and around place du 3 Septembre 1934, including the Banque du Tunisie which has an ATM, as does the STB on place du Gouvernorate.

POST & TELEPHONE

There are Taxiphone offices all around the town centre.
Main post office (ave Habib Bourguiba) Just south of the medina.

TOURIST INFORMATION

ONTT tourist office (☎ 461 960; rue de l'Indépendence; ☼ 8am-1pm & 3-5.45pm Mon-Thu, 8.30am-1.30pm Fri-Sat) Opposite the Bourguiba Mosque.

Sights & Activities

MEDINA

Monastir's medina was largely demolished after independence in an ill-considered rush to modernise the town in keeping with its status as the birthplace of the president. Thankfully the *ribat* survived, as did the **Great Mosque**. Built in the 9th century, it's a severe Aghlabid creation, apart from the graceful horseshoe arches at the northern end. The Roman columns supporting these arches and those of the prayer hall (closed to non-Muslims) were salvaged from the ruins of ancient Ruspina.

The **walls** in the western part of the medina remain largely intact and are dotted with some interesting old gates. The finest is **Bab el-Gharbi**, at the centre of the western wall. It was built by the Hafsids in the 15th century. **Bab Tunis**, in the northwest corner, was built in 1780 while the main southern gate, **Bab Briqcha**, was built by the Ottomans at the end of the 17th century.

The **Costume Museum** (rue de l'Indépendence; ☼ 9am-1pm & 3-7pm Tue-Sat summer, 9am-4pm winter; admission TD1.1) is around the corner from the tourist office and worth a quick look.

RIBAT

Monastir's star attraction is its immaculately preserved **ribat complex** (admission TD2.1, plus camera TD1; ☼ 8am-7pm summer, 8.30am-5.30pm winter), regarded as the country's finest example of Islamic military architecture. Its seemingly chaotic design with labyrinthine passageways and staircases are legacies of the *ribat*'s many periods of construction and

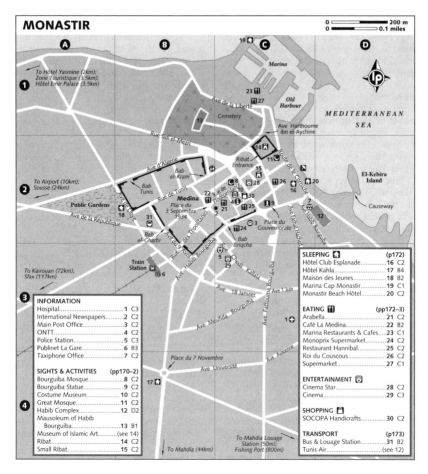

MONASTIR

renovation. The consequence is an evocative structure devoid of any uniformity.

The original *ribat*, known as the Ribat de Harthama, was built in AD 796. Its original scope would have occupied only the central courtyard and museum area. The oldest remaining sections (though heavily restored) include the *nador* (watch tower) and the area around its base, all of which date from the 8th to 10th centuries.

The walls as they currently appear were begun by the Aghlabids at the end of the 9th century and completed in the 11th century. They contained built-in accommodation for defenders and the small courtyard behind the museum is known as the women's *ribat*, with its own prayer room and accommodation.

The walls have been remodelled many times since, notably in the 17th century when the octagonal corner towers were added.

There are excellent views of the town and the coastline from the ramparts and the top of the nador; those suffering from vertigo should tread carefully.

The *ribat*'s prayer room houses a **Museum of Islamic Art**. Apart from early Arab coins and pottery, the collection includes an interesting map of Monastir's medina before independence and early photos of the town.

And if it all looks familiar, that's because the complex is a great favourite of film directors in search of accessible Islamic architecture. Many scenes from *Monty Python's Life of Brian* were filmed here, including hundreds of Tunisian extras laughing at Biggus Dickus. Franco Zeffirelli also came here to shoot scenes for his *Life of Christ*, and Monastir again became Jerusalem in *Jesus of Nazareth*.

BEACHES

Conveniently, the best beach is just across route de la Corniche from the *ribat*. It's quite a sight to emerge from the water and find yourself confronted by the imposing *ribat*. There's also a smaller, quieter beach immediately southeast of El-Kebira Island.

One reader reported that women were likely to be harassed at this beach and that the sand was filled with rubbish, although it was clean when we visited. If you do swim here, wear something on your feet, although preferably not sandals and socks.

The reasonable beaches west of town are dominated by the resort hotels of the zone touristique.

MAUSOLEUM OF HABIB BOURGUIBA

The **Mausoleum of Habib Bourguiba** (admission free) and his family is a must-see. Reached via a long, paved walkway, the gold-and-green cupolas are superb as are the marble courtyard, green-tiled arches and elegant eastern door. The mausoleum houses tombs of the family and a small display of items which belonged to the great man. If it's open, climb the small staircase on the southern side of the building to a first-floor interior balcony from where you can appreciate the full extravagance of the mausoleum's interior.

Opening times are erratic, but the mausoleum usually closes by 3pm. If the main gate is closed, walk around the fence to the small gate on the northern side.

Sleeping
BUDGET & MID-RANGE

Monastir is not a budget destination.

Maison des Jeunes (☎ 461 216; ave de Libye; dm TD5) This is Monastir's only cheap accommodation. It's just along from the bus station and offers all the comforts of an army barracks, although it has had a lick of paint.

Hôtel Kahla (☎ 464 586; fax 467 881; ave Habib Bourguiba; s/d TD20/30) A bit out on a limb south of town and a long walk from the beach, this is nonetheless a touch cheaper than the waterfront hotels. The rooms are decent but uninspiring.

Hôtel Monastir Beach (☎ 464 766; fax 463 594; s/d TD27/40; ﷯) This hotel lives up to its name – it runs the length of the main town beach, set beneath the footpath of Route de la Corniche. The rooms are a bit natty but clean. Every room has large French doors which open onto the beach; ideal if proximity to the water is your thing.

Hôtel Yasmine (☎ 501 546; route de la Falaise; s/d TD40/60) This excellent small family-run pension, 2km west of town, has attractive rooms, patchy bathrooms, good restaurant and it's just across the road from a good beach.

TOP END

Hôtel Club Esplanade (☎ 460 146; fax 460 050; route de la Corniche; s/d TD45/60, full board TD55/80; ﷯ ﷯) Three-star and terrific value if you can get a room. The location is ideal and the rooms are nicely kept. Ask for a room at the front with a balcony and sea view; they cost no more.

Marina Cap Monastir (☎ 462 305; marina@ planet.tn; Marina complex; d TD106, 4/6/8-bed apartments TD115/133/172; ﷯ ﷯) This extensive complex doesn't have the class of Port el-Kantaoui (north of Sousse), but it's close to town and laid-out around a yacht-filled harbour. The rooms are tidy and quiet and they offer good weekly rates.

Most of the resort hotels are located along the beaches west of town all the way from Monastir to Skanes, 8km away. They're quite removed from the town and they're really only good value if you book as part of a package.

Eating

All places here are open for lunch and dinner.

The **Café La Medina** (place du 3 Septembre 1934) is a popular place with bargain *briqs* (TD1.2), salads from TD2 and main courses from TD3. There's a choice of pizzas from TD2 and Gulf octopus salad (TD2.5). The service is friendly and the servings large enough. **Arabella** across the road is similar.

The **Roi du Couscous**, on the beach side of place du Gouvernorate, has couscous of the day for TD3.

Restaurant Hannibal, tucked away in the southeastern corner of the medina, is a popular spot with a rooftop terrace overlooking the medina. You can eat well here for TD15 per person.

The best restaurants are clustered together out at the marina. They're all good and it's a matter of which ambience suits your mood. Choices include **Le Grill** (☎ 462 136) and the **Restaurant Marina** (☎ 461 449). Reckon on TD30 per person, plus wine.

Self-caterers can head for the Monoprix supermarket, next to the post office.

Getting There & Away

AIR
Monastir's airport handles a lot of international traffic, but no domestic flights.

The **Tunis Air** office (☎ 468 189; route de la Corniche) is in the Habib Complex.

BUS
The bus station is at the western edge of the medina. There are services to Sousse (TD1.3, 30 minutes) every 30 minutes and to Mahdia (TD1.8, one hour) hourly.

CAR
Avis (☎ 521 031), **Europcar** (☎ 521 314) and **Hertz** (☎ 521 300) are all based at Monastir's airport.

LOUAGE
Louages to Sousse (TD1.2), Kairouan (TD4.4) and Tunis (TD7.5) leave from next to the bus station. Louages to Mahdia leave from their own station on the southeastern side of town.

TRAIN
There are 16 trains a day (less often in winter) to Sousse (2nd/1st class TD1/1.3, 30 minutes) and eight to Mahdia (TD1.7/2.4, one hour).

There's also one train a day to Tunis (2nd/1st/confort class TD7.4/9.5/10.1, three hours).

Getting Around

TO/FROM THE AIRPORT
Monastir's airport is at Skanes, 10km west of town on the road to Sousse. The trip costs about TD4.5 by taxi from the town centre. You can also get to the airport on any of the trains between Monastir and Sousse; L'Aeroport station is 200m from the airport terminal.

KAIROUAN   القيروان
☎ 77 / pop 118,000
Kairouan, 57km west of Sousse, is one of the seven holy cities of Islam, its mosque is the oldest in North Africa and its medina a charming blue, white and green evocation of life as it once was.

It's also Tunisia's most conservative city and, as such, can appear a little bemused and over-excited by the arrival of day-tripping tourists from the coast. But Kairouan has always been a place of travellers, whether here for trade or the purposes of pilgrimage, a city accustomed to strange people from far-off lands. Modern Kairouan is no exception, and in this sense there's something fundamentally Tunisian about the place – Islamic to its core and with deep roots in tradition, but adapted to the commercial necessities of the modern world. Whether you're here for the day or able to stay for a couple of nights, Kairouan is not to be missed.

History
It was in Kairouan that Islam gained its first foothold in the Maghreb. The original Arab settlement lasted only a few years before it was destroyed by a Berber rebellion. It was re-established in AD 694 by Hassan ibn Nooman and has been Islamic ever since.

THE FOUNDING OF KAIROUAN

The origins of many cities in North Africa (eg Ghadames in neighbouring Libya) centre around the chance discovery of wells. As a modern traveller on the barren plains of the Maghreb, you'll appreciate why such sites were chosen for cities. But Kairouan was different.

Kairouan was founded in AD 670 by the Arab general Okba ibn Nafaa al-Fihri and takes its name from the Arabic word *qayrawan*, meaning 'military camp'. According to legend, the site for the city was chosen after Okba's horse stumbled on a golden goblet that lay buried in the sands. The goblet turned out to be one that had mysteriously disappeared from Mecca some years previously. When it was picked up, water sprang from the ground – supplied, it was concluded, by the same source that supplied the holy well of Zem-Zem in Mecca. The legend survives at Bir Barouta in the heart of the medina.

KAIROUAN

0 ————————— 400 m
0 ————————— 0.2 miles

A · **B** · **C** · **D**

1

Some Minor Roads Not Depicted

To Hôtel Amina (1km);
Sousse (57km);
Hammamet (97km);
Tunis (155km)

Aghlabid
Basins

7 **●11**

Place
7 Novembre

↑21

🛏30

Ave Ali Belhouane

0 ————— 200 m
0 ————— 0.1 miles

↑25

ⓢ9

16

Ville
Nouvelle

🛏36

16
🛏16

9 Avril

26

↑27

🛏33

34
🛏

8 ⓢ

29

Rue de la Victoire

ⓢ

6

🛏32

Rue Habib Thameur

2

Ave Ibn el-Aghlab

Ave Ibn el-Jazzar

3 ✚

Rue Ennahassine

Cemetery

19 ©

To Bus & Louage Stations (300m);
Sbeitla (107km); Makthar (114km)

Ave Ahmed Tlili

Ave el-Moez Ibn Badis

Rue Essaadia

Ave Zama el-Belaoui

3

Rue Oum el-Mouminin Aïcha

Cemetery

Ave el-Imam Sahnoun

Rue Sidi Abdelkada

Rue Oum Yadh

© 13

Rue Okba Ibn Nafâa

Bab
Essayouri

↑22

Rue el-Bakri

↑23

Rue de la Kasbah

Rue de Jerba

Rue el-Kartadjni

Rue el-Essayouri

Bab
el-Khoukha

4

To Louage Station (400m);
Bus Station (500m);
Sbeitla (107km)

24 ↑ Market

Rue de Tunis

Bab Tunis

Rue Ibn Nej

Ave Zama

Rue Sidi Ghaïd

18 ©

Rue Ibn Zoubeir

Rue Zryeb

Rue Abou Nawas

Rue Sabah Sousi

Rue Dael-Bey

Rue el-Khadhraoui

Rue Bab Jedid

Ave Novembre

Rue des
Tailleurs

Souq el-
Blaghia

37 ▭

5 ✦

20 ↑
🛏28
31

38
Souq

10 ●

Place
Zarrouk

Rue de la Mosquée des Trois Portes

15

Bab el-Monkas

Ave de Kortoba

Rue el-Kedidi

Bou Chmali

5

Rue Hannibal

Rue Ibn Aria

Rue Rab Essalam

Ave Tarek Ibn Zayed

Rue de la Victoire

Rue Ali el-Barak

Ave Ali Zouaoui

Rue Sidi Abdel Noumen

Rue Ali Bent Amrial

🛏35

17

Place des
Martyrs

Bab ech Chouhada

14
12 Ave Assad ibn Fourat

Bab Jedid

To Sousse
(68km)

6

Cemetery

Rue de la Liberté

Rue de Zeroud

Ave Ali Belhouane

Ave Ali Zouaoui

Ave du 20 Mars

Ave de la République

Ave de Mahdia

See Inset

Ville
Nouvelle

Rue Habib Thameur

Rue 2 Mars 1934

Rue Hssein en-Noomain

To Maison des
Jeunes (500m)

To Raqqada (9km);
Sfax (136km)

To El-Jem (69km)

The city's golden age began when it became the capital of the Aghlabid dynasty in AD 909. Although they preferred to rule from their palace at Raqqada, 9km south of Kairouan, it was the Aghlabids who endowed the city with its most important historic buildings, most notably the Great Mosque.

Kairouan fell to the Fatimids in AD 909, and declined after the capital was moved to Mahdia. Its fortunes hit rock bottom when it was sacked in 1057 during the Hilalian invasions (p160). It never regained its position of political pre-eminence but it retained its significance as a seat of Islamic scholarship and holy city of Islam.

Orientation

Life in Kairouan revolves around the medina at the centre of town and the ville nouvelle to the south. The two meet at the large open space (place des Martyrs) outside the medina's main southern gate, the Bab ech Chouhada. The medina's principal street, ave 7 Novembre, runs northwest from here to the main northern gate, Bab Tunis.

Information

INTERNET ACCESS
Publitel (Hôtel el-Menema; TD1.5 per hr) Claims to be open 24 hours but don't count on it.

MONEY
There are branches of all the major banks on the streets south of place des Martyrs.
Banque du Tunisie (cnr ave de la République & ave Hamda Lâaouani) ATM.
BIAT (rue de la Victoire) ATM.
UIB (ave Hamda Lâaouani) Near place des Martyrs, ATM.

POST & TELEPHONE
Taxiphone offices are everywhere.
Main post office Southwest of Bab ech Chouhada.

TOURIST INFORMATION
ONTT tourist office (☎ 221 797; place des Martyrs; ⏰ 8am-4pm) South of the medina. Don't expect to come away from here much the wiser, and you may feel that you're getting in the way of more urgent business.
Syndicat d'initiative (cnr ave Ibn el-Jazzar and ave Ibn el-Aghlab; ⏰ 8am-6pm summer, 8.30am-5.30pm winter) On the northern edge of town. Infinitely more friendly and marginally more helpful than the ONTT.

Sights
MEDINA
Kairouan's medina feels like no other in the country. Its façades are enchanting with white walls offset by pale blue or green arches, balconies and shutters. It's a wonderful place to wander and admire the wealth of religious monuments which stand alongside decaying but elegant merchant houses, ramshackle covered souqs and carpet shops. The main thoroughfare, ave 7 Novembre, has all of these things and a clamour for the tourist dollar that doesn't extend much further into the medina.

The first walls of the medina were built towards the end of the 8th century, but those you'll see today date mainly from the 18th century. Of the numerous gates, the oldest is **Bab el-Khoukha**, which features a horseshoe arch supported by columns. It was built in 1706.

Great Mosque
The **Great Mosque** (admission multiple-site ticket; ⏰ 8am-2pm Sat-Thu, 8am-noon Fri), in the northeast corner of the medina, is North Africa's holiest Islamic site. It's also known as Sidi Okba Mosque, after the founder of Kairouan who built the first mosque here in AD 670. The original version was completely destroyed, and most of what stands today was built by the Aghlabids in the 9th century.

ENTRY TICKETS & GUIDES

Most of the sites in Kairouan can be visited on a single ticket, which can be purchased at the Great Mosque, the syndicat d'initiative or the Zaouia of Sidi Sahab. The tickets (TD4.2) are valid for the Great Mosque, the Aghlabid Basins, the Zaouia of Sidi Sahab, the Zaouia of Sidi Amor Abbada, Bir Barouta, the Zaouia of Sidi Abid el-Ghariani and the Raqqada Islamic Art Museum (see Sights, beginning previous page). The ticket is valid only for one day and one entry per site. The camera permit (TD1) is valid at all of the sites mentioned.

If you want a guide to show you around, you can arrange one through the syndicat d'initiative. These guys carry accreditation, with photos, and they know their stuff. They charge TD15 for a tour of all the major sites. They all speak Arabic and French; some also speak English and/or German. Some of the accredited guides double as low-key lookouts for carpet shops.

The exterior, with its buttressed walls, has a typically unadorned Aghlabid design. Impressions change once you step into the huge marble-paved courtyard, surrounded by an arched colonnade. The courtyard was designed for water catchment, and the paving slopes towards an intricately decorated central drainage hole which delivers the collected rainwater into the 9th-century cisterns below. The decorations were designed to filter dust from the water. The marble rims of the two wells both have deep rope grooves worn by centuries of hauling water up from the depths.

The northwestern end of the courtyard is dominated by a square three-tiered minaret. The lowest level was built in AD 728. At the base of the minaret, note the two Roman slabs (one upside down) bearing Latin inscriptions.

The prayer hall is at the southern end of the courtyard. The enormous, studded wooden doors date from 1829; the carved panels above them are particularly fine. Non-Muslims are not allowed inside, but the doors are left open to allow a glimpse of the interior. The 414 pillars that support the horseshoe arches and roof were, like those of the colonnade, originally Roman or Byzantine, salvaged from Carthage and Hadrumètum (Sousse), and no two are the same. At the far end of the hall, it's just possible to make out the precious 9th-century tiles behind the mihrab (prayer niche in the mosque wall which indicates the direction of Mecca) between two red marble columns. The tiles were imported from Baghdad along with the wood for the richly adorned *minbar* (pulpit) next to it.

Visitors must be appropriately dressed; robes are available at the entrance. Entry is through the main gate on rue Okba ibn Nafaa. The other eight gates are closed to non-Muslims.

For an overview of the Great Mosque, it's worth taking in the view from the roof of a neighbouring carpet shop on rue Okba ibn Nafaa. The owners will cheekily claim that the view is included in the price of the entry ticket; so too is a period spent inspecting carpets.

Zaouia of Sidi Abid el-Ghariani

Just inside the Bab ech Chouhada, the restored **Zaouia of Sidi Abid el-Ghariani** (rue Sidi el-Ghariani; admission multiple-site ticket) dates from the 14th century and contains some fine woodcarving and stuccowork. The *zaouia* also houses the tomb of the Hafsid sultan Moulay Hassan who ruled from 1525 to 1543. There are no official opening hours, but you're most likely to find it open in the morning.

Maison du Gouverneur

This 18th-century residence of the former beys or pashas of Kairouan is an exquisitely restored medina house and an extravagant counterpoint to the austerity of the Aghlabids. The interior is a sumptuous combination of cedar and teak, marble latticework, plaster moulding and elegant tiled arches adorning the entrance hall, harem and reception hall where the governor received official guests and held meetings. The house doubles, of course, as a carpet shop; after watching a woman demonstrate the painstaking art of carpet making (women make the carpets, men sell them), you'll be expected to view the carpets. If you only experience the carpet ritual once in Kairouan, make it here.

The building is signposted as 'Tapis-Sabra' and is generally open 8am to 5pm daily. Admission is free (unless you buy a carpet).

Bir Barouta

The **Bir Barouta** (admission multiple-entry ticket), just north of ave Ali Belhouane, was built by the Ottoman ruler Mohammed Bey in 1676 to surround the well that features in the city's foundation legend. Its waters are supposedly linked to the well of Zem-Zem in Mecca. The scene itself is a little staged for the uninitiated with a blinkered camel turning the wheel to draw water from the well for people to taste. That said, this is an important religious moment for most visitors, many of whom genuinely believe that the well is connected to Mecca.

It's up to you whether you drink the water, but at least one Lonely Planet author suffered an upset stomach the day after doing so.

Mosque of the Three Doors

The **Mosque of the Three Doors** (rue de la Mosquée des Trois Portes), 250m northeast of the Bir Barouta, was founded in AD 866 by Mohammed bin Kairoun el-Maafri, a holy man from the Spanish city of Cordoba. The interior is closed to non-Muslims, but the main feature is the elaborate façade, with its strong Andalusian influences. The mosque's three arched doorways are topped by intricate friezes of Kufic script (two of which name the mosque's founder) interspersed with floral reliefs and crowned with a carved cornice. It's well worth a detour.

AGHLABID BASINS

These **cisterns** (ave Ibn el-Aghlab; admission multiple-site ticket; ⊗ 7.30am-6.30pm summer, 8.30am-6pm winter) were built by the Aghlabids in the 9th century. Water was delivered by aqueduct from the hills 36km west of Kairouan into the smaller settling basin and then into the enormous main holding basin, which was 5m deep and 128m in diameter. In the centre of the main pool was a pavilion where the rulers could come to relax on summer evenings. The basins are more of historic than aesthetic interest.

ZAOUIA OF SIDI SAHAB

This extensive **zaouia** (ave Zama el Belaoui; admission multiple-site ticket; ⊗ 7.30am-6.30pm), about 1.5km northwest of the medina, houses the tomb of Abu Zama el-Belaoui, a *sahab* (companion) of the Prophet Mohammed. He was known as the barber because he always carried three hairs from the Prophet's beard with him, and the *zaouia* is sometimes referred to as the Mosque of the Barber. While the original mausoleum dates back to the 7th century AD, most of what stands today was added at the end of the 17th century. The additions include a *funduq* to house pilgrims, a medersa and a mosque.

The entrance to the zaouia is along an unusually decorative marble passageway that leads to a stunning white central courtyard. Sidi Sahab's mausoleum is in the northwestern corner, topped by a cupola added in 1629. Non-Muslims are not permitted to enter. The small room on the opposite side of the courtyard contains the tomb of the architect of the Great Mosque.

ZAOUIA OF SIDI AMOR ABBADA

This **zaouia** (off rue Sidi Gaid; admission multiple-site ticket; ⊗ 7.30am-6.30pm), identifiable by its seven white cupolas, was built in 1860 around the tomb of Sidi Amor Abbada, a local blacksmith with a gift for prophecy. He specialised in the production of oversized things, like a set of giant anchors (now standing north of place des Martyrs) that were supposed to secure Kairouan to the earth.

ONAT MUSEUM

The **ONAT Museum** (ave Ali Zouaoui; admission free; ⊗ 9am-1pm & 3-6pm Mon-Thu, 9am-1pm Fri & Sat) houses a collection of rugs. It could be missed, although these are the people who accredit all carpets sold in Kairouan; if you plan to buy one, look here at the various styles.

Sleeping

BUDGET

Maison des Jeunes (☎ 228 239; ave de Fes; dm TD4) The city's youth hostel, about 1km southeast of the medina, is cheap and uninviting.

Hôtel Sabra (☎ 230 263; place des Martyrs; s/d TD9/18, d with private bathroom TD20) Conveniently located opposite the Bab ech Chouhada, the Sabra is popular and deservedly so with simple, tidy rooms and staff used to dealing with travellers. There's a *hammam* (bathhouse) and the views from the roof terrace (where you can sleep in summer) are spectacular. The front rooms also have views but can be noisy.

Hôtel el-Menema (☎ 225 003; fax 226 182; ave el-Moez ibn Badis; s/d with breakfast TD10/20; 🖵) This small, modern hotel north of the medina is terrific value with good, spacious rooms, some with balcony. Highly recommended.

Hôtel Les Aghlabites (☎ 230 880; off place de Tunis; s/d TD8/16) This converted *funduq* north of the medina isn't in the most inviting part of town, but the rooms are fine and some open onto a large, tiled courtyard set back from the street. Some rooms come with a dodgy bathroom at no extra cost.

Hôtel Barouta (no phone; ave 7 Novembre; s/d TD6/12) The only place to stay in the medina, this is only for those for whom price is everything. Rooms are basic, mattresses sag almost to the floor and women will feel uncomfortable here. Some rooms have balconies overlooking the medina's main thoroughfare – a good vantage point to watch the world go by.

MID-RANGE

All hotels listed below come with air-con and prices include breakfast.

Hôtel Splendid (☎ 230 041; fax 230 829; rue 9 Avril; s/d TD26.5/39) This place once lived up to its name but is now ageing, and not doing so particularly gracefully. It is inhabited by surly staff. However, some of the rooms at the front (especially Nos 104 and 105) are still spacious, comfortable and with a hint of character.

Tunisia Hôtel (☎ 231 775; fax 231 597; ave de la République; s/d TD20/40) This good older-style hotel is about 400m south of the medina. Ask to see a few rooms as some are better than others, but they're generally not bad for the price, if a little dark.

Hôtel Continental (☎ 221 135; fax 229 900; ave Ibn el-Aghlab; s/d TD39/58) This is a quiet three-star hotel on the northern edge of town. The rooms are quite nice, the bathrooms are ageing rapidly and it's a long, hot walk into town. The return journey might be made more bearable if they filled the swimming pool.

TOP END

Hôtel la Kasbah (☎ 237 301; kasbah.kairouan@gnet.tn; ave Ibn el-Jazzar; s/d TD59/86; 🌐 🖵) Occupying the old kasbah in the northern section of the medina, this is a fantastic place to stay. The whole place has a touch of class and the rooms are elegant without being overdone.

The large pool in the central courtyard is heated.

Hôtel Amina (☎ 225 466; fax 225 411; ave Ibn el-Aghlab; s/d TD45/65; 🌐 🖵) The second-best hotel in town, it's still depressingly remote from the rest of town. Otherwise it's a comfortable, modern three-star hotel with decent rooms.

Eating
PATISSERIES

Kairouan is famous for a date-filled semolina cake soaked in honey called *makhroud*, which can be found everywhere. Expect to pay 100 mills a piece.

Segni (ave 7 Novembre) This is the best place to sample *makhroud* and other local specialties. Signed only in Arabic in the middle of the medina, Segni's interior is a wonderful example of a traditional medina shop.

Other places to try include the outdoor stalls just off the main thoroughfare near the arch, or the brightly lit and modern **Patisserie Rabaoui Kairouan** (rue Soukina bint el-Hassan).

RESTAURANTS

The streets south of the medina are the place to go looking for a cheap meal; all places listed here open for lunch and dinner.

Restaurant Sabra (ave de la République; salads TD1.3; mains from TD2.5; set meals TD7) Next to the Tunisia Hôtel, this is friendly and a good place to start. The décor is simple and the food is reasonable; couscous is plentiful and good.

Restaurant Karawan (rue Soukina bint el-Hassan; set meals TD8) An excellent choice – spotlessly clean, friendly and consistently good food. The menu contains all the usual salads, couscous, tajines and *briqs*, but they do them well.

Roi Roi du Couscous (ave Ali Zouaoui; mains around TD4) Filled with men and smoke, but (or perhaps because) this is one place where you can get alcohol – liquor licences are hard to come by in Kairouan. The food's OK but nothing more.

Restaurant de la Jeunesse (ave 7 Novembre; mains around TD6) A good place in the heart of the medina, the waiters here are friendly and the food good and varied (the beans with lamb are especially good), but beware of overcharging.

Picolomondo (ave ibn el-Jazzar; pizzas from TD2.5) This is a good place to rest on your way to

JUST LOOK, NO BUY

Viewing vast numbers of carpets and kilims is as much a part of the Kairouan experience as visiting the Great Mosque. However averse you might be to the idea, you're likely at some stage to find yourself in a carpet shop. Resistance is futile. The secret is to accept the hospitality, enjoy the ceremony and not feel in the least obliged to buy – easier said than done.

The process starts with a passing glance as you walk through one of the medina's lanes. You're invited inside and offered sweet tea or Turkish coffee while you sit around and discuss the fact that the salesman (they're all men and all very charming) has a brother or uncle living in your country and indeed, what providence, sold a carpet, a very beautiful carpet, from his private collection, to one of your countrymen just last week.

While you wait for your drinks, why not look, looking is free, just for the pleasure of your eyes. Choices are unfurled by a boy, while another brings tea and coffee which is too hot to drink quickly. You ask a price and are told in a conspiratorial whisper that, because you have not come as part of a group, you will be offered a 30% discount. You're an honoured guest in Tunisia and hospitality demands such things.

The ones you don't like are rolled up and stacked against a wall. The designs are explained and more young men arrive to hold the carpets at viewing level. They might even try to burn the carpet with a cigarette lighter to show its durability. Suddenly the room is filled with young men at your service. Carpets are expertly rolled into tiny bundles to show how easily they will fit in your bag for carrying home.

This is the point at which you might decide that carpet-buying is not for you. You say that you want to think about it. The salesman, possibly now casting furtive glances in the direction of the shop owner, is suddenly serious, knowing full well that the vast majority of tourists never return despite promises to do so, knowing even better that most visitors to Kairouan will be leaving on the next bus out of town. Prices drop. They might even do so dramatically. Looks of sadness will be exchanged that such beautiful carpets must be let go for such a price. As you walk out the door – you might be left to find your own way out as hospitality evaporates – you might hear dark mutterings and grim curses directed towards you. More likely, you'll look over your shoulder and see the salesman deflated on a chair, like a child who has lost his toy.

If you do decide to stay, bargain and buy, most of what the salesmen say about their carpets is true (apart from the price) – they are a wonderful keepsake to remember your journey. Your carpet is wrapped before you can reconsider. You hand over your credit card. The salesman looks aggrieved one last time. Cash is not possible, madam? Credit cards involve too much paperwork, sir. You might be able to get a few dinars more off the price for breach of contract, offset by requests for tips for the boys.

You leave with your carpet under your arm and walk past all the other carpet dealers who'll tell you that you paid too much. You can't help but smile at the whole performance. Rest assured, the man who sold you the carpet is smiling too.

or from the Aghlabid pools. The pizzas are nothing to write home about but are tasty nonetheless.

SELF-CATERING

Self-caterers can head for the supermarket on ave de Mahdia. Lots of fruit is grown around Kairouan; you'll find whatever's in season at the stalls around place de Tunis, just north of the medina.

Drinking

There are plenty of outdoor places to enjoy a coffee, soft drink, mint tea or a *sheesha*

(water pipe). Most popular in the evenings are the tables strewn around place des Martyrs.

For a rather more traditional experience head to the **Turkish Coffeehouse** (ave 7 Novembre), which is almost a century old; you'll find it has the atmosphere and earthy elegance to match.

If you're looking for bars with an all-male ambience, head to the main round-about south of the medina on ave Ali Zouaoui, next to the Roi Roi du Couscous restaurant. For a quieter beer, try the **Hotel Splendid**.

Shopping

Kairouan is the carpet capital of the country. If you're in the market for a carpet, this is a good place to do your shopping.

There are two basic types of carpet: knotted and woven. The traditional (pre-Islamic) carpet industry was based on the weaving of *mergoums* and *kilims*. *Mergoums* feature very bright, geometric designs, with bold use of reds, purples, blues and other vivid colours. Kilims use traditional Berber motifs on a woven background. Both are reasonably cheap to buy. The Berber *guetiffa* is another type of knotted carpet: thick-pile and normally cream coloured, with Berber motifs.

The best known of the knotted carpets are the classical (Persian-style) Kairouan carpets. This style of carpet-making was first introduced to Tunisia by the Turks. Legend has it that the first knotted carpet to be made in Tunisia was by the daughter of the Turkish governor of Kairouan.

Knotted carpets are priced according to the number of knots per square metre. On the back of each carpet is a small certificate containing the dimensions and type of carpet. Official prices are:

10x10	10,000 knots per sq metre	TD100-150 per sq metre
12x12	14,000 knots per sq metre	TD100-150 per sq metre
20x20	40,000 knots per sq metre	TD170-220 per sq metre
30x30	90,000 knots per sq metre	TD270-350 per sq metre
40x40	160,000 knots per sq metre	TD320-450 per sq metre
50x50	250,000 knots per sq metre (Usually silk)	TD1300-1600 per sq metre
kilims	TD150-200	

To see carpets being made without the hard sell, the **Centre des Traditions et des Métiers d'Art de Kairouan**, just north of Bir Barouta on a side street leading to the souqs, was set up by ONAT to promote local handicrafts. The rooms upstairs are set up to demonstrate traditional techniques for weaving, embroidery and carpet making. The artisans are usually happy to show you how it's done.

Another option is to attend the carpet auctions where Berber women sell their carpets to shop-owners. You may even be able to bid if you speak Arabic. It all takes place in the Souq el-Blaghija, with most of the action between 11am and 1pm on a Saturday. Needless to say, the carpet dealers will make you feel as unwelcome as possible, just in case you realise the extent of their profit margins.

Getting There & Around

The bus and louage stations are next to each other about 300m west of the Zaouia of Sidi Sahab. A taxi from the centre of town to place des Martyrs costs about TD1 on the meter but many taxi drivers ask three times that.

Note that for El-Jem, you'll have to go via Sousse.

BUS

Most of the services are operated by the national line, SNTRI, which has its own booking office in the terminal, together with an information board displaying destinations and departure times.

Destination	Fare	Duration	Frequency (per day)
Douz	TD17.9	7 hrs	1
Gabès	TD9.4	4¼ hrs	5
Gafsa	TD9.4	3 hrs	6
Jerba	TD14.4	5 hrs	2
Kasserine	TD7.2	2½ hrs	1
Kélibia	TD7.2	3 hrs	1
Medenine	TD12.3	5¼ hrs	1
Nabeul	TD5	2¼ hrs	3
Nefta	TD13.8	7½ hrs	2
Tozeur	TD13	4½ hrs	3
Tunis	TD7.5	3 hrs	hourly

Other destinations are served by regional companies with separate booking offices at the terminal. They include: Sousse (TD3, 1½ hours, every 30 minutes 6.30am to 7.30pm), three buses a day to Sfax (TD5.5, two hours) and two to Makthar (TD4.5, 1¾ hours).

LOUAGE

There are frequent departures to Sousse (TD3.5), Sfax (TD6.7) and Tunis (TD7.4), and occasional services to Makthar (TD4.8), Sbeitla (TD5.7) and Hammamet (TD4.5).

AROUND KAIROUAN

Raqqada Islamic Art Museum (9.30am-4.30pm Tue-Sun; entry on multiple-site ticket) occupies a former presidential palace at Raqqada, 9km south of Kairouan; take any transport heading to Sfax. Exhibits on display here include a model of the Great Mosque of Kairouan, a faithfully reproduced plaster copy of the mihrab and lots of calligraphy. There are ambitious plans for expansion, until which time it's probably not worth the effort.

EL-JEM الجم

☎ 73 / pop 14,000

There can be few more remarkable sights in Tunisia than the first glimpse of El-Jem, the ancient colosseum dwarfing the matchbox buildings of the modern town. Built on a low plateau halfway between Sousse and Sfax, the colosseum is the most impressive Roman monument in Africa.

History

E-Jem's colosseum was once the crowning glory of ancient Thysdrus, a thriving market town that grew up at the junction of the Sahel's lucrative trade routes during the 1st century AD and which derived its wealth from the olive oil produced in the area. Thysdrus, a town of sumptuous villas, reached the peak of its prosperity in the 2nd and 3rd centuries AD.

In the 17th century, the troops of Mohammed Bey blasted a hole in the western wall to flush out local tribesmen and the breach was widened during another rebellion in 1850.

Orientation & Information

Ave Habib Bourguiba runs from the colosseum to the train station on the southern edge of town. The post office and only bank are southwest of here on ave Fahdel ben Achour (the road to Sfax).

Sights

COLOSSEUM

This World Heritage-listed **colosseum** (admission TD4.2, plus camera TD1; ☼ 7am-7pm summer, 8am-5pm winter) was the third largest in the Roman world; it was 138m long by 114m wide, with three tiers of seating 30m high. Its seating capacity has been estimated at 30,000 – considerably more than the population of the town itself.

The colosseum is believed to have been built between AD 230 and 238, and is generally attributed to the African proconsul Gordian, a local landowner and patron. Stone for construction had to be hauled all the way from the quarries at Sullectum (modern Salakta), 30km away on the coast, and water had to be brought 15km by underground aqueduct from the hills northwest of town.

In AD 238, Gordian was declared emperor of Rome here during an ill-fated rebellion against the Emperor Maximus. Gordian reportedly committed suicide in the amphitheatre when it became obvious that the rebellion was doomed.

The colosseum later doubled as a last line of defence. The Berber princess Al-Kahina was besieged here by Arab forces at the end of the 7th century. According to legend, the colosseum was linked by tunnel to the coastal town of Salakta, enabling Al-Kahina to torment her besiegers by waving fresh fish from the top of the walls (see the boxed text, p204).

When you enter the colosseum for the first time, you'll be struck by the indulgent grandeur of the Roman vision. The south side of the amphitheatre is the most intact, allowing a sense of how the seats swept

---

THE ROMAN SENSE OF FUN

If you've seen *Gladiator*, you'll have an idea of what a day out at the colosseum was all about. But the spectacle of warriors fighting to the death was only the highpoint at the end of a long day which was not for the faint-hearted.

Typical prematch entertainment consisted of hunting rabbits and small rodents in the morning followed by shackled criminals being left to the mercies of the lions. At least the Christians, who followed the criminals, were allowed into the arena free of shackles although few escaped. All of this was a mere precursor to the main event – the epic contests of the gladiators.

Such bloody performances were not only about entertainment, and owe much to the 'bread and circuses' theory. If the people were kept at once sated and distracted by the sight of men and wild animals dying in distress, they were less inclined to question the excesses and misrule of the Roman administration.

SEEING THE COLOSSEUM AT SUNSET

The best time to see the colosseum is at sunset when the sun bathes the amphitheatre's interior in golden light. But for independent travellers this is more difficult than it should be.

One option is to charter a private taxi. As you'll need to pay for the driver to return home anyway, it can be a good idea to take a taxi from Mahdia (around TD30 return) or Sousse or Sfax (both around TD35).

The other option is to visit from Sfax and return on the 8.57pm train. If you're quick (and the train is late), you might also catch the 7.13pm train to Sousse. Check current departure times at the stations in Sousse and Sfax before setting out.

Either that or get up (very) early and catch a louage from Mahdia or Sousse (they start filling from 6am) and content yourself with the almost-as-impressive sunrise.

---

down from the upper tiers to the marble-walled arena, beneath which ran arched corridors. To see how the colosseum must once have appeared, check out the artist's impression displayed just inside the entrance gate.

You can still climb up to the upper seating levels and gaze down on the arena. It's also possible to explore the two long underground passageways that were used to hold animals, gladiators and other unfortunates in their last moments before they were thrust into the arena to provide entertainment for the masses. It was here that many spent their last lonely minutes, listening to 30,000 people baying for their blood.

To get a relatively uninterrupted view back towards the colosseum, take any of the streets behind the colosseum, heading north.

MUSEUM
El-Jem's **museum** (admission colosseum ticket; ⏲ 7am-7pm summer, 8am-5pm winter) is 1km south of the amphitheatre on the road to Sfax. If you can, avoid visiting this museum in a hurry. It houses a small but exceptionally beautiful collection of mosaics which are superbly rendered. Highlights include a splendid array of scenes from the colosseum, a dramatic depiction of Dionysius astride a tiger and the delightful if quixotic Genius of the Year.

OTHER SITES
The colosseum was not the first amphitheatre to be built at Thysdrus. Opposite the museum and across the railway line to the east are the ruins of an earlier amphitheatre, dug into a low hill. There's also a second area of Roman villas to the north

of the colosseum, signposted off ave Farhat Hached, the road to Sousse.

Festivals & Events
From mid-July until early August, the colosseum is transformed into a splendid floodlit venue for the **El-Jem International Symphonic Music Festival** (☎ 631 163; contact@festivaleljem.com). You can buy tickets (TD10.5 to TD27) and find a programme of events at the tourist office in Sousse. The tourist office in Tunis organises an evening bus to and from the colosseum (see p67 for contact details).

Sleeping & Eating
At the time of research, El-Jem had to be visited on a day trip (see following) as the town's only hotel, the Hôtel Julius next to the train station, was closed.

The only alternative is the **Hôtel Club Ksar El-Jem** (☎ 632 800; s/d TD25/40; ✕ ⛱), 5km north of town on the road to Sousse. The rooms are pleasant enough but getting transport in and out of town can be a problem.

The **Restaurant Le Bonheur** (⏲ lunch & dinner), 200m west of the train station, offers a small selection of traditional dishes like spicy couscous with chicken (TD4).

Getting There & Away
The louage station is 500m west of the train station along ave Hedi Chaker. The most frequent departures are to Mahdia (TD1.9), but there are also semiregular departures for Tunis (TD8.8), Sousse (TD3.3) and Sfax (TD3.3). For Kairouan, you'll need to change at Souassi. The last louage has usually left the station by 7.15pm and often well before.

Buses leave from outside the train station. A lot of SNTRI buses pass through town, but they're often full. There are buses to Tunis (TD9.5, three hours, four daily), Sousse (TD3.1, 1¼ hours), Sfax (TD3, 1¼ hours) and Mahdia (TD2, one hour).

There are trains north to Sousse (TD4.4 in 1st class, one hour) and Tunis (TD10.3, three hours), and south to Sfax (TD4.2, one hour), but only a couple in each direction are at decent times and of any use to colosseum visitors.

MAHDIA   المهدية
☎ 73 / pop 45,000

Mahdia is a delightful place, resembling a small fishing village from the northern Mediterranean grafted onto a wonderful old Arab town. It's the sort of place to spend a few days resting from the rigours of life on the road. Mahdia occupies a narrow peninsula with no room for expansion, ensuring that money can be made from the *zone touristique,* which stretches along the coast to the north of town, without Mahdia selling its soul. The result is an ancient town which is home to a healthy proportion of young people who feel no need to seek their fortunes elsewhere. Whether sitting under the shade of the trees in the wonderful place du Caire or rambling through the compact medina, chances are that you'll end up staying longer than you'd planned.

History
Mahdia was founded as a port in AD 916 by the first Fatimid caliph, Obeid Allah, known as El-Mahdi, who used Mahdia's narrow rugged peninsula as a coastal base from which to plan his attack on his ultimate goal, Cairo, and as an easily defensible refuge for his minority Shiite followers.

The original Fatimid city was protected by a massive wall, up to 10m thick, that cut across the peninsula at its narrowest point, where the Skifa el-Kahla now stands. A smaller wall encircled the remainder of the peninsula. The area within these walls was a royal compound, reserved for the Mahdi and his entourage while his subjects lived outside the walls.

When the Fatimids abandoned Mahdia in AD 947, the inhabitants of Zawila moved inside the walls. The present medina was well established by the time the famous historian Ibn Khaldun visited in the 14th century

and reported that Mahdia had become the wealthiest city on the Barbary Coast.

The medina remains a residential area, but the majority of the town's 30,000 inhabitants have reversed the trend of their ancestors and now live in the modern suburbs that spread west from Skifa el-Kahla.

Information
There's a small **tourist office** (☎ 681 098) just inside the medina, through the Skifa el-Kahla. There was a reasonable range of brochures when we visited but even the exact location of the bus station was a mystery.

The **post office** (ave Habib Bourguiba) is about 650m west of the medina. The BIAT (with ATM) is right outside the Skifa el-Kahla.

Friday is market day in Mahdia.

Sights & Activities
MEDINA
Mahdia's quiet medina stretches out along the peninsula from the Skifa el-Kahla to the lighthouse on Cap d'Afrique, 1.5km to the east. It's a place to wander and follow whichever enticing narrow, cobbled lane takes your fancy.

Skifa el-Kahla
The **Skifa el-Kahla**, a massive fortified gate and one of Tunisia's finest, is all that survives of the original Fatimid city. Entry is through a narrow, vaulted passageway, almost 50m long, that was once protected by a series of gates – one of them a suitably oversized iron portcullis. On market day, the interior is lined with impromptu stalls; it's just possible to picture yourself entering an ancient town little changed in centuries. For the view from the top of the gate, you'll need to enter the museum adjacent to the Skifa.

Place du Caire
The compact **place du Caire** is Mahdia at its best. The outdoor cafés under the generous shade of trees and vines are the perfect place to relax and contemplate the ornate arched doorway and octagonal minaret on the southern side of the square. They belong to the **Mosque of Mustapha Hamza**, built in 1772 when the square was the centre of the town's wealthy Turkish quarter. There are also some wonderful old Mahdia houses to admire.

MAHDIA

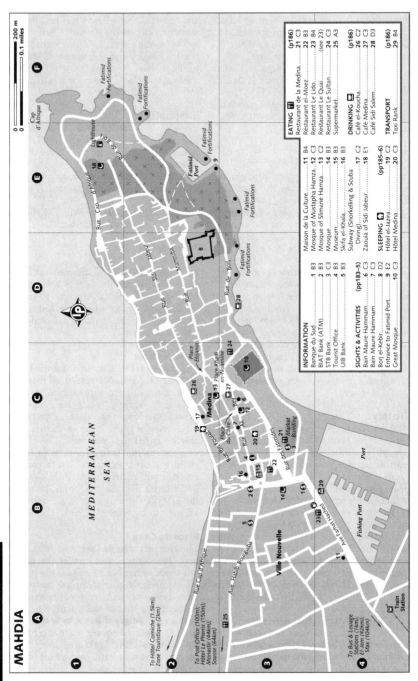

Great Mosque
The **Great Mosque** stands on the northern side of place Khadi en-Noamine. What you see today is a modern replica of the original Fatimid mosque, built by Obeid Allah in AD 921, which was destroyed when retreating Spanish troops blew up the city walls in 1554. Non-Muslims are allowed into the courtyard outside prayer times.

Borj El-Kebir
The **Borj el-Kebir** (admission TD1.1; ◯ 9am-1pm & 4-7pm Sat-Thu summer, 9am-4pm Sat-Thu winter) is a large fortress standing on the highest point of the peninsula, rising above the medina with a brooding and unadorned severity. It was built in the 16th century on the ruins of an earlier Fatimid structure. There's not much to see inside, but the views from the ramparts are well worth the entry fee. It's also aesthetically pleasing, as much for its simplicity as the clear evidence of its original purpose.

Fatimid Fortifications
Fragments of the original **Fatimid walls** dot the shoreline from near the Great Mosque all the way to Cap D'Afrique, and provide just enough hints to imagine a walled town protected from sea-borne invasion. The **Fatimid port** remains in evidence here, as do the crumbling pillars which once flanked the entrance and dominated the harbour's defences. If you're having difficulty imagining what it must have been like, the Borj el-Kebir contains an artist's representation of Mahdia in Fatimid times.

MUSEUM
The **museum** (admission TD1.1; ◯ 8.30am-5.30pm Tue-Sat), just south of the Skifa el-Kahla, is small but excellent. The ground floor has three superb, expansive mosaics and nicely displayed marble statues dating from 3rd-century El-Jem. There are also oil lamps which once illuminated the corridors of the colosseum at El-Jem.

Upstairs are cedar panels adorned with Kufic script from the Great Mosque at Kairouan, as well as local costumes and coins from more recent Tunisian history.

Before leaving, don't forget to climb to the top of the Skifa el-Kahla for the best views over the medina.

BEACHES
Mahdia's main beach is northwest of town and is fronted by the big hotels of the zone touristique; you can use the beach even if you're not staying at one of the hotels. Local kids make do with swimming off the rocks that run along rue Cap d'Afrique.

The waters here are as clear and blue as anywhere in the Mediterranean. To take a closer look, head to **Subway** (☎ 696 492; subway@topnet.tn; rue Cap D'Afrique) where they can arrange snorkelling (TD15 per hour) or diving (TD35 per dive). They cater to beginners (to whom they offer a 'baptism in the sea') and experienced divers (a 35m to 48m wreck dive).

Sleeping
BUDGET
Hôtel el-Jazira (☎ 681 629; fax 680 274; 36 rue Ibn Fourat; s/d with shared bathroom TD9/18) On the seafront on the northern side of the peninsula, this is a very good choice with friendly, helpful management and simple rooms. Some rooms and the shared toilets look out over the water. There's a table and chairs on the roof, where you can sit and enjoy the view.

Hôtel Medina (☎ 694 664; fax 691 422; rue el-Kaem; s/d with shared bathroom TD12/24) In the centre of the medina, this is newer and similarly good, although try and get a room upstairs. The rooms are well kept and quiet.

Hôtel Corniche (☎ /fax 694 201; route de la Corniche; s/d TD14/28, with sea view TD16/32) A stone's throw from the beach about 1.5km northwest of the medina, this place lacks the medina atmosphere and some rooms are definitely nicer than others.

MID-RANGE & TOP END
With one exception, Mahdia's more expensive hotels are spread along the beaches in the zone touristique which starts about 2.5km northwest of the medina. They're quite removed from the town and are designed to provide all that you need without leaving – beach, swimming pools, restaurants and high levels of comfort. As elsewhere in Tunisia, they're packed in summer and dead in winter.

Hôtel Le Phenix (☎ 690 101; www.phenixmahdia.com; ave Habib Bourguiba, s/d TD120/180; ◯ ◯) This four-star boutique hotel offers spacious and semiluxurious rooms and terrific views from the rooftop swimming pool. Just

700m west of the medina, this is the only upmarket hotel within striking distance of the medina although it's not on the beach. It's a new and friendly place with a more intimate atmosphere than the beachfront hotels in the zone touristique. It also has wheelchair access.

Eating

RESTAURANTS

Restaurant el-Moez, between the Skifa el-Kahla and the markets, is a cheerful place with large servings of daily specials which can include *mloukhia* (lamb in thick sauce made from ground herbs) and *kammounia* (a spicy stew made with lots of cumin). Unfortunately, the quality of the food can be patchy and the choice of dishes shrinks by the evening. Expect to pay around TD5 per person including drinks.

Don't be put off by the basic décor at the excellent **Restaurant de la Medina**, situated at the rear of the market building by the port. It's next to the fish markets, and fish features prominently on the menu. The grilled fish (sardines or red mullet) are excellent as is the *kammounia* (both around TD5).

Another place to try is the air-con **Restaurant Le Sultan**, just east of the Grand Mosque, where pizzas cost TD3.5.

Facing the port along ave Farhat Hached, are the **Restaurant Le Lido** and **Restaurant Le Quai** (Chez Farhat) which offer pleasant outdoor dining and alcohol, although the quality is nothing special; expect to pay TD10 per person plus drinks.

SELF-CATERING

The produce section of the market building is the best bet for self-caterers. The only **supermarket** (ave Habib Bourguiba) is about 400m west of the Skifa el-Kahla.

Drinking

The cafés in place du Caire are wonderful for a coffee or cool (nonalcoholic) drink at any time of the day or evening. They serve a limited range of pastries for breakfast. **Café Medina** on place Khadi en-Noamine is also a lovely spot under the palm trees, while on the north side of the medina, head for the pleasant **Café el-Koucha** which is especially good for breakfast and croissants.

Café Sidi Salem overlooks the Mediterranean on the south side of the medina and tumbles down the hill as if you were in the Greek Islands. It's good at any time of the day for a drink or bite to eat. In summer, it also attracts the young men and women of Mahdia; whether they're preening, flirting or just hanging out, it's fascinating to sit and watch.

Getting There & Away

BUS

The bus station is next to the louage station, about 1km southwest of the train station. Most people prefer louages or the train.

There are regular departures to Sousse (TD3.1, 1½ hours) and El-Jem (TD2.4, one hour).

LOUAGE

The louage station, also 1km southwest of the train station, has noticeboards listing fares. Regular departures include Sousse (TD2.9; 1½ hours), El-Jem (TD1.9, one hour), Monastir (TD2; 1¼ hours), Sfax (TD4.8; two hours) and Tunis (TD8.8; four hours). For Kairouan, change at Sousse.

TRAIN

The train station is just west of the port on ave Farhat Hached. There are 16 trains a day to Monastir (one hour, 1st/2nd class TD2.5/1.8) and Sousse (1¾ hours; TD3.3/2.4).

There's also a daily service to Tunis (four hours; TD10.3/7.7).

Getting Around

A taxi from the louage station to the medina should cost no more than TD2.

SFAX صفاقس

☎ 74 / pop 270,000

Sfax, 266km south of Tunis and the second-largest city in the country, is home to Tunisia's finest living and working medina. It's largely bypassed by package groups and the absence of hype makes it a pleasant place to spend a couple of days.

Paul Theroux recorded his impressions of Sfax in *The Pillars of Hercules*. Tunisians had advised him not to go because it had 'lacked colour', but he came away pleasantly surprised by the laid-back city he found.

History

The coast around Sfax has been settled since Phoenician times, but none of the towns amounted to very much until Sfax was established by the Arabs at the beginning of the 8th century AD. The city's massive stone ramparts were built by the Aghlabids in the middle of 9th century AD. They proved effective enough for the city to hold out against the Hilalian invasions in the 11th century (see p160), and Sfax emerged as the major city in the south of Tunisia. In the 14th century, it controlled a stretch of coastline reaching as far as Tripoli in Libya and it remained largely independent of the central government in Tunis until the beginning of the 17th century.

The French built the ville nouvelle in the 19th century and developed the port to handle the export of phosphate from the mines at Gafsa.

Orientation

While modern Sfax fans out over a wide area, most services that will be used by travellers are located in the ville nouvelle between the medina and the port. The main street, ave Habib Bourguiba, runs southeast through the town centre from the train station.

THE LIFE OF THE MEDINA

Despite their chaotic appearance, medinas were laid out according to strict Islamic principles, thought to have originated in 8th century Baghdad. Their layout is carefully adapted to the rigours of the climate. The deep, narrow streets keep the sun's rays from the centre during the day, and draw in the cool evening air during the night. Earth, stone and wood were used to absorb water, which then evaporates and cools the surrounding air.

Medinas also served a military purpose, surrounding the city with fortified, crenellated walls and towers (Sfax's are among the best preserved in Tunisia), elaborate gates (babs or skifas) designed to impress as much as to regulate entry to the city, and fortresses occupied by Islamic warriors.

Inside the walls, the heart of any medina was the city's main mosque, normally known as the jami el-kebir or Great Mosque. This should be located at the exact centre of the medina, as is the case in Sfax and Tunis. Radiating out from the Great Mosque were the souqs – still today the heartbeat of any medina. Closest to the mosque were purveyors of the 'noble trades': vendors of candles, incense and other objects used in the rites of worship. Next to them were the booksellers, venerated in Muslim cultures, and the vendors of leather goods. These were followed by the clothing and textile stalls, long the domain of the richest and most powerful merchants.

The hierarchy then descended through furnishings, domestic goods and utensils. Finally, on the city perimeter and away from the piety of the mosque, the caravans used to assemble and here were found the ironmongers, blacksmiths and the other craftsmen and vendors serving the caravan trade.

The funduqs (caravanserais or inns) were important features of any medina. Here, traders, nomads, pilgrims and scholars stayed while in town, usually on their route elsewhere (eg Kairouan or Mecca). Traditionally, an unadorned façade provided a doorway wide enough to allow camels or heavily laden beasts to enter. The central courtyard was open to the sky and surrounded by a number of stalls, bays or niches. The ground floor housed shops, warehouses, teahouses and stabling for the animals; the 2nd floor accommodated the travellers. The Fun-duq des Forgerons in Sfax is an evocative example.

Apart from these buildings around which the public life of the city revolved, most of the medina was the domain of residential quarters. The Tunisian town house, known as the dar or interior courtyard house, has remained largely unaltered for 3000 years. The principal feature is a central courtyard, around which are grouped suites of rooms in a symmetrical pattern. In the wealthier houses, service areas were often tacked on to one side. The courtyard was designed to keep the house light and cool as well provide a space for communal family life. Rooms could be used interchangeably for eating, relaxing and sleeping. The hottest part of the day is spent in the cool of the courtyard, and at night, the roof terrace can be used as a sleeping area. Sfax's Dar Jellouli Museum is a fine example of just such a house.

The street façade is usually just a plain wall, and the only opening is the entrance door. Any other openings are small, grilled and above the line of vision of passers-by, reflecting the strict demarcation of public and private life in Islamic society.

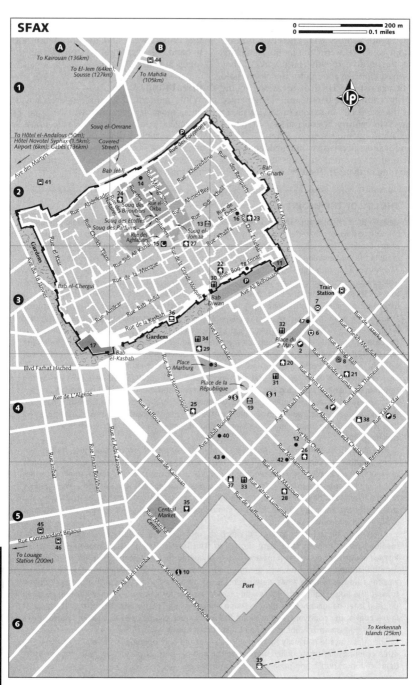

SFAX

0 _____ 200 m
0 _____ 0.1 miles

To Kairouan (136km)

To El-Jem (64km);
Sousse (127km)

To Mahdia
(105km)

44

Souq el-Omrane

To Hôtel el-Andalous (50m);
Hôtel Novotel Syphax (1.5km);
Airport (6km); Gabès (136km)

Covered
Street

Ave des Martyrs

Rue des Forgerons

Bab Jebli

Bab
el-Gharbi

41

Rue Abdelkader

Souq des Bijoutiers

24

14

Rue Mongi Slim

Rue El-Okba

Rue Kheireddine

Rue des Remparts

Ahmed Bey

Sidi Khelil

Rue de la Driba

Ave de l'Armée

Souq des Étoffes

Souq des Parfums

Rue des Aghlabites

Rue Sidi Ali Karray

13

16

23

Souq el-
Jomaa

15

27

Rue Cheikh Tijani

Rue el-Kar

Rue du 18 Janvier

Bab el-Chergui

Rue Amilcar

Rue Bab Jedid

Rue de la Mecque

Rue de la Grand Mosque

22

30

18

11

Rue Borj Ennat

Gardens

Bab
el-Kasbah

17

Bab
Diwan

Rue Ali Belhouane

Train
Station

7

Rue de Tazarka

Rue Bab el Jedid

Rue de la Kasbah

36

Gardens

34

29

Rue Dag Hammarskjold

Place
Marburg

3

Place du
2 Mars

32

47

6

2

Rue Cheikh Mezdich

Rue Wong Bull

8

Rue Alexandre Dumas

Rue Haffouz

Rue Abi Zaroûk

Place de la
République

25

9

19

20

31

1

Rue Salem Harzallah

21

Rue Habib Thameur

Rue Imbat

Rue Imam Boukhari

Ave de L'Algérie

Rue Habib Bourguiba

40

43

12

26

4

Ave Hedi Chaker

Ave Ali Bach Hamba

Rue Aboulkacem ech Chabbi

38

Rue Tahar Sfar

5

Rue Haffouz

Rue de Kairouan

42

Rue Mohammed Ali

37

33

28

Rue Patrice Lumumba

Rue Habib Maâroub

Rue de Remada

45

46

Rue Commandant Bejaoui

To Louage
Station (200m)

Central
Market

35

Rue Marché
Central

Ave Ali Bach Hamba

Ave Mohammed Hedi Khefacha

10

Port

Blvd Farhat Hached

To Kerkennah
Islands (25km)

39

**KAIROUAN & THE
CENTRAL COAST**

INFORMATION		Mausoleum of Sidi Amar		Restaurant au Bec Fin	32 C3
BIAT Bank (ATM)	1 C4	Kammoun	18 C3	Restaurant Chez Nous	33 C5
French Consulate	2 C3	Town Hall & Archaeological		Restaurant Le Corail	34 B3
International Newspapers	3 C4	Museum	19 C4		
Italian Consulate	4 D4			DRINKING	(p191)
Libyan Consulate	5 D4	SLEEPING	(pp190–1)	Bar	35 B5
Police Station	6 D3	Hôtel Abou Nawas Sfax	20 C4	Café Maure Diwan	36 B3
Post Office	7 D3	Hôtel Alexander	21 D4		
Publinet	8 D4	Hôtel Besbes	22 C3	SHOPPING	(p191)
STB Bank (ATM)	9 C4	Hôtel de la Paix	(see 21)	Club Noveca	37 C5
Tourist Office	10 B6	Hôtel du Sud	23 C2	ONAT	38 D4
		Hôtel el-Mokhtar	(see 22)		
SIGHTS & ACTIVITIES	(pp189–90)	Hôtel Ennasr	24 B2	TRANSPORT	(pp191–2)
Association de Sauvegarde de la		Hôtel La Colisée	25 B4	Ferries to Kerkennah Islands	39 C6
Medina	(see 11)	Hôtel Les Oliviers	26 C4	Hertz	40 C4
Borj Ennar	11 C3	Hôtel Medina	27 B2	Local Buses	41 A2
Children's Playground	12 C4	Hôtel Mondial	28 C5	Location 2000	42 C4
Dar Jellouli Museum	13 B2	Hôtel Thyna	29 B3	Mattei Rent-a-Car	43 C4
Funduq des Forgerons	14 B2			Northern Bus Station	44 B1
Great Mosque	15 B2	EATING	(p191)	SNTRI Bus Station	45 A5
Hammam Sultan	16 C2	Cheap Restaurants	30 C3	Southern Bus Station	46 A5
Kasbah	17 A3	Monoprix Supermarket	31 C4	Tunis Air	47 C3

Information

INTERNET ACCESS
Publinet (7 ave Ali Bach Hamba; TD2 per hr; ☺ 8am-midnight) Slowish connections.

MEDIA
Foreign newspapers are sold at the kiosk on the northern side of place Marburg.

MONEY
All the Tunisian banks here have branches either on ave Habib Bourguiba or ave Hedi Chaker.
BIAT (ave Hedi Chaker) ATM.
STB (place de la République) ATM.

POST
Post office (ave Habib Bourguiba) Occupies an entire block just west of the train station.

TOURIST INFORMATION
Tourist office (☎ 211 040; ave Mohammed Hedi Khefecha, ☺ 9am-1pm & 3-5.30pm Mon-Thu, 9am-1.30pm Fri & Sat) Out by the port. There's more information here than is first apparent, including bus, train and ferry timetables.

Sights & Activities

MEDINA
The medina is the reason that people come to Sfax, and for many travellers it's the best in the country. Apart from the imposing walls, it lacks the monumental grandeur of Sousse or Kairouan, but its considerable charm lies in the fact that the medina is remarkably untouched by tourism.

The main thoroughfares are narrow and crowded with stalls and local shoppers, while away to the northeast and southwest wind quiet, twisting lanes where you can admire the flourishes of iron balconies and window frames, ornate doors and the sound of artisans from an upstairs window.

If you need a bath, the **Hammam Sultan** (rue de la Driba; TD1.5; ☺ women noon-4pm; men 4pm-midnight) is near the Dar Jellouli Museum in the heart of the medina. It's a good earthy place for a scrub.

Any exploration of the medina is bound to start at the medina's main southern gate, the triple-arched **Bab Diwan**. This gate was added in 1306, and stands in the middle of the most impressive section of the **ramparts**.

To the north is the ornate eastern wall of the **Great Mosque** (closed to non-Muslims), founded by the Aghlabids in the middle of the 9th century AD. The eastern wall is the only section that's visible, as the other sides are hidden by souqs. The elaborate sandstone **minaret**, a smaller replica of the three-tiered square minaret at Kairouan, was added by the Fatimids in AD 988. It's best viewed from rue des Aghlabites, to the north of the mosque; take the stairs next to the entrance of the teahouse for the best view.

Further north is the wonderful world of the **covered souqs**. The main souq heading north is the celebrated **Souq des Etoffes**, which was used as the setting for the Cairo markets in the film *The English Patient*.

Souq des Etoffes emerges on rue des Teinturiers, where the dyers once carried on their business. If you keep going until you hit rue Abdelkader, which runs inside the medina's northern wall, you'll get to the delightful **Bab Jebli**, one of the original Aghlabid gates.

KAIROUAN & THE CENTRAL COAST

Nearby, the **Funduq des Forgerons** no longer functions as a *funduq*, but still serves as a base for the city's *forgerons* (blacksmiths). It's like walking back a century in time, into a world of blackened faces, smoking fires, red-hot metal and constant hammering. Climb up to the 1st floor for good views down into the courtyard. This is the most recognisable of the sites used for *The English Patient*.

The **Dar Jellouli Museum** (☺ 9.30am-4.30pm Tue-Sat; admission TD1.100, plus photography permit TD1) is in a classic courtyard house, built by the wealthy Jellouli merchant family in the 17th century, and is filled with beautiful carved wood panels, rich tile decoration and ornate stuccowork. The displays include traditional costumes and jewellery, but the building is the star attraction.

The **Borj Ennar** is a small fort added in the 17th century to protect the southeastern corner of the medina, and is now the headquarters of the Association de Sauvegarde de la Medina, the group responsible for preserving the medina. They have a good map of the medina showing all 69 mosques and all sites of historical interest.

West along rue Borj Ennar, the minaret on the left after 50m belongs to the **Mausoleum of Sidi Amar Kammoun**, built at the start of the 14th century. To the west is the **kasbah**. Built by the Aghlabids, it began life as a watch tower but was steadily expanded into a kasbah over the centuries.

VILLE NOUVELLE

The ville nouvelle of Sfax has a hint of sophistication lacking in some of the other coastal towns.

The focal point is the **place de la République**, which is fronted by a number of superb French-era buildings at the junction of ave Hedi Chaker and ave Habib Bourguiba. The grand building on the southern side of the square is the **town hall**. As well as housing the city's bureaucrats, it's also the home of the **archaeological museum** (☺ 8.30am-3pm summer, 8.30am-1pm & 3-6pm winter; admission TD1.1, plus photography permit TD1). It houses some impressive finds from nearby Roman sites.

Other architectural highlights in the area include the fine **French consulate** at 13 ave Habib Bourguiba, and the **police station** at No 11 – no photos at either place, though.

Sleeping

BUDGET

The cheapest places are found in the medina. All budget places listed here have shared bathrooms unless stated.

Hôtel Ennasr (☎ 211 037; 100 rue des Notaires; s/d TD10/14) Near Bab Jebli on the northern edge of the medina, this is the best by far. It's a tidy place with tiled rooms and good views from the rooftop terrace. Staff are friendly once they get going, and after the shops of the medina shut down it's nice and quiet.

Hôtel Medina (☎ 220 354; 53 rue Mongi Slim; d TD8) This is the next best choice in the medina. The rooms are simple but well kept and the elderly management are polite in a gracious, old-school kind of way. It can be difficult to find amid the shops so ask directions.

On a sliding scale downwards to the grim but very cheap end of the scale, there are some basic places just inside Bab Diwan along rue Borj Ennar. The less bleak among them include **Hôtel Besbes** and **Hôtel el-Mokhtar** and the quieter **Hôtel du Sud** (rue Dar Essebal); all charge TD3 to TD6 per person.

Hôtel de la Paix (☎ 296 437; fax 298 463; 17 rue Alexandre Dumas; s TD9, s/d with private bathroom TD14/20) Located in the ville nouvelle, this is the most popular budget place but they've upped their prices without a concomitant rise in quality. Rooms are simple and reasonably well kept; those with balcony are better but fill up fast.

MID-RANGE

Hôtel Thyna (☎ 225 317; fax 225 773; 37 rue Habib Maazoun; s/d with breakfast & TV TD30/46; ☒) After a recent facelift, this is probably the best overall package in the mid-range category. Good rooms and bathrooms are combined with an ideal location, friendly staff and a lovely breakfast/coffee room.

Hôtel Mondial (☎ 226 620; fax 299 350; 46 rue Habib Maazoun; s/d TD15/25; ☒) This is the cheapest in this category and, as such, not bad value. Rooms are simple and spartan but spacious; air-con costs no extra. Staff are idiosyncratic but friendly.

Hôtel Alexander (☎ 221 613; 21 rue Alexandre Dumas; s/d with breakfast TD20/30) Ageing slowly, this place still has character. The high-ceilinged rooms (most with balcony) are light and airy even if the plaster is starting to peel and the antique lift is a thing of beauty rather than functionality. Overall it's pretty good value.

Hôtel La Colisée (☎ 227 800; fax 299 350; 32 ave Taieb Mehiri; s/d with breakfast TD30/45) The rooms here are a touch better kept than those at the Alexander but some are dark and don't have balconies so probably not worth the extra dinars.

Hôtel el-Andalous (☎ 405 406; fax 406 425; ave des Martyrs; s/d TD35/50; ❄) Northwest of the medina this place also has good rooms but suffers from being a bit away from the action.

TOP END

Prices include breakfast.

Hôtel Novotel Syphax (☎ 243 333; fax 245 226; ave des Martyrs; s/d with breakfast TD75/90), 1.5km west of the medina on the way to the airport, is Sfax's top hotel. It's a modern hotel with semiluxurious rooms, a pool and good restaurant. It's a long way from anywhere, but if you're paying this much, you can probably afford a taxi.

Hôtel Abou Nawas Sfax (☎ 225 700; sfax@ abounawas.com.tn; 15 ave Habib Bourguiba; s/d TD105/ 135; ❄ ▣) Right in the middle of town and much more convenient, the rooms here are spacious and attractive but not quite worth what they ask.

Eating

There's a cluster of cheap restaurants on the right just inside the medina's Bab Diwan. All are signed only in Arabic and are very popular, with locals tucking into dishes like beans in spicy sauce with chicken (TD2.2) or couscous with lamb (TD2.5). Another cheap restaurant in the medina is the one on rue des Notaires, 50m south of the Hôtel Ennasr.

Restaurant au Bec Fin (place du 2 Mars; ❄ lunch & dinner; starters TD2, mains from TD3) Slightly less frenetic than the medina restaurants, this is nonetheless popular and wins our vote for the best *ojja* in Sfax (it's the garlic that does it; the *ojja crevette* is TD3.5). Other favourites include the octopus salad (TD4) and *spaghetti aux fruits de mer* (TD4). The service is fast and friendly and the food consistently good.

Hôtel Alexander (❄ lunch & dinner; starters from TD2.5, mains from TD5) A decent hotel restaurant (although the 1970s retro décor and Bryan Adams can be a tad claustrophobic), here you can get a huge plate of *spaghetti aux fruits de mer* for TD4.2 and you can wash it down with a cold beer (TD2).

Restaurant Chez Nous (☎ 227 128; 28 rue Patrice Lumumba; ❄ lunch & dinner; salads from TD2.5, mains from TD7) This stylish restaurant does a set menu for TD9, or an extensive á la carte menu featuring loads of seafood; count on TD20 per person, plus wine. There are many highlights on the menu, not the least of which are the *marmite au fruits de mer* and *tajine fruits de mer* (both TD10).

Restaurant Le Corail (☎ 227 301; 39 rue Habib Maazoun; ❄ lunch & dinner; starters TD4, mains from TD7) This is a great choice next to the Hôtel Thyna. The ambience is a touch more intimate than the others and the food is nicely prepared.

SELF-CATERING

There's a **Monoprix supermarket** (rue Aboulkacem ech Chabbi; ❄ 8.30am-2pm, 4.30-8pm).

Drinking

Café Maure Diwan (off rue de la Kasbah; ❄ 6am-midnight) This is one of the highlights of Sfax. Cut into the medina wall between Bab Diwan and Bab el-Kasbah, it's an atmospheric place to spend an afternoon or an hour, smoking the *sheesha* (TD2), looking out on the walls and ville nouvelle or enjoying the house specialty – *thé au pignons et menthe* (mint tea with pine nuts; TD1).

Shopping

The shops in the **Souq des Etoffes** stock a range of Berber rugs, blankets and other handicrafts from the villages of the Gafsa region. The shop owners here seem to take the view that they're more likely to secure a sale if they don't scare tourists away with absurdly high first prices – and it works! It's a refreshing change from Kairouan, although you won't have the same selection to choose from.

ONAT (❄ 8am-1pm, 5-8pm Mon-Sat) has a good crafts shop on the southern part of rue Salem Harzallah.

Club Noveca (☎ 296 920, 78 rue de Haffouz; ❄ 8.30am-8.30pm Mon-Sat & noon-3pm Sun) is a good music shop selling CDs and cassettes with a small but well-chosen selection of Arab and other international music.

Getting There & Away

AIR

Tuninter (Tunis Air; ☎ 228 028; 4 ave de l'Armée) has two flights a week between Tunis and Sfax (TD50/100, 45 minutes).

BOAT

Soretrak (☎ 498 216, ave Mohammed Hedi Khefecha) ferries for the Kerkennah Islands leave from the southwestern corner of the port. There are eleven crossings a day in summer, four in winter. Timetables are displayed at the port and at the tourist office. The trip costs 800 mills for passengers and TD4 for a car. The crossing takes about 1¼ hours in good weather and there can be long queues to take a vehicle across in summer. In summer, the last boat back from the islands leaves around 8.45pm.

BUS

All buses leave from southwest of the medina on rue Commandant Bejaoui. SNTRI is on the north side of the road, while the depot for the local company Soretras is to the south.

SNTRI also operates a daily international bus service to Tripoli, in Libya (TD17.8, seven hours); ask at the SNTRI office for the latest departure times.

Destination	Fare	Duration	Frequency (per day)
Douz	TD12	5hrs	2
El-Jem	TD3	1¼hrs	10
Gabès	TD6.3	2hrs	10
Houmt Souq (Jerba)	TD10.5	5hrs	3
Medenine	TD9.2	3hrs	2
Sousse	TD6.1	2hrs	10
Tataouine	TD11.7	4hrs	2
Tunis	TD11.8	5hrs	8

Soretras operates a busy intercity schedule, including hourly services to Mahdia (TD2.7) and three daily buses to Kairouan (TD5.5).

CAR

You're more likely to find good deals at smaller local companies like **Mattei** (Ada; ☎ 296 404; 18 rue Patrice Lumumba) or **Location 2000** (☎ 221 763; ave Habib Thameur). **Hertz** (☎ 228 626; 47 ave Habib Bourguiba) is nearby.

LOUAGE

Louages leave from the large walled compound at the junction of rue Commandant Bejaoui and rue de Maurianie, 200m west of the bus stations. There are frequent departures to Gabès (TD5.9), Sousse (TD5.9) and Tunis (TD10.9). Other destinations include El-Jem (TD3.2), Mahdia (TD4.8) and Jerba (TD11.2).

There are also louages to Tripoli (TD30). These vehicles are yellow and white, and often have Libyan markings.

TRAIN

There are three trains a day south to Gabès (three hours) and one late-night train to Gafsa (3½ hours) and Metlaoui (4¼ hours). Heading north, there are five trains daily to El-Jem (one hour), four to Sousse (two hours) and six to Tunis (3½ hours).

Destination	2nd class	1st class	Comfort
El-Jem	TD3.1	TD4.1	TD4.4
Gabès	TD5.3	TD7.2	TD7.9
Gafsa	TD7	TD9.4	TD10.1
Sousse	TD4.9	TD6.5	TD6.9
Tunis	TD9.1	TD11.8	TD12.6

Getting Around

TO/FROM THE AIRPORT

The **airport** (☎ 278 000) is 6km from town on the Gafsa road at Thyna – TD3.5 by taxi.

KERKENNAH ISLANDS حزير قرقنة

☎ 74 / pop 16,000

It's hard to get too excited about this cluster of nine islands 25km east of Sfax. Once used as a place of exile, the islands have a rather desolate air about them. They're flat and featureless – the highest point is only 13m above sea level. The islands remain almost untouched by tourism and that's their only real attraction. The islanders would prefer to keep it that way, and voted against a multimillion dinar Kuwaiti proposal to build a massive hotel complex northeast of Sidi Frej.

The islanders still use traditional fish traps made from palm fronds. Lines of fronds are stuck in the sea bed in a 'V' shape, and the fish are then driven into this large funnel and into a small trap at the end.

Orientation

The two main islands, **Île Gharbi** and **Île Chergui**, are connected by a small causeway dating back to Roman times.

Most of the population lives on Chergui. The only place of any consequence is the

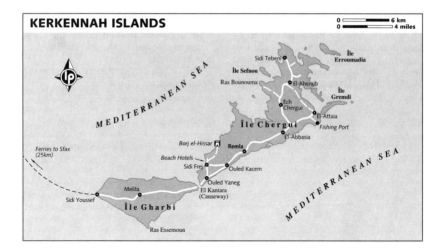

small town of **Remla**, the administrative and service 'capital' of the islands.

Information

There's a branch of the **UIBC bank** in Remla, on the road leading down to the sea next to the Hôtel el-Jazira, or change money at one of the hotels.

Borj el-Hissar

Borj el-Hissar is an old fort on the coast, about 3km north of the hotels at Sidi Frej. It's well worth the 40-minute walk; it's clearly signposted from near the Hôtel Le Grand. The small fort itself was built by the Spanish in the 16th century, but Roman ruins surround the fort. You get the feeling that you are stumbling across something previously undiscovered, with mosaics covered by sand and ruins disappearing into the sea.

Beaches

The sea is very shallow around here – you can walk out 100m before your knees get wet so it's ideal for kids. The best beach is at Ras Bounouma, northeast of Sidi Frej, but there's no public transport.

Sleeping & Eating

REMLA

Hôtel el-Jazira (☎ 481 058; per person incl breakfast TD8) The only hotel in Remla, this is opposite the bus station on the main street through town and it's pretty basic. The El-Jazira also has a restaurant and the only bar on the islands.

The **Restaurant La Sirène** is next to the Hôtel el-Jazira. It has a shady terrace overlooking the sea and does meals for around TD15, plus wine.

SIDI FREJ

Hôtel Cercina (☎ 489 953; fax 489 878; s/d TD30/45) Just 200m from the bus stop at the junction of the road to Remla, this place is OK if you can get one of the bungalows overlooking the sea, but most of the accommodation is in depressing little cylindrical concrete huts.

Hôtel Le Grand (☎ 489 864, fax 489 866, s/d TD45/60) This two-star place, about 800m east of the bus stop, is the undisputed top address on the islands and is booked out by the charter trade in summer. Facilities include tennis courts and a swimming pool.

The best restaurant in the hotel strip is at **Hôtel Cercina**. Ask for the local specialty, a thick, spicy octopus soup called *tchich* (TD2).

Getting There & Away

See opposite page for details of ferries between Sfax and Sidi Youssef.

Getting Around

BICYCLE

The flat terrain is ideal for cycling. Most of the hotels rent out bicycles (TD1.5 per hour, TD10 per day).

BUS

There's a small network of buses connecting the villages of the islands and at least two or three meet each ferry; all go to Remla. One (with a 'hotel' sign in the window) goes via Sidi Frej (TD1). There are buses from Remla and the Sidi Frej junction to Sidi Youssef departing about an hour before the ferry. Times are posted in the bus-station window in Remla.

The Remla bus station is opposite the Hôtel el-Jazira.

Southern Tunisia

CONTENTS

Spend as much time as you can in southern Tunisia; it's home to the awe-inspiring Sahara desert and the hospitable Berber people, who have built some of the finest and most unusual indigenous architecture in Africa.

Matmata is most people's first taste of the different world that awaits; its lunar landscapes and underground troglodyte homes were used to such bizarre effect in the *Star Wars* movies. Not far away, Tataouine stands at the heart of the Ksour. This region is also a favourite of the makers of *Star Wars*, with its rich treasure trove of hilltop Berber villages and abundance of other-worldly ksour (fortified strongholds).

The wonderful landscapes of the Sahara in Tunisia's southwest begin with the massive oases or *palmeraies* (oases) and taper to the sea of sand of the Grand Erg Oriental, crossing desolate, shimmering *chotts* (salt pans) along the way.

Ksar Ghilane boasts a desert ksar, an oasis fed by hot springs and some of the best scenery in the country, which has also been used by film producers – many scenes from *The English Patient* were shot here. To the south and west are the amazing sand dunes of the Grand Sud, and Tunisia's most southerly settlements.

A laid-back place to start your desert journey is Douz, a friendly, hospitable town which has the largest palm-grove in Tunisia. But you could also start in Tozeur, which has a distinctive old quarter made all of brick, the second-largest *palmeraie* in the country, a fascinating museum and savvy tour operators ready to take you to the mountain oasis villages near the Algerian border or deep into the Saharan south.

HIGHLIGHTS

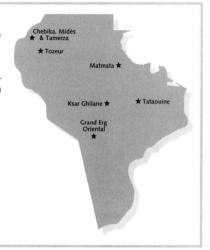

- **Camel-trekking** (p219) through the dunes of the Grand Erg Oriental, the ultimate Saharan experience
- Exploring the outstanding mountain oasis villages of **Chebika**, **Midès** and **Tamerza** (p229)
- Walking around the intricate, traditional brickwork of Tozeur's **old quarter** (p225)
- Visiting the weird and wonderful underground troglodyte homes (and *Star Wars* sets) of **Matmata** (p202)
- Savouring early-morning visits to the **ksour** (fortified strongholds; p208) around Tataouine
- Swimming in the **hot springs** (p222) at the oasis of Ksar Ghilane

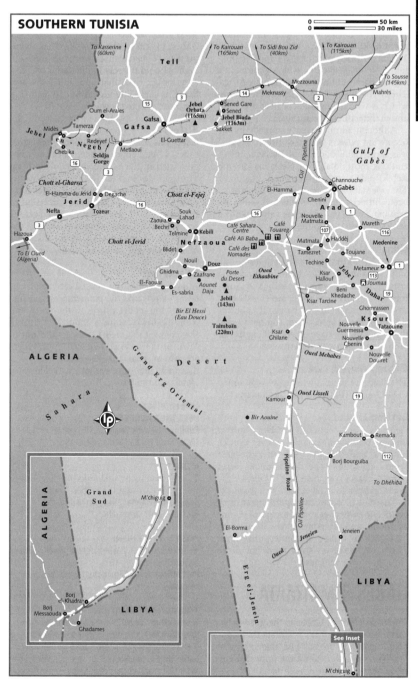

SOUTHERN TUNISIA

0 ——— 50 km
0 ——— 30 miles

To Kasserine (60km)

Tell

To Kairouan (165km) *To Sidi Bou Zid (40km)* *To Kairouan (115km)*

Mezzouna

To Sousse (145km)

Mahrès

14 Meknassy

3 **Jebel Orbata** (1165m) Sened Gare
Sened
Jebel Biada (1163m) 2 1

15

Oum el-Araies

Midès Tamerza **Gafsa**
Jebel Redeyef El-Guettar Sakket

15 *Oil Pipeline*

Gulf of Gabès

en Negeb Chebika Metlaoui
Seldja Gorge

16

Ghannouche
Gabès

3 El-Hamma

Chott el-Gharsa El-Hamma du Jérid Degache **Chott el-Fejej**
Jerid

Chenini **Arad**
Nouvelle 1
Matmata

Nefta Tozeur 16

Souk Lahad

16 Mareth

Hazoua **Chott el-Jerid** Zaouia Bechri Telmine Kebili Café Sahara
Centre Café Touareg
Café Ali Baba
Café des
Nomades Matmata 107 Haddèj

116

Medenine

3 Blidet **Nefzaoua**

To El Oued (Algeria)

Nouil Douz Tamezret Toujane

Techine **Jebel**

Ghidma Zaafrane Porte du Desert
El-Faouar Es-sabria Aounet Daja **Jebil** (143m) *Oued Ethaabine*

Ksar Hallouf 113 Metameur 1

Joumaa **Dahar**
Beni Khedache
Ksar Tarcine 19

Bir El Hessi (Eau Douce)

Taimbaïn (220m)

Ghomrassen **Ksour**
Nouvelle Tataouine
Guermessa
Nouvelle
Chenini

Ksar Ghilane *Oued Mehabes*

Nouvelle Douiret

ALGERIA **Desert**

Grand Erg Oriental

Oued Lisseli

Kamour 19

Sahara

• Bir Aouine

Kambout Remada

Borj Bourguiba 112

To Dhéhiba

Grand Sud

M'chiguig

Pipeline Road *Oil Pipeline* Jeneien Jeneien

ALGERIA

El-Borma *Oued*

Erg ej-Jeneien

LIBYA

Borj el-Khadra

Borj Messaouda **LIBYA**

Ghadames

See Inset

M'chiguig

History

Southern Tunisia was the southernmost point of Roman Africa, with towns such as Tozeur forming part of the Limes Tripolitanus – a defensive line which guarded the southwestern boundaries of Roman Africa. The Berbers were largely left to themselves which is why strongholds of Berber culture and architecture have survived.

Although administered nominally by the occupying powers of the north, the region was largely the domain of Berber confederations, most notably the Nefzaoua (around Kebili) and Ouergherma (around Tataouine). The orientation of the south has also always been different, facing as much towards the arriving and departing trade caravans from across the desert as to the coast.

Climate

Spring and autumn are the best times to visit, although tour operators claim that the season lasts from late September to early May. Summer is the worst time and camel treks are restricted to overnight excursions. It's also the season of the sirocco, a hot, southerly wind that can blow for days on end, filling the air (and lungs) with fine, desert sand.

Getting There & Away

The major southern towns are well connected to the rest of Tunisia by bus and louage.

Getting Around

Getting around the south involves a mix of louage, bus, *camionnette* (pick-up truck), hitching and (for Ksar Ghilane, the area around Tataouine, and the mountain oases around Tozeur) organised 4WD tour; see the Douz, Tozeur and Gabès sections for details.

There are no direct public-transport connections between the towns of Douz, Matmata and Tataouine; you'll need to backtrack to Gabès to connect the three. There are, however, good roads for those with their own vehicles.

GABÈS & MATMATA

The oasis town of Gabès is the gateway to Tunisia's south, but it's Matmata that most people come to see, to lose themselves in *Star Wars* nostalgia amid the improbability of underground Berber architecture.

GABÈS
قابس

☎ 75 / pop 110,000

Gabès, 137km southwest of Sfax, has an impressive *palmeraie* that's worth an overnight night stop on the way to the Ksour or Jerba. Any longer than that and you'll discover that this sprawling industrial city is one of the most polluted towns in Tunisia.

History

Gabès has been inhabited since prehistoric times. Little happened here until the town grew rich in the 14th century as the main Tunisian destination for the great camel caravans that brought gold and slaves from across the Sahara. The French invasion of the Sahara in the 19th century killed off the caravans and Gabès slipped back into obscurity. It boomed again after the discovery of oil in the gulf in the mid-20th century.

Orientation

Although Gabès is a coastal city, its orientation is towards the *palmeraie* which surrounds the modern town to the north and west; the town centre is about 2km inland, skirted by the Oued Gabès to the north. Most of the services required by travellers are on or near the two main east–west thoroughfares – ave Farhat Hached and ave Habib Bourguiba.

Information

INTERNET ACCESS

Publinet (ave Habib Bourguiba; TD1.5 per hr; ⊗ 8am-10pm) On the first floor of the Gabès Centre.

MONEY

There's a cluster of banks on ave Habib Bourguiba around the Gabès Centre.

Banque de l'Habitat (ave Farhat Hached) ATM.

BIAT (ave Farhat Hached) ATM.

POST & TELEPHONE

You can use any of the Taxiphone offices around town.

Post office (ave Habib Bourguiba) Centrally located, telephones.

TOURIST INFORMATION

Tourist office (☎ 270 254; cnr ave Farhat Hached & ave Habib Bourguiba; ⊗ 7.30am-1.30pm & 5-7pm Mon-Sat) Doesn't see many tourists but does a better job than many that do. There's a complete list of bus departures, hotel prices and an old Lonely Planet map of the town posted on the door.

GABÈS

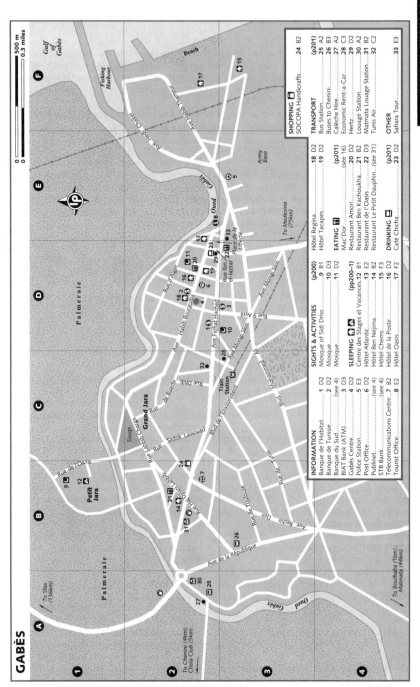

INFORMATION
Banque de l'Habitat...................	1 D2
Banque de Tunisie......................	2 D2
Banque du Sud...........................	(see 4)
BIAT Bank (ATM)........................	3 D3
Gabès Centre...............................	4 D2
Police Station..............................	5 E3
Post Office....................................	6 D2
Publinet......................................	(see 4)
STB Bank.....................................	(see 4)
Telecommunications Centre........	7 B2
Tourist Office..............................	8 E2

SIGHTS & ACTIVITIES   (p200)
Mosque of Sidi Driss...................	9 B1
Mosque...	10 D3
Mosque...	11 D2

SLEEPING [icons]   (pp200–1)
Centre des Stages et Vacances..	12 B1
Hôtel Atlantic..............................	13 E2
Hôtel Ben Nejima........................	14 B2
Hôtel Chems................................	15 F3
Hôtel de la Poste.........................	16 D2
Hôtel Oasis..................................	17 F2
Hôtel Regina................................	18 D2
Hôtel Tacapes..............................	19 D2

EATING [icon]   (p201)
Mac'Dof.......................................	(see 16)
Restaurant Amori.........................	20 D2
Restaurant Ben Kachoukha........	21 B2
Restaurant de l'Oasis..................	22 D3
Restaurant Le Petit Dauphin.......	(see 31)

DRINKING [icon]   (p201)
Café Chicha..................................	23 D2

SHOPPING [icon]
SOCOPA Handicrafts...................	24 B2

TRANSPORT   (p201)
Bus Station..................................	25 A2
Buses to Chenini.........................	26 B3
Calèche Hire................................	27 A2
Economic Rent-a-Car..................	28 C3
Hertz..	29 D2
Louage Station............................	30 A2
Matmata Louage Station............	31 B2
Tunis Air......................................	32 C2

OTHER
Sahara Tour.................................	33 E3

HENNA

Gabès is well known for its high-quality henna, which is made by grinding the dried leaves of the henna tree *(Laussonia inermis)*, a small evergreen native to the region. Gabès' henna produces a deep red-brown dye. Berber women use it to decorate their hands and feet, as well as to colour and condition their hair. You'll see henna powder for sale in the souqs, piled up in colourful green pyramids. Henna costs about TD1.500 for 100g.

If you want a henna tattoo, ask any of the stall holders around the souq on rue Lahbib Charga or in the *palmeraie* village of Chenini. Prices vary as wildly as the designs.

Palmeraie

The *palmeraie* stretches inland along the Oued Gabès. It begins on the coast at **Ghannouche** and ends more than 4km west of Gabès at the village of **Chenini** (not to be confused with Chenini near Tataouine – see p210). This western section is the most interesting (and least polluted) part.

Walking is the best way to explore although some travellers have reported having to dodge stone-throwing children. You can follow the shortcut used by the *calèches* (horse-drawn carriages), crossing the *oued* (dry riverbed) by the bridge behind the bus station and turning left onto the Chenini road. The road then twists and turns through the *palmeraie* to El-Aouadid, where a left turn leads down to Chenini. It's a pleasant walk of about one hour. The *palmeraie* looks its best during the pomegranate season in November and December, when the trees are weighed down with huge ruby-red fruit.

Chenini itself has not much more to offer other than loads of souvenir stalls. A path (negotiable by bicycle) heads off around the back of a partially reconstructed Roman dam and winds through the *palmeraie* to the Chela Club tucked away in the palms (see p201). It's about a 20-minute walk and you can continue along the *oued* to the end of the valley. Climb up the small escarpment for a view of the surrounding area.

To get back to Gabès from Chenini, the No 7 bus runs between the village and rue Haj Djilani Lahbib, or pay around TD2.5 for a taxi. Horse-drawn carriages (TD10), which leave from behind the bus station, are a popular alternative to walking.

Jara

The Jara is the old district that straddles the *oued* on the northern edge of town. The **Petit Jara**, amid the palm trees north of the *oued*, is the oldest part of town. The **Mosque of Sidi Driss**, at the far end of rue de l'Oasis, dates back to the 11th century. The old market, where the slaves once were sold, is in **Grand Jara**, south of the *oued*.

Tours

Sahara Tour (☎ 270 930; fax 270 222; ave Farhat Hached) is a well-run company offering 4WD and camel safaris into the Sahara. They organise anything from one day excursions (from TD50 per person) to seven-day expeditions (around TD200 per 4WD per day) which range as far as Tozeur and Ksar Ghilane.

Sleeping

BUDGET

Centre des Stages et Vacances (☎ 270 271; dm TD5, camping TD2.5) Located in the *palmeraie* in the old district of Petit Jara, this holiday-camp version of a *maison des jeunes* (government-run youth hostel) has the usual spartan dorms as well as shady camp sites.

Hôtel Ben Nejima (☎ 271 591; fax 221 062; cnr ave Farhat Hached & rue Haj Djilani Lahbib; s/d TD9/14) This is the best budget accommodation in town with tidy, spacious rooms, some with balcony. It's convenient to the *palmeraie* and transport.

Hôtel de la Poste (☎ 270 718; ave Habib Bourguiba; s/d TD6/12) This place is more basic with saggy beds which don't see too many travellers, but it is close to the centre of town and fine for a night.

MID-RANGE

Prices here include breakfast.

Hôtel Regina (☎ 272 095; fax 221 710; ave Habib Bourguiba; s/d with private bathroom TD11.5/15) The Regina, opposite the Gabès Centre, is an excellent choice and it's where most travellers head. It's a quiet location with helpful staff and rooms arranged around a courtyard. Most rooms have a ceiling fan.

Interior of troglodyte dwelling (p202),
Matmata

View from the ksar (Berber stronghold; p210),
Chenini

Desert sunrise, near Douz (p215)

Old walled town (p229), Tamerza

Changing colours, Tozeur (p223)

Swimming pool, La Corbeille (p230), Nefta

Ruined Berber village of Guermessa (p209)

Hôtel Atlantic (☎ 220 034; fax 221 358; ave Habib Bourguiba; s/d TD14.5/23; 🔧) This ageing one-star French place has a fine colonial façade and good rooms for the price.

Hôtel Tacapes (☎ 270 701; fax 271 601; ave Habib Bourguiba; s/d TD28.5/37; 🔧) A step up in price and quality, the rooms here come with satellite TV, but are unspectacular and probably not worth the extra; it's still worth a look.

Chela Club (☎ 227 442; fax 227 446; s/d TD20/30) Chela Club is in the *palmeraie* 5km west of the bus and louage station. It's a bit naff and run-down, but if you've only come to Gabès to see the *palmeraie*, this is the place to stay.

TOP END
Hôtel Oasis (☎ 270 381; fax 271 749; off ave Habib Thameur; s/d TD55/90; ste from TD250; 🔧 🏊) A pleasant place which fronts onto Gabès' depressing beach. The rooms are tasteful, except for the large suites which could be described as modern Tunisian kitsch. There's a thermal swimming pool, bar and it's popular with tour groups.

Hôtel Chems (☎ 270 547; fax 274 485; off ave Habib Thameur; s/d TD60/90; 🔧 🏊) Similarly comfortable, with good rooms. The staff seem to take a long time to warm up and when it's not busy the whole place has an abandoned air.

Eating
Restaurant Le Petit Dauphin (ave Farhat Hached; ✺ breakfast, lunch & dinner; starters from TD1, mains around TD3.5) This wins the prize for the friendliest owner in Gabès – Fathi serves up consistently good food and loves to sit and chat to travellers when he can escape from the kitchen. The small restaurant spills into the Matmata louage station so it's a perfect place to wait.

Restaurant Ben Kachoukha (☎ 220 387; rue Haj Djilani Lahbib; ✺ breakfast, lunch & dinner; starters from TD1.5, mains from TD3) This restaurant might lack the personal touch of Le Petit Dauphin but is nonetheless popular, especially for the grilled fish (TD5).

Restaurant Amori (ave Habib Bourguiba; ✺ lunch & dinner; set menus TD5) The set menus here (a mix of travellers' favourites and local staples) are good value.

Mac'Dor (ave Habib Bourguiba; ✺ lunch & dinner) This busy little place does hearty *shwarmas* (sliced meat in pita-type bread; TD1.3) where you can choose the ingredients. It also does pizzas.

Restaurant de l'Oasis (☎ 270 098; ave Farhat Hached; ✺ lunch & dinner; set menus TD9, mains TD7-10) Here you'll find the best food in town and a touch of class not found elsewhere. The set menus are good value, but there are plenty of á la carte seafood tempters (TD8 to TD10).

Drinking
Café Chicha (cnr ave Habib Bourguiba & ave Farhat Hached) This good coffeehouse is in the pleasant place de la Liberté. The setting, with its intricate tiling, is a cut above the rest, while the outdoor tables are a lovely spot to pass a summer's evening.

Shopping
Gabès is a major centre for straw goods – baskets, hats, fans and mats. There's plenty to choose from in the souqs off rue Lahbib Charga in the Grand Jara district.

Getting There & Away
BUS
At least three companies operate out of the bus station at the western end of town. Daily departures include: Tozeur (TD8.1), Jerba (TD6), Sfax (TD6.3), Sousse (TD7.9), Tunis (TD17), Tataouine (TD6), Medenine (TD3.7), Douz (TD5.8), Matmata (TD1.7) and Gafsa (TD6.2).

LOUAGE
The louage station adjoins the bus station, with departures for Kebili (TD5.5), Jerba (TD5.4), Medenine (TD3.6), Sfax (TD6.2), Sousse (TD11), Tunis (TD16), Douz (TD6.9) and Tozeur (TD9.1). Things quieten down considerably as the afternoon wears on.

For Matmata, louages leave from a separate lot along ave Farhat Hached. Services go to Nouvelle Matmata (TD1.2) where you'll have to change to old Matmata (a further 600 mills).

TRAIN
The train station is just off ave Mongi Slim, a five-minute walk from ave Habib Bourguiba. There are four trains daily to Tunis (TD16.2, six hours), with the most convenient departures at 10.05am and 4.10pm.

MATMATA   مطماطة
☎ 75 / pop 1000
It's easy to understand why the makers of the science fiction epic *Star Wars* picked

Matmata, 45km southwest of Gabès, as the home planet of Luke Skywalker. Surrounded by a barren, eroded landscape of fissures and craters, the Berbers of Matmata went underground centuries ago to escape the summer heat. Although conventional modern buildings are now in the majority, the town still boasts hundreds of the troglodyte pit homes; visiting these unique dwellings is one of the more unusual highlights of Tunisia.

The combination of *Star Wars* memorabilia and unusual architecture draws large numbers of tour buses on excursions from the coast. Even with this inundation, it's still possible to soak up the silence as an antidote to the clamour of the coastal cities.

There are licensed guides who charge TD10 for a guided tour of the village or TD15 for tours of both Matmata and Tamezret (you'll have to provide the transport to Tamezret). You can reach the guides through the syndicat d'initiative or ask at your hotel.

Orientation & Information

The road from Gabès descends into Matmata from the north and continues through town to the east as the back road to Medenine. In the centre of town, Ave de la Environnement branches off to the west towards Tamezret and Douz. All of the town's attractions are on or just off these two main thoroughfares.

The closest bank is the Banque Nationale Agricole in Matmata Nouvelle, 15km away. If you find yourself stuck, ask at any of the mid-range or top end hotels who might be able to help. The post office is in the centre of town, opposite the turn-off to Douz. The small **syndicat d'initiative** (☎ 230 114) is just downhill from the bus station, at the turn-off to the Hôtel Kousseila. Staff are singularly unhelpful.

Troglodyte Homes

Matmata's underground homes are easily accessible to travellers. The best places to start are the three budget hotels. The **Hôtel Sidi Driss** is spread over five pit courtyards, all connected by underground tunnels. Bits of the set are still in place from the original *Star Wars* movie (the courtyard to the right as you enter). The hotel was used again in *The Phantom Menace, Attack of the Clones* and *Episode IV – A New Hope*. Make sure you climb up behind the hotel to look down into the pits from above.

Of the other hotels, **Hôtel Les Berbères** has great tunnels although much is of recent construction, while **Hôtel Marhala** is more simple, not lime-washed and perhaps more true to a simple Matmata dwelling.

Another option for viewing the pit dwellings is the small **Musée Berber**, run by local women who have displays of carpet-making and traditional keys – because doors are secured by long, wooden bolts that disappear into the wall, these keys are up to a foot long, and open the door by releasing the bolt through a keyhole in the wall. The long, sloping entrance tunnel is one of the best in town. It's all quite rustic and unadorned, wherein lies its charm. Opening

---

THE TROGLODYTE HOMES OF MATMATA

There's nowhere on earth quite like Matmata, where a local saying claims that 'the living live under the dead'.

Underground houses provided respite from cold winters and hot summers and were a place of refuge to which the area's inhabitants could retreat when threatened by invasion – the houses were invisible to all but those within a few hundred metres.

The living quarters were at the base of a dramatic circular pit of about 5m to 10m radius cut 5m to 10m deep into the earth, forming a pleasant courtyard. Sometimes, stone walls were built in the courtyard to buttress the clay and sandstone against landslides during heavy rain. Rooms were tunnelled out from the sides and lime-washed. They generally comprised living rooms, kitchen, bedrooms and storage areas – houses were once home to as many as three families and the larger houses have two or three connected courtyards. The main entrance was usually through a narrow tunnel leading from ground level down into the courtyard.

Other villages in the region contain underground pit homes, but none are as extensive nor accessible as those at Matmata.

hours are unpredictable but mornings are the best times. A donation of TD1 to TD2 is appropriate.

You could also take up the offers of the Matmata kids to visit private homes. They'll invariably find you as you wander around town. You'll be pressured to buy a souvenir or pay an entry fee (TD2 to TD5). The people of Matmata get little enough privacy so visiting by invitation is infinitely more respectful than seeking them out on your own.

There are also a couple set up for tourists on the last 3km into town from Gabès.

Sleeping
BUDGET
The town's three budget hotels are traditional troglodyte dwellings.

Hôtel Sidi Driss (☎ 240 005; fax 240 265; per person with breakfast/half board TD12/17) The best of the below-ground hotels is the famous Sidi Driss, along the road south from opposite the bus station. There are only a couple of double rooms; some rooms have as many as eight beds. The only problem with staying here is that busloads of tour groups traipse through the hotel until late afternoon.

Hôtel Marhala (☎ 240 015; fax 240 109; s/d with breakfast TD13.5/18, half board TD15/22) One in a chain run by the Touring Club de Tunisie, this has rooms which are clean and quieter, although a touch more basic.

Hôtel Les Berbères (☎ 240 024; fax 240 097; off ave de l'Environnement; per person with breakfast/half board TD10/14) The final troglodyte option is another labyrinthine place with simple rooms and friendly staff. The sleeping quarters here are recent additions.

MID-RANGE & TOP END
All of the hotels in this category are above ground and prices include breakfast.

Hôtel Matmata (☎ 240 066; fax 240 177; s/d TD26/36, half board TD30/44; ⚡ ⚡) A modern, well-run place. The brick-vaulted rooms are attractive and there's a good restaurant and bar which get packed with tour groups at lunchtime.

Hôtel Kousseila (☎ 240 355; fax 240 265; s/d TD45/64, half board TD50/74; ⚡) This comfortable three-star place in the middle of town, down the hill from the bus station, is popular with tour groups and often booked out in summer.

Hôtel Ksar Amazigh (☎ 240 088; fax 240 173; s/d TD35/50, half board TD40/60; ⚡ ⚡) Not the friendliest place in town, but this hotel, 1.5km out of town on the Tamezret road, does have good rooms and a great position overlooking the Oued Barrak.

Hôtel Diar el Berber (☎ 240 274; fax 240 144; route de Tamazret; s/d TD50/70, half board TD60/90; ⚡ ⚡) A classy place 1.8km west of town that offers great views over the mountains from the poolside terrace. The good rooms, built in mock-traditional barrel-vaulted style, come with satellite TV.

Eating
Matmata's restaurants are nothing to get excited about. Food seems to be something of an inconvenience at **Chez Abdoul**, almost opposite the post office in the centre of town; meals cost around TD6. They're a bit more forthcoming 50m down the hill at **Restaurant Ben Khalifa**. The nameless restaurant next to the Café de la Victoire by the bus station does omelette, chips and salad for TD2.

For a troglodyte eating experience with a tourist menu (heavy on the couscous), you could do worse than **Restaurant Dalia** (meals TD6-10), signposted off the road to Tamezret 1.5km west of town.

If you're staying the night, you're better off taking a room with half board.

Getting There & Away
The bus and louage stations are in the centre of town. Louages run throughout the day to Nouvelle Matmata (650 mills), from where louages go to Gabès (TD1.2). This is the only way to get to Douz or Tataouine without your own transport.

There are seven buses a day to Gabès (TD1.7), as well as two afternoon buses to Tamezret (900 mills) which return to Matmata an hour later, although check with the driver before setting out. There are also two to Techine (900 mills) and one evening SNTRI bus to Tunis (TD18.6, eight hours).

AROUND MATMATA
Haddèj   حدّاج
The village of Haddèj, 3km northeast of Matmata, is much less developed. It was here that the crucifixion scene in *Monty Python's Life of Brian* was filmed.

Although many pit homes were abandoned after the severe floods of 1969, you may be invited into underground homes – a good chance to sit and chat with the locals. The main attraction is an underground olive press, where big millstones are turned by a camel in an impossibly small space. There's also a press operated by weights and levers.

GETTING THERE & AWAY
The road to Haddèj is signposted to the east 4km north of Matmata on the road to Gabès. There's no public transport from old Matmata, but there are occasional buses and *camionnettes* to and from Nouvelle Matmata. Otherwise, catch a bus as far as Tijma and walk the remaining 3km to Haddèj.

If the weather is favourable, there's an excellent walk back to Matmata along the mule track which cuts directly through the hills. It takes about 1½ hours at a steady pace. Ask the locals in Haddèj to point it out to you, as it's not obvious where it starts. Once you are on it, it's well trodden and easy to follow.

Tamezret   تمزرات
Few tourists make it out to the quiet little village of Tamezret, which overlooks the Nefzaoua plains from its commanding hilltop position 13km west of Matmata.

The houses here are built above ground, using the abundant local rock. The old quarter, above the bus stop, is a maze of alleyways that wind around the hillside. There are two afternoon buses from Matmata.

An excellent sealed road continues from Tamezret to Douz, 97km further west.

East of Matmata
There is some dramatic country east of Matmata on the back road to Medenine.

It's a good sealed road as far as the turn-off to **Techine**, 12km to the southeast of Matmata. Techine is a smaller version of Matmata, minus the tour buses; you'll find plenty of volunteers for the job of leading the way to the pit homes, which are unusual for their built-in furniture. There are two afternoon buses from Matmata to Techine (900 mills).

THE BERBERS
The Berbers, the indigenous people of North Africa, got their name (the Greek *barbarikos* means 'foreign') from the Arabs who arrived at the end of the 7th century and sought to distinguish the Berbers from those who had adopted Roman/Byzantine culture. The ancient Egyptians knew them as the Libou (nomads); the Greeks called them Libyans, as did the Phoenicians; and the Romans called them Africans.

Ethnically, the Berbers are a cultural melting pot – the result of successive waves of immigration from the Near East, sub-Saharan Africa and southern Europe. By the time the Phoenicians arrived in the 10th century BC, these diverse peoples had adopted a uniform language and culture.

Berber territory was divided up into tribal confederations. Northern Tunisia was the territory of the Numidians, founders of the cities of Bulla Regia, Sicca (El-Kef) and Thugga (Dougga). Other tribes had settled in the major oases of the south, while others lived a semi-nomadic pastoral existence.

Although conquered many times through history, the Berbers proved hard to repress. Military resistance to Roman rule continued until AD 24, and later resurfaced in the 4th century. They were probably at the peak of their political and military power when the Arabs arrived. The Berbers greatest success against these latest invaders was the capture of Kairouan which became the base for a short-lived Berber kingdom until 689.

The next wave of rebellion was led by Al-Kahina, a legendary figure in Berber lore. The widow of a tribal chief from the Aures Mountains in Algeria, she defeated Hassan bin Nooman at Tebessa in 695 and pushed back the Arab armies as far as Gabès, before fighting her last stand in the colosseum of El-Jem (p181). More trouble was to follow in the form of Berber-led Kharijite rebellions that flared intermittently over the following 250 years, but effective resistance to Arab rule ended with the Hilalian invasions in the 11th century.

Tunisia's Berbers have become all but totally assimilated with the Arab population. Berber customs, however, continue to survive – particularly in rural areas. Many women still wear the traditional *bakhnoug* (shawl) and *assaba* (headband) and tattoo their faces with ancient tribal symbols; men still favour the *burnous*, a hooded woollen cape.

You'll need your own transport if you want to continue further east. The road runs through some wild hill country, much of it covered by esparto grass, which the locals gather and use for making all sorts of things, from mats to mule harnesses (see Esparto Grass, p154). It finally emerges at **Toujane**, 23km southeast of Matmata. This extraordinary place of stone houses spread around a hillside and beneath the ruins of an old kasbah, is cut by a gorge that leads down to the coastal plain. It's very photogenic, particularly in the early-morning light.

A 4WD is necessary to continue on the back road from Toujane to Medenine, 38km to the southeast, but there's a good sealed road northeast from Toujane to the town

of **Mareth**, on the main road from Gabès to Medenine, and which has a **World War II Museum**.

An alternative is to turn northwest at **Ain Tounine**, 4km north of Toujane, and head back to Matmata Nouvelle, passing the charming stone village of **Ben Zeiten** on the way.

THE KSOUR القصور

The ksour district, centred on the rugged hills of the Jebel Dahar, is a weird and wonderful landscape dotted with ruined villages perched on hilltops and evocative ksour (the singular is ksar), the wonderfully

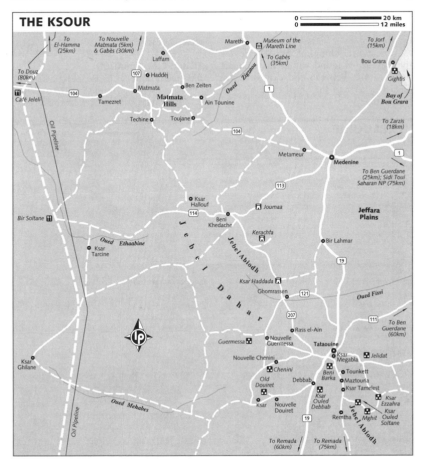

THE KSOUR

idiosyncratic fortified granaries that are the region's trademark. It's a region not to be missed.

The Dahar has long been a stronghold of Berber culture – ever since the semi-nomadic Berber tribes who inhabited the Jeffara were driven into the hills by the Hilalian invasions of the 11th century. The villages around here are among the last places where the local Berber language, Chelha, can be heard. With the deaths of elderly speakers, the language too is dying out.

TATAOUINE
تطاوين

☎ 75 / pop 58,000

Tataouine is the ideal base for visiting the ksour and exploring the nearby hills. The town itself has few attractions of its own, but the surrounding sights more than make up for it.

Almost everything of importance for the traveller is found within the compact town centre, between the east–west ave Hedi Chaker and the small clocktower in the north.

Information

INTERNET ACCESS

Both these places claim to be open 24 hours, but we didn't pass by at 4am to check.

Ksournet (rue Habib Mestaoui; TD2 per hr) Opposite the clocktower.

Publinet (ave Hedi Chaker; TD1.5 per hr) Next to the Hôtel La Gazelle.

MONEY

Most major banks have offices in town and all change money.

Banque de l'Habitat (ave Farhat Hached) ATM.

Banque du Sud (ave Farhat Hached). ATM.

BNA (ave 2 Mars). ATM.

POST & TELEPHONE

There are plenty of Taxiphone offices around the town centre.

Post office (Ave Hedi Chaker) Opposite the southern end of ave Habib Bourguiba.

TOURIST INFORMATION

ONTT tourist office (☎ 850 686; ave Habib Bourguiba; ⏱ 7.30am-1pm & 3-6pm summer, 8am-12.30pm daily & 3-5.30pm Sat-Thu winter) At the northern end of town.

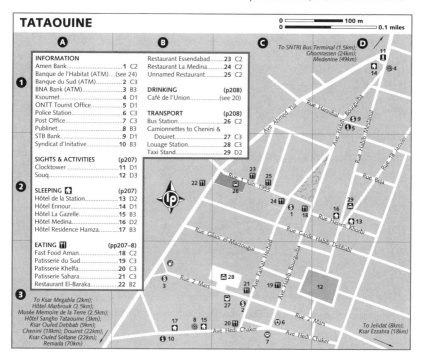

TATAOUINE

0 —————— 100 m
0 —————— 0.1 miles

INFORMATION
Amen Bank............................1 C2
Banque de l'Habitat (ATM)....(see 24)
Banque du Sud (ATM)............2 C3
BNA Bank (ATM)....................3 B3
Ksournet................................4 D1
ONTT Tourist Office..............5 D1
Police Station.......................6 C3
Post Office............................7 C3
Publinet................................8 D1
STB Bank..............................9 D1
Syndicat d'Initative..............10 B3

SIGHTS & ACTIVITIES (p207)
Clocktower 11 D1
Souq....................................12 D3

SLEEPING (p207)
Hôtel de la Station...............13 D2
Hôtel Ennour........................14 D1
Hôtel La Gazelle...................15 B3
Hôtel Medina........................16 D2
Hôtel Residence Hamza........17 B3

EATING (pp207–8)
Fast Food Aman....................18 C2
Patisserie du Sud..................19 C3
Patisserie Khelfa...................20 C3
Patisserie Sahara..................21 C3
Restaurant El-Baraka............22 B2

Restaurant Essendabad.......23 C2
Restaurant La Medina..........24 C2
Unnamed Restaurant...........25 C2

DRINKING (p208)
Café de l'Union.................(see 20)

TRANSPORT (p208)
Bus Station..........................26 C2
Camionnettes to Chenini &
Douiret..............................27 C3
Louage Station....................28 C3
Taxi Stand...........................29 D2

To SNTRI Bus Terminal (1.5km);
Ghomrassen (24km);
Medenine (49km)

To Ksar Megabla (2km);
Hôtel Marbrouk (2.5km);
Musée Mémoire de la Terre (3km);
Hôtel Sangho Tataouine (3km);
Ksar Ouled Debbab (9km);
Chenini (18km); Douiret (22km);
Ksar Ouled Soltane (22km);
Remada (70km)

To Jelidat (8km);
Ksar Ezzahra (18km)

Syndicat d'initiative (☎ 850 850; ave Hedi Chaker) Small but helpful, open the same hours as the tourist office.

Sights & Activities

KSAR MEGABLA

This small ksar, about 2km from the town centre, is a good place to start your exploration of the ksour, although much of the façade is no longer intact. It does, however, retain glimpses of its original character which can be lacking in some of the more heavily restored ksour. The villagers still keep their livestock in the cells and the courtyard can be uneven underfoot. Ksar Megabla is signposted to the right off the Remada road; it takes about one hour to walk up there from the main road.

MUSÉE MEMOIRE DE LA TERRE

Such is the other-worldly quality of the landscape and architecture around Tataouine that it should come as no surprise that dinosaurs were once prevalent here. This small **museum** (Memory of the Earth Museum; route de Chenini; admission TD1.5), 2.5km south of town, houses an interesting range of fossils and dinosaur models. There's a large dinosaur sculpture on the hill above the museum.

The museum keeps irregular opening hours – officially 9.30am to 4pm Tuesday to Saturday, but that doesn't mean that it's open at these times.

MARKETS

If you're in town on Monday or Thursday, don't miss the lively markets held in the souq at the southern end of ave Habib Mestaoui.

Sleeping

Surprisingly for a place of its popularity, Tataouine is not blessed with great accommodation. That said, there's at least one good option to suit most budgets.

BUDGET

Hôtel Ennour (☎ 860 131; ave Ahmed Tlili; s/d TD3/6) These are the cheapest beds in town. Some of them are habitable though most sag, cleanliness is not a priority and it's not an option women travellers will enjoy.

Hôtel de la Station (☎ 860 104; rue 18 Janvier; s/d TD5/10) Very close to the centre of town, this is a typical Tunisian cheapie – passably clean, friendly enough and an OK place to leave your bags for those counting their dinars.

The **Hôtel Medina** (☎ 860 999; rue Habib Mestaoui; s/d TD5/10) Directly opposite and a similar standard, the Medina's shared toilets can be a bit grim and the plumbing's a disaster, but otherwise the rooms are basic, moderately clean and rarely occupied.

Hôtel Residence Hamza (☎ 863 506; ave Hedi Chaker; s/d with breakfast TD12/17) This is by far the best budget choice if you have a few extra dinars in your pocket. The owners are friendly and the rooms (some with balcony) are pleasant and well maintained.

MID-RANGE & TOP END

Prices for the following places include breakfast and air-con.

Hôtel La Gazelle (☎ 860 009; fax 862 860; ave Hedi Chaker, s/d TD30.5/43; ▨) Two-star and central, this is the only mid-range option in town. The rooms are fine for the price if a little sterile and some of the bathrooms are in need of maintenance, but overall it's well run.

Hôtel Mabrouk (☎ 862 805; fax 850 100; route de Chenini; s/d TD40/60; ▨) Around 2.5km southwest of town on the road to Chenini, the Mabrouk's a bit out on a limb, but also quiet and the rooms have a touch more character than most.

Hôtel Sangho Tataouine (☎ 860 124; fax 862 177; off route de Chenini; s/d TD71/102; ▨ ▨) Tataouine's finest is 3km southwest of town. It's stylish, occupying a large, walled compound, and the bungalow-style rooms are tastefully decorated in traditional style, with lots of antique oddments and old photos. There's a good restaurant.

Eating

Eating in Tataouine is more a functional than pleasurable experience – think greasy spoon rather than chef's hat.

For bargain, good-sized *briqs* (pastries; 400 mills) with a hint of onion, it's hard to beat the small unnamed restaurant just along from the bus station on rue 1 Juin 1955; look for the orange-and-yellow awning outside.

A few doors to the west, **Restaurant Essendabad** was temporarily closed when we visited, but normally it has a range of daily specials that includes a delicious, thick *chorba* (soup) for 800 mills.

Among the other cheapies worth trying are **Restaurant La Medina** and **Fast Food Aman**, both on the same street, and **Restaurant el-Baraka** (ave Ahmed Tili). Expect to pay TD2 for *poulet roti*; the menus don't extend much further.

The hotel restaurants have the best food. **Hôtel La Gazelle** (☺ lunch & dinner; starters from TD2.5, mains TD6) is reasonable value with friendly waiters who are keen to talk.

Hôtel Sangho Tataouine also has a pleasant poolside restaurant, but they're reluctant to open it to non-hotel guests. Your chances improve if you dress nicely. Count on around TD15 per person.

PATISSERIES
All of Tataouine's many patisseries sell the local specialty, *corne de gazelle* (350 mills) – a pastry case, shaped like a gazelle's horn, filled with chopped nuts and soaked in honey. Good places to try are **Patisserie Khlefa** (ave Hedi Chaker) which is popular with tour groups, the more rustic **Patisserie Sahara** (ave Farhat Hached) or **Patisserie du Sud** (ave Habib Bourguiba).

Drinking
Sitting in outdoor cafés throughout the day is a favourite pastime for Tunisian men, but they do it with particular enthusiasm in Tataouine. The only one where you may be tempted to join them is **Café de l'Union** (ave Hedi Chaker) which has good shade and sees enough tourists for women to be welcome.

Hôtel La Gazelle has the only bar in town. Cold beers cost TD2, there are some outdoor tables and it can get quite rowdy if the size of the security staff are anything to go by.

Getting There & Away
BUS
The bus station occupies the large compound at the western end of rue 1 Juin 1955. There are four daily buses to Medenine (TD2.2, one hour), one to Houmt Souq (Jerba; TD6.4, 2½ hours) and six to Ghomrassen (TD1, 30 minutes); the last bus back from Ghomrassen leaves at 4.30pm. There's a daily bus southeast to Beni Barka, Maztouria and Ksar Ouled Soltane (TD1, 45 minutes), leaving town at 6am, and returning at 6pm.

SNTRI runs three daily air-con buses to Tunis (TD22.4, eight hours) which travel via Gabès (TD6.4, two hours), Sfax (TD11.4,

four hours) and Sousse (TD16, 6½ hours). They leave from the SNTRI terminal 1.5km north of town on the road to Medenine.

CAMIONNETTE
Camionnettes leave from opposite the louage station on rue 2 Mars with fairly regular departures for Chenini (TD1), Douiret (TD1.3) and Maztouria (TD1); some continue to Ksar Ouled Soltane (TD1.4). The earlier you set off the better as the system slows down around noon and is virtually nonexistent after 3pm.

LOUAGE
Louages leave from a compound on the northern side of rue 2 Mars. There are regular departures for Medenine (TD2.2) and Remada (TD3.8), and occasional services to Jerba (TD6.5), Ghomrassen (TD1.2) and Tunis (TD22.6). For Matmata, change at Gabès.

AROUND TATAOUINE
West of Tataouine is home to evocative and centuries-old Berber and Arab villages clinging to hilltops with a few ksour dotted among them. South of Tataouine, in the low hills of the Jebel Abiodh, is somewhat different, more Arab than Berber and home to some of Tunisia's best ksour.

GETTING AROUND
The best way of getting to all of the sites, unless you have your own vehicle, is to charter a taxi. Rates quoted by taxi drivers vary wildly, but count on TD60/30 for a day/half day. This gives you more freedom to stop where and for how long you want. A good half day could take in Ksar Haddada, Guermessa, Chenini and Douiret, or a loop through the ksour south of Tataouine.

The alternative is a mixture of *camionnette*, bus and hitching. Given the infrequency of transport in this part of the world, you'd need to set out early and you'd be lucky to see more than two sites in a day by public transport.

Berber Villages & Ksar Haddada   غمراسن
GHOMRASSEN
Ghomrassen, 24km northwest of Tataouine, is the main town of the Jebel Demmer. Once the stronghold of the powerful Ouergherma federation, which ruled from here until it

---

HILLTOP VILLAGES

Southern Tunisia's oldest surviving settlements are the spectacular hilltop villages built to take advantage of the region's dramatic rocky outcrops. The outcrops are formed by alternate layers of soft and hard rock, which have weathered into a series of natural terraces.

They are dotted with natural caves, which became a place of a refuge for Berber tribes who were forced to flee the plains by the Hilalian invasions of the 11th century. The caves were extended into houses by tunnelling rooms into the soft rock, and further expanded by the addition of walled courtyards at the front. The highpoint of the villages was occupied by a ksar, where the food supplies and valuables of the village were stored, while the village itself stretched out along the terraces below.

The best examples of Berber hilltop villages are those of Chenini, Guermessa and Douiret.

---

moved to Medenine in the 17th century, Ghomrassen now has transport services to Guermessa and Ksar Haddada.

The old part of town, to the south on the way to Guermessa, is a fine place to wander, spread along a gorge carved out by a broad *oued*, and protected by the ramshackle walls of the old **kalaa** (Berber hill fort) on both sides. It does have a couple of ksour in the vicinity, notably the **Ksar Rosfa** which affords fine views over the surrounds and **Ksar Bani Ghedir**, north of town, which is a typical one-storey plains ksar. Ask directions for both in town.

The modern town has a bank, shops and a couple of restaurants – but no hotels.

The best day for getting transport to Ghomrassen is Friday, when the market draws traders from all over the region. Otherwise, there are six buses a day to Tataouine (TD1, 30 minutes), and five to Medenine (TD2, one hour), as well as services to Guermessa (500 mills, 15 minutes) and Ksar Haddada.

KSAR HADDADA   قصر حدادة
Ksar Haddada, 5km north of Ghomrassen, is an amazing place that draws a steady stream of visitors who marvel at the maze of small alleyways and courtyards. Until recently, a restored section of the ksar was occupied by the fabulous Hôtel Ksar Haddada which became a place of pilgrimage for *Star Wars* fans following its appearance in *Star Wars IV – A New Hope*. The orange door jams were part of the set.

It's also a sad example of what happens after film crews leave. The hotel has now closed and the place is slowly falling apart, as the maintenance bill was too much for the operators.

Despite this, it's a special place. The old palm doors are superb and it's a wonderful site for exploring and reliving all those *Star Wars* memories.

There are occasional buses from Ghomrassen, but it's quicker to stand by the road and flag down whatever comes your way.

GUERMESSA   قرمزا
Guermessa, 8km southwest of Ghomrassen, is a spectacular ruined Berber village. The modern inhabitants long ago abandoned the old hilltop in favour of a modern village on the plains below. The beautiful and abandoned stone village makes exemplary use of the region's fortresslike hills and spreads across two peaks, linked by a narrow causeway. The larger peak is topped by a ruined *kalaa* (Berber fort). Less intact than some of the other villages, old Guermessa gives an impression of the village slowly merging back into the mountain, an effect which the photogenic white mosque below merely highlights. Guermessa remains relatively undiscovered by large numbers of visitors.

You need a 4WD to drive up to the site, which can be reached via the road to Ksar Ghilane and Douz, signposted to the east 1km north of the modern village. The turn-off to the site is 3km along this road, and loops back to Guermessa. This approach provides a great view. If you're walking, take plenty of water.

You might find the occasional bus to Nouvelle Guermessa from Ghomrassen, but the best option is to charter a taxi from Tataouine (see p208) and combine your visit with one to Chenini and Douiret.

The most direct road from Guermessa to Chenini is 4WD only.

THE SEVEN SLEEPERS

The area around Tataouine lends itself to legend and fairytale, whether in dramatic hilltop villages or improbable ksour architecture that has drawn the directors of Hollywood.

One local fable is not out of place in such company. Beyond the white mosque of Chenini, a 20-minute walk leads to a mosque and a series of strange 5m-long grave mounds known locally as the graves of the Seven Sleepers. According to local legend, seven Christians (and a dog) went into hiding in a nearby cave to escape persecution by the Romans. They slept for 400 years and awoke to find a world of Islam, long devoid of Romans. While they had slept, their bodies had continued to grow until they were 4m tall. They awoke only to die almost immediately, which must have been quite disappointing. To compensate, the story goes that, before dying, the men converted to Islam, assuring them of their place in paradise.

CHENINI   شنني

Chenini, 18km west of Tataouine, is the best known of the hill villages and is another superb spot. It's also the most visited and can get quite crowded.

The ruins of the original kalaa, dating from the 12th century AD, stand at the junction of two ridges. The settlement tumbles down and out from here, built into the rock along a series of small terraces that lead around the steep hillside. The houses consist of a cave room, which has a fenced front courtyard containing one or two more rooms. Some of the highlights include doors made from palm trunk, and the interior of some cave rooms contain the faded remnants of decorative paintwork and carvings on the roof. Some of the doorways here are so small as to require a contortionist's flexibility to enter. The ksar is still used to store grain and the village even has a few occupants (unlike the other villages), although most of Chenini's inhabitants have moved to the modern settlement of Nouvelle Chenini.

A path leads up from the road to a beautiful white mosque situated on a saddle between the two ridges.

To get the most of your visit, it can be worth allowing one of the village children to show you around, as some of the features can be hard to find. There are a few cafés serving cold drinks and snacks in the village.

Camionnettes from Tataouine stop at Nouvelle Chenini; sometimes it's possible to persuade the driver to continue the last 2km to the ruins.

There's a good sealed road south to Douiret, following the course of an *oued* (river) through the hills to Nouvelle Douiret. The road north from Chenini to Guermessa is best tackled by 4WD.

DOUIRET   دويرات

Ancient Douiret is really something, with its crumbling ksar perched high on the spur of a hill above a dazzling whitewashed mosque and white marabout (holy man or saint) tombs dotting the plains. As at Chenini, the houses are built into the rock along terraces that follow the contour lines around the hill. The main terrace leads south for 1km to more houses, some of which are still occupied. Most of old Douiret is abandoned, and you can explore the ruins at your leisure. Look out for some of the ornate carved doorways and Berber designs painted on the walls. Stairs lead up the hill next to the mosque and the higher you climb, the better the views.

Most of the time you'll have the place to yourself.

Douiret is 22km southwest of Tataouine. The road is signposted from Debbab, 9km south of Tataouine on the road to Remada. Unless you've chartered a taxi, transport to Douiret is a bit hit-or-miss. Early morning is the best time to catch a *camionnette* from Tataouine, but they normally go only as far as Nouvelle Douiret, 1.5km before old Douiret. You may be able to persuade the driver to take you the rest of the way, but you'll certainly have to walk back afterwards to find a ride to Tataouine.

Ksour

KSAR OULED DEBBAB   قصر أولاد دباب

This huge ksar sits on a low hill just east of the modern village of Debbab, 9km south of Tataouine on the Remada road. It was occupied until quite recently and most of the buildings are still in good condition. There's a sealed road leading up to the entrance gate from Debbab; the walk takes about 20 minutes.

KSAR OULED SOLTANE

قصر أولاد صلطان

Ksar Ouled Soltane, 22km southeast of Tataouine, has the best set of *ghorfas* in the south, rising a dizzying four storeys around two courtyards. The *ghorfas* have been fully renovated to give some sense of how they must once have appeared. It's a terrific place which should not be missed. The lower courtyard is used as a stage for performances during the Festival of the Ksour in late November.

The views of the sunset from here are wonderful, but don't get here too late or the courtyards will be quite dark. There's a small, friendly café in one of the *ghorfas*.

The only bus to Ksar Ouled Soltane (TD1, 40 minutes) leaves Tataouine at 6am; *camionnettes* are a better bet. There are occasional services to Ksar Ouled Soltane, but plenty to Maztouria. There's quite a lot of traffic along this road, so hitching shouldn't be a problem.

OTHER KSOUR

On the way between Tataouine and Ksar Ouled Soltane, it's worth looking in at the **Ksar Beni Barka** and **Ksar Tamelest**, which are more modest than Ksar Ouled Soltane, but nonetheless interesting examples of small village ksour.

If you have your own transport, you can continue on beyond Ksar Ouled Soltane, southeast to **Mghit**, which also has its own little ksar.

The road turns northeast to **Ksar Ezzahra**, which almost rivals Ouled Soltane as the best ksar in the region. It is almost uniformly four-storeys with two courtyards, many staircases and multi-layered tiers. Because it's further from Tataouine, you'll have the place to yourself. The small section of dirt road between Mghit and Ksar Ezzahra is easily traversed by conventional vehicle.

The road continues beyond Ksar Ezzahra to Tataouine. En route back to town, don't

---

THE KSAR

The structure that typifies Berber architecture is the ksar (plural ksour), the traditional fortified granary built by the region's tribes. Its design reflects the main priority of its builders – to preserve and protect the precious grain crops produced in good seasons. Ksour were usually built on natural defensive positions, and occupy some spectacular ridge and hilltop locations.

A single ksar consists of many *ghorfas* – long, narrow, barrel-vaulted rooms built of stone and gypsum and finished with a mud render. The *ghorfas* themselves were like caves, with a single tiny door opening onto the courtyard. The very low humidity of this arid region, combined with the cool conditions inside the ksar, meant that grain could be kept for years in the *ghorfas* without deteriorating. The storage areas were sealed with doors made of palm trunks and warded off insects, thieves and inclement weather alike. Sometimes a caretaker, often a local religious figure, regulated how much could be taken by the owners during times of scarcity. Its purpose was, therefore, akin to a modern bank and prevented the crop-holders from squandering their resources through a system of enforced saving and stockpiling.

Entry to the courtyard was by a single fortified gate or *skifa*. The *ghorfas* were stacked three or four storeys high and access to the upper levels was by a narrow staircase. Where no such staircase existed, precarious stone steps were built into the walls. The tree branches protruding from the top of the upper *ghorfas* were part of a pulley system, allowing the *ghorfas* to be filled and emptied without having to carry the grain up the difficult stairs.

Although the practice varied from town to town, in general each *ghorfa* belonged to a particular family or group of families. Grains like barley and wheat were usually kept in the rooms above the ground with olive oil stored in underground chambers.

The oldest examples of ksour are to be found occupying the highest peaks of the ancient hilltop villages west of Tataouine, but these are in poor condition. Most of the best examples are more recent constructions dating from the 15th and 16th centuries, built by Arab settlers who had adopted Berber traditions.

miss the expansive ruined complex of *ghorfas* at **Ksar Jelidet**.

MEDENINE   مدنين

☎ 75 / pop 56,000

The only reason to come to Medenine, 76km southeast of Gabès, is for a good ksar and connecting transport, or as a base for trips to the villages of the Jebel Demmer to the southeast. Otherwise, it's a dull, modern town.

Orientation & Information

The main street is ave Habib Bourguiba, which runs north–south through the centre of town.

The **post office** (place des Martyrs) is south of the town centre, although most other things

of importance – banks (with ATMs), hotels and restaurants – are north of the *oued*. There's a **Publinet** office (⏰ 8am-midnight; TD1.5 per hr) just west of place 7 Novembre.

Ksar Medenine

Medenine's only attraction is its old ksar, on ave 7 Novembre, built by the Ouergherma Federation in the 17th century following the decision to leave the mountain stronghold of Ghomrassen and assert authority over the plains. It's in fine condition, and the *ghorfas* surrounding the courtyard are draped with Berber carpets from souvenir shops.

The ruins of two other ksour are to the north, in varying stages of disrepair, and not all are open.

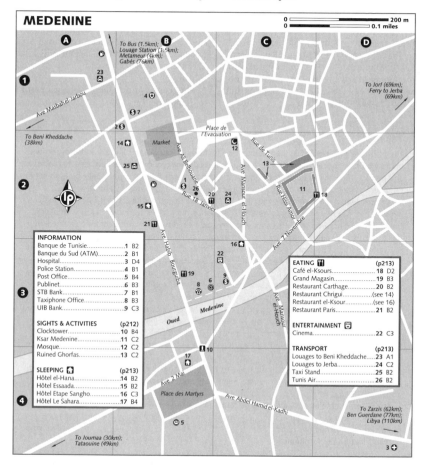

Sleeping

Hôtel Essaada (☎ 640 300; ave Habib Bourguiba; s/d TD6/8; with private bathroom TD7/10) The best budget option with rooms around a courtyard set back from the street. They're a bit airless but well-kept (including the shared toilets) and it's a laid-back place.

Hôtel el-Hana (☎ 640 690; ave Habib Bourguiba; dm TD4, s/d with shared bathroom TD6/8) Just to the north, this place is a touch more basic but fine for a night.

Hôtel Le Sahara (☎ 640 007; ave 2 Mai; s/d with breakfast TD20/30) Don't be put off by the exterior – it's much better than it looks. Rooms (some with balcony and TV) are light and airy and staff are friendly, but you don't expect the bathrooms to smell for this price.

Hôtel Etape Sangho (☎ 643 878; fax 640 550; place 7 Novembre; s/d with breakfast TD37/56; ⊠) Come here for the nicest rooms in town, especially those with balconies on the upper floors. The management seems to recognise that they're a touch overpriced and routinely offer them for TD30/44 when things are quiet, which is often.

Eating

There are plenty of good, cheap restaurants around town. **Restaurant Chrigui** (ave Habib Bourguiba), in the same building as Hôtel el-Hana, is a popular place with outdoor tables and a good range of daily specials such as couscous, chicken dishes and *merguez* (spicy sausages), all for around TD2.

Others with similar food include **Restaurant Paris** (ave Habib Bourguiba), where the *chorba* (soup; TD1) is tasty; **Restaurant Carthage** (rue 18 Janvier), a good place to wait while your louage to Jerba fills; while **Restaurant el-Ksour** (off rue 18 Janvier), is the best choice for breakfast and has a pleasant seating area.

The restaurant at the **Hôtel Etape Sangho** (⊠ lunch & dinner; starters TD2, mains from TD5.5) is the most upmarket with reasonable food, bow-tied waiters and cold beer.

For a drink in atmospheric surrounds, try the **Café el-Ksours** at the entrance to the Ksar Medenine. Sewer smells cost no extra.

Self-caterers can stock up on supplies at the **Grand Magasin** supermarket (ave Habib Bourguiba).

Getting There & Away

BUS

All services leave from the new bus station 1.5km north of town on the Gabès road.

SNTRI has seven buses daily to Tunis. The buses via Kairouan are quicker and cheaper (TD18.4, seven hours) than those via Sfax, El-Jem and Sousse. Getting a seat in summer can be difficult because only one service originates in Medenine.

There are frequent local buses to Jerba; services via the ferries at Jorf are faster and cheaper (TD3.1, 1½ hours) than those via Zarzis and the causeway (TD4.6, 2½ hours). Four buses daily head to Tataouine (TD2.2, one hour), and Gabès (TD3.7, 1¼ hours).

Local services include two daily buses to Metameur (500 mills, 15 minutes) and Beni Kheddache (TD1.6, 45 minutes).

LOUAGE

Louages to the north and Tataouine (TD2.2) leave from next to the bus station. Gabès (TD3.6) is the main destination. Louages to Jerba (TD4.2) leave from the centre of town, the small street linking rue 18 Janvier and ave Mansour el-Houch.

Louages for Beni Kheddache (TD1.5) leave from ave Masbah el-Jarbou.

AROUND MEDENINE
Metameur متامر

The small village of Metameur, 4km west of Medenine, has **Le Café Metameur** (☎ 640 294) which is set in the renovated *ghorfas* of a 17th-century ksar. It's a favourite of tour groups but a nice detour if you're exploring the area. The café is clearly visible from the Gabès–Medenine road, 1km to the east, on a low hill above the modern village. A taxi from Medenine costs about TD3 or there are two daily buses.

Ksar Joumaa قصر جومة

Joumaa, 30km southwest of Medenine, is as good a ksar as you could hope to find, and one of the few that's easily accessible by public transport.

The ksar is strung out along a narrow spur to the east of the modern village of Joumaa, the first place you come to after climbing the escarpment on the road to Beni Kheddache. The best approach is via a rough track signposted to the left about 1km before Joumaa on the road from Medenine. It's easy to spend an hour or so exploring the many *ghorfas*. Look out for unusual motifs on some of the ceilings. An archway leads to an inner courtyard and the ruins of the old *kalaa*.

Buses and louages running between Medenine and Beni Kheddache pass through Joumaa.

Beni Kheddache بني خداش

Beni Kheddache, 36km southwest of Medenine, is the main town of the northern Jebel Demmer. The run-down remnants of the town's old ksar are signposted on the way into the village, but there are better ksour in other towns, most notably Tataouine. There are two buses a day to Medenine (TD1.6, 45 minutes) and more frequent louages (TD1.5).

The road southwest to Ksar Ghilane is best left to 4WDs, but there are good roads northwest to Ksar Hallouf and south to Ksar Haddada and Ghomrassen.

Ksar Hallouf قصر حلوف

☎ 75

Ksar Hallouf, 14km northwest of Beni Kheddache, provides a great opportunity for travellers to escape from the modern world for a few days. The ksar, which overlooks a small modern village, has been converted into the wonderful **Relais Touristique de Ksar Hallouf** (☎ 637 148; fax 637 320; d TD12), with accommodation in a small restored section of *ghorfas*. It's run by a very friendly local family. The conditions are basic – there are mattresses on the floor, cold showers and squat toilets – but it's worth it for the opportunity to wake up in such superb surroundings.

The road to Ksar Hallouf is clearly signposted from the centre of Beni Kheddache. There are a couple of unsignposted forks in the road along the way; take the right fork both times. The first 10km is a good sealed road, which finishes at an army base; the final 4km of dirt road presents no problems for conventional vehicles. A taxi from Beni Kheddache costs TD5.

Gightis قطيس

The Roman port of **Gightis** (admission TD1.1, plus camera TD1; ☒ 8am-noon & 3-7pm summer, 8.30am-5.30pm winter), 20km south of Jorf on the back road from Medenine, is one of Tunisia's least-visited ancient sites.

Established by the Phoenicians, Gightis became a busy port during Roman times, exporting gold, ivory and slaves delivered by trans-Saharan caravans. Most of the buildings date from the 2nd century AD and are spread around the ancient capitol and forum. The site lay buried until the early 20th century and is relatively undeveloped. It's a lovely spot for a stroll, with clumps of palms and acacia trees dotting the coast above the gleaming waters of the Gulf of Bou Grara.

Don't worry if the site appears closed – the guardian lives opposite and will emerge.

GETTING THERE & AWAY

Buses and louages between Houmt Souq and Medenine can drop you at the site, which is just south of the tiny modern village of Bou Grara. You'll have to pay the full fare for Houmt Souq to Medenine if you catch a louage. Getting away is more difficult; you may have a long wait for a bus, and louages are likely to be full. The local practice is to flag down whatever comes by.

THE SAHARA صحراي

There are few more spectacular sights than the dunes of the Grand Erg Oriental, one of the Sahara's most expansive sand seas. The *erg* (sand sea) begins about 50km south of Douz and extends almost 500km southwest into neighbouring Algeria. Here you'll find the Sahara you've always dreamed of, with the sands turned orange and golden by the setting sun and surrounded by silence.

All along the Sahara's northern perimeter are oasis towns huddled amid vast *palmeraies*, fed by underground water and producing the finest dates in Tunisia. Conveniently, the best of these oases are the towns of Douz and Tozeur from where desert expeditions are most easily launched.

The Sahara and its northern hinterland are also the home of the Berbers. With the decline of the Roman Empire, tribes began to move in from the south at the end of the 4th century AD, bringing with them the first camels to be seen in Tunisia. The Berbers and their camels are still there, 16 centuries later and many continue to live a seminomadic existence in the south around Douz.

If you're planning to explore the Sahara in your own vehicle, a guide is strongly recommended.

KEBILI   فبلي

☎ 75 / pop 19,000

Kebili, north of Douz, is the main town and administrative centre of the Nefzaoua region. Few travellers pause any longer than it takes to catch the next bus or louage, which is a shame because there's more to Kebili than the dusty modern town centre.

Orientation & Information

The Gabès–Tozeur road crosses the northern half of town. Ave Habib Bourguiba runs south to Douz from the major junction on the eastern side of town. The main street, ave 7 Novembre, runs parallel about 500m further west.

Facilities include a post office and **bank** (☉ for changing money 9am-noon). Both are around the junction of the Gabès-Tozeur road and ave Habib Bourguiba.

Ancienne Kebili

The abandoned town of Ancienne Kebili crumbles away in obscurity in the *palmeraie* to the south of the modern town. To get there, head south towards Douz on ave Bourguiba for about 10 minutes until you reach the **hot springs** on the left. The springs feed a *hammam* (bathhouse) and pool complex. The houses may be collapsing, but the gardens are neatly tended. The **mosque** is still in use, and an ancient **koubba** (shrine) has been given a coat of blue paint.

Opposite the springs is a signposted track that winds through the *palmeraie* to the old town.

Sleeping & Eating

Hôtel Ben Said (☎ 491 573; ave Habib Bourguiba; s/d with shared bathroom TD6/10), 400m south of the Gabès–Tozeur road, is the only habitable budget choice, with clean rooms that are fine for a night.

Stepping up a few notches, the **Hôtel Kitam** (☎ 491 338; fax 491 076; route de Gabès; s/d TD30/40; ⌘) is a reasonable, modern two-star hotel on the road into town. A more interesting option is the **Hôtel Fort des Autruches** (☎ 490 933; fax 491 117; s/d with breakfast TD34/50, half board TD44/70; ⌘ ⌘), which occupies an old fort on the southeastern side of town. It's a pleasant spot with a swimming pool (that's sometimes filled), friendly management and good value rooms. Prices are similar at the **Hôtel de l'Oasis Dar Kebili** (☎ 490 654) which is next door.

The **Hôtel Les Dunes de Nefzaoua** (☎ 480 675; fax 480 653; s/d with breakfast TD50/70; half board TD55/75), 22km west of town near the village of Bechri, is only an option if you have your own transport. The turn-off south to Bechri is clearly signposted in the small village of Zaouia. You'll come to the hotel, which is popular with tour groups, after about 2km. It has a fantastic setting on the edge of the Chott el-Jerid and an inviting swimming pool.

The **Restaurant Kheireddine**, between the louage stations, is the best bet for a cheap meal. You'll find *briqs* from 600 mills, *chorba* for TD1 and main courses from TD1.5. There are a few other cheap eateries around the louage station.

Getting There & Away

BUS

The bus station is no more than an office on the main street, near the junction with the Gabès–Tozeur road. There are frequent buses to Douz (TD1.3, 30 minutes) as well as regular departures for Tozeur and Gabès. The SNTRI office is 100m away on the opposite side of the dusty square.

LOUAGE

Louages to Gabès (TD5.5) and Tozeur (TD4.6) leave from the street running between place de l'Independence and ave Habib Bourguiba, although those to Douz (TD1.5) leave from one block further south.

DOUZ   دوز

☎ 75 / pop 28,000

If you arrive in Douz in the middle of a summer's afternoon, when heat and silence become one and are almost intolerable, you'll wonder why you've come. Resist the temptation to take the first louage out of town, because this is a place like no other in Tunisia. Find a place to rest in the shade because, like all desert towns, Douz sleeps during the day, only to come alive at night when people and a cool breeze return to the streets. That's the other thing about Douz: its people are a desert people for whom friendliness and hospitality are by no means a lost art.

The town centre is probably the most backpacker-friendly place in Tunisia, with some great accommodation and plenty of small restaurants. Douz is Tunisia's most popular gateway to the Sahara and it makes a good base from which to organise camel trekking (see Desert Expeditions, p219) and other desert activities. Every Thursday, the old souq is home to the colourful weekly market; it's worth arranging to be here just to see it.

Orientation

Douz isn't big enough to get lost in. The town centre is laid out in a rough grid around the souq. Ave des Martyrs leads west from the town centre to place des Martyrs. Roads lead south from here through the *palmeraie* and towards the zone touristique.

Information

INTERNET ACCESS

Publinet (Map p216; cnr rue 20 Mars & rue el-Hounine; TD1.5 per hr; 8am-midnight) Reasonable connections.

MONEY

The post office has an exchange counter as do most hotels in the zone touristique.
Banque du Sud (Map p216; route de Kebili) ATM.
STB bank (Map p216; ave Taieb Mehiri)

POST

Post office (Map p216; ave Taieb Mehiri) Just west of the town centre. It has an exchange counter.

TOURIST INFORMATION

ONTT tourist office (Map p217; ☎ 470 351; place des

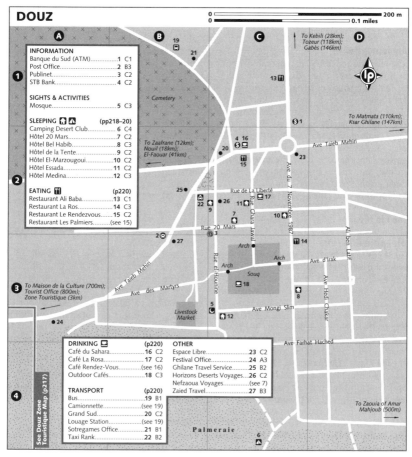

DOUZ

0 ——— 200 m
0 ——— 0.1 miles

INFORMATION	
Banque du Sud (ATM)	1 C1
Post Office	2 B3
Publinet	3 C2
STB Bank	4 C2

SIGHTS & ACTIVITIES	
Mosque	5 C3

SLEEPING	(pp218–20)
Camping Desert Club	6 C4
Hôtel 20 Mars	7 C2
Hôtel Bel Habib	8 C3
Hôtel de la Tente	9 C2
Hôtel El-Marzougoui	10 C2
Hôtel Essada	11 C2
Hôtel Medina	12 C3

EATING	(p220)
Restaurant Ali Baba	13 C1
Restaurant La Ros	14 C3
Restaurant Le Rendezvous	15 C2
Restaurant Les Palmiers	(see 15)

DRINKING	(p220)
Café du Sahara	16 C2
Café La Rosa	17 C2
Café Rendez-Vous	(see 16)
Outdoor Cafés	18 C3

TRANSPORT	(p220)
Bus	19 B1
Camionnette	(see 19)
Grand Sud	20 C2
Louage Station	(see 19)
Sotregames Office	21 B1
Taxi Rank	22 B2

OTHER	
Espace Libre	23 C2
Festival Office	24 A3
Ghilane Travel Service	25 B2
Horizons Deserts Voyages	26 C2
Nefzaoua Voyages	(see 7)
Zaied Travel	27 B3

To Kebili (28km);
Tozeur (118km);
Gabès (146km)

To Matmata (110km);
Ksar Ghilane (147km)

Cemetery

To Zaafrane (12km);
Nouil (18km);
El-Faouar (41km)

Ave Taieb Mehiri

Ave du 7 Novembre

Rue Chara Jawal

Ave 7 Novembre 1987

Rue de La Liberté

Rue 20 Mars

Arch

Arch

Souq

Arch

Ave d'Irak

Ali ben Latif

Ave Hedi Chaker

To Maison de la Culture (700m);
Tourist Office (800m);
Zone Touristique (3km)

Ave Taieb Mehiri

Ave des Martyrs

Rue el-Hounine

Livestock
Market

Ave Mongi Slim

Ave Farhat Hached

To Zaouia of Amar
Mahjoub (500m)

See Douz Zone
Touristique Map (p217)

Palmeraie

Martyrs; 8.30am-1pm & 3-5.45pm Jul-Aug, 8.30am-1.30pm & 3-5.45pm Sun-Thu, 8.30am-1.30pm Fri-Sat Sep-Jun) Helpful in giving recommended prices for camel expeditions.

Syndicat d'initiative (Map p217; ☎ 470 341) Two doors away from the tourist office, open the same hours.

Sights & Activities

MUSÈE DU SAHARA

This small folk **museum** (Map p217; place des Martyrs; admission TD1.1; 7-11am & 4-7pm Tue-Sun Jun-Aug, 9am-4.30pm Tue-Sat Sep-May) has a good collection of regional costumes, a mock nomad tent and an interesting section explaining the tattoos worn by local women. There is also information on camel husbandry and a section on desert plants. It's definitely worth a visit.

PALMERAIE

The *palmeraie* is the largest of all the Tunisian desert oases, with almost half a million palm trees. A wonderfully productive place, it turns out a remarkable assortment of fruit and vegetables – as well as prized *deglat ennour* (finger of light) dates.

The best way to explore it is to walk out along one of the two roads leading south through the *palmeraie* from the western end of ave des Martyrs. The roads link up at the zone touristique.

DESERT ACTIVITIES

The Sahara desert proper (see The Sahara, p215) starts 50km south of the zone touristique. Unless you're planning a longer excursion into the desert, the action centres around the **great dune**. It's nothing compared to the sand seas of the Grand Erg Oriental, but is a gentle introduction for those with little time.

Tours

Some of the officially recognised (and better) agencies include:

Espace Libre (Map p216; ☎ 470 620; fax 470 622; cnr ave Taieb Mehri & ave du 7 Novembre)
Ghilane Travel Services (Map p216; ☎ 470 692; gts@planet.tn; 38 ave Taieb Mehiri)
Horizons Deserts Voyages (Map p216; ☎ /fax 470 088; h.desert@planet.tn; 8 rue el-Hounine)
Nefzaoua Voyages (Map p216; ☎ 472 920; nefzaoua@planet.tn; rue 20 Mars)
Zaied Travel (Map p216; ☎ 455 014; fax 470 584; ave Taieb Mehiri)

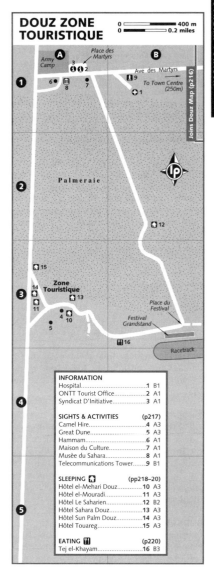

DOUZ ZONE TOURISTIQUE

0 ____ 400 m
0 ____ 0.2 miles

Festivals & Events

The main event on the Douz calendar is the **Sahara Festival**, which is normally held at the beginning of November – although the dates can be hard to track down. It's one of the few genuine festivals in the country, and draws large numbers of domestic visitors as well as foreign tourists.

THE DEPENDABLE DATE

Until recent times, life in the Sahara was almost entirely dependent on one remarkable plant, the date palm *(Phoenix dactylifera)*.

So important was it to desert life that the traditional way of assessing the size of an oasis was in terms of the number of palm trees it could support, rather than the number of people.

As well as producing dates for food, its trunk can be used for building, or hollowed out to channel water. Its branches are used for roofs and fences, while the tough leaf fibres can be woven into mats and ropes and the woody fruiting stems make good brooms. Nothing goes to waste. Even the date pits are used: in the old days, they were roasted and ground to make an ersatz coffee; today they are ground up as animal fodder.

The very presence of the date palm is an indicator of the desert's most precious resource, water. The date palm is very specific in its climatic requirements. There is an old Arab saying that it likes 'its feet in heaven and its head in hell', a reference to the tree's need for very high summer temperatures and lots of water – about 500L a day in summer.

There are more than 100 varieties of date. The finest is known as the *deglat ennour* (finger of light), so called because the flesh is almost translucent. It constitutes 50% of all plantings in Tunisia.

If you can, be in Douz in October when the best dates are harvested and freely available around town.

Most of the action takes place around place du Festival, where a special grandstand has been erected to handle the big crowds who come to watch the displays of traditional desert sports, such as camel racing and hunting with greyhoundlike Saluki dogs.

The festivities also include colourful parades and music in the town centre, and evening poetry readings and concerts at the Maison du Culture.

Sleeping

All of the budget and a couple of mid-range places are in or around the town centre; the more upmarket hotels are in the zone touristique, 3.5km southwest of town, facing the desert on the edge of the enormous *palmeraie*. There's great value to be found in all categories.

BUDGET

Camping Desert Club (☎ /fax 470 575; brahim2020@ yahoo.fr; off ave du 7 Novembre; per person TD4; motorbike/ car/campervan TD2/3/4) Set among the palm trees south of the Douz town centre, this is one of the best campsites in Tunisia. If you don't have a tent, there are mattresses available inside a Berber tent. There's also an Italian/ Tunisian restaurant. Showers here are free, but expect to pay for electricity (TD1), water (TD2) and use of a washing machine (TD5). The gates are closed to cars between 11pm and 7am.

Hôtel Essada (Map p216; ☎ 470 824; rue Ghara Jawal; per person TD5) The basic Essada has some of the cheapest beds in town which are a bit run-down but clean.

Hôtel de la Tente (Map p216; ☎ /fax 470 468; rue el-Hounine; per person TD5, with shower TD7.5, with shower & toilet TD10) This is a better choice with a range of good rooms (those on the roof are best) and helpful management. It's excellent value.

Hôtel Bel Habib (Map p216; ☎ /fax 471 115; off ave du 7 Novembre; s/d TD7/14, with private bathroom TD10/20) This is also very good although some of the rooms without bathroom are a bit cell-like. Those with bathroom are much better and some have balconies. There's also a small restaurant.

Hôtel el-Marzougoui (Map p216; ☎ /fax 473 030; ave du 7 Novembre; per person without/with shower TD8/ 10) Another similarly good choice, there are rooms with views over the souq area.

MID-RANGE

Hôtel 20 Mars (Map p216; ☎ 470 269; hotel20mars@ planet.tn; rue 20 Mars; s/d TD11/16, with shower TD13/18, with shower & toilet TD15/20) This place is in the mid-range category by virtue of its quality as much as its price – if only more places in Tunisia were this good value. The hotel's recently renovated rooms with brick-vaulted ceilings are set around a small tree-filled courtyard and are spotless and very pleasant. The management here is also super-friendly.

Hôtel Medina (Map p216; ☎ 470 010; rue el-Hounine; per person without/with bathroom & air-con TD10/15; ⊠) Equally good, the medina's rooms are a touch older but most are larger and the air-con is a big selling point. Also highly recommended.

Hôtel Le Saharien (Map p217; ☎ 471 337; hotoasis@gnet.tn; s/d with breakfast TD46/72; ⊠ ⊠) In the heart of the *palmeraie* on the road to place du Festival, this is a touch more run-down than the places in the zone touristique but still good value, especially the rooms in the southern wing. There are several swimming pools, including an indoor thermal one.

TOP END

All top-end hotels have a bar, *hammam* and restaurant. Prices include breakfast. It's worth booking ahead in summer.

Hôtel Touareg (Map p217; ☎ 470 057; fax 470 313; s/d 50/70; half board TD65/100) Built in the image of an old-style kasbah, complete with crenellations, this well-run place has a palm-covered 'island' in the middle of the swimming pool and comfortable rooms.

Hôtel Sun Palm Douz (Map p217; ☎ 470 123; fax 470 525; s/d TD64/94; half board TD72/102; ⊠ ⊠) Pleasant rather than spectacular, the rooms here are comfortable and spacious.

Hôtel el-Mouradi (Map p217; ☎ 470 303; elmouradi.douz@planet.tn, s/d TD70/104, half board TD82/128; ⊠ ⊠) A four-star venue which is suitably a step up in style though not a huge one in price.

Hôtel Sahara Douz (Map p217; ☎ 470 864; saharadouz@planet.tn; s/d TD55/80, half board TD65/100; ⊠ ⊠) Rooms here come with more character than most; it's one of the better choices.

DESERT EXPEDITIONS

Camel trekking is big business in Douz and everyone from restaurant waiters to taxi drivers have a friend with a camel ready to take you into the desert at a moment's notice. If you come in summer, only overnight excursions are possible.

The possibilities start with one-hour rides, available in the morning and late afternoon at the zone touristique. You'll probably have to bargain hard to get the official rate of TD4 per hour, unless you arrange your ride through the ONTT tourist office. If you've never been on a camel before, it's a good idea to try a short ride before signing up for a longer trek. Camel riding is not for everyone, and some people decide that one hour is enough!

Overnight treks are equally easy to organise; longer treks generally require 24-hours notice. The biggest problem is choosing between the range of treks on offer. The tourist office advises travellers to stay clear of the town's many unlicensed guides, pointing out that they are uninsured and unaccountable if problems arise. Some of the ten registered tour companies are listed under the Tours section (p217).

In practice, many independent travellers end up using unlicensed guides operating through one of the hotels in town. Most charge TD35 for overnight treks (the official tourist office rate is TD25) or TD40 per day for longer treks. You could try bargaining, but you run the risk of operators taking short cuts with food and water.

These treks leave Douz in the afternoon, and involve about four hours riding before pitching camp at sunset. Guides prepare an evening meal of damper bread, cooked in the ashes of a camp fire, and stew, before bedding down beneath the stars (blankets provided on request). An early breakfast of damper and jam is followed by the return ride, arriving in Douz mid-morning. Sometimes a visit to a village or Berber encampment is included.

The main complaint about these treks is that the desert immediately south of Douz isn't very interesting. The real desert, the Grand Erg Oriental, is a long way further south.

Longer expeditions can range as far as Ksar Ghilane (seven to ten days). If you don't have that much time, most companies arrange overnight 4WD trips to Ksar Ghilane, leaving Douz around 4pm and arriving back mid-morning the following day. Count on around TD200 to TD250 per 4WD per day.

You'll need to be properly equipped to go trekking. Essential items include a sensible hat which you can secure to your head, sunscreen and sunglasses. Long trousers are a good idea to prevent your legs getting chafed. Cameras and watches should be kept wrapped in a plastic bag to protect them from the very fine Saharan sand that gets into everything.

Hôtel Mehari Douz (Map p216; ☎ 471 088; fax 589; s/d TD62/94, half-board TD72/104; ❄ ☒) One of the original zone touristique hotels, the Mehari Douz is still a good choice and one of the closest to the great dune.

Eating

Douz has plenty of budget restaurants, all of which are open for lunch and dinner.

Restaurant La Rosa (Map p216; ave du 7 Novembre 1987) Probably the pick of the cheapies, this place has friendly waiters, simple but well-cooked food and a good range of dishes for less than TD3.

Restaurant Ali Baba (Map p216; route de Kebili) About 100m north of the roundabout, this is another traveller-friendly place although it gets mixed reviews from readers. It has good outdoor seating in a courtyard garden at the back. Couscous with spicy sauce (TD2.5) is the house specialty.

Restaurant Les Palmiers (Map p216; ave Taieb Mehri) Les Palmiers is similar to the other two and worth trying if you fancy a change of scenery.

Restaurant Le Rendezvous (Map p216; ☎ 470 802; ave Taieb Mehri; starters from TD1.5, mains from TD3.5) A step up in price and quality; the eating area has a bit more polish and you'll find a bit more meat on your chicken.

Tej el-Khayem (Map p217; ☎ 472 446; zone touristique; starters from TD2.5, mains TD6.5-12) Terrific venue facing the desert. You can eat indoors, in a Berber tent or out on the sand and they organise belly-dancing and more traditional dances for groups. This is a great place to try the camel (TD12) or, if there are 10 of you and you order 24 hours in advance, the *coucha agneau* – a local speciality of meat cooked underground in *gargoulette* (pottery). They also serve wine (from TD7) and beer (TD2).

Drinking

In the evening, the best place for a coffee or mint tea are the outdoor tables in the open square of the souq.

The **Café Rendez-Vous** (Map p216) and **Café du Sahara** (Map p216), almost side-by-side on ave Taieb Mehiri, are the favourite meeting places for the men of Douz and good spots to check out the comings and goings. **Café La Rosa** (Map p216; Rue Ghara Jawal) has a quiet courtyard at the back where you can enjoy a coffee away from the crowds.

Shopping

There are numerous shops around town which sell Saharan sandals (comfortable slip-on shoes made from camel skin). The tourist versions normally come decorated with palm motifs etc. The prices vary from TD14 to TD20, depending on the level of decoration and quality. All around the souq and surrounding streets, you'll find Berber rugs, sand roses, Tuareg jewellery and a range of other pots and pieces.

Getting There & Away
BUS

SNTRI has two air-con services a day to Tunis (TD23, eight hours). The 6am service goes via Tozeur, Gafsa and Kairouan (TD17.1, seven hours), and the 9pm service goes via Gabès (TD6.9, 2½ hours), Sfax (TD11.5, five hours) and Sousse (TD16.3, 6½ hours).

Regional company Sotregames has daily buses to Kebili (TD1.3, 30 minutes), Tozeur (TD4.7, three hours) and Gabès (TD5.7, three hours). There are also five daily buses to Zaafrane (550 mils), Sabria (TD1.4) and El-Faouar.

CAR & MOTORCYCLE

Lots of money has been spent upgrading the road between Douz and Matmata, 110km to the east. There are several small cafés along the way. The pipeline road to Ksar Ghilane intersects the Douz–Matmata road 66km east of Douz.

LOUAGE & CAMIONNETTE

There are regular departures to Kebili (TD1.5) and Gabès (TD6.9), but none to Tozeur or Matmata – change at Kebili or Gabès respectively. There are also regular *camionnettes* to Zaafrane (600 mills) and the other oases south of Douz.

Getting Around
BICYCLE

Bicycles can be rented (TD2.5 per hour) from **Grand Sud** (☎ 471 777; ave Taieb Mehri).

TAXIS

The best place to find taxis is on rue de la Liberté, near the corner with ave Taieb Mehri. A trip from the centre of town to the zone touristique shouldn't cost more than TD2.

AROOUND DOUZ

☎ 75

A sealed road runs southwest from Douz to a string of smaller oases, which are bases for the region's semi-nomadic tribes who prefer life in the desert to the concrete-block settlements provided by the government.

Zaafrane   زعفران

The small oasis town of Zaafrane, about 12km southwest of Douz, has emerged as the camel-trekking capital of Tunisia in the past few years. The town is home to the Adhara tribe, which has found tourism to be a good way of turning desert skills into an income.

The town itself is not particularly attractive – a collection of utilitarian block houses, but it's on the edge of some interesting country.

The only hotel, **Hôtel Zaafrane** (☎ /fax 491 720; s/d with breakfast TD23/32, half-board TD27/36), is a good and friendly place. The hotel has the only restaurant and bar in Zaafrane.

There are regular buses from Douz, as well as frequent *camionnettes* (600 mills). The flow of traffic dries up around 4pm and there's never anything much on Friday afternoons.

Beyond Zaafrane

The road continues from Zaafrane to **El-Faouar**, 41km southwest of Douz. This is the region's second-largest oasis, after Douz, with a population approaching 6000. It's also the source of the bulk of the 'sand roses' that are sold at souvenir stalls throughout the country. The best day to visit El-Faouar is Friday, when the market comes to town.

The three-star **Hôtel Faouar** (☎ 460 531; fax 460 576; s/d with breakfast TD40/60, full board TD50/80) is signposted to the left on the road into town from Zaafrane. As well as the standard swimming pool, they also offer dune skiing (TD10) on nearby dunes.

There's a back road that loops north from Zaafrane to Kebili via the oasis villages of **Nouil** and **Blidet**. The turn-off is just west of Zaafrane on the road to El-Faouar. Nouil is nothing much, but Blidet has a great setting on the edge of the Chott el-Jerid. Blidet can be reached by bus and *camionnette* from Kebili. The **Campement Touristique Saharien** (☎ 494 714; fax 491 918; per person half board TD12) has accommodation in nomad-style tents.

THE GREAT DESERT

The Sahara desert stretches from the Atlantic to the Red Sea, covering, at last count, more than 9.065 million sq km or 3.5 million sq miles, passing across 15 degrees of latitude in the process. This vast space is home to just over two million people and encompasses large parts of Mauritania, Morocco, Algeria, Libya, Tunisia, Mali, Niger, Chad, Egypt, Sudan and a small slice of Burkina Faso.

The Sahara is home to haunting mountain ranges, particularly in southern Algeria, Libya, northern Niger and Chad where the Sahara reaches its high point at Emi Koussi, 3415 metres above sea level. Most of the Sahara is a high plateau, while the Qattara Depression of northwestern Egypt is its lowest point, 133 metres below sea level.

Contrary to popular myth, as little as one-ninth of the Sahara's surface is covered with sand. Some of the unimaginably beautiful sand seas nonetheless cover areas larger than many European countries and the Grand Erg Oriental, which straddles Algeria and southern Tunisia, is both one of the largest and one of the most stunning.

In ancient times, the Sahara was the domain of camel caravans numbering up to 30,000 beasts and carrying salt (which once traded ounce for ounce with gold), gold and slaves from the heart of Africa to the northern coast and beyond. Tunisian oasis towns such as Gabès, Tozeur and Gafsa grew rich on the trade.

The Sahara is a place of myth and legend – the silent gravitas of its many moods, the beauty of its diverse landscapes. You can get a taste with a fleeting visit, but the Sahara rewards those who linger, as Antoine de Saint-Exupéry observed: 'If at first it is merely emptiness and silence, that is because it does not open itself to transient lovers.'

Above all, the Sahara is home to its once-nomadic people, primarily Berbers, Tuareg and Tubu, who alone understand the Sahara's lure. The Nigerian Tuareg writer Mano Dayak wrote that the desert could not be described, but could only be lived.

SOUTH INTO THE SAHARA

The country immediately south of Douz is flat and fairly featureless; low dunes interspersed with small *chotts*. The first point of interest is the evocative abandoned village of **Aounet Rajah**, about 15km southwest of Douz, which has all but disappeared beneath a large dune. A small domed marabout tomb at the crest is the only building that remains intact; elsewhere all that remains are the tops of old walls poking from the sand.

Officially, the desert begins at La Porte du Desert, about 20km south of Douz. This gleaming white crenellated arch is visible from miles around.

Tour companies refer to this area as *jebel* (small mountain), which is the low hill nearby. It is the starting point for trips to **Taimbaïn** (pronounced Tembayine), 5km further south. Taimbaïn itself is a large, crescent-shaped outcrop of rock that offers magnificent views from its summit (220m). The main attraction is the journey through some magnificent dune country, crossing three great walls of gleaming white sand that the wind has thrown up like defensive ramparts around Taimbaïn.

KSAR GHILANE قصر غلان

☎ 75

The remote oasis of Ksar Ghilane, 138km southeast of Douz, is an amazing spot with a desert ksar and surrounded by the stunning dunes of the Grand Erg Oriental – this is some of the finest desert scenery in Tunisia.

The ksar is the ancient Roman fort of Tisavar, once a desert outpost on the Limes Tripolitanus defensive line. It was modified and renamed by the local Berber tribespeople in the 16th century. The ksar now lies abandoned on a low hill about 2km west of a magical little oasis where hot springs feed a small swimming hole shaded by graceful tamarisk trees. There are impressive dunes between the oasis and Tisavar, particularly once you get among them. They're wonderful at sunset and sunrise.

There are cafés around the swimming hole, but no shops or other facilities.

It was also here that many of the scenes for *The English Patient* were filmed and it's not hard to see why.

Accessible by overnight 4WD excursion from Tozeur or Douz, Ksar Ghilane is where you'll understand the power of the Sahara's lure.

Camel Rides

Locals charge TD15 for the 1½-hour return journey from the oasis to the fort. Evening is the best time, when the setting sun produces some stunning plays of light and shadow across the dunes.

Sleeping & Eating

Camping is tolerated around the fringe of the oasis, but most visitors use one of the camp sites. All offer beds in large nomadstyle tents as well as providing areas for pitching tents. All also have restaurants.

The pick of them is **Camping Ghilane** (☎ 470 750; per person TD7), ideally located next to the hot springs on the northern edge of the oasis. A three-course evening meal costs an extra TD6.

Other options include **Camping Paradise** (☎ 620 570), in the middle of the *palmeraie*, and **Camping L'Erg** (☎ 01-860 799), in the desert to the south.

The extraordinary **Hôtel Pansea** (☎ 621 870, 900 506; www.pansea.com/ksar.html; s/d TD118/130; 🌊 🍴) is a fabulous place. Situated on the edge of Grand Erg Oriental, the internationally renowned Pansea has air-con linen tents with private bathrooms, a swimming pool, restaurant and a decided touch of class. This is one of the best places in the country for a splurge.

Getting There & Away

There's no public transport to Ksar Ghilane and this remote spot is only accessible by 4WD along the pipeline road which runs south from El-Hamma, on the Gabès–Kebili road, all the way to Borj el-Khadra.

If you have a 4WD, there are several other possibilities, including the roads from Beni Kheddache, Guermessa and Douiret (see The Ksour, p205).

AROUND KSAR GHILANE

There are a couple of interesting diversions off the pipeline road between Ksar Ghilane and the Douz–Matmata road.

Most popular is **Bir Soltane**, where a small stone dome surrounds an ancient well. Centuries of use has cut deep rope grooves into the well-head. The only other building here is the nearby National Guard post, which uses a windmill to draw its water. Bir Soltane is about 2km west of the pipeline road, reached by signposted tracks both north and south of the **Café Bir Soltane**, 32km south of the Douz–Matmata road.

Hardly anyone heads out to **Ksar Tarcine**, about 12km southeast of Bir Soltane. This remote outpost began life as part of the Roman Limes Tripolitanus – when it was called Centenarium Tibubuci. As occurred with Ksar Ghilane, it was later modified by local Berber tribes and is now in ruins. It stands on a rise overlooking the broad bed of the Oued Ethaabine, which stretches away towards the Jebel Dahar range, silhouetted to the east. There's a well on the bank of the *oued*, as well as some cisterns.

Access is from the road to Beni Kheddache, which is signposted to the east off the pipeline road 500m south of the Café Bir Soltane. Keep going along here for 8km until you reach a small settlement with a well and a few struggling saplings. The turn-off to Ksar Tarcine is signposted to the south just beyond the settlement.

GRAND SUD لجنوب الكبيرا

The desert south and west of Ksar Ghilane is remote Saharan country which brings many rewards for those who venture deep into this largely uninhabited area. Tunisia's southernmost settlement is **Borj el-Khadra**, 292km south of Kamour. The pipeline road to reach it curves around the edge of the Grand Erg Oriental, across barren steppe country dotted with great outcrops of weathered rock and crisscrossed by the boulder-strewn beds of *oueds* that might flow only once in a hundred years. There's very little along the way save the odd military post. Borj el-Khadra itself comprises no more than a small military garrison and airfield. Sadly, it's impossible to continue to the legendary Libyan oasis of Ghadames, just across the border.

Dunes – seriously large ones – are the main reason tourists come to this part of world. Some of the best examples are found between **Bir Aouine** and **El-Borma**, and this trek is popular with the tour operators in Douz.

This is border country and much of the area lies within a military zone so you need a permit to continue beyond **Kamour**, on the pipeline road 110km south of the Douz–Matmata road, and **Kambout**, about 10km

east of Remada. Unless you're travelling as part of a group, you will need to apply in person to the governorate in Tataouine; ask about the current situation at the **syndicat d'initiative** (☎ 75-850 850) in Tataouine. The permit takes two days to process.

If you're heading for the Grand Sud, the best access is from Remada, 70km south of Tataouine.

TOZEUR & THE JERID

Tozeur is one of the undoubted highlights of Tunisia with its distinctive brick old town and the second largest *palmeraie* in the country. It makes a pleasant base for exploring the stunning towns (such as Nefta, Tamerza, Chebika and Midès) close to the Algerian border.

The Jerid, which these towns occupy, is the narrow strip of land between the region's two major salt lakes, the Chott el-Jerid and the Chott el-Gharsa. It has long been one of the most important agricultural districts in Tunisia and the oases around here are famous for their high-quality dates. The harvest is in October which is a good time to visit the area; the weather is cooling down and there's lots of activity.

TOZEUR توزر

☎ 76 / pop 33,500

Tozeur is one place where southern Tunisia comes alive and it's an excellent base for excursions into the fascinating surrounding country. Not surprisingly, it's one of the most popular travel destinations in Tunisia with its expansive palm groves, the labyrinthine Ouled el-Hadef with its distinctive traditional brickwork and the excellent Dar Charait Museum. Even getting here is a unique experience – the road from Kebili crosses the desolate *chott* (salt pans) by causeway.

History

The oasis at Tozeur has been inhabited since Capsian (see p22) times (from 8000 BC). It developed into the small Roman town of Thuzuros which lay within the *palmeraie*, around the area now occupied by the district of Bled el-Hader. Tozeur's prosperity peaked during the age of the great trans-Saharan camel caravans, between the 14th and 19th centuries.

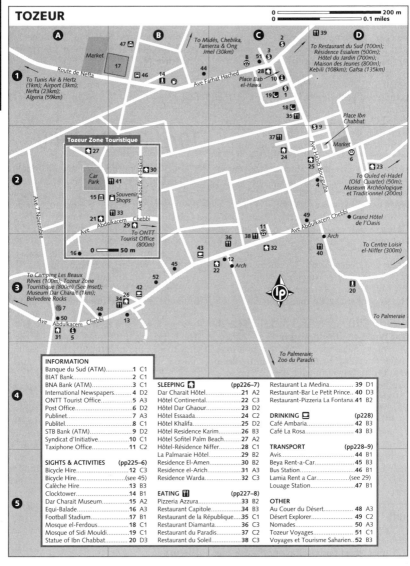

TOZEUR

0 ——————— 200 m
0 ——————— 0.1 miles

INFORMATION
Banque du Sud (ATM)................**1** C1	
BIAT Bank............................**2** C1	
BNA Bank (ATM)....................**3** C1	
International Newspapers..........**4** D2	
ONTT Tourist Office...............**5** A3	
Post Office.........................**6** D2	
Publinet............................**7** A3	
Publitel.............................**8** C1	
STB Bank (ATM)....................**9** D2	
Syndicat d'Initiative..............**10** C1	
Taxiphone Office..................**11** C2	

SIGHTS & ACTIVITIES (pp225–6)
Bicycle Hire.........................**12** C3	
Bicycle Hire.....................(see **45**)	
Calèche Hire........................**13** B3	
Clocktower.........................**14** B1	
Dar Charait Museum................**15** A2	
Equi-Balade.........................**16** A3	
Football Stadium...................**17** B1	
Mosque el-Ferdous.................**18** A3	
Mosque of Sidi Mouldi.............**19** C1	
Statue of Ibn Chabbat............**20** D3	

SLEEPING (pp226–7)
Dar Charait Hôtel...................**21** A2	
Hôtel Continental...................**22** C3	
Hôtel Dar Ghaour..................**23** D2	
Hôtel Essaada.......................**24** C2	
Hôtel Khalifa.........................**25** D2	
Hôtel Residence Karim.............**26** A3	
Hôtel Sofitel Palm Beach...........**27** A2	
Hôtel-Résidence Niffer.............**28** C1	
La Palmaraie Hôtel..................**29** B2	
Residence El-Amen.................**30** B2	
Residence el-Arich..................**31** A3	
Residence Warda...................**32** C3	

EATING (pp227–8)
Pizzeria Azzura.....................**33** B2	
Restaurant Capitole................**34** B3	
Restaurant de la République.......**35** C1	
Restaurant Diamanta...............**36** C3	
Restaurant du Paradis..............**37** C2	
Restaurant du Soleil................**38** C3	

Restaurant La Medina..............**39** D1	
Restaurant-Bar Le Petit Prince..**40** D3	
Restaurant-Pizzeria La Fontana.**41** B2	

DRINKING (p228)
Café Ambaria.......................**42** B3	
Café La Rosa........................**43** B3	

TRANSPORT (pp228–9)
Avis....................................**44** B1	
Beya Rent-a-Car...................**45** B3	
Bus Station..........................**46** B1	
Lamia Rent a Car................(see **29**)	
Louage Station......................**47** B1	

OTHER
Au Couer du Désert................**48** A3	
Désert Explorer.....................**49** C2	
Nomades............................**50** A3	
Tozeur Voyages.....................**51** C1	
Voyages et Tourisme Saharien...**52** B3	

Orientation

It's easy to find your way around Tozeur because there are only three main streets: Ave Abdulkacem Chebbi, which runs along the edge of the *palmeraie* on the southern side of town; ave Farhat Hached, which skirts the northern edge of town; and ave Habib Bourguiba, which links the two.

Information

INTERNET ACCESS

Publinet (11 ave de 7 Novembre; 24 hr; TD2 per hr) Connections can be patchy.

MEDIA

A kiosk on ave Habib Bourguiba has English-language and other international newspapers.

CHOTT EL-JERID

The Chott el-Jerid is an immense salt lake covering an area of almost 5000 sq km, the bulk of it stretching away to the horizon south of the Kebili–Tozeur road and part of a system of salt lakes that stretches deep into Algeria from the Gulf of Gabès. The Chott el-Jerid is a scene of desolation – dry for the greater part of the year, when the flat, flat surface stretching to the horizon becomes blistered and shimmers in the heat. It was here that Luke Skywalker contemplated the two moons in the first *Star Wars* movie. The Kebili–Tozeur road crosses the northern reaches of the *chott* on a 2m-high causeway – it's a trip not to be missed. At times, the wind-driven salt piles up into great drifts by the roadside – creating the impression that you're driving through a snowfield. Just one litre of water can yield as much as 1kg of salt. Mirages are common, and if you've picked a sunny day to cross you may see some deceptive optical effects.

MONEY

You'll find branches of all the major Tunisian banks around the town centre. Those with ATMs include STB, Banque de Tunisie, Banque du Sud and BNA. Amen Bank has an exchange counter inside the entrance to the Dar Charait Museum.

POST & TELEPHONE

There are telephone offices all over town, including an (allegedly) 24-hour Publitel office on ave Farhat Hached opposite place Bab el-Hawa.

Post office (off place Ibn Chabbat) By the market.

TOURIST INFORMATION

ONTT office (☎ 454 088; ave Abdulkacem Chebbi; ⏲ 7.30am-1.30pm & 5-8pm Jul-Aug, 8.30am-1pm & 3.30-6pm Sun-Thu & 8.30am-1.30pm Fri-Sat Sep-Jun) Between the town centre and the zone touristique.

Syndicat d'initiative (☎ 462 034; place Bab el-Hawa)

Sights & Activities

DAR CHARAIT MUSEUM

The **museum** (ave Abdulkacem Chebbi; admission TD3.4, plus camera TD1.7; ⏲ 8am-midnight) is part of the impressive Dar Charait complex. The building in which the museum is housed is an extravagant reproduction of an old palace and contains collections of pottery, jewellery, costumes and other antiques, as well as an art gallery. Throughout the rooms off the splendid main courtyard is a series of replicas of scenes from Tunisian life, past and present. They include the bedroom of the last bey (provincial governor in the Ottoman Empire), a palace scene, a typical kitchen, a *hammam*, wedding scenes and a Bedouin tent. The museum attendants, dressed as servants of the bey, set the tone for the museum.

The complex also includes attractions aimed at children. 'Dar Zaman – 3000 years of Tunisian History' features scenes from the nation's long history using some good models. 'La Medina – 1001 Nights' is a theme park full of cartoon characters. Both are open the same hours as the museum and each charges TD5 admission.

The whole complex is tastefully lit at night which is a good time to visit.

PALMERAIE

Tozeur's *palmeraie* is the second largest in the country with at least 200,000 palm trees (locals claim twice that number) spread over an area of more than 10 sq km. It's a classic example of tiered oasis agriculture. The system is watered by more than 200 springs that produce almost 60 million litres of water a day, distributed around the various holdings under a complex system devised by the mathematician Ibn Chabbat in the 13th century AD.

The best way to explore the *palmeraie* is on foot. Take the road that runs south off ave Abdulkacem Chebbi next to the Hôtel Continental and follow the signs to the Zoo du Paradis. After about 500m the road passes the old quarter of **Bled el-Hader**, thought to be the site of ancient Thuzuros. The mosque in the main square dates from the 11th century, while the minaret (mosque tower) stands on the square base of an old Roman tower.

Further on is the village of **Abbes**, where the tomb of marabout (holy man) Sidi Bou Lifa stands in the shade of an enormous jubube (Chinese date) tree. There are lots of paths leading off into the *palmeraie* along the irrigation canals. It's delightfully cool among all the vegetation.

If you want to see more of the oasis, you can hire bicycles from a number of places around town (see p228). Thus equipped, you can complete a loop through the *palmeraie* that emerges further west on ave Abdulkacem Chebbi near the Grand Hôtel de l'Oasis.

OULED EL-HADEF
The town's delightful old quarter was built in the 14th century AD to house the El-Hadef clan, which had grown rich on the proceeds of the caravan trade. The area is a maze of narrow, covered alleys and small squares. It's famous for its amazing traditional brickwork, which uses protruding bricks to create intricate geometric patterns in relief. The style is found only here and in nearby Nefta.

The easiest entrance to the Ouled el-Hadef is from ave de Kairouan. Follow the signs pointing to the small **Museum Archéologique et Traditionnel** (admission TD1.1; ☼ 8am-noon & 3-6.30pm Tue-Sun), which occupies the old Kobba of Sidi Bou Aissa. It houses a small collection of local finds, costumes and displays on local culture.

Like the medinas further north in Tunisia, wandering through the Ouled el-Hadef is a journey of discovery best made by getting lost. The most well-preserved sections are east of the museum, including the house of the former governor (Dar Bey).

Although outside the boundaries of the old town, the brick minarets of the **Mosque of Sidi Mouldi** and **Mosque el Ferdous** on ave Habib Bourguiba are very attractive.

BELVEDERE ROCKS
A sandy track running south off the Route Touristique near the Dar Charait Museum leads to the Belvedere Rocks. Steps have been cut into the highest rock, giving access to a spectacular sunset view over the oasis and the *chott*. It's a pleasant 20-minute walk. The recent landscaping has taken away somewhat from the beauty of the natural setting, but not entirely; look for the likeness of Abdulkacem Chebbi.

ZOOS
The owners of the **Zoo du Paradis** (admission TD1), which is on the southern side of the *palmeraie*, must have a strange vision of paradise if the depressingly small cages are

anything to go by. The star turn is a Coca-Cola–drinking camel.

HORSE-RIDING
Equi-Balade (☎ 452 613; fax 462 857; off ave Abdulkacem Chebbi), based on the road leading out to the Belvedere Rocks, charges TD15/25 for one/two hour excursions on horseback, or TD45 for a half-day trip.

Tours
There are dozens of travel agencies around town. Some of the better ones include:
Au Coeur du Désert (☎ 453 660; aucoeur.dudesert@gnet.tn; ave Abdulkacem Chebbi)
Desert Explorer (☎ 460 950; fax 460 900; ave Abdulkacem Chebbi)
Nomades (☎ 453 423; 196 ave Abdulkacem Chebbi)
Tozeur Voyages (☎ 452 203; fax 452 038; 58 ave Farhat Hached)
Voyages et Tourisme Saharien (VTS; ☎ 460 300; fax 463 300; 128 ave Abdulkacem Chebbi 128)

For details of available excursions and prices on offer by these agencies, see p229.

Sleeping
BUDGET
Camping Les Beaux Réves (☎ 453 331; campingbeaureves@voila.fr; ave Abdulkacem Chebbi; per person in tent/bungalow TD5/7, showers TD1.5) This is a good, shady site 250m west of the tourist office and backing onto the *palmeraie*. Staff are friendly and helpful.

Maison des Jeunes (☎ 452 335; route de Gafsa; dm TD4) Tozeur's youth hostel is opposite the police station about 800m northeast of the town centre, and is only for the dedicated. The dorms here are basic and sometimes clean.

Hôtel Essaada (☎ 460 097; off ave Habib Bourguiba; per person TD5, cold shower TD0.5) Central and basic, this one's only for those for whom price is everything. Some rooms have balconies, although the sheets could be cleaner.

Hôtel Khalifa (☎ 454 858; ave Habib Bourguiba; per person TD7.5) The Khalifa isn't a whole lot better and the only rooms with windows overlook busy ave Habib Bourguiba. Things not to expect here: service with a smile, clean sheets and comfortable beds.

Residence Essalem (☎ 462 881; ave de l'Environnement; s/d with shower TD6.5/7, with shower & toilet TD7/14) Far and away the best budget choice in Tozeur, the rooms here are simple but clean and the owners are friendly. It's 150m past the roundabout at the western end of ave Farhat Hached.

MID-RANGE

All prices in this category include breakfast.

Hôtel Residence Karim (☎ /fax 454 574; fax 463 499; 150 ave Abdulkacem Chebbi; s TD13-20, d TD22-29; ✵) This deservedly popular hotel is well accustomed to the needs of travellers and the architecture is very attractive with shady courtyards. The tiled rooms are a little small but others are spacious so ask to see a few.

Residence Warda (☎ 452 597; fax 452 744; 29 ave Abdulkacem Chebbi; s/d TD13/20, with private bathroom TD15/25) The Warda is another travellers' favourite although their attention to detail sometimes wavers. It's still a good choice with tidy, decent-sized rooms.

Residence el-Arich (☎ 462 644; elarichtozeur@ yahoo.fr; 93 ave Abdulkacem Chebbi; s TD18-21, d TD30-33; ✵) Also very well run and gets great reports from travellers. Rooms are pleasant, spacious and airy and staff very welcoming. An excellent choice.

Residence el-Amen (☎ 463 522; amentozeur@ yahoo.fr; 10 ave Taoufik el-Hakim; s TD15-19, d TD25-29; 4-bed apartment TD45, 6-bed studio TD70; ✵) This excellent new family-run venture is out in the zone touristique. The owners are friendly, the rooms tidy and spacious and it's quiet. Highly recommended.

Hôtel-Résidence Niffer (☎ 460 610; fax 461 900; Pl Bab el-Hawa; s/d TD13/20) Simple, spacious rooms are the order of the day here and it's convenient for the old town.

Hôtel Dar Ghaouar (☎ /fax 452 666; ave de Kairouan; s/d TD15/30) The closest hotel to the old town is also not a bad choice although the swimming pool was empty when we visited.

Hôtel du Jardin (☎ 454 196; medmoncef@voila.fr; ave de l'Environnement; s/d TD25/40) Quiet, about 1km east of town on the road to Kebili, and set among gardens with pleasant rooms and a good restaurant.

TOP END

Tozeur has dozens of upmarket hotels, most of which are out in the zone touristique. By European standards, they're reasonable value. All prices include breakfast.

Hôtel Continental (☎ 461 411; fax 452 109; 79 ave Abdulkacem Chebbi; s/d TD43/70; ✵ ✵) The cheapest top end place is an older establishment and some of the rooms (and bathrooms)

have been better maintained than others. However, it isn't bad value and is set in shady gardens.

La Palmaraie Hotel (☎ 454 599; fax 454 839; ave Abdulkacem Chebbi; s/d TD110/150; ✵ ✵) A four-star venue with nicely appointed rooms, a gym, tennis court and children's playroom.

Dar Charait Hotel (☎ 454 888; melia.dar.cherait@ solmelia.com; s/d TD145/220; ✵ ✵) Five-star and adjoining the museum, the Dar Charait has loads of character, with much of the interior decoration faithful to an old-style opulence.

Hôtel Sofitel Palm Beach (☎ 453 111; palmbeach .tozeur@gnet.tn; s/d TD180/240; ✵ ✵) Also five-star, the Palm Beach has all of the accompanying class and elegance that you'd expect for this price.

Eating

Tozeur is better served by cheap restaurants than most places. All are open for lunch and dinner.

Restaurant du Paradis (off ave Habib Bourguiba) A couple of doors along from the Hôtel Essaada, this is a quaint, tiny eatery run by two very polite older guys. The prices are old-fashioned, too, with *chorba* (800 mills) and couscous with sauce (TD2).

Restaurant du Soleil (☎ 454 220; 58 ave Abdulkacem Chebbi; starters from TD1.5, mains from TD4) An extensive menu with a couple of vegetarian dishes. The service is attentive and it's a good place to try camel steak (TD6) because you generally don't have to pre-order it as in other restaurants. They also do pizzas (TD5 to TD7) and sandwiches (TD1.5 to TD2).

Restaurant de la République (☎ 452 354; 108 ave Habib Bourguiba; starters from TD2, mains from TD4) Tucked away in an arcade next to the Mosque el-Ferdous, this is another good place with a pleasant eating area and decent food.

Other good venues include: **Restaurant Capitole** (☎ 463 477; 152 ave Abdulkacem Chebbi; starters from TD1.5, mains from TD3) which is great value, popular with local families and a good place to try *metabgha* (Berber pizza; TD3, pre-order only); **Restaurant Diamanta** (ave Abdulkacem Chebbi; starters TD1.5, mains from TD3.5) which is often packed out with local workers at lunch time; and the quiet **Restaurant La Medina** (☎ 454 426; ave Farhat Hached; starters TD1.5, mains from TD3.5), 100m northeast of place Bab el-Hawa.

There are a couple of pizzerias opposite the entrance to the Dar Charait Museum.

Pizzeria Azzura (pizzas from TD4) gets great reports from travellers.

Restaurant Pizzeria La Fontana (☎ 462 776; pizzas TD2.5-8, pasta from TD3), a few doors north, is also pleasant.

Restaurant Les Andalous (Hôtel du Jardin) is a classy choice and is rated as the one of the best restaurants in the south with a small but carefully selected menu. Allow TD15 per person plus wine; it's worth it.

Restaurant-Bar Le Petit Prince (☎ 452 518; off ave Abdulkacem Chebbi; mains TD6-14) is also more upmarket and very pleasant. The menu here has both European and Tunisian specialties and the dining area under the palm trees is lovely in the evening. What drink to choose from the extensive list is the hardest thing about eating here.

Handy for a snack and very much a part of the Tozeur experience are the dates available in the market. The best dates are harvested in October, but you'll usually find something on offer throughout summer. For reasonable quality, expect to pay TD3 per kg, although the best method is to taste before you buy.

Drinking

There are plenty of outdoor *sheesha* (water pipe) and coffeehouses around the town centre.

Café La Rosa (ave Abdulkacem Chebbi) This busy café spills over onto the street and can get rowdy in the evenings but it's pleasant enough if you don't mind the choir of all-male voices.

Café Ambaria (ave Abdulkacem Chebbi) A cut above the rest in terms of décor and service, although again it's mostly all men. It's less busy during the day. *Sheesha* cost TD1.2 and they have a real live coffee machine if you're craving an espresso or cappuccino (each 270 mills).

Centre Loisir el-Niffer (☉ 9.30am-1am) Set deep in the *palmeraie*, this is a great place for a *sheesha* (TD1 to TD2) under the palm trees, or a coffee or cool drink. There's a swimming pool (TD3) and a few courting couples and families sitting at the tables spread throughout the garden. To get here, take the road past the Restaurant-Bar Le Petit Prince and follow the signs (about 700m).

Getting There & Away

AIR

Tuninter runs five flights a week to Tunis (TD56/107 one way/return). The airport handles a growing number of international flights, mainly charters from Europe. The **Tunis Air** (☎ 452 127) office is out towards the airport along the Nefta road.

BUS

There are five air-con SNTRI buses a day to Tunis (TD18.9, seven hours), travelling via Gafsa (TD4.5, 1½ hours) and Kairouan (TD12.4, 4½ hours). SNTRI also has a service to Sousse (TD14.7, 5¾ hours) in the morning.

Regional services include six buses a day to Gafsa (TD4), five to Nefta (TD1.1) and two to Tamerza (TD3). There are also daily buses to Douz (TD4.8, three hours) and Gabès (TD8, 4½ hours).

CAR

There are half a dozen car-rental outlets in town. You'll find better deals at local agencies like **Lamia Rent a Car** (☎ 462 433), opposite La Palmeraie Hotel in the zone touristique, and **Beya Rent a Car** (☎ 462 211; 146 ave Abdulkacem Chebbi).

International agencies include **Avis** (☎ 453 547; 96 ave Farhat Hached) and **Hertz** (☎ 450 214; route de Nefta), out towards the airport.

LOUAGE

The louage station has regular departures to Nefta (TD1.2), Gafsa (TD4.3) and Kebili (TD4.5). There are also occasional louages to Tamerza (TD3.3) and Gabès (TD9.5).

Getting Around

TO/FROM THE AIRPORT

Tozeur's taxis don't have meters – the fare depends on your bargaining skills and how wealthy you look. Most charge around TD5 for the 4km trip, although some ask as much as TD10 late at night.

BICYCLE

Bicycles can be rented from numerous places, including a couple along ave Abdulkacem Chebbi and from the Taxiphone office opposite the Dar Charait complex at the zone touristique. Rates range from TD2 to TD3.5 per hour. Motor-scooters cost around TD10 per hour.

CALÈCHE
Calèches can be hired from opposite the Hôtel Karim for TD10 per hour.

AROUND TOZEUR
There are plenty of worthwhile excursions which can be made from Tozeur; see the table below. Almost all the hotels in Tozeur, as well as the tour agencies (see p226) can organise such trips.

Destination	Duration	Cost (per person)
Tamerza, Chebika & Midès	4 hrs	TD30
Nefta & Ong Jemal	3-4 hrs	TD30
Kebili, Douz & La Porte du Désert	½ day	TD60
Lezard Rouge (see p235)	½ day	TD35
Ksar Ghilane, Douz & Matmata	2 days	TD120
Ksar Ghilane, Douz, Tataouine & Matmata	3 days	TD150

The half-day excursions are best done in the afternoon, as in the morning most 4WD vehicles are booked out by the tour buses which roll into town. Also, if you're on your own, you may need to wait a day or two for enough other travellers to arrive so as to make the trip viable for the operators. And one final thing: no matter when you go, each site will be inundated with convoys of 4WD vehicles. It just comes with the territory in this part of the world.

Mountain Oases
☎ 76

The beautiful, ancient Berber villages of Tamerza, Midès and Chebika are near the Algerian border in the rugged Jebel en-Negeb ranges, 60km north of Tozeur. They were part of the Limes Tripolitanus defensive line developed by the Romans to keep out marauding Saharan tribes.

The villages were abandoned after the region was hit by 22 days of torrential rain in 1969. The freak rains turned the earthen houses into mud, and villagers moved to new settlements that were hastily built nearby.

CHEBIKA شبيكة
This village, 59km north of Tozeur, is on the southern edge of the mountain range and overlooks the Chott el-Gharsa. The *palmeraie* is visible for miles – a great slash of green set against the barren mountains. Old Chebika is up the hill behind the *palmeraie*, next to a small spring-fed stream. The best way to explore is to climb up through the deserted village to the narrow cleft in the rock from where there are great views over the oasis. On the other side of the rock, steps lead down into a pretty little canyon fed by a spring and with a tiny waterfall. The path follows the gorge back up to the town.

Drinks and a few snacks are available at the foot of old Chebika.

TAMERZA تمغزة
Nestled in a small valley in the heart of the mountains 75km north of Tozeur, Tamerza is the largest of the villages. The shell of the **old walled town** is about 1km east of new Tamerza (a characterless modern sprawl). Strung out along a ridge on the southern bank of the Oued Horchane, this is one of the most photogenic old villages in Tunisia set against the backdrop of the rugged mountain range and with the *palmeraie* to the west. Sadly, the excursions from Tamerza usually only stop briefly for photos from across the valley.

Tamerza's water comes from a spring that rises in the hills south of old Tamerza. The spring supplies water to the old town and then to an extensive *palmeraie*, which locals claim produces the finest dates in Tunisia.

If you're on a half day trip, most of your time will be spent at one of the town's small waterfalls (bring your swimmers) and there's considerable novelty value to be swimming in such a barren landscape.

Tamerza has two hotels, as well as a bank and a few small shops. The **Hôtel Les Cascades** (☎ 485 322; s/d TD20/25) has a great setting, at the edge of the *palmeraie*, next to a small waterfall but the rooms are uninviting and cost too much.

Hôtel Tamerza Palace (☎ 453 722; fax 453 845; route de Midès; s/d TD90/130; ✶ ☒) overlooks the old town and is a splendid choice with great views from some rooms and from the swimming pool terrace.

Tamerza has several restaurants, most of which cater to tour groups. The tiny **Restaurant de Tamerza**, on the right on the road leading down to the Hôtel Les Cascades, turns out a filling bowl of couscous with vegetables for TD2.8. The restaurant at the **Hôtel Tamerza Palace** does a three-course set menu for TD12.

Tamerza is the only one of the three oasis villages with public transport. There are two SNTRI buses a day from Tunis (TD22, seven hours), three buses a day from Gafsa (TD4, 2½ hours) and two from Tozeur (TD3, 1½ hours).

MIDÈS ميداس

Midès, 6km north of Tamerza and only 1km from the Algerian border, boasts a stunning setting; it's perched high above a dramatic gorge that was previously employed as the town's southern fortification. The gorge has been used a setting for many movies, including *The English Patient*. You can walk down into the canyon if you have time.

There are two places at Midès calling themselves camping grounds. Neither has any set fees or facilities – just a patch of ground on which to pitch a tent. You need to take your own food, or you can buy meals from local families. Drinks are available at the souvenir stalls at the top of the canyon.

Ong Jemal عنق الجمال

Ong Jemal (Neck of the Camel) is a popular spot for watching the sunset out over the sand dunes. The name derives from an unusual rock formation, shaped, not surprisingly, like the neck and head of a camel, overlooking the barren plains. Not far away, is a line of sand dunes where *The English Patient* crew indulged in lots of billowing sand-blown romantic stuff. Drivers of 4WDs love this spot for exhilarating descents of the dunes and it's a stunning place to watch the sunset.

Just over a hill to the west is **Mos Espa**, a very well preserved *Star Wars* set. This was Darth Maul's lookout in *The Phantom Menace*, and the location for his and Qui-Gon's tussle, as well as lots of pod-race scenes. It's remarkably intact and one of the best *Star Wars* sites in the country. Film crews spent four and a half months here (including building the now-decaying road) for 12 minutes of footage.

Visiting this remote spot, around 30km north of Nefta, is only possible as part of an organised tour from Tozeur.

NEFTA نفطة

☎ 76 / pop 22,000

The oasis of Nefta, 23km west of Tozeur, is a smaller version of Tozeur, although its sunken *palmeraie* is unlike any other. Like in Tozeur, there are some very good examples of distinctive ornamental brickwork in the old town.

Nefta is also the home of Sufism in Tunisia, and there are a couple of important religious sites here (see the boxed text, p232).

Orientation & Information

Nefta's main street, ave Habib Bourguiba, is also the main Tozeur–Algeria road. The route de la Corbeille does a loop around the *corbeille* off ave Habib Bourguiba.

The small **syndicat d'initiative** (☎ 430 236) is on the right as you come into town from Tozeur, just before the ring-road junction. The guys who staff the office are there primarily to promote their services as guides (TD15 for a two-hour tour of Nefta, full day TD40 plus vehicle, four-hour camel rides TD24).

There's also a post office and a branch of the UIB bank.

Sights & Activities

LA CORBEILLE

La Corbeille (literally 'basket'), the deep palm-filled gully that takes up much of the northern part of town and cuts the town in two, is the highlight of Nefta. It measures almost 1km across at its widest point and is about 40m deep. The best views are from the northwestern side. Here you can take in the setting over a coffee at the Café de la Corbeille or Café Maure el-Khazen, which both have terraces overlooking the *corbeille*.

Below the cafés is a large spring-fed concrete pool, a popular swimming spot with local kids. The *corbeille* contracts to a narrow gorge which leads to the main *palmeraie* on the southern side of town.

EL-BAYADHA

The cafés at the northwestern edge of the *corbeille* are a good starting point for a walk through the old El-Bayadha neighbourhood, which lies to the southwest. Many of the houses here were badly damaged by heavy rain in 1990, which also caused several landslides around the edge of the *corbeille*. Just about every other building

NEFTA

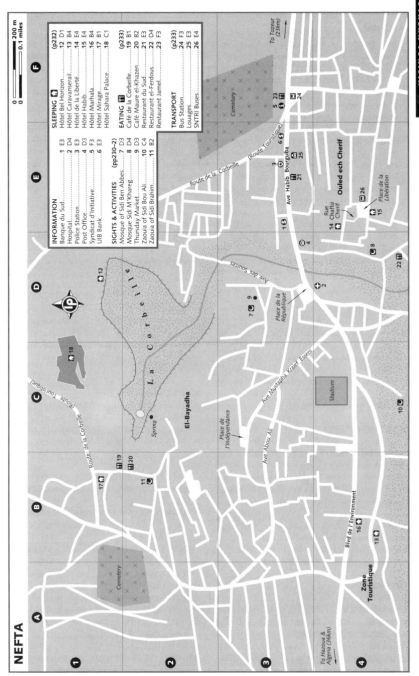

0   200 m
0   0.1 miles

INFORMATION
Banque du Sud	1	E3
Hospital	2	D4
Police Station	3	E3
Post Office	4	D3
Syndicat d'Initiative	5	F3
UIB Bank	6	E3

SIGHTS & ACTIVITIES (pp230–2)
Mosque of Sidi Ben Abbes	7	D3
Mosque Sidi M'Khareg	8	D4
Thursday Market	9	D3
Zaouia of Sidi Bou Ali	10	C4
Zaouia of Sidi Brahim	11	B2

SLEEPING (p232)
Hôtel Bel Horizon	12	D1
Hôtel Caravanserail	13	B4
Hôtel de la Liberté	14	E4
Hôtel Habib	15	E4
Hôtel Marhala	16	B4
Hôtel Mirage	17	B1
Hôtel Sahara Palace	18	C1

EATING (p233)
Café de la Corbeille	19	B1
Café Maure el-Khazen	20	B2
Restaurant du Sud	21	E3
Restaurant el-Ferdous	22	D4
Restaurant Jamel	23	F3

TRANSPORT (p233)
Bus Station	24	F3
Louages	25	E3
SNTRI Buses	26	E4

To Tozeur (23km)

Cemetery

Route de la Corbeille (Route Touristique)

Ave Habib Bourguba

Ouled ech Cherif

Rue Chaffai Cherif

Place de la Libération

Ave des Sources

Place de la République

La Corbeille

Spring

El-Bayadha

Place de l'Indépendance

Ave Mustapha Kraief Esseni

Ave Abou Ali

Stadium

Cemetery

Route de la Corbeille (Route Touristique)

Blvd de l'Environment

Zone Touristique

To Hazoua & Algeria (36km)

SUFISM

The Islamic order of Sufism was formed by ascetics who wished to achieve a mystical communion with God through spiritual development rather than through the study of the Quran. The name derives from *suf*, meaning 'wool', referring to the simple cord they wore as a belt.

The orders tend to gather at the mosque or tomb of their holy man (or *wali*, a term loosely translated as 'holy man or saint') and follow a particular *tariq* (path), or way of worshipping. A particular aspect of Berber Sufism in North Africa is maraboutism – the worship of a holy man endowed with magical powers.

For orthodox Muslims, veneration of the saint is tantamount to worship of an idol, although Sufis would not see it that way. The *wali* is a 'friend' (the more literal meaning of the word) of God and so an intermediary. The great *moussems* (pilgrimages) to the tombs of such saints are more a celebration of the triumph of the spirit than an act of worship of a particular saint. Despite the conflict with religious orthodoxy, Sufis are largely tolerated because they were generally prepared to make concessions to local rites and superstitions, as a result of which they were able to attract large numbers of people who had not otherwise embraced Islam.

Sufis, of which there are literally hundreds of different orders, were renowned for their peculiar devotional practices which range from the dances of whirling dervishes to more ecstatic and extreme demonstrations of self-mutilation (pushing skewers into their cheeks, eating glass or walking on coals) to bring them closer to God.

The Sufis held positions of power in Tunisia, particularly in rural areas, following the breakdown of Almohad rule in the 13th century.

---

in El-Bayadha seems to have some level of religious significance. The most important of them is the **Zaouia of Sidi Brahim**, where the Sufi saint and some of his followers are buried. The zaouia is 100m south of the cafés. There's an open space opposite the Mosque of Sidi Ben Abbes, off ave des Sources at the eastern edge of El-Bayadha, where Nefta's Thursday market is staged.

OULED ECH CHERIF

The best preserved of Nefta's old districts is the **Ouled ech Cherif**. To get there, follow the signs to the Hôtel Habib on the main road leading south next to the bus station. The layout is very similar to the Ouled el-Hadef in Tozeur, with winding, vaulted alleyways and some stunning examples of traditional brick designs. Check out the street that runs west off place de la Libération to the *palmeraie*, emerging next to the quarter's principal mosque, the **Mosque of Sidi M'Khareg**.

Sleeping
BUDGET
Hôtel de la Liberté (☎ 430 643; off place de la Libération; per person TD5) Nefta's cheapest hotel is friendly and set among the winding alleys of the Ouled ech Cherif; some locals know it as the Hôtel Mahmoud. It's a basic old hotel built around a vine-filled central courtyard.

Hôtel Habib (☎ 430 497; place de la Libération; per person with breakfast TD7.5) The Habib's owners seem to have spent the decoration budget on signs directing people to the hotel. What awaits are gloomy rooms and friendly staff.

MID-RANGE & TOP END
All prices here include breakfast.

Hôtel Mirage (☎ 430 622; fax 430 644; s/d TD15/25) This shabby one-star hotel on the northwestern side of the *corbeille*, has re-opened after 'renovation' – of which there is no evidence.

There's a small cluster of big hotels in the small zone touristique on the southwestern side of town.

Hôtel Marhala (☎ 430 027; fax 430 511; s/d TD40/56; ✎ ✇) The two-star Marhala is clean, comfortable and simple.

Hôtel Bel Horizon (☎ 430 328; fax 430 500; s/d TD50/64; ✎ ✇) With an extra star and north of the *corbeille*, the Bel Horizon is another good choice in this price range.

Hôtel Caravanserail (☎ 430 355; fax 430 344; s/d TD75/100; ✎ ✇) This is the most luxurious of a cluster of hotels in the area.

Hôtel Sahara Palace (☎ 432 005; www.sangho.com; s/d TD135/200) This five-star place is the best hotel in town. Rooms are luxurious and the views over the *corbeille* are superb.

Eating

The sum total of Nefta's eateries is a few basic restaurants on ave Habib Bourguiba near the bus station and around place de la Libération, plus the hotel restaurants. The best of the cheapies is the **Restaurant Jamel**, next to the tourist office. It does a delicious *chorba* (TD1) and a range of daily specials like spicy beans with chicken (TD2). Next to the louage station, the **Restaurant du Sud** has couscous for TD2.

The **Restaurant el-Ferdous** is a popular bar/restaurant in the *palmeraie*. It's a quiet spot to have lunch, but gets rowdy in the evenings.

Getting There & Away

BUS

SNTRI has two daily buses to Tunis (TD20, seven hours).

Regional services operate from the bus station on the southern side of ave Habib Bourguiba. There are five buses to Tozeur (TD1.1, 30 minutes) and six a day to Gafsa (TD5, three hours).

LOUAGE

Louages leave from outside the restaurants on ave Habib Bourguiba. You won't have to wait long for a ride to Tozeur (TD1.2).

GAFSA　　　　　　قفصة

☎ 76 / pop 82,000

Despite its long history, modern Gafsa is one of the least-inspiring towns in Tunisia. The town is, however, the hub of the region's transport network and historically significant as the site of Capsa (see p22), which was captured and destroyed by the Roman consul Marius in 107 BC as part of the campaign against the Numidian king Jugurtha (see p24). It went on to become an important Roman town.

Information

There's a small **tourist office** (☎ 221 664; ⊗ 8am–1pm & 3-5.45pm Mon-Thu, 8.30am-1.30pm Fri-Sat) in the small square by the Roman Pools.

The **post office** (ave Habib Bourguiba) is 150m north of the kasbah. There are plenty of Taxiphone offices around the town centre.

The most central place for Internet is **L'Univers de l'Internet** (ave Abdulkacem Chebbi; ☎ 8.30am-midnight; TD1.2 per hr).

All the major banks have branches around Jardin du 7 Novembre in the centre of town. Most have ATMs.

Sights

The twin **Roman Pools** (Piscines Romaine) are Gafsa's main attraction and it's a pleasant spot although you've seen all there is to see after a few minutes. Apart from the entertainment provided by local children diving, note the Latin inscriptions just above water level in the eastern pool. The pools are located at the southern end of ave Habib Bourguiba. Sadly, the pleasant café overlooking the site was closed when we visited and is unlikely to reopen.

Beside the entrance to the pools is a small **museum** (admission TD1.1; ⊗ 7.30am-12.30pm & 3-7pm Tue-Sun Apr–mid-Sep, 9am-4.30pm mid-Sep–Mar) which houses, among other things, a couple of large mosaics from ancient Capsa.

Sleeping

BUDGET

There are lots of cheap hotels in the area around the bus station but most of them are best avoided.

Hôtel Tunis (☎ 221 660; ave 2 Mars; s/d TD6/8, showers TD1.5) This is a rare thing in Tunisia – a cheapie that has been renovated in the last five years. Rooms are simple but clean and quite well kept. It's the best choice.

Hôtel de la République (☎ 221 807; rue Ali Belhaouane; s/d TD5.5/7, showers TD1.5) Of the others, this one around the corner from the bus station is the only one worth trying. Rooms are basic but fine for a night; ask for one away from the street if you want to sleep beyond 6am.

MID-RANGE

Prices listed here include breakfast.

Hôtel Maamoun (☎ 226 701; fax 226 440; ave Jamel Abdennaceur; s/d TD55/80; ▨ ▣) Just south of the main market square, this hotel is probably the best, but only if they offer their reduced rates of TD25/40. Rooms are large and comfortable if ageing and the service is good.

Hôtel Gafsa (☎ 224 000; fax 224 747; rue Ahmed Snoussi; s/d TD27.5/40) Nearby, this is also a good if declining establishment where the rooms are a touch smaller than those at the Maamoun.

Hôtel Lune (☎ 220 218; fax 220 980; rue Jamel Abdennaceur; s/d TD20/30) A one-star hotel, about

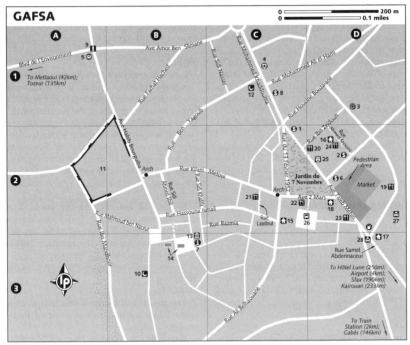

GAFSA

To Metlaoui (42km);
Tozeur (135km)

Jardin du
7 Novembre

Pedestrian
Area

Market

Rue Samel
Abdennaceur

To Hôtel Lune (250m);
Airport (4km);
Sfax (190km);
Kairouan (233km)

To Train
Station (2km);
Gabès (146km)

INFORMATION	
Banque de l'Habitat (ATM)	1 C2
Banque du Sud (ATM)	2 D2
L'Univers de l'Internet	3 D1
Police Station	4 C1
Post Office	5 A1
STB Bank (ATM)	6 D2
Tourist Office	7 B3
UIB Bank	8 C1

SIGHTS & ACTIVITIES	(p233)
Clocktower	9 A1
Grand Mosque	10 B3
Kasbah	11 A2

Mosque of Sidi Bou Yacoub	12 C1
Museum	13 B3
Roman Pools	14 B3

SLEEPING	(pp233–4)
Hôtel de la République	15 C2
Hôtel Gafsa	16 D2
Hôtel Maamoun	17 D2
Hôtel Tunis	18 D2

EATING	(p234)
Cheap Restaurants	(see 21)
Magasin General	19 D2
Patisserie	20 D2

Patisserie	(see 22)
Restaurant Abid	21 C2
Restaurant Erriadh	22 C2
Restaurant Le Paradis	23 D2
Restaurant Semiramis	24 D2

ENTERTAINMENT	
Cinema	25 D2

TRANSPORT	(pp234–5)
Bus Station	26 C2
Louage Station	27 D2
Taxi Rank	28 D3

300m south of the Maamoun. Has spacious rooms, though it's a bit removed from the town centre.

Eating

There are lots of small restaurants around the bus station, especially clustered on Rue Laadoul. The pick of them is the fast and friendly **Restaurant Abid** (⏰ lunch & dinner) which has an extensive menu of local dishes, including *kammounia* (meat stew with lots of cumin) (TD2.500). It's often packed out at lunchtime with locals – always a good sign.

Of the other cheapies, **Restaurant Erriadh** (ave 2 Mars) next to the bus station is good,

while chicken is the (only) order of the day at **Restaurant Le Paradis** (ave Taieb Mehri). A couple of **patisseries** are dotted around the centre.

If you want to drink wine with your meal, try the **Restaurant Semiramis** (rue Ahmed Snoussi, mains from TD4), below the Hôtel Gafsa, or the restaurant at the **Hôtel Maamoun** (mains from TD10); the latter gets overrun with large bus groups at lunchtime.

Getting There & Away
AIR

Tuninter flies to Tunis twice a week (TD50/100 one way/return). The airport is 4km northeast of town; taxis cost TD2.5.

BUS

The bus station in the centre of town has ticket windows for booking.

SNTRI runs at least five buses a day to Tunis (TD16, 5½ hours), most of which go via Kairouan (TD9.3, three hours).

The local company, Sotregafsa, drives an amazing collection of wrecks eight times a day to Tozeur (TD4.3, two hours) and Nefta (TD4.9, 2½ hours), as well as services to Gabès (TD6, 2½ hours, three daily), Kasserine (TD4.6, 1¾ hours, two daily), and Sfax (TD7.7, 3½ hours, three daily). There are also nine buses to Metlaoui (TD2, 45 minutes); three of these continue via Redeyef to Tamerza (TD4.1, 2½ hours).

LOUAGE

There are regular louage departures from Gafsa for Metlaoui (TD2) and Tozeur (TD4.4). Other possibilities include Tunis (TD15.4), Sfax (TD8.7), Sousse (TD12.4) and Gabès (TD6.6). There are occasional direct services to Kasserine (TD5), otherwise change at Feriana.

TRAIN

The station is 3km south of town and about TD1.5 by taxi. The only departures are a night train to Tunis, and a morning service to Metlaoui – at 5am.

AROUND GAFSA
Metlaoui & the Seldja Gorge   متلوي و شالجة

☎ 76

Metlaoui is a drab, dusty town 42km southwest of Gafsa that exists almost entirely because of phosphate mining. The only reason to come here is because it's the starting point for rides through the Seldja Gorge on the Lezard Rouge (Red Lizard) train.

LEZARD ROUGE

Built in 1910, the Lezard Rouge was once used by the bey of Tunis for journeys between Tunis and his summer palace at Hammam Lif. It was given a complete refit by the national railway company SNCFT in 1995, and put back to work transporting tourists in style. The gorge features some weird and wonderful rock formations as it follows the path carved out by the Oued Seldja.

The 1½-hour return journey leaves Metlaoui at 10.30am on Monday, Friday and Sunday and at 10am on Tuesday and Thursday. It's a good idea to contact the **Bureau de Lezard Rouge** in Metlaoui (☎ 241 469, fax 241 604) or the tourist office in Tozeur to check that the train is running; reservations are highly recommended. The return fare is TD20.

TOURS

Tour companies in Tozeur (p226) offer the trip on the Lezard Rouge as a half-day tour for TD35, which is good value and probably the best option.

SLEEPING & EATING

Hôtel Ennacim (☎ 241 920; route de Tozeur; s/d TD9/13), 1km or so from the centre of town on the road to Tozeur, is very shabby. The place survives because it has the only bar in town (also somewhere to steer clear of).

Hôtel Seldja (☎ 241 570; fax 241 486; s/d TD30/40), in the centre of town, is much more comfortable and has a good restaurant popular with tour buses at lunchtime.

GETTING THERE & AWAY

All transport between Gafsa and Tozeur pass through Metlaoui and there are regular louages to Gafsa and Tozeur.

COMPENSATION DAMS

For centuries, the inhabitants of the villages around Gafsa have scraped together a living from the arid landscape through a traditional dry-land farming technique known as compensation dams (*jesseur* in Arabic). The dams are rough stone walls built across watercourses and backfilled with soil, producing a pocket of land that gets the maximum benefit from any flow of water from seasonal rains. The water, held up by the wall of the dam, soaks down through the soil before flowing to the next dam further downstream.

The dams vary in size from tiny pockets of soil growing a patch of wheat to half-hectare plots with fruit trees and vegetable gardens. These dams are also a feature of the landscape in the hills around Matmata.

East of Gafsa

There are half a dozen traditional Berber villages east of Gafsa and spread along the mountain range that runs south of the Gafsa–Sfax road. Most of them are very difficult to get to unless you have a 4WD. The most accessible is **Sened**, 10km south of modern Sened Gare and spread along the banks of a river in the hills below Jebel Biada (1163m). The houses are built of stone and are still in reasonable condition. People have lived around here for thousands of years – the escarpment behind the village is dotted with caves.

Jerba

JERBA

Jerba is a special place, an enchanting combination of superb beaches, a religious and ethnic mix unlike anywhere else in Tunisia, and traditional whitewashed architecture that echoes with the cries of a North African bazaar.

You could easily spend a week here. In summer you can enjoy kicking back and relaxing in the sun on Sidi Mahres beach, while in winter there are flocks of pink flamingos just north of the beach at Flamingo Point. Whatever time of year you're here, allow ample time for exploring the island's interior where Jerba's unique fortresslike architecture – distinctive above- and below-ground mosques found nowhere else, crumbling fortified homesteads and small weaver's workshops – is found in small villages under the palm trees. Jerba is home to one of the last remaining Jewish communities in North Africa, with their synagogue at Erriadh, as well as an equally unusual population of Ibadis.

North of Houmt Souq, the old Jerba meets the new where the luxury marina complex (under construction) overlooks the ancient and down-at-heel fishing port, where traditional techniques haven't changed since the days of the Phoenicians. Not far away, the Borj Ghazi Mustapha overlooks the ocean with little evidence to suggest its grisly past.

But it's in Houmt Souq, the island's largest town, that you'll want to spend as much time as you can. It's full of beguiling covered souqs, ancient *funduqs* (caravanserais) set around a central courtyard and now converted into hotels, and an outdoor café and restaurant culture that is the perfect place to soak up the slow pace of life on this idyllic island.

HIGHLIGHTS

- Staying at one of the enchanting old **funduqs** (p243) in Houmt Souq
- Lazing on the sands of **Sidi Mahres beach** (p248)
- Visiting the ancient Jewish community at the **El-Ghriba synagogue** (p246) in Erriadh

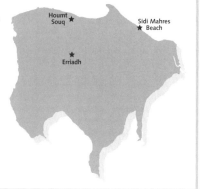

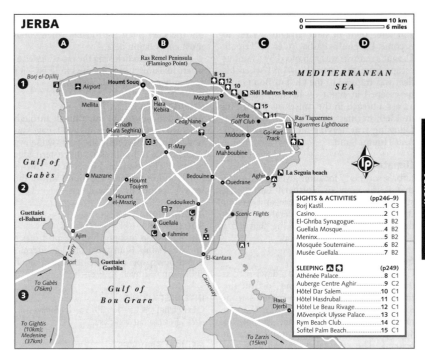

History

Jerba's history is the story of Berbers and schismatic Islamic sects, a place of refuge for pirates as well as those fleeing persecution.

Local Berber tribes were well established when the Phoenicians arrived on the scene about 2700 years ago. Among them were the Gerbitani of Gerba (near modern Houmt Souq). The Phoenicians established settlements at Meninx (modern El-Kantara) on Jerba and at Gightis on the mainland.

Jerba was one of the first places to fall to the Arabs on their march into Tunisia, but it later became a stronghold and refuge of the Kharijites in the wake of the Kharijite rebellion and subsequent Fatimid backlash that erupted across North Africa in AD 740. They belonged to the Ibadite sect of Kharijism (see the boxed text, p39) and were largely responsible for the huge number of mosques on the island – 213 in all.

Jerba later became a home base for some of the Mediterranean's most renowned

---

THE LAND OF THE LOTUS-EATERS

According to legend, Jerba is the Land of the Lotus-Eaters, where Ulysses paused in the course of the *Odyssey* and had a lot of trouble persuading his crew to get back on board. Today's islanders are said to be descendants of these people.

In a passage that more than a few visitors to Jerba can relate to, Homer wrote that after landing in 'the country of the Lotus-Eaters' and being given flowering food by the natives, his companions did not want to leave or even remember the way home.

These days there's scarcely a lotus to be found anywhere on the island, although many visitors to Jerba wish that they could forget the way home. Even louage drivers, not normally the most poetic of men, seem to have eaten of the lotus. When we boarded our louage to Jerba, the driver told us: 'You are going to the island of dreams'.

pirates, including the Barbarossa brothers and later their offsider Dragut – later to become Dargouth Pasha, ruler of Tripoli. Dragut's renown was enhanced by a famous escape from the Spanish in 1551 when his fleet was trapped in the Gulf of Bou Grara; he escaped at night by hauling the ships across a breach in the causeway. Returning in 1560, he massacred Spanish forces the following year, leaving the Tower of Skulls near Houmt Souq.

Climate

Jerba's southerly location gives it a climate that is the envy of Northern Europe. In summer it catches a sea breeze, and even in the middle of winter, temperatures rarely drop below 15°C, guaranteeing that it's a great place to visit year-round.

Getting There & Away

Car ferries operate 24 hours a day between the Jerban port of Ajim and Jorf on the mainland, leaving every 30 minutes from 6.30am to 9.30pm; hourly from 9.30pm to 11.30pm; two-hourly from 11.30pm to 4.30am and hourly again from 4.30am to 6.30am. The trip takes 15 minutes and the fare is 600 mills for a car. Passengers travel free.

The alternative – which is more expensive and time-consuming – is the longer main road from Houmt Souq to Zarzis along the old Roman causeway linking El-Kantara and the mainland.

Getting Around

Getting around the island depends upon what best suits your budget and time frame. Local bus, bicycle or motor scooter, taxi or hire car are all options (see p245).

HOUMT SOUQ   حومة السّوق

☎ 75 / pop 70,000

Jerba's main town rivals the beaches as the island's main attraction. With its distinctive and uniformly whitewashed architecture (see the boxed text, p242), attractive small squares and maze of narrow, winding streets, it has a beguiling charm and is unlike anywhere else in Tunisia. Houmt Souq has always been a market town and the selection of handicrafts on offer in its delightful covered souqs is among the best in the country. But being lost in a quiet lane of

the old town when the call to prayer drowns out the sales pitch is probably when you'll most enjoy being here.

If you've been drinking the tap water elsewhere in Tunisia, give it a miss in Jerba – it's very salty and of dubious safety.

Orientation

Ave Habib Bourguiba runs north through the town centre from the bus and louage stations and finishes near the port, while ave Abdelhamid el-Kadhi skirts the eastern edge of town. The souqs and most of the town's hotels and restaurants are found within the large V formed by these streets.

Information

BOOKSHOPS

The bookshop just north of the post office on ave Habib Bourguiba stocks international newspapers, magazines and a small collection of novels in French.

INTERNET ACCESS

Cyber Planet (☎ 8am-1am; TD1.5 per hr) Northwest of place Sidi Brahim; fast connections.

MEDICAL SERVICES

Clinique Dar ech-Chifa (☎ 650 441; fax 652 215; off ave Abdelhamid el-Kadhi) Private clinic northeast of town.
Hospital (☎ 650 018) Large regional facility about 500m southeast of the town centre on the road to Midoun.

MONEY

All the major banks have branches around the town centre and most have ATMs. There's always one bank rostered to be open on Saturday and Sunday; the *syndicat d'initiative* can tell you which one.

POST & TELEPHONE

There are dozens of Taxiphone offices around the town centre.
Main post office (ave Habib Bourguiba)

TOURIST INFORMATION

ONTT tourist office (☎ 650 016; blvd de l'Environment; ☼ 8.30am-1pm & 3-5.45pm Mon-Thu, 8.30am-1.30pm Fri-Sat) Out on the beach road, about a 15-minute walk from the centre. Staff are moderately helpful.
Syndicat d'initiative (☎ 650 915; ave Habib Bourguiba; ☼ 9am-1pm & 3.30-6pm Mon-Sat) Set back from the street, behind the two large maps of the island opposite place Mongi Bali.

HOUMT SOUQ

0 — 200 m
0 — 0.1 miles

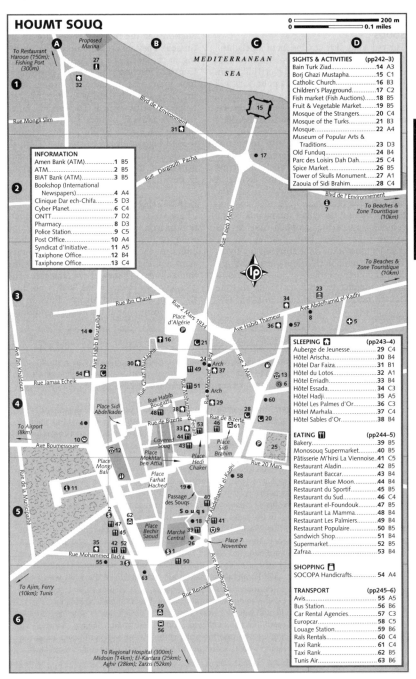

MEDITERRANEAN SEA

Blvd de l'Environnement

JERBA

INFORMATION
Amen Bank (ATM).........................1 B5
ATM..2 B5
BIAT Bank (ATM)...........................3 B5
Bookshop (International
  Newspapers)...............................4 A4
Clinique Dar ech-Chifa..................5 D3
Cyber Planet..................................6 C4
ONTT...7 D2
Pharmacy.......................................8 D3
Police Station.................................9 C5
Post Office....................................10 A4
Syndicat d'Initiative.....................11 A5
Taxiphone Office..........................12 B4
Taxiphone Office..........................13 C4

SIGHTS & ACTIVITIES (pp242–3)
Bain Turk Ziad..............................14 A3
Borj Ghazi Mustapha....................15 C1
Catholic Church............................16 B3
Children's Playground..................17 C2
Fish market (Fish Auctions)..........18 B5
Fruit & Vegetable Market.............19 B5
Mosque of the Strangers..............20 C4
Mosque of the Turks.....................21 B3
Mosque...22 A4
Museum of Popular Arts &
  Traditions...................................23 D3
Old Funduq...................................24 B4
Parc des Loisirs Dah Dah..............25 C4
Spice Market.................................26 B5
Tower of Skulls Monument..........27 A1
Zaouia of Sidi Brahim...................28 C4

To Beaches &
Zone Touristique
(10km)

To Beaches &
Zone Touristique
(10km)

SLEEPING (pp243–4)
Auberge de Jeunesse....................29 C4
Hôtel Arischa...............................30 B4
Hôtel Dar Faiza............................31 B1
Hôtel du Lotos.............................32 A1
Hôtel Erriadh................................33 B4
Hôtel Essada.................................34 C3
Hôtel Hadji...................................35 A5
Hôtel Les Palmes d'Or..................36 C3
Hôtel Marhala...............................37 C4
Hôtel Sables d'Or.........................38 B4

EATING (pp244–5)
Bakery..39 B5
Monosouq Supermarket...............40 B5
Pâtisserie M'hirsi La Viennoise.....41 C5
Restaurant Aladin.........................42 B4
Restaurant Baccar........................43 B4
Restaurant Blue Moon..................44 B4
Restaurant du Sportif...................45 B5
Restaurant du Sud........................46 C4
Restaurant el-Foundouk...............47 B5
Restaurant La Mamma..................48 B4
Restaurant Les Palmiers................49 B4
Restaurant Populaire....................50 B5
Sandwich Shop.............................51 B4
Supermarket.................................52 B5
Zafraa...53 B4

SHOPPING
SOCOPA Handicrafts.................... 54 A4

TRANSPORT (pp245–6)
Avis...55 A5
Bus Station...................................56 B6
Car Rental Agencies.....................57 C3
Europcar.......................................58 C5
Louage Station.............................59 B6
Raïs Rentals..................................60 C4
Taxi Rank......................................61 C4
Taxi Rank......................................62 B5
Tunis Air.......................................63 B6

Sights & Activities

SOUQS

The old souq district consists of a delightful tangle of narrow alleys and open squares with cafés. In the shops you'll find everything from Gabès basketwork to Guellala pottery, as well as the usual carpets, *sheeshas* (water pipes), sandals and miniature bird cages. The owners are used to dealing with tourists who don't bargain too hard, so prices can be high.

The old town is filled with some fine examples of traditional Jerban architecture, including white walls enclosing living quarters and domes dotting the skyline. A particular feature of the old town are the *funduqs* (caravanserais), former lodging houses for the travelling merchants of the camel caravans that stopped here in Ottoman times when Houmt Souq was the island's most important entrepôt for trade. They were built on two floors surrounding a central courtyard; the top floor had rooms for the merchants, while their animals were housed below. Some of these *funduqs* have been turned into excellent hotels.

For a break from tourist Jerba, the daily auctions at the **fish market** are not to be missed. They take place late in the morning in the northeast corner of the Marché Central. Auctioneers – born performers to a man – sit on elevated thrones touting strings of fish handed to them by their helpers and fishermen. The bidders range from restaurant owners to local women buying fish for the family. Fishing is Jerba's second-biggest money earner and it can all get delightfully frenetic. Close by, the **spice market** and the **fruit-and-vegetable market** are more sedate but still worth a look.

ISLAMIC MONUMENTS

There are some interesting Islamic monuments around town. On the edge of the souq is the **Zaouia of Sidi Ibrahim**, which contains the tomb of the 17th-century saint. On the other side of the road is the multi-domed **Mosque of the Strangers**. The 18th-century **Mosque of the Turks** is north of the souq on place d'Algérie. Built in the same fortress style as the island's traditional

---

JERBAN ARCHITECTURE

Jerba's highly distinctive fortress architecture reflects the island's long history as a stronghold of the fiercely autonomous Ibadite sect (see the boxed text, p39). The constant fear of attack encouraged the development of a bunker mentality, and the landscape is dotted with what look like defensive battlements.

The architecture also reflects the islanders' preoccupation with water conservation, and with keeping cool during the long, hot summers. Rooftops and courtyards were designed to channel rainwater into underground *impluviums* (tanks), providing both a water supply and a cool foundation. Thick rendered walls built of mud and stone provided further insulation. Finally, buildings were painted a brilliant white to deflect the summer sun.

Nothing typifies Jerban architecture quite like the mosque. These squat, square buildings positively bristle with defiance and with their heavily buttressed walls and minimalist decoration, they look more like forts than places of worship. The finest examples are the mosque at El-May – it stands in the middle of a large paved compound, dotted with hatches where you can check out the water level in the tanks below – and the one south of Guellala.

Menzels are traditional fortified homesteads. The island once boasted hundreds of them, but most have now been abandoned. There are still some good examples to be seen beside the main road between Ajim and Houmt Souq, and around El-May in the centre of the island. They were all built to a standard design, with a defensive wall enclosing a large rectangular central compound entered by a single gate. Rooms were built around the inside of the walls which had square towers at the corners. The top storeys of these towers were used as summer bedrooms, with window grates to let in the evening breezes and slatted floors for extra ventilation.

Known as *harout*, the traditional weaver's workshops have a design that is simplicity itself: a long, barrel-vaulted *ghorfa* (room) built half below ground for insulation. They are characterised by a triangular front, extending well beyond the walls of the *ghorfa*, and buttressing along the outer walls. There's a good example to be found in the grounds of the Museum of Popular Arts & Traditions in Houmt Souq.

JERBA

THE OCTOPUS CATCHERS

On this island which has been transformed by tourism, not everything has changed. The most distinctive features of Houmt Souq's fishing harbour are the great piles of terracotta pots shaped like Roman amphorae. Each bears its own mark signifying the local octopus fisherman who uses it in a traditional technique known as *gargoulette* that has changed little from Phoenician times. The 45cm to 50cm pots are tied together and cast out on long lines; they sink to the bottom and are left there for the octopus to discover. The slow-learning octopus mistakes the pot for its favourite underwater rocky nook or cranny, and obligingly crawls into the pot, only to be caught when the pots are hauled to the surface.

mosques, the only clue to its Turkish origins is the distinctive Ottoman minaret. All of these monuments are closed to non-Muslims but can be admired from outside.

MUSEUM OF POPULAR ARTS & TRADITIONS

This fine little **museum** (☎ 650 540; ave Abdelhamid el-Kadhi; admission TD2.1, plus camera TD1; ⊙ 8am-noon & 3-7pm Sat-Thu summer, 9.30am-4.30pm Sat-Thu winter) occupies the Zaouia of Sidi Zitouni, under the eucalyptus trees about 200m from the town centre. It houses a good collection of local costumes as well as pottery and jewellery. The room housing the latter still has the original terracotta domed tile ceiling as well as superbly intricate latticework design around the base. Indeed, the building itself is as interesting as the exhibits, with courtyards, arches and underground workshops. The ticket office is the small traditional weaver's hut near the entrance.

BORJ GHAZI MUSTAPHA

The town's old **fort** (Borj el-Kebir; admission TD1.1, plus camera TD1; ⊙ 8am-noon & 3-7pm Sat-Thu summer, 9.30am-4.30pm Sat-Thu winter) is on the coast 600m north of the Mosque of the Turks. It was built by the Aragonese in the 13th century on the rubble of a 9th century Aghlabid *ribat* (fortified monastery). It was extended early in the 16th century.

The fort was the scene of a massacre in 1560 when a Turkish fleet under Dragut (see p240) captured the fort and put the Spanish garrison to the sword. The skulls of the victims were stacked up on the shoreline 500m west of the fort as a grim reminder to others not to mess with Dragut. This macabre Tower of Skulls stood for almost 300 years until it was dismantled in 1848. A simple monument now stands in its place, although a drawing in the room next to the fort's entrance shows how it must have appeared.

The fort's interior has dozens of rooms and a mosque crammed into a small space. The ramparts are accessible and offer good views along the coast. Look for the mounds of cannonballs, both stone and rusting iron, that have been found in the course of restoration.

FISHING PORT

Houmt Souq's busy little fishing port is at the northern end of ave Habib Bourguiba, a 15-minute walk from town. It's delightfully down-at-heel, although that's set to change with the completion of the marina complex around the harbour (see the boxed text, p248). Early mornings are the busiest and best times to visit.

Festivals & Events

The Ulysses Festival is held in July to August. This is strictly for tourists and includes events like a Miss Ulysses beauty contest. Ask at any of the tourist offices (see p240) for details.

Sleeping

Houmt Souq has an excellent range of accommodation, although all of the top-end options are out at the zone touristique (see p249). Prices here include breakfast unless stated.

BUDGET

For camping on the island, head to Aghir, 28km southeast of Houmt Souq (p249).

Auberge de Jeunesse (☎ 650 619; rue Moncef Bey; dm TD6) Houmt Souq's excellent youth hostel occupies an old *funduq* in a quiet lane close to the centre. It's as good as hostels get, with friendly staff, and it's open throughout the day, although there's a three-day limit on stays in the high season. Breakfast is available for TD1.

Hôtel Arischa (☎ 650 384; rue Ghazi Mustapha; s/d TD15/20, with private bathroom TD20/28) Just north of the souq, this is one of the best *funduqs*, with a flower-filled courtyard and attractive barrel-vaulted rooms which are spacious and keep quite cool in summer.

Hôtel Marhala (☎ 650 146; fax 653 317; rue Moncef Bey; s/d TD16/26) Owned by the Touring Club de Tunisie, the Marhala also has barrel-vaulted rooms, although some are a bit bare and claustrophobic. Otherwise, it is very good value and the courtyard is arguably the best of the *funduqs*.

Hôtel Sables d'Or (☎ 650 423; rue Mohammed Ferjani; s/d TD12/22) Not a *funduq* but instead a delightful old Houmt Souq house, this place is very well kept (including the shared toilets), quite stylish and very good for the price.

MID-RANGE

Hôtel Erriadh (☎ 650 756; fax 650 487; rue Mohammed Ferjani; s TD17.5-22.5, d TD26-30; 🞕) Just north of the souq, the Erriadh is only a small step up in price but it's a lovely place and the most upmarket of the old *funduqs*. The large rooms have loads of character and are set around a pleasant courtyard.

Hôtel Hadji (☎ 650 630; fax 652 221; 44 rue Mohammed Badra; s TD17-22, d TD28-33; 🞕) It lacks the charm of the hotels in the souq area, but the rooms are spacious, light and airy, if a little soulless.

Hôtel Les Palmes d'Or (☎ 653 369; 84 ave Abdelhamid el-Kadhi; s/d TD30/50; 🞕) The bright, modern and comfortable rooms with satellite TV are among the best in town. The staff are eager to please.

Hôtel Essada (☎ 651 422; fax 652 048; ave Habib Thameur; s/d TD20/30; 🞕) They don't get many tourists here but the building is nicely decorated and the rooms worth seeking out if the other mid-range options are full.

There are two good places facing the beach on blvd de l'Environment to the west of the fort. They're quiet but it's a long, hot walk into town and the coast here is a bit grotty.

Hôtel du Lotos (☎ 650 026; fax 651 127; blvd de l'Environment; s/d TD23/36) Opposite the Tower of Skulls monument, this was the original tourist hotel on the island and still has a quiet, decaying charm. The rooms are huge, with correspondingly large balconies, staff are friendly and there's a bar.

Hôtel Dar Faiza (☎ 650 083; fax 651 763; s/d TD33.5/53; 🞕) This quiet retreat has accommodation spread through gardens at the rear of the main hotel building. It also has one of the better restaurants on the island. The rooms are large if nothing special.

Eating

The streets of Houmt Souq are filled with cafés and restaurants to suit every budget. All are open for lunch and dinner unless stated.

For a hearty snack, try the tiny sandwich shop on rue Mohammed Ferjani, just south of place d'Algérie, which stuffs baguettes with your choice of fillings for between 500 mills and TD1. It's very popular with locals.

Restaurant La Mamma (signed only in Arabic) A tiny rough-and-ready place on rue Habib Bougatfa, it does a roaring trade at lunchtime, with local workers tucking into such staples as *lablabi* and *chorba* (soup; both 800 mills). It also has daily specials like spicy, Tunisian-style macaroni for TD1.5.

Restaurant Populaire (☎ 653 823; ave Abdelhamid el-Kadhi; starters TD1, mains from TD2.5) This tiny, earthy place behind the Marché Central is good value for money. Its Tunisian specialties include *kammounia* (meat stew with lots of cumin) and *mloukhia* (meat stew).

Restaurant Les Palmiers (place d'Algérie; starters from TD1.5, mains from TD3) Les Palmiers is always busy with Tunisians and tourists attracted by good food at prices up to four times cheaper than the restaurants on place Hedi Chaker. The *chorba* (TD1.5) is good, *briqs* cost less than a dinar and seafood starts at a very reasonable TD4.

Restaurant du Sportif (ave Habib Bourguiba; starters from 500 mills, mains from TD2.5) Even cheaper than Les Palmiers and with a similar selection, it can be difficult to get a table here at lunchtime.

Restaurant el-Foundouk (☎ 653 238; off ave Habib Bourguiba; salads TD2.5, mains from TD4) Set back from the road in a courtyard, this place is just a touch more atmospheric than others in town in this price range. The food is fine, including the Jerban rice (TD5).

Restaurant Aladin (☎ 621 191; ave Mohammed Badra; starters TD1.5; mains from TD3) This cheery little place is good for affordable seafood. Among the highlights is octopus cooked in its own ink (TD3.5).

Patisserie M'hirsi La Viennoise (ave Abdelhamid el-Kadhi; ☯ breakfast, lunch & dinner) An amazing range of cakes and pastries.

For more upmarket restaurants, head to place Hedi Chaker. They all offer similar menus (heavy on the seafood) and pleasant surrounds, but expect to pay a minimum of TD10 for most dishes; always check the price before ordering, especially where fish prices are listed by weight. That said, the atmosphere is pleasant on a summer's evening and the food is generally good.

Among those surrounding place Hedi Chaker: **Restaurant Baccar** (☎ 650 708) gets good reports, has good service and its specialty (*spaghetti au fruits de mer*; TD10) is huge; **Restaurant Blue Moon** (☎ 650 559) does the fish really well; while **Restaurant du Sud** (☎ 650 479), between place Hedi Chaker and place Sidi Brahim, is a touch less pricey and not quite as picturesque, but highlights on the menu do include *briq au fruits de mer* (TD4.5) and *calamar grillé* (TD7).

Most of the tables in the actual square belong to **Zafraa** which is reasonably priced and great for large sandwiches (TD2), pizzas (from TD3) and fresh fruit juices (from TD2), with a lovely seating area under the vines. If crêpes (TD1.5) are your thing, it's a good breakfast alternative to the bread, butter and jam breakfasts served by most hotels.

Of the hotel restaurants, one of the most popular with locals for seafood is downstairs at the **Hôtel Arischa** (mains around TD10), with good food backed up by friendly service and a very reasonably priced wine list, while the restaurant at the **Hôtel Dar Faiza** (set menu TD8) is another favourite and it has an outdoor terrace.

Restaurant Haroon (☎ 650 488) Out by the fishing harbour, this place is a touch more classy than the rest. Allow TD25 plus wine, or opt for the three-course menu (TD15).

Getting There & Away
AIR
Jerba's airport, near the village of Mellita in the northwest, handles a busy schedule of international flights with a constant flow of charter flights from Europe (see p268). **Tunis Air** (☎ 653 102) has an office on ave Habib Bourguiba and four flights a day to Tunis (TD65 one way, one hour) in summer.

BUS
The bus station is at the southern end of ave Habib Bourguiba. Scheduled departures are listed on a board above the ticket windows.

SNTRI runs at least three air-con services a day to Tunis (TD23). Two of these travel via Kairouan (TD13.7, six hours) and take eight hours; the other service goes via Sfax (TD11, five hours) and Sousse (TD16.3, seven hours) and takes nine hours. All SNTRI services stop at Gabès (TD6.1, 2½ hours).

The regional company, Sotregames, has five buses a day to Medenine. Make sure you catch one of the services that travels via the Ajim–Jorf ferry. These services cost TD3.2 and take 1½ hours; services via Zarzis take an hour longer and cost TD4.6. Two of these buses continue to Tataouine (TD5.1, 2½ hours). The afternoon service travels via Zarzis, stretching the journey time to 3½ hours and the fare is TD6.4.

There are three buses a day to Gabès (TD6.1, three hours). One service continues to Matmata (TD6.5, three hours).

LOUAGE
Louages leave from opposite the entrance to the bus station. There are frequent departures for Gabès (TD5.4) and Medenine (TD4.4), and some services to Tataouine (TD6.5). Occasional louages leave for Tunis, Sfax and Sousse.

Getting Around
TO/FROM THE AIRPORT
The airport is 8km west of Houmt Souq, past the village of Mellita. There are three buses (570 mills) a day from the central bus station, which makes it unlikely that a bus will suit your departure time. Taxis cost about TD3.5 from Houmt Souq, or TD8.5 from the zone touristique.

BICYCLE & MOPED
For those with a more energetic bent, a bicycle or motor scooter will give you more independence in exploring the island and won't blow the budget. When you're riding a moped you're unlikely to be covered by your insurance policy. Be extremely careful, especially out in the smaller inland villages where young children, wayward cyclists and suicidal dogs can be a real hazard. On the plus side, the roads on Jerba are very flat. **Raïs Rentals** (☎ 650 303; ave Abdelhamid el-Kadhi), north of the Mosque of the Strangers, has a good selection of bikes and motor scooters. Bicycles/50cc-scooters cost TD10/45 per day.

JERBA

BUS

For those with lots of time but not so much money, the cheapest way to get around the island is the reasonably extensive local bus network which operates from Houmt Souq to Guellala (800 mills, nine daily, 30 minutes) via Erriadh (450 mills); Cedouikech (600 mills, seven daily); the zone touristique (750 mills, 14 daily); and Midoun (800 mills, 12 daily, 30 minutes) among other villages. There's a timetable and a colour-coded route map of the services above the ticket windows in the bus station in Houmt Souq.

CAR RENTAL

Another option is to rent a car, but it's really only good value if you do so for a few days and plan to explore further afield. All the companies have offices in Houmt Souq and out at the airport. The offices in town include **Avis** (☎ 650 151; ave Mohammed Badra) and **Europcar** (☎ 650 357; ave Abdelhamid el-Kadhi). It's worth hunting around for deals at the cluster of local companies at the northern end of ave Abdelhamid el-Kadhi.

TAXI

If time is more important than saving money, renting a taxi can be a good way to see the island. Rates start at TD10 per hour, but you may be able to bargain for less. Taxi drivers know the island inside out, but do have a tendency to take you to where they think you should go rather than where you want; be firm. There are two taxi ranks in Houmt Souq – on ave Habib Bourguiba in the centre of town and place Sidi Brahim. Some of the big hotels in the zone touristique have their own taxi ranks.

ERRIADH (HARA SEGHIRA)   الرّياض
☎ 75

Erriadh (or Hara Seghira) is around 7km south of Houmt Souq and is well worth a visit for its ancient synagogue. Although there's little else to see in town, it's also home to Jerba's best hotel.

El-Ghriba Synagogue

The most important synagogue on Jerba is **El-Ghriba** (The Miracle; admission TD1; ☼ 7.30am-6pm Sun-Fri), signposted 1km south of the town. It's the oldest mosque in North Africa and a major place of pilgrimage during the Pass-over Festival, when Jews come to pay tribute to the grand master of the Talmud, Shimon Bar Yashai, who died more than 400 years ago. As part of the festivities, local Jews

---

THE JEWS OF JERBA

The Jewish community dates its arrival in Jerba either from 586 BC, following Nebuchadnezzar's conquest of Jerusalem, or from the Roman sacking of the same city in AD 71; either way this makes it one of the oldest Jewish communities in the world outside Israel. Some historians, however, argue that many Jerban Jews are descended from Berbers who converted to Judaism. Over the centuries the community also received several influxes of Jews fleeing from persecution in Spain, Italy and Palestine.

In the 19th century, Jews in Jerba were required to wear distinctive clothes: black pantaloons, black skull cap and sleeveless blue shirts. Discrimination ended with the arrival of the French in 1881. The community was known for being staunchly traditional, like its neighbours the Kharijite Muslims, and it rejected financial and educational aid from the rest of the Jewish world. Communities of Jerban Jews settled all over southern Tunisia, usually working as blacksmiths famed for their jewellery, but returned to the island for the summer and for religious festivals.

Most Jerban Jews emigrated to Israel after the 1956 and 1967 Arab–Israeli wars; after centuries of relative peace, the clash between Arab and Israeli nationalism made their position untenable across North Africa. The community also suffered during WWII, when the Germans extorted 50kg of gold as a communal fine.

The Jewish community on Jerba now numbers only a few hundred. The community's survival on Jerba was called into question in April 2002 when a truck bomb exploded at the synagogue, killing 19 people in an event locals call 'Le Catastrophe'. Muslim and Jewish locals are quick to point out that the two communities have lived in harmony alongside one another for generations, pointing the finger at external elements for the bombing. Security at the site is now as tight as you'll see in Tunisia (independent travellers may be asked for identification).

and pilgrims carry the community's holy books through the town.

The site dates back to 586 BC, although the present building was constructed early in the 20th century. The original synagogue is thought to have been founded here after a holy stone fell from heaven at the site and a mysterious woman appeared to direct the construction of the synagogue. It is also believed that when the last Jew leaves Jerba, the keys to the synagogue will return to heaven.

The interior is an attractive combination of blue tilework and sombre wooden furniture. The inner sanctuary, with its elevated pulpit, is said to contain one of the oldest Torahs (Jewish holy book) in the world. Numerous silver plaques from pilgrims adorn the eastern wall.

Sleeping & Eating

Dar Dhiafa (☎ 671 166; d TD170, ste TD210-250; ⌘) is one of the most enchanting hotels in Tunisia. It's a classy adaptation of local architecture, with arches, alcoves, antique tiles, fountains, courtyards and domes complementing the supremely comfortable and beautifully decorated rooms. The owners are welcoming but discreet and facilities include a *hammam*, Moorish café and an excellent restaurant. The hotel is well signposted in town.

Getting There & Away

Buses from Houmt Souq to Guellala go past the synagogue (450 mills).

GUELLALA قلّالة

☎ 75

This village on the south coast is known for its pottery, and a dozen or so workshops and galleries line the main road. The selection is much the same as you'll see in Houmt Souq but you're more likely here to be getting the genuine article rather than an imitation.

Cave d'Ali Berbere

Be sure to check out the Cave d'Ali Berbere, on the southeastern edge of town. Ali is an endearing old guy who claims that the cave, supported by a series of stone arches, dates back to Roman times. He'll demonstrate pottery-making as it used to be done, climb into a massive amphora to show how Ali

Baba and his 40 thieves were able to hide and take you to an ancient underground olive press. There's no entrance fee but a tip is both appreciated and deserved.

Guellala Mosque

The waterfront mosque 1.5km south of town is a fine example of Jerban Islamic architecture, and a favourite spot to watch the sunset.

Musée Guellala

This impressive new **museum** (Museum of Guellala; ☎ 761 114; admission TD5, plus camera TD3; ☽ 8am-11pm summer, 8am-6pm winter) is one of the best (and most expensive) folklore museums in the country. Modern reproductions of Jerban architecture are used to house nearly 50 scenes of traditional life, ranging from weddings (the depilation scene graphically captures the pain of hair removal!), the solemn rite of circumcision, Sufi dancers and olive pressing. The mannequins are well displayed with music piped through the rooms, and there are labels in four languages. There are also displays of wedding costumes from around Tunisia. The museum, around 1.5km east of town on the road to Cedouikech, occupies one of the highest points on the island, affording fine views over Guellala and down to the Gulf of Bou Grara. It's also signed as the Musée du Patrimonie.

Getting There & Away

There are seven buses a day between Guellala and Houmt Souq (800 mills, 30 minutes).

GUELLALA TO THE ZONE TOURISTIQUE

The most interesting road northeast of Guellala runs through the quiet town of **Cedouikech**, notable for its subterranean mosque, the **mosquée souterraine** or Louta Mosque, with only the white domes visible above ground. It was an Ibadite mosque and dates from the 12th century. Continuing northeast takes you to **Mahboubine**, where the Turkish or El-Kaatib Mosque is worth stopping for. The road from here to Midoun is a good place to see examples of traditional *menzels* along the roadside.

Midoun itself is the island's second-largest town and is really only of passing interest for its busy Friday market. The town also stages a traditional Jerban wedding ceremony for the benefit of tourists every Tuesday at 4pm. For local food, the **Restaurant de l'Orient** has couscous for TD2, while the **Restaurant Le Khalife** (☎ 657 860), on ave Salah ben Youssef, is an upmarket fish restaurant.

Another worthwhile detour is to the oasis of **Cedghiane**. It's in the most fertile part of the island, with an ample supply of sweet artesian water, which has allowed the development of traditional, tiered desert oasis agriculture. Tall palms provide shade for citrus and pomegranate trees, which in turn protect vegetable crops. The huge *menzels* (Jerban dwellings) of the area are evidence that this was once an important settlement, but most are in ruins.

ZONE TOURISTIQUE
☎ 75

Jerba's zone touristique occupies most of the island's eastern coast. **Sidi Mahres** is a splendid sweep of golden sand. It begins east of the low-lying Ras Remel Peninsula, which protrudes from the middle of the north coast 10km east of Houmt Souq. The peninsula is known as **Flamingo Point** because of the large number of flamingos that gather there in winter. Sidi Mahres beach then continues east all the way to **Ras Taguermes**, the cape at Jerba's eastern tip. A long sand spit extends south from the cape, enclosing a large lagoon.

South of here on the east coast is **La Seguia**. The hotels are further apart here, and the beaches less crowded.

Most of the beaches are the private domain of the hotels, but there are some small public beaches (ask for la plage populaire; the only ones left for locals) just south of the Mövenpick Resort.

The road running along the coast behind the hotels has a range of restaurants, souvenir shops and bicycle/scooter-hire places.

Activities
In addition to lying on the beach or by the pool, there is a range of water-sports for the more energetic. Equipment is available for hotel guests at most of the hotels, including windsurfers (TD5 per hour), pedalos (TD5) and catamarans (TD20), and you can also try your hand at parasailing.

JERBA AND TOURISM

The at-times-difficult relationship between tourism and traditional Tunisian society is nowhere more evident than on Jerba, particularly in Houmt Souq and the zone touristique. Environmentally, ground water has become less drinkable and agriculture less tenable as supplies are exhausted by thirsty resorts and other tourist infrastructure on the island. For many of the older inhabitants of Jerba, the tourism inundation has also been profoundly alienating, with liberal displays of flesh putting the best beaches out of bounds for Tunisian families, and prices pushed ever higher to catch the tourist euro.

The most visible example of the impact of tourism upon traditional life can be found at the fishing harbour north of Houmt Souq, where local fishermen have been following millennia-old techniques passed down from father to son. But rising behind the little harbour is a new luxury marina complex modelled on those at Monastir and Port el-Kantaoui. Slated for completion in 2005, the harbour is likely to be transformed into the domain of wealthy yachters, while the fishermen will be shunted further along the coast.

Traditional ways survive in the Berber-speaking Ibadite villages of the south, like Guellala and Cedouikech, but they're fading as young people are drawn away to jobs in the tourist business.

Tourism has also brought good things to Jerba, including a renewed interest in preserving the architectural heritage of the island, the revival of the manufacturing of traditional handicrafts and the providing of much-needed jobs; government statistics suggest that every hotel bed in Tunisia supports 1.1 direct local jobs.

Your impact is likely to be diminished if you avoid the temptation to fly through the souq, make a couple of rapid-fire purchases and eat at a restaurant visited only by tourists, only to hasten back to your hotel. Take the time to talk to locals – whether it's the youngster who serves you breakfast, the vendor who sells you the stuffed camel or the old men sitting in the cafés frequented only by locals. Chances are that they'll appreciate someone taking the time to stop and listen to a different story of Jerba.

More land-based alternatives include bowling alleys, go-karting (TD8 for 10 laps) and a decent golf course. **Jerba Golf Club** (☎ 659 055; djerba.golfclub@planet.tn; 9/18 holes TD28/ 48, club hire TD12) is 17km east of Houmt Souq. Tee-off times must be booked in advance.

Less an activity than an indulgence, Jerba's **casino** (☺ 6pm-5am) only accepts foreign currency.

Sleeping & Eating

At last count, there were 107 hotels lining the Jerban coast. They're usually booked out in summer and really only worthwhile if you book as part of a package; independent travellers will pay full rates on the offchance that there's a room free. At the top end of the market, most are impressive complexes containing one or two swimming pools, private beaches, massage centres, tennis courts, nightclubs, bars, restaurants, coffee shops, boutiques and a programme of daily activities to keep guests entertained.

At the time of writing, there were seven five-star resorts, all of which quoted summer rates of around TD150/200 for a single/ double; all come close to the last word in modern, beachside luxury. They include the **Athénée Palace** (☎ 757 600) and **Mövenpick Ulysse Palace** (☎ 758 777) at the northern end of Sidi Mahres beach, down to the **Sofitel Palm Beach** (☎ 757 777) and **Hôtel Hasdrubal** (☎ 657 650). Not five-star, but still very good, is the **Rym Beach Club** (☎ 657 614) down near Ras Taguermes.

An option that may be open to independent travellers is to stay in one of the two-star places, which tend not to be booked quite so heavily. Most are close to the beach but not right on it, and offer more personal, pension-style accommodation. Expect to pay around TD50/80 for a single/double. Ones to try include **Hôtel Dar Salem** (☎ /fax 757 667), pitched towards families rather than tour groups, and **Hôtel Le Beau Rivage** (☎ 757 130; fax 758 123).

Auberge Centre Aghir (☎ 657 366; dm without breakfast TD2; tent TD2.5) is the best place on the island for campers. It's on the beach at Aghir at the junction of the Midoun road 28km southeast of Houmt Souq. It's simple but adequate. To get there from Houmt Souq, catch the bus (TD1, 40 minutes) to Club Med via Midoun.

SOUTHEASTERN COAST

There are a few sites of minor interest along Jerba's quiet southeastern coast. The **Borj Kastil** is a reconstructed Roman fort visible on a narrow peninsula southwest of La Seguia. It's a lonely spot not accessible by car, but worth seeing if you're on a bike.

Around the uninspiring town of **El-Kantara** are the meagre ruins of Roman **Meninx**, an ancient trading post. Many of the ruins are visible from the road, especially west and north of El-Kantara. The old Roman causeway links Jerba to the mainland.

JERBA

Directory

CONTENTS

ACCOMMODATION

From basic boltholes to five-star resorts, Tunisia has accommodation to suit just about everyone. Throughout this book, accommodation is generally divided into three price categories – budget, mid-range and top end.

Although it can vary a little from town to town, budget accommodation includes camping, youth hostels and cheap hotels where a bed will usually range from TD2.5 per person to TD15 for a double. At the lower end of this price range, your few dinars won't get you much more than a bed in a dorm or a bare room without windows and with shared bathroom facilities; at the upper end of the budget range you may get a private bathroom and some of the places are quite pleasant. Lone women travellers will feel uncomfortable in the cheapest of the cheapies.

Mid-range accommodation can start at TD15 and rise to TD40 for a double. For this price range, you'll almost always have a private bathroom, a bit more space so that you don't end up tripping over your backpack every time you get off the bed, and standards of cleanliness that some budget places clearly can't afford.

For top-end rates (from TD40 up to TD180 for a double), you have a right to

---

PRACTICALITIES

Newspapers & Magazines
La Presse (www.lapresse.tn) and *Le Temps* (French-language newspapers); *Assabah* (www.tunisie.com/Assabah) and *Al-Houria* (Arabic dailies); *Tunisia News* (an English-language weekly); (two-day-old) major European & US papers; (week-old) *Time* and *Newsweek*

Radio
Local French-language radio station (98FM; www.radiotunis.com); BBC World Service on shortwave (15.070MHz & 12.095MHz)

TV
French-language TV station (30 minutes of news at 8pm daily; www.tunisiatv.com); satellite TV (CNN etc) in top-end hotels

Video Systems
Like Europe and Australia, Tunisia uses PAL, which is incompatible with the North American and Japanese NTSC system

Electricity
Almost universal and reliable; supply is 220V; wall plugs have two round pins (as in Europe)

Weights & Measures
Tunisia uses the metric system (weight in kilograms, distance in metres); conversion charts on inside back cover of this book

expect semiluxurious rooms with satellite TV, fluffy white towels, direct-dial telephone, a bath and a swimming pool; some also have beauty parlours and a *hammam* (bathhouse).

Camping

Camping has not really caught on in Tunisia and facilities tend to be pretty basic. Most charge about TD4 to TD7 per person and some in the south have Bedouin tents where you can sleep if you don't have your own tent. Showers are either free or no more than TD1.5, while those with cars and campervans will pay a few extra dinars for water and electricity. The best campsites are those in Tozeur (p226), Ksar Ghilane (p222) and Douz (p218).

Campsites apart, it should be possible to camp anywhere as long as you obtain the permission of the landowner. Sleeping out on the beach is the accepted thing in the north at Raf Raf and Ghar el-Melh. The same does not apply, however, to the beaches in the resort areas of the Cap Bon Peninsula, Jerba and Sousse.

Hostels

Hostels fall into two categories: *auberges de jeunesse*, affiliated to Hostelling International; and government-run *maisons des jeunes*. They couldn't be more different.

The *auberges de jeunesse* are thoroughly recommended. Most have prime locations, such as a converted palace in the Tunis medina (p76) and an old *funduq* (caravanserai) in Houmt Souq on Jerba (p243). Others are at Remel Plage (p118) outside Bizerte and at the beach in Nabeul (p104).

They generally charge about TD4 to TD6 per night, with breakfast available for TD1 and other meals for TD3 each. Their popularity means that most impose a three-night limit during the high season.

There's no reason for time limits at the *maisons des jeunes*. Almost without exception (see Ain Draham, p128), they are characterless concrete boxes with all the charm of an army barracks. Almost every town has one, normally stuck out in the middle of nowhere and hard to get to without private transport. The only reason to mention them is that in some towns they're the only budget accommodation option. They all charge around TD4 for a dorm bed.

There are a couple of places where the *maison des jeunes* concept has evolved into a scheme called *centre des stages et vacances*, which are holiday camps that combine hostel and camp site. These are located on the beach at Aghir on Jerba (p249), in the oasis at Gabès (p200) and north of Kélibia on Cap Bon (p106). Camping charges are TD2.5 per person plus 500 mills per tent. Power and hot showers are available for a few dinars extra.

Hotels

Tunisian hotels fall into two main categories: classified hotels, which have been awarded between one and five stars under the government's rating system; and nonclassified hotels, which haven't. The latter are indicated by the initials NC (*nonclassifié*) on the accommodation lists handed out by tourist offices.

The majority of the budget places recommended in this book are nonclassified and some are very good. The cheapest are in the medinas of the major cities. They're basic, often with no showers, and you pay for a bed in a shared room. These hotels are totally unsuitable for women travellers.

The one- and two-star hotels tend to be smaller, older hotels, often built in colonial times. They're generally clean, if a little run-down, and are popular with local business travellers and tourists who want a decent double room with private bathroom and hot water. A three-star rating usually indicates a hotel built to cater for tour groups. Four- and five-star hotels are of international standard with all the usual facilities.

Hotel prices are normally listed according to three seasons – *haute* (high), *moyenne* (middle) and *basse* (low). High season usually corresponds with European summer and Christmas holidays and runs from 1 July to 15 September. Low season is from 1 November to 15 March, and the rest is middle season. Generally low-season prices for top-end places are between 30% and 60% less than the rates during high season. Differences are less marked at mid-range places and are only a few dinars cheaper at budget hotels. Throughout this book, prices listed are high-season rates unless otherwise stated.

At classified hotels, the room rates include breakfast; at nonclassified hotels, breakfast is often quoted separately, so ask. You'll soon tire of the typical hotel breakfast which consists of coffee, French bread, butter and jam. Occasionally, you may be lucky enough to be offered a croissant. Hotels that cater for package groups normally offer a buffet breakfast.

Resorts

Tunisia's coastline is awash with resort-style hotels, most of which are clustered together in what's known as a *zone touristique*. These are not aimed at the independent traveller, for whom the prices quoted are the full five- or four-star rates – still cheaper than European prices but expensive for Tunisia. The overwhelming number of people who stay at resorts do so as part of an airfare-and-accommodation package where prices are great value. Most resorts will have bars, restaurants, at least one swimming pool, travel desk and a number of shops, as well as one or two of a *hammam*, games room, private beach, gym and activities club. The most popular resorts are those at Hammamet (p98), Sousse (p166), Port el-Kantaoui (p169), Monastir (p172) and Jerba (p249).

ACTIVITIES

Tunisia is more for seeing than for doing but there is a range of activities for the more energetic among you. Apart from lazing on the beach, the most popular pastimes for visitors are camel trekking, 4WD excursions into the Sahara and water sports.

Beaches

Tunisia's tourist industry is built around its beaches. Hammamet's prime attraction is a glorious curve of golden sand, which begins in the shadow of a picturesque old kasbah (fort) and stretches away as far as the eye can see. There are more good beaches on the Cap Bon Peninsula, all along the central coast and the best beach in the south is Sidi Mahres on Jerba.

There are also some fine spots in the north of the country. The beaches at Raf Raf and Sidi Ali el-Mekki, between Tunis and Bizerte, are very popular with Tunisian holiday-makers. Cap Serrat, at the centre of the rugged north coast, shelters a glorious sandy bay that's all but deserted for most of the year. More accessible is Montezah Beach

at Tabarka, set against the backdrop of the densely forested Kroumirie Mountains.

For an itinerary based around the best Tunisian beaches, see p16.

Bird-Watching

Tunisia is a good place to see an interesting variety of birds, ranging from rarities such as Audouin's gull to local species such as Levaillant's woodpecker and Moussier's redstart.

Spring and autumn are the best times to see a wide range of migratory birds resting on their way elsewhere. In winter, the wetlands of the World Heritage–listed Ichkeul National Park (see the boxed text, p122) in the north, are home to more than 200,000 migratory waterfowl from all over Europe, including the rare greylag goose. Winter is also the time for flamingos who visit the northeast coast of Jerba and the Korba Lagoon on Cap Bon Peninsula.

May and June in El-Haouaria on Cap Bon is the last chance to see the migratory species as they wait to catch the wind to Europe.

For more information about birds in Tunisia, see p46.

Camel Trekking

The Saharan town of Douz is the place to go camel trekking (see the boxed text, p219 for details). You can organise anything from a one-hour ride (TD4) to an eight-day, oasis-hopping trek to Ksar Ghilane and back (from TD40 per day).

Diving & Water Sports

The best place to go diving or snorkelling is Tabarka on the north coast (see p125 for details), which has three good diving centres. Other places to try include Mahdia (see p185), Hammamet (p97) and Port el-Kantaoui (p169). At each place, there are agencies which organise trips, rent equipment and run courses for beginners.

Prices for snorkelling start from TD15 per hour, while diving costs about TD35 per dive.

The beaches of the big tourist resorts (Hammamet, Sousse, Monastir and Jerba) are the places to go for water sports. You'll find a whole range of activities from windsurfing to water-skiing and paddle-boats to parasailing.

Dune Skiing

Although exhilarating descents on skis down a sand dune should in theory be possible everywhere in the Sahara, only in the tiny oasis village of El-Faouar, 30km southwest of Douz, has the idea caught on to the extent of equipment being available (see p253).

4WD

The most popular way of exploring the desert, particularly for those with little time, is by 4WD. Although the resort hotels on the coast can make the arrangements, independent travellers will find the best agencies in Douz (p217), Tozeur (p226) and Gabès (p200). Costs start from TD200 per 4WD per day. The most popular expedition is from Douz to Ksar Ghilane. For more information, see the Desert Expeditions boxed text (p219).

Golf

Quite a few people come to Tunisia to play golf, particularly in winter when the fairways of northern Europe are covered in snow.

Hammamet is the best served, with two beautifully manicured courses to choose from. There are also good lay-outs at Jerba, Port el-Kantaoui (Sousse), Tabarka and Tunis. Green fees average about TD45 for 18 holes. Golfers of any standard are welcome at Tabarka, but elsewhere players need to show proof of their handicap.

It's very rare to encounter a Tunisian who has played golf, which is looked on as a game for wealthy foreigners.

Hammams

The Tunisian *hammam* (public bathhouse) experience is just about vigorous enough to qualify as an activity and should be tried at least once. Just about every town has one.

The standard TD1 to TD2 service includes a rubdown with a *kassa*, a coarse mitten that is used to remove the grime and dead skin after your stint in the steam room. It's usually possible to have a massage as well. It's a good idea to bring along a towel and shorts for moving around the *hammam*. The idea is to wear a pair of underpants while washing, so bring a second dry pair. And be warned – a rubdown with the *kassa* and massage are not for the faint-hearted; it can be quite vigorous.

For a description of the *hammam* experience see the boxed text, p73.

Hiking/Trekking

Tunisia is just waking up to the possibilities for trekking. The Kroumirie Mountains forests around Ain Draham have enormous potential as a trekking destination; the region is stunningly beautiful and conditions are perfect for walking in spring and autumn. The potential is limited by the lack of the sort of detailed maps you need in order to venture off the beaten track by yourself.

See p128 for more details.

Horse Riding

Sitting astride a horse is an excellent way to see the landscape. Horse riding is available in Tabarka, Hammamet and Tozeur.

Sailing

Tourist authorities have been promoting the country as a destination for yachting. The main attraction seems to be the cost of winter berthing compared with prices in the northern Mediterranean. The largest marinas are at Monastir, Port el-Kantaoui, Sidi Bou Saïd, Tabarka and Zarzis. For information on sailing in Tunisia, go to www.noonsite.com/Countries/Tunisia.sailing.

BUSINESS HOURS

See the inside cover for a summary of the country-wide opening hours for shops, post offices, banks, offices and restaurants. The opening hours for tourist offices are listed under each city throughout the book.

CHILDREN

Tunisians love children. Everyone finds Tunisians friendly, but it's multiplied for those travelling with kids. The extended family is the centre of Tunisian life and children are included in all that goes on – except perhaps the male ritual of sitting in cafés smoking the *sheesha* (water pipe). Expect to be stopped in the street, to have your child admired and doted upon and to have an extra special effort made to make sure you're comfortable. If you have the good fortune to be invited to a Tunisian wedding, you'll discover children are only marginally less feted than the bride and groom (see the boxed text, p35).

See p16 for our favourite Tunisian destinations for children.

Practicalities

Although the long-lasting benefits of travelling with children almost always outweigh the hassles, there are a few practical matters to bear in mind.

Airlines usually allow children up to two years old to fly for 10% of the adult fare, although a few may allow them to fly for free. Reputable international airlines usually provide nappies (diapers), tissues, talcum powder and all the other paraphernalia needed to keep babies clean, dry and half-happy. For children between the ages of two and 12, the fare on international flights is usually 50% of the regular fare or 67% of a discounted fare.

Breastfeeding is a private affair in Tunisia; doing it in public will attract lots of stares. Safety seats in hire cars are more likely to be available from international companies, while high-chairs in restaurants are only occasionally available.

Baby products (baby food, nappies etc) are widely available although they can be expensive, at least in the sense of being no cheaper than comparable brands in Europe. Many recognised brands are available in Tunisia, but expect to find them only in larger cities. If you prefer to stick to your favourite brand, you'd be better off bringing supplies with you. As one reader reported:

I have been having a fabulous time touring Tunisia with my hubby and 10-month-old son and as we have been here for a month we most certainly have had the opportunity to get off the beaten track with great success... If travelling with a baby I would definitely suggest bringing all the baby food you think you will need because it is very expensive here at TD2 for a jar; baby wipes are also expensive at TD14 for a pack of 72 wipes.

Elizabeth Ben Hassine, Australia

For more comprehensive advice on the dos and don'ts of travelling with children, pick up a copy of Lonely Planet's *Travel with Children* by Cathy Lanigan.

Sights & Activities

There are relatively few organised forms of entertainment for children. That said, most of the resort hotels have some form of children's entertainment or playground (and many have child-care services). Public playgrounds feature in some Tunisian towns and are marked on maps where relevant in this book. Impromptu football games spring up on just about any open patch of ground most evenings; everyone's welcome.

CLIMATE CHARTS

Northern Tunisia has a typical Mediterranean climate, with hot, dry summers and

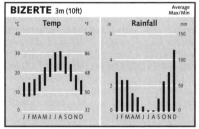

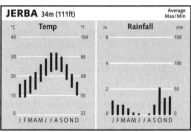

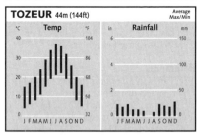

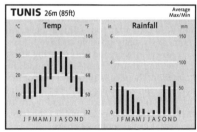

wet winters which are quite mild by northern European standards. The mountains of the northwest occasionally get snow. The further south you go, the hotter and drier it gets. Annual rainfall ranges from 1000mm in the north down to 150mm in the south, although some Saharan areas go for years without rain. Desert nights can get very cold.

COURSES

The Institut Bourguiba des Langues Vivantes in Tunis runs courses in classical and Tunisian Arabic (see p75 for details).

CUSTOMS

Searches of tourist baggage at Tunisia's airports are almost nonexistent. This is in stark contrast to the situation for those arriving with their car by boat, where every bag is likely to be opened and searched, a process which can take hours as you fill out forms listing valuable items. Apart from prohibited goods (drugs, excessive amounts of alcohol), officials are also keen to ensure that you don't intend to sell goods from Europe while in Tunisia – hence the list which you'll be asked for on departure from the country.

The duty-free allowance is 400 cigarettes, 2L of wine, 1L of spirits and 250ml of perfume.

DANGERS & ANNOYANCES

Tunisia is a generally safe place to travel and attacks on Westerners are extremely rare. One notable exception was in April 2002, when a suicide bomber blew himself and 19 others up at Erriadh's El-Ghriba Synagogue on the island of Jerba. The Tunisian government has spent decades cracking down on Islamic fundamentalism and such acts, claimed by Al-Qaeda, are extremely rare, but always do your research before going to Tunisia to get an idea of the risks as assessed by Western intelligence services.

Carpet Touts

Tunisian shopkeepers will never die wondering, but most take no for an answer. One place where they may wear you down is Kairouan where carpets and carpet tours abound (see the boxed text on p179 for a light-hearted look at the carpet-buying process). They're persistent rather than threatening.

GOVERNMENT TRAVEL WARNINGS

Before setting out, it's always a good idea to check on the prevailing safety and health situation in Tunisia. Most governments have travel advisory services detailing potential pitfalls and areas to avoid. Some of these include:

- Australian Department of Foreign Affairs & Trade (☎ 02-6261 1111; www.dfat.gov.au/consular/advice/)
- Canadian Department of Foreign Affairs & International Trade (☎ 1-800-267-6788; www.voyage.gc.ca/dest/index.asp)
- New Zealand Ministry of Foreign Affairs & Trade (☎ 04-439 8000; www.mft.govt.nz/travel/)
- UK Foreign and Commonwealth Office (☎ 0870-6060290; www.fco.gov.uk/travel)
- US Department of State (☎ 202-647-4000; www.travel.state.gov/travel_warnings.html)

Mines

Although unexploded mines are not widespread, you do need to be careful not to stray off the road in the area around Le Kef (see p146 for more details).

Mosquitoes

In some of the oasis towns in the south of the country (such as Tataouine, Tozeur and, to a lesser extent, Douz), sleeping with your window wide open is a good way to wake up the next morning covered in mosquito bites.

Sexual Harassment

Both female and male travellers have reported varying degrees of sexual harassment. For men, this seems to take place mostly in *hammams*, whereas women will soon realise that this is a frequent occurrence wherever you are (see p266 for more details).

Stone-Throwing Children

We have received some reports from readers of children throwing stones, particularly in some of the ksour around Tataouine and in the *palmeraie* (palm groves) around Gabès. Don't throw back.

Theft

Tunisia has very low levels of street crime. Still, it pays to take precautions, particularly in busy areas like the medinas of Tunis and Sousse. There have also been a few reports of beach thefts, so don't leave your belongings unattended on the sand. Crimes such as mugging are very rare.

The best place to keep your valuables (passport, travellers cheques, credit cards etc) is under your clothes in contact with your skin where, hopefully, you will be aware of an alien hand before it's too late. Most people opt for a moneybelt, while others prefer a leather pouch hung around the neck. Whichever method you choose, put your valuables in a plastic bag first, otherwise they'll get soaked in sweat as you wander around in the heat of the day and after a few days they'll end up looking like they've been through a (none-too-clean) washing machine.

DISABLED TRAVELLERS

If mobility is a problem, the hard fact is that most Tunisian hotels, museums and tourist sites are not wheelchair-friendly. However, take heart in the knowledge that disabled people do come to Tunisia and that the absence of infrastructure is somewhat compensated for by the friendliness and willingness to help of most Tunisians. Nonetheless, the trip will need careful planning, so get as much information as you can before you go. The British-based organisation Radar (Royal Association for Disability and Rehabilitation) publishes a useful guide called *Holidays & Travel Abroad: A Guide for Disabled People*. It's available from **Radar** (☎ 020-7637 5400; 25 Mortimer St, London W1N 8AB).

DISCOUNT CARDS
Hostel Cards

You need to be a member of Hostelling International (HI) if you want to stay at any of Tunisia's four affiliated hostels (see p251 for more details). You can join on the spot at the hostel in Tunis (p76).

Student & Youth Cards

There are no advertised discounts for student cards, although it never hurts to ask. One traveller reported being given free admission to some of the ancient sites on flashing a student card – probably because the site guardian mistook the card for some sort of official document. Some Internet cafés will offer a small discount for students.

EMBASSIES & CONSULATES

It's important to realise what your own embassy can and can't do. Generally speaking, it won't help much in emergencies if the trouble you're in is remotely your own fault. Embassies will not be sympathetic if you end up in jail after committing a crime locally, even if such actions are legal in your own country. In genuine emergencies you might get some assistance, but only if other channels have been exhausted (the embassy would expect you to have insurance). If you have all your money and documents stolen, it might assist with getting a new passport.

On the more positive side, some embassies post useful warning notices about local dangers or potential problems.

Tunisian Embassies & Consulates

Following is a list of Tunisian embassies and consulates abroad:

Algeria Algiers (☎ 2-69 20 857; rue Ammar Rahmani, El-Biar, 16000)
Australia Sydney (☎ 02-9363 5588; GPO Box 801, Double Bay, NSW 2028)
Belgium Brussels (☎ 2-771 7395; 278 ave De Tervueren, 1150)
Canada Ontario (☎ 613-237 0330; 515 O'Connor St, Ottawa, Ontario K1S 3P8)
Egypt Cairo (☎ 2-340 3940; 26 Sharia al-Jazirah, Zamalek, 11211 Cairo)
France Paris (☎ 01 45 55 95 98; 25 rue Barbet de Jouy, 75007); Lyon (☎ 04 78 93 42 87; 14 ave du Maréchal Foch, 69453); Marseilles (☎ 04 91 50 28 68; 8 blvd d'Athènes, 13001); Nice (☎ 04 93 96 81 81; 18 ave des Fleurs, 06000); Toulouse (☎ 05 61 63 61 61; 19 allé Jean Jaurès, 31000)
Germany Berlin (☎ 30-4 72 20 64/7) 110 Esplanade 12, 1100); Düsseldorf (☎ 211-37 10 07; 7-9 Graf Adolf Platz, 4000); Hamburg (☎ 40-2 20 17 56; Overbeckstrasse 19, 2000, 76); Munich (☎ 89-55 45 51; Adimstrasse 4, 8000, 19)
Italy Rome (☎ 06-860 42 82; Via Asmara 5, 00199); Palerm (☎ 091-32 89 26; 24 Piazza Ignazio Florio, 90100)
Japan Tokyo (☎ 3-3353 4111; 1-18-8 Wakaba Cho, Shinjuku-Ku, 160)
Libya Tripoli (☎ 21-607161; Ave Jehara, Sharia Bin Ashur, 3160)

Morocco Rabat (☎ 7-730 576; 6 Rue de Fès)
Netherlands The Hague (☎ 7-351 22 51; Gentenstraat 98, 2587 HX)
South Africa Pretoria (☎ 12-342 6283; 850 Church St, Arcadia, 0007)
UK London (☎ 020-7584 8117; 29 Princes Gate, SW7 1QG)
USA Washington DC (☎ 202-862 1850; 1515 Massachusetts Ave NW, 20005)

Embassies & Consulates in Tunisia

There is a large selection of foreign embassies concentrated in the capital, Tunis (telephone area code ☎ 71), including the following:

Algeria (Map p68; ☎ 783 166, fax 788 804; 18 rue du Niger, 1002 Tunis)
Australia The Canadian embassy in Tunis handles consular affairs in Tunisia for the Australian government
Austria (☎ 751 091; fax 767 824; 6 rue Ibn Hamdiss, 1004 El-Menzah)
Belgium (☎ 781 655; fax 792 797; 47 rue du 1 Juin, 1002 Tunis)
Canada (Map p68; ☎ 796 577; fax 792 371; 3 rue du Sénégal, 1002 Tunis)
Denmark (☎ 792 600; fax 790 797; 5 rue de Mauritanie, 1002 Tunis)
Egypt (Map p68; ☎ 791 181; fax 794 389; ave Mohammed V, 1002 Tunis)
France (Map pp70-2; ☎ 105 111; fax 105 191; 1 place de l'Indépendance, ave Habib Bourguiba, 1000 Tunis) Consulate (Map pp70-2; ☎ 333 027; 1 rue de Hollande, 1000 Tunis)
Germany (☎ 786 455; fax 788 242; 1 rue el-Hamra, 1002 Tunis)
Italy (Map pp70-2; ☎ 341 811; fax 354 155; 3 rue de Russie, 1000 Tunis)
Japan (☎ 791 251; fax 786 725; 10 rue Mahmoud el-Matri, 1002 Tunis)
Libya (☎ 781 913; fax 795 338; 48 rue du 1 Juin, 1002 Tunis); Consulate (☎ 285 402; fax 280 586; 74 ave Mohammed V, 1002 Tunis)
Morocco (☎ 782 775; fax 787 103; rue du 1 Juin, 1002 Tunis); Consulate (☎ 784 442; fax 783 627; 26 rue Ibn Mandhour, Notre Dame, 1002 Tunis)
Netherlands (☎ 799 442; fax 785 557; 8 rue de Meycen, 1002 Tunis)
South Africa (☎ 798 449; fax 791 742; 7 rue Achtart, 1002 Tunis)
Spain (☎ 782 217; fax 786 267; 22 rue Dr Ernest Conseil, 1002 Tunis)
UK (Map pp70-2; ☎ 341 444; fax 354 877; 5 place de la Victoire, 1000 Tunis); Consulate (Map p68; ☎ 793 322; fax 792 644; 141-143 ave de la Liberté, 1002 Tunis)
USA (☎ 107 000; fax 962 115; Zone Nord-Est des Berges de Lac Nord de Tunis 2045, La Goulette)

FESTIVALS & EVENTS

Tunisia's calendar is chock full of festivals, celebrating everything from octopus fishing to the wheat harvest.

The high point in the festival year comes in July and August with the opportunity to see performances of classical music and drama at some of the country's best-known ancient sites. The **El-Jem International Symphonic Music Festival** (www.festivaleljem.com) uses the town's magnificent floodlit colosseum to great effect, while the **Carthage International Festival** (www.festival-carthage.com.tn) features classical drama at the Roman theatres of Carthage and Dougga. The **Hammamet International Festival**, held in August, also attracts an impressive cast of international musicians, theatre groups and movies.

The **Tabarka International Jazz Festival**, staged in early July, is an event that has grown considerably in stature in recent years. Tabarka also hosts a **rai festival** in June, a **world music festival** in late August and **Latin music** in early September, not to mention an **international festival** throughout July and August.

Another festival to seek out is the **Sahara Festival** in Douz, held at the beginning of November. It features camel racing and displays of traditional desert skills as well as music, parades and poetry reading. Tozeur stages the **Oasis Festival** the following week.

Other festivals include:

MARCH
Octopus Festival (Kerkennah) Features people dressed up in octopus costumes.

JUNE
Falconry Festival (El-Haouaria) Features displays of falconry by local enthusiasts.

JULY
Festival of Malouf (Testour) Performances of Tunisia's musical emblem, *malouf*.

AUGUST
International Short Film Festival (Kélibia) Showcases the fine tradition of Tunisian movie-making.

OCTOBER
Carthage International Film Festival Biennial, even-numbered years in Tunisia, every other year this prestigious festival is held in Ouagadougou (Burkina Faso); two weeks of films from around the world, with an emphasis on Arab and African cinema.

NOVEMBER
Festival of the Ksour (Tataouine) Includes performances of Berber dance at nearby Ksar Ouled Soltane.

You'll find a full list of festivals, complete with dates, on the ONTT's website: www.tourismtunisia.com/culture/festivals.

For those keen to see as many festivals as possible, see the itinerary on p17.

FOOD
For a comprehensive insight into Tunisian food written by an expert on the subject, see p48.

Vegetarians can find it difficult to find purely vegetarian dishes, as the idea of not eating meat or fish is anathema to many Tunisians. As one vegetarian traveller pointed out:

I did not find it that complicated – but most of the time you end up eating couscous where the meat was picked out and the sandwich places are everywhere where you can pick out the ingredients.
Rainer Hamet, Austria

Throughout this book, restaurant information includes whether the restaurant is open for breakfast, lunch and/or dinner. For more information about meal times in Tunisia, see the inside front cover. Throughout the book, we also provide a range of prices for starter dishes and main courses or the average cost of a meal at each restaurant.

GAY & LESBIAN TRAVELLERS
While the lifestyle in Tunisia is generally liberal by Islamic standards, Tunisian society has yet to come to terms with overt homosexuality, which remains illegal under Tunisian law – in theory you can go to jail and/or be fined. However, although it's not openly admitted or shown, male homosexuality remains relatively common (men are occasionally propositioned in *hammams*) and there is a long tradition of male gay travellers going to Tunisia. These days Tunisians seem relatively easygoing on the subject and certainly in touristy places they are finding it less bizarre to see gay couples. In some of the more touristy areas, local 'beach gigolos' looking to pick up foreign men are not unheard of. Regardless of your sexual orientation, discretion is the key.

HOLIDAYS
Some of the secular public holidays in Tunisia, such as Women's Day and Evacuation Day, pass without notice. On others (particularly Islamic holidays), everything closes and comes to a halt (although transport still runs). On some long weekends, such as the Eid al-Fitr (celebrating the end of Ramadan), public transport gets strained to the limit as everyone tries to get home for the festival.

As the Gregorian (Western) and Islamic calendars are of different lengths, the Islamic holidays fall 11 days earlier every Western calendar year. For more details on the Islamic calendar and holidays, see p39.

Ramadan is the main holiday to watch out for, because for the whole month the opening hours of everything (as well as the patience of many officials) are disrupted.

ISLAMIC HOLIDAYS

Hejira Year	Ras as-Sana	Moulid an-Nabi	Ramadan Begins	Eid al-Fitr	Eid al-Adha
1425	22.02.04	01.05.04	14.10.04	13.11.04	21.01.05
1426	11.02.05	20.04.05	03.10.05	02.11.05	10.01.06
1427	31.01.06	09.04.06	22.09.06	22.10.06	30.12.06
1428	20.01.07	29.03.07	11.09.07	11.10.07	19.12.07

OTHER PUBLIC HOLIDAYS
- **New Year's** Day 1 January
- **Independence Day** 20 March
- **Youth Day** 21 March
- **Martyrs' Day** 9 April
- **Labour Day** 1 May
- **Republic Day** 25 July
- **Public Holiday** 3 August
- **Womens Day** 13 August
- **Evacuation Day** 15 October
- **Anniversary of Ben Ali's Accession** 7 November

INSURANCE
Travel Insurance
A travel insurance policy to cover theft, loss, cancellations and medical problems is a good idea. Some policies specifically exclude dangerous activities, which can include scuba diving, motorcycling, even trekking.

You may prefer a policy that pays doctors or hospitals directly rather than you having to pay on the spot and claim later. If you have to claim later ensure you keep all documentation.

Check that the policy covers ambulances or an emergency flight home.

For more information on issues relating to health, see the Health chapter (p278), while for details on car insurance see p275.

INTERNET ACCESS

Public access to the Internet in Tunisia is handled by Publinet, which has Internet cafés in just about every medium-sized town in the country; addresses are listed throughout this book. The quality of the connections varies – some are painfully slow, others reasonable, none are super-fast. The normal cost of one hour's surfing is TD1.5 to TD2.

There are a couple of very important things to remember about the Internet in Tunisia before setting out. At the time of research, hotmail accounts were not accessible in Tunisia after having been blocked by the government. If your normal account is hotmail, it may be worth setting up an alternative web-based email (eg Yahoo; www.yahoo.com) before you go. Other web pages considered subversive or corrupting are also blocked; ask the Publinet staff if you're having problems.

If you need to access your home email account, you'll need to carry three pieces of information with you: your incoming (POP or IMAP) mail server name, your account name and your password. With this information, you should be able to access your Internet mail account from any Net-connected machine in the world.

If you're travelling with a portable computer, Internet access from your hotel room is difficult in Tunisia and possible only in top-end hotels. Most international ISPs with global roaming facilities don't have agreements with Tunisian service providers. You may also need to buy a reputable 'global' modem before you leave home, or buy a local PC-card modem; contact **Planet Tunisie** (☎ 71-847 373; www.planet.tn; French only), Tunisia's service provider. However, unless you're in the country for an extended time, it's not worth the hassle.

If you intend to use your computer in your hotel room, always check that there are wall sockets as even a few mid-range hotels don't have any.

See Internet Resources, p11, for a list of useful websites relating to Tunisia.

FIGHTING THE TUNISIAN KEYBOARD

Your first encounter with a Tunisian computer keyboard is likely to be a frustrating one, especially for touch-typers. The bulk of the letters are where you always thought they were but there are just enough which aren't to throw you completely. The more important things to realise are:

- The letters 'a' and 'q' have swapped places
- The letters 'z' and 'w' have also done a swap
- The letter 'm' is located on the far right of the middle row
- If you're trying to insert the '@' symbol for an email address, use the 'Alt Gr' key plus the number '0'
- Numbers require the shift key (very annoying)
- dash ('-') can be accomplished with '6' (without using the shift key)
- The apostrophe also doesn't require the shift key; simply press '4'
- A full stop needs the shift key plus ';'

---

ekno Communication Service

Lonely Planet's ekno global communication service offers an online travel vault, where you can securely store all your important documents. You can join online at www.ekno.lonelyplanet.com, where you will find local access numbers for the 24-hour customer-service centre as well as updates on new features.

LEGAL MATTERS

As a visitor to Tunisia, it's unlikely that you'll encounter any difficulties with the Tunisian police, who will routinely turn a blind eye to minor indiscretions by tourists, and you'll certainly be treated much more leniently than locals in such cases. We've never heard of incidents of tourists being approached by police or asked for identification. The only exception was at Erriadh's El-Ghriba Synagogue in Jerba, scene of an April 2002 bombing, where independent travellers may be asked to show identification and be asked a few questions.

Police leniency towards tourists doesn't extend to more serious offences; drug laws are very strict and possession of even the smallest amount of cannabis resin is punishable by one year in jail and/or a hefty fine. In Tunisia, the legal age for voting, driving, drinking and having sex is 20 years old; in the last case, the dictates of traditional family mores render the legal position somewhat irrelevant.

MAPS

If you plan on driving in Tunisia, it's a good idea to buy a map before you go. The Michelin *Tunisia 956* or *744* (1:800,000) is probably the best, although Freytag & Berndt's *Tunisia* (1:800,000) is also comprehensive.

The best locally produced maps come from the Tunisian Office de la Topographie et de la Cartographie (OTC). It produces the *Carte Touristique et Routiére* (1:750,000), which is the most up-to-date road map around. The OTC also produces a series of street maps of major cities, including Tunis, Sfax and Sousse (all 1:10,000); Kairouan (1:8000); and Hammamet and Nabeul (1:5000). Unfortunately, the only place where you could buy these maps at the time of research was at the OTC office in Tunis (see p66 for details), as the OTC office in Sousse was closed.

The government-run Office National du Tourisme Tunisien (ONTT) hands out a reasonable (and free) 1:1,000,000 road map of the country, but it's more of general use than a helpful navigational tool. Most local ONTT offices also hand out free town maps. They range from the useful to the barely comprehensible.

MEN TRAVELLERS

Travelling as a man in Tunisia involves few special pitfalls and is certainly easier than travelling as a woman (see p266).

In most Arab countries the only people you'll get to speak with are men, but Tunisian women enjoy greater freedom and often enjoy talking to foreigners, whether male or female. As a result, male travellers will find opportunities to get an alternative insight from those offered by Tunisian men. Although men should never be the one to initiate contact with a Tunisian woman, proximity in shops and particularly on transport will often lead to the women starting a conversation as one reader reported:

> I was really surprised that Arab women and girls did talk to me, in a strange way for sure, talking sometimes about love immediately, or women in their 20s, 30s like teens in Europe.
> *Rainer Hamet, Austria*

We have received some letters from male readers who experienced some low-level sexual harassment from other men in *hammams*.

MONEY

The unit of currency is the Tunisian dinar (TD), which is divided into 1000 millimes (mills). There are five, 10, 20, 50, 100 and 500 mills coins and one- and five-dinar coins. Dinar notes come in denominations of five, 10, 20 and 30. Changing the larger notes is not usually a problem, but can be so in small shops.

The TD is a soft currency, which means that exchange rates are fixed artificially by the government. The dinar cannot be traded on currency markets and it's illegal to import or export it, so you won't be able to equip yourself with any local currency before you arrive. It's not necessary to declare your foreign currency on arrival.

Within the country, the euro, UK pound and US dollars are readily exchangeable, while the Canadian dollar and Japanese yen should be fine in most banks. Australian and New Zealand dollars and South African rand are not accepted. Exchange rates are regulated, so the rate is the same everywhere.

Tunisian banks will usually want to see your passport when you change money, especially for travellers cheques. Post offices change cash only.

When leaving the country, you can re-exchange up to 30% of the amount you changed into dinars, up to a limit of TD100. You need to produce bank receipts to prove you changed the money in the first place.

ATMs

ATMs are found in almost all medium-sized town large enough to support a bank, and certainly in all the tourist areas. If you've got MasterCard or Visa, there are plenty of places to withdraw money. Many of them will allow you to access international savings accounts; look for the Cirrus or Visa Electron logo. However, ATMs are often out of order so always check the information on the screen before putting in your card.

Cash

Nothing beats cash for convenience – or for risk. If you lose it, it's gone for good and very few travel insurers will come to your rescue. Those who do will normally limit the amount to about US$300. Don't carry too much cash on you at any one time; use travellers cheques or your ATM card to withdraw as much cash as you think you'll need for a few days at a time. It's also a good idea to set aside a small amount of cash, say US$50, as an emergency stash.

Credit Cards

Credit cards are an accepted part of the commercial scene in Tunisia, especially in major towns and tourist areas. They can be used to pay for a wide range of goods and services such as upmarket meals and accommodation, car hire and souvenir shopping.

The main credit cards are MasterCard and Visa (Access in the UK), both of which are widely accepted in Tunisia. They can also be used as cash cards to draw dinars from the ATMs of affiliated Tunisian banks in the same way as at home. Daily withdrawal limits are set by the issuing bank. Cash advances are given in local currency only. Both companies say they can replace a lost card in Tunisia within 24 hours, and will supply you with a phone number in your home country that you can call, reverse charges, in an emergency; ask your bank for details.

The main charge cards are Amex and Diners Club, which are accepted in tourist areas, but unheard of elsewhere.

Tipping

Tipping is not a requirement but small change is often appreciated by underpaid waiters in restaurants; cafés and local restaurants put out a saucer for customers to throw their small change into. Waiters in tourist restaurants are accustomed to tips: 10% is plenty. Taxi drivers do not usually expect tips from locals, but often round up the fare for travellers.

Travellers Cheques

The main reason for carrying your funds as travellers cheques rather than cash is the protection they offer against theft. They are, however, losing popularity as more and more travellers opt to leave their money in a bank at home and withdraw it at ATMs as they travel.

American Express (Amex), Visa and Thomas Cook cheques are widely accepted and have efficient replacement policies. Maintaining a record of the cheque numbers and when you use them is vital when it comes to replacing lost cheques. Keep this record separate from the cheques themselves. US dollars and euros are the best currencies. The Banque Nationale Agricole (BNA) insists on being shown the customer purchase record.

Banks charge a standard 351 mills commission per travellers cheque and the larger hotels take slightly more.

Note that STB Bank is the only bank which can be relied upon to change travellers cheques in smaller towns.

PHOTOGRAPHY
Film & Equipment

Name-brand film such as Kodak and Fuji is widely available and reasonably priced. Expect to pay about TD4.5 for 24-exposure 100 ASA film, and TD5.5 for 36 exposures. Slide film is increasingly available in more touristy areas (expect around TD10 for a 36-exposure 100 ASA roll) but always check the expiry date. Never buy film which has been sitting in a shop window in the sun.

Photographing People

You should always ask permission before taking photographs of people. While Tunisians expect every tourist to carry a camera, most don't like to have the lens turned on them. This applies particularly to Tunisian women and to people in rural areas.

Restrictions

It's forbidden to take photographs of airfields, military installations, police stations and government buildings.

Technical Tips

For detailed technical advice, get a copy of Lonely Planet's *Travel Photography: A Guide to Taking Better Pictures*, written by internationally renowned travel photographer,

Richard I'Anson. It's full colour throughout and designed to take on the road.

POST

Post offices are known as PTTs. See the inside front cover for post office opening times.

Air-mail letters cost 750 mills to Europe and 800 mills to Australia and the Americas; postcards are 100 mills cheaper. You can buy stamps at post offices, major hotels and some general stores and newsstands.

Receiving Mail

Mail can be received poste restante at any post office in Tunisia. It should be addressed clearly, with your family name in capitals. Address mail to: (Your Name), Poste Restante, PTT Central, City Name, Postcode, Tunisia. Ask the clerks to check under your given name as well if you think you are missing mail. There's a collection fee of 200 mills per letter.

Sending Mail

The Tunisian postal service is slow but reliable. Letters to/from Europe generally take about a week to arrive; for further afield expect about two weeks. If you want to ensure that your mail gets through quickly, the Rapide Poste service guarantees to deliver anywhere in Europe within two working days (TD25), or within four working days to the Americas, Asia and Oceania (TD30). The service is available from all post offices. Posting your letter from a big city post office will ensure it arrives more quickly.

Parcels that weigh less than 2kg can be sent by ordinary mail. Larger parcels should be taken, unwrapped for inspection, to the special parcel counter. There you will be required to indicate clearly if you want to send something by surface mail.

SHOPPING
What to Buy
CHECHIAS

Chechias are the small, red felt hats worn by older Tunisian men. The *chechia* souq in Tunis (p69) is the obvious place to look for them. Quality varies, but an average price is around TD6.

COPPER & BRASS

Beaten copper and brass items are also popular and widely available. Beaten plates, which range in size from a saucer to a coffee table, make good souvenirs, although transporting the larger ones can be a problem.

ESPARTO GOODS

Rectangular, woven esparto baskets are practical and cheap. Some are pretty tacky, with pictures of camels and 'typical desert scenes' woven into them, but there are plenty of other more simple designs. Hats and fans are other popular choices. Most of the esparto items come from Gabès and Jerba in the south of the country. See the boxed text (p154) for more details.

JEWELLERY

Arabic jewellery (and particularly gold jewellery) is often too gaudy and ornate for Western tastes. The Hand of Fatima (daughter of the Prophet) or *khomsa* is a traditional Arabic motif used in many different forms and in varying sizes, from small earrings to large neck pendants, and is usually made of silver. In pre-Islamic times this same design represented Baal, the protector of the Carthaginians.

Other traditional pieces of jewellery include the *hedeyed*, which are finely engraved, wide bracelets made of gold or silver, and *kholkal*, which are similar, but worn around the ankle. In Carthaginian times *kholkal* were commonly worn to signify chastity; today they're still a symbol of fidelity and are often part of a bride's dowry.

The quality of pure silver and gold jewellery can be established by the official stamps used to grade all work. The quality of unstamped items is immediately suspect. The stamps in use are: the horse's head (the Carthaginian symbol for money and used to mark all 18-carat gold jewellery); the scorpion (all nine carat gold jewellery); grape clusters (silver graded at 900 mills per gram); and the Negro head (poorer-quality silver graded at 800 mills per gram).

LEATHER

Kairouan is the country's leading producer of leather goods, supplying the nation's souvenir shops with belts, wallets, purses and handbags embossed with camels and palm trees.

Other articles for sale include traditional pieces such as camel and donkey saddles, water skins and cartridge pouches.

In Douz and elsewhere in the south, you'll also come across comfortable sandals made from camel leather.

OILS & PERFUME
The Cap Bon Peninsula is famous for the production of essential oils, especially orange blossom and geranium. Most of the output goes to the international perfume market, but some is kept and used to make the cheap scented oils that are sold in tourist shops everywhere. Prices start at TD1.50for 5ml.

POTTERY & CERAMICS
Tunisia has long been associated with the art of pottery. The main centres of production are Nabeul (p105) and the town of Guellala (p247) on Jerba. The workshops in these places turn out a variety of styles from simple terracotta to elegant Andalusian-style vases and dinner settings.

The Berber villages around the small northern town of Sejnane (p122) are famous for a primitive style of pottery known as Sejnane ware, producing unusual moulded bowls and animal figures decorated with traditional motifs.

RUGS & CARPETS
These are among the most readily available souvenirs and, although they're not cheap, there are some really beautiful ones for sale. The main carpet-selling centres are Tunis, Kairouan, Tozeur and Jerba. For details on the various types of carpets available and official prices in these main centres, see p108 and the boxed text on p179.

In addition to those types of carpets available in Kairouan, *allouchas* are a type of thick-pile Berber woven rug, spun by hand in wool. They feature natural tones and are decorated with simple traditional Berber motifs. Look for them in Ain Draham, where they are produced by a small women's cooperative called Les Tapis de Kroumirie. (See the boxed text on p129 for more details.) They are also sold in Tunis at Main des Femmes, above the Banque de l'Habitat in Ave Habib Bourguiba.

All these types of carpets are sold at the government-run Socopa emporiums (see this page for details) found in all the major tourist centres. They have been inspected by the Organisation National de l'Artisanat

(ONAT) and classified according to type and number of knots. They come with an affixed label giving this information.

SAND ROSES
Sand roses are the specialty of southern Tunisia, although they're sold all over the country. They are formed of gypsum, which has dissolved from the sand and then crystallised into spectacular patterns that resemble flower petals.

They range from about 5cm in diameter up to the size of a large watermelon. They do make good cheap souvenirs, but carting around a great chunk of gypsum for weeks on end isn't much fun.

SHEESHAS
The ubiquitous water pipes come in all shapes and sizes and are readily available from souqs and tourist shops. They range in price from around TD4 for a small, cheap one up to TD70 for a good quality, full-size version.

Where to Shop
You'll find that all the items previously listed are available from souvenir shops everywhere in the country.

The problem is finding the right price. The tourist shops in the big medinas are the worst place to start, especially if you have no idea what you should be paying. First prices are sometimes 10 times higher than the real price.

The best place to start is at one of the government-run Société de Commercialisation des Produits de l'Artisanats (Socopa) emporiums found in all the major tourist centres. Expert bargainers may be able to find cheaper prices elsewhere, but not the guarantee of quality that Socopa provides. Sales staff in these shops are paid to assist shoppers, not to apply hard-sell techniques. Even if you don't buy, it's a good idea to visit a Socopa shop just to see what constitutes a reasonable price before heading to the medina.

If you do opt to shop in the medina, be careful – many a TD100 carpet has been sold for TD500 on the (considerable) strength of a complimentary cup of mint tea.

MARKETS
Town and village life often revolves around the weekly markets. Market day is a good

MARKET DAYS

Day	Location
Monday	Ain Draham, El-Jem, Houmt Souq, Kairouan, Kélibia, Matmata and Tataouine
Tuesday	Ghardimao, Kasserine and Kebili
Wednesday	Gafsa, Jendouba and Sbeitla
Thursday	Douz, Hammamet, Le Kef, Nefta, Remla (Kerkennah), Sejnane and Tebersouk
Friday	El-Haouaria, Mahdia, Nabeul, Sfax, Tabarka, Tamerza, Zaghouan
Saturday	Ben Guerdane, El-Fahs, Gabès and Monastir
Sunday	Hammam Lif, Le Kef

day to be in a town as it will be far more lively than usual with traders and shoppers from all around the region.

Some markets have become real tourist traps; nevertheless, it is on market days that there is the best selection of stuff for sale from quality handicrafts to fairly mundane household goods. For the dates of the main market days in Tunisia's main towns, see the boxed text above.

BARGAINING
Handicrafts are about the only items you'll have to bargain for in Tunisia. To be good at bargaining, you need to enjoy the banter. Once you get the hang of it, it can be a lot of fun, and a lot better for your wallet. If you don't like bargaining, you're better off buying your souvenirs from the Socopa stores (see p263 for details).

SOLO TRAVELLERS
Travelling around Tunisia on your own should present few problems, although it's clearly easier for men than for women (see p266).

Prices for single rooms are rarely half the price of a double so it's obviously cheaper if you hook up with other solo travellers and share a room.

The most difficult aspect of travelling alone presents itself when you want to rent a taxi for the day in places like Tataouine (p208) and Jerba (p237), or a 4WD in Tozeur (p229) or Douz (p221), to explore the surrounding sites that are not accessible by public transport. Sharing a taxi reduces costs considerably (the price quoted by taxi drivers is for the taxi, regardless of the number of people), while 4WD tours or expeditions are so prohibitive (around TD250 per 4WD per day) that the only

option is to wait until enough people turn up wanting to take the same trip. This can involve a few days of waiting around, particularly during the low season; always ask around a number of agencies to increase your chances.

Unless you're on one of the private hotel beaches, travelling alone means having no-one to watch your belongings on the beach while you go for a swim – petty theft can be a problem on some of the busier public beaches, so leave any valuables locked up in your hotel.

Solo travellers will encounter a lot of incomprehension and curiosity as it's quite rare for Tunisians to travel without a friend. This is especially the case for women.

TELEPHONE & FAX
The telephone system is fairly modern and easy to operate. Few people have a phone at home, so there are lots of public telephones, known as Taxiphones. They accept 100-millime, 500-millime and one-dinar coins. An attempt to introduce cardphones appears to have fizzled out.

See the inside front cover, as well as the relevant city or town sections, for a list of local telephone codes.

Fax
Almost every classified hotel has a fax machine. It costs less to use the public facilities available at the telephone offices and some post offices in major towns. Telegrams can be sent from any post office.

International Calls
All public telephones can be used for international direct dialling. Some places advertise themselves as International Taxiphones; all it means is that the meters ac-

cept only 500-millime and one-dinar coins. International codes and charges per minute are listed in the table below. Rates are 10% cheaper between 8pm and 6am.

Country	Code	Cost
Algeria	☎ 213	TD0.7
Australia	☎ 61	TD1.2
France	☎ 33	TD1.1
Germany	☎ 49	TD1.1
Italy	☎ 39	TD1.1
Morocco	☎ 212	TD0.7
New Zealand	☎ 64	TD1.2
UK	☎ 44	TD1.1
USA/Canada	☎ 011	TD2

Local Calls
Local calls cost 100 mills for two minutes, so you'll need a few to have a conversation.

Taxiphone offices keep a copy of the recently updated national telephone directory, published in both Arabic and French, and have information on international area codes and charges.

Mobile Phones
Mobile phones of most European carriers function in Tunisia, although it's a bit more hit-and-miss with North American and Australian mobile companies. Contact your phone company before setting out to check that they have reciprocal arrangements with a Tunisian company and to make sure you don't have to activate a global roaming facility. Coverage is almost universal throughout the country, save for more remote desert locations such as Ksar Ghilane. At the time of writing, it was not possible to get a local mobile card without paying for an expensive contract with a local company (around TD100); ask at any mobile-phone store.

TIME
Tunisia is one hour ahead of GMT/UTC from October to April, and two hours ahead of GMT/UTC from May to September. That means that when it's noon in Tunisia in July, the time elsewhere is:
- Cairo – 1pm
- London – 2pm
- Paris – 1pm
- New York – 7am
- Sydney – 9pm

TOILETS
You will still come across the occasional squat toilet, but most places frequented by tourists have Western-style, sit-down toilets – as do most modern Tunisian homes.

Public toilets are almost unheard of, except in places like airports and major bus and train stations. If you're caught short, the best bet is to go to a café, but you'll be expected to buy something for the privilege of using their facilities, unless it's really busy and they don't notice.

TOURIST INFORMATION
The government-run **Office National du Tourisme Tunisien** (ONTT; www.tourismtunisia.com) handles tourist information. The standard of service from tourist offices inside Tunisia varies from efficient to friendly-but-of-little-use, all the way down to totally apathetic. Most can supply no more than glossy brochures in half a dozen languages and a map. Some can supply a list of hotels and prices, and one or two have transport information.

Many towns also have municipal tourist offices, called *syndicats d'initiative*, which tend to open only in the high season.

For details of the various tourist offices around the country, see the relevant city and town entries throughout the book.

The ONTT's foreign representatives tend to be much better equipped, and more enthusiastic, than their domestic counterparts. See www.tourismtunisia.com/adresses/international.html for a full listing of overseas addresses, which include the following:

Belgium Brussels (☎ 2-511 11 42; tourismetunisien@skynet.be; Galerie Ravenstein 60, 1000)
Canada Montreal (☎ 514-397 1182; tunisinfo@qc.aira.com; 1253 McGill College, Quebec H3 B2 Y5)
France Paris (☎ 01 47 42 72 67; ontt@wanadoo.fr; 32, Ave de l'Opéra, 75002); Lyon (☎ 04 78 52 35 86; 12, rue de Séze, 69006)
Germany Berlin (☎ 30-885 0457; Kurfuerstendamm 171, 10707); Düsseldorf (☎ 211-880 0644; Flingerstrasse 66 23, 40213); Frankfurt am Main (☎ 69- 297 0640); Munich (☎ 29-16 36 85; Burgerstrasse 12, 80331)
Italy Rome (☎ 06-42 01 01 49; Via Calabria 25, 00187); Milan (☎ 02-86 45 30-44; Via Baracchini 10, 20123)
Netherlands Amsterdam (☎ 20-622 4971; info@worldonline.nl; Muntplein 2111, 1012 WR)
Spain Madrid (☎ 91 548 14 35; tunezturismo@mad.servicom.es; Plaza de Espana 18, Torre de Madrid, 28008)

UK London (☎ 020-7224 5598; tntolondon@aol.com; 77A Wigmore St, W1H 9LJ)
USA Washington DC (☎ 202-862 18 50; ezzedine@ix.net com.com; 1515 Massachussets Ave, 20005)

VISAS

Visas are not a problem for most visitors to Tunisia. Nationals of most Western European countries can stay up to three months without a visa – you just collect a stamp in your passport at the point of entry. Americans, Canadians, Germans and Japanese can stay for up to four months.

Australians and South Africans can get a three-month visa at the airport for TD3. There's a separate counter for visas so don't join the queue for an entry stamp until you've been to the visa desk. At most entry points, you'll need to leave your passport at the visa counter and talk your way through immigration and customs (without your passport) to reach a bank to change money and all the way back through to pay the visa fee and collect your passport. It's usually easy enough but can take a while.

Other nationalities need to apply before they arrive; the visa costs around US$6.50 or 6 euros, takes three to four weeks in person or six weeks via post, and the length of stay is up to the embassy.

Israeli nationals are not allowed into Tunisia.

Visa Extensions

Extending a visa is a process to be avoided. Applications can be made only at the Interior Ministry on Ave Habib Bourguiba in Tunis. They cost TD1.5 to TD10 (payable only in 'timbres fiscales', revenue stamps available from post offices) and take up to 10 days to issue. You'll need two photos, and may need bank receipts and a *facture* (receipt) from your hotel, for starters.

Visas for Onward Travel

The Algerian and Libyan embassies in Tunis do not issue visas. If you want to visit either of these countries from Tunisia, you should apply to the Algerian or Libyan embassy/consulate in your home country. Australians and New Zealanders can apply in London. Don't leave it until the last minute – it can be a lengthy process.

WOMEN TRAVELLERS
What to Expect

Prior to marriage, Tunisian men have little opportunity to hang out with women, and the expense of getting married means that, for many, this mixing of the sexes is delayed frustratingly further. Foreign women exist outside the social structure, and hence are seen as an entirely separate species, tantalisingly related to the free-and-easy types that may be spotted on satellite TV or in foreign films.

Sexual harassment is par for the course (though nothing like in Egypt) and the tidal waves of testosterone that you encounter in some places can be a bit intimidating. Harassment usually takes the form of being stared at or subjected to slimy chat-up strategies. Don't be surprised to receive proposals of marriage and declarations of undying love (or considerably less noble suggestions). Physical harassment is very rare; it may happen in a crowded medina, but it's unlikely to occur elsewhere.

Among those women who wrote to us were the following two alternative perspectives:

As a 19-year-old white, blonde-haired female, I was harassed constantly. School children followed me around the museum in Sousse, men grabbed my hair and tried to grope me, and I was always shouted at. All of this harassment was in spite of the fact that I dressed extremely conservatively. I feel that this is in part due to the fact that I was travelling with my mother, without a male present. You should advise young, fair-skinned women to travel with a male or not go at all.

Jennifer Sudick

We quickly learnt to be on our guards. Although Tunisians are a very friendly bunch and most will bend over backwards to please you, at times the stares, calls and propositions were overwhelming and discouraging. However, that said, we never felt in danger and learnt that a firm 'no' or simply walking away was all that was needed. We were disappointed not to be able to communicate more with the local women (at times, we weren't even sure if they existed) and we wish that

we had a better overall understanding of women in an Islamic culture… Our two weeks in Tunisia have been fantastic. The amazing things we've seen, tasted, heard, and experienced definitely outweigh any negatives. A country not to be missed.
Ruth Gould & Monique Menard, Australia

The country's beach resorts are the territory of Casanovas, who spend their summers attempting to charm their way into the bedrooms of female tourists. Some foreign women do have holiday romances with local men and the mythology arising from these encounters fuels the expectations of many a local man. If you do decide to take things further, follow safe-sex practices at all times (see p282).

Strategies

You can try a few strategies to reduce your hassle quota.

Most Tunisian men will be befriending you with one intention in mind, but this doesn't mean that you must ignore every man. Most of the men are just trying their luck and are harmless and genuinely friendly. The simple and obvious rule is to be careful. If you get a bad vibe then get away. If you don't want to chat, don't be afraid of ignoring people or telling them that you're busy (or on your way to meeting a friend). The best way to respond is in good humour as most men will immediately leave you alone if you ask them too.

The best policy is to ignore sexist remarks and sound effects, and sunglasses are a good way of avoiding eye contact. It's advisable to sit next to other women on buses and louages, sit in the back seat of taxis, and avoid staying in cheap medina hotels. If someone does touch you, '*harem alek*' (Arabic for 'shame on you') is a useful phrase.

Dressing modestly – cover your shoulders, upper arms and legs, and a headscarf can be useful to indicate modesty – can make a difference and you'll gain more respect by doing so, especially in rural areas. That said, dressing conservatively doesn't mean that you won't be hassled. What local women are wearing is also a reasonable guide to prevailing attitudes wherever you are – you can get away with a lot more in Hammamet, Sousse and Jerba than in the villages of the interior.

A wedding ring might be a deterrent, as may photos of your husband and children, either real or borrowed.

Transport

CONTENTS

THINGS CHANGE...

The information in this chapter is particularly vulnerable to change. Check directly with the airline or a travel agent to make sure you understand how a fare (and ticket you may buy) works and be aware of the security requirements for international travel. Shop carefully. The details given in this chapter should be regarded as pointers and are not a substitute for your own careful, up-to-date research.

GETTING THERE & AWAY

ENTERING THE COUNTRY

Most of the bureaucratic obstacles to entering the country have been stripped away. Arriving by air is by far the easiest entry, with immigration and customs completed with a minimum of fuss. It takes longer for those who have to apply for a visa on arrival (see p266 for details), but is still relatively easy. On board your flight to Tunisia, you should be given an arrivals card (keep the departures section until you leave the country as it will be stamped on arrival) which asks for all of the usual passport details; on the 'Address in Tunisia' section, simply choose any hotel from this book.

Those arriving by sea with a car can expect a tedious three- to four-hour wait as bags and vehicles will be searched thoroughly. If the boat is running late, that can mean being released into the deserted streets of Tunisia in the wee hours of the night.

Land borders with Algeria and Libya are not really an option as most are closed to foreigners, with the exception of Ras al-Jedir in Libya; expect long queues of vehicles.

Passport

Tunisian immigration officers (and embassy officials) will take a dim view of Israeli stamps or any evidence that you have visited Israel, and you won't be allowed in if your passport bears such evidence. Israeli passport holders are not allowed into the country. For more details on visa requirements see p266.

AIR
Airports & Airlines

There are six airports handling international traffic in Tunisia:

7 Novembre-Tabarka (TBJ; ☎ 78-644 100)
Jerba-Zarzis (DJE; ☎ 75-650 233)
Monastir-Habib Bourguiba (MIR; ☎ 73-460 300)
Sfax-Thyna (SFA; ☎ 74-241 740)
Tozeur-Nefta (TOE; ☎ 76-450 342)
Tunis-Carthage (TUN; ☎ 71-755 000)

The national carrier is **Tunis Air** (☎ 71-330 100, www.tunisair.com.tn; 48 ave Habib Bourguiba, Tunis). It has offices throughout the country and an excellent safety record (see www.airsafetyonline.com/safetycenter/reportcard.shtml for details).

Other airlines flying to and from Tunisia are:
Aeroflot (☎ 71-845 831; www.aeroflot.org/; 42 ave Hedi Chaker, Tunis) Hub: Moscow
Air Belgium International (Sobelair; www.air-belgium.be/index.htm) Hub: Brussels

Air Berlin (www.airberlin.com) Hub: Berlin
Air Europa (www.air-europa.com) Hub: Mallorca
Air France (☎ 71-355 422; www.airfrance.com; 1 rue d'Athènes, Tunis) Hub: Paris
Air Holland (www.airholland.nl) Hub: Amsterdam
Air Malta (☎ 71-703 299; www.airmalta.com; Complexe Ariana Centre, Ariana) Hub: Valletta
Alitalia (☎ 71-331 377; www.alitalia.com; 17 ave Habib Thameur) Hub: Rome
British Airways (☎ 71-330 046; www.british-airways.com; 17 ave Habib Bourguiba, Tunis) Hub: London
EgyptAir (☎ 71-341 182; www.egyptair.com.eg/docs/home.asp; 49 ave Habib Bourguiba, Tunis) Hub: Cairo
Eurofly (www.eurofly.it) Hub: Milan
GB Airways (www.gbairways.com) Hub: London
Iberia (☎ 71-840 238; www.iberia.com) Hub: Madrid
Interflug (www.interflug.de) Hub: Frankfurt
Lufthansa Airlines (☎ 71-941 344; www.lufthansa.com; ave Ouled Haffouz, Tunis) Hub: Frankfurt
Luxair (www.luxair.lu/en) Hub: Luxemburg
Nouvelair (☎ 73-520 600; www.nouvelair.com) Hub: Monastir
Royal Air Maroc (☎ 71-351 377; www.royalairmaroc.com; 16 ave Habib Bourguiba, Tunis) Hub: Casablanca
Royal Jordanian (www.rja.com.jo) Hub: Amman
Turkish Airlines (☎ 71-787 033; www.turkishairlines.com; ave Ouled Hafouz, Tunis) Hub: Istanbul

Tickets

If you're looking for bargain air fares, go to a travel agency rather than directly to the airline, which generally only sells fares at the official listed price. One exception to this rule is the expanding number of 'no-frills' carriers operating in the USA and northwest Europe, which sell direct to travellers (many of them sell tickets over the Internet).

Some reliable online flight-booking sites include:

- www.airnet.co.uk
- www.cheapflights.co.uk
- www.ebookers.co.uk
- www.lastminute.com
- www.opodo.com
- www.travelocity.co.uk

However, online super-fast fare generators are no substitute for a travel agency that knows all about special deals and can offer advice on other aspects of your trip.

Tickets to Tunisia are also invariably cheaper if you buy some sort of flight-and-accommodation package through a travel agency.

From Africa & the Middle East

EgyptAir and Tunis Air both operate between Cairo and Tunis (from TD400), while Royal Air Maroc and Tunis Air share the route between Tunis and Casablanca (from around TD350). Royal Jordanian Airlines also connects Tunis with Amman which has good connections throughout the Middle East.

Recommended agencies in the region include:

Al-Rais Travels (www.alrais.com; Dubai)
Egypt Panorama Tours (☎ 2-359 0200; www.eptours.com; Cairo)
Orion-Tour (www.oriontour.com; Istanbul)

Tunisia is not well connected with sub-Saharan Africa and you'll need to change in Cairo or Casablanca.

From Australia & New Zealand

There are no direct flights between Australia or New Zealand and Tunisia. The easiest option is to first travel to Europe with one of the major European airlines with good connections to Tunisia, and then fly to Tunis as a side trip. Possibile airlines include Alitalia, Air France and Lufthansa, which often have good deals using Singapore Airlines, Qantas or Thai Airways International between Australia and Southeast Asia.

STA Travel (☎ 1300 733 035; www.statravel.com.au) and **Flight Centre** (☎ 133 133; www.flightcentre.com.au) are both good places to check on ticket prices. Both agencies have offices throughout Australia; call or visit the websites for office locations. For online bookings, try www.travel.com.au.

In New Zealand, both **Flight Centre** (☎ 0800 243 544; www.flightcentre.co.nz) and **STA Travel** (☎ 0508 782 872; www.statravel.co.nz) have branches throughout the country. The site www.travel.co.nz is recommended for online bookings.

From Canada

There are no direct flights to or from Canada to Tunisia. You can either use one of the major European airlines and take a connecting flight to Tunis, or fly to Europe as cheaply as possible and then shop around.

Travel Cuts (☎ 800-667-2887; www.travelcuts.com) is Canada's national student travel agency.

For online bookings try www.expedia.ca and www.travelocity.ca.

From Continental Europe

Just about any European travel agency that's worth its salt can drum up a cheap airfare-and-accommodation package to Tunisia. Expect to be paying at least 350 euros for a simple return flight in the high season. Charter flights are much cheaper; you may get tickets for as little as 250 euros in the high season for a return flight plus an extra 100 to 150 euros for seven nights' accommodation, although the deals vary widely.

FRANCE

Not surprisingly, France has better flight connections to Tunisia than anywhere else in Europe. Air France and Tunis Air between them have regular flights to Tunis, Sfax and Tozeur from Paris, Lyon, Marseille, Nice and Bordeaux.

Recommended agencies include:

Anyway (☎ 0892 893 892; www.anyway.fr)

Lastminute (☎ 0892 705 000; www.lastminute.fr)

Nouvelles Frontières (☎ 0825 000 747; www.nouvelles-frontieres.fr)

OTU Voyages (www.otu.fr) This agency specialises in student and youth travellers.

Voyageurs du Monde (☎ 01 40 15 11 15; www.vdm.com)

GERMANY

Recommended agencies include:

Expedia (www.expedia.de)

Just Travel (☎ 089 747 3330; www.justtravel.de)

Lastminute (☎ 01805 284 366; www.lastminute.de)

STA Travel (☎ 01805 456 422; www.statravel.de) For travellers under the age of 26.

ITALY

One recommended agency is **CTS Viaggi** (☎ 06 462 0431; www.cts.it), specialising in student and youth travel.

THE NETHERLANDS

One recommended agency is **Airfair** (☎ 020 620 5121; www.airfair.nl).

SPAIN

Recommended agencies include **Barcelo Viajes** (☎ 90 211 6226; www.barceloviajes.com) and **Nouvelles Frontières** (☎ 90 217 0979). Air Europa flies directly from Madrid to Tunis.

From the UK

GB Airways (a subsidiary of British Airways) and Tunis Air both operate scheduled flights from London to Tunis, although London is a good place to pick up cheap deals with other airlines. Expect to pay from around UK£240/275 for a low-/high-season fare, although high-season fares can sell for as low as UK£180.

Charter flights offer a much wider choice of departure points, and most tickets are for a two-week stay. The Office National du Tourisme Tunisien (ONTT; see p265 for details) has a list of operators.

Discount air travel is big business in London. Advertisements for travel agencies appear in the travel pages of the weekend broadsheet newspapers, in *Time Out*, the *Evening Standard* and *TNT*.

Recommended travel agencies include the following:

Bridge the World (☎ 0870 444 7474; www.b-t-w.co.uk)

Flight Centre (☎ 0870 890 8099; www.flightcentre.co.uk)

Flightbookers (☎ 0870 010 7000; www.ebookers.com)

North-South Travel (☎ 01245 608 291; www.northsouthtravel.co.uk) North-South Travel donates part of its profit to projects in the developing world.

Quest Travel (☎ 0870 442 3542; www.questtravel.com)

STA Travel (☎ 0870 160 0599; www.statravel.co.uk) For travellers under the age of 26.

Trailfinders (www.trailfinders.co.uk)

Travel Bag (☎ 0870 890 1456; www.travelbag.co.uk)

From the USA

New York has both the cheapest airfares and the largest choice of airlines. The cheapest option is to buy a discount ticket to Europe and then to shop around, but there's not much point in doing this unless you want to spend a few days hanging around. London is the best place to head for.

Discount travel agents in the USA are known as consolidators. San Francisco is the ticket consolidator capital of America, although some good deals can be found in Los Angeles, New York and other big cities.

The following agencies are recommended for online bookings:

- www.cheaptickets.com
- www.expedia.com
- www.itn.net
- www.lowestfare.com
- www.orbitz.com
- www.sta.com (travellers under 26)
- www.travelocity.com

LAND
Border Crossings
The only land border crossing open to foreigners is between Tunisia and Libya at Ras al-Jedir. All other crossings from Tunisia to Libya or Algeria were closed to foreigners at the time of research.

Car & Motorcycle
Crossing by ferry from Italy or France is a popular option. If you're arriving by sea (see this page) you could end up entering Tunisia in the middle of the night when few petrol stations are open – don't arrive with an empty tank.

Drivers of cars and riders of motorcycles will need the vehicle's registration papers, liability insurance and a driver's licence (preferably an international drivers' permit in addition to their domestic licence, although usually the latter is sufficient). There's no need for a *carnet de passage en douane* (which is effectively a passport for the vehicle and acts as a temporary waiver of import duty). Contact your local automobile association for up-to-date details about the documentation required. See p274 for information about driving in Tunisia.

From Algeria
Algeria has been effectively out of bounds to travellers since the start of the civil war in early 1993. The conflict has forced the cancellation of all bus and train services between the two countries.

Louages (shared taxis) are the only form of public transport still operating between the two countries. They operate from place Sidi Bou Mendil in the Tunis medina to Annaba (TD22) and Constantine (TD30).

From Libya
The only crossing point open to foreigners is at Ras al-Jedir, 33km east of Ben Guerdane. For a tourist, the main obstacle is obtaining a visa. It's difficult for an individual to get a visa; the best approach is to use a tour company specialising in trips to Libya.

There are daily buses to Tripoli from the southern bus station in Tunis. The trip costs TD29.6 and takes up to 16 hours. There are also daily services from Sfax (TD17.8, 10 to 12 hours).

Louages are faster and more convenient than the buses. There are regular services to

Tripoli via Ras al-Jedir from many Tunisian towns, including Tunis, Sfax, Gabès, Medenine, Houmt Souq and Ben Guerdane. The louages that work these routes are yellow with a white stripe.

SEA
There are year-round ferry connections between Tunis and Italy or France. The ferries are heavily booked in summer, so book well in advance.

Shipping agents and ferry companies which operate on these routes include:

Compagnie Tunisienne de Navigation (CTN; www.ctn.com.tn/index.html) Tunis (Map pp70-2; ☎ 71-322 802; fax 354 855; 122 rue de Yougoslavie); Marseille (☎ 04 91 56 32 00; fax 04 91 56 36 36; 61 blvd des Dames)
Linee Lauro (www.viamare.com)Tunis (Map pp70-2; ☎ 71-347 015; fax 330 902; carthage.tours@gnet.tn; Carthage Tours, 59 ave Habib Bourguiba); La Spezia (☎ 0187-507 031; fax 509 255; Ufficio Imbarco, Molo 48); Naples (☎ 081-551 3352; fax 552 4329; prenotazioni@lauro.it; Piazza Municipio 88); Trapani (☎ /fax 0923-24073; Ufficio Imbarco, Statione Marittima)
SNCM Tunis (Map pp70-2; ☎ 71-338 222; www.sncm.fr; 47 ave Farhat Hached)
Tirrenia Navigazione (www.tirrenia.it) Trapani (☎ 0923-21896; Salvo Viaggi, Corso Italia 48); Genoa (☎ 010-275 8041; fax 269 82 55; Stazione Marittima Ponte Colombo); Tunis (Map pp70-2; Carthage Tours; ☎ 344 066; 59 ave Habib Bourguiba)
Viamare Travel London (☎ 020-7431 4560, www.viamare.com; Graphic House, 2 Sumatra Rd, London NW6 1PU)

From Italy
Throughout the year, ferries run between Tunis and the Italian ports of Genoa, Naples and Trapani (in Sicily) with summer (July to September) services to and from La Spezia. Viamare Travel has a full listing of services and fares.

GENOA–TUNIS
The route between Tunis and the northern Italian port of Genoa is operated by CTN. The frequency of services ranges from four a month in winter to one every couple of days in July and August. The trip costs around 110 euros one way and takes between 22 and 24 hours.

LA SPEZIA–TUNIS
Linee Lauro runs a weekly service between Tunis and La Spezia, about 100km

southeast of Genoa. One-way passenger fares start from 90/130 euros in low/high season up to 135/175 euros for the most comfortable cabin. Small cars cost from 170/230 euros and the journey can take 24 to 29 hours.

NAPLES–TUNIS
Linee Lauro operates nine boats a week on this route in July and August, and at least one a week at other times. Passenger fares for low/high season start from 80/120 euros, while cars start from around 150/200 euros. The trip takes 17 hours.

TRAPANI–TUNIS
Both Linee Lauro and Tirrenia Navigazione operate between Trapani and Tunis. Both companies sail at least once a week, although the day varies. The trip for passengers costs from 40/60 euros in low/high season and around 90/110 euros for a small car. The trip lasts 10 hours.

From France
CTN and the French company SNCM operate ferries year round between Marseille and Tunis. Between them there are at least two ferries a week, even in the middle of winter. There are sailings almost every day between late June and the middle of November. The trip costs around 150 euros one way and takes 24 hours. For small vehicles it costs about 300 euros one way.

SNCM also operates a weekly service from Bastia, on the island of Corsica, between late May and mid-September.

GETTING AROUND

Tunisia has a well-developed transport network which includes buses, louages (shared taxis), trains and ferries. Just about every town of any consequence has daily connections with Tunis.

AIR
Tunisia's domestic air network is fairly limited.

Domestic flights are operated by Tunis Air subsidiary Tuninter (UG) which, like its parent company, has a good safety record. Tuninter can be contacted through any Tunis Air office.

There are flights between Tunis and Gafsa (one way TD50), Jerba (up to four daily in summer; TD65), Sfax (TD50) and Tozeur (TD56). There are no domestic flights to either Monastir or Tabarka.

BICYCLE
Tunisia is developing a good reputation as a destination for cycling fans. The road network is extensive and well maintained and most of the country's roads are flat, although it's too hot in summer and can get very cold in winter in the north. For the rest of the year conditions are ideal. It's also possible to put a bike on the train if you want to skip a long stretch or get yourself back to Tunis. All louages are equipped with roof racks and can also carry bikes.

The downside of riding a bike in Tunisia is that you share the road with what can be heavy traffic on some of the coastal routes. Most Tunisian drivers aren't accustomed to driving alongside cyclists (some barely manage to avoid larger vehicles). Bicycle lanes are nonexistent and most roads are two-lane stretches of tarmac with little evidence of a road shoulder.

If you want a decent touring bike, you should bring your own; check with the airline before buying your ticket to see if you can check your bicycle in as checked baggage.

One note of caution: before you leave home, go over your bike with a fine-toothed comb and fill your repair kit with every imaginable spare as you won't necessarily be able to buy spares for your machine if it breaks down in the middle of nowhere.

Hire
There are a few places that rent bicycles and it can be a great way to explore a town, especially if it's spread over a large distance. This is particularly the case with the massive palmeraies (palm groves) in the far south of the country. Most charge between TD2.5 and TD4 per hour, but you can usually negotiate cheaper day or half-day rates. Never take the first bike offered to you – instead check through the bikes to find the best one, and make sure that the brakes work.

BOAT
There are two regular scheduled ferry services in Tunisia. The first connects Sfax with the Kerkennah Islands (see p192), about

TOP 10 TIPS FOR GETTING AROUND TUNISIA

Travelling around Tunisia is generally hassle-free, but there are some things you can do to avoid getting stranded or getting out at the other end with no circulation, and to show the locals that you're as savvy as they are:

- A 1st-class train ticket on a popular route in summer doesn't mean you have a reserved seat; first-class carriages have quotas for standing passengers so get there early and fight for your (or any) seat.
- Always check whether the bus you're waiting for originates elsewhere; if so, chances are it will be full when it arrives.
- In the old louages (Peugeot station wagons), avoid the back seats unless you're under five feet tall.
- In the new louages (eight-seater 'people-mover' vans), avoid the middle front seat where the combination of dashboard, radio and gearstick can play havoc with knees.
- In the new louages, don't choose a back seat until you've seen how much luggage will be piled in behind you; suitcases have been known to considerably diminish head space.
- Don't expect louages to run after 7pm.
- If the sun is sinking low, always consider paying for the last louage seat(s) or sharing the cost with other passengers; it's better than not leaving at all or arriving late at night.
- If you want to see the El-Jem colosseum at sunset, see the boxed text on p182.
- Expect touts hawking camel treks to accost you somewhere between the louage station and your hotel when you arrive in Douz – there's no way to avoid them, but you're better off not taking the first offer; be polite but firm.
- Don't ask the Mahdia tourist office staff for the location of the town's bus station.

25km off the coast. In summer, there are up to 11 crossings daily, dropping to four in winter.

The second service runs from Jorf on the mainland to Ajim on the island of Jerba (p240) throughout the day and night.

BUS

The national and regional bus companies normally operate from a communal bus station (ask for the *gare routière*) although there are exceptions (eg Tabarka and Tataouine).

Buses are definitely the way to travel if you're on a longer journey and you manage to board the bus at its point of origin, as they leave at set times (unlike louages which leave when full).

National Buses

The national bus company, the Société Nationale du Transport Rural et Interurbain (referred to as SNTRI and pronounced 'sintry'), operates daily air-conditioned buses from Tunis to just about every town in the country. The frequency of services ranges from one bus a day (small towns) to 10 a day to major cities (like Sousse and Sfax). The green-and-white buses run pretty much to schedule, and they're fast, comfortable and not too expensive.

In summer, many of the long-distance departures are at night to avoid the heat of the day, which means you don't get to see any of the country you're travelling through. Booking ahead is usually recommended.

Regional Buses

In addition to the national company there are regional bus companies operating services within a particular region and to nearby cities outside the region.

These buses are reliable enough, but most have seen better days; they're also slow and are never air-conditioned. Coverage of routes is good; in some cases, they're the only form of transport to smaller towns. The only way to be sure of bus schedules is to go to the bus station and ask. Some larger towns are served by two or three regional companies.

Costs

Buses are usually slightly more expensive than louages, but it's definitely worth it for the comfort on long-haul travel. Sample long-distance fares from Tunis include Jerba (TD23), Sfax (TD11.8) and Tozeur (TD18.9).

Reservations

Almost every bus station has an SNTRI booking office where reservations can be made. Regional companies maintain similar windows but they often open only an hour or so before departure, so advance reservations can be difficult.

CAMIONNETTE

Camionnettes (pick-ups) go where buses and louages fear to tread. There aren't many of them and they make few pretensions to comfort, but they're indispensable if you want to get to some of the out-of-the-way places in the south (especially around Tataouine). Try to establish what the locals are paying before you pay and remember that they don't operate much beyond mid-afternoon.

CAR & MOTORCYCLE
Automobile Associations

The **Touring Club de Tunisie** (☎ 71-323 114; fax 324 834; 15 rue d'Allemagne, Tunis 1000) has reciprocal arrangements with many European automobile clubs, including the UK's Automobile Association. If your car conks out, they can direct you to an affiliated breakdown service.

Bring Your Own Vehicle

For an explanation of the documents required if you're bringing your car into Tunisia, see p271.

Driving Licence

National driving licences are sufficient for driving (or hiring a car) in Tunisia, but international driving permits are also acceptable and recommended if you come from a country outside Western Europe.

Fuel & Spare Parts

Fuel is inexpensive by European standards and prices are the same everywhere: 430 mills per litre for diesel, 730 mills per litre for super (high octane), 690 mills per litre for regular (low octane) and 710 mills per litre for two-stroke mix. Unleaded fuel (760 mills per litre) is still something of a rarity outside the major towns.

Spare parts are generally available in Tunisia for most well-known European cars (especially French ones), but that really only applies in larger towns; get your car comprehensively serviced before leaving your home country.

If you're bringing your own motorcycle, make sure you carry some basic spare parts. These are virtually impossible to find within the country; few people in Tunisia own motorcycles.

Hire
CAR

Hire cars can be a great way to see more of the country at your own pace, but they're so expensive that they're not a realistic option unless you're travelling in a small group.

Typical rental charges by international car-rental agencies for the smallest cars (eg Fiat Uno) start at about TD45 per day plus 250 mills per kilometre or TD54 per day for unlimited kilometres and a minimum of seven days. On top of these rates you'll have to pay 18% tax, insurance for at least TD8 per day, contract fees etc. Medium-sized cars (Renault Clio or VW Polo) cost about TD65 per day plus 350 mills per kilometre, or TD450 per week with unlimited kilometres.

You'll find the best deals at local companies, which have more scope for negotiation. In winter, it should be possible to find someone willing to hire a Renault Clio for less than TD350 per week. Tunis, Sfax and Houmt Souq (on Jerba) are the best places to look for bargains.

A deposit of roughly the equivalent of the rental is required (unless you're paying by credit card). Rental companies require that drivers be aged over 21 and hold a driving licence that has been valid for at least a year.

When you hire the car, make sure that an accident report form has been included with the car's papers; in the event of an accident, both parties involved must complete the form. If the form is not completed, you may be liable for the costs, regardless of whether you have paid for insurance or not.

WITH A SMILE AND A WAVE

All along Tunisia's roads you'll come across policemen keeping watch over the nation's safety. While that may be reassuring, not all Tunisians see it that way. Anyone who has spent any time in a louage will know the ritual well.

As the driver approaches the intersection or police checkpoint, or an area where his local knowledge tells him that there may be one, he slows the car almost to walking speed, puts on his seat belt and asks front-seat passengers to do the same. At a snail's pace, he draws near, pretending not to look at the police, yet unable to take his eyes off them. When he catches their eye and receives the shrug indicating permission to pass, the driver smiles innocently and waves genially in the direction of the men in uniform, all the while muttering dark curses about scorpions under his breath.

As a driver in Tunisia, you'd be well advised to follow the same procedure (except that you should wear your seatbelt at all times), although before you curse the police, remember that your status as a foreigner almost always guarantees you unimpeded passage.

MOTORCYCLE

A few places rent scooters or mopeds for which no licence or insurance is required, although for a machine of more than 50cc you need to be over 21 and to have held a valid motorcycle licence for more than one year.

Insurance

If you have insurance with a European company, ask them before setting out for a 'Green Card' extension to your home insurance cover; this will provide third-party cover in both Tunisia and Morocco. If you haven't done this before leaving home, ask for insurance forms from the customs police (who may or may not have them).

Road Conditions

Tunisia has an excellent road network. All but the most minor roads are tar sealed and well maintained. Potholes are more common in the south but even there they're quite rare. Many of the roads that are marked as unsealed on maps have now been sealed, particularly in the south where the army has heavily involved itself in the road-building effort. Of the unsealed roads in the south, most are graded regularly and can usually be negotiated easily enough with a conventional 2WD vehicle (see the regional chapters for more details).

There is only one *péage* (toll road) in Tunisia – the new A1 expressway between Tunis and Msaken, south of Sousse. The trip costs TD2.4 by car. There are plans to extend the system north to Bizerte and south to Sfax and Gabès.

Police officers rarely stop foreigners, but it's best to make sure you have your passport and car registration papers handy at all times.

Road Hazards

Tunisian drivers are generally well behaved, and drive fairly predictably and safely, although overtaking manoeuvres are often launched with little regard for what's coming the other way. For someone used to driving in Western Europe, the worst thing is not the cars but the moped riders, who weave suicidally in and out of traffic, and pedestrians, who think they have an inalienable right to walk on the road regardless of traffic conditions. In country towns, watch out for animals and small children making unexpected forays onto the road.

Road Rules

The road rules in Tunisia are much the same as in continental Europe. You drive on the right and overtake on the left. Speed limits are 50km/h in built-up areas and 90km/h on the open road. The only exception is on the toll road from Tunis to Sousse, where the speed limit is 110km/h.

The regulation that causes the most problems for tourists is the one giving priority to traffic coming from the right in built-up areas. This also extends to roundabouts, where you are obliged to give way to traffic approaching from the right even if you are already at the roundabout.

The special intersections for turning left off major roads are another curiosity of Tunisian driving. Instead of using a turning lane in the centre of the road, the Tunisian system involves a special lane leading off to the right which loops back and crosses the main road at right angles. It can be very confusing if you're driving along looking for a sign pointing to the left – and then find a sign telling you to turn right!

Seat belts are not compulsory in cities or towns, but are obligatory for front-seat passengers on the open road. That said, it's highly recommended to wear seat belts at all times.

It's almost unheard of for a tourist to be booked – unless the infringement causes an accident, when the police are obliged to act.

HITCHING

Although many people do hitch (especially in the south), it is not an entirely safe method of transport and you do so at your own risk. It is strongly recommended that women do not attempt to hitch without a male companion.

LOCAL TRANSPORT

Most towns are compact enough to get around on foot. The problem comes in summer, when it's too hot to walk far during the day.

Taxis are the best alternative. They can be found in all but the smallest towns and are cheap by European standards. The day rate (tariff A or tariff 1) applies from 5am to 8pm; flag fall is 340 mills, and fares work out at about 500 mills per kilometre. At night the flag fall is 510 mills and fares are 50% higher.

Major towns like Sousse, Sfax and Tunis have local bus networks. Tunis also has a modern (tram) network and a suburban train line (TGM) connecting the city centre with the northern suburbs.

Some towns, including Gabès, Houmt Souq, Nabeul and Tozeur, have *calèches* (horse-drawn carriages) for hire. All charge TD10 per hour.

LOUAGE

Louages (long-distance shared taxis) are the workhorses of the Tunisian road and are by far the simplest and fastest way to get from A to B, as one traveller reported:

Generally, I think using louages should be much stronger recommended as the bus system is erratic, seat reservation seems impossible and fares are almost identical. The best practice is as follows: head for the bus station, and if the bus departure for your destination is more than one hour away, head for the louage station: it is highly unlikely that you'll have to wait more than 45 minutes.

George Kouseras, Greece

Whereas buses leave to a timetable, louages leave when full. They seldom take long to fill up, although don't leave your run too late – most louages stop running after 7pm, sometimes earlier.

In most towns, the louage station is close to, or combined with, the bus station, enabling you to choose between the services. At the louage stations, drivers stand by their vehicles and call out their destinations. A foreigner is sure to be asked their destination and given assistance. It's often a good idea to ask the fare before you get in. If you think you're being ripped off, ask to see the list of tariffs (set by the government) that all drivers are required to carry.

Most of the old Peugeot or Renault station wagons (with an extra bench seat in the back and licensed to carry five passengers) are being rapidly replaced by more comfortable 'people mover' vans which are licensed to carry eight passengers. Fares are quoted *par place* (per person). There are no discounts for children.

Although some louages are licensed to operate nationwide, most can operate only within their local government area on a specific route. The town name on the roof of each louage indicates where it's licensed, which is not necessarily where it's going.

TOURS

Most sites in Tunisia can be reached by public transport so there's little need for an organised tour in the conventional sense of seeing most of the country in a tour bus. There are, however, two types of tour that will be of use to travellers.

The first is the Sahara desert tour. Indeed, unless you have your own vehicle, a tour is the only way to see the desert. Options range from overnight camel treks to week-long 4WD expeditions. Douz (p217) is the main base for launching desert tours, although good operators also work from Tozeur (p226) and Gabès (p200). Many resort hotels from the coast (especially Jerba) can also make the arrangements for desert exploration. For more information on what sort of trip is possible, see the boxed text on p219.

The second types of tour is the day trip. This usually involves a hotel rounding up enough people to make the trip viable. This is a popular way of visiting Matmata, the oasis villages near Tozeur or the Roman cities inland from Tabarka.

Chartering a taxi privately is a popular do-it-yourself alternative for exploring Jerba or the Berber villages and ksour around Tataouine.

ECOTOURS

Ecotourism is a relatively new concept in Tunisia, and guides with a good understanding of ecology are hard to find. The Tunisian government is working with the World Bank to open up the national parks for ecotourism, but this was yet to bear fruit at the time of research.

One company to seek out is **Becasse** (☎ 71-960 314; fax 960 249; becasse@planet.tn), which specialises in small-group tours to areas of outstanding natural interest. Becasse's international affiliate is **Visit Tunisia** (www.visit -tunisia.com/interne/partners.htm).

TRAIN

Travelling by train is the most comfortable way to get around (unless it's busy and you have to stand). Trains are run by the Société Nationale des Chemins de Fer Tunisiens (SNCFT). The rail network is extensive (though not comprehensive) and is modern, efficient and generally punctual.

The main train line runs north–south between Tunis and Gabès via Sousse and Sfax, and there are frequent services along this route. One train per day branches off at Mahres, south of Sfax, to Gafsa and Metlaoui. There are also lines to Bizerte, via Mateur; Ghardimao, via Jendouba; and Kalaat Khasba (halfway between Le Kef and Kasserine).

Cap Bon is serviced by a branch line between Bir Bou Regba and Nabeul, while the Metro du Sahel network operates south from Sousse to Monastir and Mahdia. Both these lines are linked to the main north–south line. Other rail lines shown on maps are for freight only.

For train enthusiasts, the *Lezard Rouge* (Red Lizard) is a restored train that belonged to the former bey, who used it to go on pleasure trips into the mountains. It runs between Metlaoui and Redeyef daily, offering great views of the Seldja Gorge. For more details, see p235.

Classes

Passenger trains offer three classes: 2nd, 1st and *confort*. Second class costs about the same as a bus, and is normally packed, with everything from people and produce to livestock. It's a circus that can be fun to experience for a short journey. Unless you get on at the point of origin and have sharp elbows, you're unlikely to find a seat.

First class, which costs about 40% more than 2nd class, has reclining, upholstered seats, and a better chance of actually sitting in one. *Confort* costs a bit more again, but doesn't offer much more than 1st class apart from a smaller, slightly more exclusive compartment. Most mainline trains have a restaurant car, which sends out a regular supply of sandwiches, soft drinks and coffee.

Costs

Sample fares from Tunis include Sousse (TD6), Sfax (TD9.2), Gafsa (TD13.4) and Bizerte (TD3.5).

Reservations

The trains can get crowded in summer, especially going south. To get a seat, it's a good idea to make a reservation the day before which can be done at train stations in any medium-sized towns around the country.

Health by Dr Caroline Evans

Prevention is the key to staying healthy while travelling in Tunisia. A little planning before departure, particularly for pre-existing illnesses, will save you trouble later: see your dentist before a long trip to sort out any loose fillings; carry a spare pair of contact lenses and glasses and take your optical prescription with you. Infectious diseases can and do occur in Tunisia, but they are extremely rare. Medical facilities can be excellent in large cities, but in remoter areas may be more basic.

BEFORE YOU GO

It's tempting to leave it all to the last minute – don't! Many vaccines don't ensure immunity for two weeks, so visit a doctor four to eight weeks before departure. Ask your doctor for an International Certificate of Vaccination (otherwise known as the yellow booklet), which will list all the vaccinations you've received. This is mandatory for countries that require proof of yellow fever vaccination upon entry, but it's a good idea to carry it wherever you travel.

Travellers can register with the International Association for Medical Advice to Travellers (IMAT; www.iamat.org). Their website can help travellers to find a doctor with recognised training. Those heading off to very remote areas may like to do a first aid course (Red Cross and St John's Ambulance can help) or attend a remote medicine first-aid course such as offered by the Royal Geographical Society (www.rgs.org).

Bring medications in their original, clearly labelled, containers. A signed and dated letter from your physician describing your medical conditions and medications, including generic names, is also a good idea. If carrying syringes or needles, be sure to have a physician's letter documenting their medical necessity.

INSURANCE

Find out in advance if your insurance plan will make payments directly to providers or reimburse you later for overseas health expenditures (in many countries doctors expect payment in cash); it's also worth ensuring that your travel insurance will cover repatriation home, or to better medical facilities elsewhere. Your insurance company may be able to locate the nearest source of medical help, or you can ask at your hotel. In an emergency contact your embassy or consulate. Your travel insurance will not usually cover you for any dental work other than emergency treatment. Not all insurance covers emergency aeromedical evacuation home or to a hospital in a major city, which may be the only way to get medical attention for a serious emergency.

RECOMMENDED VACCINATIONS

The World Health Organization recommends that all travellers regardless of the region they are travelling in should be covered for diphtheria, tetanus, measles, mumps, rubella and polio, as well as hepatitis B. While making preparations to travel, take the opportunity to ensure that all of your routine vaccination cover is complete. The consequences of these diseases can be severe and there is a small risk of contacting them in Tunisia.

MEDICAL CHECKLIST

Following is a list of other items you should consider packing in your medical kit.

- Antibiotics if travelling off the beaten track
- Antidiarrhoeal drugs (eg loperamide)
- Acetaminophen (Tylenol) or aspirin
- Anti-inflammatory drugs (eg ibuprofen)
- Antihistamines (for hay fever and allergic reactions)
- Antibacterial ointment (eg Bactroban) for cuts and abrasions
- Steroid cream or cortisone (allergic rashes)
- Bandages, gauze, gauze rolls
- Adhesive or paper tape
- Scissors, safety pins, tweezers
- Thermometer
- Pocket knife
- DEET-containing insect repellent for the skin
- Permethrin-containing insect spray for clothing, tents, and bed nets
- Sun block
- Oral rehydration salts
- Iodine tablets (for water purification)
- Syringes and sterile needles if travelling to remote areas

ONLINE RESOURCES

There is a wealth of travel health advice on the Internet. For further information, the Lonely Planet website at www.lonelyplanet.com is a good place to start. The World Health Organization publishes a superb book, *International Travel and Health*, which is revised annually and is available online at no cost at www.who.int/ith/. Another website of general interest is MD Travel Health at www.mdtravelhealth.com, which provides complete travel health recommendations for every country, updated daily, also at no cost. The Centers for Disease Control

and Prevention website at www.cdc.gov is a very useful source of traveller's health information.

FURTHER READING

Lonely Planet's *Healthy Travel* is packed with useful information including pretrip planning, emergency first aid, immunisation and disease information and what to do if you get sick on the road. Other recommended references include *Traveller's Health* by Dr Richard Dawood (Oxford University Press), *International Travel Health Guide* by Stuart R Rose, MD (Travel Medicine Inc) and *The Travellers' Good Health Guide* by Ted Lankester (Sheldon Press), an especially useful health guide for volunteers and long-term expatriates working in the Middle East.

IN TRANSIT

DEEP VEIN THROMBOSIS (DVT)

Deep vein thrombosis occurs when blood clots form in the legs during plane flights, chiefly because of prolonged immobility. The longer the flight, the greater the risk. Though most blood clots are reabsorbed uneventfully, some may break off and travel through the blood vessels to the lungs, where they may cause life-threatening complications.

The chief symptom of deep vein thrombosis is swelling or pain of the foot, ankle, or calf, usually but not always on just one side. When a blood clot travels to the lungs, it may cause chest pain and difficulty breathing. Travellers with any of these symptoms should immediately seek medical attention.

To prevent the development of deep vein thrombosis on long flights you should walk about the cabin, perform isometric compressions of the leg muscles (ie contract the leg muscles while sitting), drink plenty of fluids, and avoid alcohol and tobacco.

JET LAG & MOTION SICKNESS

Jet lag is common when crossing more than five time zones; it results in insomnia, fatigue, malaise or nausea. To avoid jet lag try drinking plenty of fluids (nonalcoholic) and eating light meals. Upon arrival, seek

It's usually a good idea to consult your government's travel health website before departure, if one is available:

Australia: www.dfat.gov.au/travel/
Canada: www.travelhealth.gc.ca
United Kingdom: www.doh.gov.uk/traveladvice/
United States: www.cdc.gov/travel/

HEALTH

exposure to natural sunlight and readjust your schedule (for meals, sleep, etc) as soon as possible.

Antihistamines such as dimenhydrinate (Dramamine) and meclizine (Antivert, Bonine) are usually the first choice for treating motion sickness. Their main side effect is drowsiness. A herbal alternative is ginger, which works like a charm for some people.

IN TUNISIA

AVAILABILITY & COST OF HEALTHCARE

The health care system in Tunisia varies. Medical care can be excellent in larger towns (eg Tunis, Sousse, Sfax and Houmt Souq, where many of the doctors completed their studies in Europe). Reciprocal arrangements with countries rarely exist and you should be prepared to pay for all medical and dental treatment.

Medical care is not always readily available outside major cities. Medicine, and even sterile dressings or intravenous fluids, may need to be bought from a local pharmacy. Nursing care may be limited or rudimentary as this is something families and friends are expected to provide. The travel assistance provided by your insurance may be able to locate the nearest source of medical help, otherwise ask at your hotel. In an emergency contact your embassy or consulate.

Standards of dental care are variable and there is an increased risk of hepatitis B and HIV transmission via poorly sterilised equipment. And keep in mind that your travel insurance will not usually cover you for anything other than emergency dental treatment.

For minor illnesses such as diarrhoea, pharmacists can often provide valuable advice and sell over-the-counter medication. They can also advise when more specialised help is needed.

INFECTIOUS DISEASES
Diptheria
Diphtheria is spread through close respiratory contact. It causes a high temperature and severe sore throat. Sometimes a membrane forms across the throat requiring a tracheostomy to prevent suffocation. Vac-

cination is recommended for those likely to be in close contact with the local population in infected areas. The vaccine is given as an injection alone, or with tetanus, and lasts 10 years.

Hepatitis A
Hepatitis A is spread through contaminated food (particularly shellfish) and water. It causes jaundice, and although it is rarely fatal, can cause prolonged lethargy and delayed recovery. Symptoms include dark urine, a yellow colour to the whites of the eyes, fever and abdominal pain. Hepatitis A vaccine (Avaxim, VAQTA, Havrix) is given as an injection: a single dose will give protection for up to a year while a booster 12 months later will provide a subsequent 10 years of protection. Hepatitis A and typhoid vaccines can also be given as a single dose vaccine, hepatyrix or viatim.

Hepatitis B
Infected blood, contaminated needles and sexual intercourse can all transmit hepatitis B. It can cause jaundice, and affects the liver, occasionally causing liver failure. All travellers should make this a routine vaccination. (Many countries now give a hepatitis B vaccination as part of routine childhood vaccination.) The vaccine is given singly, or at the same time as the hepatitis A vaccine (hepatyrix). A course will give protection for at least five years. It can be given over four weeks, or six months.

HIV
HIV is spread via infected blood and blood products, sexual intercourse with an infected partner and from an infected mother to her newborn child. It can be spread through 'blood to blood' contacts such as contaminated instruments during medical, dental, acupuncture and other body piercing procedures and sharing used intravenous needles.

Poliomyelitis
This disease is generally spread through contaminated food and water. It is one of the vaccines given in childhood and should be boosted every 10 years, either orally (a drop on the tongue), or as an injection. Polio may be carried asymptomatically, although it can cause a transient fever and,

in rare cases, potentially permanent muscle weakness or paralysis.

Rabies

Spread through bites or licks on broken skin from an infected animal, rabies is fatal. Animal handlers should be vaccinated, as should those travelling to remote areas where a reliable source of post-bite vaccine is not available within 24 hours. Three injections are needed over a month. If you have not been vaccinated you will need a course of five injections starting within 24 hours or as soon as possible after the injury. Vaccination does not provide you with immunity, it merely buys you more time to seek appropriate medical help.

Tuberculosis

Tuberculosis (TB) is spread through close respiratory contact and occasionally through infected milk or milk products. BCG vaccine is recommended for those likely to be mixing closely with the local population. It is more important for those visiting family or planning on a long stay, and those employed as teachers and health-care workers. TB can be asymptomatic, although symptoms can include cough, weight loss or fever months or even years after exposure. An x-ray is the best way to confirm if you have TB. BCG gives a moderate degree of protection against TB. It causes a small permanent scar at the site of injection, and is usually only given in specialised chest clinics. As it's a live vaccine it should not be given to pregnant women or immunocompromised individuals. The BCG vaccine is not available in all countries.

Typhoid

This is spread through food or water that has been contaminated by infected human faeces. The first symptom is usually fever or a pink rash on the abdomen. Septicaemia (blood poisoning) may also occur. Typhoid vaccine (typhim Vi, typherix) will give protection for three years. In some countries, the oral vaccine Vivotif is also available.

ENVIRONMENTAL HAZARDS
Heat Illness

Heat exhaustion occurs following heavy sweating and excessive fluid loss with inadequate replacement of fluids and salt. This is particularly common in hot climates when taking unaccustomed exercise before full acclimatisation. Symptoms include headache, dizziness and tiredness. Dehydration is already happening by the time you feel thirsty – aim to drink sufficient water such that you produce pale, diluted urine. The treatment of heat exhaustion consists of fluid replacement with water and/or fruit juice, and cooling by cold water and fans. The treatment of the salt loss component consists of salty fluids as in soup or Bovril, and adding a little more table salt to foods than usual.

Heat stroke is much more serious. This occurs when the body's heat-regulating mechanism breaks down. Excessive rise in body temperature leads to sweating ceasing, irrational and hyperactive behaviour and eventually loss of consciousness and death. Rapid cooling by spraying the body with water and fanning is an ideal treatment. Emergency fluid and electrolyte replacement by intravenous drip is usually also required.

Insect Bites & Stings

Mosquitoes may not carry malaria but can cause irritation and infected bites. Using DEET-based insect repellents will prevent bites. Mosquitos also spread dengue fever.

Bees and wasps only cause real problems to those with a severe allergy (anaphylaxis). If you have a severe allergy to bee or wasp stings you should carry an adrenaline injection or similar.

Sand flies are found around the Mediterranean beaches. They usually only cause a nasty itchy bite but can carry a rare skin disorder called cutaneous leishmaniasis. Bites may be prevented by using DEET-based repellents.

Scorpions are frequently found in arid or dry climates. They can cause a painful bite which is rarely life threatening.

Bed bugs are often found in hostels and cheap hotels. They lead to very itchy lumpy bites. Spraying the mattress with an appropriate insect killer will do a good job of getting rid of them.

Scabies are also frequently found in cheap accommodation. These tiny mites live in the skin, particularly between the fingers. They cause an intensely itchy rash.

HEALTH

Scabies is easily treated with lotion from a pharmacy; people who you come into contact with also need treating to avoid the spread of scabies between asymptomatic carriers.

Snake Bites
Avoid getting bitten – do not walk barefoot or stick your hand into holes or cracks. Half of those bitten by venomous snakes are not actually injected with poison (envenomed). If bitten by a snake, do not panic. Immobilise the bitten limb with a splint (eg a stick) and apply a bandage over the site, firm pressure, similar to a bandage over a sprain. Do not apply a tourniquet, or cut or suck the bite. Get the victim to medical help as soon as possible so that antivenin can be given if necessary.

Travellers' Diarrhoea
To prevent diarrhoea, avoid tap water unless it has been boiled, filtered, or chemically disinfected (iodine tablets); only eat fresh fruits or vegetables if cooked or if you have peeled them yourself; be wary of dairy products that might contain unpasteurised milk. Buffet meals are risky, food should be piping hot; food freshly cooked in front of you in a busy restaurant is more likely to be safe.

If you develop diarrhoea, be sure to drink plenty of fluids, preferably an oral rehydration solution containing lots of salt and sugar. A few loose stools don't require treatment, but if you start having more than four or five stools a day you should start taking an antibiotic (usually a quinolone drug) and an antidiarrhoeal agent (such as loperamide). If diarrhoea is bloody or persists for more than 72 hours or is accompanied by fever, shaking chills or severe abdominal pain you should seek medical attention.

Water
Tap water is safe to drink throughout Tunisia, with the notable exception of Jerba where salt water has seeped into underground water sources; stick to bottled water or boil water for ten minutes, use water purification tablets or a filter. Do not drink water from rivers or lakes, as this may contain bacteria or viruses that can cause diarrhoea or vomiting.

TRAVELLING WITH CHILDREN
All travellers with children should know how to treat minor ailments and when to seek medical treatment. Make sure the children are up to date with routine vaccinations, and discuss possible travel vaccines well before departure as some vaccines are not suitable for children aged under a year.

In hot, moist climates any wound or break in the skin may lead to infection. The area should be cleaned and then kept dry and clean. Remember to avoid contaminated food and water. If your child is vomiting or experiencing diarrhoea, lost fluid and salts must be replaced. It may be helpful to take rehydration powders for reconstituting with boiled water. Ask your doctor about this.

Children should be encouraged to avoid dogs or other mammals because of the risk of rabies and other diseases. Any bite, scratch or lick from a warm blooded, furry animal should immediately be thoroughly cleaned. If there is any possibility that the animal is infected with rabies, immediate medical assistance should be sought.

WOMEN'S HEALTH
Emotional stress, exhaustion and travelling through different time zones can all contribute to an upset in the menstrual pattern. If using oral contraceptives, remember some antibiotics, diarrhoea and vomiting can stop the pill from working and lead to the risk of pregnancy, so remember to take condoms with you just in case (they're readily available over the counter in pharmacies in Tunisia). Condoms should be kept in a cool dry place or they may crack and perish.

Emergency contraception is most effective if taken within 24 hours after unprotected sex. See the International Planned Parent Federation website (www.ippf.org) for details about the availability of contraception in Tunisia. Tampons are usually only found in supermarkets, and can be hard to find outside medium-sized towns.

Travelling during pregnancy is usually possible but there are important things to consider. Have a medical check-up before embarking on your trip. The most risky times for travel are during the first 12 weeks of pregnancy, when miscarriage is most likely, and after 30 weeks, when complications such as high blood pressure and premature delivery can occur. Most airlines will not accept a traveller after 28 to 32 weeks of pregnancy, and long haul flights in the later stages can be very uncomfortable. Antenatal facilities should be relied on only in larger cities. Taking written records of the pregnancy including details of your blood group are likely to be helpful if you need medical attention while away. Ensure your insurance policy covers pregnancy delivery and postnatal care, but remember insurance policies are only as good as the facilities available.

HEALTH

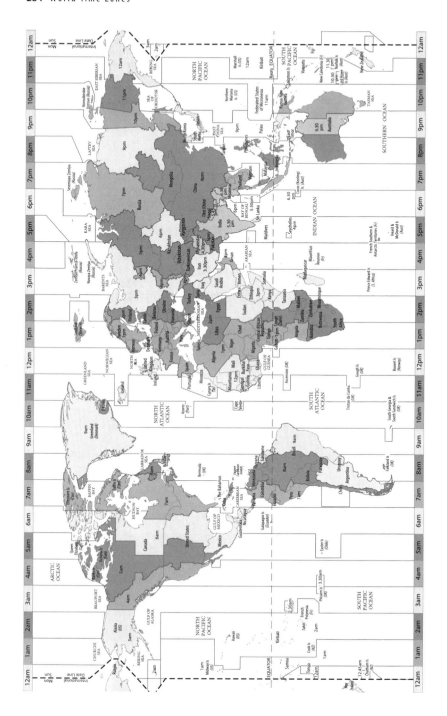

Language

CONTENTS

While Arabic is the official language in Tunisia, in all but the most remote rural communities there will always be someone who speaks French, and most signs throughout the country are written in both Arabic and French.

ARABIC

Tunisian Arabic belongs to a dialect known as Western Colloquial Arabic. The popularity of Egyptian movies and music ensures that most Tunisians understand the Egyptian dialect well. There is no dictionary or

phrasebook specifically for Tunisian Arabic, but this language guide includes some of the most common words and phrases; they are predominantly in Egyptian Arabic, but Tunisian variants are used where the differences are significant. For a more comprehensive guide to Arabic, get a copy of Lonely Planet's *Egyptian Arabic phrasebook*.

More specialised or educated language tends to be much the same across the Arab world, although pronunciation varies considerably. The spread of radio and television have increased all Arabs' exposure to and understanding of what is commonly known as Modern Standard Arabic (MSA). MSA, which has grown from the classical language of the Quran and poetry, is the written and spoken lingua franca of the Arab world. It's the language of radio, television and the press, and also the majority of modern Arabic literature.

Foreign students of the language constantly face the dilemma of whether to learn MSA first (which could mean waiting a while before being able to talk with the locals) and then a chosen dialect, or simply to acquire spoken competence in the latter. Dialects supposedly have no written form (the argument goes it would be like writing in Cockney or Strine), although there's no reason why they could not avail themselves of the same script used for the standard language. If this leaves you with a headache, you'll have some idea of why so few non-Arabs or non-Muslims embark on the study of this complex tongue!

That said, you'll break down many barriers by having a go, and if you take the time to learn even a few words and phrases, you'll discover and experience much more while travelling through the country.

Arabic uses masculine and femine forms, which are indicated in this language guide by (m) and (f) respectively, or separated by a slash (m/f) if both forms are given.

TRANSLITERATION

Converting what for most outsiders is just a bunch of squiggles into meaningful words (ie those written using the Roman alphabet)

THE STANDARD ARABIC ALPHABET

Final	Medial	Initial	Alone	Transliteration	Pronunciation
‍ا			ا	ā/aa	as in 'father'/as the long 'a' in 'ma'am'
ب	ب	ب	ب	b	as in 'bet'
ت	ت	ت	ت	t	as in 'ten'
ث	ث	ث	ث	th	as in 'thin'
ج	ج	ج	ج	j/zh	as in 'jet'/as the 's' in 'measure'
ح	ح	ح	ح	H	a strongly whispered 'h', like a sigh of relief
خ	خ	خ	خ	kh	as the 'ch' in Scottish *loch*
د			د	d	as in 'dim'
ذ			ذ	dh	as the 'th' in 'this'; also as **d** or **z**
ر			ر	r	a rolled 'r', as in the Spanish word *caro*
ز			ز	z	as in 'zip'
س	س	س	س	s	as in 'so', never as in 'wisdom'
ش	ش	ش	ش	sh	as in 'ship'
ص	ص	ص	ص	ṣ	emphatic 's'
ض	ض	ض	ض	ḍ	emphatic 'd'
ط	ط	ط	ط	ṭ	emphatic 't'
ظ	ظ	ظ	ظ	ẓ	emphatic 'z'
ع	ع	ع	ع	'	the Arabic letter *'ayn*; pronounce as a glottal stop – like the closing of the throat before saying 'Oh-oh!' (see Other Sounds on p287)
غ	غ	غ	غ	gh	a guttural sound like Parisian 'r'
ف	ف	ف	ف	f	as in 'far'
ق	ق	ق	ق	q	a strongly guttural 'k' sound; also often pronounced as a glottal stop
ك	ك	ك	ك	k	as in 'king'
ل	ل	ل	ل	l	as in 'lamb'
م	م	م	م	m	as in 'me'
ن	ن	ن	ن	n	as in 'name'
ه	ه	ه	ه	h	as in 'ham'
و			و	w	as in 'wet'; or
				oo	long, as in 'food'; or
				ow	as in 'how'
ي	ي	ي	ي	y	as in 'yes'; or
				ee	as the 'e' in 'ear', only softer; or
				ai/ay	as in 'aisle'/as the 'ay' in 'day'

Vowels Not all Arabic vowel sounds are represented in the alphabet. For more information on the vowel sounds used in this language guide, see Pronunciation on p287.

Emphatic Consonants To simplify the transliteration system used in this book, the emphatic consonants have not been included.

is a tricky business – in fact, no really satisfactory system of transliteration has been established, and probably never will be. For this book, an attempt has been made to standardise some spellings of place names and the like.

There is only one article in Arabic: *al* (the). It's also sometimes written as 'il' or 'el' and sometimes modifies to reflect the first consonant of the following noun, eg in Saladin's name, *Salah ad-Din* (righteousness of the faith), the 'al' has been modified to 'ad' before the 'd' of 'Din'.

The long history of French in Tunisia has meant that transliterations will often reflect French pronunciation. This is particularly evident with the letter combination 'ch', which in French is pronounced as the 'sh' in English 'she' (eg *cher*, meaning 'dear'), but in English would almost invariably be pronounced as the 'ch' in church'.

The letters **q** and **k** have caused enormous problems, and have been interchanged willy-nilly in transliteration. For a long time, Iraq (which in Arabic is spelled with what can only be described in English using its nearest equivalent: 'q') was written, even by scholars, as 'Irak'. Other examples of an Arabic **q** receiving such treatment are *souq* (market), often written 'souk' and *qasr* (castle), sometimes written 'kasr'. It's a bit like spelling English 'as she is spoke' – imagine the results if Australians, Americans, Scots and Londoners were all given free rein to write as they pronounce!

PRONUNCIATION

Pronunciation of Arabic can be somewhat tongue-tying for someone unfamiliar with the intonation and combination of sounds. Pronounce the transliterated words and phrases slowly and clearly.

The following guide should help, but it isn't complete because the myriad rules governing pronunciation and vowel use are too extensive to be covered here.

Vowels

a	as in 'had' (sometimes very short)
aa	like the long 'a' sound in 'ma'am'
ā	as the 'a' in 'father'
e	as in 'bet' (sometimes very short)
ee	as in 'beer', only softer
i	as in 'hit'
o	as in 'hot'
oo	as in 'food'
u	as in 'put'

Diphthongs

ow	as in 'how'
ai	as in 'aisle'
ay	as in 'day'

Consonants

Pronunciation for all Arabic consonants is covered in the alphabet table on p286. Note that when double consonants occur in transliterations, each consonant is pronounced. For example, *il-Hammam* (bathhouse) is pronounced 'il-ham-maam'.

Other Sounds

Arabic has two sounds that are very tricky for non-Arabs to produce, the 'ayn and the glottal stop. The letter 'ayn represents a sound with no English equivalent that comes even close – it is similar to the glottal stop (which is not actually represented in the alphabet) but the muscles at the back of the throat are gagged more forcefully and air is allowed to escape, creating a sound that has been described as reminiscent of someone being strangled! In many transliteration systems 'ayn is represented by an opening quotation mark, and the glottal stop by a closing quotation mark. To make the transliterations in this language guide (and throughout the rest of the book) easier to use, we have not distinguished between the glottal stop and the 'ayn, using the closing quotation mark to represent both sounds. You'll find that Arab speakers will probably understand you a lot better than if you tried to cover both sounds.

ACCOMMODATION

I'm looking for a ...	*ana badowwar 'ala ...*
pension	*bansyon*
hotel	*otayl*
youth hostel	*oberzh dar shabāb*

Where can I find a cheap hotel?
ala'ee otayl rakhees fayn?
What is the address?
il 'unwān ey?
Could you write the address, please?
mumkin tiktib/tiktibee il' unwān men fadhlek? (m/f)
Do you have rooms available?
'andak/'andik ghuraf fadya? (m/f)

LANGUAGE

I'd like (a) ...	ana 'aiz/'aiza ... (m/f)
I'd like to book (a) ...	'aiz aHjaz ... low samaHt (m)
	'aiza aHjaz ... low samaHtee (f)
bed	sireer
single room	ghurfa li wāHid
double room	ghurfa bi sirir muzdawaj
room with	ghurfa bi sirirain
two beds	
room with	ghurfa bi Hammām khās
a bathroom	
room with air-	ghurfa bi kleemateezasiyon/
con/fan	marwaha
bed in a dorm	ghurfa mushtarika

in the name of ...	bi 'ism ...
date	tareekh
from (date) to (date)	min yom (...) li yom (...)
credit card ...	kredit kard ...
number	raqm
expiry date	tareekh al-'intiha'

How much is it ...?	gedaesh/bikam ...?
per night	li laila waHida
per person	lil fard

Do you have any cheaper rooms?
  fee ghuraf arkhas?
May I see the room?
  (wash) yimkin lee nshoof al-ghurfa?
Where is the bathroom?
  fayn il Hammaam?
I'm/We're leaving today.
  (ana Hamshi/iHna Hanimshi) innharda.

CONVERSATION & ESSENTIALS

Arabic is more formal than English, especially with greetings; thus even the simplest greetings, such as 'hello', vary according to when and how they're used. In addition, each greeting requires a certain response that varies according to whether it is being said to a male, female or group of people.

Hello.	as-salām 'alaykum (literally:
	'peace be upon you') or
	assalāma
(response)	wa 'alaykum as-salām ('and
	upon you be peace')
Goodbye.	ma' as-salāma ('go in safety') or
	bi'salāma
Good morning.	sabaH al-khayr
(response)	sabaH an-noor
Good evening.	masa' al-khayr
(response)	masa' an-noor
Welcome.	marhaba

How are you?	ashnu'a walek?
I'm fine, thank you.	labes (al-Hamdu lillah)
Yes.	eeyeh (or na'am – more formal)
No.	la'
Please.	men fadhlek
Thank you (very	bari kelorfik or shukran (jazilan)
much).	
Excuse me.	sa'mahni
That's fine. (You're	la shukran 'ala wajib
welcome)	
Sorry. (ie forgive me)	'assif
What's your name?	ma'howa ismok?
My name is ...	ismee ...
Pleased to meet you.	tasharrafna (pol)
(when first meeting)	fursa sa'eeda (inf)
Where are you from?	min een enta/entee? (m/f)
I'm/We're from ...	ana/eHna min ...
I like/don't like ...	ana baHibb/mabaHibbish
Just a minute.	da'ee'a waHida

A useful word to know is *imshee*, which means 'Go away'. Use this when you are being besieged by children. Don't use it on adults; instead, just say, *la' shukran* (No thanks).

DIRECTIONS

Where is ...?	fayn ...?
Go straight ahead.	'ala tool
Turn left.	Howid yasarl
Turn right.	Howid yameen

SIGNS	
Entrance	مدخل
Exit	خروج
Information	معلومات
Open	مفتوح
Closed	مغلق
Prohibited	ممنوع
Police	شرطة
Men's Toilet	حمام للرجال
Women's Toilet	حمام للنساء
Hospital	مستشفي

at the (next) corner	'alal nasya (illi jaiya)
at the traffic lights	'and il ishāra
behind	wara
in front of	'uddaam
far (from)	ba'eed ('an)
near (to)	'urai-ib (min)
opposite	muqabbal

here	*huna*
there	*hunaak*
this address	*al-'anwaan da*
north	*shamaal*
south	*janoob*
east	*sharq*
west	*gharb*
beach	*al blaaj/ash-shātta*
bridge	*kubri*
castle/palace	*al-qasr*
my hotel	*al-otayl betaa'ee*
island	*jazeera*
main square	*al-maidaan ar-ra'eesi*
mosque	*al-jaam'*
museum	*al-matHaf*
old city	*al-medeena*
ruins	*asār*
sea	*baHr*
square	*midān*
street	*ash-shaari'*
tower	*burj*
university	*al-jam'a*
village	*al-qarya*

EMERGENCIES – ARABIC

Help!	*el-Ha'nee!*
There's been an accident.	*fee hadsa!*
I'm lost.	*ana (tāyih/tāyha)* (m/f)
Go away!	*imshee!*
Call a doctor!	*itassal/ee bi-doktoor!* (m/f)
Call the police!	*itassal bil-bolees!*
I've been robbed.	*ana itsara't*
Where are the toilets?	*fayn at-twalet?*

HEALTH

I'm ill.	*ana 'aiyān/a* (m/f)
My friend is ill.	*sadeeqi 'ayan*
It hurts here.	*biyuja'ni hina*
I'm ...	*'andee ...*
asthmatic	*azmit raboo*
diabetic	*is sukkar*
epileptic	*sara'*
I'm allergic ...	*'andee Hasasiyya ...*
to antibiotics	*min mudād Haiowi*
to aspirin	*min asbireen*
to penicillin	*min binisileen*
to bees	*min naHl*
to nuts	*min mukassarāt*

antiseptic	*mutahhir*
aspirin	*asbireen*
condoms	*'aazil zakary (kaboot,* slang)
contraceptive	*wasā'il mana' il Haml*
diarrhoea	*is-haal*
fever	*sukhoona*
headache	*sudā'*
hospital	*mustashfa*
medicine	*dowa*
pharmacy	*farmasyan*
pregnant	*Haamel*
prescription	*roshetta*
sanitary napkins	*fuwat saHiyya*
stomachache	*waja' fil batn*
sunblock cream	*kreym did ish shams*
tampons	*tambax*

LANGUAGE DIFFICULTIES

Do you speak English?
enta bititkallim ingleezee? (to a man)
entee bititkallimee ingleezee? (to a woman)
Does anyone here speak English?
fee Hadd biyitkallim ingleezee?
How do you say ... in Arabic?
izzai a'ool ... bil 'arabee?
What does ... mean?
ya'ni ... ey?
I understand.
fhemt
I don't understand.
ma fhemtesh
Please write it down.
mumkin tiktibuh/tiktibeeh? (m/f)
Can you show me (on the map)?
mumkin tiwarreeni ('alal khareeta)?

NUMBERS

Arabic numerals are simple to learn and, unlike the written language, run from left to right. Pay attention to the order of the words in numbers from 21 to 99. When followed by a noun, the pronunciation of *miyya* changes to *meet* for the numbers 100 and 300 to 900, and the noun is always used in its singular form.

0	*sifr*	٠
1	*waaHid*	١
2	*itneen*	٢
3	*talaata*	٣
4	*arba'a*	٤
5	*khamsa*	٥
6	*sitta*	٦
7	*saba'a*	٧

LANGUAGE

8	tamanya	٨
9	tissa'	٩
10	'ashara	١٠
11	wāHidash	١١
12	itna'ash	١٢
13	talattash	١٣
14	arba'atash	١٤
15	khamastash	١٥
16	sitt'ash	١٦
17	saba'atash	١٧
18	tamantash	١٨
19	tissa'atash	١٩
20	'ashreen	٢٠
21	wāHid wa 'ashreen	٢١
22	itneen wa 'ashreen	٢٢
30	talateen	٣٠
40	arba'een	٤٠
50	khamseen	٥٠
60	sitteen	٦٠
70	saba'een	٧٠
80	tamaneen	٨٠
90	tissa'een	٩٠
100	miyya (meet before a noun)	١٠٠
200	miyyateen	٢٠٠
1000	'alf	١٠٠٠
2000	'alfayn	٢٠٠٠

| How many? | kam wāHid? |

PAPERWORK

name	ism
nationality	jinsiyya
date/place of birth	tareekh/maHal il milād
sex (gender)	jins
passport	basboor or jowaz is safar
visa	ta'sheera

QUESTION WORDS

Who?	meen?
What?	ey?
When?	imta?
Where?	fayn?
How?	izzay?
Which?	ayy?

SHOPPING & SERVICES

I'd like to buy ...	'aiz/'aiza ashteri ... (m/f)
How much is it?	(gedaesh/bikam) da?
I don't like it.	mish 'ajibni
May I look at it?	mumkin ashoofu?
I'm just looking.	batfarraj bas
It's cheap.	da rakhees
It's too expensive.	da ghaalee awee
No more than ...	mish aktār min ...
I'll take it.	'akhudha

Can you give me ...?	mumkin tiddeeni ...?
a discount	takhfeed
a good price	sa'r kwayyis

Do you accept ...?	bitakhud/ee ...? (m/f)
credit cards	kredit kard
traveller cheques	sheekāt siyaHiyyai

more	aktar
less	a'all
bigger	akbar
smaller	asghar

I'm looking for ...	ana badawwar 'ala
a bank	banka
the bazaar/market	as-sooq
the chemist/	al-farmasyan
pharmacy	
the city centre	wust al-balad
the (...) embassy	as-sifāra (...)
the post office	boosta/maktab al-bareed
the telephone	centraal it-telifonaat
centre	
the tourist office	maktab as-siyaHa

I want to change ...	ana 'aiz/aiza asrif ... (m/f)
money	fuloos
travellers cheques	sheekaat siyaHiyya

TIME & DATES

What time is it?	saa'a kam?
It's (8 o'clock).	(saa'a tamanya)
morning	sabaH
afternoon	fil-asheeya
in the evening	masa'
today	al-yoom
tomorrow	ghaddan
yesterday	al-bereH
day	nahar
month	shahr
week	usbu'
year	'am
early	bakree
late	mu'attaguiz
daily	kull yom

Monday	(nhar) al-itneen
Tuesday	(nhar) at-talata
Wednesday	(nhar) al-arbaa
Thursday	(nhar) al-khamees
Friday	(nhar) al-juma
Saturday	(nhar) as-sabt
Sunday	(nhar) al-aHad

LANGUAGE

January	yanâyir
February	fibrâyir
March	mâris
April	abreel
May	mâyu
June	yunyu
July	yulyu
August	aghustus
September	sibtimbir
October	uktoobir
November	nufimbir
December	disimbir

TRANSPORT
Public Transport

When does the ... leave/arrive?	emta qiyam/wusuul ...?
boat	as-safeena
bus/coach	al-otobees/kar
ferry	ma'adiya
plane	al-tayyâra
train	al-qitar

I'd like a ... ticket.	'aiz/'ayza ... tazkarit (m/f)
one-way	zihaab
return	'owda
1st-class	daraja oola
2nd-class	daraja tanya

I want to go to ...
ureed an adhaba ila ...
The train has been cancelled/delayed.
il atr it'akhkhar/itlagha
Which bus goes to ...?
ey kar yamshee ila ...?
Does this bus go to ...?
yamshee had al-kar ila ...?
Please tell me when we arrive in ...
men fadhlek, ullee emta Hanoosel ...
What is the fare to ...?
mahowa assir ila ...?
Stop here, please.
qif honamen, men fadhlek
Wait!
intadhirnee!

the first	il awwil/oola (m/f)
the last	il aakhir
the next	illli jayy
airport	matâr
bus station	maHattat al-otobees
bus stop	mawqif al-otobees
city	al-medeena
platform number	raseef nimra
ticket office	maktab at-tazkara

timetable	jadwal
train station	maHattat al-qitar

Private Transport

I'd like to hire a/an ...	'aiz/'aiza a'ajjâr ... (m/f)
car	sayara
4WD	jeep
motorbike	mutusikl
bicycle	'ajala
camel	jamal
donkey	Humâr
horse	Husân

ROAD SIGNS

Stop	قف
No Entry	ممنوع الدخول
No Parking	ممنوع الوقوف
Danger	خطر
Slow Down	هادي السرعة
One Way	إتجاه واحد

Is this the road to ...?
itaree' da yiwassi li ...?
(How long) Can I park here?
mumkin arkin hina (addi ay)?
Where do I pay?
adfa'a fayn?
I need a mechanic.
miHtaj/a mekaneeki (m/f)
The car/motorbike has broken down (at ...)
as-sayara/al-mutusikl it'âlit 'and ...
The car/motorbike won't start.
as-sayara/al-mutusikl mish bitdoor
I have a flat tyre.
il kawitsh nayim
I've run out of petrol.
il benzeen khilis
I've had an accident.
kan 'andee hadsa
Where's a service station?
fayn maHattet benzeen?
Please fill it up.
fawwilha, low samaHt
I'd like (30) litres.
'aiz/'aiza (talateen) litr (m/f)

diesel	solâr
leaded petrol	tamaneen (regular)
	tisa'een (super)
unleaded petrol	min ghair rusâs or
	khamsa wa tisa'een

TRAVEL WITH CHILDREN

Is there a/an ...?	*fee ...?*
I need a/an	*'aiz/'aiza ... (m/f)*
car baby seat	*kursi arabiyya li tifl*
child-minding service	*khidmat ra'ai-it tifl*
children's menu	*menai lil atfāl*
(disposable) nappies/diapers	*bambers*
formula (milk)	*laban mujafaf lil baybi*
(English-speaking) babysitter	*jalisat atfāl (bititkallim ingileezi)*
highchair	*kursi lil-atfāl*
potty	*asriyya*
stroller	*arabiyyat atfal*

Do you mind if I breastfeed here?
mumkin aradda'a hina?

Are children allowed?
masmooH bistiHaab il atfāl?

FRENCH

Almost everybody in Tunisia speaks French, so if the thought of getting your mind around Arabic is too much, it'd be a good investment to learn a little French instead.

In French, an important distinction is made between *tu* and *vous*, which both mean 'you'. The informal *tu* is only used when addressing people you know well, or children. When addressing an adult who is not a personal friend, *vous* should be used unless the person invites you to use *tu*.

ACCOMMODATION

I'm looking for a ...	*Je cherche ...*	zher shersh ...
campground	*un camping*	un kom·peeng
guesthouse	*une pension (de famille)*	ewn pon·syon (der fa·mee·ler)
hotel	*un hôtel*	un o·tel
youth hostel	*une auberge de jeunesse*	ewn o·berzh der zher·nes

Where is a cheap hotel?
Où est-ce qu'on peut trouver un hôtel pas cher?
oo es·kon per troo·vay un o·tel pa shair

What is the address?
Quelle est l'adresse?
kel e la·dres

Could you write it down, please?
Est-ce que vous pourriez l'écrire, s'il vous plaît?
e·sker voo poo·ryay lay·kreer seel voo play

Do you have any rooms available?
Est-ce que vous avez des chambres libres?
e·sker voo·za·vay day shom·brer lee·brer

I'd like (a) ...	*Je voudrais ...*	zher voo·dray ...
single room	*une chambre à un lit*	ewn shom·brer a un lee
double-bed room	*une chambre avec un grand lit*	ewn shom·brer a·vek un gron lee
twin room with two beds	*une chambre avec des lits jumeaux*	ewn shom·brer a·vek day lee zhew·mo
room with a bathroom	*une chambre avec une salle de bains*	ewn shom·brer a·vek ewn sal der bun
to share a dorm	*coucher dans un dortoir*	koo·sher don zun dor·twa

---

MAKING A RESERVATION

(for phone or written requests)

To ...	*A l'attention de ...*
From ...	*De la part de ...*
Date	*Date*
I'd like to book ...	*Je voudrais réserver ... (see the list under Accommodation for bed and room options)*
in the name of ...	*au nom de ...*
from ... (date) **to ...**	*du ... au ...*
credit card number	*carte de crédit numéro*
expiry date	*date d'expiration*
Please confirm availability and price.	*Veuillez confirmer la disponibilité et le prix.*

How much is it ...?	*Quel est le prix ...?*	kel e ler pree ...
per night	*par nuit*	par nwee
per person	*par personne*	par per·son

May I see the room?
Est-ce que je peux voir la chambre?
es·ker zher per vwa la shom·brer

Where is the bathroom?
Où est la salle de bains? oo e la sal der bun

Where is the toilet?
Où sont les toilettes? oo·son lay twa·let

I'm leaving today.
Je pars aujourd'hui. zher par o·zhoor·dwee

We're leaving today.
Nous partons aujourd'hui. noo par·ton o·zhoor·dwee

CONVERSATION & ESSENTIALS

Hello.	*Bonjour.*	bon·zhoor
Goodbye.	*Au revoir.*	o·rer·vwa
Yes.	*Oui.*	wee
No.	*Non.*	no
Please.	*S'il vous plaît.*	seel voo play
Thank you.	*Merci.*	mair·see
You're welcome.	*Je vous en prie.*	zher voo·zon pree
	De rien. (inf)	der ree·en
Excuse me.	*Excuse-moi.*	ek·skew·zay·mwa
Sorry. (forgive me)	*Pardon.*	par·don

What's your name?
Comment vous appelez-vous? (pol)	ko·mon voo·za·pay·lay voo
Comment tu t'appelles? (inf)	ko·mon tew ta·pel

My name is ...
Je m'appelle ...	zher ma·pel ...

Where are you from?
De quel pays êtes-vous?	der kel pay·ee et·voo
De quel pays es-tu? (inf)	der kel pay·ee e·tew

I'm from ...
Je viens de ...	zher vyen der ...

I like ...
J'aime ...	zhem ...

I don't like ...
Je n'aime pas ...	zher nem pa ...

Just a minute.
Une minute.	ewn mee·newt

DIRECTIONS

Where is ...?
Où est ...?	oo e ...

Go straight ahead.
Continuez tout droit.	kon·teen·way too drwa

Turn left.
Tournez à gauche.	toor·nay a gosh

Turn right.
Tournez à droite.	toor·nay a drwa

at the corner
au coin	o kwun

at the traffic lights
aux feux	o fer

behind	*derrière*	dair·ryair
in front of	*devant*	der·von
far (from)	*loin (de)*	lwun (der)
near (to)	*près (de)*	pray (der)
opposite	*en face de*	on fas der
beach	*la plage*	la plazh
bridge	*le pont*	ler pon
castle	*le château*	ler sha·to

island	*l'île*	leel
lake	*le lac*	ler lak
main square	*la place centrale*	la plas son·tral
museum	*le musée*	ler mew·zay
old city (town)	*la vieille ville*	la vyay veel
palace	*le palais*	ler pa·lay
ruins	*les ruines*	lay rween
sea	*la mer*	la mair
square	*la place*	la plas
tourist office	*l'office de tourisme*	lo·fees der too·rees·mer

EMERGENCIES – FRENCH

Help!
Au secours!	o skoor

There's been an accident!
Il y a eu un accident!	eel ya ew un ak·see·don

I'm lost.
Je me suis égaré/e. (m/f)	zhe me swee·zay·ga·ray

Leave me alone!
Fichez-moi la paix!	fee·shay·mwa la pay

Call ...!
	Appelez ...!	a·play ...
a doctor	*un médecin*	un mayd·sun
the police	*la police*	la po·lees

HEALTH

I'm ill.	*Je suis malade.*	zher swee ma·lad
It hurts here.	*J'ai une douleur ici.*	zhay ewn doo·ler ee·see

I'm ...
	Je suis ...	zher swee ...
asthmatic	*asthmatique*	(z)as·ma·teek
diabetic	*diabétique*	dee·a·bay·teek
epileptic	*épileptique*	(z)ay·pee·lep·teek

I'm allergic to ...
	Je suis allergique ...	zher swee za·lair·zheek ...
antibiotics	*aux antibiotiques*	o zon·tee·byo·teek
aspirin	*à l'aspirine*	a las·pee·reen
bees	*aux abeilles*	o za·bay·yer
nuts	*aux noix*	o nwa
peanuts	*aux cacahuètes*	o ka·ka·wet
penicillin	*à la pénicilline*	a la pay·nee·see·leen

antiseptic	*l'antiseptique*	lon·tee·sep·teek
aspirin	*l'aspirine*	las·pee·reen
condoms	*des préservatifs*	day pray·zair·va·teef
contraceptive	*le contraceptif*	ler kon·tra·sep·teef
diarrhoea	*la diarrhée*	la dya·ray
medicine	*le médicament*	ler may·dee·ka·mon
nausea	*la nausée*	la no·zay
sunblock cream	*la crème solaire*	la krem so·lair

LANGUAGE

| tampons | *des tampons* | day tom·pon |
| | *hygiéniques* | ee·zhen·eek |

LANGUAGE DIFFICULTIES

Do you speak English?
Parlez-vous anglais? par·lay·voo ong·lay

Does anyone here speak English?
Y a-t-il quelqu'un qui ya·teel kel·kung kee
parle anglais? par long·glay

How do you say ... in French?
Comment est-ce qu'on ko·mon es·kon
dit ... en français? dee ... on fron·say

What does ... mean?
Que veut dire ...? ker ver deer ...

I understand.
Je comprends. zher kom·pron

I don't understand.
Je ne comprends pas. zher ner kom·pron pa

Could you write it down, please?
Est-ce que vous pouvez es·ker voo poo·vay
l'écrire? lay·kreer

Can you show me (on the map)?
Pouvez-vous m'indiquer poo·vay·voo mun·dee·kay
(sur la carte)? (sewr la kart)

NUMBERS

0	*zero*	zay·ro
1	*un*	un
2	*deux*	der
3	*trois*	trwa
4	*quatre*	ka·trer
5	*cinq*	sungk
6	*six*	sees
7	*sept*	set
8	*huit*	weet
9	*neuf*	nerf
10	*dix*	dees
11	*onze*	onz
12	*douze*	dooz
13	*treize*	trez
14	*quatorze*	ka·torz
15	*quinze*	kunz
16	*seize*	sez
17	*dix-sept*	dee·set
18	*dix-huit*	dee·zweet
19	*dix-neuf*	deez·nerf
20	*vingt*	vung
21	*vingt et un*	vung tay un
22	*vingt-deux*	vung·der
30	*trente*	tront
40	*quarante*	ka·ront
50	*cinquante*	sung·kont
60	*soixante*	swa·sont
70	*soixante-dix*	swa·son·dees

80	*quatre-vingts*	ka·trer·vung
90	*quatre-vingt-dix*	ka·trer·vung·dees
100	*cent*	son
1000	*mille*	meel
2000	*deux mille*	der meel

PAPERWORK

name	*nom*	nom
nationality	*nationalité*	na·syo·na·lee·tay
date/place	*date/place*	dat/plas
of birth	*de naissance*	der nay·sons
sex/gender	*sexe*	seks
passport	*passeport*	pas·por
visa	*visa*	vee·za

QUESTION WORDS

Who?	*Qui?*	kee
What?	*Quoi?*	kwa
What is it?	*Qu'est-ce que*	kes·ker
	c'est?	say
When?	*Quand?*	kon
Where?	*Où?*	oo
Which?	*Quel/Quelle?*	kel
Why?	*Pourquoi?*	poor·kwa
How?	*Comment?*	ko·mon

SHOPPING & SERVICES

I'd like to buy ...
Je voudrais acheter ... zher voo·dray ash·tay ...

How much is it?
C'est combien? say kom·byun

I don't like it.
Cela ne me plaît pas. ser·la ner mer play pa

May I look at it?
Est-ce que je peux le voir? es·ker zher per ler vwar

I'm just looking.
Je regarde. zher rer·gard

It's cheap.
Ce n'est pas cher. ser nay pa shair

It's too expensive.
C'est trop cher. say tro shair

I'll take it.
Je le prends. zher ler pron

Can I pay by ...?	*Est-ce que je peux*	es·ker zher per
	payer avec ...?	pay·yay a·vek ...
credit card	*ma carte de*	ma kart der
	crédit	kray·dee
travellers	*des chèques*	day shek
cheques	*de voyage*	der vwa·yazh

more	*plus*	plew
less	*moins*	mwa
smaller	*plus petit*	plew per·tee
bigger	*plus grand*	plew gron

I'm looking for ...	Je cherche ...	zhe shersh ...
a bank	une banque	ewn bonk
the ... embassy	l'ambassade de ...	lam·ba·sahd der ...
the hospital	l'hôpital	lo·pee·tal
the market	le marché	ler mar·shay
the police	la police	la po·lees
the post office	le bureau de poste	ler bew·ro der post
a public phone	une cabine téléphonique	ewn ka·been tay·lay·fo·neek
a public toilet	les toilettes	lay twa·let
the telephone centre	la centrale téléphonique	la san·tral tay·lay·fo·neek

TIME & DATES

What time is it?	Quelle heure est-il?	kel er e til
It's (8) o'clock.	Il est (huit) heures.	il e (weet) er
It's half past ...	Il est (...) heures et demie.	il e (...) er e day·mee
in the morning	du matin	dew ma·tun
in the afternoon	de l'après-midi	der la·pray·mee·dee
in the evening	du soir	dew swar
today	aujourd'hui	o·zhoor·dwee
tomorrow	demain	der·mun
yesterday	hier	yair

Monday	lundi	lun·dee
Tuesday	mardi	mar·dee
Wednesday	mercredi	mair·krer·dee
Thursday	jeudi	zher·dee
Friday	vendredi	von·drer·dee
Saturday	samedi	sam·dee
Sunday	dimanche	dee·monsh

January	janvier	zhon·vyay
February	février	fayv·ryay
March	mars	mars
April	avril	a·vreel
May	mai	may
June	juin	zhwun
July	juillet	zhwee·yay
August	août	oot
September	septembre	sep·tom·brer
October	octobre	ok·to·brer
November	novembre	no·vom·brer
December	décembre	day·som·brer

TRANSPORT
Public Transport

What time does ... leave/arrive?	À quelle heure part/arrive ...?	a kel er par/a·reev ...
boat	le bateau	ler ba·to
bus	le bus	ler bews
plane	l'avion	la·vyon
train	le train	ler trun

I'd like a ... ticket.	Je voudrais un billet ...	zher voo·dray un bee·yay ...
one way	simple	sum·pler
return	aller et retour	a·lay ay rer·toor
1st class	de première classe	der prem·yair klas
2nd class	de deuxième classe	der der·zyem klas

I want to go to ...
Je voudrais aller à ...   zher voo·dray a·lay a ...
The train has been delayed.
Le train est en retard.   ler trun et on rer·tar
The train has been cancelled.
Le train a été annulé.   ler trun a ay·tay a·new·lay

the first	le premier (m)	ler prer·myay
	la première (f)	la prer·myair
the last	le dernier (m)	ler dair·nyay
	la dernière (f)	la dair·nyair
platform number	le numéro de quai	ler new·may·ro der kay
ticket office	le guichet	ler gee·shay
timetable	l'horaire	lo·rair
train station	la gare	la gar

Private Transport

I'd like to hire a/an...	Je voudrais louer ...	zher voo·dray loo·way ...
car	une voiture	ewn vwa·tewr
4WD	un quatre-quatre	un kat·kat
motorbike	une moto	ewn mo·to
bicycle	un vélo	un vay·lo
camel	un chameau	un sha·mol
donkey	un âne	un an
horse	un cheval	un she·val

Is this the road to ...?
C'est la route pour ...?   say la root poor ...
Where's a service station?
Où est-ce qu'il y a une station-service?   oo es·keel ya ewn sta·syon·ser·vees
Please fill it up.
Le plein, s'il vous plaît.   ler plun seel voo play
I'd like ... litres.
Je voudrais ... litres.   zher voo·dray ... lee·trer

petrol/gas	essence	ay·sons
unleaded	sans plomb	son plom
leaded	au plomb	o plom
diesel	diesel	dyay·zel

(How long) Can I park here?
(Combien de temps) Est-ce que je peux stationner ici?   (kom·byun der tom) es·ker zher per sta·syo·nay ee·see?

Where do I pay?
  Où est-ce que je paie? oo es·ker zher pay?

I need a mechanic.
  J'ai besoin d'un zhay ber·zwun dun
  mécanicien. may·ka·nee·syun

The car/motorbike has broken down (at ...)
  La voiture moto est la vwa·tewr/mo·to ay
  tombée en panne (à ...) tom·bay on pan (a ...)

The car/motorbike won't start.
  La voiture/moto ne veut la vwa·tewr/mo·to ner ver
  pas démarrer. pa day·ma·ray

I have a flat tyre.
  Mon pneu est à plat. mom pner ay ta pla

I've run out of petrol.
  Je suis en panne zher swee zon pan
  d'essence. day·sons

I had an accident.
  J'ai eu un accident. zhay ew un ak·see·don

TRAVEL WITH CHILDREN

Is there (a/an) ...?
Y a-t-il ...?
ya teel ...

  baby change room
  un endroit pour un on·drwa poor
  changer le bébé shon·zhay ler bay·bay

  car baby seat
  un siège-enfant un syezh·on·fon

  child-minding service
  une garderie ewn gar·dree

  children's menu
  un menu pour enfant un mer·new poor on·fon

  disposable nappies/diapers
  couches-culottes koosh·kew·lot

  formula (milk)
  lait maternisé lay ma·ter·nee·zay

  (English-speaking) babysitter
  une babysitter (qui ewn ba·bee·see·ter (kee
  parle anglais) parl ong·glay)

  highchair
  une chaise haute dewn shay zot

  potty
  un pot de bébé un po der bay·bay

  stroller
  une poussette ewn poo·set

Do you mind if I breastfeed here?
  Cela vous dérange si ser·la voo day·ron·zhe see
  j'allaite mon bébé ici? zha·lay·ter mon bay·bay ee·see

Are children allowed?
  Les enfants sont permis? lay zon·fon son pair·mee

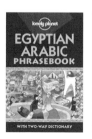

LANGUAGE

Glossary

This glossary includes terms and abbreviations you may come across during your travels in Tunisia. Where appropriate, the capital letter in brackets indicates whether the terms are French (F) or Arabic (A).

A

Abbasids – Baghdad-based ruling dynasty (AD 749–1258) of the Arab/Islamic Empire

Africa Proconsularis – Roman province of Africa

agha – a military commander or a title of respect (in the Ottoman Empire)

Aghlabids – Arab dynasty based in Kairouan who ruled Tunisia (AD 800–909)

ain (A) – water source or spring

Allah (A) – Muslim name for God

alloucha (A) – thick-pile, woven, woollen Berber rug

Almohads – Berber rulers of Spain and North Africa (1130–1269)

Almoravids – dynasty of Berbers from the Sahara, reigned from 1061 to 1106 in Morocco and the Maghreb, and later in Andalusia, after 1086.

ASM – Association de Sauvegarde de la Medina; group charged with preserving the medinas of a number of Tunisian towns

assaba (A) – headband worn by Berber women

auberge de jeunesse (F) – youth hostel affiliated to Hostelling International

B

bab (A) – city gate

bakhnoug (A) – traditional shawl worn by Berber women

Barbary Coast – European term for the Mediterranean coast of North Africa in the 16th to 19th centuries

basilica – Roman building used for public administration; early Christian church

Berbers – indigenous (non-Arab) people of North Africa

bey – provincial governor in the Ottoman Empire; rulers of Tunisia from the 17th century until independence in 1957

boissons gazeuses (F) – carbonated drinks

borj (A) – fort (literally 'tower')

boukha (A) – local spirit made from figs

brochette (F) – kebab

burnous (A) – hooded winter cape worn by men

buvette (F) – refreshment room or stall

C

calèche (F) – horse-drawn carriage

caliph – Islamic ruler, originally referred to the successors of the Prophet Mohammed

camionnette (F) – small pick-up used as a taxi

capitol – main temple of a Roman town, usually situated in the forum

caravanserai – see *funduq*

casse-croûte (F) – Tunisian fast food; a sandwich made from half a French loaf stuffed with a variety of fillings

centre des stages et des vacances (F) – holiday camps

chechia (A) – red felt hat

chorba (A) – soup

chott (A) – salt lake or marsh

confort (F) – class above 1st class on passenger trains

corniche (F) – coastal road

corsairs – pirates, especially those who operated on the North African coast from the 16th to the 19th century

couscous – semolina granules, the staple food of Tunisia

D

dar (A) – town house or palace

deglat ennour (A) – a type of date (literally 'finger of light')

destour (A) – literally 'constitution' but also name for Habib Bourguiba's political party before independence

dey – the Ottoman army's equivalent of a sergeant; rulers of Tunisia in the 16th century

diwan – assembly (in the Ottoman Empire)

E

eid (A) – feast

Eid al-Adha (A) – feast of Sacrifice marking the pilgrimage to Mecca; sometimes called Eid al-Kebir

Eid al-Fitr (A) – feast of the Breaking of the Fast, celebrated at the end of Ramadan

emir – military commander or governor

erg – sand sea; desert

F

Fatimids – Muslim dynasty (AD 909-1171) who defeated the *Aghlabids* and ruled Tunisia from Mahdia from AD 909 to 969

forum – open space at the centre of Roman towns

fouta (A) – cotton bath towel provided in a *hammam*

funduq (A) – former lodging houses or inns for the travelling merchants of the camel caravans, also known as *caravanserai*; Arab word for hotel

G

gare routière (F) – bus station

gargotte (F) – cheap restaurant that serves basic food

gargoulette (F) – pottery amphora used in traditional octopus catching technique used on Jerba

ghar (A) – cave

ghorfa (A) – literally, room; especially a long, barrel-vaulted room built to store grain
guetiffa – a thick-pile, knotted Berber carpet

H

Hafsids – rulers of *Ifriqiyya* from the 13th to the 16th century
haj (A) – the pilgrimage to the holy sites in and around Mecca, the pinnacle of a devout Muslim's life
hammam (A) – public bathhouse
harissa (A) – spicy chilli paste
harout (A) – traditional Jerban weaver's workshop
hedeyed (A) – finely engraved, wide bracelets made of gold or silver
hejab (A) – woman's veil or headscarf
Hejira (A) – Mohammed's flight from Mecca in AD 622; also the name of the Muslim calendar
Hilalian tribes – tribes of Upper Egypt who invaded the Maghreb in the 11th century, causing great destruction
Hizb al-Nahda – Renaissance Party, the main Islamic opposition party
Husseinites – dynasty of *beys* who ruled Tunisia from 1705 to 1957

I

Ibadites – an offshoot of the *Kharijite* sect found only on Jerba, in the villages of the M'Zab Valley in Algeria and in Oman
ibn (A) – son of
Ifriqiyya – Arab province of North Africa, including Tunisia and parts of Libya
iftar (A) – (also spelt 'ftur') the breaking of the day's fast during *Ramadan*
imam (A) – religious teacher

J

jami (A) – the main district mosque
janissary – infantryman in the Ottoman army
jebel (A) – hill or mountain
jihad (A) – holy war

K

kalaa (A) – Berber hill fort
kasbah (A) – fort or citadel
kassa (A) – a coarse mitten used in the steam room of a *hammam*
Kharijites – puritanical Islamic sect, which broke away from the mainstream *Sunnis* in AD 657 and inspired Berber rebellions from the 8th to the 10th century
kholkal (A) – gold or silver anklets
khomsa (A) – hand-of-Fatima motif
khutba (A) – weekly sermon in the mosque
kilim (A) – woven rug decorated with typical Berber motifs
ksar (A) – (plural *ksour*) a fortified Berber stronghold consisting of many *ghorfas*
ksibah (A) – small fort

kuttab (A) – Quranic primary school

L

Limes Tripolitanus – the defensive line developed by the Romans in southern Tunisia
louage (F) – shared long-distance taxi

M

Maghreb – term used to describe northwest Africa, including Morocco, Algeria and Tunisia
maison des jeunes (F) – government-run youth hostel
malouf (A) – musical form that originated in Andalusia and adopted as traditional Tunisian music
marabout (A) – Muslim holy man or saint
masjid (A) – small local mosque
medersa (A) – Quranic school
medina (A) – city; the old quarter of Tunisian towns and cities
menzel (A) – fortified family dwelling found on Jerba
mergoum (A) – woven carpet with geometric designs
mihrab (A) – vaulted niche in a mosque, which indicates the direction of Mecca
minaret – tower of a mosque from which the *muezzin* calls the faithful to prayer
minbar (A) – the pulpit in a mosque
mouloud (A) – *Maghreb* term for the Moulid an-Nabi, the feast celebrating the birth of the Prophet Mohammed
moussem (A) – pilgrimage to a shrine or to a tomb of a *marabout*
muezzin (A) – mosque official who calls the faithful to prayer
Muradites – line of Tunisian *beys*, ruling from the 17th to 18th century

N

nador (A) – watch tower
Numidians – tribe from present-day Algeria, once controlled Northern Tunisia; founders of the cities of Bulla Regia, Sicca (El-Kef) and Thugga (Dougga)

O

ONAT – the Office National de l'Artisanat Tunisien; government-run fixed-price craft shops
ONTT – Office National du Tourisme Tunisien; government-run national tourist office
Ottoman Empire – former Turkish Empire, of which Tunisia was part; based in Constantinople from the late 13th century to the end of WWI
oud – lute
oued (A) – river; also dry riverbed
Ouergherma (A) – 17th-century Berber confederation which ruled from Medenine

P

palmeraie (F) – palm grove; the area around an oasis where date palms, vegetables and fruit are grown

pasha – provincial governor or high official in the Ottoman Empire

patisserie (F) – cake and pastry shop

pension (F) – guesthouse

Phoenicians – a great sea-faring nation, based in modern Lebanon, which dominated trade in the Mediterranean in the 1st millennium BC; founders of Carthage

PSD – Parti Socialiste Destourien (called the Neo-Destour Party before 1964); the first nationalist party in Tunisia

Punic – the Phoenician culture that evolved in North Africa

Punic Wars – three wars waged between Rome and Carthage in the 3rd and 2nd centuries BC, resulting in the destruction of Carthage by the Romans in 146 BC

Q

qibla (A) – the direction of Mecca in a mosque, indicated by the *mihrab*

qubba (A) – domed roof

Quran (A) – the holy book of Islam

R

Ramadan – ninth month of the Muslim year, a time of fasting

razzegoui (A) – a large white grape that ripens to a pink blush

RCD – Rassemblement Constitutionel Democratique; President Ben Ali's ruling party

ribat (A) – fortified Islamic monastery

rôtisserie (F) – basic restaurant serving roast chicken

S

Sahel – eastern part of central Tunisia occupying the large, fertile coastal bulge between the Gulf of Hammamet and the Gulf of Gabès

sand rose – crystallised gypsum found in desert and sold as souvenirs

sebkha (A) – salt flat or coastal marshland

Sharia'a (F) – Quranic law

sheesha (A) – water pipe used to smoke tobacco

Shiite – one of two main Islamic sects (see also *Sunni*); its followers believe that the true *imams* are descended from Ali

sidi (A) – saint

skifa (A) – gate

SNCFT – Société Nationale des Chemins de Fer Tunisiens; the national railway company

SNTRI – the Société Nationale du Transport Interurbain; the national bus company

souq (A) – market

stele – grave stone

Sufi – follower of Islamic mystical orders that emphasise dancing, chanting and trances to attain unity with God

Sunni – the main Islamic sect (see also *Shiite*) derived from followers of the *Ummayyad* caliphate

syndicat d'initiative (F) – municipal tourist office

T

Taxiphone – public telephone

Tell – the high plains of the Tunisian Dorsale, in central Tunisia

thibarine – a local spirit from the village of Thibar near Dougga

tophet – sacrificial site

tourbet (A) – mausoleum

U

Ummayyads – first great dynasty of Arab Muslim rulers (AD 661–750), based in Damascus

Z

zaouia (A) – a complex surrounding the tomb of a saint

zone touristique (F) – tourist strip

Behind the Scenes

THIS BOOK

The 3rd edition of *Tunisia* was prepared in Lonely Planet's Melbourne office. The first two editions were written by David Willett. This edition was researched by Anthony Ham and Abigail Hole. Rafik Tlatli wrote the Food & Drink chapter and Dr Caroline Evans wrote the Health chapter.

THANKS FROM THE AUTHORS

Anthony Ham My special thanks to Faouzi Bouali in Tozeur who taught me so much about the south; Ahmed and Mohammed in Douz who showed me again the hospitality of the desert; and Fathi and his daughter in Gabès who always had a welcoming smile. Thanks also to Mohammed (Sfax), Ali (Tataouine), Sonia (Jerba), Ibrahim (Kairouan), Miled (Ksar Ouled Soltane) and Salem (Kerkennah) and to fellow travellers including Francesco Ruffino, Elena Venturi, Tom and the crew in Matmata, Emmanuel (for his translations) and all the readers who took the time to write in with suggestions. An extra special thank you to Simon Westcott who was great company and brought such wisdom and insight to the book. My co-author Abi was a dream to work with, as were Lynne Preston and Will Gourlay back in the Lonely Planet office. In Australia, thanks as always to Jan, Ron, Lisa, Greg, Alex, Greta and Damien for reminding me how much I miss them. In Madrid, *muchisimas gracias* to Alberto, Marina, Beatriz and all my wonderful Spanish friends. And above all to my partner Marina, who held the fort while I was away, welcomed me home so wonderfully and said yes when I asked her to marry me.

Abigail Hole Many thanks to all at the very helpful Tunisia Tourist Board in London; to Rafik Tlatli; to Ginnie, Sumeet, Sophia and Tom; to Kais in Bizerte; to Khaled in Hammamet; to Mohammed Chihi and to Wahid in Le Kef; to Anthony Ham, Lynne Preston and Will Gourlay; and to Kate James, Margedd Heliosz and Julie Sheridan.

CREDITS

Series Publishing Manager Virginia Maxwell oversaw the redevelopment of the country guides series with help from Maria Donohoe, and she also steered development of this title. The series was designed by James Hardy, with mapping development by Paul Piaia. The series development team included Shahara Ahmed, Susie Ashworth, Gerilyn Attebery, Jenny Blake, Anna Bolger, Verity Campbell, Erin Corrigan, Nadine Fogale, Dave McClymont, Leonie Mugavin, Rachel Peart, Lynne Preston and Howard Ralley.

This edition was commissioned and developed in Lonely Planet's Melbourne office by Lynne Preston, and taken through to production by Will Gourlay. Cartography for this guide was developed by Julie Sheridan and Shahara Ahmed. Overseeing the project were project manager Rachel Imeson, managing editor Brigitte Ellemor and managing cartographers Shahara Ahmed and James Ellis. Editing was coordinated by Kate James with assistance from Margedd Heliosz, Sally Steward and Linda Suttie. Cartography was coordinated by Julie Sheridan, who also put together the colour map, with assistance from Christopher Crook and Paul Bazalicki. Natasha Velleley created the back-cover

---

THE LONELY PLANET STORY

The story begins with a classic travel adventure: Tony and Maureen Wheeler's 1972 journey across Europe and Asia to Australia. There was no useful information about the overland trail then, so Tony and Maureen published the first Lonely Planet guidebook to meet a growing need.

From a kitchen table, Lonely Planet has grown to become the largest independent travel publisher in the world, with offices in Melbourne (Australia), Oakland (USA), London (UK) and Paris (France).

Today Lonely Planet guidebooks cover the globe. There is an ever-growing list of books and information in a variety of media. Some things haven't changed. The main aim is still to make it possible for adventurous travellers to get out there – to explore and better understand the world.

At Lonely Planet we believe travellers can make a positive contribution to the countries they visit – if they respect their host communities and spend their money wisely.

SEND US YOUR FEEDBACK

We love to hear from travellers – your comments keep us on our toes and help make our books better. Our well-travelled team reads every word on what you loved or loathed about this book. Although we cannot reply individually to postal submissions, we always guarantee that your feedback goes straight to the appropriate authors, in time for the next edition. Each person who sends us information is thanked in the next edition – and the most useful submissions are rewarded with a free book.

To send us your updates – and find out about LP events, newsletters and travel news – visit our award-winning website: **www.lonelyplanet.com**.

Note: We may edit, reproduce and incorporate your comments in Lonely Planet products such as guidebooks, websites and digital products, so let us know if you don't want your comments reproduced or your name acknowledged. For a copy of our privacy policy visit www.lonelyplanet.com/privacy.

map. Andrew Ostroff prepared the colour pages and also laid out the book. The cover was designed by James Hardy and the cover artwork was done by Brendan Dempsey. Quentin Frayne compiled the Language chapter.

THANKS FROM LONELY PLANET

Many thanks to the travellers who used the last edition and wrote to us with helpful hints, useful advice and interesting anecdotes:
A Jenny Amor, John Anderson, Sarah Andrews, Jonathan Antill, Daniel Auger **B** DL Baker, Gord Barentsen, Lisa Barnes, Rosa Maria Perales Barrero, Sandra & Wendy Bebbington, Elizabeth Ben Hassine, Carlo Beraha, Lavinia Beraha, Tim Bewer, Andrzej Bielecki, Lisa Blair, Han Blankstein, Virginia Bloch-Jorgensen, Brian W Boag, Geert Boeije, Jean-Thomas Boily, Hatem Bouattour, Dimitris Boukogiannis, Inge Bouwman, J Butcher **C** Gerald Cadieux, Karen Carlsen, Melissa Carr, Jamie Carstairs, Robert & Isabella Cesen, David Chaudoir, Shuming Chen, Yee Cheng, Jessica Chloros, Heidi Clemmenson, Renee Cole, Cathrine Cook, Cam Cooper, Luis Costa, Brian Cruickshank **D** Ake Dahllof, Niklas Damm, Karsten Dax, Malgorzata Dera, Romain Desrousseaux, Roupen Deuvletian, Jeff Doyle, Andreas Drechsler, Odree Ducharme **E** PA Edney, Dave Eggelton, Vanessa Elliott-Smith **F** Paul Fatt, Patricia A Felch, Joan Ferrer, Claudia Flynn, Angela Fountain, Richard N Frye **G** Elisabetta Galasso, Marco Garrone, Ruth Gould, Ann Graham, Linda Gregory **H** Emmy Hahurji, Rainer Hamet, Solange Hando, Haider Haraghi, Jan Havranek, Emma Holmbro, Jenny Horwood, Kevin Hudson, Antje Huick, Valerie M Hume **I** Christine Ingemorsen **J** George Jackson, Rok Jarc, Sally Jennings, Mark Jonas, Kate Jones, Kevin Jordon **K** Wilfried Kaib, Tasa Kampouroudi, M Idrees Kayani, Colin Kenworthy, Chris Knutson, Chris Kostopoulos, George Kouseras, David Krivanek, Gloria Kuo, Peter Kurze **L** Robb Lawton, Adrian Lay, David Lee, Chung-Chu Leung, Anja Lieder, Paul Lindsay-Addy, Amanda Little, Alessandro Liverani, Ellen Livermore, Peter Loeskow, Sven Lotzvie, Catherine Lucas **M** Clark Madrosen, A Magnus, Anabelle Martelli, Alison McCormick, PAP Miller, Nissim Mizrahi, Andrew Moncrieff, Marie-Claire Muir, Gabe Murtagh, Andrea Mussa, EP Mycroft, Imogen C Myers **N** R Naiman, R & J Naiman **P** André Paillard, Wim Pannecoucke, Emily Peckham, David Petrie, RC Pietri, Lori Plotkin, John Porter, Jean Potter, Pat Pyner **Q** Paul Quenby **R** Loretta Rafter, Anne Rees, Nancy Refki, Philipp Renggli, Rosemarie Richards, Tony Robinson, Claudia Gaffino Rossi, Angela Rowe, Nerea Rozas **S** Kevin Salvage, EM Sanford, Aidan Santer, Nathalie Schmelz, Jeff Sejer, Ken Shaw, Philippe Sibelly, Mario Silva, Peter Simpson, Jennifer Smith, Neil Smith, Sally Smith, Chris Stephenson, Kurt Stevens, Alison Stirling, Jennifer Sudick **T** Kris Terauds, Marius Throndsen, Michel Thuriaux, Dimitris Tsouflidis **V** Ronald van Engers, Rene Van Havene, Lieven Van Keer, Dominiek Vansteenkiste, Thomas Vaughan, Marianne Verhaagen, Sabine Verhelst, Armijn Verweij, Jens von Scheele **W** Chelly Wael, Rosamund Wastell, Frank Watson, Peter & Betty Watson-Kay, Nate Wessler, Troy West, Jan Williamson, Shane Wilson, Louise Winspear **Z** Greg & Sylvie Zibell, Felix Zimmermann

306

Index

INDEX

INDEX

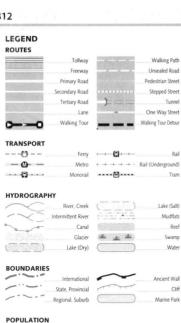

LEGEND

ROUTES

.... Tollway
.... Freeway
.... Primary Road
.... Secondary Road
.... Tertiary Road
.... Lane
.... Walking Tour

.... Walking Path
.... Unsealed Road
.... Pedestrian Street
.... Stepped Street
.... Tunnel
.... One Way Street
.... Walking Tour Detour

TRANSPORT

.... Ferry
.... Metro
.... Monorail

.... Rail
.... Rail (Underground)
.... Tram

HYDROGRAPHY

.... River, Creek
.... Intermittent River
.... Canal
.... Glacier
.... Lake (Dry)

.... Lake (Salt)
.... Mudflats
.... Reef
.... Swamp
.... Water

BOUNDARIES

.... International
.... State, Provincial
.... Regional, Suburb

.... Ancient Wall
.... Cliff
.... Marine Park

POPULATION

◎ **CAPITAL (NATIONAL)**
● .... **Large City**
○ .... Small City

◉ .... **CAPITAL (STATE)**
● .... **Medium City**
○ .... Town, Village

AREA FEATURES

.... Area of Interest
.... Beach, Desert
.... Building
+ + + Cemetery, Christian
× × × Cemetery, Other
.... Forest

.... Land
.... Mall
.... Market
.... Park
.... Sports
.... Urban

SYMBOLS

SIGHTS/ACTIVITIES
Beach
Buddhist
Castle, Fortress
Christian
Confician
Diving, Snorkeling
Hindu
Islamic
Jain
Jewish
Monument
Museum, Gallery
Picnic Area
Point of Interest
Ruin
Shinto
Sikh
Skiing
Taoist
Winery, Vineyard
Zoo, Bird Sanctuary

INFORMATION
Bank, ATM
Embassy/Consulate
Hospital, Medical
Information
Internet Facilities
Parking Area
Petrol Station
Police Station
Post Office, GPO
Telephone
Toilets

SLEEPING
Sleeping
Camping

EATING
Eating

DRINKING
Drinking
Café

ENTERTAINMENT
Entertainment

SHOPPING
Shopping

TRANSPORT
Airport, Airfield
Border Crossing
Bus Station
Cycling, Bicycle Path
General Transport
Taxi Rank
Trail Head

GEOGRAPHIC
Hazard
Lighthouse
Lookout
Mountain, Volcano
National Park
Oasis
Pass, Canyon
River Flow
Shelter, Hut
Spot Height
Waterfall

NOTE: Not all symbols displayed above appear in this guide.

LONELY PLANET OFFICES

Australia
Head Office
Locked Bag 1, Footscray, Victoria 3011
☎ 03 8379 8000, fax 03 8379 8111
talk2us@lonelyplanet.com.au

USA
150 Linden St, Oakland, CA 94607
☎ 510 893 8555, toll free 800 275 8555
fax 510 893 8572, info@lonelyplanet.com

UK
72–82 Rosebery Ave,
Clerkenwell, London EC1R 4RW
☎ 020 7841 9000, fax 020 7841 9001
go@lonelyplanet.co.uk

France
1 rue du Dahomey, 75011 Paris
☎ 01 55 25 33 00, fax 01 55 25 33 01
bip@lonelyplanet.fr, www.lonelyplanet.fr

Published by Lonely Planet Publications Pty Ltd
ABN 36 005 607 983

Lonely Planet 2004 ©

photographers as indicated 2004 ©

Cover photographs by Lonely Planet Images: Palm trees and sand dunes near Douz, Wayne Walton (front); Central courtyard of the Zaouia of Sidi Abid el-Ghariani in Kairouan, Geoff Stringer (back). Many of the images in this guide are available for licensing from Lonely Planet Images: www.lonelyplanetimages.com.

Printed through Colorcraft Ltd, Hong Kong.
Printed in China

Although the authors and Lonely Planet have taken all reasonable care in preparing this book, we make no warranty about the accuracy or completeness of its content and, to the maximum extent permitted, disclaim all liability arising from its use.